12-99

KT-216-104

The South East Essex
College of Arts & Technology
Carnarvon Road, Southend-on-Sea, Essex SS2 6LS
Phone 0702 220400

30130504254576

OR
11/07 X

SHL
942.05
GUY

TUDOR ENGLAND

John Guy is Professor of Modern History and Head of
the School of History and International Relations at the
University of St Andrews. He is the author of many books
on the Tudor period, and is a contributor to *The Oxford
Illustrated History of Britain*.

0006434459 9 0010

Tudor England

JOHN GUY

OXFORD
UNIVERSITY PRESS

OXFORD
UNIVERSITY PRESS

Great Clarendon Street, Oxford OX2 6DP

Oxford University Press is a department of the University of Oxford.
It furthers the University's objective of excellence in research, scholarship,
and education by publishing worldwide in

Oxford New York

Athens Auckland Bangkok Bogotá Buenos Aires Calcutta
Cape Town Chennai Dar es Salaam Delhi Florence Hong Kong Istanbul
Karachi Kuala Lumpur Madrid Melbourne Mexico City Mumbai
Nairobi Paris São Paulo Singapore Taipei Tokyo Toronto Warsaw

with associated companies in Berlin Ibadan

Oxford is a registered trade mark of Oxford University Press
in the UK and in certain other countries

© John Guy 1988

First published by Oxford University Press 1988
First issued as an Oxford University Press paperback 1990

All rights reserved. No part of this publication may be reproduced,
stored in a retrieval system, or transmitted, in any form or by any means,
without the prior permission in writing of Oxford University Press,
or as expressly permitted by law, or under terms agreed with the appropriate
reprographics rights organization. Enquiries concerning reproduction
outside the scope of the above should be sent to the Rights Department,
Oxford University Press, at the address above

You must not circulate this book in any other binding or cover
and you must impose this same condition on any acquirer

British Library Cataloguing in Publication Data

Data available

Library of Congress Cataloging in Publication Data

Guy, John.
Tudor England/John Guy.
Bibliography: p.
Includes index.
1. Great Britain—History—Tudors, 1485–1603.
2. England—Civilization—16th century.
3. Tudor, House of. I. Title.
DA315.G89 1988 942.05—dc19 88-5371

ISBN 0-19-285213-2

13 15 17 19 20 18 16 14

Printed and bound in Great Britain by
Cox & Wyman Ltd,
Reading, Berkshire

For Rachel, Richard, and Emma

PREFACE

THIS book stems from relatively simple and possibly naïve ambitions. I have attempted to write a clear narrative account of the period of English history from 1460 to the death of Elizabeth I in a manner equally accessible to the general reader and to the student. Second, I wished to provide a comprehensive and up-to-date synthesis of the vast amount of recent research on Tudor history which has appeared during the last thirty years. Inevitably the book became rather longer than I had planned, and even a long book has to be selective. I have therefore conceived my work essentially as a political and religious narrative with analytical discussion of main themes. I have also written chapters on the economy and society, the theory and development of the state, and political culture, which are intended as contexts for the bulk of the book. I plainly had to choose main themes if my work was not to become impossibly long. Though my selection may not be to everyone's taste, it nevertheless remains true that those topics and debates which I regard as most interesting and important turn out to be complementary to the most recent surveys by David Palliser, Penry Williams, and Joyce Youings. In particular, while numerous surveys have appeared on the early Tudors, of which that of most consummate skill is by Sir Geoffrey Elton, no up-to-date narrative which traverses the full period up to Elizabeth's death has appeared for many years, despite the quite radical rethinking during the last decade of such central topics as the progress of the Reformation, the 'revolution in government', and the strengths and weaknesses of Tudor politics and government, including local government. I firmly maintain that the Tudor period and its institutions must be considered as a whole if the significance of either the Henrician Age or the Elizabethan Age is to be properly understood, and my argument in this book reflects this conviction. Lastly, since the demands of legitimate historical debate have obliged me to disagree with several aspects of Sir Geoffrey Elton's magisterial account of Thomas Cromwell and his reforms, I must make plain my loyalty and respect for my former teacher.

In writing this book I have incurred innumerable and pervasive debts to the work of other Tudor scholars. I am deeply grateful for all the help I have received, and have endeavoured to make full and specific acknowledgements in my notes and select bibliography. It is somewhat invidious to attempt to summarize so many obligations in a few prefatory lines, but I cannot fail to record that I am heavily indebted to the work of Simon Adams, Jim Alsop, George Bernard, Margaret Bowker, Susan Brigden, Michael Bush, Christopher Coleman, Patrick Collinson, Margaret Condon, Cliff Davies, Geoff Dickens, Steve Ellis, Geoffrey Elton, Alistair Fox, Michael Graves, Peter Gwyn, Chris Haigh, Dale Hoak, Ronald Hutton, Eric Ives, Mervyn James, Norman Jones, Jennifer Loach, David Loades, Wallace MacCaffrey, Diarmaid MacCulloch, Richard Marius, Tom Mayer, Helen Miller, Virginia Murphy, Graham Nicholson, Rex Pogson, Jack Scarisbrick, Roger Schofield, Joe Slavin, Hassell Smith, David Starkey, Greg Walker, R. B. Wernham, Bob Whiting, and Penry Williams. I gladly acknowledge the further help received from the many British and North American dissertations cited in the notes. Also I am particularly indebted to David Starkey's unpublished papers read at Bristol University, the Folger Institute, and the 101st Annual Conference of the American Historical Association, which first set me thinking upon altered lines concerning the Pilgrimage of Grace, the Council, and the role of the nobles at Court at the time of the Eltham Ordinance and during the 1530s. For many helpful and suggestive comments on drafts of the typescript, I am deeply grateful to Alistair Fox, Rachel Guy, and John Morrill, as well as to an anonymous publisher's reader. Rachel Guy and Hilary Walford kindly assisted with finalizing the typescript, proof-reading, and making the index. The genealogical table was prepared by Rachel Guy, who with Richard Guy performed heroic labours on our photocopier. Manuscripts in the Public Record Office, British Library, Folger Shakespeare Library, Washington DC, Huntington Library, San Marino, California, and Department of Special Collections, Spencer Library, University of Kansas, are cited by generous permission of the authorities. Finally, sincere thanks are due to the publisher for permitting extensions both of the length of the book and of the date of its delivery.

CONTENTS

LIST OF ILLUSTRATIONS

between pp. 208–9, 368–9

The author and publisher gratefully acknowledge permission to reproduce illustrations from the following: the National Portrait Gallery (nos. 1–8, 12, 16–17, 20–7, 34); the Society of Antiquaries of London (no. 9, copyright reserved; no. 11); the Ashmolean Museum, Oxford (no. 10); the Courtauld Institute of Art (no. 13, Longleat collection; no. 14, Lambeth Palace collection; no. 15, Petworth collection); the Mansell Collection (no. 18); the British Library (no. 19); the Guildhall Library, London (no. 28, copyright reserved); the Rijksmuseum, Amsterdam (no. 29); the Bodleian Library, Oxford (no. 30); the National Gallery of Ireland (no. 31); the Sherborne Castle Estates (no. 32); *Country Life* (no. 33, copyright reserved).

ABBREVIATIONS

APC	*Acts of the Privy Council of England*, ed. J. R. Dasent *et al.* (NS; 46 vols.; London, 1890–1964).
BL	British Library
CSPD	*Calendar of State Papers, Domestic*
CSPF	*Calendar of State Papers, Foreign*
CSPI	*Calendar of State Papers, Ireland*
CW	*The Complete Works of St Thomas More* (15 vols.; New Haven, Conn., 1963–).
EHD	*English Historical Documents*, ed. D. C. Douglas *et al.* (12 vols.; London, 1953–77).
LP	*Letters and Papers, Foreign and Domestic, of the Reign of Henry VIII*, ed. J. S. Brewer, J. Gairdner, R. H. Brodie, *et al.* (21 vols. and *Addenda*; London, 1862–1932).
MS	Manuscript
PRO	Public Record Office
St. Pap.	*State Papers during the Reign of Henry VIII* (11 vols.; Record Commission, London, 1830–52).

Manuscripts preserved at the PRO are quoted by the call number there in use. The descriptions of the classes referred to are as follows:

C 193	Chancery, Crown Office, Miscellaneous Books
C 244	Chancery, Files, Corpus Cum Causa
C 254	Chancery, Files, Dedimus Potestatem
E 36	Exchequer, Treasury of the Receipt, Miscellaneous Books
E 159	Exchequer, King's Remembrancer, Memoranda Rolls
E 192	Exchequer, King's Remembrancer, Private Collections
LC 2	Lord Chamberlain's Department, Office of Robes, Special Events
PC 2	Privy Council Office, Registers
SP 1	State Papers, Henry VIII, General Series

SP 2	State Papers, Henry VIII, Folio Volumes
SP 6	State Papers, Henry VIII, Theological Tracts
SP 10	State Papers, Domestic, Edward VI
SP 11	State Papers, Domestic, Mary
SP 12	State Papers, Domestic, Elizabeth I
STAC 1	Star Chamber Proceedings, Henry VII
STAC 2	Star Chamber Proceedings, Henry VIII
STAC 10	Star Chamber Proceedings, Miscellaneous

In giving dates, the Old Style has been retained, but the year is assumed to have begun on 1 January. In quotations, abbreviations have been extended, and modern spelling and punctuation adopted, with the result that capitals have occasionally been supplied where there is none in the original and vice-versa.

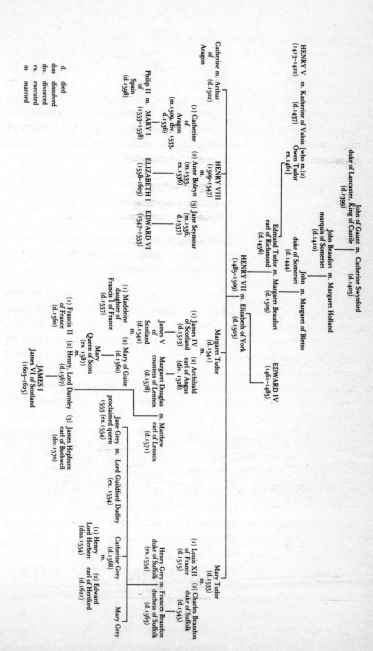

John of Gaunt m. Catherine Swynford
duke of Lancaster, King of Castile
(d.1399)

John Beaufort m. Margaret Holland
marquis of Somerset
(d.1410)

John m. Margaret of Bletso
duke of Somerset
(d.1444)

Edmund Tudor m. Margaret Beaufort
earl of Richmond
(d.1456) (d.1509)

HENRY V m. Katherine of Valois [who m.(2)
(1413–1422) (d.1437) Owen Tudor
ex. 1461]

HENRY VII m. Elizabeth of York
(1485–1509) (d.1503)

Catherine m. Arthur
of (d.1502)
Aragon

(1) Catherine (2) Anne Boleyn (3) Jane Seymour
of (m.1533, (m.1536,
Aragon ex.1536) d.1537)
(m.1509, div. 1533, m.
d.1536) HENRY VIII
(1509–1547)

Philip II m. MARY I ELIZABETH I EDWARD VI
of (1553–1558) (1558–1603) (1547–1553)
Spain
(d.1598)

Margaret Tudor
(d.1541)
m.

(1) James IV (2) Archibald
of Scotland earl of Angus
(d.1513) (div. 1528)
m.

James V Margaret Douglas m. Matthew
of countess of Lennox earl of Lennox
Scotland (d.1578) (d.1571)
(d.1542)
m.

(1) Madeleine (2) Mary of Guise
daughter of (d.1560)
Francis I of France
(d.1537)

Mary
Queen of Scots
(ex. 1587)

(1) Francis II (2) Henry, Lord Darnley (3) James Hepburn
of France (d.1567) earl of Bothwell
(d.1560) (div.1570)

JAMES I
James VI of Scotland
(1603–1625)

EDWARD IV
(1461–1483)

Mary Tudor
(d.1533)
m.

(1) Louis XII (2) Charles Brandon
of France duke of Suffolk
(d.1515) (d.1545)

Henry Grey m. Frances Brandon
duke of Suffolk duchess of Suffolk
(ex.1554) (d.1563)

Jane Grey m. Lord Guildford Dudley
proclaimed queen (ex. 1554)
1553 (ex.1554)

Catherine Grey Mary Grey
(d.1568)
m.

(1) Henry (2) Edward
Lord Herbert earl of Hertford
(diss.1554) (d.1621)

d. died
diss. dissolved
div. divorced
ex. executed
m married

1

THE ADVENT OF THE TUDORS

WHATEVER survives the test of time, the achievements of the Tudors must be assessed critically. They manufactured panegyric and manipulated prophecies: Bernard André's *Life of Henry VII*, Polydore Vergil's *English History*, and Edward Hall's *The Union of the Two Noble and Illustrious Families of Lancaster and York* epitomize what Grafton and Holinshed popularized and Shakespeare made immortal. The Galfridian prophecy was invoked in 1485: Bosworth was foretold when an angel visited Cadwalader to inform him that the British would recover their lands from the Saxons. Henry VII claimed descent from Cadwalader, so the king's champion at the coronation banquet rode a horse trapped with his arms. Henry claimed, too, that he was divinely ordained to quell political turbulence by marrying the daughter of Edward IV. As Hall explained, the 'old divided controversy' was 'buried and perpetually extinct' by this union. Or, as Shakespeare put it:

> We will unite the white rose and the red:
> Smile, heaven, upon this fair conjunction,
> That long hath frowned upon their enmity!
> .   .   .   .   .   .
> Now civil wounds are stopped, peace lives again:
> That she may long live here, God say Amen!
> (*Richard III*, v. iv. 32–4, 53–4)

Yet the 'Wars of the Roses', in the sense that the tussles of a thirty-year period were a single dynastic conflict between the houses of Lancaster and York, were a myth. In reality, Court factionalism moved into the provinces as rival nobles raised their affinities in armed engagements in which participants aligned themselves to best advantage. Chroniclers exaggerated the dynastic element in the 'wars' and the length and scale of the fighting: the aggregate period of active campaigning was only a year or so. But more casualties and damage resulted than is

sometimes claimed. There were fourteen pitched battles and
numerous skirmishes: three thousand men were slain at the battle
of Mortimer's Cross alone (1461). In total thirty-eight peers were
killed, though fewer noble families were extinguished by the
'wars' than by biological causes such as infertility or infant
mortality. To judge from private correspondence, the 'wars'
barely occurred. Non-combatants were nevertheless troubled:
overseas trade was damaged, towns feared the sack, social
tensions were increased, and some gentry took the opportunity
to settle private quarrels violently. Moreover, there was
psychological damage. We recall the advice of John, third Lord
Mountjoy, to his sons: 'to live rightwisely and never to take the
state of baron upon them if they may lay it from them, nor to
desire to be great about princes, for it is dangerous.'[1]

Three 'wars' erupted in the wake of Henry VI's mental
breakdown in 1453. The first (1455–61) followed the lapse of
the duke of York's first protectorate after Christmas 1454. It
was an armed political struggle for power at Court and in the
counties that only became dynastic in October 1460, when York
claimed the throne before Parliament as 'heir' of Richard II.
Slain at the battle of Wakefield (30 December), he was succeeded
by his son, who, after victory at Towton Moor (29 March 1461),
was crowned Edward IV. By 1464 this king blazed glorious. But
his marriage to Elizabeth Wydeville split the Yorkist party and
provoked the second 'war'. Although Richard Neville, earl of
Warwick, had been York's chief ally in 1459–61, he joined
Edward's feckless brother George, duke of Clarence, in a revolt
(1469–70). Warwick and Clarence sought the aid of Louis XI
of France, who wished to undo Edward IV's foreign policy and
therefore helped to equip and transport to England a Lancastrian
army in order to restore Henry VI (a prisoner in the Tower since
1465). Outflanked at first, Edward fled to Alkmaar in the Low
Countries, but returned with an army in March 1471 to
reconquer his realm. He first defeated and killed Warwick at
the battle of Barnet (14 April), and then routed a second
Lancastrian force at Tewkesbury (4 May). Prince Edward,
Henry VI's heir, was killed at Tewkesbury, and, within hours
of Edward's return to London, Henry VI died at the Tower.

Edward IV restored royal authority during his second reign,
but eleven weeks after his death his twelve-year-old son

Edward V was deposed by his uncle, Richard, duke of Gloucester (26 June 1483). Although the nobility acquiesced in Richard's usurpation, an underground network of those who feared or hated him quickly formed, and within four months Henry Stafford, duke of Buckingham, spearheaded rebellion. Henry Tudor, then an obscure exile, whose claim to the throne was through his mother Margaret Beaufort from John of Gaunt and Catherine Swynford, was the stated beneficiary of this revolt, which Richard crushed. Whether Buckingham had intended to claim the throne himself is unknown, but rumours of the murder of Edward IV's sons by Richard at the Tower paved the way for Henry's invasion. Supported by key defectors and with material assistance from Charles VIII of France, he landed close to Milford Haven on 7 August 1485. Attracting sympathetic forces as he marched into England via Shrewsbury, Stafford, and Lichfield, he obliged Richard III to advance to Leicester. By Sunday, 21 August, both sides were encamped in the vicinity of Ambien Hill, 2 miles from Market Bosworth, but the battle next day has been the subject of endless debate — there have been as many different accounts as there are historians. What we know is that in mid-conflict Richard tried to win the day by killing Henry in personal combat. With a loyal squadron of his household, he swept through to Henry's immediate bodyguard, striking down his standard-bearer and engaging Sir John Cheyney. At this moment his horse died under him. And then Sir William Stanley's intervention on Henry's side proved decisive. 'Alone', reports Polydore Vergil, Richard III 'was killed fighting manfully in the press of his enemies.' However, it was Henry's second victory over the Yorkist pretender Lambert Simnel at the battle of Stoke (16 June 1487) that concluded this third 'war'. Thereafter Henry protected himself by a combination of international diplomacy and internal security measures.

Important as are these facts, they form a subtext to Bosworth's significance. Tudor propaganda implies that the battle marked a new beginning in English history, but the more the question of Tudor originality has been explored, the less satisfactory this approach has seemed. If we test the Tudors against the benchmark of modern statecraft, we shall either be pulled back into the Middle Ages, to Magna Carta and the Provisions of Oxford, and to the political crises of Edward II, Richard II, and

Henry VI, or shall be invited on to the Civil War and
Protectorate, to the Convention Parliament and Bill of Rights,
or beyond to the age of Walpole. Bosworth was a landmark in
dynastic history, but Tudor rule must be seen in perspective.
We can neither forget its debt to Yorkist government and
administration, nor ignore the impact of the Renaissance on
English religion and political thought.

Late in 1470 or early in 1471, after the readeption of Henry VI
but before the battle of Barnet, Sir John Fortescue, who also
wrote *The Governance of England*, addressed a memorandum to
the earl of Warwick. Cast in the form of articles 'for the good
publique of the realm', the document called for refoundation
of the monarchy along lines suggested by Henry VI's critics in
Parliament during the 1450s.[2] Fortescue was not especially
perspicacious as a political analyst but his account summarizes
the main issues, and he had the benefit of inside knowledge, since
Henry VI had appointed him chief justice of king's bench in
1442. He left England in 1461 to become the nominal chancellor
of the Lancastrian government in exile. Making his peace with
Edward IV in 1471, he was admitted to his Council and wrote,
or more likely recast, *The Governance* as an advice book for him.
This tract repeated the ideas of the memorandum.[3]

   Since Fortescue knew that the Crown must check its financial
decline, he proposed retrenchment and re-endowment. He
demonstrated that political stability and the king's capacity to
maintain his estate were linked: the king should be able to pay
his officials and meet normal expenditure without having to
borrow at high interest rates. *The Governance* was less explicit on
income than expenditure, but the most important royal revenues
were the receipts from Crown lands, the profits of justice, customs
duties, and income accruing from the king's standing as a feudal
lord. Although direct taxes augmented these revenues in time
of emergency, taxation needed parliamentary consent by the
middle of the fourteenth century. The Crown might exact 'loans'
in lieu of taxes but this method generated political friction; it
was best avoided if the monarchy was weak. Fortescue divided
expenditure into two categories: 'ordinary' charges and
'extraordinary' ones. 'Ordinary' expenses were those of the royal
household and wardrobe, the salaries of councillors and officials,

and the costs of maintaining the law courts, king's houses, castles, and garrisons at Calais, in Ireland, and on the Scottish border. Parliament expected the king to pay these costs himself, but in emergencies the 'extraordinary' costs of defence and diplomacy by convention deserved relief. So, while Fortescue held that average (i.e. annually recurring) 'extraordinary' charges should be paid for by the Crown, he agreed that expenditure *above the average* was properly met by taxation. 'If there fall a case over much exorbitant,' he wrote, 'then it shall be reason, and also necessary, that all the realm bear for that case a singular charge.'

The decline of fifteenth-century monarchy was largely financial: the Crown's deficit on its current account in 1433 was £16,000 per annum. Income was only £34,000 per annum, despite accumulated charges and debts totalling £225,000.[4] But charges and debts had swelled to £372,000 by 1450, while annual income actually dropped. These figures exclude revenues of the duchy of Lancaster amounting to £2,500 annually in 1433. Still the prospect was slim that the king could 'live of his own' in the sense of meeting the full costs of normal government out of his regular revenues. That he should 'live of his own' nevertheless became Parliament's slogan under Henry IV and Henry VI, a slogan revived under the early Stuarts. Factionalism underpinned this demand: when 'reformers' asserted the need to remove vested interests from behind the throne, they usually meant to step there themselves. Richard, duke of York, is the classic example.

Yet two measures were advocated. One was the resumption of grants made out of royal revenues in the past; the other was the limitation of the king's power to alienate them in the future. The priorities adopted in managing the Crown estates in the thirteenth and fourteenth centuries had been first the needs of the royal family, second the reward of royal servants, and only third a contribution to government finance. And usually nothing was left for the last. So in Henry IV's reign a faction in Parliament called for resumption into the king's hands of all the lands which he and his predecessors had ever held since 1366. Grants of royal lands and of their profits were not in future to be given in lieu of salaries, fees, and annuities, but the Crown estates were to be at the disposal of the exchequer to meet the normal expenses of government. In practice, Henry IV

sidestepped such attempts at 'reform', and his son Henry V ruled
with obsessive and impressive vigour: like Henry VII he checked
his accounts personally. Indeed, since there was little alienation
of Crown land outside the circle of the royal family between 1404
and 1437, parliamentary criticism of the 'abuse' of royal lands
died down.

The collapse of Henry VI's government after 1449 was,
however, the signal for renewed attacks on the management of
the Crown lands. After 1437 Henry VI alienated Crown lands
at an unprecedented rate and entrusted important business to
coteries of courtiers. His generosity and partiality sparked new
factional rivalry. In particular, his reign was scarred by failure
in the Hundred Years War — every English possession in France
except Calais was lost. Acts of resumption between 1450 and
1456 were Parliament's riposte, but the results were ambiguous.
It is not clear how much money was saved; in fact more harm
than good may have been done by depriving the king of his
patronage, for largesse was the legitimate means whereby kings
demonstrated their power at the centre and traded influence in
the counties. When Parliament resisted demands for taxation,
a crisis was reached.

So Edward IV staked his career on reversing the monarchy's
decline. He claimed that he would 'live of his own' and not
'charge my subjects but in great and urgent causes concerning
more the weal of themself, and also the defence of them and of
this my realm, rather than mine own pleasure'. Fortescue
meanwhile urged wholesale cancellation of existing royal grants
by Crown-inspired acts of resumption; the vetting by the Council
of future grants to check that they were necessary; and safeguards
whereby offices and rewards would only be given to the king's
sworn servants — no one should hold two offices except a trusted
courtier who might have the keepership of a park as well as his
household position. The last of these proposals was impractical:
to have restricted the Crown's patronage to its servants would
have curtailed royal influence in the counties. But Fortescue
highlighted the main point: the dilapidation of the king's estate
had gone too far; the need was for 'a new foundation of his
Crown'. Edward IV and Henry VII shared his view. Whether
or not they read *The Governance*, seven acts of resumption between
1461 and 1495 restored some of their revenues.[5]

Also 397 dynastic attainders during the civil wars ensured the forfeiture of large estates to the Crown. Attainders were public and parliamentary condemnations for treason or rebellion that were also convenient weapons of political proscription. Verdicts by common law or the law of arms were given statutory force in order to extend the Crown's rights to forfeitures. The victim was deemed a traitor by authority of Parliament when he was slain or fled in battle against the king or otherwise convicted. The method guaranteed the confiscation of his lands and goods by the Crown, and 'corruption of blood', which disinherited his family and deprived his heirs of entailed land that would otherwise have escaped forfeiture. After 1459 attainders were used to exact revenge and to secure the property of defeated opponents: Edward IV's 113 attainders after Towton brought him lands and stewardships worth between £18,000 and £30,000 per annum. Among estates forfeited during this round of proscription were those of two dukes, five earls, one viscount, and six barons, as well as several dozen gentry. Yet care was needed to ensure that attainders were not used excessively, and many were reversed at varying later dates—though rarely in full—in favour of heirs who had shown loyalty to the regime. Reconciliation was as important as coercion in an age without a police force or standing army, when government remained a partnership between the magnates and the Crown. The nobility were the leaders of the political community; their territorial power and personal authority were vital to the running of the country. Attainders thus became as much a method of political control as one of fiscal advantage.[6]

It used to be argued that Edward IV and Henry VII launched calculated attacks on the power of the nobility after 1461, but this view is refuted by the fact that 84 per cent of noble attainders were reversed. The problem created by Henry VI was less that of overmighty subjects than of an undermighty king. It is possible that Edward IV tried to divide the nobility and gentry at the level of county government, undermining established networks of political affinity in favour of Crown domination. King John had driven a wedge between nobility and gentry in 1215—the trick was not new. But Edward's policy on reversing attainders was consistent: figures for knights and esquires show that 79 and 76 per cent of attainders among those respective social groups were reversed, which squares with the figure for the nobility. Only at a social level outside the governing elite were figures for reversals lower: for yeomen, clerics, and merchants they were 47, 36, and 29 per cent respectively. Obscurity was thus no protection: the lower a person's rank the more difficult it was to secure restoration in law and lands. The time taken for heirs to obtain reversals varied: Edward IV reversed forty-two of his 140 attainders, but forty-three heirs had to wait for Henry VII's reign. One was restored to favour by Richard III, leaving fifty-four of Edward's attainders unreversed. Of Richard III's hundred attainders, ninety-nine were reversed after Bosworth. Henry VII relented in respect of forty-six of the 138 persons attainted in Parliament during his reign. Finally six more heirs were restored under Henry VIII, leaving 86 unrestored.[7]

The effect of these measures upon the Crown's finances is hard to quantify. Acts of attainder tightened the king's political grip but they did not do much more. If proscriptions had been permanent, vast inheritances would have escheated to the Crown: attainders would have made the major contribution to the augmentation of income before Henry VIII dissolved the religious houses. Yet, although proceeds of sales and sums taken from the attainted before restoration of their lands were considerable, some forfeited estates always had to be shared with the victors after each stage of the civil wars. So attainders kept pressure off the Crown's meagre resources in the short term, but long-term endowment was beyond their range. Seven noble and seventeen knightly inheritances at most were retained by the Crown. The remaining 119 estates that were kept were those of esquires, clerics, yeomen, and merchants—lands of relatively small value. It is, however, true that the Yorkists and Henry VII administered their assets more efficiently than their predecessors. Except during a brief interlude after Bosworth, they adopted the latest management techniques of the great baronial estates, transferring Crown lands from the control of the exchequer, which farmed them out at fixed rents, to that of surveyors, receivers, and auditors, who specialized in maximizing income.[8] The key figure was the receiver, who was responsible for collecting rents, making new leases, expelling bad tenants, and authorizing repairs. He accounted personally in the king's chamber, which under Edward IV and Henry VII turned into the financial department of the royal household. The king's coffers in the chamber became the main treasury, and other revenues began to be transferred there, such as foreign pensions, loans and benevolences, and some taxation too. To store money in the king's coffers was more or less to keep it under the royal bed. There was nothing advanced about this system except that it worked: the exchequer was given a subordinate status and did not fully recover its dominance in royal finance until 1554, though customs duties and sheriffs' accounts continued to be received and audited there.

Edward IV began this 'land revenue' experiment in 1461, Richard III continued and extended his brother's policy, and the system was adopted and perfected by Henry VII after 1487. So it was from the chamber that these kings appointed officials, struck bargains for the sale of forfeited estates and the wardship of heirs during their minorities, compounded for feudal dues, and generally oversaw their finances. Often transactions would be completed informally: Edward IV several times took accounts verbally, and Henry VII examined and signed chamber accounts himself, and then discharged the accountants without further reckoning. But no king could oversee everything personally, and trusted councillors and intimates played a prominent role in the wider process of auditing land revenues. Whether flexibility in the taking of accounts offered rewards greater than straightforward convenience is doubtful, but the central question had been tackled—the need to extract every last penny from the Crown's estates.

English royal finance bristles with difficulties, but some indication of the rate and extent of recovery after 1461 can be given.[9] Of Henry VI's net income in 1432–3, £10,500 came from land revenues and £26,000 from customs. Exact comparison with the income of Edward IV is impossible, because no accounts of the Yorkist chamber have survived, but during the last eight years of his reign net income from land was about £20,000 per annum and from customs £35,000 per annum. Richard III's cash receipts from land rose to between £22,000 and £25,000 per annum, plus another £4,600 or so from sources linked to land. In other words, cash receipts from land doubled under Yorkist rule. The arithmetic does not reveal what proportions of extra income came from increased efficiency rather than from escheats and forfeitures; it cannot calculate the Crown's total resources, which included direct taxation, benevolences, and foreign pensions; but an estimate of Edward IV's total income in his last year is between £90,000 and £93,000. He was thus the first king of England since Henry II to die solvent. Net receipts from land may have dropped sharply at the beginning of Henry VII's reign, but had recovered by 1492–5 to £11,000 per annum. Receipts then rose spectacularly when the full impact of Henry VII's chamber finance was experienced: royal income from all sources averaged £104,800 per annum in 1502–5. This figure comes from John Heron's record of chamber receipts and is reliable. Land revenues brought a net cash yield of £40,000 per annum, customs realized the same amount but not all in cash, and lay and clerical taxation supplied an average of £13,600 per annum. By the end of the reign total revenue was £113,000 per annum: land revenues went as high as £42,000 annually in 1504–9. So Henry VII perfected Yorkist techniques once he had appreciated their significance. In line with current practices, he managed his estates efficiently.

Yet stability could not be achieved by financial recovery alone. Edward IV and Henry VII were successful rulers in great part because they availed themselves of the services of hard-working and experienced councillors, and the striking feature of their mutual approach was continuity. Out of forty of Edward IV's councillors who were still alive after 1485, twenty-two became councillors to Henry VII, notably John Morton, Thomas Rotheram, and John Dynham; and twenty of Richard III's councillors served the new dynasty, of whom Rotheram and Dynham were again two. Henry VII's Council was attended by fifteen close relatives of various Yorkist councillors, including the Bourchiers and Wydevilles. Others, such as Sir Richard Croft and Richard Empson, had likewise served the Yorkists. These men were added to the nucleus of a council which Henry had brought with him from exile in Brittany and France. Edward IV had 124 councillors between 1461 and 1483, but subtracting diplomats the number is 105. Before the revolts of 1469–70, sixty councillors were active: 20 nobles, 25 ecclesiastics, 11 officials, and 4 others. During his second reign eighty-eight councillors served: 21 nobles, 35 ecclesiastics, 23 officials, and 9 others.

Henry VII had 227 councillors between 1485 and 1509: 43 nobles, 61 ecclesiastics, 45 courtiers, 49 officials, and 27 lawyers. The division among various groups is similar to that of Edward IV's Council but it is the continuity of personnel that surprises.[10]

The functions of the Council were threefold: to advise the king on matters of policy, to administer the realm, and to adjudicate disputes.[11] Councillors had, however, a wide remit: consultation and the consent of the realm were vital to the smooth working of the political process, and councillors had the task of assessing opinion in an age when rumour and prophecy were ubiquitous. Opinion was most thoroughly tested in time of Parliament, but Parliaments were not regularly in session under the Yorkists and early Tudors until the Reformation Parliament assembled in 1529. Councillors thus worked to the mutual benefit of king and realm: they took the political temperature and assumed administrative responsibility; they built up networks of contacts at Court and in the provinces, making themselves the eyes and ears of the prince as well as his executives. In the Rainbow Portrait of Elizabeth I at Hatfield House, the queen's golden cloak is adorned with eyes and ears, but not mouths. This symbolizes the role of her councillors, chiefly William Cecil, Lord Burghley. As Sir John Davies (1569–1626) wrote: 'many things she sees and hears through them but the Judgement and Election are her own.'

Under Edward IV and Henry VII the Council became a real governing institution. Its members therefore had to work efficiently, and Fortescue, stressing the point, anticipated Wolsey, Thomas Cromwell, and Cecil by recommending reform. He knew from experience that large aristocratic councils bred faction and were riddled with private vested interests. To enable the Council to function as an executive board he urged the exclusion of magnates who claimed a councillor's place by virtue of high birth alone (*consiliarii nati*), and proposed that twelve clerics and twelve laymen be appointed to a standing or 'continual' council on grounds of ability. In advocating this reconstruction he assumed that the great officers of state would automatically serve on the Council. Otherwise his intention was that councillors should be 'the wisest and best disposed men that can be found in all the parts of this land', though to satisfy honour four bishops and four nobles were to serve for a year on the Council in turn, making a total of thirty-two members.[12] Lastly, Fortescue emphasized that his general principle was to create a Council equipped to foster the 'public good' of the realm, a theme that reappeared in the writings of Thomas More, Thomas Elyot, and Thomas Starkey.

Yet the crucial element in Fortescue's scheme was his desire to reduce the household element in government — the 'men of [the king's] chamber [and] of his household'. Since Richard II's minority, efforts had several times been made in Parliament to appoint named persons to membership of the Council to assist the great officers. But this reflected the politics of the period and was less an attempt to reform the Council than to pack it with the clients of faction leaders. So Fortescue's scheme was not parliamentary: his idea mirrored Edward IV's decision to make his Council his premier ruling instrument. The rise of the executive King's Council under Edward IV, Henry VII, and Henry VIII was cumulative. By the beginning of Elizabeth's reign the reconstituted Privy Council operated as a corporate board of leading office-holders, implementing its decisions by means of letters signed by seven or eight councillors ordering things to be done, and acting as the decisive authority in routine financial administration, religious enforcement, military organization, socio-economic policy, and local government. But constitutional tradition bisected this development. The old baronial theory that 'representatives' from among those normally summoned to Parliament should be consulted at times of political crisis remained entrenched. This theory could be used to attack ministers and councillors, and formed a prominent part of the manifesto of the Pilgrims of Grace in 1536. Burghley even deferred to it during the crisis of 1584 when it was feared Elizabeth might be assassinated. So the Council worked in co-operation with Parliament; except in 1491, 1525, 1544–6, and 1594–9, no attempt was made to levy non-parliamentary taxation in the Tudor period. Fortescue wrote that an English king does not tax his subjects nor change the laws 'without the grant or assent of his whole realm expressed in Parliament'; this by 1461 was firm convention. And it implied strength not weakness. As Henry VIII explained in 1542: 'We at no time stand so highly in our estate royal, as in time of Parliament, wherein we as head, and you as members, are conjoined and knit together into one body politic.' But the boundaries of Parliament's power were established politically: whether the whole realm in Parliament could legitimize Henry VIII's supremacy over the church was disputed by More, who lost the argument and his head.[13]

Since the monarchy's refoundation began in 1461 and was resumed by the Tudors, who at first used similar administrative methods and even many of the same councillors, it is fruitless to maintain that Bosworth marked a new dawn. Of course, this does not mean that administrative continuity was total: Henry VII's foreign and ecclesiastical policies had novel aspects, while the fiscal intensity of his rule was distinctive. Politics from 1455 to 1500 were volatile, violent, and pre-emptive; the dynastic swings of 1461, 1470–1, and 1485 speak for themselves. Yet this situation was not unique. Although he had expelled the English from Paris, Charles VII's nobility plotted against him in 1437, 1440, and 1446: there was mayhem and misrule in many parts of France. So Charles (1422–61) reorganized his army — something the English monarchy neglected to do — and strengthened his finances: *tailles* (poll taxes) and *aides* (sales taxes) were revived and collected without parliamentary consent. Louis XI (1461–83) continued this work, provoking civil war in 1465. The War of the Public Weal was stirred by malcontents who — like Warwick and Clarence in 1469 — adopted 'commonwealth' as their platform. Claude de Seyssel (citing Roman history) wrote: 'men unable to get the management of great affairs . . . by merit, beneficence, and authority of the senate found chances to win the favour of the people by persuading them to self-indulgent courses on the pretext of the common weal' — this might have been Fortescue speaking![14]

The aims of Charles VII, Louis XI, Edward IV, and Henry VII can be summarized in a sentence: they wished to control their realms and to create administrative machinery to channel disposable wealth into royal coffers. Yet by recommending this, Fortescue contradicted himself when he wrote of England as a 'mixed' monarchy (*regnum politicum et regale*), unlike Louis XI's France. He forgot that, if the re-endowment of the Crown proved successful, the 'regal' element would overtake the 'political'. This started to happen under Henry VII and Henry VIII, but sales of Crown lands during the 1540s restored the balance: by 1547 two-thirds of the ex-religious property was alienated, while further grants by Edward VI and Mary brought the figure to three-quarters. After Henry VIII's death the king could not 'live of his own' despite the great spoliation. So the wheel turned full circle.

Since centralization and an effective bureaucracy took priority under Edward IV, Fortescue was doubtless unaware of his inconsistency. Court methods remained crucial, if only because the monarch's person was the regime's most spectacular asset. The fifteenth century was the age of household government. 'National' institutions such as the exchequer and chancery had long existed under the Crown but had tended to become inflexible. The emphasis shifted towards 'intimate' administration based on the royal household. So Edward IV and Henry VII directed the 'land revenue' experiment from the chamber; Henry VIII turned the king's coffers into his deposit treasury for the proceeds of the dissolved religious houses; and Francis I tried to create a central cash reserve based on the king's coffers as well as a new official, the *trésorier de l'Épargne*, to replace his outdated financial system. But in the mid-sixteenth century the trend was reversed. In particular, the exchequer was streamlined and the executive Privy Council assumed responsibility for routine financial administration acting as a corporate board. Both cash reserves and accounting procedures were removed from the household and reabsorbed into the exchequer. So, whereas Edward IV and Henry VII were involved on an almost daily basis in the minutiae of revenue-raising and cash disbursement, Elizabeth exercised little immediate supervision over cashflow and accounting: these decisions and operations were controlled by Burghley and the Privy Council, though the queen decided in principle how her revenue would be managed.[15]

An issue not discussed by Fortescue was peacetime taxation. Did the king's subjects have a duty to meet the escalating costs of normal government through taxation when the 'ordinary' revenue of the Crown was insufficient? Attempts had first been made to obtain taxes for non-military purposes in the 1380s and 1390s, but they sparked resistance. Henry IV, whose charges and mounting debts twice forced him to plead necessity before

Parliament, made renewed efforts. But the principle was not established that taxation should be authorized for the maintenance of normal government. Such radical ideas were, however, ventilated during the sixteenth century: peacetime taxation was secured between 1534 and 1555. Thereafter taxation was still associated with maintenance of the royal estate, but a sign of Elizabeth's conservatism was her emphasis on the fact or threat of war. The principle of taxation in recognition of beneficial rule alone was eschewed.[16] Yet Elizabeth insisted that taxation be available for 'essential' purposes, and, when Lord Keeper Bacon argued in Parliament that all 'extraordinary' costs had always been relieved by taxation, he repudiated Fortescue's claim that only 'extraordinary' expenditure *above the usual average* was chargeable to taxation.

The Renaissance is a movement often misunderstood. Assumptions about the 'rebirth' of art, architecture, and letters, the 'novel' attempts of scholars to Christianize pagan authors, and the association of the civic republicanism of Italian cities such as Florence and Venice with political liberty and the dignity and perfectibility of man are too simplistic. The idea that the Christian and classical components of western civilization could be fused into a more harmonious and valid interpretation of the world and of man permeated the Middle Ages but, after Dante and Petrarch, it was articulated more vigorously and self-consciously. Yet the spirit of the Renaissance came later to England than to Italy; it was less manifest in the fine arts than in humane letters or grammar; and it was received largely at second-hand, travelling from Burgundy and France, not directly from Italy. Only with Wolsey's and Henry VIII's artistic patronage was the balance adjusted somewhat. Humanism understood in the strict sense of the study of humane letters reached England in the fifteenth century, where it was purified by scholars in London, Oxford, and Cambridge who emphasized Platonism and the study of Greek literature as the means of better understanding and writing. This group was a small minority whose views were controversial; during the 1510s and 1520s they were challenged to the 'war of the grammarians' by hardline Latinists in the universities (Wolsey and Thomas More intervened more than once on the side of the 'Greeks').

They were, however, influential. Those who migrated to the young Henry VIII's Court included John Colet, Thomas Linacre, William Lily, Richard Pace, Cuthbert Tunstall, and More himself. Three humanists of the next generation, Thomas Elyot, Thomas Starkey, and Richard Moryson, were on the fringes of this group: Elyot was a Platonist, but Starkey and Moryson were inspired by Italian civic republicanism.

The humanists were not, of course, the first to emphasize the value of classical learning. Chaucer had quoted Ovid and the Roman poets as well as the Italian poet Boccaccio, and John Gower showed familiarity with the *Secreta secretorum* attributed to Aristotle, but the forerunners of humanism tended to cite the classics as mere *exempla* or as fuel for their allegorical interpretations. Change came during the fifteenth century, although the earliest humanists were patrons rather than practitioners, bishops and nobles who fostered the careers of scholars, collected interesting books and manuscripts, and donated them to college or monastic libraries. Humphrey, duke of Gloucester (1391–1447), was the most significant patron: advised by Piero del Monte, an Italian humanist who had come to England as a papal tax collector, he assembled a library that included translations of Plato, Aristotle, and Plutarch, the works of Livy, Caesar, Cicero, and Suetonius, and modern humanist treatises by Petrarch, Salutati, Poggio, Bruni, and others. The duke's literary patronage included Tito Livio Frulovisi, Antonio Beccaria, Leonardo Bruni (translator of Aristotle's *Politics*), Pier Candido Decembrio (translator of Plato's *Republic*), and John Lydgate (who knew the work of Dante, Petrarch, and Boccaccio as well as Greek and Roman authors). His influence persuaded Oxford University to include the *Nova rhetorica* of Cicero, the *Metamorphoses* of Ovid, and the works of Virgil as alternative set books for the study of rhetoric, and between 1439 and 1444 he presented 280 volumes to the university for public use. These books served to stimulate the new and to revive much of the older learning.[17]

Another Oxford benefactor was William Grey, later bishop of Ely (d. 1478), who attended the lectures of Guarino da Verona at Ferrara and besides studying the classics took a keen interest in philosophy. He moved to Rome, where he came into contact with leading humanists and, despite his preference for theology, collected classical and modern humanist manuscripts, employing his own scribes when necessary. He presented 200 manuscripts to Balliol College and was instrumental in financing the construction of the library there. He also presented books to Peterhouse at Cambridge and his patronage extended to Niccolò Perotti and to two Englishmen, John Free and John Gunthorpe, whose studies at Ferrara he financed. Free, whom John Tiptoft, earl of Worcester, also patronized, taught medicine but was equally renowned for his knowledge of philosophy and civil law. His command of Greek was exceptional, and he translated, lectured, and wrote rhetorical treatises in the style characteristic of Italian humanism. His translation of the *Calvitii encomium* of Synesius of Cyrene, a satire on the sophists in the form of a eulogy on baldness, was later printed in the same edition as Erasmus's *Praise of Folly* at Basle.[18]

The exchange was reciprocal and several Italian scholars taught at Oxford and Cambridge. Stefano Surigone lectured on grammar and rhetoric between 1454 and 1471, Cornelio Vitelli was praelector in Greek at New College in 1475, and lecturers at Cambridge included Lorenzo da Savona in 1478 and Caio Auberino in 1483–4. Free, who died in 1465, was the first Englishman to reach Italian standards of classical scholarship. But more significant than individuals were organized centres of study, for the major preoccupation of the humanists was education. Some 114 endowed schools functioned in England by 1499, of which eighty-five were founded after 1450. The first humanist centre to have a grammar school attached to it was Magdalen College, Oxford, founded by William of Waynflete, bishop of Winchester (1447–86)—he set Wolsey an example by suppressing religious houses to help meet the cost. Magdalen took a great stride forward in educational organization and grammar was the foundation of the school curriculum: teachers and former students quickly monopolized the writing of set books for school use. John Anwykyll, the first master, printed passages in English translation from the plays of Terence for his pupils in 1483 and the same year published the *Compendium totius grammaticae*, an abridgement of treatises by Perotti and Valla. Other Magdalen men who compiled grammar books were John Stanbridge, William Lily, and Robert Whittington. In fact, Lily's *Grammar*, originally written for pupils at St Paul's School, was proclaimed the official textbook for use in schools throughout the realm by Henry VIII in 1543.

Although the Council of Vienne (1311-12) had directed that provision should be made for the teaching of Greek at Oxford, the university had done little to give effect to this recommendation. So Magdalen and, later, Corpus Christi College, founded by Richard Fox, filled the gap, and those teaching or learning the rudiments in Oxford included men as diverse as Colet, John Stokesley, William Tyndale, Thomas More, and Reginald Pole. Although in the minority, Greek studies were sufficiently active to attract Erasmus to Oxford in 1499. Magdalen's lead was also followed at St Paul's School in London, which Colet refounded in 1508-10. The curriculum was to comprise Latin and Greek texts 'and good authors such as have the very Roman eloquence joined with wisdom, especially Christian authors that wrote their wisdom with clean and chaste Latin'. Excluded was the 'Latin adulterate' of scholasticism, the 'abusion which the later blind world brought in which more rather may be called blotterature than literature'.[19]

Colet travelled to France and Italy in the mid-1490s. Linacre had preceded him ten years before and William Grocyn, who began at Winchester and New College, studied in Florence between 1488 and 1491. They alone of their group mastered Greek at the Italian source. Colet, attracted by the Platonism of Marsilio Ficino and Pico della Mirandola, applied his learning to Bible study. His method, like Ficino's, mirrored Plotinus and the later Platonists, though it also respected Aristotle and his medieval commentators. Colet lectured at Oxford on the Epistles of St Paul in 1497-8, when his exposition broke new ground: he stressed the historical circumstances in which the Epistles were composed, treated St Paul as an individual personality, and adumbrated belief in a personal and redemptive Christ. These were exciting ideas at a time when the Lady Margaret Professor of Divinity was lecturing on the 'Quodlibets' of Duns Scotus.[20] The message of salvation was clearly stated and Thomas More, who submitted himself to Colet's spiritual direction, owed much to him, as did Erasmus of Rotterdam, whom most English humanists adopted as their European mentor. Erasmus, who visited England several times between 1499 and 1517, exclaimed, 'When Colet speaks I might be listening to Plato!'[21]

Together they fused the evangelical piety of the Netherlands with Christian Platonism. But the Englishmen's relationship with Erasmus was idealized; it contained inherent contradictions. Erasmus aspired to 'peace of mind' and 'moderate reform' through the application and development of critical insight and the power of humane letters. He eschewed politics; some said he was a dreamer. Colet, More, Tunstall, and Pace, by contrast, became councillors to Henry VIII: they resolved to enter politics and Erasmus disapproved, predicting the misfortunes that befell those who put their trust in princes.

English humanism had another important facet—the humanist study of law. This began in Italy with Valla's proof that the Donation of Constantine was false: the document granting spiritual and temporal authority over the Western Empire to Pope Sylvester I had been forged in the eighth or ninth century. Valla's attack was philological and historical rather than specifically legal, but historicism and legalism were virtually inseparable and attempts to cleanse the Augean stables of law at French and Italian universities were paralleled by developments in England at the inns of court.[22] English law was essentially common or customary law reinforced by acts of Parliament; it was both written and unwritten. The written elements were to be found in the records of the courts of law, in printed statutes, and on the rolls of Parliament; the unwritten corpus of law was enshrined upon the collective memory of the legal profession, in the minds of judges, practitioners, and officials, and was expounded and decided by pleadings and judgments in the course of specific litigation.

Despite popular prejudice against lawyers, the study of law was far from inimical to English humanists and both More and Elyot were legally educated. True, provision of legal education at the inns of court was not new in the fifteenth century, since 'readings' or lectures given during the Lent and summer vacations were already established. But by 1460 elaborate moots or mock trials were being held to teach students the correct forms of pleading, and 'readings' had expanded into complete courses of lectures lasting three to four weeks, two hours a day, four days a week. The term 'reading' itself became a misnomer, for the delivery of a prepared script was replaced by seminars on a set text in which judges and benchers in the audience engaged the 'reader' in debate while students listened or took notes.[23] Both Fortescue in *De laudibus legum anglie* and Elyot in *The Book Named the Governor* observed the new system in operation, Elyot comparing the techniques of legal debate to those of ancient rhetoric and suggesting that the study of English law was the perfect way to complete the education of young gentlemen.[24] His advice was accepted during the second half of the sixteenth century, when the inns of court assumed the role of a third university.

The consequences of intellectual revival at the inns of court can be seen in the later years of the fifteenth century. For the first time since Henry II's reign lawyers began to innovate on a wide scale from within their profession: in chancery and king's bench novel procedures were devised to tackle contemporary needs in cases of disputed title to land, inheritance, debt, breach of contract, promises to perform acts or services, deceit, nuisance, defamation, and the sale of goods.[25] These innovations were the internal reforms of judges, lawyers, and court officials, and they mirrored the humanists' conviction that the law had to be changed to meet current social conditions, not that litigants should try to make their pleas fit outdated law. Next, lawyers gained self-conscious perception of their 'common erudition' and began formulating principles whereby their law was systematically expounded, and written and unwritten law was assimilated. Attention was not, however, confined to secular law: common lawyers examined canon and papal law too. Although the substance of English law owed little to Roman law, most practitioners were acquainted with both systems and in the climate of humanism a number seized upon points of conflict between common and canon law. They advanced arguments designed to harmonize these twin species of law, for in certain areas of overlap, for example debt, restitution, bastardy, and the age of legal majority, the laws of church and state contradicted each other. The opinion of a vocal minority at the inns of court was that similar decisions should be given in similar types of lawsuit in both royal and church courts, and that the canon law should defer to common law. This type of theory was immensely important because it could amount, with royal support, to political ideology, and the demand that canon law should yield to common law was, in fact, a hallmark of Henry VIII's platform during the Reformation.

The impact of humanism upon English thought and religion during this period must be seen in perspective. Humanism was only an option for the select few and its historical importance properly derives from its educational role in challenging scholasticism and the papacy. The Yorkist and early Tudor period was characterized for the majority of English people by traditional forms of religious devotion: liturgical worship, mysticism, pilgrimages, the veneration of images, prayers to the Virgin Mary and local saints, miracles, and prophetic revelations.[26] The most popular devotional writers were still the fourteenth-century mystics: Richard Rolle, Walter Hilton, Margery Kempe, Dame Julian of Norwich, and the anonymous author of *The Cloud of Unknowing*. In fact, more manuscripts of Rolle's works are extant than of any other pre-Reformation writer. These mystics marked a reaction against the learned theology and philosophy of the universities: St Thomas à Kempis was their inspiration, not St Thomas Aquinas. But their emphasis on the contemplative life and pursuit of perfection cast them as the lay equivalents of monastic instructors. Their devotion to the Passion of Christ and the Holy Name of Jesus was intense and orthodox, unlike that of the heretical Lollards. Their common preoccupations were with death, judgement, heaven, and hell; the doctrine of tribulation and the need to follow Christ's example; the virtues of silence and solitude, of obedience, patience, meekness, and love; and the concept of life as a battle between grace and nature, or between the temptations of the flesh and God's will. In an age when the monastic life was seen as the ideal expression of Christianity, lay men and women emulated its pattern to the best of their abilities, either as individuals or members of a household.

Lay piety was also expressed in a highly materialistic form before the Reformation. Almost two-thirds of English parish churches were built or rebuilt during the fifteenth century. Spectacular examples of the wealth poured into church building in this period which can still be seen include St Mary Redcliffe in Bristol, St Peter Mancroft in Norwich, and the East Anglian 'wool' churches. There were innumerable gifts to monastic houses and nunneries; to furnish parish churches; to purchase rich vestments, plate, and jewels; and to adorn images and shrines. Chantries, hospitals, religious guilds, and alphabet schools were endowed by pious lay people. Votive and requiem masses were likewise purchased, while smaller legacies bought 'lights' or candles to burn in memory of deceased persons. Religious guilds or confraternities played a constructive role in the life of the whole community assisting social cohesion: they were associations of lay and clerical persons integrated by sex as well as social status. Women made up perhaps half the total membership and single as well as married women could belong.[27] Guilds chiefly undertook, in the name of the Trinity, the Virgin Mary, or a saint, to provide members with solemn funerals and requiem masses for their souls, but they also repaired bridges and highways, provided fresh water facilities and conduits in towns such as Bristol, Norwich, and Ashburton, offered members business contacts or proto-banking facilities, paid midwives, looked after town clocks, and played a prominent part in civic ceremonial and the rituals of the communal year. At Henry VII's formal entry into Bristol in 1487, for example, an elephant with a clockwork Resurrection scene on its back was provided.

Yet the pre-Reformation church was dominated by the clergy and did not permit the laity an active part in its administration or public worship. What little people could hear of the mass through the chancel screen was lost on all but the handful who could understand Latin. Worshippers went to adore the consecrated elements but were not expected to communicate more than three times a year. When they received communion, they partook of the bread alone; and men and women communicated separately except at nuptial masses. Preaching was not so rare in the parishes as is sometimes alleged, but most sermons of which we have any knowledge were stale, hackneyed, and uninspiring. Either allegorical or anecdotal, packed with violent fantasies and pagan narratives, they could have done little to teach congregations the principles of Christianity, though some preachers adequately explained the meaning of Easter and the penitential system of the church.[28] Sermons were doubtless best in London, where two-thirds of the clergy were graduates. In the provinces, however, the parish clergy might be less well educated than some of their parishioners. Roughly one-fifth of clergy in the diocese of Canterbury between 1454 and 1486 were graduates, while only one-tenth of the parochial incumbents of Surrey at this time had degrees. Of a total of 1,429 men presented to benefices in the diocese of Lincoln between 1495 and 1520, 261 were graduates, while, out of 1,454 presentees in the diocese of Norwich between 1503 and 1528, 256 had degrees. In fact, the numbers of graduates were steadily rising, though whether this improved the parochial ministry until the numbers of clergy with degrees comprised a much higher proportion of the total is arguable. It was educated priests who were most likely to be absentees on the grounds that they were required for secular or diocesan adminis-tration, and few clergy were graduates in theology, which was the best training for pastoral work. Of clerical graduates in Lincoln diocese, 35 per cent held degrees in arts, another 35 per cent in canon or civil law, and only 11 per cent in theology.[29]

To assess the professional standards of non-graduate clergy is difficult, since most of our information comes from reports filed during episcopal or archidiaconal visitations. Such reports, of course, were made only when priests had failed to meet the norms the parish expected and when the laity were more anxious about standards than their pastors. On the other hand, the comments found in literary sources are largely stylized. While 'Sloth the Parson' in Langland's *Vision of Piers Plowman* preferred to eat, sleep, or lie in bed with his mistress until mass was over, was ignorant of the Lord's Prayer and canon law, and was unable to construe a single verse of the Psalms and explain it to his parishioners — his speciality was tracking hares — this was poetic fiction.[30] The popular butts of literary satire were clergy and lawyers; indeed Langland's source was the *Oculus sacerdotis* of William Page, the fourteenth-century homilist:

And many are the priests, in these days, who neither know the law of God, nor teach others. But giving themselves up to sloth, they spend their time upon banquetings and carousals, they covet earthly things, they grow wise in earthly things, constantly in the streets, rarely in the church, slow to investigate the faults of their parishioners, ready to track the footprints of hares or some other wild beast . . . More freely do they offer food to a dog than to a poor man; more wait upon them at table than at mass; they wish to have men servants and maid servants with them, but not clerics.[31]

Canon law required priests to preach at least four times a year, visit the sick, say the daily liturgies, and hear the confessions of parishioners at least once a year. They were to lead upright lives, dress suitably, avoid inns and brothels, and ensure that their relations with women were above reproach. In practice, there were priests who failed to hold services at the proper times, who did not preach, and whose habits were aggressive — the rector of Addington in Northamptonshire, cited before the Lincoln consistory court in 1526, had two children by his cook and marched about the village in chain-mail. But the vast majority of clergy said their daily offices properly, though whether they preached or visited the sick is arguable. More conspicuous were their morals, for it was all too easy for a priest to behave like other villagers: to make a mistress of his housekeeper, and to spend the day cultivating his glebe. Although few charges were brought in church courts for offences of this type before Henry VIII's reign, 12.5 per cent of parochial incumbents in the diocese of Lincoln were reported as 'having a woman' by 1520. One-fifth of these priests were not suspected of incontinence, but another fifth were definitely suspected or convicted, while there were many other cases of immorality.[32] Moreover, poorer clergy attempted to augment their stipends by farming and thereby focused attention on the church's main economic problem, for many benefices (chiefly in the north) were inadequately endowed; indeed pluralism might be *necesssary* if a priest was to be supported. Other livings in stark contrast were valuable, even marketable commodities which lay patrons treated as pieces of disposable property. If, however, the bishops resisted ruthless patrons by rejecting unsuitable candidates for preferment when they could, many inadequately ordained or pastorally unfit candidates still met the basic legal requirements or came armed with papal dispensations.[33] So the pre-Reformation church was free of major scandals, but such abuses as non-residence, pluralism, concubinage, and the parochial clergy's neglect to repair chancels continued to attract attention. Also tithes disputes, probate and mortuary fees, charges for saying mass on special occasions, and unduly harsh treatment of suspects in heresy cases could become flashpoints. Indeed, although its nature and fashionable extent were transformed when Henry VIII's first divorce reached the parliamentary agenda, anticlericalism did exist at the advent of the Tudors, though on a far smaller scale than in Germany.

What can be said with confidence is that heretics were vastly outnumbered by orthodox English people in the fifteenth century, though the exact size of the Lollard community is elusive. Their founder, John Wyclif (*c.*1329–84) was an Oxford scholastic philosopher and theologian who had entered the service of John of Gaunt, and who accordingly escaped trial in the church courts when a university commission found him guilty of teaching erroneous doctrines. His earliest followers were intellectuals, while his demands that the clergy confine themselves to their pastoral duties, his support for an English translation of the Bible, and repeated attacks on church property won the attention of certain politicians who at first protected Lollard preachers and then provided havens for the copying of Lollard manuscripts. But Sir John Oldcastle's revolt (1414) marked a turning-point, since it cemented the link between heresy, sedition, and treason already recognized in Europe, and enabled the bishops to initiate the systematic persecution that canon law authorized, but for which secular co-operation had previously been lacking.[34]

There had been little heresy in England before Wyclif and few heretics burned before 1401. An Albigensian was burned at London as early as 1210, while in 1222 an apostate deacon who had turned Jew for love of a Jewish woman was degraded at a provincial council at Oxford and delivered to the sheriff, who burned him. Otherwise, the only reported cases were those upon the heresy statutes of Richard II, Henry IV, and Henry V. Legislation against Lollardy in 1382 condemned heretical sermons and commanded sheriffs and others to assist the bishops by arresting and imprisoning suspects to be tried in the church courts: the context was the Peasants' Revolt in the previous year. The statute *De heretico comburendo* was enacted in 1401 to permit the burning of Lollards who refused to abjure their opinions or who had relapsed into heresy after previous abjuration and penance; this was the first English lay enactment that settled the secular arm's duty to burn heretics properly convicted in church courts. Lastly, an act of 1414 required a wide range of secular officers and judges, sheriffs, JPs, and municipal officials to assist the bishops in the task of detecting and suppressing heresy. It also provided for the forfeiture to the Crown of the lands and goods of convicted heretics, and empowered the justices of king's bench, the assize judges, and JPs to detect heresy by the secular procedures of presentment and indictment, though persons accused were to be handed to the bishops or their commissaries for trial in the church courts within ten days.[35]

That the heresy law was enforced in the century before the Reformation is clear from the records of trials between 1423 and 1522. Evidence survives of 544 trials in this period which resulted in 375 abjurations, 19 canonical purgations, and 29 (possibly 34) burnings. (The outcome of the remaining cases is unknown.)[36] Of course, these figures are minima—the records of the church courts before the Reformation are generally quite defective. Yet it is plain that, quantitatively, heresy was not a serious threat before the break with Rome, though whether it was a threat qualitatively is harder to judge, since the later fifteenth century saw a resurgence of popular Lollardy in specific regions. These were notably Essex, Kent, the Chilterns, the Thames valley, the Midlands, parts of East Anglia, the towns of Bristol, Coventry, and Colchester, and the wards of Coleman Street, Cripplegate, Cordwainer, and Cheap in London. Later Lollards whose backgrounds can be traced were mainly artisans—weavers, tailors, glovers, and skinners—or middlemen in the textile trade. But in Coventry some leading citizens and a former mayor were sympathizers, and in London there were Lollards among the civic and mercantile classes too. Indeed, by the early sixteenth century the London Lollards seem to have regarded themselves as the pioneers of southern dissent, an outlook justified by the fact that their networks of communication were to prove as useful for the dissemination of Lutheran books in the 1520s as for their own Bible translations and sermon cycles earlier.[37]

How far the Lollards were forerunners of the Protestant Reformation is arguable. They variously attacked papal authority, transubstantiation in the Eucharist, the veneration of images, clerical endowments, purgatory, indulgences, pilgrimages, and the use of music during the liturgy. They argued that Scripture was the sole authority for faith, preached sermons, and circulated Bible translations and religious tracts among their number. When the early Protestants ran across them, however, the two groups did not always agree.[38] Yet, if divergent strands appeared within Lollardy, and if Wyclif's teachings were diluted beyond recognition at popular level, in a quite different respect the Oxford reformer was ahead of his time. For his repeated insistence that the 'reformation of the church' was a political matter in the first instance was proved correct by Henry VIII. Like the German emperors during the Investiture Contest, Wyclif distinguished between the popes of the primitive church and their successors: in the earliest age of Christianity power had been exercised by lay priest–kings, while popes and clergy had been content to preach true doctrine and administer the sacraments. He therefore advocated a re-creation of the apostolic church in which tyrant–priests would be redeemed into holiness and deprived of their power by secular rulers.[39] Like Henry VIII he visualized the state in terms of the ruler's sovereignty and demanded the dissolution of the religious orders on the grounds that sovereignty cannot tolerate the existence of independent ecclesiastical corporations. All men should be equal as subjects under the Crown; the new order of society, born out of the reformation, would be one in which citizens obeyed the lay prince as priest and king.

Wyclif failed because his patron John of Gaunt would not imperil the stability of the realm by adopting a radical policy and because the weakness of the Crown and factional nature of politics during Richard II's minority precluded united action. (By contrast Henry VIII acted decisively once he had backed the radicals.) Yet the idea that reformation was a revolution by the head itself, an administrative act imposed from above by a right-minded government, was as prophetic as the association of the true state with sovereignty. In this respect, Wyclif's ideas sprang out of the circumstances of the Great Schism when the Catholic Church lost ground to nationalism. But, although England was a more centralized, less pluralist society than France, national identity developed late, and was a result, rather than the cause, of the Protestant Reformation. That there was a keen sense of 'Englishness' or 'nationhood' in the fifteenth century is plain, but there was no concept of England as a nation state. At the Council of Constance (1414–18) Henry V's delegates had highlighted the language, territory, and blood bonds of the English in arguing the case for separate voting rights. If, however, these were some distinctive features of nationality, 'abuttals' or boundaries became more important as Henry VI's loss of continental possessions made its impact. England's identity was soon associated with her coastline. A poem written in 1436, 'The Libel of English Policy', which was a plea for naval protection of English trade, concluded:

> Keep then the sea about in special,
> Which of England is the round wall,
> As though England were likened to a city,
> And the wall environ were the sea.[40]

The anonymous author of *The Commodities of England* (1451) reiterated that England was recognized by her natural frontiers and separate languages—he cited English, Welsh, and Cornish—but geographical, linguistic, or racial 'nationality' could never be tantamount to national sovereignty as long as the English church retained its separate legislatures and judiciary which claimed to be, within their areas of competence, independent of the Crown.[41]

It is true that fifteenth-century England had an accepted political theory: the realm was governed by a monarch who was the superior legislator but who could neither make law himself nor tax his subjects without their consent in Parliament.[42] The Anglo-papal Compromise of Avranches (1172) had, however, secured the church's right to self-regulation, and the jurisdictional independence of the Convocations of Canterbury and York, and of the ecclesiastical courts, had been enshrined in the opening clause of Magna Carta. King John had granted, 'for us and our heirs in perpetuity, that the English church shall be free, and shall have its rights undiminished and its liberties unimpaired'. This concession had received many royal confirmations. Politics came into play when spiritual jurisdiction touched the temporal rights of Crown and laity: Parliament had blocked papal provisions and controversial canons in the reigns of Edward III, Richard II, Henry IV, and Henry V. Yet *causes célèbres* did not make good law, and the weight of opinion was overwhelmingly in favour of the status quo and against sudden change. As Wyclif complained, the arguments against change were relentless: that *reformatio* would cause upheaval; that even then it might not succeed; that the time was not right; that present conditions were inappropriate. He met 'the normal responses made by any bureaucracy to a reformer who wanted to change things and do it in a hurry'.[43] John of Gaunt thought it was worse to risk the stability of the realm than to deflower the king's daughter. So the established juristic framework whereby parallel powers in church and state coexisted and owed allegiance to king and pope respectively ensured that the idea of England as a unitary state remained anachronistic before the 1530s, and whether Henry VIII's break with Rome itself amounted to an expression of unitary sovereignty is a question that will need to be investigated.

THE CONDITION OF ENGLAND

ENGLAND and Wales were predominantly agrarian societies, subject after 1520 to sustained population pressure. Obvious opportunities sprang from the enhanced level of demand that stimulated the development of capitalistic agriculture and a more commercialized industrial economy, but inflation, speculation in land and foodstuffs, unemployment, poverty, vagrancy, and urban squalor were the inevitable consequences of the sudden rise in population. The power of the state was negligible when faced by demographic, economic, and social changes, but we can take a relatively optimistic view of the period for one overriding reason: some regional crises apart, Tudor England managed to feed itself. A major national subsistence calamity was avoided.

It is true that higher rates of mortality followed bad harvests in 1519–21, 1527–9, 1544–5, 1549–51, 1554–6, 1586–7, and 1594–7, the most serious crop failures being in 1555–6 and 1596–7. In fact, as the effect of a bad harvest in any particular year lasted until the next good or average crop was gathered, the severest dearths lasted from 1555 to 1557, and 1596 to 1598. The former was especially harsh because it coincided with an influenza epidemic which began in 1555 and peaked in 1557–9. Then, when the harvests of 1596 and 1597 were ruined by too much rain, the worst famine of the century hit upland parishes and those in the valleys of areas of mixed agriculture which the rain had most affected. However, the north Midlands, Essex, and the south-west were largely spared in 1557–9, while in 1596–8 relatively few parishes in eastern England and the central Midlands suffered starvation, and relatively few in the south-east.[1]

In addition to crises caused by harvest failure, bubonic plague, pneumonia, smallpox, and a viral disease called 'the sweat' created short-term emergencies at least once per decade. But that plague epidemics were becoming localized in extent after the ravages of the Black Death is suggested by the fact that major outbreaks in Devon in 1546–7 and 1589–93, and in Staffordshire in 1593, did not spread to neighbouring villages, while in the 1520s and 1590s it seems that the worst outbreaks were centred on London. Of course, at some time or another most areas were afflicted by plague or influenza which wiped out 10 per cent or more of the population. But the principal centres of plague outbreaks were London, the Thames estuary, and the hinterlands of Colchester, Ipswich, and Norwich. These more densely populated areas were especially vulnerable because animal wastes in drains and excreta deposited in the streets attracted rats and flies. So, whereas mortality caused by harvest failure tended to hit hardest the upland regions where crops were grown under marginal conditions or where grains had to be purchased, these same regions were usually spared plague owing to their isolation. By contrast, whereas famine spared many parishes in the south-east and East Anglia which had local food supplies and convenient access to imported grain from abroad, the insanitary towns, mixed farming lowlands, and areas with well-developed communications were most at risk from plague.[2]

So, while dearth and disease proved devastating for the affected areas, especially for the towns of the 1590s, mass mortality on the national scale witnessed during the fourteenth century was absent even during the influenza epidemic of 1555–9. True, in addition to its other difficulties, Mary's regime faced the most serious mortality crisis since the Black Death: the population dropped by 200,000, or by 6 per cent. But, since some regions were relatively lightly affected, it is not proved that this was a national crisis in terms of its geographical extent. Also population growth was only temporarily interrupted. Indeed, the chronology, intensity, and restricted geographical range of famine in the sixteenth century suggest that starvation crises in England were abating, rather than worsening, over time, while epidemics took fewer victims than before in proportion to the expansion of population. The countryside escaped crisis during two-thirds of Elizabeth's reign and the rural population remained in surplus. When the towns suffered an excess of deaths over births, this surplus was sufficient both to increase the numbers who stayed on the land and to compensate for urban losses by migration to towns.

The matter is debatable, but there is much to be said for the
view that England was economically healthier, more expansive,
and more optimistic under the Tudors than at any time since
the Roman occupation of Britain. Recovery of population after
the ravages of the Black Death had been slow — slower than in
France, Germany, Switzerland, and some Italian cities. The
process of economic revitalization in pre-industrial societies was
basically one of recovery of population, and figures will be useful.
Before the famine of 1315–17 and the Black Death (1348–9),
the population of England and Wales was between 4 million and
5 million, perhaps as high as 5.5 million or 6 million, but by
1377 successive disasters had reduced it to 2.5 million. By 1450
there had been a further decline to 2 million but the population
stabilized at this level until gradual recovery began towards the
end of the century. Yet the figure for England (without Wales)
was still no higher than 2.26 million in 1525. Furthermore,
population growth was at first slow and discontinuous, and was
perhaps restricted to particular areas only. Not until 1520 did
growth accelerate but after 1525 it did so rapidly (see table 1).
Between 1525 and 1541 the English population grew extremely
fast, an impressive burst of expansion after long inertia. This rate
of growth slackened off somewhat after 1541, but the population
still continued to increase, with a reversal only in the late 1550s,
to reach 4.10 million in 1601. In addition, the population of
Wales rose from about 210,000 in 1500 to 380,000 by 1603.

TABLE 1. *English population totals, 1525–1601*

Year	Population total in millions
1525	2.26
1541	2.77
1551	3.01
1561	2.98
1571	3.27
1581	3.59
1591	3.89
1601	4.10

Source: E. A. Wrigley and R. S. Schofield, *The Population History of England,
1541–1871: A Reconstruction* (London, 1981), 531–2, 568.

These changes were the result of a complex process. The stagnation of fifteenth-century population was partly caused by disease in both towns and countryside, but two more important factors were low fertility and family limitation via late marriage. It seems that many couples delayed marriage until at least their mid-twenties, whereas at the time of the 1377 poll tax women had generally married in their mid- or late-teens. Population decline before 1500 was thus due to low birth-rates as well as high death-rates: it has been estimated from wills that 24.2 per cent of all males died unmarried during the period 1430–80, whilst 49 per cent of those who did marry died without a male heir.[3] Yet these conditions created a bubble of artificial prosperity: farm rents were discounted because tenants were so elusive and lords abandoned direct cultivation of their demesnes, which were leased to tenants on favourable terms. Rents were low, too, on peasants' customary holdings, labour services were commuted, and servile villeinage had virtually disappeared in England by 1500 except in parts of East Anglia. Money wages had risen to reflect the contraction of the wage-labour force after 1349 and food prices fell in real terms in response to reduced market demand. Perhaps this prosperity brought about increased fertility or perhaps there was a fall in the age of marriage. It does appear that by the 1480s a higher proportion of the population was marrying, which must have contributed to the rising birth-rate. Despite bad harvests in 1519–21, 1527–9, and 1544–5, fertility was high by 1550, when the evidence of parish registers is fully available. Demographers also calculate that expectation of life at birth was better after 1564 than before, though it varied from 41.7 years in 1581 to 35.5 years in 1591. In fact, between 1564 and 1586 mortality was less severe than it would be again before the end of the Napoleonic Wars: life expectancy at birth was roughly thirty-eight years. Although this should not obscure the fact that many children died in infancy while others lived to be fifty and a few to be ninety, the central portion of Elizabeth's reign was spared a crisis: the annual death-rate was never higher than 2.68 per cent of the population.[4] Acceleration in the growth of population was therefore possible: rising birth-rates after 1500 were complemented by gradual reductions in the severity of mortality.

Yet the geographical distribution of population was uneven,

since in an agrarian economy people lived largely where the land was able to support them. Ninety per cent of the Tudor population lived in the countryside and the remainder dwelt in towns, but three-quarters lived to the south and east of a line drawn from the Severn to the Humber. Although few farmers were completely self-reliant and increasing numbers were using markets for the sale or exchange of agricultural surpluses, every region or area had to have its basic means of support: some each of arable, pastoral, and woodland farming. The local emphasis on either crop growing or grass production varied with climate, soil, and slope, but in general the south-east part of the country contained the main regions of arable and mixed farming, and of rural industry. The northern counties contained pockets of arable farming, but here and in Wales, as well as in Devon and Cornwall to the far south-west, there were vast areas of open pasture, moorlands, and mountains where settlement was sparse. A useful dividing line can be drawn between Teesmouth and Weymouth: this distinguishes the more densely populated southern and eastern counties, where farming of grain and livestock predominated, from the pastoral regions to the north and west, where sheep, horses, and cattle were reared. There are obvious exceptions to this generalization: the rich grazing lands of the Fens and wood pastures of the Kent and Sussex Weald were pastoral enclaves in the south-east, and the mixed-farming areas of Herefordshire and the Welsh borderlands produced grain in the north-west.

The largest towns outside London were Norwich, Bristol, Exeter, York, Coventry, Salisbury, and King's Lynn, but by Henry VIII's reign none had a population in excess of 12,000 except London, which may have had 60,000 inhabitants. Norwich had 12,000 inhabitants, Bristol 10,000, Exeter, York, and Salisbury 8,000 each, Coventry 7,500, and King's Lynn 4,500. The populations of smaller towns such as Oxford, Cambridge, Ipswich, Canterbury, Colchester, and Yarmouth ranged from 2,600 to 5,000, but other towns were much smaller: Sheffield had 2,200 people and Stafford 1,550 as late as 1620. Unlike continental cities, no Tudor provincial town ever exceeded a population of 20,000, but Norwich reached 18,000 before it was hit by plague in 1579. Approximately 10 per cent of the Tudor population lived in towns, but half of this number was always accounted for by London. These proportions remained constant throughout the sixteenth century: London's population rose to 215,000 by 1603 and the aggregate for the provincial towns more or less kept pace. At the end of Elizabeth's reign Norwich had 15,000 inhabitants, Bristol 12,000, York 11,500, Exeter and Newcastle upon Tyne 9,000 each, and King's Lynn, Coventry, Salisbury, Plymouth, Oxford, Cambridge, Ipswich, Canterbury, Colchester, Yarmouth, Shrewsbury, Worcester, and Chester had populations of between 5,000 and 8,500. There were, however, considerable variations in the rates of growth of provincial towns during the sixteenth century: sustained growth was confined to established centres or to places where economic development was fastest, for instance Norwich, York, Newcastle upon Tyne, King's Lynn, and Yarmouth.

Population changes created increased market demand for agricultural commodities, with a consequent rise in prices that was exacerbated by short-term crises in 1555–9 and 1596–8 (see table 2). The period after 1520–9 was characterized by an increase both of agricultural prices as a whole and of grain prices

TABLE 2. *Index of agricultural prices, 1480–1609* (1450–99 = 100)

Decade	Average all grain prices	Average all animal products	Average wool prices
1480–9	114	107	113
1490–9	97	101	96
1500–9	112	102	93
1510–9	115	118	119
1520–9	154	105	111
1530–9	161	127	122
1540–9	187	159	153
1550–9	348	213	206
1560–9	316	236	205
1570–9	370	257	234
1580–9	454	295	225
1590–9	590	372	315
1600–9	560	387	348

Source: J. Thirsk (ed.), *The Agrarian History of England and Wales*, iv. *1500–1640* (Cambridge, 1967), 861–2.

relative to wool prices. Prices of animal products generally—
milk and cream, butter, cheese, eggs, wool, sheepskins, cattle
hides, etc.— rose faster than wool prices but not as fast as those
of wheat, barley, oats, and rye. Between 1450 and 1520 the
movement of wool prices had been commensurate with those
of grain. This reflected lack of population pressure and the
strength of cloth exports; cheaper grain prices perhaps also
enhanced the purchasing power of domestic consumers thereby
boosting home demand for textiles. But the rise in population
brought about two major changes. First, it created an upsurge
in demand for cereals, which gave farmers able to produce
surpluses for the market an opportunity to make huge profits.
Next, wool production lost some of its glitter, since the increased
demand for beef and mutton from wealthier households made
meat production a more profitable use of pasture.

The commercialization of agriculture must not be
exaggerated.[5] Market conditions after 1520 offered efficient
farmers the chance to practise capitalism, since internal and
coastal transport were adequate to move foodstuffs to and from
urban centres. The demands of London and the larger provincial
towns were a powerful magnet, but the pace of change was slow.
Agricultural efficiency was restricted and productivity low. There
was a shortage of land for cereal crops and commercial and
peasant farmers were in competition for what converted pasture
and reclaimed land were available. Intermittent hostility
prevailed, too, between the arable and pastoral sectors. Although
the two were basically complementary, since dung was essential
to grain production if soil was not to be exhausted, many sheep
pastures provided cloth to pay for luxury imports for the wealthy,
and cloth exports did not assist food supplies. So pamphleteers
argued that sheep farmers exacerbated the declining standard
of living that the majority of people suddenly experienced.
Certainly the impact of the sudden crescendo in demand for food,
and pressure on available resources after 1520, was as painful
as it was, arguably, beneficial as an economic stimulant. For
land hunger led to soaring rents, especially for new tenancies.
In the south some rents increased tenfold between 1510 and the
Civil War. In the Midlands the rent of meadowland rose fourfold
between 1540 and 1585, and that of arable land even more. Only
in the north were increases less, in areas where customary rights

enabled tenants to resist landlords' efforts to raise their incomes. Probably rent increases were worst in places where landowners amalgamated two or more adjacent farms for profit at the expense of outgoing tenants, a process condemned in Parliament and the pulpit as the chief cause of rural depopulation; and when commons were enclosed and wasteland reclaimed by landlords or squatters, peasant grazing rights were often extinguished too. The opinion of pamphleteers and preachers that the active land market nurtured a new entrepreneurial class of capitalists grinding the faces of the poor is hyperbole. Yet it is fair to say that not all landowners, claimants, and squatters were entirely scrupulous in their attitudes: a vigorous market arose among dealers in defective titles to land, with resulting harassment of many legitimate occupiers.

Most distress sprang, however, from inflation and unemployment. High agricultural prices gave farmers the incentive to produce crops for sale in the dearest markets rather than for the satisfaction of rural subsistence. Rising population put intense strain on the markets themselves, especially urban ones: demand for food often outstripped supply. So most urban markets were forced to promulgate stringent regulations whereby local purchasers were given preference over non-residents and outside speculators.[6] The price rise was in real terms more adverse than it appears, since population growth ensured that labour was plentiful and cheap, and wages low. Inexorably the pool of available labour exceeded available employment opportunities: average wages and living standards declined accordingly. Men and women were prepared to do a day's work for little more than board wages; able-bodied persons, many of whom were peasants displaced by rising rents or the enclosure of commons, drifted in waves to the towns in quest of work.

The fortunes of wage-earning consumers are shown in table 3; the calculations are based on the fluctuating costs of composite units of essential foodstuffs and manufactured goods such as textiles that made up an average family shopping basket in southern England at different times. Three indexes are available: first, the price index of the composite basket of consumables; second, the price index expressed in terms of the purchasing power of a building craftsman in southern England; third, the price index in terms of the purchasing power of an agricultural labourer in southern England. No one supposes that these indexes were standard for the entire labour force, but they serve as indicators of the severity of the rising household expenses of the majority of Tudor people. In the century after Henry VIII's accession the average prices of essential consumables rose by over 400 per cent. The figures given in table 3 are, however, decennial averages: individual years experienced greater volatility of price movements. The index stood at the 100 or so level until 1513, when it rose to 120. A gradual rise to 169 had occurred by 1530, and a further crescendo to 231 was attained by 1547, the year of Henry VIII's death. In 1555 the index reached 270, but two years later it hit 409, which was partly due to the effects of currency debasements as well as to the influenza epidemic. By the accession of Elizabeth I the index had recovered to an average of 230. It climbed again thereafter, but more steadily: 300 in

TABLE 3. *Price of consumables and wage-rates in southern England, 1480–1609*

(1) price of composite unit of consumables (1451–75 = 100)
(2) purchasing power of the wage-rate of a building craftsman
   (1450–99 = 100)
(3) purchasing power of the wage-rate of an agricultural labourer
   (1450–99 = 100)

Decade	(1)	(2)	(3)
1480–9	116	93	86
1490–9	101	103	104
1500–9	104	96	97
1510–9	111	88	89
1520–9	148	76	80
1530–9	155	68	80
1540–9	192	70	71
1550–9	289	51	59
1560–9	279	62	66
1570–9	315	64	69
1580–9	357	57	57
1590–9	472	47	49
1600–9	475	46	50

Sources: (1) E. H. Phelps Brown and S. V. Hopkins, *Economica*, NS 23 (Nov. 1956). (2) & (3) J. Thirsk (ed.), *The Agrarian History of England and Wales*, iv. *1500–1640* (Cambridge, 1967), 865.

1570, 342 in 1580, and 396 in 1590. But the later 1590s witnessed widespread dearth and regional epidemics: the index read 515 in 1595, 685 in 1598, and only settled back to 459 in 1600.

The index expressed in terms of purchasing power gives an equally sober impression of the vicissitudes of Tudor life. A steady decline in the value of a building craftsman's wages occurred between 1500 and 1540, the commodity equivalent falling by some 30 per cent over these years. The index fell again in the 1550s, but recovered in the next decade to a position equivalent to two-thirds of its value in 1500. It then remained more or less stable until the 1590s, when figures for individual years become more eloquent than decennial averages: the index collapsed to 39 in 1595, and to 29 in 1597. By 1603 it had recovered to a figure of 45, which meant that industrial wages had dropped by more than half since 1500. Fluctuations in agricultural wages were roughly commensurate with those of the building craftsman, except that the decline in purchasing power took longer to work through the system. But agricultural wages were less volatile than industrial wages since the farm labourer was able to secure higher rates of pay for seasonal work such as mowing, haymaking, and harvesting. He was also able to benefit from payments in kind, which, like the meat and drink offered to servants in wealthy households, were of increasing value at a time when the cost of foodstuffs was rising.

The data presented in tables 1–3 establish the most fundamental truth about Tudor England. When the rise in population is matched with the indexes of prices and wages, it becomes plain that the trends are correlated: living standards declined as the population rose; wage-rates recovered and grain prices abated temporarily after population growth was cut back in 1555–60; but living standards steadily dropped again to plummet towards the end of the century. Currency debasements, sudden movements in exchange rates, and cumulative increases in the size of the wage-labour force must have had distorting effects, but when a basic pattern is sought it seems that population trends, rather than government policies, capitalist entrepreneurs, European imports of American silver, the more rapid circulation of money, or even debasements, were the primary motor of economic fortunes. Government expenditure on warfare and fortifications during the 1540s, foreign borrowing, and debasements worsened inflation and unemployment: the cost of Henry VIII's later wars and those of Protector Somerset was some £3½ million. Since the combined net yields of taxation and proceeds from sales of ex-religious lands fell short of this figure, the currency was debased, the Crown's profit being in excess of £1 million. True, monetarist explanations of the price rise based on the theory that increase in the money supply forced up prices have secondary value. Spanish silver from the New World formed a high proportion of the bullion stocks of the Tower mint in the few years of Elizabeth's reign with relevant extant records. Also privateering and piracy brought in substantial sums.[7] Yet even monetarist explanations owe something to population growth: the rise of European populations that stimulated demand and output helped to increase the need for money that made mining more profitable, though demand was met, too, by the increasing velocity of circulation of existing coin.

If, however, population growth was the crucial determinant of economic fortunes, the argument is reinforced that Tudor England's greatest success was its ability to feed itself. Commercialized agriculture responded to the pressure on the food supply, but the condition of England after 1500 was not strictly Malthusian. Thomas Malthus, who wrote his *Essay on the Principle of Population* in 1798, listed positive and preventative checks as the traditional means whereby populations were kept in balance with available resources of food.[8] Positive checks involved mass mortality and abrupt reversal of population growth. Preventative checks included declining fertility, contraception, and fewer or later marriages. But there were no mortality crises under the Tudors that were national in geographical extent, nor did preventative checks reverse population growth. Instead they preserved the equilibrium needed for long-term expansion of population. The relationship between price movements and mortality was flexible during the sixteenth century: high prices generated increased mortality only for two or three years at a time, and then there was a compensating reaction. The net or cumulative effect upon population figures over five years was zero. Next, mortality had a strong negative effect at first upon fertility due mainly to foetal mortality and fewer conceptions, but after ten months fertility rebounded sharply for a period of some twenty-six months thereby compensating for the earlier drop in the birth-rate. Thirdly, mortality had a short-term negative effect upon nuptiality, but after two months remarriages accelerated and the total effect was firmly positive.[9] There was, too, a declining level of permanent celibacy in society which may have been connected with the Protestant Reformation. So Malthus was right to explain Tudor inflation in terms of population growth, but was wrong to assume that preventative checks were cutting back population in the absence of subsistence mortality. The distinctive feature of Tudor population history was that a higher birth-rate coincided with increased life expectancy.

An optimistic view of the period, therefore, has sufficiently firm foundations. The sixteenth century saw the evolution of the pre-industrial political economy: an accommodation between population and resources, economics and politics, ambition and rationality. The national subsistence crises of the Middle Ages were replaced by a system of low-pressure equilibrium. Yet progress had its price. Agricultural improvement promoted economic growth at the cost of peasant distress; increased production generated prosperity for landlords and impoverishment for wage-earners. The main dynamic of change was growth, but the effect was to polarize society. A growing divergence emerged in the living standards of rich and poor between 1500 and 1640, and the scramble for agricultural profits undermined traditional ideals of good lordship and social responsibility. The upper strata of society — peers, gentry, yeomen, and the urban elite — became richer, but the poor became poorer. While the diet of the upper strata improved, their houses were bigger and more comfortable than before, and their furniture and tableware rose to new levels of sophistication, the diet of the poor deteriorated, and they lived in bare cottages or rural hovels and in squalid overcrowded suburbs in the towns.[10]

Some of this was remarked upon at the time. In his *Description of England*, written in the 1560s, William Harrison noted the changes that the old men of his Essex village had observed in their lifetime. The 'multitude of chimneys lately erected' signalled

the arrival of the Elizabethan mansion; the 'great amendment
of lodging' meant more comfortable bedding; and 'the exchange
of vessel' meant the substitution of pewter plates and silver or
tin spoons for wooden ones. Changes for the worse included
diminished ecclesiastical and gentry hospitality, the rise of rents
from £4 per annum to £40, £50, or £100, the oppression of
tenants and copyholders, and the rise of interest rates above 10
per cent.[11] Contemporary perceptions of social change did not,
however, include that of the peasant as a productive resource.
Yet economic growth was linked to the means of production,
which was mostly manual labour. The wage-labourer was an
essential resource and in Tudor England the proportion, as well
as the number, of men and women who worked for wages
increased. Displaced peasants formed a migratory work-force
obtaining seasonal employment according to the opportunities
available in agriculture or local industries. A large number moved
into regions of pastoral agriculture as cottagers in the fens, forests,
and wastelands upon which animals could be raised, seeking work
from merchant entrepreneurs who found them a convenient pool
of labour under the 'putting-out' system. The weaving districts
of Norfolk, Suffolk, and Essex attracted these settlers as did the
mining, woodcrafts, and iron industry of the Forest of Dean and
the coal industry of the Tyne valley. Other migrants moved to
towns, especially to London, which absorbed 5,600 persons a
year between 1560 and 1625. But the worst-managed pool of
itinerant labour were the homeless and unemployed: masterless
men and women who roamed the countryside seeking a living
and, if they could not find it, begged or resorted out of necessity
to theft.[12]

It is difficult to estimate what proportion of the population
was poor since poverty is a relative concept and the tyranny of
the price index was not ubiquitous. The number of people
entirely dependent on wages was much less than half the total
population, even by 1603. Multiple occupations, seasonal work,
and cottage industries complemented wage-labour in the
countryside, while town-dwellers grew vegetables, kept animals,
and brewed beer, except in the confines of London. Perhaps two-
fifths of the population were on the margin of subsistence, but
Harrison estimated the number of vagrants or 'sturdy beggars'
at 10,000, and an official survey in 1569 put the figure at

13,000 — a mere 0.4 per cent of the population. Yet in the minds of property owners the poor were not a resource, but a threat. They were idle and delinquent; they preferred begging and stealing to a hard day's work; they migrated not to seek employment, but to take advantage of urban and parish welfare schemes. Both central government and local magistrates feared the dangers of vagrancy, especially at times of dearth or political crisis: their immediate mental responses were to assume that people were unemployed because they were idle, and then to deem 'wilful' unemployment to be criminal. In *A Remedy for Sedition*, written in 1536, Richard Moryson gave the classic analysis:

How much ground is lost in England? How much corn might we carry into other countries if we would use the commodities of our realm? How many heaths be there that would bear other fruits than shrubs, brakes, broom, and fern if they were well handled? How many cities are decayed, how many towns that are now hamlets, quite down, that would stand if the third part of England did not live idly? Towns would up again if crafts were set up. There are few nations, but many be idle. Yet I think there is not two of the greatest nations in Christendom that hath half so many that live without crafts as little England hath.[13]

The belief that destitution was culpable was modified as the century progressed: positive as well as negative thinking came into play. The Statute of Artificers (1563) and multiple Poor Law enactments between 1536 and 1601 achieved the transition between traditional attitudes, whereby the poor's function was to furnish others with opportunities for acts of charity, and rationalized secular relief schemes modelled on the welfare projects successfully pioneered in the cities of France, Germany, Italy, and the Low Countries, and based on the principle that involuntary unemployment and poverty should be ameliorated by apprenticeships and parish rates.[14] True, assurance of labour discipline was as fundamental to the new outlook as provision of public doles for the deserving poor. Also nothing was attempted in Parliament that was not already well established in the more enlightened towns: the experiments of London, Hull, Norwich, Ipswich, and York underpinned positive thought.[15] Likewise the motivation behind the codifying legislation of 1598 and 1601 was as much fear of vagrancy and urban food riots as altruism. Harrison, however, articulated the new approach when he cited three categories of destitution: that by 'impotency' or dependency; that by casualty or misfortune; and that by idleness or neglect. The distinction between voluntary and involuntary poverty was medieval, but it was reasserted during the sixteenth century as indiscriminate charity and begging were restricted throughout Europe in the interests of public order. Harrison argued that the involuntary poor were to be relieved by community action as Scripture commanded, but the voluntary poor were 'thieves and caterpillars in the commonwealth and by the Word of God not permitted to eat'. Vagrants and idle beggars did 'but lick the sweat from the true labourers' brows and bereave the godly poor of that which is due unto them'.[16]

Social polarization did not, however, preclude social mobility. A vigorous land market, agricultural commercialization, and the expansion of education provided openings for young men to advance themselves. Advancement through education without gentle birth was probably less easy after 1560 than before, but women had fewest means of improving their position save by marriage because institutions and the law discriminated against them. Some women served as churchwardens, manorial officials, or school teachers, but common law regarded wives as *femmes couvertes*: their legal existence was vested in their husbands. True, the Elizabethan court of chancery began to offer women relief in respect of their rights of inheritance and rights to property settled on them at marriage. Common and municipal law allowed widows to hold land and to trade in their own right. London permitted married women to trade separately from their husbands within the city limits. But discrimination was otherwise severe: single women were especially vulnerable, while literature stereotyped women as 'scolds' or gossips. So social mobility must be seen in perspective. The chance of a significant upgrading in status was confined to males able to obtain enough land, gain entry to an urban elite, or enter one of the professions, and to persons able to engineer a marriage well above their existing standing. Time had also to elapse before a rise in status was cemented: some said three generations were needed but wealth, connections, and local politics played the decisive role.

The question of status is complicated by the fact that economic status was not equivalent to social status. Prosperity was the test of the former, but gentility of the latter. Often the two overlapped, as in the case of landowners, but sometimes they did not. The professions are the obvious example: clergy, lawyers, university graduates, medical practitioners, military officers, and government officials ranked as gentlemen. But yeomen, lesser merchants, craftsmen, and scriveners did not, even though they might enjoy comparable wealth. Urban status was especially ambiguous. Persons holding superior civic office were generally accorded gentle status, and greater merchants were regarded as gentry if they had invested in land—the practical test of gentility—but livery company men, substantial haberdashers, and clothiers were not regarded as gentry if they lacked land.

Political status, too, had its own framework. The 'political nation' comprised the nobility, senior clergy, gentry, and some other enfranchised persons. In the countryside the greater and lesser gentry and wealthier yeomanry served as local magistrates, tax collectors, and muster commissioners. Persons possessed of freehold land worth 40s. or more per annum were entitled to vote in parliamentary elections, though few elections were in fact contested before the seventeenth century. So the lines of political demarcation between greater yeomen and lesser gentry were blurred; some husbandmen even became exceptions to the custom excluding the common people from electoral participation when inflation caused the value of their freeholds to exceed 40s. Yet some greater yeomen were disfranchised because they were leaseholders not freeholders. By comparison the urban franchise was both more and less than that of the countryside. Citizens were admitted to the 'freedom' of their town by patrimony, apprenticeship, or purchase, after which they had the right to stand for civic office and to elect some two or three dozen town councillors. In practice, however, town government was less democratic than it appeared: conciliar membership shrank under the Tudors and intermarriage between elite families was so common that in the smaller towns most councillors were in some way related to each other. Furthermore, they were invariably the citizens in control of local trade. The mayor and a dozen or so aldermen were chosen by these councillors and the town's MPs were often named by the mayor and aldermen with or without the councillors. Since the mayor and aldermen doubled as commissioners of the peace, tax collectors, and muster commissioners when required by the Crown, and since they administered justice both in the civic courts and at quarter sessions, most towns were in practice oligarchical.[17] Their chief concerns were economic regulation and the preservation of their vested interests; their leaders could appear dictatorial and unrepresentative, and superior office tended to be confined within the same circle of notables for decades at a time.

The limitations upon upward mobility are best seen in terms of the patterns of landownership and distribution of honours.[18] The premier members of lay society were the peers: although they numbered only 42 in 1509, 51 in 1547, 56 in 1553, 63 in 1559, and 55 in 1603, they held very roughly 10 per cent of the land available for cultivation. In addition, peers were unique in society because admission to their ranks was controlled by the monarch and regulated by the rules of primogeniture. New peerage creations were few under Henry VII and Henry VIII, except between 1529 and 1540. Wolsey's fall and the summoning of the Reformation Parliament produced the largest number: Henry VIII created seven new barons and promoted three existing peers. He was motivated by politics: the additional number reversed the numerical balance in the House of Lords so as to give lay peers, rather than prelates, a majority of votes. Thereafter, Henry VIII was relatively generous with new creations, but the number of attainders during his reign, coupled with biological failures in the male line, prevented numbers rising significantly. At his death in 1547 there were only nine more peers than at his accession. But most were 'new' nobles: half the barons owed their rank to Henry, while, of seventeen peers of the rank of viscount or above, only six titles did not derive from him. The great majority of new creations elevated successful courtiers or soldiers: in this sense there was potential for upward mobility on merit, but a man's chances of ennoblement by that route remained slim.

By contrast, Elizabeth created or revived only eighteen peerages. Her policy was to maintain the peerage as a select caste for men of ancient lineage. Francis Naunton wrote, 'a concurrence of old blood with fidelity [was] a mixture which ever sorted with the queen's nature'. There were only ten 'new' creations during her reign, and most of the beneficiaries already possessed peerage connections, noble ancestry, or kinship with the queen. The exceptions were Lord Burghley and Lord Compton. In addition, five former titles were restored; Reginald Grey was permitted to resume the earldom of Kent (which his grandfather had resigned on account of his poverty); and two titles were inherited via the female line. In January 1589 Elizabeth contemplated some expansion. Burghley wrote: 'Her Majesty, finding a great want of noblemen for Parliament, is minded to create some earls and barons.' But nothing was done at the time, and the queen's grants of honour did not even compensate for losses due to failures of the male line and attainders: the size of the peerage dropped slightly during her reign.

Knighthood was usually conferred upon the dozen or so leading gentry families of each county but numbers fluctuated considerably. In 1490 there were some 375 knights, a figure which climbed to 600 by 1558, fell back to 300 by 1583, and recovered to 550 by 1603. Although knighthood had originally involved military obligation, this aspect was muted in the sixteenth century. Harrison noted that persons who possessed freehold land worth £40 per annum might be 'enforced into the taking of that degree' by the Crown, and Sir Thomas Smith observed that knights were 'most commonly [made] according to the yearly revenue of their lands being able to maintain that estate'. But Elizabeth was sparing in her dubbing of English knights despite the upward aspirations of many landed families. Creations during her war years were ostensibly fairly large, but many of these knights were dubbed in Ireland or on the battlefield by the lord deputy or the lord general. Many were volunteer soldiers or 'adventurers' who then swaggered about London as knights while their fathers in the country were still esquires. It was said that the earl of Essex angered Elizabeth as much because he created eighty-one knights during his inglorious Irish expedition of 1599 as because he failed to defeat Tyrone.

An average landed estate for a knight was roughly 6,000 acres in 1524, and the group as a whole owned perhaps 8 per cent of the cultivated area by the accession of Elizabeth. Precise calculations are impossible, but, if the landed estates of English peers and knights are aggregated, they amount to roughly 3–4 million acres, or somewhere between 15 and 20 per cent of the

20 million or so acres under cultivation. The two groups together formed a largely homogeneous elite with a common outlook derived from their substantial interest as landowners.

Esquires and 'mere' gentry were far more numerous, while the latter was the only principal status group that could in practice be entered without some form of royal or noble intervention. Esquires were the eldest sons of knights, and their eldest sons in succession; the younger sons of barons or their heirs; male persons invested esquire by the Crown; JPs and others called to magistracy in their counties; and gentry otherwise qualified by wealth and position. By contrast, gentlemen were less easily defined. Although the College of Heralds made some effort to preserve the use of coat armour from complete debasement, the recognition of friends and neighbours usually counted for as much as notions derived from the law of arms and theories about the right to use coats of arms. Harrison explained:

Whosoever studieth the laws of the realm, whoso abideth in the university giving his mind to his book, or professeth physic and the liberal sciences, or, beside his service in the room of a captain in the wars or good counsel given at home, whereby his commonwealth is benefited, can live without manual labour, and thereto is able and will bear the port, charge, and countenance of a gentleman, he shall for money have a coat and arms bestowed upon him by heralds (who in the charter of the same do of custom pretend antiquity and service and many gay things), and thereunto being made so good cheap, be called master, which is the title that men give to esquires and gentlemen, and reputed for a gentleman ever after. Which is so much the less to be disallowed of for that the prince doth lose nothing by it, the gentleman being so much subject to taxes and public payments as is the yeoman or husbandman, which he likewise doth bear the gladlier for the saving of his reputation . . . No man hath hurt by it but himself who peradventure will go in wider buskins than his legs will bear or, as our proverb saith, now and then bear a bigger sail than his boat is able to sustain.[19]

There were approximately five thousand gentry families in 1540 and perhaps fifteen thousand in 1640. Superficially the number had increased threefold at a time when the population had only doubled. However, the success or failure of these landowners depended on their adaptability, or vulnerability, to capitalistic agriculture; moreover, landowners likely to prosper were prima facie greater yeomen, particularly yeomen–freeholders, who were immune from rent rises. Figures are hard to obtain but, in 1600, Thomas Wilson estimated the numbers of freeholders in England and Wales at 'about the number of 80,000, as I have seen in the sheriffs' books'.[20] His figure is, in fact, too high if it is supposed to exclude gentry: but even if the number of non-gentry freeholders were reduced to 60,000, which might be taken as a reasonable estimate of the numbers of greater yeomen who were freeholders with an average of 70–80 acres each, it is clear that only a small proportion of these farmers had to 'bear the port' of gentlemen for the 'rise of the gentry' to be conveniently explained.

This matter is more complex because there was downward, as well as upward, social mobility. Noble and gentry families died out or became impoverished as well as rose: in Yorkshire there were 557 gentry families in 1558, 641 in 1603, and 679 in 1642, but the 'net increase' of 122 families hides the fact that another 181 families became extinct in the male line, 64 left the county, and 30 vanished without trace.[21] In general, the families that rose with most obvious good fortune between 1540 and 1640 were those of politicians with access to the profits of office: William Petre, Nicholas Bacon, William Cecil, Robert Cecil, Lionel Cranfield, Thomas Wentworth, and others. Other families rose spectacularly upon fortunes made in business in the City of London, or in the legal profession, rather than in landowning. Yet, whereas by Henry VII's reign middling and lesser gentry held some 25 per cent of the cultivated land, by 1640 they owned nearly half. By comparison the holdings of yeomen, husbandmen, and secure copyholders increased marginally during the same period: from some 20 per cent to between 25 and 33 per cent of the land. (The main losers of land between 1500 and 1640 were the church and Crown.)[22] It follows that, if the numbers of gentry increased threefold, but the amount of land they controlled only doubled, then the average size of gentry estates must have decreased.[23] Since, however, many Tudor yeomen must have risen into gentry ranks on the strength of farming profits, this is what one would expect. The majority of seventeenth-century gentry owned estates of 1,000 acres or less—many had considerably less—and in the long run the economic mobility of individual landed families was a more crucial determinant than their social status, though the two issues are obviously inseparable. If, however, economic fortunes made the running, this reinforces an opinion that, in the Renaissance, 'gentility was a concept in search of a role in society'.[24]

The industrial and commercial sectors of the economy were small in relation to agriculture but they, too, were affected by the growth of population. Rising home and export demand, after 1470, encouraged increased output and some division of labour, but industrial growth was barely sustained between 1550 and 1603. Too little is known about home demand for firm conclusions to be drawn, but it seems that the pool of surplus labour caused by population expansion, the decline in purchasing power of wage-earners, and the fact that some two-fifths of the population were on the margin of subsistence, combined to depress industrial demand and gave merchant entrepreneurs insufficient incentive to raise output, seek organizational change or technical innovation, or practise import substitution on a wide scale.[25]

Consumer demand was mainly for a restricted range of products: woollen textiles and leather goods, building materials, and agricultural and household implements. In 1500 the leading towns still had important cloth industries but, during the fourteenth and fifteenth centuries, cloth manufacture had largely shifted to the market towns and villages of Norfolk, Suffolk, and Essex, the Weald of Kent, Gloucestershire, Wiltshire, Somerset, and Devon, and the West Riding of Yorkshire. These rural centres developed not because they were convenient for local supplies of wool — sheep farming in the Weald was negligible — but because cloth manufacture was labour-intensive, some fifteen people taking a week to produce a single undyed cloth of medium quality measuring 12 yards by 1¾ yards. Elastic supplies of labour were the key to the economics of the industry, and expansion continued under Henry VII and Henry VIII in those areas where cheap labour was available either for daily wages or, more usually, for work at home at piece-work rates. But the crescendo in output was curtailed in the 1550s: between 1470 and 1550 cloth exports had tripled, averaging some 130,000 broadcloths per annum in the period 1547–53, though the expansion was at the expense of exports of raw wool. In fact the currency debasements of Henry VIII and Edward VI, which made English exports cheaper, created artificial booms in 1544–6 and 1550–1, but exports retreated in 1551–2 as the coinage was revalued. Yet retreat was not drastic: stability rather than collapse was achieved by 1560, when cloth exports averaged some 110,000 broadcloths per annum, a level maintained for most of Elizabeth's reign.

Although English cloth-making techniques remained largely traditional, some technical improvements were achieved by native manufacturers, and the arrival of Protestant weavers from the Netherlands fleeing Philip II's Inquisition and military offensives in the 1560s and 1570s encouraged the manufacture of a wider range of products. Whole colonies of immigrants settled in the towns of Kent and East Anglia: in Norwich they may have formed almost one-third of the population by the early 1580s. The immigrants already had trading links with Mediterranean markets (which English merchants neglected before the Dutch revolt in favour of Antwerp), since their comparatively colourful and lightweight fabrics were more attractive to southern Europeans than the heavier English cloths. Their fabrics were generally hybrid: mixtures either of woollen and worsted yarns or even of worsted and silk. They were cheaper and sometimes less durable than English broadcloth, thus enhancing both initial and replacement demand. In short, the 'new draperies', as they were called, were the products that English clothiers needed to attract new customers at home and abroad, and from 1570 onwards textiles variously called bays, says, perpetuanas, shaloons, grosgraines, serges, etc., were manufactured, though a significant impact on exports was not achieved until the seventeenth century.

Leather was the second most important manufacturing industry: much tanning was done in the countryside, but the manufacture of shoes, saddlery, gloves, purses, and clothing mostly took place in the towns. The building industry was dependent upon supplies of timber, the main material for constructing houses, ships, carts, and industrial equipment, but stone was used for house building from the late-sixteenth century onwards, and brick for royal palaces, mansions, and great houses. Shortage of timber meant that there was a growing tendency to substitute the products of mine and quarry for those of the forest: coal began to replace wood and charcoal as fuel, and the coal and iron industries were among the few to introduce significant technical improvements during the Tudor period.

Investment in agricultural hardware and domestic utensils stimulated the metal industries: nails, bolts, hinges, locks, ploughing and harrowing equipment, and lead for windows and roofs. There was higher demand for household utensils: pots and pans of copper and brass; pewter plates, drinking vessels and candlesticks; cutlery and glassware; and table and bed linen. Wealthy landowners and merchants built town houses and country seats with long galleries, ornate chimney-pieces, decorative plasterwork, oak and walnut furniture, tapestries, carpets, paintings, silver plate, pewter, brass, and glassware. Extravagant dress, conspicuous consumption, and the advent of coaches characterized London high society by the end of Elizabeth's reign, but most luxury goods were imported: demand in the capital city, high in itself, was generally too low overall to justify home manufacture in lieu of imports. Glassware and small metal goods, especially cutlery, were exceptions, and imports of these gave way to home-manufactured products by the 1590s.[26] At the other end of the social scale, however, it is unlikely that the urban and rural poor sought domestic comforts beyond food and clothing: salt and soap were doubtless regarded as luxuries.

HENRY VII

FEW in English history have ascended the throne with less experience of government than did Henry VII after the battle of Bosworth. Henry's victory, itself little short of miraculous, was preceded by fourteen years of impoverished exile in Brittany and France; before that his youth had been spent in Wales and he may not have visited England more than once. Of course, the Yorkists had begun the 'refoundation' of the monarchy: Edward IV and Richard III pointed the way with Crown-inspired acts of resumption and attainder, the 'land revenue' experiment, and chamber finance, and they had developed the Council as a real governing institution. But personal methods of rule had a drawback: they pivoted on the Court and Council, which automatically dissolved upon the king's death. Each monarch necessarily had to appoint his own councillors and construct his household. This process took time and required shrewd judgement. Henry VII was vulnerable to inexperience during the early years of his reign: he had to train himself in kingship while establishing his dynasty, and it is unlikely that he had a moment's ease before his second victory over the Yorkists at the battle of Stoke (16 June 1487).

Henry VII's reign falls into three fairly distinct phases. From 1485 to about 1492 Richard Fox, king's secretary and from 1487 keeper of the privy seal and bishop of Exeter, was in charge of administration. Finance was centred on the exchequer, with whose officials Fox dealt by writs and letters under the privy seal. After 1487 the Yorkist financial system began to be revived, but it was not until 1492 that significant revenues were diverted from the exchequer into the chamber and king's coffers. In this phase, too, the French annexation of Brittany caused Henry VII to engage in military action, but Anglo-French relations were defined, after a short siege of Boulogne, by the treaty of Étaples in 1492. Henry's project for an Anglo-Spanish dynastic alliance was meanwhile ventilated.

The second phase ran from 1492 to 1503. This period was dominated by the administration of Reynold Bray, who transformed the chamber into the hub of a governmental and fiscal nexus that penetrated to the most distant parts of the land, recording receipts, issues, bonds, obligations, and debts, and dealing only in cash. Bray as chief general auditor after the king and as chancellor of the duchy of Lancaster was also responsible for fostering a tribunal named the Council Learned in the Law—a conciliar court based on the duchy chamber but acting with the full authority of the Council—that supervised matters connected with the king's prerogative and acted, in effect, as the Crown's agency of enforcement. This body had come into formal existence by 1498–9. In diplomacy Henry VII managed to emerge as a significant European monarch in this phase, since the invasion of Italy by Charles VIII of France in 1494 resulted in Henry's inclusion in the defensive Holy League of 1496 alongside Ferdinand of Aragon, the Emperor Maximilian I, and Pope Alexander VI. Henry negotiated an important treaty with the Burgundian Netherlands too, and in September 1497 achieved the truce of Ayton with Scotland. Renewed in 1499, this was cemented in 1502 as the first Anglo-Scottish peace treaty since 1328. Henry's diplomacy with Spain came to fruition in November 1501, when the marriage of his son, Prince Arthur, to Catherine of Aragon was celebrated in London. Although Arthur died in April 1502, discussions soon began for Catherine's marriage to Prince Henry, while the marriage of James IV of Scotland to Henry VII's daughter Margaret took place in August 1503.

The third phase of Henry VII's reign ran from Bray's death in 1503 to the king's in 1509. These were the years of Henry's most personal rule, when he used his signature on warrants and state papers to short-circuit long-established bureaucratic procedures.[1] By 1507–8 more grants of lands and offices were being authorized by 'immediate warrants' (as they were called) than by due process of the signet and privy seal.[2] Henry VII also attended far fewer Council meetings in this period than before. This reflected the fact that he increasingly delegated fiscal and enforcement business to the Council Learned in the Law, where Richard Empson and Edmund Dudley had succeeded Bray. And he also established another administrative tribunal acting as a conciliar court of audit, where Robert Southwell and Roger Laybourne presided. These men were Henry's personal agents whom he trusted: they acted with the full authority and jurisdiction of the Council but were responsible solely to the king, who ordered and checked their work in the chamber and privy chamber at Court. So, whereas Henry VII had adopted Yorkist methods in his first phase, he transmuted them somewhat in his last years, since his fiscalism sometimes reduced the business of government to pecuniary transactions in which the need to pay, outbid, and enforce prerogative rights overrode moral authority and, if not legality, justice.

Mortality dominated foreign policy in this third phase. Elizabeth of York died in February 1503, which meant that Henry was a widower who could attempt a further dynastic union via marriage on his own account. Henry's plans for a second marriage proved fruitless but, under terms settled in June 1503, he agreed that marriage be contracted between Catherine of Aragon and Prince Henry. Yet the treaty noted that a full papal dispensation would be needed because Catherine, through her marriage to Arthur, had become related to Prince Henry in the first degree of affinity. In fact, the requisite bulls were obtained, but the marriage was postponed until some weeks after Henry VII's death. The reason was that he shifted to an Anglo-Burgundian policy on the death of Isabella of Castile, though the untimely death of Archduke Philip in September 1506 caused a readjustment towards France.[3]

Henry VII's immediate concerns when he came to the throne were the security and stability of Tudor rule. Always he acted resolutely and promptly, dating his reign as beginning on 21 August 1485, the day before Bosworth, for the purpose of attainting his opponents, but for other purposes his regnal years began on the anniversary of the battle itself. Elizabeth of York, daughter of Edward IV, was brought out of the Tower, and preparations were made for the coronation, for the summoning of Parliament, and for the reconstruction of the Council and royal household. Writs were issued for Parliament to assemble on 7 November 1485; the coronation was held on 30 October. Councillors and judges were appointed during September and had much to do by way of rewards, arrests, appointments of minor officials, and parliamentary draftsmanship between then and January 1486. Henry chose the leading members of his Council and household from three obvious groups: those whose aid and counsel he had received in Brittany and France; those who had supported him at Bosworth; and those who had participated in the duke of Buckingham's unsuccessful revolt against Richard III in October 1483. He selected some of Buckingham's former retainers and servants too, but experience of government was at a premium and he had to choose many former Yorkists as councillors and officials. However, throughout his reign Henry chose men solely on the basis of competence and willingness to serve the Tudor regime; it would be misleading to think the terms 'Lancastrian' and 'Yorkist' bore any resemblance to modern party affiliations. 'Loyalty and ability were the only criteria of service — mighty lord, bishop, doctor of canon or civil law, or official, all were there, but only at the king's will.'[4]

Henry VII's chief officers of state were John Morton (lord chancellor, archbishop of Canterbury, and cardinal from 1493), who died in 1500; John, Lord Dynham (lord treasurer), who died in 1501; Richard Fox (keeper of the privy seal and, successively, bishop of Exeter, Bath and Wells, Durham, and Winchester); John de Vere, earl of Oxford (lord great chamberlain, and admiral); and Thomas, Lord Stanley (the king's stepfather, earl of Derby, and constable), who died in 1504.[5] Equally important were those of Henry's Council who managed his fiscal and enforcement policies: Bray, whose brainchild was to be the Council Learned, was singled out as the king's financial administrator and property manager almost immediately; Thomas Lovell served as chancellor of the exchequer, treasurer of the household, and as Speaker in Henry's first Parliament; Giles, Lord Daubeney, was master of the mint, chamberlain of the household from 1495, and commanded the forces that suppressed the Cornish Rising; Richard Guildford acted as master of the ordnance (i.e. minister of defence) and comptroller of the household; John Riseley, knight of the body, was one of the regime's most assiduous councillors, holding minor offices only but acting, in effect, as a minister without portfolio.

Henry VII assured his security by calculated precaution and

by acknowledging no debts save political service. He married Elizabeth of York five months after Bosworth, fulfilling a promise made in 1483 and providing the essential palliative to those Yorkist defectors who had joined him against Richard III in the first place—the ensuing births of Arthur in 1486, Margaret in 1489, Henry in 1491, and Mary in 1496 also solved the succession question. Next, Henry made a determined effort to put the command of castles and garrisons, as well as wider control of military organization, in the hands of trusted courtiers, and he launched selective attacks on the magnates if he felt that they were exercising their territorial power to his disparagement. For example, when the Stanleys abused their position in the north-west, the whole family was bound in recognizances for future good conduct: Sir William, whose intervention at Bosworth had saved Henry's day, had communicated with the pretender Perkin Warbeck; he was convicted of high treason, while both James and Edward Stanley were tried for illegal retaining, Edward's indictment being annotated by Henry—proof of royal intervention in the case.[6] Also star-chamber proceedings against Thomas, Lord Dacre, Henry, Lord Clifford, and others for feuding along the Scottish border were managed by the king, who examined the defendants himself, scribbling his notes on the back of the bill of articles.[7] Thomas, marquis of Dorset, was in 1492 bound in a cluster of obligations and feoffments which, if put into effect, would have secured his disinheritance. Lastly, Lord Daubeney was mulcted for embezzlement as lieutenant of Calais and compelled to surrender his French pension to the king.

Of the revolts faced by Henry VII, the most serious were those with dynastic intentions. The imposture of Lambert Simnel as the imprisoned nephew of Edward IV, Edward, earl of Warwick, however exotic, was even more menacing, because it occurred within two years of Bosworth.[8] Perkin Warbeck's imposture as Edward IV's younger son, Richard of York, during the 1490s was more easily contained, despite Scottish and European intervention. Simnel was routed at the battle of Stoke: his promoters were slain or imprisoned, and the young imposter was taken into the royal household as a servant. Warbeck fell into Henry's hands in October 1497; before long he had abused the king's leniency and so was hanged (23 November 1499).

A week later the life of the real earl of Warwick was forfeited for alleged treason. But it was another seven years before Henry's diplomacy secured the capture of Edward IV's nephew, Edmund de la Pole, earl of Suffolk. Being the Yorkist heir, Suffolk was in exile in the Low Countries, but the Archduke Philip delivered him to Henry in March 1506 to complete the Anglo-Burgundian *rapprochement*. Suffolk was incarcerated in the Tower until May 1513, when he was executed by Henry VIII.

Yet the dynastic threat to the Tudor regime must not be exaggerated. The striking feature of the period is not the prevalence but the absence of males of the royal blood: 'Unlike the situation under Edward IV, there was no centre within the King's kindred for rival political tensions and no obvious focus for political discontent.'[9] It is true, the supporters of Simnel and Warbeck dressed their ambitions in dynastic garb, but the most important revolt in Henry VII's reign, the Cornish Rising of 1497, was not dynastic. On the contrary, it was sparked by the parliamentary grant of that year to finance an invasion of Scotland provoked by James IV's aid for Warbeck — this before the truce of Ayton altered Henry VII's plans. The tax revolt erupted in the south-west because Cornishmen refused to underwrite a campaign against Scotland for which, they believed, a scutage or land tax levied in the north was the correct source of finance. Some 15,000 rebels marched via Exeter, Salisbury, and Winchester to Kent; the gentry rallied, London was called to arms, and the expedition to Scotland cancelled. The rebels took their stand in a pitched battle on Blackheath (17 June). More than a thousand were slain and the rest fled or were captured. The three ringleaders, Thomas Flamank, a Bodmin lawyer, Michael Joseph, a blacksmith, and James Touchet, Lord Audley, were sent to the Tower, tried for treason, and executed, their dismembered heads being set upon poles on London bridge.[10]

Since Henry VII governed England as his private estate through his Council and household, Parliament played no role at all in policy-making but acted as a working instrument of government underpinned by feudal notions whereby vassals offered suit of court, rather than by the Roman principle of *amicitia*, or friendship, which characterized the Council's less formal deliberations. Legislation and taxation were the functions of Parliament, from the Crown's standpoint at any rate, and that attitude was sustained throughout Henry VII's seven Parliaments. 'The precedents already set over the previous century or so were followed; there were no significant innovations in procedure, so far as we know; no change in composition or electoral arrangements; few legislative measures enacted were of any great importance.'[11]

But it is mistaken to suppose that Henry's view of Parliament meant that he did not consult his subjects. Despite his fiscalism and personal methods of rule, he attempted to govern consensually, consulting as widely as any other Tudor while keeping executive power in his own hands. He summoned five Great Councils between 1487 and 1502 to take advice and seek authority in principle for war and taxation. (Great Councils were plenary assemblies of nobles and councillors summoned to meet the political, financial, diplomatic, and ceremonial needs of the king and his realm.) In fact, whereas Parliament under Henry VII was restricted to enacting legislation, granting money, and validating or reversing attainders, the king used Great Councils to make major political decisions and bind representatives of the nation to support them. At least twice burgesses attended, too, as in the French *conseil général des notables*. In France, according to the views of theorists, the king was supposed to consult a great council of the estates on matters affecting the whole realm. 'This gathering', wrote Claude de Seyssel, 'is not called an ordinary council. On the contrary, it is an occasional assembly which should not be undertaken except when the circumstances require it.' Members included the princes of the blood, the bishops, the great officers of state, and other officials and councillors, and provincial representatives were to be summoned when important business affecting everyone arose, for instance a declaration of war. Henry VII may have subscribed to this theory, which he possibly encountered while in exile. At any rate, he sometimes took his desire for consensus to unusual lengths, since he did not curtail his 1492 French campaign without assembling 'in his field beside Boulogne all the lords, estates, counsellors, and captains of his army' and 'debated this matter with them sundry ways'. He gathered them 'in one whole counsell', and made them sign documents pleading with him to agree the retreat into

England; the list was headed by twenty-one peers, followed by king's councillors below the peerage rank.[12]

Henry VII's Parliaments sat between November 1485 and March 1486; November and December 1487; January 1489 and February 1490; October 1491 and March 1492; October and December 1495; January and March 1497; and January and April 1504. Three of these Parliaments had more than one session with breaks between: hence Parliament sat in all for seventy-two weeks during the twenty-three years and eight months of the reign. The first Parliament declared Henry's title to the throne, reversed some Yorkist attainders and attainted Richard III and his men, granted the king the subsidy on wool and that of tunnage and poundage for life, passed an act of resumption, and enacted legislation designed to reinforce stability and the public peace. The most important measure concerned the king's title: the Crown was assured to Henry and his legitimate heirs, though the act did no more than legally validate his 'hereditary' title and the verdict, at Bosworth, of the God of battles. The other significant act was the grant of customs duties for life. The duties applied to imports and exports: Henry VII collected some £900,000 from this source during his reign, half from London.

Each of the remaining six Parliaments made some kind of financial provision. The recognized tax was the fifteenth and tenth, which in the early fourteenth century had been assessed directly on the value of movable goods but which, in 1334, had been converted into fixed sums due from each vill or borough; thereafter each fifteenth and tenth produced an assured net yield to the Crown of £29,500. Grants of fifteenths and tenths to Henry VII in 1487, 1489–90, 1491–2, and 1497 thus represented the standard form of taxation levied since 1334 and one which was continually resorted to alongside other methods until 1624—these taxes yielded £203,000 during the reign.[13] Fifteenths and tenths were, however, stereotyped taxes; they did not reflect any longer the true distribution of wealth in England, and Henry VII decided to raise some more efficient taxes if he could. Seven such grants involving direct assessment of taxpayers' wealth had been granted by Parliament before 1485, but two of these experiments had to be abandoned. In a new effort to raise revenue Henry VII secured the grant of a poll tax on aliens in 1487 and obtained the grant of an open-ended

subsidy to maintain a force of ten thousand archers for a year
in 1489; but the second tax failed to raise more than £27,000—a
quarter of what had been expected. Although this failure was
so bad as to discourage further attempts to levy a directly assessed
subsidy for twenty-five years, compromise forms of taxation were
adopted in 1497 and 1504. In 1497 Parliament was asked to grant
£120,000 in the form of two fifteenths and tenths, plus an aid
or subsidy to be collected by direct assessment. In other words,
the total yield was to be assured to the Crown, but the burden
of outdated assessments was to be partially lifted. And this
experiment was successful. Lastly, Parliament in 1504 granted
a subsidy of £30,000, to be assessed and collected as in 1497.
Behind this grant lay the one example of haggling during
Henry VII's reign. The king, it seems, had originally wanted
two feudal aids, perhaps to provide a subterfuge for exploiting
his prerogative rights and to justify the compilation of a new
record of lands held of the Crown *in capite*—a sort of Tudor
Domesday Book.[14] William Roper's story of Thomas More's
political baptism as 'leader of the opposition' to Henry's proposal
is, however, apocryphal.[15] Henry VII's net receipts from the
subsidies of his reign were £80,000.

The legislation of Henry VII's Parliaments has been considerably overrated. Writing *The History of the Reign of Henry VII*
during the summer of 1621, Francis Bacon opined: 'his times
for good commonwealth's laws did excel'; his laws were 'the pre-
eminent virtue and merit of this king'.[16] Addressed to James I
by a fallen minister, these were relevant comments upon the
legislative stalemate of the 1620s, but had little to do with
Henry VII's statutes—even though it is upon Bacon's statements
that Henry's reputation as a legislator has been grounded. Of
Henry's 192 statutes some 40 were acts of resumption, attainder
or restitution; 31 regulated trade, prices, and wages; 22 modified
the common law; 19 were personal acts affecting only the
individuals specified; 14 strengthened law enforcement; 13
conferred pardons or privileges; 12 made fiscal provisions; 7
concerned JPs; 5 dealt with church matters; and the rest were
miscellaneous, casting little light on Henry VII or his policy.[17]
Yet even the main acts do not look very impressive: they boil
down to those concerning law enforcement, JPs, and the church.

An act of 1487 created a small tribunal comprising three

leading officers of state, the two chief justices, and two other
councillors, who were to enforce summarily existing legislation
against rioting, retaining, and the corruption of justice, for
instance bribing jurors.[18] The new tribunal sat in star chamber
but was distinct from the separate court of star chamber, the
judges of which were all the king's councillors, not just the few
named in the act. In 1495 another tribunal was erected to punish
perjury, but neither tribunal actually heard many cases.[19] In
the same year a statute of limitations reassured Yorkists who
had so far escaped attainders that no further proceedings would
be taken against them in respect of actions before 1485, but
treason after Bosworth was naturally not exempt — the purpose
of this act was to heal old wounds and to reiterate, if reiteration
was necessary, that the question of the Tudor succession
was closed.

Minor reforms to the civil and criminal law had little practical
impact (most were related to aspects of procedure) and were not
always what they seemed: an act against hunting in disguise,
for instance, was not meant to reduce violence but to conserve
deer. Unlawful retaining, riot, rout, illegal assembly,
maintenance, embracery, and false verdicts by jurors were
attacked by statute, but even Henry's 'great' statute of 1504
against unlawful retaining (19 Henry VII, c. 14) basically
repeated earlier legislation since 1399. Also the act was
temporary, to run for the term of the king's life and no longer;
and there were few government prosecutions under *any* of
Henry's criminal statutes during his reign.

In fact, crime was meant to be tackled locally. So Henry VII's
criminal legislation was directed at JPs. It regulated their taking
of recognizances for keeping the peace; limited the granting of
bail to suspected felons; required JPs to review the empanelling
of juries and inquests by sheriffs; and obliged them to enforce
the vagrancy and game laws. Purely administrative tasks were
also assigned to JPs. They were to help assess subsidies; to
enquire into usury and defaults in weights and measures; to
regulate alehouses; to examine complaints against tax collectors;
and to administer the sumptuary laws and statutes against dicing
and unlawful games. JPs could try felonies at quarter sessions
by 1485, but were newly authorized to punish lesser crimes on
information without indictment; they were empowered to

summon suspected rioters to face trial, or to commit them to
gaol pending trial; they were to supervise inquiries into unlawful
retainers and were to certify the names of any offenders into
king's bench; and they were to examine complaints of extortion
levelled against sheriffs, undersheriffs, and sheriffs' clerks.
Without doubt these measures enhanced the role of JPs as local
administrators and criminal judges. Indeed JPs were steadily
rising in importance as Crown-appointed officials who, though
unsalaried, were nevertheless strategically responsible for
supervising a wide range of tasks and, somewhat randomly, for
the public prosecution of crime. By the end of Henry VII's reign
they had superseded the sheriff and the feudal lord as
administrative agents.

The fact remained that the need was less for new legislation
than for the means to enforce existing law. A fifteenth-century
epigram lamented:

> Many laws and little right,
> Many acts of Parliament,
> And few kept with true intent.[20]

And the same point was made by Chief Justice Hussey at a
meeting of all the judges at Blackfriars in 1485. 'The law', he
said, 'will never be well executed until all the lords spiritual and
temporal are of one accord, for the love and dread they have
for God or for the king, or both, to execute them effectually.'[21]
Here the role of JPs was crucial. The need was to appoint reliable
men with local knowledge, legal expertise, and sufficient social
weight to command authority. In this respect Henry VII's most
significant contribution may have been his shift towards direct
reliance on lesser gentry as JPs. Like Edward IV he sought to
weaken the ties which had traditionally linked the local interests
of the nobility and gentry, and which encouraged corruption of
justice. He also split some existing affinities, and appointed new
JPs who were courtiers or middling gentry, including professional
lawyers and even, sometimes, non-residents of the shire, in an
attempt to construct Crown affinities. He did not complete this
process, but Wolsey continued the work by similar means and
there was a perceptible shift before the Reformation towards
the idea of a Crown-controlled magistracy, although it was
Henry VIII's need to defend the break with Rome in the 1530s that

produced the most serious Tudor attempts at centralized law
enforcement.[22]

Henry VII's ecclesiastical legislation was also related to law
enforcement. A statute of 1485 authorized bishops to punish by
imprisonment priests, clerks, monks, and friars convicted by
canon law of sexual offences, but the most important measure
was the act of 1489 that provided that a layman could only enjoy
the privilege of benefit of clergy once.[23] Benefit of clergy was
a concession obtained in the wake of the dispute between
Henry II and Thomas Becket: the principle was that the secular
court was not allowed to punish a criminal who proved himself
a clerk, but the privilege had long been extended to literate
laymen. This extension had arisen so as to give the judges
the option of leniency over the death penalty, but the technique
had backfired with the invention of printing—anyone who
could obtain a psalter and read or memorize the so-called
'neck-verse' (for verse 1 or 14 of Psalm 55 was usually chosen
by the judges) could escape hanging. Indeed it was established
precedent that, if a man was a slow reader who spelled out the
letters first and then put them together, this sufficed, and it was
even enough for the prisoner to learn to read in gaol after his
arrest![24] The 1489 statute thus limited the privilege to a single
escape for the laity and, to ensure against evasion, those found
guilty of homicide were to be branded on the thumb with the
letter 'M', and other felons with a 'T'. Persons tried a second
time were disallowed benefit of clergy unless they produced
letters of ordination; other legislation even disallowed genuine
clergy benefit for a second felonious attempt. Surviving branding
irons show this legislation was enforced, but its wider significance
was that it was the first Tudor encroachment by act of Parliament
upon the traditional liberties of the church.

Yet Henry VII restored law and order after the Wars of the Roses
less by judicature than by inventing swords of Damocles.[25]
As Dudley later confessed, the king wished 'to have many
persons in his danger at his pleasure'.[26] He compelled leading
figures at Court and in the counties to enter into bonds,
recognizances, or obligations (i.e. legally enforceable contracts
with stiff financial penalties) obliging them to remain loyal to
the Crown or to perform specified duties on pain of forfeiture.

Parties were called upon to be bound 'for his grace would have them so made'. And that Henry personally supervised the system is shown by a note in one of John Heron's chamber books 'about certain persons which are not yet through with the king's grace. And his said grace hath a list of their names.'[27] It is true, Henry VII's bonds and recognizances often related to genuine debts owed to the Crown. But many hundreds were political: they required the nobility and gentry to behave in ways determined by the king without reference to the courts of law. Henry's bonds had penalty clauses with forfeits ranging from £100 to £10,000. Though the full penalty would normally be compounded for a large fine, the king's calculated purpose was to hold the magnates at his mercy and to short-circuit due process of common law.[28] If a person was deemed to have misbehaved, the offender would simply be sued for debt on his bond — it was impossible to litigate over the nature or extent of the supposed offence. In other words, Henry VII used bonds to enforce compliance and defeat the law in the way that King John and Richard II had used blank charters, and the system was self-perpetuating, because the consequence of a forfeit bond was a further recognizance for the payment of a fine by instalments.[29] Henry's system may have been politically necessary, but without much doubt it was morally dubious. Whether or not the means justified the ends is a question that has no easy answer.

Polydore Vergil, a visiting collector of papal taxes, whom Henry himself commissioned to write a history of England, made two comments. The first concerned Henry's exemplary treatment of his elite.

The king wished (as he said) to keep all Englishmen obedient through fear, and he considered that whenever they gave him offence they were actuated by their great wealth. . . . All of his subjects who were men of substance when found guilty of whatever fault he harshly fined in order by a penalty which especially deprives of their fortunes not only the men themselves but even their descendants, to make the population less well able to undertake any upheaval and to discourage at the same time all offences.[30]

It is indeed likely that, by means of bonds, Henry VII, in effect, disabled his nobility. Of 62 peerage families alive during the reign, some 46 were at the king's mercy: 7 were under attainder,

36 were bound by obligations or recognizances, of whom 5 at least were heavily fined, and 3 were under constraint by other means. Only 16 families were left alone.[31]

Henry rigorously exploited his prerogative feudal rights too. He issued commissions in all directions and the hunt for revenue led to the appointment, in 1508, of Edward Belknap as surveyor of the king's prerogative. All possible means were used: wardships, escheats, reliefs, licences for the marriage of the king's wards and widows, and searches for concealed lands (i.e. lands legally held *in capite* of the Crown but the facts of tenure concealed from the king's officials). Infractions were meticulously ferreted out despite the administrative complexities: cases were tracked through the legal records going back for decades. In 1505–6, for instance, the commissioners for concealed lands filed ninety-three returns alleging alienations, minorities, idiocies, and intrusions—one case went back over forty years.[32] For landowners these techniques were a two-edged sword: not only did they have to compound promptly for their outstanding dues, but their lands might be seized temporarily by the Crown pending legal proceedings, which meant they also forfeited their own feudal income. If anyone protested too loudly, he would be dragged through the courts, vulnerable to 'the extremity of the law'.

Polydore's second comment concerned Henry's later years. He argued that the first of the Tudors began to practise rapacity.

For he began to treat his people with more harshness and severity than had been his custom, in order (as he himself asserted) to ensure they remained more thoroughly and entirely in obedience to him. The people themselves had another explanation for his action, for they considered they were suffering not on account of their own sins but on account of the greed of their monarch. It is not indeed clear whether at the start it was greed; but afterwards greed did become apparent.[33]

The debate concerning Henry's alleged rapacity still rages, but it is not fruitful since it is not disputed that the king used every available procedure of government to get money. Some of his methods may have been improper, most were undignified, but what was at stake was politics rather than plain rapacity.[34]

On the other hand, the character of Henry's government changed with the rise to prominence of the Council Learned in the Law after 1500.[35] This body comprised some of Henry's most powerful and intimate courtiers: Bray, Empson, Dudley, James Hobart (attorney-general), Thomas Lucas (solicitor-general), John Mordaunt (chancellor of the duchy), and Humphrey Coningsby and Robert Brudenell (king's serjeants). It met in the chamber of the duchy of Lancaster at Westminster, where it formed a specialized board distinct from the King's Council as a whole. Its function was to maintain the king's causes, fiscal and feudal, and exploit his prerogative rights by whatever means were necessary. So members met more or less daily, and were exclusively concerned with enforcement. They interrupted, overrode, or anticipated decisions of the common-law courts, and the board's jurisdiction in contempt enabled it to function as an administrative tribunal untramelled by lack of penal sanctions. By 1500 it was the Council Learned which decided when and where to prosecute evaders of feudal taxes and other Crown rights. And it was this body that increasingly kept the paperwork and put the teeth into Henry VII's system of bonds and recognizances. 'It was a hegemony which, combined with its use of legal process and recognizance, fed by a system of information and enquiry, and governed by astute and searching legal minds and a steady tenacity of purpose, enabled it so to dominate the whole domestic scene in the last decade of the reign.'[36]

The rule of Henry VII and the Council Learned after 1500 was personal monarchy at its height. But did Henry stretch his prerogative too far? It seems that he did in three specific but limited spheres, and the effect was to erode the accepted channels of government and patronage; convention was cast aside by the scale of Henry's use of recognizances, his management of inquisitions *post mortem*, and his sale of offices. In these spheres there was something in the charge of fiscal excess.

There was nothing new about the disciplinary use of financial instruments but Henry's system of recognizances was so extensive that 'it must have created an atmosphere of chronic watchfulness, suspicion, and fear'.[37] Under the Yorkists only one peer gave more than one recognizance, but under Henry VII the number giving several rose to twenty-three: eleven gave 5 or more, two gave as many as 12, and Lord Mountjoy gave 23. Gentry and clergy were also bound, and a large bundle of recognizances was dispatched to Dudley in 1505 to sue for the king's profit. A prisoner in the Tower after Henry's death, Dudley confessed that on eighty-four occasions the king had imposed excessive burdens upon his subjects; persons had been compelled to enter into recognizances in unjust amounts, their true offences considered. A number had been bound, without any condition, in simple and absolute bonds.[38] 'It were', he declared, 'against reason and good conscience, these manner of bonds should be reputed as perfect debts,' and mistakes obviously could arise; among Lord Dacre's complaints was that Empson and Dudley had wrongly turned a recognizance of 3,000 marks into a debt payable at Michaelmas. Dudley said of Henry, 'I think verily his inward mind was never to use them.' This remark indicates that the king's real purpose was to enforce obedience through fiscal coercion in the circumstances of a new dynasty; but if 'watchfulness, suspicion, and fear' were indeed the result, Henry's methods may have smacked of pre-emptive overkill.

His management of inquisitions *post mortem*, too, was pre-emptive. The purpose of these inquests was to establish, by means of juries, whether the king had any rights as tenant-in-chief over the estates of deceased landowners. If the jury found such rights, the lands were immediately taken into the king's hands pending the payment, by the heir apparent, of the necessary feudal taxes. And if the heir was a minor the inquest established the king's right to his marriage, wardship, relief, etc. It is clear that Empson and Dudley sometimes bullied juries at inquests falsely to find lands to be held in chief of the Crown, but these manoeuvres, it appears, were not evidence of rapacity.[39] No financial loss could accrue to the subject, because wronged landowners had a legal remedy either by petition of right, which disclosed new facts not known to the inquest, or by *monstrans de droit*, which relied on the facts as found. The remedy was called traverse: the facts determined at the inquest were denied and the verdict reversed. Any lost profits were returned to the landowner at this stage. Traverses were dealt with by the common-law process of the court of chancery, an obscure but important side of that department's work. The evidence is incomplete but of the fifty cases extant for Henry's reign, in twenty-one instances the Crown conceded the truth of the traverse without delay, and in five cases it admitted, without equivocation, that the inquest was 'feigned'.

In other words, Henry's technique was to shoot first and ask questions afterwards. The confused state of late-fifteenth-century land law and the tax-avoidance to which landowners were prone encouraged the Council Learned to guarantee the Crown the benefit of the doubt, but there was no attempt to restrict or impede procedure by traverse. Henry's aggression at inquests was, however, a break with the past.

Too little is known about sales of offices for firm conclusions to be drawn, but again, in breach of custom Henry VII sold sensitive offices as well as minor ones. English rulers, unlike the kings of France, avoided the blatant sale of royal authority for cash, but among existing office-holders and would-be officials there was some traffic by sale and purchase. Yet Henry was sometimes venal, demanding a premium from anyone appointed to an office of profit. He twice sold the chief justiceship of the court of common pleas for 500 marks (£333).[40] On one of these occasions John Shaa gave 200 marks and an obligation for £200 that Thomas Frowick should be appointed. The merit was that Henry retained a lever he could exert upon the purchaser and thus, indirectly, upon the judge. Next, Lord Daubeney bid the fee of the Speaker of the House of Commons (£100) that Robert Sheffield should have the post, but he was outdone by Bray's bid for Thomas Englefield, who was elected. The record of the first bid was struck through and a memorandum of the second noted in Henry's own hand; the 'election' was handled by Thomas Lovell.[41] Dr John Yonge paid £1,000 upon appointment as master of the rolls; John Erneley was charged £100 for the post of attorney-general; and William Esyngton gave £166 to be attorney-general to the duchy of Lancaster for life, but the grant was held to have been voided in 1509 by the king's death. Minor officials like clerks of the peace paid between £13 and £26, though all these 'sales' must be seen in perspective: his councillors did not buy their offices, nor is it likely that royal grace had ever been entirely free in English history, but Henry VII overturned convention by selling judicial office.

Bacon believed that Henry VII amassed treasure worth £1,800,000, but this is pure myth. Although his revenue from all sources averaged £104,800 per annum in 1502–5, reaching £113,000 per annum by 1509, Henry had been forced to borrow money, raise 'loans' under the signet, and was granted a

benevolence by a Great Council in July 1491. After his chamber
system of finance got into gear, he purchased jewellery, plate,
cloth of gold, etc., and he spent large sums on building. He
rebuilt royal houses at Woodstock, Langley, and Sheen, and
started new works at Woking and Hanworth. The rebuilding
of Sheen began in 1495 and was completed in 1501, when the
king renamed the palace 'Richmond'. His outlay there alone
exceeded £20,000. Between 1491 and 1509 he spent between
£200,000 and £300,000 on jewels and plate — the safest form of
'investment'; but at his death the chamber cash balance was
exhausted. The receipts of Henry VIII had to be used to pay
his father's debts. Perhaps Henry's legacy of plate was worth
two years' gross yield of his revenue?

The likely explanation of Bacon's fable lies in the basic
principle of chamber finance — its receipts were in cash. Whereas
income into the exchequer came as 'assignments', or credits by
tally from local receivers who collected the money and then
disbursed it direct to those the government wished to pay, chamber
receipts came in coin. By European standards Henry VII's
income was comparatively small, but the vast revenues of
Louis XII of France, for instance, were also managed on the
basis of decentralized debit finance. Doubtless it was the glint
of gold in the coffers of his chamber that started the rumour of
Henry's hoard. 'Louis was rich on paper, and that impresses
historians; Henry was rich in cash, and that impressed
contemporaries.'[42]

The ecclesiastical policy of Henry VII raises more intractable
questions. The king was conventionally, even ostentatiously
pious; he founded three religious houses and contributed to
church building and poor relief. He was not personally interested
in theology, but piety was a useful prop to his status and he built
a chapel at the east end of Westminster Abbey to contain his
tomb, endowing ten thousand masses for his soul. He was also
intolerant of heresy, seventy-three suspects being put on trial
in the church courts during his reign, of whom (according to
John Foxe's *Acts and Monuments*) eleven were burned. In
particular, relations between church and state and king and pope
were good, something for which Archbishop Morton was most
likely responsible. For Morton, as well as being one of Henry's

trusted intimates, had visited Rome shortly before Bosworth and secured a promise of support which was implemented decisively once Henry was victorious. Thus the necessary papal dispensation for the king's marriage to Elizabeth of York was quickly granted (it was necessary because both were descended from John of Gaunt). And Innocent VIII issued a bull which pronounced excommunication against persons challenging the marriage or Henry's claim to the throne (27 March 1486). The special relationship had ended by 1489, but relations between king and pope remained smooth, with isolated exceptions, possibly because the papacy needed money and hoped for an English subsidy. Yet it hoped in vain, since, although Henry VII levied clerical taxation at a rate unseen since Henry V's reign, he did so for his own benefit, preparing the way for Henry VIII and Wolsey and sending only £4,000 to Rome.[43]

On the other hand, Henry VII did not renew Edward IV's 1462 confirmation of the church's privileges and customs, though Edward had never enforced the charter's terms and it does not appear that Morton sought a Tudor reissue. And some jurisdictional issues arose. In a reading at the inns of court Thomas Kebell, in 1485, asserted that 'if all the prelates should make a provincial constitution, it would be void, because they cannot change the law of the land'. He meant that English canons were invalid if they contradicted prevailing statute and common law, and the jurisdiction of the church courts in cases of debt and contract had already been attacked by writs of prohibition awarded by king's bench.[44] Some months later the judges were asked to rule upon the validity of the pope's excommunication of some Englishmen who had seized alum from Florentine merchants in England. But Chief Justice Hussey answered by citing precedents of the repudiation of papal jurisdiction in England. Of course, Henry VII at once assured Innocent that as a newcomer to the throne he was reluctant to interfere with due process of law, but this was rhetoric.[45]

Also in 1486 the privilege of ecclesiastical sanctuary was attacked. Sanctuaries were places, usually churches, in which fugitives from justice could find asylum: some places could give permanent refuge although in most sanctuaries the fugitive could legally be starved into submission after forty days. Sanctuary had been mostly respected during the fifteenth century, though

there had been isolated violations by Edward IV and Richard III.
During the hearing of Humphrey Stafford's case for alleged
treason, however, Henry's judges ruled that only the king could
grant sanctuary for treason, and that neither prescription (i.e.
long use of sanctuary) nor a papal bull could amplify a royal
grant. Some judges even argued that no one could grant such
privileges. So it is a sign of willingness on the part of the
Renaissance papacy to co-operate pragmatically with the secular
rulers of Europe that Innocent issued a bull, confirmed by
Alexander VI and Julius II, withdrawing the privilege from
second offenders, tightening control of sanctuaries, and
permitting the Crown to station guards outside.[46] The reform
of the worst ecclesiastical abuses was on the papal agenda in the
interests of protecting genuine privileges, though the judges'
decision of 1486 paved the way for abolition of sanctuary in the
reign of Henry VIII.

Archbishop Morton, meanwhile, obtained bulls from Innocent
to conduct visitations of certain religious houses exempt from
episcopal jurisdiction.[47] In 1493–4 Henry's Council acted
against persons seeking papal bulls without royal permission.[48]
William Walker had accepted provision to the archdeaconry of
St David's without royal assent and had managed to have his
bishop, Hugh Pavy, excommunicated. The abbot of Holy Cross
in Ireland was sworn not to obtain bulls from Rome to the
prejudice of the king. Few bishops, too, thought it worthwhile
to seek secular aid against excommunicates in the last years of
the reign: the total of seventy-six significations for 1500–9 was
the lowest for any decade since 1250. And judicial appeals to
Rome fell sharply, despite a revival in Edward IV's reign.[49]

The Statutes of Provisors and *Praemunire* were the chief
legislation of the Middle Ages regulating ecclesiastical
jurisdiction.[50] They were designed to prohibit the exercise of
papal authority on points prejudicial to the rights and interests
of the king and, when enforced, they defeated canon law. The
Yorkists had not much invoked these acts; Richard III had even
allowed that, if an action already begun in a church court raised
an issue triable at common law, the case was notwithstanding
to be tried by canon law. But Henry VII reversed this policy
and, in contrast with Lancastrian application of the statutes, it
was the king's legal counsel who promoted attacks on the church

courts by actions of *praemunire*, not private litigants. Since the penalties of *praemunire* were life imprisonment and loss of property to the Crown, the matter was important. James Hobart, attorney-general and member of the Council Learned, was prominent in these *praemunire* cases: he began prosecutions in king's bench and, as a JP in Norfolk and Suffolk, he urged defendants in the church courts to file charges against their ecclesiastical judges at quarter sessions. He also allowed Henry VII's legislation that empowered JPs to receive cases on information without indictment to be applied to *praemunire*. And Dudley listed ecclesiastical cases in his confession: seventeen out of the eighty-four persons unjustly treated by Henry VII were churchmen and, in at least two instances, a *praemunire* action was responsible.[51]

In addition to *praemunire* actions, many private litigants were granted writs of prohibition in the reign of Henry VII to prevent the hearing in church courts of cases touching common law. A torrent of cases was brought to king's bench against ecclesiastical judges who, allegedly, had encroached upon royal jurisdiction. In fact, few of these private cases came to judgment and further research will be needed to explain their immediate significance. When, however, it is remembered that it was the application of *praemunire* to the political situation of 1529 that destroyed Wolsey, the long-term relevance of king's-bench proceedings is apparent.[52]

Lastly, Henry VII changed the character of the bench of bishops to the extent that he enervated its religious leadership. Edward IV's later preferments had shown the beginning of a change from Henry VI's policy: appointments began to favour lawyers at the expense of theologians, and a bishopric began to become a reward for administrative services. But Henry VII's policy marked a real shift. 'Of the 16 bishops first appointed to English sees by Edward IV, eight (50%) were doctors learned in the law, and six (38%) were theologians. Of 27 similar appointments made by Henry VII, 16 were lawyers, mostly learned in the civil law (57%), and only six (21%) were theologians.'[53] Most of Henry's theologians, too, were administrators — this transformation of the episcopal bench was a deliberate strategy. Moreover, service to the state, even to the detriment of the church, was required of his bishops.

William Smith, bishop of Lincoln, vainly petitioned to be allowed
to leave the marches of Wales in order to undertake pastoral
work; Richard Redman, of Exeter, had to *buy* permission to
reside in his diocese at the rate of £100 per annum![54] Non-
resident Italians were appointed to the bishoprics of Worcester
and Bath for political services at Rome. And Henry was as severe
with his bishops as with his nobility: even Richard Fox had to
pay £2,000 for a pardon. Most bishops paid heavily for the
restitution of their temporalities, whilst all were subject to fiscal
feudalism and the hunt for revenue following searches among
'old precedents' in the exchequer.[55]

Throughout his reign Henry VII's foreign policy was defensive:
he reacted to external events in order to secure his Crown and
dynasty.[56] Initially in debt to Brittany and France, he had to
neutralize the capacity of France, Spain, Burgundy, and Scotland
to profit from Yorkist claimants and safeguard his northern
border with Scotland. So his first moves were designed to win
time. Truces with France and Scotland were ratified and a
commercial treaty negotiated with Brittany, while talks began
for the betrothal of Prince Arthur and Catherine of Aragon in
March 1488. By the treaty of Medina del Campo (27 March
1489), Aragon and Castile were closed to Yorkist pretenders and
a future marriage alliance projected. Yet what Henry especially
needed was an alliance with the Burgundian Netherlands, the
chief market for English exports and springboard for Yorkists.
The Austrian Habsburg Archduke Maximilian (king of the
Romans from 1486; Holy Roman Emperor from 1493; regent
during the minority of his son Philip) was only prepared,
however, to renew Edward IV's treaty for a year. Harassed at
home by widespread disaffection among the Flemish cities, he
lacked the power to curb the Yorkist intrigues of his mother-in-
law the dowager Duchess Margaret, Edward IV's sister, whose
dower lands gave her the means to take independent action. Also
he was distracted by his need to defend Austrian Habsburg lands
against the Hungarians.

Henry VII's first major decision was reluctantly to aid Brittany
by the treaty of Redon (14 February 1489) when Charles VIII
of France overtly threatened to annex the duchy. Six thousand
English troops were sent under Lord Daubeney's command. The

Bretons, however, were themselves divided, while their Habsburg and Spanish allies were unreliable. When in the face of defeat Anne of Brittany married Charles VIII (6 December 1491), the reunification of France begun by Joan of Arc and Charles VII was virtually completed. Henry VII therefore made a show of strength: he asserted his claim to the French Crown, although his intention was to repeat Edward IV's pecuniary treaty of Picquigny (18 August 1475). And he succeeded. In the autumn of 1492 he marched into the Boulonnais at the head of an army of twenty-six thousand men, but negotiated the treaty of Étaples after a campaign of only thirty-three days. Charles VIII undertook to withdraw his support for Perkin Warbeck and other Yorkist claimants; to reimburse the arrears of Edward IV's pension due by the earlier treaty; and to indemnify the costs of Henry's interventions in Brittany (£124,000) by remitting twice-yearly instalments of £25,000.

In fact, Charles VIII was eager to begin his Italian adventures. His victories encouraged the European states to forge defensive alliances. So the treaty of Medina del Campo was confirmed; England joined the Holy League; and the truce of Ayton was agreed with James IV of Scotland. Although James did not abandon the 'Auld Alliance' with France, he married Henry VII's daughter Margaret in August 1503. The *Magnus Intercursus* meanwhile closed the Low Countries to the Yorkists (24 February 1496). This treaty was the culmination of lengthy economic warfare. Henry's patience with Maximilian over his aid to Perkin Warbeck snapped at the end of 1493; English trade with Antwerp and the Low Countries was therefore diverted to Calais; Maximilian and Philip retaliated with a counter-embargo in May 1494. Accordingly the treaty combined political and commercial clauses: trade was restored on the old terms on condition that each government did not harbour the other's rebels, while Maximilian and Philip promised that the Duchess Margaret should forfeit her dower lands if she disobeyed. Although new disruptions occurred when Philip tried to impose a new import duty on cloth, the *Magnus Intercursus* was confirmed by a second treaty in May 1499.

The same month Catherine of Aragon married Prince Arthur by proxy. She finally arrived in England in October 1501 and the marriage was celebrated in person on 14 November. But

Arthur died at Ludlow on 2 April 1502. Ten months later
Elizabeth of York did not recover from giving birth to a
daughter — the child also died. Although Spain tried to reclaim
Catherine's dowry in a tactical move, little time was lost in
starting negotiations for her marriage to Prince Henry. Then
other deaths complicated the picture, so that, despite the arrival
of the necessary papal dispensation by March 1505, the marriage
treaty was not put into effect during Henry VII's lifetime.

Isabella of Castile died in November 1504. Although the union
of the two Spanish kingdoms had been achieved by the marriage
of Ferdinand of Aragon and Isabella, Spain seemed to be
breaking apart after Isabella's death, for Ferdinand and the
Archduke Philip became competitors for the regency of Castile
(Philip's claim was by right of his wife Joanna, daughter of
Ferdinand and Isabella). This meant that the two allies upon
whom Henry VII depended for insurance against France had
become rivals. His reaction was to engineer an Anglo-
Burgundian *rapprochement*: he 'lent' Philip £138,000 in 1505 to
aid his attempt to claim Castile — a total of £342,000 had been
provided by 1509.[57] Ferdinand's response was to turn to France
by the treaty of Blois (October 1505): he married Louis XII's
niece the following March. Louis and Ferdinand were therefore
aligned against Philip, Maximilian, and Henry VII. Castile was
the prize and the Low Countries the bait. So when in January
1506 Philip and Joanna were blown ashore near Weymouth *en
route* for Castile, Henry VII entertained them for three months!
The resulting treaty of Windsor (9 February) was Henry's
rejoinder to the treaty of Blois. First, he recognized Philip as king
of Castile and pledged himself (within limits) to assist him should
anyone invade his present or future dominions. Second, the two
parties promised mutual defence and refused to countenance the
other's rebels. Next, by a second treaty, Philip and Joanna
undertook to arrange Henry's marriage to Philip's sister
Margaret of Savoy, then the effective governor of the Low
Countries. Finally, Philip authorized the commercial negotiations
that led to the *Malus Intercursus* (30 April 1506), so called by the
Flemings because it was markedly favourable to England.
However, the treaty never came into effect.

Philip died in September 1506, and his death robbed Henry of
his bargains. The Low Countries passed to Philip's six-year-old

son Charles, while Ferdinand reasserted himself as regent of Castile by confining Joanna to virtual imprisonment on grounds of insanity. Although Henry seriously contemplated an Anglo-Burgundian-Spanish alliance by proposing marriage to Joanna and putting Catherine of Aragon's nuptials back on the agenda, he played safe in the end, settling for a triple *entente* between England, the Netherlands, and France. Marriage was therefore planned between the young Archduke Charles (later Charles V) and Henry's younger daughter Mary, and between Prince Henry and Margaret of Angoulême, sister to Francis, heir presumptive of France. Yet the cockpit of European diplomacy had become Italy, where Louis XII broke with Venice and reached an understanding with Ferdinand. So when in December 1508 the League of Cambrai was formed, its members were the pope, Louis XII, Maximilian, Charles, and Ferdinand. But although Henry was left out, he was not isolated: all parties to the alliance cultivated England's friendship, so her interests were secure unless she revived Henry V's claim to the French Crown.

The cultural climate under Henry VII is hard to assess. Edward IV and Richard III were book collectors and patrons of learning, and Henry and Margaret Beaufort, his mother, emulated them. Henry added the office of royal librarian to his household and built a library at Richmond. Yet humanism barely penetrated the royal establishment: Henry's library contained few English or Latin works but was filled with French vernacular writings — the works of Froissart, Chartier, Christine de Pisan, and others. Prose romances were well represented along with French translations of classical texts, and it appears that both Henry VII and Henry VIII collected books without humanistic direction. Their emphasis was on 'learned' or 'poetic' chivalry, and neither king was interested in Greek or Latin for its own sake.[58]

The striking cultural shift of the period was the increased output of the printing presses. Henry VII appointed a king's printer from 1504 and two Norman Frenchmen resident in London held the post: William Faques (from 1504) and Richard Pynson (from 1508). Wynkyn de Worde, from Wörth in Alsace, acted as printer to Margaret Beaufort. He had been Caxton's assistant from the time of the introduction of printing into

England in 1476, and inherited Caxton's premises and printing materials in 1491.[59]

The rise of domestic printing galvanized change: it acted as a catalyst, speeding and transforming existing channels so that, in the long term, a more demanding, individualistic, and better informed culture was created. Writing in Elizabeth's reign, John Foxe, the Protestant martyrologist, spoke of 'the excellent art of Printing . . . whereby great increase of learning and knowledge, with innumerable commodities else have ensued, and daily do ensue to the life of man, and especially to the furtherance of true religion'.[60] It was not accidental that the European Reformation coincided with the rise of printing technology; in England, Henry VIII's quarrel with the pope offered printers the ideal opportunity to develop their trade in religious and controversial literature. The output of books steadily climbed: whereas Caxton printed only 107 items between 1476 and 1491, during the 1520s 550 titles were printed in England, 739 during the 1530s, 928 during the 1540s, and 1,040 during the 1550s.[61] True, the size of editions was small: as late as 1563 the government asked for 300 copies of a work intended for a foreign as well as a home market. In fact, 600–700 copies was a large print run, though the first edition of Tyndale's English *New Testament* (1525) exceptionally numbered 3,000 copies. Yet books were regarded as common property in the Renaissance and were not hidden away by individual owners unless heretical. Knowledge was regarded as 'a gift of God and cannot be sold': this medieval idea was fortified by Christ's injunction 'Freely ye have received, freely give' (Matt. 10: 8). Sometimes ownership inscriptions would appear in the form 'Liber Ricardi Pace et Amicorum' — 'The book of Richard Pace and his friends'. Like modern periodicals, therefore, the circulation was much larger than the print run, and, in a culture in which ideas were transmitted orally as much as, or more than, by the written word, the influence of books was even greater than the circulation.

Henry VII's reign was distinguished by sober statesmanship. Bosworth's victor was a stabilizer: he could be ruthless and severe, but was neither bloodthirsty nor egoistical. By comparison with Henry V, Edward IV, and Henry VIII, he appears shadowy

and remote. In fact, he kept his distance, sharing this quality
with Henry IV, Henry VI, and Mary, Queen of Scots, though
not to extremes.[62] In 1492 he personally led his 'army royal'
to France in the knowledge that the nobility (and Parliament)
exalted kings who defended their honour while belittling those
who (like Henry VI) eschewed chivalric obligation. Henry also
attempted to centralize English politics. The Tudor Court began
to exercise magnetic influence, and, if much territorial power
still lay in the hands of regional magnates, faction was tamed
by recognizance and the exaction of royal prerogative rights by
the Council Learned. Lastly, Henry's diplomacy and security
measures guaranteed his dynasty's survival. The turbulence of
the fifteenth century was quelled: the way was cleared for Wolsey
and Thomas Cromwell. Yet Henry's acumen was the dynamic
force—not divine right, as his propaganda claimed. Like
Charles II—though this was the only similarity between them—
he did not wish to go on his travels again.

WOLSEY'S ASCENDANCY

OWING to Prince Arthur's death, Henry VII was succeeded on 22 April 1509 by his younger son, who, under pressure from the Council, began his reign by marrying Catherine of Aragon, his brother's widow. This union had momentous consequences later but, at the time, it fulfilled Henry VII's treaty obligation. Henry VIII continued by executing Empson and Dudley. His accession was followed by a political backlash, springing from resentment of Henry VII's Council Learned, and of his system of bonds, recognizances, and obligations. Some common lawyers also opposed the informality of the Yorkist–Tudor 'land revenue' experiment. Since the receivers of Crown lands rendered their accounts in the king's chamber, they bypassed not only the financial but also the legal procedures of the exchequer. This caused mounting concern: it was not clear whether such methods were fully grounded in the law of the land, and therefore whether they were valid. Furthermore, the decisions of the Council Learned and chamber officials were not formally entered in the records of any of the courts of common law but were often verbal or jotted down into notebooks. These questions were debated by councillors and common-law judges in October and November 1509, when it was resolved that the so-called 'by-courts' of the experiment should be abolished. In the words of the Council register: 'it was thought to the said Council and judges expedient and necessary to annul the said courts that they be no more used.'[1]

The register spoke the truth: 'expediency' ruled at the accession of Henry VIII. By an act of his first Parliament, which met in January–February 1510, chamber finance was put on a statutory footing and left to continue more or less as before. But the Council Learned was abolished as a specialist arm of the Council, and the general surveyors of Crown lands were subjected to the normal processes of the exchequer, losing the power to take recognizances for due performance of an office or for the payments of debts. Also in November 1509 the general commissions of *oyer et terminer* (i.e. special assizes throughout the realm to redress grievances) that the Council had ordered in July 1509 were stopped. Although many grievances had been brought before the commissioners, the majority of complaints had been trivial: 'few criminal causes or other for which such commissions should be granted were there sued.'[2] The reaction against Henry VII's government was emotional and unsupported by hard evidence; Empson and Dudley were convicted of treason in show trials but bills in Parliament to attaint them got nowhere. They were imprisoned for a year, then beheaded; the executions were a calculated ploy to enable the new regime to profit from the stability won by Henry VII without incurring any of its attendant stigma. To complete the charade a few of Henry VII's bonds were cancelled, on the grounds that they 'were made without any cause, reasonable or lawful . . . by the undue means of certain of the learned council of our said late father thereunto driven, contrary to law, reason and good conscience'.[3] The measure was a sop to Cerberus, but it worked; no one complained that Henry VIII's government omitted to cancel the bulk of the outstanding bonds, many of which did not expire until the 1520s. Yet Henry VIII showed his mind by these proceedings; something of his ruthlessness was revealed even though he was barely eighteen years of age at his accession.

Henry VIII's character was fascinating, threatening, and sometimes morbid. His egoism, self-righteousness, and capacity to brood sprang from the fusion of an able but second-rate mind with what looks suspiciously like an inferiority complex. Henry VII had restored stability and royal authority, but it may have been for reasons of character, as much as policy, that his son resolved to augment his regal power. As his reign unfolded, Henry VIII added 'imperial' concepts of kingship to existing 'feudal' ones; he sought to give the words *rex imperator* a meaning unseen since the days of the Roman Empire. He was eager, too, to conquer — to emulate the glorious victories of the Black Prince and Henry V, to quest after the golden fleece that was the French Crown. He wished, in fact, to revive the Hundred Years War, despite the success of Valois France in consolidating its territory and the shift of emphasis of European politics towards Italy and Spain. Repeatedly the efforts of his more constructive councillors were bedevilled, and overthrown, by his chivalric dreams, and by costly wars that wasted men, money, and equipment. If, however, humanist criticism of warfare by Colet, Erasmus, and Thomas More is well known, it should not be forgotten that 'honour' in the Renaissance was necessarily defended in the last resort by battle. 'Honour' was the cornerstone of aristocratic culture; sovereign rulers argued that unlike their subjects they lacked 'superiors' from whom redress of grievances might be sought, and so had no choice but to accept the 'arbitrament' of war when diplomacy failed. Also war was the 'sport of kings'. By competing dynastically and territorially with his European counterparts, especially Francis I, Henry VIII acknowledged settled convention and, even more obviously, popular demand. His reign saw the boldest and most extensive invasions of France since the reign of Henry V. In fact, only a minority of contemporaries had any sense of the serious long-term economic damage that Renaissance warfare could inflict.

Since Henry VIII enjoyed 'pastime with good company', as he claimed in a song he wrote himself, he was less consistently arbiter of his policy than his father. He found writing state papers 'both tedious and painful'; like Edward IV, but unlike Henry VII, he participated fully in the disport of his Court. Yet he wielded decisive influence on important topics, for instance diplomacy, the invasion of France, the tactics of his first divorce, the definition of the royal supremacy, and the theology of the Church of England during the 1540s. That Wolsey and Thomas Cromwell enjoyed prime-ministerial ascendancy on the scale often attributed to them is illusory, though both largely controlled the implementation of policy as executives once it was decided. True, Henry allowed his Council the freedom to initiate policy on many matters, far more so than Henry VII or Elizabeth I. At certain times councillors enjoyed wide latitude, though they always operated within the limits of Henry's trust and confidence: there were ministers but not prime ministers. And if ministers pursued policies unapproved by the king, they did so at their peril, or behind his back when he was busy with private matters. But the ease of access to his presence that Henry permitted courtiers, rival councillors, and foreign ambassadors alike ensured he did not long remain ignorant of vital political developments. His Court perambulated southern England and

the Midlands, but communications with London and
Westminster were maintained on a daily, if not twice-daily
basis. Henry's ministers and courtiers were engaged in
constant political intrigue and competition for patronage and
advancement, but the king remained the ultimate source of power.

Henry, not Wolsey or Cromwell, was therefore in charge. But,
though his decisions made and broke wives, councillors, and
factions, he listened to his intimates far more than he supposed
and was influenced and even manipulated by the prevailing
balance at Court. Whereas tradition has the king jesting, 'If I
thought my cap knew my counsel, I would cast it into the fire
and burn it,'[4] Henry in reality wore his heart on his sleeve.
Indeed, John Foxe, despite blatant Protestant bias, hit several
nails on the head when he wrote:

So long as Queen Anne, Thomas Cromwell, Archbishop Cranmer,
Master Denny, Doctor Butts, with such like were about him, and could
prevail with him, what organ of Christ's glory did more good in the
church than he? . . . Thus, while good counsel was about him, and
could be heard, the king did much good. So again, when sinister and
wicked counsel, under subtle and crafty pretences, had gotten once
the foot in, thrusting truth and verity out of the prince's ears, how
much religion and all good things went prosperously forward before,
so much, on the contrary side, all revolted backward again.[5]

Thomas Wolsey, Henry's first minister, enjoyed greater freedom
than his successor, Cromwell. This was because the young Henry
intervened less before 1527 (possibly 1525) than afterwards. The
turning-point in this respect was the king's first divorce
campaign, which began in earnest in the summer of 1527 when
Henry himself seized the initiative from an absent Wolsey in
soliciting support and orchestrating the debate.[6] If, however,
Henry's pastimes distracted him more during the first half of
his reign, it was precisely because he was satisfied with Wolsey.
Indeed, this implies that Wolsey, who has been depicted as *alter
rex* (i.e. 'second king') as much as minister, was far more the
loyal servant of the Crown than conventional historiography has
suggested.[7] Wolsey first took his seat on the Council in June
1510. Born in 1472, he was the son of an Ipswich butcher; seeking
preferment in the church, he graduated BA at Magdalen College,

Oxford, and was elected a fellow of the college in 1497. Ordained priest in 1498, he became bursar of Magdalen but was accused of appropriating funds to the completion of Magdalen tower without proper authority. Although it is usually claimed that this behaviour exemplified his approach to government, it is more likely that the story is apocryphal, a smear on Wolsey following his support for Richard Mayhew, the absentee president of Magdalen, in an academic squabble.

After 1501 Wolsey was appointed to several benefices in plurality and was successively chaplain to Archbishop Henry Deane and to Sir Richard Nanfan, deputy of Calais. Nanfan recommended him to Henry VII in 1507 and the king made him a royal chaplain, sending him on diplomatic missions to Scotland and Flanders and appointing him dean of both Lincoln and Hereford cathedrals. Wolsey became almoner to Henry VIII in November 1509 and five months later succeeded Thomas Ruthal as registrar of the Order of the Garter. But the breakthrough was his seat on the Council. His mentor was Richard Fox, who had returned to the limelight on Henry VIII's accession. Fox was lord privy seal but he needed assistance, and Wolsey proved his flair for administration during Henry VIII's early wars against France. An Anglo-Spanish campaign of 1512 to recover Aquitaine was unsuccessful, but Wolsey in 1513 co-ordinated Henry VIII's invasion of northern France that resulted in the occupation of Thérouanne and Tournai. These conquests were of little strategic value—Thomas Cromwell called them 'ungracious dogholes' during the Parliament of 1523—but they pleased the king. And in September 1513 the earl of Surrey defeated the Scots, with whom Louis XII had concluded a league, at the battle of Flodden. The elite of Scotland—the king, three bishops, eleven earls, fifteen lords, and some ten thousand men—were slain.

Henry VIII followed war by diplomacy. In August 1514 Wolsey negotiated a treaty whereby Henry and Louis XII swore a peace to last until a year after the death of either, Henry recovered his pension due under the treaty of Étaples, and Louis married Henry's younger sister Mary. 'I was the author of the peace,' bragged Wolsey. But the boast was true and he immediately exchanged the bishopric of Lincoln, given to him in February 1514, for the vacant archbishopric of York.

Pope Leo X had already granted him the bishopric of Tournai, but Wolsey found it impossible in practice to collect his revenues in the face of competition from a rival French bishop-elect.

Wolsey's success in arranging the Anglo-French marriage showed his ability to conduct diplomacy. Seductive charm was partly the key to Tudor ministerial prowess, and George Cavendish, Wolsey's contemporary biographer, attributed to him 'a special gift of natural eloquence with a filed tongue to pronounce the same'. He was thus 'able with the same to persuade and allure all men to his purpose'.[8] When the older councillors, bred under Henry VII, complained that his son was too wedded to pleasure and suggested that he attend Council meetings more regularly, Wolsey, to Henry VIII's delight, counselled the exact opposite. Cavendish claimed Wolsey openly offered to relieve Henry of the weight of public affairs; it seems unlikely but Wolsey got his way by whatever means. 'Thus the almoner ruled all them that before ruled him.'[9]

Wolsey, like Disraeli, had no guiding political principles. He was flexible and opportunist; he thought in European terms and on the grand scale; and he was the consummate politician. His policies had the effect of centralizing English politics: the firm rule of Henry VII was continued by different means, and political attention was focused on Westminster and the king's Court, rather than on the territorial feuds of magnates and men of worship. Wolsey interfered constantly in the affairs of the nobility, leading gentry, and citizens of London, and demanded the attendance of many of them at Court. He packed his own household, too, with great men, rivalling the king—to the point that the poet John Skelton quipped:

> Why come ye nat to court?
> To which court?
> To the king's court?
> Or to Hampton Court?[10]

Hampton Court was, of course, Wolsey's sumptuous palace on the Thames.

Wolsey's centralizing vision was an important step towards the emergence of national identity under the Tudors, but the minister himself was both good and bad. While recent research has confounded the truth of most of Skelton's attacks,[11] it can scarcely be denied that Wolsey's buildings, chapels, art collections, and projected tomb, as well as the style and size of his household, marked conscious attempts to rival Henry. Foreign envoys described Wolsey as a 'second king' almost all of the time, and not simply when he was playing the diplomatic game as Henry's surrogate abroad. If, as can be argued, he was merely acting as the king's loyal servant, so later did Thomas Cromwell and William Cecil, neither of whom required such conspicuous wealth, pomp, and circumstance. It must be said that the complaints of Skelton, John Palsgrave, and the authors of the articles laid before the House of Lords in December 1529 attacking Wolsey's arrogance and misrule were part of a ruthless campaign to attaint him after his dismissal as lord chancellor. Far too much weight and attention are conventionally given to them. Wolsey had some powerful enemies who plotted his death once the king's favour was lost. On the other hand, a number of the charges, if absurdly exaggerated, contained elements of truth. Wolsey had tended to arrogate power to himself in the Council, depriving the king of attendant councillors at Court. His fiscalism became counterproductive between 1522 and 1525, showing Tudor government at its most ambitious and least effective. In the 1523 Parliament he was arrogant and maladroit. The Anglo-French peace of 1525 was a political mistake (opposed by influential nobles). Lastly, Wolsey often declined to delegate or finish things he had begun, thereby clogging up the administrative machine.

After centuries of vilification Wolsey's reputation is in the process of rehabilitation, and yet a sense of proportion must be retained. If he was creative and, with minor blemishes, constructive in star chamber, in Parliament he was arrogant and insensitive. His fiscal policy lost touch with reality, while he treated domestic government generally as a series of cavalry charges. What he started, he rarely completed; he worked in fits and starts, stimulated by the scent of political advantage rather than sustained concern that policy should be seen through. As lord chancellor he sought better law enforcement, justice for the poor, and the Crown's re-endowment through regular taxation, but he met with mixed success; in particular he defied accepted constitutional wisdom by attempting to levy taxation without parliamentary consent. In short, he was strong on rhetoric but weak on results. Contrary to the version of tradition, he obtained the Council's support for his actions. Indeed, it has been suggested that Wolsey's biggest failure, the Amicable Grant, was loyally backed by the dukes of Norfolk and Suffolk, the earl of Shrewsbury, Cuthbert Tunstall (bishop of London), Thomas More, and other councillors, as well as by the judges.[12] But it is equally true that Wolsey thought irrelevant the views of everyone except Henry VIII, or brushed them aside because he presumed them hostile, wrong, or ignorant. In diplomacy he endeavoured to establish a European concert for the purposes of peace, but was constrained, through Henry VIII's will and sheer opportunism, to advocate war. His object, in any case, was less peace than power and glory: honour for his royal master and himself. And his confidence in his own abilities sometimes moved him to an almost callous optimism, as in star chamber where despite advice he became a plaintiffs' judge as well as litigants' chancellor.

Of course, if Wolsey were merely following Henry VIII's specific orders, the picture would look very different. Indeed, Wolsey consistently maintained the posture of the king's loyal executive; this was not simply a matter of tact or presentation: it was strictly true. But, although Henry was in charge of *overall* policy and occasionally fumed that he 'would be obeyed, whosoever spake to the contrary', only in the broadest respects was he taking independent decisions whilst Wolsey's career was at its height, though he kept a much tighter rein on patronage (including ecclesiastical patronage) than is sometimes supposed. True, Henry was attentive to Wolsey's letters: he read them carefully, and answered all outstanding questions; he retained his own independent sources of information, and enjoyed catching out Wolsey's sources from time to time. But until the summer of 1527 it was Wolsey who almost invariably calculated the available options and ranked them for royal consideration; who established the parameters of each successive debate; who controlled the flow of official information; who selected the king's secretaries, middle-rank officials, and JPs; and who promulgated decisions he himself had largely shaped, if not strictly taken. In the domestic sphere fiscal policy in the early 1520s was inevitably dictated by Henry's invasion schemes and campaigns of 1522 and 1523, yet the king's specific responsibility for Wolsey's 'loans' of 1522–3 and the Amicable Grant has never been documented. And in foreign affairs, though Henry's responsibility for the broad outline of his policy is not in doubt, more than mere details were left to Wolsey. To foreign ambassadors, Henry seemed largely consistent: he was bent on conquering new territory in France, an objective which in principle Wolsey shared, but about which in practice he reserved judgement.[13] Wolsey always saw ambassadors first, replying to them *extempore*. What he said was normally repeated unchanged by Henry at a later interview. Only rarely did Henry and Wolsey disagree, as in the summer of 1521, when Wolsey was at Calais and thus unable to ride to Court, or in the spring of 1522, when Wolsey urged a combined attack on the French navy at anchor in various ports, but Henry apparently thought the plan too risky.[14] So king and minister routinely worked in harmonious concert. Yet to explain away Wolsey's greed, monopolistic tendencies, and frequent bullying tactics on the grounds that they were not only useful to Henry's service, but indulged deliberately as a matter of royal policy, is to say more than we can know.

It is, however, true that Henry saw the diplomatic value of Wolsey's arrogation of power. He reported the Anglo-French peace to the pope on 12 August 1514, and in another letter dated the same day he asked Leo to make Wolsey a cardinal, saying he could achieve nothing without him, and that he esteemed him above his dearest friends.[15] In fact, Wolsey had not been shy to anticipate Henry's letter through his own agents, who had been lobbying the pope since May. But objections were raised to Wolsey's candidature. It was rumoured, not without some foundation, that he was implicated in the poisoning at Rome of his predecessor as archbishop of York; moreover, the Italian cardinals disliked English and French prelates. It took a year's haggling in the Consistory before Leo obliged Henry. Wolsey was elected a cardinal in September 1515. His title was that of 'Saint Cecilia beyond Tiber of the Holy Church of Rome', a lucky strike, purred his agent, 'as many popes have proceeded from it'.[16]

No sooner had Wolsey learned the news than he was demanding that his cardinal's robes be sent in time for the session of Parliament scheduled for early November. 'It shall be necessary', he wrote, 'that I have the habit and hat of a cardinal, and whereas there be none here that can make the said habit . . . send to me two or three hoods of such fashion and colour as cardinals be wont to wear . . . [with] silk used by cardinals there for making of kirtles and other garments.'[17] One of the charges against Wolsey at his fall in 1529 was that the public triumph he organized for the receiving of his hat in London, which Cavendish likened to the coronation of a mighty prince, was a 'prodigal and wasteful expense' and a 'token of vainglory'.[18]

On 22 December 1515 Archbishop Warham resigned as lord chancellor. Tradition reports that Wolsey's aggression drove Warham from the scene but the fact is that this somewhat morose and inflexible prelate felt incongruous at the Court of Henry VIII. Warham had not approved of Henry's marriage to his brother's wife though, ironically, he later enraged the king by affirming its validity. He was also bogged down in a tedious dispute with the suffragan bishops of his province over probate of wills. Warham and Wolsey were rivals, but Thomas More understood Warham to have openly professed himself willing to retire.[19] Since Fox wished to withdraw in order to perform pastoral duties in his diocese of Winchester, Wolsey's succession to the chancellorship was assured. On Christmas Eve after vespers he swore his oath of office before Henry in the chapel at Eltham palace. The formalities completed, his ascendancy began, to end only when Henry's conflict with the pope rendered his position as cardinal–minister untenable.

At once Wolsey turned his attention to the court of star chamber, which within a few years was transformed into a mainstream tribunal of law enforcement and impartial justice to match the civil jurisdiction enjoyed by the court of chancery. Whereas under Henry VII only 300 or so lawsuits were initiated in star chamber (a mere 12 per annum), under Wolsey 1,685 suits (120 per annum) were filed — a workload that was the direct consequence of ministerial sponsorship. In chancery Wolsey received 535 suits per annum, as against the 500 or so petitions filed each year between 1487 and 1515 under Archbishops Morton and Warham, which suggests that he made less impact on that court. In fact, Wolsey had more important tasks to

perform than to judge chancery cases and we do not know how
often the master of the rolls deputized for him. Star chamber
was crucial, however, to Wolsey's statecraft because he rested
his reputation upon the policies he promulgated there. He sat
as a judge in the court several times a week.[20]

His first policy was his law-enforcement plan, unveiled before
Henry VIII and the Council on 2 May 1516 and reiterated in
May 1517 and October 1519. This concentrated into star
chamber the traditional enforcement jurisdiction of both the
Council and the former statutory tribunals of the reign of
Henry VII. Enforcement under Wolsey meant both the
investigation and prosecution of crime and corruption of justice
(with prosecution preferably at common law), and the stream-
lining of all existing legal machinery. He aimed to provide
impartial justice in the ordinary courts of common law, irrespective
of a litigant's social status, with the assignment to star chamber
of a firm supervisory and, if necessary, punitive power, thus
improving the efficiency of the system. This amounted to an
attack on the corrupt methods associated with 'bastard
feudalism'. And Wolsey investigated and attacked without delay
the illegal acts, abuses, and judicial malfeasance perpetrated in
their counties by the king's own councillors, JPs, and sheriffs.
He threatened Sir Andrew Windsor, a councillor and keeper
of the king's wardrobe, with the 'new law of the star chamber';
he sent Sir Robert Sheffield, another councillor who as Speaker
of the 1512 Parliament had thwarted Wolsey, to the Tower as
an accessory to felony, fined him £5,333 for 'opprobrious words',
and obliged him to confess that he arrived at this astronomical
fine only through the minister's 'charitable' mediation. He sent
the earl of Northumberland to the Fleet prison; he prosecuted
Sir William Bulmer as an illegal retainer and tried three Surrey
JPs for corruption in show trials; he even brought three *praemunire*
cases in star chamber — a unique instance of the court's use for
that purpose. He continued with a series of inquiries into the
prevalence of crime and 'enormities' against justice in the
localities, using individual councillors, the assize judges, members
of his household, and trusted JPs as the instruments by which
reliable evidence could be obtained. On receipt of news
concerning alleged offences, Wolsey acted either by summoning
the offenders into star chamber, or by appointing commissioners

of *oyer et terminer* to try cases in accordance with accepted legal procedure. He also publicized his wish to receive complaints about wrongdoing from private individuals; the concomitant of his enforcement policy thus became the facility of open access to star chamber. It was axiomatic under Wolsey that men with grievances who were unable to obtain justice at common law, especially before JPs, should be allowed to file bills in star chamber.[21] Such bills were also received in chancery but most went to star chamber.

Wolsey's second policy was to emphasize the merits of the justice of star chamber and chancery for private parties. To throw open the doors of the courts was a bold and radical move; in an age when the slogan was 'Justice is a fat fee', Wolsey proclaimed the notion that the people should have justice as a right. It must be remembered that he did so partly so that litigants might complain against those whom, like Sheffield, Wolsey wanted to hammer. But the idea was admirable save that the provision of abstract 'justice' was an almost Sisyphean task. Wolsey attracted far too much business to star chamber; his popularization policy backfired when the court's machinery became clogged with civil actions. In 1517, 1518, and 1520 Wolsey thus established a temporary series of overflow tribunals to relieve the pressure on star chamber, and in 1519 he settled a permanent judicial committee at the White Hall at Westminster. Staffed by judges chosen from among those who had formerly dealt with the suits of the poor as members of Henry VIII's household, the White Hall court became the immediate ancestor of the later court of requests. Yet even this was not enough, and Wolsey compounded the backlog of litigation by neglecting to complete the organization of star chamber during the ensuing decade, when he was distracted by war, diplomacy, and the divorce. The final organization of the court he left to his successors.[22]

Adjunct to Wolsey's policy of impartial justice was his campaign against enclosing landlords. Tudor theorists believed that enclosures brought about the decay of villages and the neglect or demolition of houses, and caused unemployment. Enclosure meant the extinction of common rights over land; hedges and fences were erected and common grazing forbidden. The change might accompany a shift from arable to pastoral husbandry and the critics assumed this to be the landowners' goal—hence the connection with unemployment. Sheep runs, the argument went, needed fewer labourers than ploughed fields. And the classic fable was that of sheep eating men, since it was easy to portray landlords as exploiters of the poor and enclosures as instruments of oppression.

The subject of enclosures belongs, of course, to a discussion of the economics of farming. In that context enclosures were, first, not widespread in the sixteenth century—half the agricultural land of England was still to be enclosed as late as 1700. Enclosing had taken place in the Middle Ages, too, without upheaval. Next, the economic gains to the enclosed region were small, perhaps no more than a 13 per cent increase in agricultural productivity, though the benefit to landowners from increased rents could be greater. Lastly, wool prices fell relative to grain prices as the sixteenth century progressed, so the long-term incentive was not, in any case, to switch from arable to sheep farming. A practice related to enclosures, however, the engrossing of farms, may have been damaging to rural employment. Engrossing meant the amalgamation of two or more farms into one, often by outside speculators who demolished superfluous farmhouses, left them to decay, or downgraded them to accommodate cottagers. The amalgamated properties were then enclosed and sold, or leased, to genuine farmers at a profit, since by depriving the community of common rights the land was worth more.

Enclosing, engrossing, and conversion of arable land to pasture were attacked by statute in 1489 and 1514–15. The acts forbade new enclosures and ordered demolished buildings to be reconstructed and land restored to tillage. Wolsey, who approached enclosures from the perspective of equity rather than economics, launched a national inquiry in 1517–18 to discover how many farmhouses had been destroyed, how much land had been enclosed, by whom, when, and where. The commissioners reported to Wolsey's chancery and it was eventually decided to proceed against 264 landlords or corporations.[23] One landowner summoned to the court of exchequer was Thomas More—ironically, since More in Book I of his *Utopia* (1516) had repeated the fable that sheep ate men. In Hilary term 1527 he pleaded that his lands in Fringford, Oxfordshire, had been returned to tillage and a house rebuilt. Seventy-four other defendants pleaded guilty and undertook to rebuild farmhouses or convert pasture back to cultivation. Others pleaded not guilty or argued that they had enclosed their land by local agreement. Some defended their actions as beneficial to the commonwealth. Many cases dragged on for years but, surprisingly, 222 cases were decided by the courts, of which 188 ended with clear verdicts — a very high proportion for Tudor litigation.

Wolsey kept his eye on the prosecutions, but it is far from proved that many convicted defendants, like More, satisfied the terms of their recognizances by removing hedges, rebuilding houses, etc. And, while the proportion of decided cases indicates that Wolsey was in earnest, his seriousness did not override his fiscalism. In the Parliament of 1523 Wolsey agreed to abandon his enclosure policy for eighteen months as part of the deal whereby he raised a subsidy worth £151,215. He even granted the landowners a complete amnesty until October 1524, something unthinkable had he sincerely regarded enclosures as the evil he claimed them to be.[24] True, the king's urgent need for money in 1523 put Wolsey on the spot. But when his amnesty is linked to our suspicion that Wolsey offered justice to the poor partly to strike back at those among the rich who were his political opponents, a more sceptical view of his philanthropy seems appropriate. In fact, there is considerable ambiguity about his domestic policy, while Tudor opinion, too, is open to more than one interpretation. When contemporaries said to Wolsey, 'there was never thing done in England more for the common weal than to redress these enormous decays of towns and making of enclosures', did they speak the truth, or indulge the minister's vanity?[25]

We must not be too hard on Wolsey since, in pre-Reformation England, councillors and local administrators were conditioned to think in moral rather than empirical terms. Sir Thomas Smith, William Cecil's mentor and a privy councillor to both Edward VI and Elizabeth, better understood Tudor economic problems. Drafting *A Discourse of the Commonweal of this Realm of England* in 1549, he set out systematically to discover the causes of people's complaints and to propose practical remedies. He wrote, 'Experience should seem to prove plainly that enclosures should be profitable and not hurtful to the Commonweal.'[26] Smith's methodology, however, contentious even in his own time, was alien thirty years earlier. The vision of pre-Reformation humanism extolled ideal forms and the nature of things, not realism and experience. Wolsey's contemporaries took their cue either from the medieval sermon and complaint literature, or from Plato's *Republic*, not Aristotle's *Politics*. Moral idealism was found wanting as social distress was exacerbated by rising population after 1520; the shift towards Aristotelian prognosis began with Cromwell's social legislation of the 1530s (the elusive question is exactly how this shift came about). But Wolsey's idealism does not excuse his tendency to leave things half-finished.

For example, he attacked from star chamber the abuses of private traders in civic markets, doing so in the interests of social responsibility. The 'just price' was still the main consideration in agricultural marketing, but traders were businessmen who, necessarily, made money at the consumer's expense. At a stroke Wolsey hauled seventy-four provincial graziers before the Council along with dozens of London butchers, but this crackdown was not followed up—nothing happened.[27] He also issued proclamations prohibiting profiteering in grain and enforcing traditional statutes regulating vagabonds and labourers.[28] Yet when in 1520 six grain speculators from Buckinghamshire were reported to him for action, he referred the complaint back to the locality, being too busy to deal with it.[29] Another swoop on traders led to one documented conviction, while only two cases were brought to Wolsey on the strength of his proclamations.[30]

In February 1518 Wolsey fixed poultry prices and investigated the scarcity of beef, mutton, and veal in London.[31] Seventeen months later he was the force behind a midnight purge of criminals, vagrants, and prostitutes within the city and its suburbs: dozens of suspects were caught and brought before the Council.[32] This successful exercise was repeated only once, because Wolsey suddenly shifted his attention to what, superficially, looks like fundamental administrative reform. He had three papers drafted for the king's attention: a dossier of measures 'the king's grace will have to be done and hath given in commandment to his cardinal to put the same in effectual execution'; matters Henry had resolved 'in his own person to debate with his Council and to see reformation to be done therein'; and 'privy remembrances'.[33]

In fact, Wolsey put the words into Henry's mouth, but the programme was no less impressive for that: the agenda was the reform of justice to eliminate abuses and corruption; the reform of finance; plans to pacify Ireland; plans to put national resources to better use in order to reduce unemployment; and the defence of the realm and repair of fortifications. A more attractive scheme could not have been devised and even John Palsgrave, Wolsey's bitterest enemy, praised it. 'Every of these enterprises were great', he wrote, 'and the least of them to our commonwealth much expedient, especially the executing of our laws made in our own days; but that they have been begun, and brought to no good end.'[34] For the truth was that Wolsey's reforming intentions in 1519 were subordinate to his political schemes. His real object was revealed in May when, under the pretence of national reform, he evicted potential rivals from the inner sanctum of Henry VIII's Court, the privy chamber, and replaced them with new, more sober attendants who were also more compliant. Wolsey also attacked the rising financial status of the privy chamber under its titular head, the groom of the stool. The groom had started to siphon off cash from the chamber, administering it beyond Wolsey's reach at Court. So Wolsey struck back: hence the talk of financial reform. He put a ceiling of £10,000 per annum on the groom's account and demanded proper book-keeping in duplicate, with monthly audits.[35] Yet criticism of Wolsey can go too far. For when in a fit of energy Henry VIII dispatched the earl of Surrey to Dublin as lieutenant in 1520, Palsgrave falsely alleged he had been 'exiled' there by Wolsey when his mission, in reality, was to inform the king 'by which means and ways your grace might reduce this land to obedience and good order'.[36] Beyond this, however, Surrey's expedition had no clear aims: he lacked the resources to tackle any problems of government, and he had only five hundred soldiers. Achieving little, he was recalled in 1522, whereupon Palsgrave spread the smear that Wolsey had taken care to prevent his 'enemy' finishing the task he was sent to perform!

Indeed, the very suggestion that Surrey was Wolsey's enemy depends upon a rumour that in May 1516 the earl was 'put out of the council chamber' along with the marquis of Dorset, Lord Bergavenny, and certain other nobles.[37] This particular story may be true, but it is not evidence that Wolsey and Surrey, son of the victor of Flodden who succeeded his father as duke of Norfolk in 1524, were uncompromising opponents. While incarcerated in the Tower in 1546, Surrey made an often-quoted statement to the effect that Wolsey confessed shortly after his fall that he 'had gone about fourteen years to have destroyed me, saying he did the same by setting upon of my lord of Suffolk, the marquis of Exeter, and my lord Sandes'.[38] Although a hoary fable, the tale is regularly retailed as evidence of Wolsey's relations with the nobility. Of course, given Wolsey's low birth, it is unlikely that these relations were especially comfortable, but when a 'great snarling' arose at Court after Wolsey had first announced his law-enforcement programme, he seemed genuinely to have been taken by surprise, for he openly accused Sir Henry Marney of starting the trouble.[39]

Whether or not Wolsey should be credited with the destruction of the duke of Buckingham is elusive. He should be absolved from pursuing a systematic vendetta against the old nobility, but it is likely that Buckingham was among those nobles who found it difficult to adapt themselves to their Tudor roles as courtiers and servants of the Crown.[40] In 1510 Buckingham had petitioned to be restored to the great hereditary office of constable of England, which he had been allowed to exercise only on the day of Henry VIII's coronation. Four years later he won his legal battle when the judges accepted that he held two manors in Gloucestershire by virtue of service as constable, therefore the king might at his pleasure invite him to exercise the office. Henry VIII, however, preferred to keep the office dormant. (According to old baronial theory, the high steward, the constable, and the earl marshal, or two of them, could 'reform' evil councillors and even impose conditions on the king.) So he refused to call the duke to perform functions that he said were 'very high and dangerous'.[41] Thus Buckingham had won a Pyrrhic victory. Perhaps, like Charles, duke of Bourbon, constable of France, he was among those who felt the contradiction between his ducal standing and a royal policy that was calculated to ensure the honourable subordination of those it increasingly regarded as 'feudal anachronisms'. Or perhaps, like some of the French nobility, he found it socially difficult to identify himself with royal power and profit from his position as a councillor. At any rate, after a star-chamber attack on his servant Sir William Bulmer for wearing the ducal livery in the king's presence in October 1519, Buckingham was heard grumbling about the king's councillors. And in November he allegedly made the threat later attributed to him, that he would kill Henry VIII as his father had been prepared to kill Richard III.

Yet if Wolsey had sought Buckingham's downfall, a suggestion for which there is no hard evidence — in fact, he had made at least one attempt to steer the duke into safer paths — Buckingham had played into his hands. For his dynastic ambition and provocative retaining precipitated an outright break with Henry VIII. When in February 1521 he sought a licence to visit his lordships in Wales with 400 armed men, it was all too reminiscent of his father's revolt against Richard III. Henry VIII wrote secretly to Wolsey, 'I would you should make good watch on the duke of Suffolk, on the duke of Buckingham, on my lord of Northumberland, on my lord of Derby, on my lord of Wiltshire, and on others which you think suspect.'[42] Whatever was afoot, it culminated in Buckingham's trial and execution for treason. For, whether properly convicted or not, this was among the few state trials of the reign in which the victim was almost certainly guilty of the basic offence with which he was charged. If Buckingham's case was controversial and upset Thomas More, it was because the evidence called against him was the hearsay of disgruntled servants and the proof of guilt would not have satisfied a modern court of law.[43]

In March 1522 Wolsey started a major national survey of England's military resources and financial capacity, a task more complex and comprehensive even than his enclosure inquiry.[44] By the end of the summer he had learned that 128,250 men were available for conscription (from twenty-eight counties), that 35,328 coats of mail were ready, and that a surprising one-third of the militia were archers. These and other details provided the necessary information to bring the militia up to date. Certainly the quasi-feudal 'system' of military obligation, whereby the Crown, nobility, and gentry mustered soldiers on a local territorial basis, needed replacement by some 'national' or uniform criteria for musters and the provision of weapons. But nothing tangible was done: this successful inquiry led to no military reorganization and the information collected was soon forgotten. On the other hand, Wolsey used the financial assessments obtained by the survey to extract so-called 'loans' amounting to the fantastic sum of £260,000 from taxpayers in 1522 and 1523. These 'loans' were not meant to be taxes, but short-term loans to the Crown due for repayment from the proceeds of the next parliamentary subsidy.[45] In fact, Wolsey expressly promised, when instructing his collectors for the first 'loan', that the money was refundable.[46] But the 'loans' were not repaid, and this may have been Wolsey's intention all along. In a rare instance of friction between Tudor government and the common lawyers, Lewis Pollard, a judge of common pleas, challenged the legality of Wolsey's action but was defeated by his opponent's 'dexterity' — the word was probably a euphemism for political power and influence over the king.[47] The episode illustrates Wolsey's creativity, but failure to repay the 'loans' aroused resentment.

Yet in the mainstream of finance Wolsey made a permanent contribution to government. Henry VII's attempt to raise directly assessed taxes to supplement fifteenths and tenths was imperfect, but Wolsey used his position as the administrator of Henry VIII's early wars to invent a more efficient system: the Tudor subsidy.[48] The secret was to abandon the idea of fixed rates and yields of tax in favour of flexible rates and accurate valuations of taxpayers' true wealth. In 1513 Wolsey laid down new principles: taxpayers were to be assessed individually on oath by local officials under the supervision of nationally appointed commissioners, who had power to examine and revise assessments. The commissioners then calculated the tax due from each individual, and in cases where taxpayers were liable to be assessed in more than one category — for example, in respect of income from lands, wages, or the capital value of their possessions — they were charged in one category only, but that was to be the one which yielded the largest amount of tax. The legal provisions of the subsidy were drafted by John Hales, a Gray's Inn lawyer who became a judge in the court of exchequer. Wolsey implemented the new system four times in 1513–15 and once in 1523. There were teething troubles, but Wolsey learned by experience and solved the technical problems. He raised £322,099 by parliamentary subsidies, not counting the 'loans' of 1522–3; separate clerical taxation yielded £240,000 between

1512 and 1529; and fifteenths and tenths, levied in 1512–17, brought in £117,936.[49]

For the first time since 1334 the Crown was raising more realistic taxation. But Wolsey's attempt to complete the re-endowment of the monarchy begun by Edward IV and Henry VII failed. The insufficiency of the Crown's revenues was obvious from the moment Henry VIII decided to resume the Hundred Years War. Government expenditure in the period 1509–20 was roughly £1.7 million, of which £1 million was spent on troops, and the purchase of ships, victuals, and ordnance. Large sums were also advanced to England's allies: aids and subsidies to the emperor took 32,000 gold florins in 1512 and £14,000 in 1513; £80,000 was advanced in 1515–16, and £13,000 loaned in 1517. Tournai, too, cost money to defend: £40,000 per annum each year between 1514 and 1518, when Wolsey sold it back to France. The Crown's cash revenues from land, however, slipped back to about £25,000 per annum once the guiding hand of Henry VII was removed. Even supposing Wolsey's aggressive taxation could have been sustained indefinitely—a false assumption—the government could not balance its books if it wished to fight wars.[50]

Henry VIII, meanwhile, was building new palaces at Bridewell in London and at New Hall near Chelmsford, and was refurbishing old ones at Eltham and Greenwich. His youthful acquisitions and building operations were not on the dazzling scale seen after 1535, when he added over thirty residences to his stock in a decade—he owned fifty houses at his death. But he spent a minimum of £40,000 at Bridewell and New Hall alone before 1525, not counting furniture, tapestries, silver, jewels, etc.

In 1521 the chamber officials were forced to borrow money to pay the wages of the royal servants. When Henry VIII renewed the war with France, campaigns by the earl of Surrey in 1522 and the duke of Suffolk a year later cost £400,000. In April 1523 Wolsey summoned Parliament, but the subsidy he secured was less than a quarter of what he first sought. He soured the atmosphere from the start by demanding supply of £800,000 on top of the £260,000 he collected by means of 'loans' in 1522–3. When the Commons mustered, Wolsey blustered 'that he would rather have his tongue plucked out of his head with a pair of pinsors' than to move Henry VIII to take less. He tried to overawe MPs by personally addressing them, but met 'a marvellous obstinate silence'; he lied that the Lords had offered the requisite taxation; he reneged on his promise of 1522 that the 'loans' would be repaid out of the proceeds of the next parliamentary subsidy.[51] True, his initial demand of taxation at the rate of 4*s.* in the £ on goods and lands was a bargaining ploy; real negotiations centred on the prospect of half that amount — that is, the basic rate used for the 'loans' of 1522–3.[52] But, while that would have been acceptable under normal conditions — Archbishop Warham had asked Parliament for £600,000 in 1512 but settled for £126,745 — Wolsey had expressly promised when collecting the first 'loan' that the money was refundable from the proceeds of the next parliamentary grant. An observer wrote: 'My lord Cardinal hath promised on his faith that the 2*s.* of the £ of loan money shall be paid with a good will and with thanks. But no day is appointed thereof.'[53] And there was the nub. Not only were the 'loans' not repaid promptly (the Crown's debt was eventually cancelled by an act of 1529 on the grounds that the 'loans' were used for the defence of the realm and might thus be deemed taxation); also a cumulative burden of taxation had arisen by 1523. It is hardly surprising that the Commons pleaded poverty when £288,814 had been levied in lay taxation between 1512 and 1517 and the 'loans' had raised £260,000. In fact, those MPs who complained that the realm lacked adequate liquidity for taxation on this scale had some right on their side.[54]

Wolsey's response was to keep Parliament sitting longer into the summer than on any other occasion between 1433 and the Long Parliament. On 13 May supply was offered at the basic rate of 2*s.* in the £ on goods and lands, but Wolsey continued the haggling. Edward Hall wrote: 'This grant was reported to the Cardinal, which therewith was sore discontent, and said, that the Lords had granted 4*s.* of the £, which was proved untrue.'[55] A revised offer on 21 May did not conclude the matter, since either Wolsey declined it, or MPs themselves had second thoughts over the Whitsun recess. In a period when counted votes were extremely rare in the House of Commons, MPs divided on a third proposal on 27 June, when the motion was defeated. Indeed, the Speaker, Thomas More, had to intervene to calm tempers so that about 6 July 'after long persuading, and privy labouring of friends' the rates of the subsidy were finalized.[56]

Yet Wolsey's reputation as a parliamentary manager plummets when we realize that the rates of tax he secured in July 1523 were only marginally better than those offered on 13 May. The Commons' first offer was spread over two years: a subsidy of 2*s*. in the £ on lands, or 2*s*. in the £ on goods worth over £20, whichever assessment yielded the greater revenue from individual taxpayers; 1*s*. 4*d*. in the £ on goods valued between £2 and £20; and a poll tax of 8*d*. on everyone else — this was to be the total amount. The final rates were 2*s*. in the £ on lands, or on goods over £20 as before; 1*s*. in the £ on goods valued between £2 and £20; and a poll tax of 8*d*. on wages of £1 to £2 per annum or goods worth £2 — these amounts were spread over two years. In the third year a surcharge of 1*s*. in the £ was to be levied on lands valued at £50 or more. And in the fourth and last year 1*s*. in the £ was due on goods worth £50 or more. The third and fourth year surcharges brought in £5,521 and £9,116 respectively.[57] So the question is whether these amounts compensated for the difference between the rates of tax offered on 13 May and the standard rates of the first two years of the final subsidy. In theory they did, but the margin was slim. Wolsey's estimated net gain from negotiating the subsidy's third and fourth year surcharges was a mere £5,139. He had haggled with Parliament for months at some political cost, but, whatever he achieved between May and July 1523, it was not a king's ransom.[58]

Perhaps the final straw was Wolsey's attempt to 'anticipate' payment of the first instalment of the 1523 subsidy on the basis of rigorous assessments. On 2 November he named commissioners to 'practise' with all persons having £40 and above in lands or goods, whose names he obtained from the returns of the 1522 military survey.[59] They were to pay their first instalment of tax immediately, instead of at the date specified in the subsidy act, using the assessments of 1522 which may have overestimated their wealth. Only 5 per cent of this 'anticipation' was paid by the due date, though 74 per cent was realized within another month. Although the subsidy was eventually levied on the basis of new and, possibly for richer taxpayers, lower valuations, it provoked dismay. Indeed, when the second instalment fell due in February 1525, late payments by the vast majority of all taxpayers signalled burgeoning resistance to Wolsey's fiscal ambitions.[60]

If, however, Wolsey learned that accurate assessments of taxpayers' wealth could not by themselves compensate for Parliament's denial of excessive rates of tax, money remained short in 1523 and Wolsey was forced to ask the king to advance £10,000 from his palace treasury towards the war effort. Aid to England's ally the duke of Bourbon cost 200,000 gold crowns in 1523 and 1524, and it was only a matter of time before a crisis occurred. The crunch came when Henry VIII wished once more to invade France in the spring of 1525: the war chest was empty. So Wolsey sent out commissioners in March and April 1525 to demand a non-parliamentary tax based on the valuations of 1522; he called it an 'amicable grant'. The clergy were asked to pay at the rate of one-third of their yearly revenues or the value of their goods above £10, or one-quarter of their revenues or goods below £10. The laity were charged according to a sliding scale: those worth above £50 per annum were to contribute 3s. 4d. in the £; those worth between £20 and £50, 2s. 8d. in the £; and those worth below £20, 1s. in the £.[61]

Wolsey's demand fired a tax rebellion. The 'loans' of 1522–3 had not been repaid and the subsidy of 1523 was still being collected. At Reading the people offered one-twelfth of their property, an offer that enraged Wolsey, who threatened to execute one of the commissioners: 'it should cost the Lord Lisle his head, and his lands should be sold to pay the king the values that . . . he had lost.'[62] In London, where Wolsey appointed himself sole commissioner for the tax, he likewise advised the mayor and aldermen: 'beware and resist not, nor ruffle not in this case, for it may fortune to cost some their heads.'[63] By the end of April Wolsey was modifying his demands and was attempting to settle for payment of a benevolence; he was told that, if mandatory, benevolences were illegal by Richard III's statute of 1484, and he finally had to accept voluntary contributions. Discontent, meanwhile, reached dangerous levels right across England. In Essex, Kent, Norfolk, Warwickshire, and Huntingdonshire the Amicable Grant provoked reactions ranging from reluctance to outright refusal, and full-scale revolt erupted in Suffolk that spread to the borders of Essex and

Cambridgeshire. The dukes of Norfolk and Suffolk mustered the East Anglian gentry; they successfully negotiated the surrender of the militants. But 10,000 men had converged on Lavenham—the most serious rebellion since 1497.[64] Even after the 'stirs' were over, the dukes were still worrying that a Suffolk revolt could have attracted surviving descendants of the old Yorkist nobility. And an eyewitness reported that the militants had only failed to do more harm because a loyal townsman had removed the clappers from the bells of Lavenham church, which were to have been rung to signal the start of the uprising.[65]

The rebellion was crushed, but the rebels had in fact won. By 13 May not only was any attempt to enforce the Amicable Grant confounded by Wolsey's resort to voluntary contributions in London, but it was also seen to be politically impossible for the Crown to levy new taxation on top of the 'loans' of 1522–3 and the subsidy of 1523. Henry and Wolsey therefore dropped the Amicable Grant in a stage-managed display of 'clemency'. The captains of the Lavenham Rising were brought before star chamber, and Wolsey ostentatiously sought their pardon and stood surety for them as a fellow-Suffolk man! He paid the expenses they had incurred in the Fleet prison, and presented each man with a piece of silver—an extraordinary scene.[66]

The failure of the Amicable Grant thus reduced considerably the fiscal potential of Henrician government. It also determined foreign policy, for there followed an Anglo-French *entente*. This in itself raised the stakes, because a section of the nobility opposed the French negotiations, and, before long, the dukes of Norfolk and Suffolk, the marquis of Exeter, and other prominent nobles were with Henry VIII at Court and were reading Wolsey's letters. Henry was dining in the privy chamber, too, which presaged a new round of Court intrigues. The French treaty ended significant warfare for England until the Scottish campaign of 1542, but this meant that the magnates returned to domestic routine at a time when Wolsey was weakened by the uproar over the Amicable Grant.[67] The idea that Wolsey and the nobility were in active political opposition is far too sweeping, but in January 1526 the cardinal was obliged to neutralize the privy chamber and attempt to frustrate the magnates' return to politics. He promulgated the Eltham Ordinance, an edict for the royal household which, under the cover of supposed reform in the interests of economy, enabled him to purge the privy chamber and claim that the time had come to reform the King's Council. He announced that twenty leading councillors should always attend the king at Court; this attendant council would have exercised immense power had it ever met, but Wolsey contrived that it did not. By ensuring the absence in London of the important office-holders on affairs of state, he reduced the body to a committee of ten and then to a subcommittee of four, providing finally that two councillors from among those permanently resident in the king's household should always be available to advise Henry and dispatch matters of justice.[68] In other words, Wolsey restored as best he could the status quo established since 1515.

Wolsey's domestic policy was overtaken by the failure of his diplomacy. At first he was triumphant, managing to erect a splendid cardboard castle. That this was built upon a void was, however, proved in 1527–9. Until that time Wolsey's basic need was to achieve European acclaim for Henry VIII; but after 1527 his enforced object was to satisfy the king's wish for papal annulment of his marriage to Catherine of Aragon.

It has been said that Wolsey's foreign policy was dominated by his support for the papacy and wish to become pope, but this looks unlikely.[69] If Rome was the key to Wolsey's strategy, why did he do so little to ingratiate himself with the Curia or to build up English representation there? Wolsey exploited Rome, but his policy was not 'papal'. He never visited Rome and strove constantly to put the papacy under a moral obligation in exchange for English support. He did not seriously become a papal candidate either. His name was discussed in 1522, when Adrian VI was elected, and in 1523, when Giulio de Medici became Clement VII, but, if his own words are to be believed, he was not in earnest. His agent wrote: 'your grace at my departing showed me precisely that ye would never meddle therewith.'[70] It is more likely that Henry urged Wolsey's candidature; if so, Wolsey made a half-hearted effort to comply, then told the king he had made the grand gesture by supporting de Medici in England's best interests.

Far more important was Henry VIII's attitude to what he considered to be his lawful claim to the French Crown. His accession was followed by a propaganda war across the Channel: the houses of Tudor and Valois vied with each other for primacy in sacerdotal sovereignty.[71] In 1515 the French republished the fifteenth-century dialogue known as the *Debate of the Heralds*. The French herald in that exchange praised the independence of his king from all overlordship, whereas, he gibed, the English king was a papal vassal—an allusion to King John's homage to Pope Innocent III in May 1213. In reply, the English exhumed and embellished the ideology of the Hundred Years War. Henry was anxious to justify his sovereignty and began to flaunt emblems of 'imperial' kingship. He placed the arched or imperial crown as a decorative motif on his gold and purple pavilion at the tournament of 1511. In 1513 the arched crown was struck on a special issue of coinage during the occupation of Tournai. And when in 1517 he was musing on the idea of succeeding the Emperor Maximilian, who had purported to be willing to resign in Henry's favour in order to gain a subsidy, Cuthbert Tunstall informed him: 'One of the chief points in the election of the emperor is that he which shall be elected must be of Germany subject to [the] Empire; whereas your grace is not . . . But the Crown of England is an Empire of itself much better than now the Empire of Rome.'[72] It should not be forgotten, however, that war with France was popular: France had been England's enemy since 1337; Calais provided a convenient European base; the king's minions preferred real war to the tournament; and England's main export trade was with the Low Countries.

Wolsey's Anglo-French peace of 1514 had crumbled on the death of Louis XII and the accession on 1 January 1515 of Francis I. Within nine months Francis had crossed the Alps and won a great victory at Marignano against the Swiss and Milanese; Wolsey spent the next three years trying to recoup the situation. He subsidized Swiss and imperial armies but was let down by his allies, who were interested in English cash, not Henry's diplomacy. At this time Wolsey's exuberance was his greatest asset: he refused to admit defeat and so emerged victorious. In 1518 he agreed new terms with France, which, by 2 October, were transformed into a dazzling European peace treaty. The pope, emperor, Spain, France, England, Scotland, Venice, Florence, and the Swiss forged, with others, a non-aggression pact with provision for mutual aid in case of hostilities. At a stroke

Wolsey made London the centre of Europe and Henry VIII its arbiter. This *coup de théâtre* was the more remarkable in that it was the pope's own plan, proposed in March, that Wolsey had snatched from under his nose. Wolsey next extorted his appointment by the pope as one of two legates *a latere* to conduct the negotiations, something he had coveted for years but failed to obtain. These powers were, in effect, vice-papal. Rarely granted save during crusades and for the conduct of papal diplomacy, the beneficiary became the pope's *alter ego*, with full rights save in matters of episcopal appointments, the summoning of general councils, the creation of new bishoprics, and certain exemptions from absolutions.

Yet Wolsey was no obvious pacifist and the European accord that the treaty of London represented was built on shifting sands.[73] When Maximilian died in January 1519, Charles of Spain and Burgundy succeeded to his title and possessions in Germany and eastern Europe. In 1520 Henry and Wolsey staged a meeting with Francis I on French territory at the Field of Cloth of Gold, a chivalric (but costly) extravaganza to outshine Henry V's victory at Agincourt and which was hailed as the eighth wonder of the world. Wolsey also met the emperor and posed as honest broker. He still needed the *rapprochement* with France but was aware of the defects of the treaty of London. The main disadvantage was the requirement to offer aid in case of hostilities: England might be dragged into a war on the losing side. By 1520–1 the loser was likely to be Francis, not Charles; Henry VIII and Wolsey therefore courted both sides, but made a secret treaty at Bruges in 1521 whereby Henry and Charles committed themselves to a 'Great Enterprise' against France to be launched before March 1523.[74] Both Henry and Wolsey, however, remained sceptical: nine months later the 'Enterprise' was postponed by the treaty of Windsor until 1524. The idea of fighting the French remained popular — when Wolsey ordered the preparation of six thousand archers in September 1521, he was told: 'Every man judgeth thereby that we shall have war against France, whereof they be most desirous.'[75] But Henry, with good reason, mistrusted his allies, whom he believed might make a separate peace or saddle him with the main costs of battle. Nevertheless, England drifted into war with France and a small expedition was led into Picardy in 1522 by the earl of Surrey, though it achieved only aimless raiding and two failed sieges.

Wolsey's diplomacy thus became opportunistic. By 1521 the French were actively supporting the claim of their candidate, the duke of Albany, heir presumptive to the Scottish throne. This turned attention to Scotland, for Albany had bragged he could overthrow Henry if Francis gave him ten thousand men, and Francis referred the idea to his Council.[76] During the Parliament of 1523 Thomas Cromwell urged the old adage, 'Who that intendeth France to win, with Scotland let him begin.' His speech mirrored debates in Henry VIII's Council which contemplated abandonment of the 'Great Enterprise' in favour of uniting the crowns of England and Scotland by conquest (June 1523). But Henry took the opinion of Lord Dacre, warden of West March, and Dacre did not think a plan to annex Scotland militarily feasible.[77] (That he was right was proved by Protector Somerset's inability to establish permanent garrisons in Scotland.) Wolsey next planned to kidnap the young James V with the connivance of his mother Margaret, Henry VIII's sister. This plot was a variation of a plan mooted the previous year by Dacre, who thought Albany's presence in Scotland might be tolerated provided the young king was in custody in England—a proposal that foreshadowed the incarceration by Elizabeth I of Mary, Queen of Scots.[78] Evidently news leaked, for Skelton jibed:

> What say ye of the Scottish king?
> That is another thing.
> He is but an youngling,
> A stalworthy stripling.
> There is a whispering and a whipling
> He should be hither brought;
> But and it were well sought,
> I trow all will be nought.[79]

What killed all these schemes was the treason of Charles, duke of Bourbon, constable of France, against Francis I. Henry's and Wolsey's policy oscillated in 1522–3 between their wish to attack France and their negotiations for peace or a papal truce. Yet immediately they were convinced that Bourbon was willing to rise in revolt, they abandoned their Scottish strategy and began shipping an army of eleven thousand troops under the duke of

Suffolk into France. The army was expected at Calais in late August 1523, while the policy switch was cemented by a league in September between the Habsburgs, Henry VIII, and Bourbon. Wolsey was especially keen on an aggressive, offensive policy at this point. While the march on Paris was still going well, he told Henry, 'there shall be never such, or like opportunity given hereafter for the attaining of France'.[80]

Yet, although Suffolk's campaign gained glimpses of brilliant success, it ended in abject failure. Getting off to a bad start owing to smallpox outbreaks, inadequate transport, the inability of Margaret of Austria (Charles V's regent in the Low Countries) to raise sufficient troops, and a disagreement over strategy, Suffolk nevertheless managed to cross the Somme and threaten Paris. But Bourbon's revolt was betrayed while Charles's Spanish troops achieved little. Francis was therefore able to throw his total resources into the defence of Paris, though in the event Suffolk did not march the last 50 miles to the capital since mutinies and drinking bouts incapacitated his forces. First, an orderly retreat became necessary; then the plan to winter in northern France and resume the assault the next spring had to be abandoned as Henry's Burgundian allies withdrew and bitterly cold weather killed men and horses alike.[81]

After Suffolk's return, plans to resume the war were consistently tempered by parallel overtures for peace. Henry's and Wolsey's commitment to the 'Great Enterprise' evaporated as cash reserves ran low. By early 1525 Wolsey was secretly ready to make terms with France. Then news suddenly arrived of Charles's triumph at the battle of Pavia (24 February); Francis I had been taken prisoner. Henry and Wolsey accordingly wished to revive and implement the 'Enterprise' immediately in order to partition France. As it seemed, Henry had never been better placed: the chances of victory no longer depended on the reliability of rebellious French nobles. 'Now is the time', the king urged visiting Burgundian diplomats, 'for the emperor and myself to devise the means of getting full satisfaction from France.'[82] But Charles was cool; he had no need to share his victory, and his attention was concentrated on Italy. In fact, Henry and Wolsey had made a fundamental miscalculation. Before Pavia, Wolsey was advising the king that, if the Habsburgs won, Henry would get the thanks on account of the money he had contributed to assist them, while, in the unlikely event of a French success, he would reap the benefits of Wolsey's secret negotiations with Francis I. The triumphant Charles was, however, not at all grateful for Henry's limited aid. Indeed, he wrote in his diary, 'the king of England does not help me as a true friend should; he does not even help me to the extent of his obligations'.[83]

So Wolsey performed his desperate *volte-face*, allying with France by the treaty of The More (30 August 1525), despite Anglo-Habsburg dynastic ties, the importance of safeguarding exports to the Low Countries, and hostile public opinion. The following year he joined the pope, France, Venice, Milan, and Florence in the anti-Habsburg League of Cognac. Against the odds he was trying to revive his role of honest broker. For, although Henry and Wolsey obtained large French pensions in 1525 — an attractive prospect once the Amicable Grant was revoked — the new strategy was a mistake. Its focus was on Italy; Henry VIII's hopes of an easy divorce were ruined when Habsburg troops mutinied and captured Rome in May 1527; and England's wool and cloth trades suffered badly when economic warfare erupted in 1528. The last straw was the defeat of France at the battle of Landriano (21 June 1529): the pope came to terms with Charles, while France and Spain made peace at Cambrai (3 August 1529). This left Charles V in control of Italy and Henry ingloriously isolated. Wolsey's star was waning fast, though Tunstall and Thomas More snatched useful crumbs from the Cambrai table when Francis I agreed to pay the arrears of Edward IV's pension and to redeem some of Charles's debts to Henry VIII. Indeed, if finance had been all that was at stake, this might have sufficed: Henry received between £20,000 and £50,000 a year from France until 1534. But the burning issue by this time was the king's demand that his marriage to Catherine of Aragon be annulled, and, in the diplomatic situation Wolsey had created, that demand was unlikely to be met by the pope.

Wolsey's most equivocal performance was as cardinal–legate. While it is unfair to say that in principle he repudiated clerical reform in the spirit of Colet and Erasmus, in practice he ended up creating a legatine despotism that paved the way for Henry VIII's 'imperial' authority over the church in the 1530s.

However, it must be said in his defence that he stood between the church and its subjection by the Crown before 1529. In 1512 and 1515 quarrels between clergy and laity over clerical immunity from secular jurisdiction had inspired a ruling by the common-law judges that clergy who appealed to Roman canons not demonstrably based on divine law or approved in advance by the king were liable to *praemunire* proceedings, and that Henry might legislate in Parliament by himself with the temporal lords and commons but without the bishops and abbots, who sat (as it was claimed) by reason of their temporal possessions. During a meeting of judges and councillors at Baynard's Castle in November 1515 Henry therefore declared: 'By the ordinance and sufferance of God we are king of England, and the kings of England in time past have never had any superior but God alone. Wherefore know you well that we shall maintain the right of our Crown and of our temporal jurisdiction as well in this point as in all others.'[84]

Henry's oracular pronouncement meant no more than that he wanted money and power: money in the form of clerical taxation and power through control of church patronage. It is unlikely that he yet had any developed theoretical sense of what the church's relationship to him should be; indeed it was not until he was presented by Edward Foxe and Thomas Cranmer with the manuscript of *Collectanea satis copiosa* in the autumn of 1530 that he gained coherent appreciation of 'his' caesaropapism. But the common-law judges had taken their opportunity to outfoot the clergy, and Wolsey attempted to defend their privileges as best he could. Kneeling before Henry at Baynard's Castle, he argued that royal prerogative had never been in question; the clergy were none the less bound on oath to defend the liberties of the church. He therefore prayed that the matter might be referred to the pope—a request Henry refused on the spot.

Henry's words indicated that he already deemed his 'superiority' to mean denial of the pope's right to infringe his territorial sovereignty, but this was nothing new. Similar claims had been made by Richard II and Henry IV, whilst the ideas of the common-law judges reflected earlier case-law. So the 'superiority' or 'supremacy' that Henry spoke of at Baynard's Castle in 1515 and in the Acts of Appeals and Supremacy of

1533-4 were fundamentally different. The first was territorial and referred to what were seen by common lawyers as 'temporal' matters, for instance the Crown's authority to monitor the reception of papal law, to administer its regalian rights, and to regulate clerical privileges in royal courts; by contrast the second was magisterial—Henry VIII's supremacy was like the Emperor Constantine's, embracing the ordering of both 'spirituals' and 'temporals' alike and affecting every aspect of the church's external life.[85]

If, however, Wolsey insulated the church from lay attacks as legate *a latere*, his centralizing policy paved the way for the break with Rome in another sense. As legate he was ubiquitous; he interfered with everyone and everything: appointments, elections, visitations, probate jurisdiction, and episcopal rights.[86] Thus in probate cases what was his as archbishop of York was his own, but of what was Warham's as archbishop of Canterbury, half was demanded by Wolsey. His fiscalism was barely subdued; bishops and archdeacons had to pay tribute to him for permission to exercise their jurisdictions and he 'farmed' the bishoprics of Salisbury, Worcester, and Llandaff, which were held by non-resident Italians, paying these bishops fixed stipends. Some of this need not have mattered; as Thomas More wrote in his *Apology* and *Debellation of Salem and Bizance*, where there had been a traitor even among the twelve Apostles, it was unrealistic to expect a perfect clergy. But in addition Wolsey held wealthy bishoprics in plurality: as well as being archbishop of York, he was bishop of Bath and Wells (1518-23), Durham (1523-9), and Winchester (1529-30). Contrary to canon law, in 1521 he secured appointment as abbot of St Albans, one of the richest abbeys in England, which he left impoverished. And he was not celibate.

Why, then, did the pope and Henry VIII permit this conduct? The answer is partly that Wolsey's service was useful to king and pope alike, and partly that Wolsey had some reforming intentions. In 1519 Richard Fox, his former mentor and an enlightened humanist sponsor, exclaimed on receipt of Wolsey's letters announcing reformation of the clergy that he 'has desired to see this day as Simeon desired to see the Messiah'.[87] Yet it is well said, 'Wolsey was under no illusion about the exercise of [his] authority being dependent on his serving the king's pleasure, and the king's pleasure was that Wolsey control the

English church in the king's interest.'[88] Whatever Wolsey's
original plans, his 'reforms' in practice amounted to four things:
(1) his visitations of the monastic clergy and statutes for the
Benedictines and Augustinians that largely reproduced the
Benedictine Constitutions of 1336; (2) his York *Provinciale* (a set
of constitutions for his own provincial clergy that was entirely
selected from the canons of his predecessors); (3) an unfinished
scheme to create thirteen new episcopal sees on monastic
foundations to bring the English dioceses into line with current
population patterns; and (4) another plan to reduce the number
of Irish archdioceses from four to two and dioceses from thirty
to nine or ten, and to appoint only English candidates to them.
Yet to dub as 'reforms' either inconclusive attempts to enforce
supposedly existing standards or ambitious but (typically)
unfinished plans to restructure the diocesan hierarchy, does not
seem entirely satisfactory. In particular, Wolsey mainly targeted
his 'reforms' at the lax discipline of the monks and friars, and
not at those areas of pastoral neglect that would be criticized
by the Reformation Parliament. It can be argued that he was
'interested more in the highly visible deterioration of the religious
[orders] than in parochial and pastoral matters'.[89] True,
Skelton's view of Wolsey as a vicious and perjured pluralist is
grotesque. But it is hard to rate his ecclesiastical policy at anything
much beyond the level of good intentions.

After the fiasco at Baynard's Castle Wolsey was eager to check
unnecessary abuses of sanctuary and of the privileges enjoyed
by minor orders of clergy, but his attitude was commensurate
with papal policy in these fields. He took a more radical line
in 1528 when he obtained from Clement VII permission to have
criminous clerks degraded with less formality than before in the
interests of public order. But his approach was narrowly defined
to minor clerks and notorious offenders. Indeed, Leo X in 1516
had denied clerical status to ordinands who did not take all the
minor orders and that of subdeacon at once, or who did not seek
an ecclesiastical benefice.[90] So Wolsey's degradations were
designed to protect, not to contradict, the privileges of *genuine*
clergy, and a reduction of clerical immunity from secular
jurisdiction was never in practice at stake.

In addition, Wolsey dissolved some thirty houses of monks,
canons, or nuns between 1524 and his fall, using the proceeds

to build colleges at Oxford and Ipswich. Inspired by the foundations of William of Waynflete and Richard Fox at Oxford, and Margaret Beaufort and John Fisher at Cambridge, he had planned institutions since 1518 'where scholars shall be brought up in virtue, and qualified for the priestly dignity'. A renowned patron of learning and, like Fox and Thomas More, an advocate of the study of Greek in the universities, Wolsey sponsored Oxford lectures in classics and theology by such distinguished scholars as John Clement, Thomas Lupset, and Juan Luis Vives. Cardinal's College, which by 1524–5 he conceived as having five hundred students, and Ipswich School, which he saw as providing students for his Oxford college, were designed on the most lavish scale. They were, indeed, Wolsey's pride and joy: he sought stone from Caen in Normandy; negotiated for the purchase of books in Rome and Venice; and planned public professorships in theology, canon law, philosophy, civil law, medicine, and classics. But he did not always proceed canonically, though infringements were minor. Wolsey spoke the truth when he assured Henry VIII, 'I have not . . . willed mine officers, to do anything concerning the said suppressions, but under such form and manner as is, and hath largely been, to the full satisfaction . . . of any person which hath . . . interest in the same.'[91] Yet he never escaped the accusation that his object was less the advancement of learning than his wish to build monuments to himself. Likewise, his refusal to convey his colleges' assets formally to them meant that they were seized by the Crown with the rest of his property in 1529. Cardinal's College was refounded on a much smaller scale by Henry VIII as King's College (later Christ Church), but Ipswich School was destroyed: all that remains is the gateway.

Whether or not Wolsey was a spiritual man is elusive. Cavendish said 'he heard most commonly every day two Masses in his privy closet'.[92] He rose at dawn to say his daily offices; his chaplain noticed that he never missed so much as one collect, 'wherein I doubt not but he deceived the opinion of divers persons'. When a crisis blew up in state business, he would work for twelve hours at a sitting never rising 'once to piss, ne yet to eat any meat'. But the work done, 'he went to Mass, and said his other divine service . . . and then went straight into a garden; and after he had walked the space of an hour or more, and there said his evensong, he went to dinner'.[93] Of course, Skelton and the rest claimed otherwise, and the answer lies somewhere between the two extremes. Wolsey was a prince of the church; such men were the automatic targets of satire and ridicule. What is certain is that his legatine powers were useful to the papacy as well as to Henry VIII. For the Renaissance papacy invariably devolved powers it was too weak to exercise itself. Although Wolsey's appointment as legate *a latere* for life in 1524 was novel, Cardinals Ximenes in Spain, Georges d'Amboise in France, and Matthew Lang in south Germany enjoyed similar prestige, and d'Amboise (1460–1515) was in a very real sense Louis XII's Wolsey. Also the papacy wanted an English subsidy, which Wolsey failed to obtain. But he persuaded Rome that he might succeed if his legatine powers were extended enough. In this way he wrested over a dozen legatine bulls from Rome by raising hopes of financial aid.[94]

Yet Wolsey's papal legacy was bound, for inherent reasons, to disturb Anglo-Roman relations. His presence curtailed the traffic to Rome in judicial appeals and dispensations, already reduced by Henry VII, and the English clergy refused to offer a papal subsidy on principle because they knew that the precedent would ensure the nomination of future legates. In particular, Wolsey's position was constitutionally anomalous. Legates *a latere* were supposed to be papal diplomats, but Wolsey was the subject and lord chancellor of Henry VIII. When Henry Beaufort had received a cardinalate and legatine commission during Henry VI's minority, his opponent Humphrey, duke of Gloucester, had him charged with *praemunire*, even though he had resigned the chancellorship before accepting the appointments. Wolsey must have realized that his own legatine commission rendered him vulnerable given the different values of the common lawyers. He may have accepted it only *because* he believed he enjoyed Henry VIII's total confidence. For his part, Henry envied the degree of control the French Crown had obtained over its prelates by the Concordat of Bologna (1516). In a striking sense, he abetted Wolsey's legacy because he wished the English church to be ruled by a royal servant. And the clergy tolerated this because it was better to be obedient to an ecclesiastical than a secular power, for Wolsey stood between the church and its subjection as papal legate.[95] None of this means that the youthful Henry VIII was as yet anti-papal: Francis I, too, was master of his realm, but he did not break with Rome. The fact of Henry's control is, however, proved by Wolsey's destruction in October 1529. When accused in the court of king's bench, England's 'vice-pope' bowed before the Statutes of Provisors and *Praemunire*. He confessed that, on the authority of bulls obtained by him from Rome which he had published contrary to the statutes, he had illegally vexed the realm, thereby incurring the penalties of *praemunire*.

Henry VIII stripped Wolsey of his assets but allowed him, at first, to retire in disgrace to Esher and then to his see of York. A year later the fallen minister was brought south for incarceration in the Tower, but he died *en route* at Leicester Abbey. 'If I had served God as diligently as I have done the King, he would not have given me over in my grey hairs.'[96] Wolsey's deathbed speech echoes down the centuries but, always, he was the master of rhetoric. He had proved himself the most gifted administrator since Hubert Walter; in this respect his critics never did him justice. And popular views of his ascendancy were forged after his fall in 1529, when it was prudent to deny that he had largely governed consensually, for if so, who were his collaborators and why had Henry VIII allowed them to go unpunished? But his vision and originality in star chamber were limited by his personality; his management of Parliament in 1523 was hamhanded; his success in realizing Henrician fiscal potential was seriously reduced by the débâcle of the Amicable Grant; he overreached himself in diplomacy; and his lasting achievement, the centralization of the English church, was unintentional. Neither evil nor quite a genius, Wolsey was brilliant but flawed. On the other hand, he was not a bigot, and was mild-mannered by some European standards. It was said of Pope Paul IV that, when he walked in slippers, he struck sparks from the cobbles, but even Palsgrave spared Wolsey that!

THE BREAK WITH ROME

WOLSEY'S fall in 1529 and the break with Rome in 1533–4 resulted from the inability of the cardinal–minister and Henry VIII to persuade Pope Clement VII to annul the king's first marriage to Catherine of Aragon in order that he might marry Anne Boleyn. It is, however, unlikely that this would have led to the Crown's supremacy over the English church, the executions of Thomas More and John Fisher, the dissolution of the religious houses, the Pilgrimage of Grace, and the rest, without the intervention of forces that transcended the immediate issues. That Henry VIII would quarrel with the pope was inevitable, because his position was uncompromising from the moment he ventilated his doubts about his marriage in the spring of 1527. An interdict on England was a serious possibility in the 1530s — Henry VIII and King John had this in common — but the context of Henry's crisis was the fragmentation of humanism, the advent of the Reformation, a crescendo of anticlericalism at the inns of court, Anne Boleyn's support for reform, and the formation of Court factions sustained by politico-religious ideology after Wolsey's removal. It was these catalysts that fused Henry VIII's interest in 'imperial' kingship with his demand for a divorce: the outcome was a political and ecclesiastical revolution which, thanks to his second chief minister, Thomas Cromwell, Henry enforced throughout his dominions.

The king's quarrel was serious because he had no legitimate male heir: the Tudor dynasty was at risk. He and Catherine had a daughter, Princess Mary (b. 1516), and he had by Elizabeth Blount an illegitimate son, Henry Fitzroy, whom he created duke of Richmond in 1525. He may have had another child by Mary Boleyn, Anne's sister, but he wanted a legitimate son. The fact that Catherine had four children who died shortly after birth only heightened his conviction that his marriage was unlawful. He argued that the text of Leviticus that prohibited a man's union with his brother's widow was divine law.[1] There was a contradictory text in the Book of Deuteronomy, but he held this to be Judaic custom, not God's law — on this matter opinion was divided.[2] And as time passed he came to think that sexual intercourse with a brother's widow was an unnatural act. So he argued that the bull of dispensation obtained by Henry VII from Pope Julius II that had authorized his marriage to his brother's widow had been improperly granted. His marriage had always been forbidden by divine and natural law, and, if Julius II had dispensed with the laws of God and nature, he had exceeded his powers and was no better than another human legislator who had abused his authority. Henry wanted Clement VII to put the matter right, but he was asking too much.

Henry thus challenged the pope's dispensing power. Before the autumn of 1530 this objection was muted in the interests of a speedy compromise with Rome, but the fact remains that his position was an affront to papal authority, an obstacle to his divorce that ran in parallel with the deadlock caused by the collapse of Wolsey's diplomacy and the emperor's stranglehold on Italy. In fact, papal annulments were not hard to obtain, if the circumstances were right. Louis XII of France secured one to marry Anne of Brittany and an annulment of the duke of Suffolk's first marriage to Margaret Mortimer was later confirmed by Clement VII. Much of Henry VIII's trouble sprang from his egoism. If it was not bad enough that in his dynasty's best interests he wished to divorce the emperor's aunt and marry a reformer, he sought a papal annulment as a matter of principle and for a reason humiliating to the papacy. Henry, moreover, was related to Anne Boleyn in the same degree of consanguinity via his former relationship with her sister as he was to Catherine via her first marriage to Prince Arthur: this raised eyebrows. Finally, Clement VII wished to do right by both parties in the suit and, when he finally revoked Henry's case to Rome, his object was partly to satisfy Charles V and partly to provide Catherine with the justice he suspected Henry would deny her if the case were to be decided by delegates in England.

So Henry put his case before public opinion: he sought the support of the leading universities of Christendom and instigated a pamphlet debate that argued the merits of his suit.[3] By 1531 he was using the printing press to publish statements of his

position; and his appeal to wider opinion made a catalytic
reaction possible, because the divorce debate coincided with
the Reformation.

The humanists had first challenged the English establishment
in 1512 when, preaching before the Canterbury Convocation,
Colet attacked clerical abuses and advocated reform of the church
from within. He compared negligent priests to heretics, quoting
St Bernard. And to the bishops he said: 'In you and in your
life we desire to read, as in lively books, how and after what
fashion we may live. Wherefore, if you will ponder and look upon
our motes, first take away the blocks out of your eyes. It is an
old proverb: "Physician, heal thyself." '4 This sermon aroused
resentment, but the humanists repeated their demand for
religious renewal, the classic expositions coming from the pens
of Erasmus and the youthful Thomas More. Erasmus best
combined the Christian and classical elements of the Renaissance;
the key to his success was his exquisite style: the medium was
as important for him as the message. He embellished his
evangelism with racy criticisms of priests and monks, superstition
and empty ritual, scholastic theologians, and even the mores of
the papacy, but was careful to insinuate and thereby avoid
dangerous statements. He published his *Handbook of a Christian
Knight* (1503), *Praise of Folly* (1511), and *Education of a Christian
Prince* (1516) before Luther challenged the papacy. Also in 1516
he published the first edition of the Greek text of the New
Testament together with a revised Latin translation. The Bible
of the medieval church, the Latin Vulgate translation, symbolized
the corruption of ecclesiastical tradition and Erasmus added notes
in which the Vulgate's errors were exposed. Scholars and
educated laymen were delighted; at last they drank the pure
waters of the fountainhead. More's *Utopia* (1516) was more
complex. Book I was an implied criticism of Erasmus's rejection
of political action as well as a critique of the somewhat naïve
political and social assumptions that many humanists
adumbrated, but Book II was in his mould. It wittily idealized
an imaginary society of pagans living on a remote island in
accordance with principles of natural virtue. The Utopians
possessed reason but lacked Christian revelation, and, by
implicitly comparing their benign social customs and enlightened

attitudes with the inferior standards, in practice, of Christian Europeans, More produced an indictment of the latter based largely on deafening silence. For the irony and scandal was that Christians had so much to learn from heathens.

Yet the humanism of Erasmus and More was fragile. Even without Luther's challenge it would have become fragmented because faith and reason in its scheme were at odds. More's solution was to argue that faith was the superior power and that Catholic beliefs must be defended because God commanded them, but Erasmus trusted human rationality and could not accept that God tested people's faith by making them believe things that Renaissance scholarship had thrown into question. Even Luther regarded Erasmus as an enemy because of his emphasis on reason. So these fissures weakened humanism and new exponents of reform caught public attention. A group of native English reformers had already outpaced the humanists by the time of Wolsey's fall. Robert Barnes, Thomas Arthur, Thomas Bilney, and their friends were evangelists who preached in East Anglia, Kent, and London.[5] They doubted papal authority and the usages of Rome but adhered to the 'Catholic Church'. More regarded them as heretics because they believed the Bible to be a superior authority to the church. In particular, they regarded cults of saints and the veneration of images as 'idolatry'; they rejected the penitential system of Catholicism in favour of faith; and they exercised a preaching ministry that held sermons to be more important than ancient rites. While they probably owed more to Lollardy than to European Protestantism, there was no straightforward move from pre-Reformation dissent into the mainstream of the Reformation. But shared opinions on image worship, pilgrimages, and clerical endowments must have brought people together.[6]

Although his role has often been exaggerated, Luther (1483–1546) influenced the early English reformers, as did his Swiss and Rhineland contemporaries Zwingli (1484–1531) and Hausschein (1482–1531). Both European and Lollard ideas complemented each other in the writings of William Tyndale, John Frith, and George Joy. The theology of grace was crucial to their thought, because they argued that salvation was God's free gift to believers. By contrast Catholics believed that grace was conveyed by the church. In the *Confessions* St Augustine had written, 'I would not have believed the Gospel had the Catholic church not moved me to it.' But Tyndale, Frith, and Joy held that the Bible was antecedent to the church. Tyndale was also converted to the Lutheran doctrine of 'justification by faith alone'. He wrote that 'the right faith springeth not of man's fantasy, neither is it in any man's power to obtain it; but it is altogether the pure gift of God poured into us freely . . . without deserving and merits, yea, and without seeking for of us'. The 'right faith' justified since it was a form of pardon that excluded human merit; an act of divine sovereignty that banished human pride and endeavour.[7]

Tyndale, Frith, and Barnes also took the 'reformed' view of predestination based on Swiss theology which was remote from Lollardy. Tyndale wrote: 'In Christ God loved us, his elect and chosen, before the world began;' the believer in Christ 'was predestinate, and ordained unto eternal life, before the world began.' Frith argued that salvation is by an election of grace — God justifies his elect — while Barnes and Joy asserted double predestination (i.e. that the reprobate are as much predestined to damnation as the elect to salvation).[8] This theology of salvation by 'election of grace' became the cornerstone of Protestantism when it was propounded by John Calvin (1509–1564) in his *Institutes* (1536 and innumerable later editions), the leading textbook of 'reformed' theology. So nothing could have been further from Erasmus's view that a man's reason was near-sovereign under God and that man had free will to choose the path of salvation or damnation.

Soon the early English reformers were questioning the Catholic doctrine of transubstantiation (i.e. the doctrine explaining how every particle of the bread and wine in the Eucharist is changed into the body and blood of Christ). But they were unable to construct a full Protestant understanding of Holy Communion, which was the achievement of Cranmer and the Swiss and Rhineland exiles under Edward VI. In his *Brief Declaration of the Sacraments* Tyndale contented himself by listing the three competing opinions of the 1530s: transubstantiation; a doctrine of the real presence (i.e. that the Eucharist was Christ's body and blood but not in every particle); and the Swiss memorialist interpretation (i.e. that Holy Communion was commemorative, Christ's death and passion being the only satisfaction for sin).

So Tyndale was England's earliest Reformation publicist. Helped financially by Humphrey Monmouth, a London merchant, he went to Germany and met Luther, then undertook to print an English New Testament (1525). More railed against the reformers in his *Dialogue Concerning Heresies* (1529) and *Confutation of Tyndale's Answer* (1532–3). In 1523 he had attacked Luther at Henry VIII's request: he recognized Protestants when he thought he saw them. Yet whether Barnes, Arthur, and Bilney were 'Protestants' is arguable, while Tyndale's chief preoccupation was to disseminate the Bible. Although many European countries had fairly accessible translations of the Bible, there was no authorized English translation and, when the bishops discussed the idea in 1530, they rejected it. They decided that Scripture was best expounded in sermons and thought access to vernacular translations nurtured heresy by encouraging people to form their own religious opinions. If, however, this attitude was partly justified by the circulation in manuscript of some Lollard Bibles, it ignored the power of the printing press. Tyndale completed his translation at Worms and, in spite of vigorous efforts by Warham, Tunstall, and More to regulate the book trade, copies quickly reached England. Successive editions in 1526, 1534, and 1535 reflected Tyndale's conviction that the Bible came first and should determine the doctrines, institutions, and ceremonies of the church. His translation was largely accurate, but the pope, the bishops, and Catholic theology were vigorously attacked in an array of marginal glosses.

In 1528 Tyndale printed his *Obedience of a Christian Man*. Like Erasmus he called the church a 'congregation' and defended the equality of all true Christians against the priesthood. But he also developed a political theory: that of a Catholic church so powerful and tenacious that only the godly king could rescue the English people from its thraldom. He adopted the position of Henry IV of Germany during the Investiture Contest: kings were anointed by God, therefore they were godly servants for the reform of the church.[9] And he moved close enough to an 'imperial' theory of kingship to catch Henry VIII's ear. He wrote of kings: 'God hath made the king in every realm judge over all, and over him is there no judge. He that judgeth the king judgeth God; and he that layeth hands on the king layeth hand on God; and he that resisteth the king resisteth God, and damneth God's law

and ordinance.'[10] But he refused to champion Henry's divorce;
indeed his *Practice of Prelates* (1530) positively denounced it. So
his direct influence on events was reduced, but he paved the way
for the king by formulating the ideas 'Truth as revealed in
Scripture' and 'We must rather obey God than men'. These
ideas became slogans in the minds of royal apologists during the
1530s, while the strength of Henry's case against the pope was
that it defined the powers of kings and church government in
terms that were Biblical.

Other reformers whom More thought dangerous were Simon
Fish and Christopher St German. Both were anticlerical common
lawyers: Fish was of Gray's Inn and St German of the Middle
Temple. Early in 1529 Fish wrote *A Supplication for the Beggars*,
a vicious satire of the wealth of the clergy that accused them of
making vast fortunes from tithes, probate and mortuary fees,
and other exactions, while living in idleness and sin, and
spreading across the country leprosy and venereal diseases caught
from whores. Fish, whose polemic Anne Boleyn is said to have
applauded, urged Henry VIII to reform the clergy by act
of Parliament.

By contrast, St German was the master of subtlety. He
proclaimed the equality of all persons under the law, but his 'law'
was English common law and statute, not canon or papal law.
So his idea that the clergy should enjoy no greater, nor less,
favour than the laity under the law challenged the independence
of the church and its courts as guaranteed by Magna Carta.[11]
But St German wielded influence, since he had written *Doctor
and Student*, the most important legal treatise between the time
of Littleton and Sir Edward Coke. Although not a Protestant
by the usual theological criteria, he was formidable in his assault
on Catholic tradition: no one else forced More to concede that
the councils of the church could err. In fact, his anticlerical
writings cogently synthesized the claims for secular supervision
of the church that common lawyers had been advancing since
Henry VIII's pronouncement in 1515 that 'the kings of England
in time past have never had any superior but God alone'. Just
as Henry appealed to legal precedent, so St German used
historical perspective to impugn benefit of clergy and the heresy
laws: scholarship had proved they were not a thousand years
old, as More liked to think. Erasmus, too, had challenged the

ferocity of heresy trials, and St German knew that few, if any, heretics had been burned in England before 1401.

In fact, St German wanted the clergy to be stripped of their power to enforce under pain of heresy doctrines not written in Scripture, and his lobbying was instrumental in securing the revision of the law in 1534.[12] He wanted Henry VIII to commission an authorized translation of the New Testament under parliamentary supervision, and he argued that the unwritten traditions and ancient rites of Catholicism need not be believed unless they were authorized by Scripture. Unlike Tyndale and Barnes, he did not hold that Scripture was antecedent to the church. In his opinion, no written Christian text was available after the Crucifixion until St Matthew wrote his gospel and, therefore, the faith had then been propagated via an oral tradition. But when faith was reduced to writing and the New Testament was validated by the church, it was no longer permissible to define the articles of belief other than by the written word, 'for else many superstitious articles and untrue inventions' might be added.[13] So St German, in theology as in *Doctor and Student*, was influenced by the Parisian conciliarist, Jean Gerson (1363–1429), who had affirmed that nothing necessary to salvation was preserved outside the canonical Scriptures.

On the evidence of the Old Testament and the practice of Anglo-Saxon kings as inferred from chronicles, St German conceded to Henry VIII the right to govern the church, but he rejected unlimited theocracy. His main platform, however, was his attack on clerical abuses and alleged racketeering, though his accusations were not based on empirical observation, for he copied lists of 'abuses' from continental conciliarist writers, notably Henry of Langenstein (1324–97).[14] This accounts for the discrepancy between his reports of clerical standards and those given by modern historians. Indeed the 'anticlerical' debate was theoretical and eristic, but it created reservoirs that Henry VIII and Thomas Cromwell could tap. The classic questions of the Middle Ages had centred on the relations between temporal and spiritual powers, but when Clement VII revoked Henry VIII's divorce suit to Rome, politics, humanism, evangelism, and legalism fused to ask the question, 'What is the state and how is it constructed?' It was Henry VIII and Parliament who gave the answer.

Henry summoned Parliament in August 1529: it met at Westminster on 4 November to begin a programme of revolutionary statute-making that required eight sessions lasting until 1536. Eustace Chapuys, Charles V's ambassador in London, thought Henry VIII all along intended to use Parliament to obtain his divorce, but his view reflected paranoia. Despite Henry's own decision to take command, no settled policy existed during the crisis years 1529-32; instead competing policies were advocated by rival factions, though Henry tried to unite his Council by selecting More as lord chancellor.

But this appointment backfired. While More was a brilliant lawyer who consolidated Wolsey's work in star chamber and chancery, he opposed the divorce. When More told the king his position, Henry at first accepted defeat with unusual grace. He told More that he would never 'put any man in ruffle or trouble of his conscience'.[15] Yet the king's 'great matter' became More's 'matter' too. As a minister of state, he had to make serious efforts to support the Crown, so at Henry's insistence he conferred with the king's spiritual counsel, who included Edward Foxe, Thomas Cranmer, Edward Lee, and Nicholas de Burgo, an Italian friar—these men were the 'think tank' working out details of the royal divorce strategy and mustering the ideas that later buttressed the Acts of Appeals and Supremacy. More read 'as far forth as my poor wit and learning served me', but to no avail. By his study, however, he learned the facts of Henry's case as presented by Foxe and Cranmer. He became privy to Henry's policy in outline, though he was excused involvement in it.

The three factions battling to control Henry's policy before More resigned in May 1532 were, first, the supporters of Catherine of Aragon; second, those radicals like Foxe and Cranmer (whom Cromwell later joined) who planned to secure the divorce by some form of unilateral action in England that ignored the pope; and, third, the conservative nobility, though this group had little to offer by way of constructive policy and was less a faction than a dominant political force.[16]

The queen's group included More, the earl of Shrewsbury, Bishop John Fisher, William Peto (head of the Franciscan Observants of Greenwich), Bishop Cuthbert Tunstall,

Nicholas Wilson (archdeacon of Oxford), and Bishops West, Clerk, and Standish. A cohesive party united against heresy and determined to defend both the queen and the Catholic Church, they acted on leaks (from More?) of impending government moves and countered them by public sermons and propagandist treatises. Fisher wrote seven or eight books against the divorce; and Peto preached that, if the divorce went ahead, the dogs would lick Henry's blood as they had Ahab's.

Less active at first in Parliament than in the Council, the queen's party was assisted in the House of Commons by members of the Queen's Head group, an inchoate band of Catholic members who dined and talked politics together at the Queen's Head Tavern. Among them were Sir George Throckmorton (whose brother later served the self-exiled nobleman and scourge of Henry VIII, Reginald Pole); Sir William Essex; Sir Marmaduke Constable; Sir William Barantyne; and Sir John Gifford. Throckmorton later confessed to engaging in parliamentary opposition at the behest of More and Fisher. More had summoned him to a little room off the Parliament chamber; interrupting a conversation with John Clerk, he called Throckmorton a good Catholic, and urged him not to be afraid to speak his conscience, though More was too discreet to speak out himself. Lastly, the queen's party was represented in the Lower House of Convocation by Peter Ligham (a friend of Fisher), Thomas Pelles, Robert Clyff, John Baker, Adam Travers, and Rowland Philips—all these men were indicted for *praemunire* by Cromwell in June 1531. More was therefore politically active as lord chancellor, arguing that it was necessary to fight if the cause was just, and opposition was politically feasible. His main object was to prevent unilateral action on the divorce, but he was also in contact with John Stokesley (bishop of London) about the assault on heresy; indeed More and Pelles, who was chancellor of Norwich diocese, concocted together a defence of Bilney's burning that few will find convincing.[17]

Allied against Catherine's party were Anne Boleyn's supporters: Cranmer, Foxe, Cromwell, Thomas Audley (Speaker of the House of Commons), and Sir George Boleyn. They saw their chance to promote radical ideas by solving the divorce crisis. Cromwell, in particular, recovered from Wolsey's fall by becoming Henry's councillor and business manager in 1531. And if the radicals were ambitious, they were not afraid to extend royal power in church and state at the clergy's expense. More said to Cromwell: 'If you will follow my poor advice, you shall, in your counsel-giving unto his grace, ever tell him what he ought to do but never what he is able to do. . . . For if a lion knew his own strength, hard were it for any man to rule him.'[18]

Yet Cromwell did not control Henry's policy before 1532. The most powerful group after Wolsey's fall comprised the dukes of Norfolk and Suffolk, the earls of Wiltshire and Sussex, Stephen Gardiner (promoted bishop of Winchester), Lord Darcy, and Lord Sandes. They had helped to destroy Wolsey and wished to please the king; but they rejected radical ideas until Henry himself adopted Cromwell's route to the divorce. Norfolk, Darcy, and Gardiner recoiled from schism; Darcy later opposed the royal supremacy and became a prime mover of the Pilgrimage of Grace. Norfolk was a religious conservative, not ashamed to say in the king's chamber that 'he had never read the Scriptures nor ever would, and it was merry in England before this New Learning came up'.[19] He led the faction on the Privy Council in 1540 that destroyed Cromwell by attacking the minister's pro-Lutheran diplomacy and helping to convince Henry VIII that his minister had advanced the radical Reformation at Calais.

Faced by stalemate, Henry VIII gave Parliament its head. The Mercers Company of London had prepared anticlerical articles attacking mortuary and probate fees, citations, and excommunications; a bill drafted by the common lawyer John Rastell attacked heresy trials; and MPs met in committee to frame petitions against clerical abuses and the church courts. Three statutes were enacted reforming mortuary and probate fees, clerical pluralism, and non-residence. The act against pluralism was especially contentious because it infringed ecclesiastical immunity from secular jurisdiction: offenders were to be prosecuted in the royal courts, and dispensations for pluralism obtained from Rome were declared null and void. To Queen Catherine's supporters this was shocking: Bishops Fisher, West, and Clerk appealed to the pope to condemn the acts as invalid. Their move shows how far they realized what was at stake. If Parliament could reform the clergy, perhaps it could instruct the bishops to pronounce the divorce? Henry VIII summoned a Great Council to Hampton Court in October 1530 to ask this very question but was rebuffed. The ultimate test, however, was pragmatic: how far could Henry govern England by anticlerical caucus rather than Catholic consensus? Could he coerce the church without provoking rebellion? St German wrote in defence of Parliament's power: 'The king in his Parliament [is] the high sovereign over the people, which hath not only charge on the bodies but also on the souls of his subjects.'[20] This virtually amounted to a full-blown theory of parliamentary sovereignty. And he said of the authors of the 1529 statutes: 'I hold it not best to reason or to make arguments whether they had authority to do that they did or not. For I suppose that no man would think that they would do anything that they had not power to do.'[21]

In January 1531 Henry VIII insisted that the clergy repeat the subsidy Wolsey had obtained from them in 1523. A triumph of fiscal ingenuity, the tax had yielded £118,840, and Henry demanded it again as a fine for the clergy's complicity in Wolsey's papal legacy. He began in king's bench, where the attorney-general charged fifteen selected clergy and one lay proctor with *praemunire* as Wolsey's accomplices, but within six months the focus of the attack had broadened to include the whole clergy of the province of Canterbury and all their registrars and scribes. Henry wanted money because the divorce campaign had brought threats of an imperial invasion from Charles V's ambassador in London, which the Council took seriously. By this time the Crown was only solvent on its current account thanks to the French pensions Wolsey had negotiated in 1525; there was no cash reserve and the king wanted money to replenish the war chest. Yet far more than money was involved. The clergy were finally 'pardoned' not for abetting Wolsey's papal legacy but for exercising their spiritual jurisdiction in church courts. The whole thrust of the king's attack was designed to put pressure on the pope and archbishop of Canterbury to take action on the divorce. In fact, this objective was crucial from the start, since the selected clergy whom Henry accused of *praemunire* included all Catherine of Aragon's episcopal supporters except Cuthbert Tunstall.

Convocation decided to pay the required taxation on 24 January, but a straw was in the wind when the prologue to the

Council's draft 'offer' on the clergy's behalf alluded to Henry VIII as 'protector and highest head' of the English church. This was in itself fairly innocuous since the Crown's role as patron and protector had always been emphasized, but the crunch came on 7 February when Henry raised the stakes and insisted that he be styled 'sole protector and supreme head of the English church and clergy' and that his 'cure' of his subjects' souls be recognized. These new demands hit Convocation like a thunderbolt. After passionate speeches from John Fisher, the first claim was diminished by the qualification 'as far as Christ's law allows', and the second claim was emasculated. As eventually conceded, the 'royal supremacy' of 1531 was so hedged about with qualifications that no one knew for sure what it meant. But Henry gained a victory in so far as he obtained taxation and a qualified new title. He had also succeeded in linking his religious policy to coercive fiscal manœuvres.[22]

By early 1531 Henry VIII saw 'his' royal supremacy as a fact rather than a novelty. He could see no objection to it, and interpreted the clergy's resistance as culpable disobedience. Perplexing at first sight, his attitude can be explained. For some months Henry had been studying a manuscript known as *Collectanea satis copiosa*. A collection of sources for pro-royal propaganda, it was prepared by members of the Boleyn faction. The work was undertaken by Edward Foxe and Thomas Cranmer during 1530; the *Collectanea* was presented to Henry in September that year. And the king read it: his handwriting is to be found in forty-six places on the manuscript. 'Ubi hic?' ('Whence does this come?') he exclaimed in marginal asides! His curiosity was aroused. Yet he applauded the document because, setting out to validate the divorce, Foxe and Cranmer had justified it from legal and historical principles, not simply personal or dynastic needs. For the first time, the righteousness of the king's case was established as an aspect of monarchic power from the Bible, traditional Catholic texts, and English histories and chronicles—the Old Testament, the Church Fathers, the Donation of Constantine, Ivo of Chartres, Hugh of St Victor, the fifteenth-century conciliarists, Anglo-Saxon laws, Geoffrey of Monmouth, and other authorities. Indeed, Foxe and Cranmer had redefined the boundaries between royal and ecclesiastical power, arguing that, ever since the conversion of the

Anglo-Saxons to Christianity, the kings of England had enjoyed secular *imperium* and spiritual supremacy like the later Roman emperors. Also the English church had *always* been a separate province of Christendom subject only to royal jurisdiction. Even the papacy had (allegedly) confirmed this. So, if this were true, Henry VIII's kingship was like that of the Emperor Constantine after his conversion to Christianity and papal jurisdiction was a usurpation. Henry's temporal sovereignty remained the same but his spiritual sovereignty was absolute. He was, in short, a theocratic king, though he did not possess the sacramental 'cure of souls' which the ordained priesthood alone might exercise. But he could summon church councils within his dominions, enforce their decrees, and define the articles of faith. In particular, he could summon the bishops, or an English church council, to pronounce his divorce, and then enforce their decision by proclamation or act of Parliament.[23]

In March 1531 More was given a most unpleasant task. He was required as lord chancellor to bolster Henry VIII's credibility by presenting to both Houses of Parliament the opinions favourable to the divorce which had been procured from various European universities. Although he viewed the duty with obvious discomfort, he began in the House of Lords, explaining that he was there to deny that Henry sought a divorce out of love for a woman rather than for genuine scruples of conscience. When he moved to the Commons, his speech was recorded by the chronicler Edward Hall, MP for Wenlock: 'You of this worshipful House, I am sure, be not so ignorant but you know well that the king our sovereign lord hath married his brother's wife, for she was both wedded and bedded with his brother Prince Arthur.'[24]

His son-in-law was right to suppose that More could only have done this at Henry's personal request. Was he right, too, that the job was embarrassing enough to make More ask Norfolk for help in resigning his office? For More's integrity was now compromised: he had been forced to associate himself with, and lend his authority to, the divorce policy. His assertion that Catherine was bedded with Arthur was highly damaging to the queen, whose whole case rested upon her assertion that her first marriage to Arthur had not been consummated, and thus was invalid.

Why then did More not resign in 1531? The answer is that he thought the factional battle in Council could still be won. The cliff-hanger was not resolved, for during 1531 Cromwell was making slow progress in the Council, while Anne Boleyn's insolence led the duke of Norfolk to suppose that Henry would shortly cast away that 'she-devil'. (And we should remember that Norfolk was Anne's uncle.) Meanwhile, More was described by Chapuys as 'the true father and protector' of Queen Catherine's interests, helping the ambassador's business forward in Council and at Court. In recognition of his services, Charles V sent a letter of appreciation to More. Written in Brussels on 11 March 1531, this reached London on the 22nd. More received word of its arrival shortly after he spoke in Parliament. But he would not accept the document. He avoided Chapuys and refused him permission to visit his house at Chelsea. Chapuys wrote to Charles: '[More] begged me for the honour of God to forbear, for although he had given already sufficient proof of his loyalty that he ought to incur no suspicion, whoever came to visit him, yet, considering the time, he ought to abstain from everything which might provoke suspicion.' And More claimed that a visit would prevent him 'speaking boldly' in matters concerning Charles and his aunt, though he assured the emperor of 'his most affectionate service'.[25]

This was one of More's most important statements. It confirms that he regarded himself as a spokesman for the queen's party in Council; that this group was sufficiently engaged in opposition to frighten More that he would be ruined should his contact with Charles V become known; and that More was anxious not to lose such influence as he had over policy—itself an admission that he did have influence still. So More had come to terms with his conscience in 1531. He had compromised himself in Parliament on the king's behalf; and with the emperor against the king's divorce. Noteworthy is that he would avoid contact with Chapuys in order to 'incur no suspicion'. From Henry VIII's point of view, More had shown unusual flexibility by speaking in Parliament. His presence may have bolstered royal hopes that More would one day be won round to supporting the divorce, which was always Henry's objective. Yet More himself must have seen the value of compliance in terms of continued influence over policy. His motive was to promote

Henry's and England's welfare *in the long term*. He used this argument when encouraging Throckmorton to opposition in Parliament. He told him that, by speaking his mind in support of the Catholic cause, he would 'deserve great reward of God' and 'thanks of the king's grace at length'.[26] Apart from confirming that for the present Henry's attitude was likely to be very different, that official policy was veering away from Catholicism, and that More was working to change that policy, the statement shows that More also held an implicit trust that Henry would eventually lose his infatuation for Anne Boleyn, and return to his senses. He would then appreciate the true worth of subjects who were the king's good servants, but God's first.

But a year later More lost both battle and war. In March 1532 Parliament passed the Act in Conditional Restraint of Annates. The payments clerics made to Rome on their appointment to benefices were to cease and, if the pope ordered an interdict, it should be ignored. This provoked an outcry and Henry had to concede a clause making the act conditional upon later confirmation. Next, Cromwell resurrected the Commons' anticlerical grievances of 1529, especially those concerning heresy trials. He brilliantly exploited the emotions of MPs to engineer, on 15 May 1532, the formal submission of the clergy to Henry VIII. Convocation was not to assemble without the king's permission; no new canons were to be enacted without royal assent; existing ones were to be vetted by a royal commission; and those prejudicial to royal prerogative were to be annulled. More resigned next day; Cromwell had brought off a coup. Yet Henry still lacked his divorce. Even if he told 'his' clergy to pronounce it, the queen would appeal to the pope unless first he broke with Rome.

In fact, there was an eight-month delay before Henry married Anne Boleyn; the reasons were the conservative nobility's dislike of royal policies and the king's continued psychological dependence on the pope. Also diplomacy overshadowed radical politics when it became known that Francis I would marry his second son, Henry, to Catherine de Medici, a relative of Clement VII. In the summer of 1532 Henry VIII renewed the Anglo-French alliance and planned to meet Francis at Calais and Boulogne, convinced that the forthcoming French marriage would prove a bargaining counter with the pope. Henry took

Anne Boleyn to Calais and, it seems, saw Francis's support as giving him sufficient security to consummate his relationship with Anne. Her suite of rooms at Calais backed on to Henry's own, while the couple took ten days to travel on their return journey from Dover to Eltham![27]

Anne was pregnant by the end of December 1532, and this enabled her to forge ahead. She knew Henry would convince himself that any child she might conceive would be a son. Moreover, the only fundamental obstacle left to her marriage was Henry's own indecision, for, though Archbishop Warham could not be pressured into defying the pope in the wake of the clergy's submission, his death in August 1532 had paved the way for Cranmer's appointment. Indeed, Anne Boleyn, Cranmer, and Thomas Cromwell were reformers of similar views and Cranmer's nomination was vital to the radical faction's success. But, despite his Cambridge connections, he was unqualified save through his support for the divorce and factional ties. Not only were his 'reformed' tendencies a positive drawback given Henry's commitment to Catholic theology, but he also had to be recalled from an embassy to Charles V at Mantua. Bishoprics, too, were normally left vacant for a year following an incumbent's death so that the Crown could collect the revenues. However, Cranmer's nomination was common knowledge by 24 January 1533, and the next day Henry and Anne were secretly married in a pre-dawn ceremony. When the celebrant asked, 'I trust you have the pope's licence?', the king replied, 'I have truly a licence . . . which if it were seen, should discharge us all.' Having only an old papal licence expressly conditional upon his marriage to Catherine being ruled invalid, Henry was disingenuous. But Cromwell was already drafting the initial instrument of schism, the Act in Restraint of Appeals, which reached the statute book in April 1533. Ending appeals to Rome, it ordered them to be heard by the English church courts and provided that appeals touching the king were to go directly to the upper house of Convocation. Catherine's appeal to the pope was not expressly mentioned; the act claimed to be a development of the Statutes of Provisors and *Praemunire*, but this was legal fiction. On the contrary, the act's preamble vigorously asserted Henry's 'imperial' kingship: England was 'an empire' governed by 'one supreme head and king'. For this the act cited the authority of 'sundry old authentic histories and chronicles'. And the 'imperial' constitution comprised three things: the king's 'whole and entire power' to govern his subjects without interference from 'any foreign princes or potentates'; the English church's national independence under the Crown; and the assertion that it was the ancient English kings and nobility who had endowed the national church 'both with honour and possessions'. Property law was administered by the secular judges, and the implication was that what the Crown had originally granted — for instance, the earliest religious houses — it could take away by acts of resumption.[28]

The link between the Act of Appeals and *Collectanea satis copiosa* is manifest — even more so if drafts of the act are examined. These alluded to a supposed letter written *c*. AD 187 by Pope Eleutherius in which he addressed the (mythical) King Lucius I of Britain as 'vicar of God' within his realm. The letter was in the *Collectanea*, which also claimed that Lucius had endowed the English church. Henry VIII drew the simplest conclusion: he scribbled on one of the drafts that recent papal jurisdiction in England was 'but only by negligence or usurpation as we take it and esteem'.[29]

Yet the Act of Appeals was a compromise document. Henry VIII asserted his royal supremacy, but Cromwell wanted the church to be subject to the king-in-Parliament, as did St German. Cromwell had attempted to engineer the clergy's submission of 1532 to Parliament, but Henry objected. In fact, Cromwell *opposed* 'imperial' kingship if 'empire' meant the Crown's absolute right to rule the church without the consent of Parliament. St German took the same view and argued the case for parliamentary sovereignty in several treatises. This ambiguity permeated the theory of the supremacy for the remainder of the Tudor period. It was disguised by the claim that royal supremacy was ordained by God's law, but the people had given Henry VIII the authority by their free votes in Parliament. Apologists from Bishop Gardiner, writing his *Oration of True Obedience* (1535), to Sir Christopher Hatton, addressing the House of Commons in 1589, took this line. But these propositions contradicted each other: if royal supremacy existed by divine law, its authority preceded, and superseded, Parliament's approval. The clergy themselves did not wish to be subject to Parliament, however, and Cranmer and Edward Foxe, as well as Henry VIII, had perhaps pressed Cromwell on this point. Either way Cromwell accepted the compromise as the price of victory in the Council. And later events revised Parliament's role to match Cromwell's vision. The supremacy was repealed by Queen Mary but re-enacted by Elizabeth I. Parliament had to be used on both occasions: Mary, in particular, was obliged to repeal the Acts of Appeals and Supremacy in order to deny them. This process served to strengthen Parliament's power.

The Act of Appeals did not pass without a fight, though this was in the Commons, not the Lords. A majority of the bishops supported the Crown in Parliament during the 1530s, perhaps because they wished to close ranks against Cromwell's threat of a parliamentary supremacy. Indeed, to politically alert bishops royal supremacy was the better of two evils: the clergy would not have to counter the approaching anticlerical backlash without the necessary filter of royal mediation. Since a majority of temporal peers also supported the Crown in the interests of social stability, the upper house was relatively easy to manage. By contrast, the bill of Appeals raised a fight in the Commons. A damaged list of some thirty-five names of MPs compiled by Cromwell survives among his papers, detailing opponents of the bill.[30] They included Sir George Throckmorton, Sir William Essex, and Sir John Gifford, members of the Queen's Head group. Also More's family circle were there, William Roper and William Daunce, as was Robert Fisher, the bishop's brother. We know that Henry VIII sent for Throckmorton, who had 'reasoned to the bill' — a polite way of saying he had opposed it. Cromwell was present at this interview, and he told Throckmorton to 'stay at home and meddle little in politics'.[31]

While Parliament debated the Act of Appeals, the prelates ruled Catherine of Aragon's marriage to be invalid. In May 1533 Cranmer annulled it and pronounced Anne Boleyn's marriage valid. Anne was crowned on Whit Sunday, 1 June, in a spectacle complete with aquatic pageants; but there were mutterings in corners, and More and the earl of Shrewsbury refused to attend the ceremony. And Henry's joy turned to sorrow when, on 7 September 1533, Anne was delivered not of a son but of a daughter, Elizabeth. In July 1533 Pope Clement VII threatened to excommunicate Henry, who replied by recalling his envoys from Rome and by confirming the Act in Conditional Restraint of Annates. He also appealed to a General Council of the church; but this was bluster.

Parliament cemented the break with Rome in 1534–6. In the spring session of 1534 the Succession Act put Cranmer's judgment into statute, commanded allegiance to Anne and her issue, and made it high treason to impugn the king's title to the Crown or slander his marriage. An Act for the Submission of the Clergy incorporated into law the surrender of 1532 and modified the Act of Appeals by giving final authority in ecclesiastical cases to lay commissioners in chancery. The Dispensations Act reiterated Henry's royal supremacy and provided that licences and dispensations should in future be sought from the English authorities. Those monasteries which, by papal privilege, were exempt from episcopal jurisdiction were placed under royal supervision, and no monk was to travel overseas to take part in general chapters of his order. Lastly, the law of heresy was relaxed to permit speaking against papal authority and, as St German had demanded, common-law safeguards were added to the procedures for conducting trials. The bishops were to observe the 'two-witness' rule prevailing at common law; trials were to be held in open court; and the king's writ was required for the burning of heretics. In his *Apology* and *Debellation* More had claimed that such provisions would render the church authorities impotent, so that heretics would 'wax bold' and the 'streets swarm full' of them.

In the second session of 1534 the Act of Supremacy defined Henry VIII's caesaropapism:

Be it enacted by authority of this present Parliament that the King our sovereign lord, his heirs and successors kings of this realm, shall be taken, accepted and reputed the only supreme head in earth of the Church of England called *Anglicana Ecclesia*, and shall have and enjoy annexed and united to the imperial crown of this realm as well the title and style thereof, as all honours, dignities, preeminences, jurisdictions, privileges, authorities, immunities, profits and commodities, to the said dignity of supreme head of the same Church belonging and appertaining.[32]

These words did not mean that Parliament had created the supremacy, which Henry always maintained was ordained by

God. The purpose of putting the supremacy into statute was to enable its enforcement by a Treason Act that also updated the law of treason. The act, the first major revision of the law since 1352, made it high treason to rebel against or threaten the royal family, even by words, or to deny their titles, or to call the king a heretic, schismatic, tyrant, infidel, or usurper. Lastly, the Act for Payment of First Fruits devised new clerical taxes at substantially higher rates than before. Between 1485 and 1534 the clergy paid £4,800 a year to Rome, but in 1535 they paid £46,052 and in 1536 £51,770 to Henry VIII.[33]

In 1536 the jurisdictional revolution was completed by the Act Extinguishing the Authority of the Bishop of Rome. This was necessary because the acts of 1533–4 had omitted to proscribe the pope's rights as a pastor or teacher who might interpret Scripture or offer moral guidance. Such rights had been affirmed by Gardiner's *Oration of True Obedience* but this standpoint could not last. The act came into force on 31 July 1536; it prohibited the exercise or defence of papal authority in any form under penalty of *praemunire*.

Yet the test of 'imperial' kingship was whether it could be imposed on the localities. By December 1534 at the latest Henry had named Cromwell his vicegerent (deputy) in spiritual affairs as well as following his advice in matters of civil government. Cromwell's first technique was to bind the nation: all adult males were to swear an oath to the terms of the Succession Act; the parish clergy had to subscribe to the statement that the pope had no greater power than any foreign bishop; the diocesan and monastic clergy had to swear to the succession, supremacy, and pruning of canon law; finally, an oath renouncing papal jurisdiction and supporting the supremacy was imposed on all ecclesiastical and lay officials, as well as on persons suing livery of lands, taking holy orders, or proceeding to a degree at the universities.

Cromwell next launched a sponsored propaganda and preaching campaign that recognized pulpit and press as the mass media of Tudor England.[34] Latin treatises were addressed to learned and European audiences; vernacular tracts began the battle for the hearts and minds of English parishioners. Often elegant, witty, and persuasive, these books injected reforming ideas into society but their main object was to encourage unity,

conformity, and obedience to royal and parliamentary authority.
Familiar themes were that papal power was usurped but royal
power divine; that England's independence was her destiny; that
clerical jurisdiction had no foundation in Scripture save in respect
of the church's sacramental life; and that canon law was not
divine but human. Government control of pulpits was attempted
through a licensing system: sermons were ordered against papal
authority and in defence of the Boleyn marriage and the
supremacy, but preachers were warned against denying the mass,
the cult of saints, purgatory, pilgrimages, miracles, or clerical
celibacy. Both in London and the country at large the ultimate
control of preaching was contested between Cromwell and
Cranmer on one side and the conservative bishops on the other.
Reformers were licensed to preach: Robert Barnes, Hugh
Latimer, Thomas Garrett, Edward Crome, Nicholas Shaxton,
and William Jerome. And through Anne Boleyn's influence
Latimer and Shaxton were made bishops. But the 'reformed'
cause had gone too far for Henry VIII's taste by 1538; Cromwell
had to silence his pulpits, and in 1539 the Act of Six Articles
forced Latimer and Shaxton to resign their sees. Barnes, Garrett,
and Jerome were burned as heretics two days after Cromwell's
execution, which shows how fine was the line between
advancement and persecution.

Other instruments of Cromwell's strategy were circular letters
and the work of JPs and assize judges.[35] In April 1535 royal
letters were sent to bishops, nobility, and JPs commanding them
to imprison clergy who continued to preach papal authority. A
barrage of circulars followed in 1535–9 ordering the detention
of dissidents, the defence of the supremacy, the erasure of the
pope's name from mass books, the observance of Cromwell's
vicegerential injunctions, the placing of the English Bible in
parish churches, the proscription of St Thomas Becket, etc. But
the key element was Cromwell's use of psychology. He told
recipients they were 'specially elected and chosen' for their tasks;
letters were individually handwritten, the printing press being
avoided so each thought his own letter unique; and Cromwell
applied a two-tier method to reinforce the impact of his orders —
letters under the king's stamp were immediately followed by
letters from the minister. Since Cromwell also threatened reprisals
against the tardy or disobedient, his call to action was shrill.

Bishops and JPs alike were charged with 'all speed and diligence' to make arrests or file reports with the Council; the replies Cromwell received requesting his 'further pleasure' testify to his success in gathering information.

But more than information was needed. Cromwell decided to set the JPs and sheriffs as watchdogs over the bishops — a policy emulated by Elizabeth's Council as part of its programme to enforce Anglicanism. With this reversal of traditional roles, the laicization of the realm was taken a stage further. The assize judges, as well as enforcing the Treason Act on circuit, were used by Cromwell to collect opinion, assess the effectiveness of JPs, and set forth the supremacy at assizes by expounding the statutes to juries. The cumulative effect was to stress Tudor efficiency and centralization, or at least the presumption of these. The eyes and ears of the government seemed to be everywhere, like those of Janus.[36]

Few people realized the significance of the distinction between royal and papal supremacy before the martyrdoms of More, Fisher, and the London Carthusians. The Treason Act came into force on 1 February 1535, but, if the Lancashire and Lincolnshire experiences are typical, the vast majority of clergy did not regard the divorce and supremacy as important issues in themselves; protests were delayed until it became clear to what purposes the supremacy would be turned.[37] It was Cromwell's vicegerency, his injunctions, statutes and proclamations aimed at the duties, incomes, and, finally, the beliefs of the Catholic clergy, that roused a surge of opposition. It was the dissolution of the monasteries that fuelled outright rebellion in Lincolnshire and the northern counties, though in London and the south-east the scale of resistance was small.

Specific episodes, however, brought individuals into the limelight. In November 1533 the Holy Maid of Kent was sent to the Tower: Elizabeth Barton was a young prophetess from Aldington (Kent) who had foretold Henry VIII's early death if he married Anne Boleyn. Although genuinely charismatic, Barton was manipulated by opponents of the divorce: Fisher was among those who listened to her, but neither Catherine of Aragon nor More would entertain any political prophecies. On 21 April 1534 Barton and four of her promoters became the first victims of the Henrician Reformation—attainted for treason without trial at common law, though the act claimed that the accused had confessed their offences before the Council.[38] Parliament had to be used because the existing treason law was inadequate. But when Cromwell introduced his new treason bill into the Commons, it met vigorous opposition: there was 'never such a sticking at the passage of any Act in the Lower House'.[39] Whether Cromwell or the Commons put the word 'maliciously' into the bill, the significance of this safeguard was contested. William Rastell, More's nephew and publisher, wrote: 'The bill was earnestly withstood, and could not be suffered to pass, unless the rigour of it were qualified with this word *maliciously*; and so not every speaking against the Supremacy to be treason, but only maliciously speaking.'[40]

This vital qualification was, however, ignored in the *causes célèbres* of Prior Houghton and the Carthusians, Fisher, and More. More's trial in July 1535 proved the most problematical because he had not expressly denied the supremacy, though he had discussed it by example, or what lawyers called 'putting of cases'. We have the record of his own words, spoken to Richard Rich in the Tower on 12 June 1535:

A King [ma]y be made by Parliament and a King deprived by Parliament to which act any [of his] Subjects being of the Parliament may give his consent, but to the case . . . [in question] a Subject cannot be bound by cause he cannot give his consent . . . [in] Parliament. Saying further that although the King were accepted in England [as supreme head] yet most Utter [i.e. foreign] parts do not affirm the same.[41]

Although More knew the efforts made by the draftsmen of the Act of Supremacy to avoid stating that Parliament had made the king supreme head of the Church of England, and to make clear that Henry VIII and his predecessors had always been supreme head, so that Parliament was simply recognizing the fact belatedly, he thought them futile. In the Tower he compared the 'restructuring' of English Christianity under the Crown to a second betrayal of Christ. But he suffered execution not for denying the supremacy outright, but for refusing to be convinced that Parliament could require assent to it when the rest of Catholic Europe said otherwise.

Yet if More would not deny the royal supremacy outright, neither would he affirm papal supremacy, for he had doubted for years claims that the papacy was divinely ordained by Christ to govern Christendom absolutely; indeed his expressed views came close to endorsing conciliarism. 'As touching . . . the primacy of the Pope,' he told Cromwell, 'I nothing meddle in the matter,' though he continued: 'Truth it is . . . I was myself some time not of the mind that the primacy of that see should be begun by the institution of God, until that I read in that matter those things that the King's Highness had written in his most famous book against the heresies of Martin Luther.'[42]

More's argument that it was Henry VIII who had taught him the primacy of the pope was a palpable hit. He admitted privately that he was 'not as thoroughly instructed on the subject as the times required'; and by 1534 saw 'no commodity' in denying the primacy—which any lawyer knows does not mean he fully affirmed it. But More's rejection of royal supremacy pushed him inexorably towards Rome. He told Cromwell in 1534 that papal primacy 'is at the least wise instituted by the corps of Christendom and for a great urgent cause in avoiding of schisms',[43] though this was to say no more than that the papacy was an institution of human convenience approved by church councils over the centuries. Indeed, it was a relatively weak statement of the pope's case. And More always spoke of papal primacy, never papal supremacy, nor papal sovereignty.

But in April 1534 More declined Henry VIII's oath of succession. He refused to approve the Boleyn marriage against his conscience, since to do so was to commit perjury: the penalty was damnation. Also the preamble to the Act of Succession abhorred papal jurisdiction, which went too far. For their refusals More, Fisher, and Nicholas Wilson were sent to the Tower, then attainted of misprision of treason (i.e. bare knowledge or 'concealment' of treason).[44] Finally, More was indicted under the Acts of Supremacy and Treason. He argued that his indictment was invalid because it was drawn upon parliamentary statutes repugnant to the common law of Christendom: he meant that Parliament had no power to enact laws that the rest of Catholic Europe rejected, if these were to bind men's consciences. He raised a crucial point that Chief Justice Fitzjames rebutted with a double negative: 'By Saint Julian, I must needs confess that if the act of Parliament be not unlawful, then is not the indictment in my conscience insufficient.'[45] This decision echoes down the centuries. But the Tudors shared St German's view of Parliament's power; More's stand was thus conservative and radical at once. It was a Catholic act of resistance to defend the church's liberty from the king-in-Parliament; a radical protest to claim freedom of conscience against what More had come to think was a totalitarian state. And he thwarted Henry VIII by mounting the scaffold under the spotlight of Europe. Moral authority was on his side; in Fisher's case less so, since he had urged Charles V to invade England.

If, however, More gained the moral victory, it was necessarily posthumous, and it is rightly asked whether his trial was fair. Certainly it was ordered by the king and implemented by Cromwell, who was fully briefed by the judges on the difficulties. Once Henry decided to avenge himself upon his former chancellor, the trial was a foregone conclusion, but the verdict may not have been. On the contrary, More's trial went badly for the government. Not only did he embarrass the judges by invoking the procedure known as motion in arrest of judgment, but also the prosecution's evidence collapsed at a crucial point. So More was finally convicted on the testimony of a single perjured witness. Since he was tried by jury, his conviction was only inevitable if the jury was rigged, but a single piece of evidence exists to suggest that it was. One juror was John Parnell, a London draper and informer who had unsuccessfully accused More of corruption after More, as lord chancellor, had decreed a chancery case against him.[46]

Anne Boleyn followed More to the scaffold within a year, her destruction the result of a rapid sequence of events. When in January 1536 she miscarried what by all accounts was a deformed foetus, Henry instantly 'knew' his second marriage to be damned: God's wrath would forever deny him sons by her. Yet Henry had his reputation to protect. By the end of the month his councillors were salvaging his honour by claiming that Anne had bewitched him. He had been 'seduced and forced into his second marriage by means of sortileges and charms'. A strategy was developed for her trial and divorce which enabled Henry publicly to deny his paternity and remarry without acknowledging the deformed foetus. Yet Anne's fall presaged Cromwell's too. Her Court enemies rallied about Jane Seymour, whom they adopted as bait. Henry VIII was hooked, but the opposition had a triple intent: to make Jane queen; to neutralize Anne's religious patronage; and to restore the Catholic Princess Mary to the succession. Cromwell was vulnerable to this resurgent factionalism on two fronts: he was the second target of the Catholic party, and Anne too mistrusted him for reopening negotiations with Charles V after Catherine of Aragon's death. In fact, Cromwell's diplomacy accelerated in the same month as Anne miscarried—a vital indicator. So Cromwell moved first, allying with Anne's opponents to persuade Henry that she had committed incest with her brother, the 'father' of the deformed foetus, and multiple adultery with her clients in the privy chamber: this way both Anne and her Court party were dragged down. On 17 May 1536 Henry Norris, groom of the stool, Lord Rochford (Anne's brother), Sir Francis Weston, William Brereton, and a musician Mark Smeaton were executed. Anne herself suffered at sunrise on the 19th: Cranmer wept, but Henry married Jane.[47]

Cromwell cemented his *putsch* by driving Princess Mary's supporters from Court on the grounds that they had plotted to restore her to the succession. He was promoted lord privy seal and then ennobled as Lord Cromwell of Wimbledon. But the most important result of these events was that the privy chamber fell under his influence. He named his own men to the vacancies there: Ralph Sadler (who also took Brereton's best estates) and Peter Mewtas were appointed in 1536, Philip Hoby by 1538, and Richard Moryson and others later. By the end of 1539 Cromwell presided over 'by far the largest and strongest Court faction'.[48]

On 12 October 1537 Jane Seymour gave birth to Henry's only legitimate son, Prince Edward; her triumph was Pyrrhic, as a Caesarian section killed her. But the dynasty was secured and not a moment too soon. The consumptive Henry Fitzroy had died in July 1536, when Princess Mary and her sister Elizabeth had also been bastardized by the Second Act of Succession, an act that guaranteed the throne to Jane's offspring and modified the Treason Act in the light of More's case by making equally heinous denial of the supremacy or keeping silence when asked to swear an opinion.

'These bloody days have broken my heart,' penned Sir

Thomas Wyatt after the *putsch*.[49] Violence was unavoidable, for
the break with Rome was a political revolution. Yet Cromwell
did not preside over a reign of terror, since no more than 883
people were tried for treason during the 1530s, 308 of whom
were executed and 21 probably so. Of these, however, 287 were
participants in rebellions, so their fate was hardly surprising.
Only 63 people died for treason by words under Cromwell's
extension of the law, and 23 of these cases followed from the
Pilgrimage of Grace. Twenty executions resulted from the Court
and dynastic coups of the decade, while the remaining victims
were convicted for acts that would probably have qualified as
treason under pre-Reformation legislation. Some 178 executions
specifically resulted from the Lincolnshire Rising and Pilgrimage
of Grace (which included 74 executions at Carlisle in 1537 when
the duke of Norfolk proclaimed martial law). And some 10 people
died in prison before trial or conviction. Yet 37 accused persons
were acquitted; 108 were pardoned after conviction; 16 were
reprieved; and 13 convictions were quashed. Also at least 212
cases of alleged treason were dropped after investigation. Indeed,
state trials apart, accusations were properly evaluated; there was
no automatic assumption of guilt save where the accused was
caught in open rebellion. Few of Henry's provincial critics were
put on trial; people were left to get on with their lives, but they
had to accept, or at any rate not deny in public, that the king
was supreme head of the church.[50]

Yet nothing could save the monasteries. While there was in
practice no thought at first of dissolving the greater religious
houses but only the smaller ones, powerful forces dictated that
there would be at least piecemeal suppressions. First, the very
idea that members of the religious orders owed an allegiance to
their parent institutions outside England was unacceptable after
the Acts of Appeals and Supremacy. Second, the regular clergy
produced more opponents of Henry VIII than any other section
of the community. Third, the criticisms of enclosed religion and
idolatry voiced by Erasmus, Tyndale, Fish, and evangelical
preachers were being assimilated into English culture; the view
that founders had intended religious houses to serve the needs
of the realm gained currency. Behind this argument lurked the
appetite of the laity for land — stimulated by rising population

and agricultural commercialization. Henry VIII, too, needed
to win the support of the local governors for his proceedings by
injections of new patronage — to appease the magnates and JPs
with a share of the spoils. But it was the Crown's own needs
that dictated the scope and timing of the dissolution. A bold plan
for a single strike against Wolsey and the wealth of the church
had been mooted in July 1529. While the Act of Appeals was
before Parliament, Henry announced his goal 'of uniting to the
Crown the lands which the Clergy of his dominions held thereof,
which lands and property his predecessors on the throne could
not alienate to his prejudice'.[51] His remark rationalized but was,
unquestionably, taken from the theory of Fortescue and the
Collectanea satis copiosa. 'Imperial' kingship implied tribute
(taxation) not resumption, but 'feudal' ideas retained their
usefulness. An anonymous proposal of the autumn of 1534
mapped a scheme for the wholesale resumption by the Crown
of all ecclesiastical endowments above parish level, to be followed
by the provision of fixed incomes for the clergy. The plan was
headed: 'Things to be moved for the king's highness for an
increase and augmentation to be had for maintenance of his most
royal estate, and for the defence of the realm.'[52] Cromwell's
task, in short, was to finalize the work of Edward IV, Henry VII,
and Wolsey; to endow the 'imperial' Crown so that stability
could be assured, the royal household and institutions of
government maintained, patronage dispensed, and foreign policy
conducted without resort to 'exquisite means' — the type of
emergency expedients that provoked domestic political friction.

Such theory underpinned the process of dissolution. In an
important sense the 'great spoliation' was only the biggest
component of a broader financial strategy. For a new round of
fiscalism had begun in 1529: first Wolsey was stripped of his
assets; then clerical taxation in 1531 raised £69,432 allowing for
an instalment of tax remitted as a quid pro quo for the Act for
Payment of First Fruits. Next, first fruits and tenths together
with other clerical taxation raised £406,103 between 1535 and
1540. The dissolution itself netted £1.3 million between August
1536 and October 1547. Lastly, parliamentary lay taxation
yielded £80,384 in 1535–7.[53] Cromwell's taxation was itself a
landmark, since both first fruits and tenths, and the Subsidy Act
of 1534, were justified on grounds not of war but of peace;

Henry VIII had for twenty-five years so capably ruled the realm 'to the high pleasure of Almighty God' that loyal subjects felt obliged to assist by offering peacetime taxation—so the argument ran. A precedent existed in Wolsey's act of 1515 granting a fifteenth and tenth; some limitation should be placed on the idea that the grant of 1534 announced a revolutionary new principle. But Cromwell's view that national taxation should be authorized for the maintenance of normal administration on a sustained basis was radical.[54] It gave a cutting edge to Fortescue's plea for the monarchy's re-endowment; it complemented Wolsey's invention of the Tudor subsidy and demand for up-to-date assessments and progressive rates of tax. And, of course, it underpinned the planned Great Contract of 1610 and the Restoration financial settlement.

Although a total of £1.3 million accrued from the dissolution between 1536 and Henry VIII's death, a distinction must be made between the rents of confiscated lands, which were true revenues, and cash derived from the sale of lands, which was the alienation of capital. The gross receipts of Henry VIII's land sales were £799,310; the gold and silver plate and jewels seized from shrines and elsewhere raised a further £79,471. An average of £82,000 per annum accrued from land sales between October 1539 and Henry VIII's death, but sales were at their height in 1544 and 1545 with totals of £164,495 and £165,459 respectively. Sales of goods and movables reached their peak in 1541–3 (£13,787). However, capital sales reduced the Crown's recurring income: rents reached their maximum in 1542 and 1543, but then fell. In 1546 they totalled £59,255, in 1547 £48,303, less than half the original monastic income. Sales, which began before Cromwell's fall in 1540, thus impugned his ability, if not his determination, to use the monastic lands as a permanent endowment of the 'imperial' Crown. By 1547 almost two-thirds of the monastic property had been alienated; further grants by Edward VI and Queen Mary brought this figure to over three-quarters by 1558; and the remaining lands were sold by Elizabeth I and the early Stuarts. Little land was given away: out of 1,593 grants in Henry VIII's reign, only sixty-nine were gifts or partly so; the bulk of grants (95.6 per cent) represented lands sold at prices based on fresh valuations. But the proceeds of sale were not invested; land, in any case, *was* the best investment.[55]

Yet cash reserves were the key to Henry VIII's strategy after Wolsey's fall. From January 1531 Cromwell started to act as an informal national treasurer: he ran government finance in 1532–6 from the funds under his control, and thereafter he managed clerical taxation and the dissolution too. So his activities completely reconstituted the Crown's financial system and overthrew the remains of the Yorkist–Tudor chamber. But change occurred less because the revenues Cromwell administered were novel than because as master of the jewels—his earliest major office—he had access to the king's coffers. These 'coffers' became the cash reserve: they comprised chests of cash stored at the back of Henry VIII's bedchamber at the palace of Whitehall, as well as at the Tower and elsewhere.[56] Although Cromwell created a new department of state and a new official to *collect* the proceeds of the dissolution and first fruits and tenths—the court of augmentations and treasurer of first fruits and tenths respectively—they were used largely for accountancy purposes. Their cash surpluses were transferred to the king's coffers.

Cromwell had established this procedure by 1536, and a year later each revenue-raising body or official—the chamber, augmentations, the treasurer of first fruits and tenths, the duchy of Lancaster, and exchequer—were ordered to file 'declarations' of income and expenditure in their offices, and then to calculate 'what the whole remainder [i.e. balance] to the King's use will yearly amount unto'. The purpose of the exercise was so 'the King's Highness may know his estate, and by means thereof may establish all his affairs; and thereby to put an order how a certain treasure yearly may be laid up for all necessities'.[57] After 1536 the king's coffers duly received £178,000 from augmentations, £96,000 from parliamentary taxation, £28,000 from the jewel house, and £60,000 from first fruits and tenths. A total of £362,000 was transferred in this way, and in 1542–7 £241,570 was placed by Henry VIII under the charge of Sir Anthony Denny, chief gentleman of the privy chamber and keeper of the palace of Whitehall and its deposit treasury.[58]

Whether or not Denny's funds were meant to be the king's war chest is a matter of debate. Certainly most of the money was disbursed during the Boulogne campaign of 1544. It had never been Cromwell's intention to squander the proceeds of the dissolution: the whole thrust of his financial policy had been to maximize the Crown's long-term income. But Cromwell was arrested in June 1540 and in July he was dead. His end stemmed from politics, his pro-Lutheran diplomacy, and support of radical reformers — yet perhaps all along his and Henry's financial intentions had conflicted?

There is, however, no doubt about Cromwell's conduct of the dissolution. In 1535 he organized an ecclesiastical census and general visitation to assess the wealth and condition of the church. His census was completed by July; *Valor ecclesiasticus* served both as a valuation of monastic assets and as a record of individual clerical incomes for taxation purposes. The visitations were delayed until September, when six canon lawyers, who were also Cromwell's men, made a whirlwind tour of religious houses armed with eighty-six articles of inquiry and twenty-five articles of injunction. Cromwell's object was partly to encourage voluntary surrenders and partly to collect incriminating data that could be used to manipulate Parliament into authorizing mandatory dissolution. He was successful: an act was secured in March 1536 which dissolved all religious houses worth under £200 per annum — some 372 institutions in England and twenty-seven in Wales fell into this category.[59] Although a number purchased exemption from the act, it was not long before the greater and remaining houses were attacked. Initially there was no plan to reduce all the greater houses; some isolated 'surrenders' were induced at the end of 1537. In the latter part of 1538, however, Cromwell and some thirty agents entered upon a systematic campaign of total dissolution. The 202 remaining institutions yielded within some sixteen months: the final deed of surrender, that of Waltham Abbey, was dated 23 March 1540.[60] Meanwhile, an act of 1539 legitimized Cromwell's proceedings by transferring the property of the greater houses to the Crown.

The long-term effects of the dissolution have often been debated by historians and may conveniently be divided into those which were planned, and those which were not. Within the former category Henry VIII eliminated the last fortresses of potential resistance to the supremacy. He founded six new dioceses upon the remains of monastic buildings and endowments — Peterborough, Gloucester, Oxford, Chester,

Bristol, and Westminster, the last being abandoned in 1550. He re-established the cathedral churches of Canterbury, Rochester, Winchester, Ely, Norwich, Worcester, Durham, and Carlisle. He also re-endowed Wolsey's college at Oxford, refounded the King's Hall Cambridge as Trinity College, and created regius chairs at both universities. Yet schemes to endow preachers, schools, colleges, hospitals, Greek and Hebrew studies, poor relief, highways, etc. were dropped. The humanist Thomas Starkey and preachers Robert Crowley and Thomas Lever criticized Henry's failure to redirect a higher proportion of the monastic wealth to schools, universities, and the poor—but fiscal needs took priority.

Of the unplanned effects, the wholesale destruction of fine Gothic buildings, melting down of medieval metalwork and jewellery, and sacking of libraries were acts of licensed vandalism. The clergy suffered an immediate decline in morale; the number of candidates for ordination dropped sharply—there was little to suggest that Henry's Reformation had much to do with spiritual life, or with God. Some seven thousand monks, nuns, and friars, their attendants and servants, were dispossessed. The Crown awarded most monks pensions proportionate to their standing and the revenues of their houses, but clerical taxes were deducted at source and only abbots and priors found themselves living among the country gentry for the rest of their days. Some abbots became bishops or deans of cathedral chapters, and some two thousand monks purchased dispensations to serve as secular clergy—making up for the drop in ordinations. Yet there must have been much hardship. The disappearance of the abbots from the House of Lords left the laity ascendant in both Houses. Landed laity, too, gained the lion's share of ecclesiastical patronage at parish level through Henry's capital sales. The monasteries had possessed two-fifths of the rights of presentation to parochial livings, rights which the Crown first subsumed, then alienated along with the lands it sold—setting a pattern that lasted for three centuries. Finally, the dissolution and its aftermath redistributed national wealth between 1535 and 1558 overwhelmingly in favour of Crown and laity, as against the church, and appreciably in favour of the nobility and gentry, as against the Crown. Very few new or substantially enlarged private estates were built up solely out of the ex-religious lands by 1558. Taking the figures for Norfolk as an example, the changing pattern of wealth distribution at Elizabeth's accession was that 4.8 per cent of the county's manors were held by the Crown; 6.5 per cent belonged to bishops, and deans and chapters; 11.4 per cent were owned by nobles; and 75.4 per cent had been acquired by the gentry. In 1535, 2.7 per cent of manors had been held by the Crown; 20 per cent had been owned by the church; 9.4 per cent were in the hands of nobles; and 64 per cent belonged to gentry families.[61] These figures suggest that the church retained one-third of its lands despite the dissolution; but the diocesan and chantry property became the Crown's prey in the 1540s and 1550s.

Since the dissolution involved the largest confiscation and redistribution of wealth since the Norman Conquest, it was bound to arouse opposition on religious and economic grounds. On 1 October 1536 the Lincolnshire Rising began at Louth and spread north; by the end of the month rebellion convulsed the northern counties from the River Don to the Scottish border: Yorkshire, Durham, Northumberland, Cumberland, Westmorland, and parts of Lancashire and Cheshire. In fact, three self-contained rebellions overlapped: the Lincolnshire Rising was over by 18 October; the Pilgrimage of Grace lasted until December 1536; and new revolts in the East Riding and north-west erupted in January–February 1537.[62]

The Pilgrimage was threatening because nobles, gentry, clergy, and people combined forces, and because they shared an ideology. Indeed this revolt was neither a clash between different social groups nor a split within the governing class, but a popular rising by northerners in general. They wore badges of the Five Wounds of Christ; they swore an oath that contradicted the Crown's oath of supremacy; and they circulated ballads connecting the theme of the church in danger to the socio-economic distress they believed would result from the loss of monastic charity:

> Alack! Alack!
> For the church sake
> Poor commons wake,
> And no marvel!

For clear it is
The decay of this
How the poor shall miss
No tongue can tell.[63]

Their oath, which was formulated by Robert Aske at York on 17 October, bound them to take up Christ's cross, to defend the Catholic Church, to strive for suppression of 'these heretics', and to expel 'villein' blood and 'evil councillors' from the King's Council: they named Cromwell, Cranmer, Audley, and Sir Richard Rich, chancellor of the court of augmentations, in their manifestos.

But while the Pilgrimage followed medieval patterns of dissent — that is, protest combined with protestations of loyalty to the king and the established order — the rebels were mistaken if they thought they could repeat the success of the East Anglian opponents of Wolsey's Amicable Grant. Henry VIII saw that his position depended on keeping face and making no concessions. The revolt was too big to condone: over thirty thousand men were involved; York and Hull were occupied; and Lord Darcy surrendered Pontefract Castle to the rebels. Henry immediately ordered the nobility to arms: the dukes of Norfolk and Suffolk, the marquis of Exeter, and the earls of Shrewsbury, Derby, Arundel, and Huntingdon. When Norfolk confronted the Pilgrims at Doncaster Bridge, his army was heavily outnumbered; conciliation was therefore necessary, though few of the Pilgrims wished to start civil war. In fact, the rebel leaders, too, saw negotiations as the route to success; so under cover of a truce Norfolk offered terms that achieved the dispersal of the rebels on 8 December, when a pardon was read by Lancaster Herald and the duke promised that the suppressed abbeys would be restored and a free Parliament summoned.

Henry VIII, however, was disingenuous and never intended to keep his word. The outbreak of new revolts in the East Riding and Lake Counties gave him an excuse to exact reprisals, and the duke of Norfolk proclaimed martial law at Carlisle. Some six thousand rebels quickly surrendered, and seventy-four were hanged on the spot. Elsewhere the common law was used: men whom Cromwell identified as rebel leaders were brought to London for interrogation and trial, and order was restored by March 1537. Leaders executed included Lords Darcy and

Hussey, Sir Robert Constable, Sir Thomas Percy, Sir Francis Bigod, Sir John Bulmer, and Aske. Clerical victims were James Cockerell of Guisborough Priory, William Wood, prior of Bridlington, Friar John Pickering, Adam Sedbar, abbot of Jervaux, and William Thirsk of Fountains Abbey.

Historians have long debated the motives of the rebels: were they spiritual, economic, or dominated by concern to protect traditional communities against Cromwell and his agents? All these motives were present in varying degrees, for a poor harvest in 1535 was followed by a disappointing one in 1536; peacetime taxation (Cromwell's subsidy of 1534) was being collected in Lincolnshire and Yorkshire when the revolts erupted; the Crown's revival of fiscal feudalism in the final session of the Reformation Parliament threatened landowners; the smaller monasteries were being dissolved; and Cromwell's vicegerential injunctions, circulars, and decision to abolish lesser saints' days were being enforced by diocesan officials and JPs. It is judiciously said, 'issues simplify and polarize' in such circumstances: defence of the Catholic Church and of the poor against the Crown 'became a single issue'.[64] If, however, rumours attacking Cromwell's centralizing and fiscal policies abounded and his agents were resented, the rebels' grievances were still chiefly religious and their cause bonded by religious imagery: the banners and badges of the Five Wounds; the ballads and marching songs; the quasi-religious oath; and the use of the term 'Pilgrimage'. 'Commonwealth' slogans provided useful stimulus, but 'true religion' was the most important rebel platform, not least because it legitimized a movement against Henry VIII's government.[65]

Was the Pilgrimage spontaneously begun by people and clergy after whom the nobles and gentry were swept along against their will, or planned in advance by nobles and gentry who used their territorial power to raise the country? Although this question has been disputed, compelling signs exist that the noble and gentry supporters of Princess Mary joined forces with Catholic lawyers from the inns of court in revolt against Cromwell's administration. This connection links Lords Darcy and Hussey, Sir Robert Constable, Robert Aske, William Stapleton, Robert Plumpton, William Babthorpe, and others.[66] In particular, Darcy and Hussey had assured Chapuys in September 1534 that,

if Charles V were to declare war, English politics would be transformed 'by the insurrection of the people, who would be joined immediately by the nobility and the clergy'.[67] In the north there were sixteen earls and other 'great gentlemen' whom they claimed supported them, and Darcy promised to 'raise the banner of the Crucifix' and put eight thousand of his tenants into the field. Yet, although Darcy, Hussey, and Aske encouraged pre-planning and the northern parochial clergy incited the people to revolt, the actual sequence of events differed from their schemes. In fact, the 'conspirators' were taken by surprise when revolt broke out in Lincolnshire. The speed with which the protest movement spread suggests, furthermore, that 'the quantity of explosive material was such that it needed very little to set it off'.[68] While Catholic factionalism divided some members of the governing elite, the mobilization and solidarity of so many northerners cannot be taken for granted. Also there were lesser disturbances in southern counties: East Anglia, Somerset, and Cornwall. So, while Court plotting shaped the form of the Pilgrimage to some degree, it does not sufficiently explain its force and extent.

Yet the rebels could only have toppled Henry VIII with the support of the leading nobility whom the king named as members of the 'emergency' Privy Council in the autumn of 1536: the dukes of Norfolk and Suffolk, the marquis of Exeter, and the earls of Shrewsbury, Sussex, and Oxford. Whereas Lords Neville, Latimer, Lumley, and the earl of Northumberland's brothers and clients joined the rebels, the five northern earls — Northumberland, Westmorland, Cumberland, Derby, and Shrewsbury — remained loyal, as did the dukes of Norfolk and Suffolk. It is true that Northumberland and Westmorland hesitated, while Norfolk, Exeter, and Derby wavered threateningly, but none saw any advantage in treason. And the key figure was Shrewsbury, who, although a former champion of Catherine of Aragon and Princess Mary and a man of advancing years, leapt into action as Henry's lieutenant to suppress the revolts despite his friendship with Darcy and Hussey.[69] Shrewsbury, Norfolk, and Suffolk simply owed too much to Henry VIII to rebel, a debt Cromwell exploited in November 1538 when he attacked Exeter and thereby extinguished the remnant of Mary's Court faction. The marquis

himself, Lord Montague, the countess of Salisbury, Sir Edward Neville, and Sir Nicholas Carew were arrested and executed for treason, but the countess of Salisbury's death was delayed until 1541.[70]

The independence of the English church was abrogated in the 1530s. The church's jurisdictional immunity recognized since the twelfth century was rescinded by Henry VIII. The clergy no longer owed allegiance to Rome, while Convocation became subject to the Crown's authority. Cromwell's enforcement strategy also accelerated the Tudor centralizing process and restoration of royal finances: the laity were ascendant in Parliament and government, and parliamentary statute and common law subordinated canon and papal law. When England secured a new status, she therefore abandoned the status quo, and Henry VIII deluded himself if he thought he could maintain Catholicism without the pope. He backed Cromwell and the radical faction in the autumn of 1532; Anne Boleyn became queen. Her evangelism, once injected into the Court, was never neutralized and politics were never quite the same. Like Cromwell she patronized scholars and protected reformers; she imported and circulated evangelical books; she played a constructive role in poor relief and advocated social reform. Despite the violence of her fall, the Reformation was not reversed in 1536: the ancient cults of saints and images came under attack; the dissolution was taken by many to imply that purgatory had been abolished; Erasmian teaching repudiated clericalism and ritualism; Cromwell's preachers were contradicting the conservative bishops; and the printing presses disseminated fresh ideas. In particular, Tyndale's slogan 'Truth as revealed in Scripture' assailed Catholic tradition, since 'Scripture' in this sense meant the Bible, not the unwritten traditions of the Roman church that More had so vigorously defended. It was no accident that a case of heresy was tried in star chamber and an alleged miracle investigated there against canonical practice, for the Catholic oral tradition could not survive the repudiation of papal authority.[71] On the other hand, it was not until Henry VIII's death that traditionalists fully realized the dangers of caesaropapism: that the power of the royal supremacy might repudiate Catholic doctrine as easily as it had broken with Rome.

HENRICIAN GOVERNMENT

'MY prayer is, that God give me no longer life, than I shall be glad to use mine office in edification, and not in destruction.'[1] So Thomas Cromwell justified himself to an episcopal critic shortly before the dissolution of the greater religious houses. And expert opinion rightly holds him to have been a remarkable statesman. Born the son of a Putney clothworker about the year 1485, he left England in unexplained circumstances at the turn of the century. Either he quarrelled with his father who was a known troublemaker, or he was himself in trouble since he later admitted to Cranmer having been a 'ruffian' in his teens. Roving Italy as an adventurer, Cromwell served as soldier or page on the defeated French side at the battle of the Garigliano (1503). He then learned trade and accountancy, being employed by Florentine bankers and Venetian and English merchants, and travelling on business to the commercial towns of Flanders. In May 1514 he was in Rome giving evidence in a lawsuit as a client of Cardinal Bainbridge, the English resident at the papal court. Then Bainbridge died (he was allegedly poisoned), whereupon Cromwell followed the cardinal's men back to England to offer his services to Wolsey.

Cromwell was a member of Wolsey's household by 1516 and his 'councillor' by 1519. Soon he was his solicitor too. He somehow became a skilled legal practitioner without a formal apprenticeship at the inns of court, and he acted independently as a lawyer, arbitrator, merchant, and moneylender as well as serving Wolsey in the 1520s. In 1523 he sat in Parliament, and the following year was admitted to Gray's Inn. After his return from Italy he married a moderately rich widow, and built up valuable connections among the legal and commercial communities of London as well as setting up his own domestic establishment. He played bowls at John Rastell's house, and was known to Thomas More—the influential merchant of Lucca, Antonio Bonvisi, was their mutual friend.

So Cromwell was a self-made man—a man of action not a university-trained intellectual like More, Cranmer, or Reginald Pole. Yet the distinction should not be overdrawn, since in Italy he discovered wide intellectual interests. He read history as well as law, spoke fluent Italian and acceptable French, and wrote Latin and some Greek. Later he patronized writers and commissioned paintings from Hans Holbein the Younger. He had a sure grasp of rhetoric and (like Wolsey) was a natural orator. He made a formidable adversary in debate, sharp enough to defeat More, John Fisher, and Stephen Gardiner in verbal tussles. But his manner was usually relaxed and always engaging. When speaking, his face lit up; his conversation sparkled; and he cast roguish oblique glances when striking aphorisms. Most important, his talent for managing men and institutions was instinctive. John Foxe remembered him as 'pregnant in wit . . . in judgment discreet, in tongue eloquent, in service faithful, in stomach courageous, in his pen active'.[2] A prodigious worker with a powerful and exact memory, Cromwell took the rounded view, was inwardly determined yet outwardly urbane. 'Nothing was so hard which with wit and industry he could not compass.' Foxe claimed that, riding to Rome in 1516–18 on business for the Guild of St Mary, Boston (Lincs.), Cromwell learned the New Testament by heart in Erasmus's version, an exercise that seemingly laid the foundations of a lifelong understanding. Indeed, this story rings true: men said in the Renaissance that they had their best ideas on horseback.

Of course, for all his ease of manner, accessibility, and capacity for friendship, Cromwell had a dangerous edge. He was a politician who got things done. A degree of ruthlessness was the corollary of his single-mindedness, as his role in the *putsch* of 1536 indicated. On the other hand, Pole's charge that as early as 1528 Cromwell was a 'Machiavellian' who held that the politician's art was to enable kings to gratify their lusts without offending public morality or religion was malicious. First, *The Prince* was not published until 1532, several years after the alleged conversation with Pole took place. Although the work was written in 1513–14, there is no evidence that Cromwell knew it before Lord Morley drew it to his attention in 1539. Second, *The Prince*'s evil reputation in the sixteenth century sprang largely from its author's anticlericalism. Lastly, *The Prince* was barely relevant

to England before the Civil War, because the work preferred
the expansionist military vigour of Rome to the stability and
permanence of Venice. The Tudors had no place for 'vigour'
at the expense of stability.[3] Though Cromwell certainly believed
that formal state planning could offer limited immunity against
the hazards of fortune, it is equally true that, far from
downgrading reason, ability, and learning as qualifications for
men to rule in favour of military 'vigour', he actually emphasized
merit to the point where the Pilgrims of Grace accused him of
preferring 'villein' to noble blood, and the bill of attainder against
him in June 1540 included the charge of *scandalum magnatum* (i.e.
that he had contrived to bring the nobility into public
disrepute).[4]

It has been argued over the last thirty years that Cromwell
achieved a 'revolution in government' during the 1530s, though
this interpretation has been attacked.[5] The 'revolution' thesis
maintains that Cromwell consciously — that is, as a matter of
principle — reduced the role of the royal household in government
and substituted instead 'national' bureaucratic administration
within departments of state under the control of a fundamentally
reorganized Privy Council. The royal household, as a result,
was driven Coriolanus-like from the stage, becoming merely 'a
department of state concerned with specialized tasks about the
king's person'. Finance 'fell to national institutions rather than
to the personal servants of the king and those household offices
which administered it before 1530'. Lastly, the Privy Council
and secretary of state 'stepped out of the household on to the
national stage'. These changes were 'crowded together so thickly
and so deliberately' between the fall of Wolsey and the fall of
Cromwell that 'only the term "revolution" can describe what
happened'. Moreover, it was Cromwell who all along masterminded 'this deliberate and profound reforming activity.'[6]

Such argument is, however, too schematic, since the
reorganized Privy Council, though more directly in executive
control than Wolsey's Council, was often subsumed politically
within the Court. Also members of the royal household continued
to play essential administrative roles throughout the early modern
period.[7] Yet the Privy Council *did* increasingly assume
corporate responsibility for Tudor government under the Crown,

especially financial and legal administration and local government. Whereas Henry VII personally managed his kingdom from his chamber and privy chamber and checked every page of his chamber accounts, Elizabeth was largely concerned only with major policy decisions and important matters of state, leaving the bulk of routine administration and financial management to members of the Privy Council, who also took the lead as governors in the counties, first as JPs and then as lords-lieutenant during the war with Spain. The essential shift *was* made from undifferentiated household administration of Crown revenue under Edward IV and Henry VII, to diversified management by means of multiple revenue departments under Henry VIII and Cromwell, and finally to corporate exchequer-based fiscal management by the Privy Council under Elizabeth.[8]

So the thesis that a Tudor 'revolution in government' took place is comprehensible when the periodization of change is extended to Elizabeth's death,. though whether the word 'revolution' is appropriate—as opposed to 'readjustment' or straightforward 'change'—is a matter of judgement. If 'revolution' is supposed to designate permanent change, it will not do. For the Tudor system tottered in the last years of James I, and collapsed under his son, when, increasingly, the Privy Council was bypassed in the making of crucial political decisions and ceased to be an effective executive arm of government.

Critics of the 'revolution' thesis have even argued that the whole concept of 'revolution' meaning fundamental change within the Tudor body politic is irrelevant. Such an approach muddies the waters, since to deny that the break with Rome was a jurisdictional revolution is unacceptable. Also the triumph of Protestantism in forcing parish Catholicism into minority status by the 1590s was a cultural revolution of the first magnitude. Naturally it is true that the shape of Tudor government was defined by the political system which underpinned it. Practical politics, and to a very considerable extent contingent events, were vital. Henrician politics increasingly focused on the Court, therefore the Privy Council lived and moved there. Cromwell was successful as a politician until 1538–9 because he responded to royal demands and immediate needs. Personal and kinship relationships, furthermore, so pervaded Tudor society that 'efficient bureaucratic' administration was neither feasible nor desirable. It is striking that Cromwell himself used personal methods, regularly short-circuiting official machinery, especially in finance.[9] Lastly, the word 'revolution' in Tudor speech did not mean the sudden overthrow of an established order of government, but merely signified the completion of a cycle or a 'turning back' to earlier practice.[10] As Francis Bacon wrote, 'Certain it is that matter is in a perpetual flux, and never at a stay.'[11]

Bacon's emphasis on the 'turning wheels of vicissitudes' was, however, born of his own disappointments. Beyond any doubt, the Tudor 'revolution' thesis as *originally* formulated has hit the buffers. But when its critics seemingly deny *any* possibility of development in government because all was 'at the throw of the dice of royal personality or ministerial calculation',[12] we have entered the world of Gulliver. True, sixteenth-century administrators had not discovered the 'laws of progress' known to the Victorian era. But change dictated by conscious state planning *was* within their mental grasp. Educational and welfare projects were being promoted throughout Europe at this time, for example at Ypres, Lyons, Venice, Wittenberg, Nuremberg, and Geneva. Both Catholics and Protestants sponsored these institutions, and the reforming ordinances of Nuremberg (1522), Ypres (1525), and Lyons (1531) were published in numerous editions and languages.[13] Cromwell's papers are littered with draft schemes and proposals for the reform of education, agriculture, trade, industry, poor relief, and the common law, while towns such as London, Norwich, and Hull introduced their own welfare projects and enforced higher standards of sanitation starting in the 1530s.

Contrary to Bacon's point of view, the Frenchman Louis Le Roy, author of *On the Vicissitude or Variety of Things* (1579), compared the achievements of his time favourably to those of ancient Greece and Rome, and exhorted that 'we aspire always to the perfection that has never yet appeared'.[14] Like many Renaissance thinkers, he believed that, when properly guided by reason, men could make a better world. When Cromwell and Cranmer justified Henry VIII's royal supremacy as a 'restoration' or 'return' to the constitution of the primitive church and a repudiation of post-Hildebrandine papal 'tyranny', they

believed the change was for the better. In More's fictional *Utopia*
the character 'Morus' argued, 'What you cannot turn to good
you must make as little bad as you can.' More's satire and
criticism nudged people to think of 'the best state of a
commonwealth'. Likewise, when St German submitted
comprehensive draft legislation to Cromwell in 1531 for reform
of the parochial clergy, canon law, poor relief, food prices, wages,
enclosures, and rural depopulation, he showed a grasp of the
essential principle that a time had come to attempt fundamental
social and administrative reform. Among his other achievements,
St German was the first theorist to propose the creation of a pay
research board to assess whether existing wages were sufficient
to support basic subsistence at a time of rising population and
living costs, though this was only one of a thousand ideas
circulating during the early Reformation.[15]

But the cornerstone of the 'revolution' controversy is the
executive Privy Council. How and when did it replace the large
and amorphous King's Council that had advised Edward IV and
Henry VII and worked under Wolsey's direction in star
chamber? Did Cromwell create it from the rib of Adam as a
fundamental act of reform?[16] Certainly the streamlined body of
office-holders that existed by the end of 1536 has been regarded
as the zenith of state planning. It permitted greater efficiency,
security, and confidentiality in central government; comprised
only working councillors; and left star chamber free to organize
itself within a decade as a specialist law court. Precedents, too,
existed for the creation of 'privy' conciliar boards emancipated
from immediate household tasks. Wolsey created an executive
privy council for Ireland in 1520 which operated independently
of the king's deputy in Dublin. By the Eltham Ordinance of 1526
he planned (at least in theory) to reduce the size of the English
Council to twenty executives, of whom those present at Court
should meet daily at 10 a.m. and 2 p.m. in the king's dining
chamber.[17] He sketched an alternative scheme for 'the division
of such matters as shall be treated by the King's Council', which
suggested reform by applying the principle of differentiation of
function to star chamber: administration and justice were to be
assigned to separate groups of councillors, leaving the principal
officers of state and household free to concentrate on the
government of the realm unhindered by the pleas of private

suitors.[18] Finally, the Calais Act of 1536 created an executive
Council for the government of the town and Calais Pale. Its
membership was fixed at eleven named office-holders sitting in
order of precedence from the deputy down to the under marshal.[19]

If, however, the 'creationist' view of the Privy Council is
superficially attractive, the balance of evidence is against it.
Cromwell assuredly contemplated reform, because in June 1534
he noted on the back of a letter, 'To remember the King for
the establishment of the Council'.[20] What this meant in practice
is elusive, but he had been responsible for implementing Council
decisions since May 1533 when he jotted down 'Remembrances
to be put into my book for things done in the Council.'[21] He
had a vested interest in defining the Council's working practices,
and doubtless had specific plans in mind. But if so, they were
overtaken by events. The political milieu was turbulent: first
Wolsey's fall and More's refusal as lord chancellor to support
Henry VIII's divorce campaign, and then the fall of Anne Boleyn
and the Pilgrimage of Grace. And these events *by themselves*
animated change. Wolsey's overthrow curtailed his emphasis on
star chamber and caused a power vacuum there. Ambitious
politicians raced to serve the king at Court, where Henry's 'select'
councillors quickly removed to the inner sanctum of the 'privy'
apartments.[22] Not since Bosworth had the need for radical
decisions and confidentiality in the Council been so pronounced.
After 1530 the dukes of Norfolk and Suffolk, the earl of Wiltshire
(Anne Boleyn's father), Lord Sandes, the earl of Sussex, Sir
William Fitzwilliam, Cromwell, and the rest were the 'political'
or 'secret' councillors who debated the divorce strategy and dealt
with Chapuys and the papal nuncio. Moreover, during the
fifteenth century the term 'privy' councillor had been used to
distinguish such 'continual' advisers at Court from members of
the Great Council or Council in star chamber. So it is
understandable that Cromwell was styled a 'privy councillor'
as early as 1533.[23] Observers could see that executive affairs
were in his hands and not in More's or Audley's in star chamber.
But, despite the use of the word 'privy', Henry VIII's 'Court'
councillors were not yet the Privy Council. The reason is that
lesser councillors, the judges, king's serjeants, and others had
not finally been excluded from Council membership, so that
formal reconstruction had not taken place.[24]

Yet the Council *was* reconstructed by the spring of 1537. A list compiled at that time shows that the Privy Council existed in size and membership. Thirteen leading office-holders plus Viscount Beauchamp, Jane Seymour's brother (the future Protector Somerset), were included. By contrast second-rank councillors were demoted, enjoying thereafter honorific status during their lifetimes as 'ordinary councillors' or councillors 'at large'. They helped perform the judicial work of star chamber until 1544 or thereabouts, and assisted privy councillors by sifting the suits and petitions of private parties at Court and channelling them as appropriate to the Privy Council, star chamber, or court of requests. But they were excluded from the Privy Council. Likewise the judges, king's serjeants, and lord mayors of London were excluded, though the senior judges still sat in star chamber as expert assessors.[25]

A number of lord mayors of London had been sworn of the Council since 1485 and an attempt has been made to reiterate the 'revolution' thesis by dating the 'Cromwellian' reconstitution of the Council to 'the middle of 1536' on the grounds that 'most lord mayors before that date, and none thereafter, can be found described as king's councillors'.[26] It is claimed that the Council must have been reconstructed before the Pilgrimage, because the lord mayor was already 'excluded'.[27] But this is at best inconclusive, at worst misleading. Only three out of twenty-one lord mayors of London can be shown to have attended a meeting of the Council between 1515 and 1536: Sir John Allen, Sir James Spencer, and (arguably) Sir Ralph Warren.[28] References to the mayors as councillors are, in any case, not above six in twenty years.[29] Although 'the middle of 1536' defines the approximate date at which a City petition received by Warren as a 'king's councillor' was considered, this evidence provides no sound basis upon which to date his exclusion from the Council. To establish the date of his *exclusion* means to show when he was told his attendance at Council meetings was no longer required, which is not achieved by citing in evidence the fact that he adjudged a victuallers' petition on the price of fish.[30]

Although the process of exclusion is the key to the reconstruction of the Council, Cromwell's correspondence is silent on the matter. In fact, it has never been explained how he accomplished 'fundamental reform' in a year which saw his

Court *putsch* in the spring and the Pilgrimage in the autumn.
Not only was his career under direct attack during the
Pilgrimage — it was his conservative enemies, after all, who
vilified him in 1540 — but also the Pilgrims challenged Henry VIII
to expel Cromwell and Cranmer from the Council as 'upstarts'
and 'heretics'! Far from the politics of 1536 smoothing a path
for conciliar reform by Cromwell, the exact opposite is the
case. The 'select' group of councillors operating since 1530
had sparked intense resentment: the leaders of the Pilgrimage
exhumed the 'medieval' debate on Council membership that
asserted the alleged duty of the monarch to share political power
with the old nobility and others born to traditional conciliar status
(*consiliarii nati*). By 1536 the issue of Council membership was
explosive, and, had Cromwell attempted 'fundamental reform'
before the outbreak of revolt, the matter could not have failed
to reach the Pilgrims' agenda.[31]

But the most striking aspect of the new Privy Council was
its ideological profile. At least half the members of the 'reformed'
Privy Council were religious conservatives opposed to Cromwell.
By 1539–40 their party was in the ascendant; Cromwell's fall
was precipitated to a great extent because he was outnumbered
at the Council board.[32] It is unthinkable that so shrewd a
politician could have stacked the cards against himself by
'creating' an executive board dominated by opponents: to do
so was tantamount to signing his own death warrant. His original
intention when he spoke of 'the establishment of the Council'
in June 1534 was seriously frustrated. Moreover, the date of the
reconstruction can be pinned down to the autumn of 1536, when
the minister's career was on the line. As soon as the revolt
erupted, Henry's 'select' councillors closed ranks as an
'emergency Council' or war cabinet. Cromwell retired to the
sidelines, though his eclipse was largely tactical — a pretence on
his and the king's part.[33] But from 14 October onwards the
Privy Council issued instructions as a corporate board to the
captains who took the field against the rebels.[34] No longer did
Cromwell write letters on the Council's behalf; they were
prepared for group signature at the board.[35] And there is proof
that the Privy Council was being organized on lines of restricted
membership. The draft of Henry VIII's answer to the rebels
for the first time listed the names: the dukes of Norfolk and Suffolk,

the marquis of Exeter, three earls, three bishops, Sandes, Fitzwilliam, and Sir William Paulet.[36]

We should add Cromwell, Audley, and Cranmer to the king's list — the overseers of the Reformation whom the rebels had singled out for attack.[37] Their omission was at first thought wise, but the fiction could not be sustained. When Henry's answer was printed for distribution to the rebels, their names *were* included. Whereas, however, Cranmer as archbishop of Canterbury was simply ranked with the bishops, the presence of Cromwell and Audley among the lay office-holders was glossed. Henry VIII was said to have 'elected and chosen' them to the Privy Council by virtue of their abilities, not their offices. He selected them 'by the advice of our whole [Privy] Council before named'.[38] (They were even said to have been 'elected and chosen' into their offices!) The snub was significant. Henry VIII proclaimed to the world that, in his first Privy Council, Cromwell and his principal assistant were little better than co-opted members.

Of course, it is hard to know who was deceiving whom. The outbreak of the Pilgrimage had caught Henry VIII unprepared; his answer aimed to mollify the rebels by balancing its sharp defence of his right to choose his own Council against its refutation of the Pilgrims' complaint that his Court was packed with 'villeins'. So his list of privy councillors merged the nobility with the leading office-holders of Court and state. The mix was almost identical to that projected by Wolsey in the Eltham Ordinance, and it met legitimate expectations. But it was incomplete: a full list is obtained by checking Henry's answer against the signatures on Privy Council letters. This reveals that four other privy councillors (including Beauchamp) served during the Pilgrimage, yielding an executive Council of nineteen members — the same number as sat when the Privy Council declared its hand after Cromwell's execution in 1540.[39]

The Privy Council therefore existed during the 1530s. Cromwell observed the birth of the elite board of office-holders which by Elizabeth's reign had assumed corporate responsibility for Tudor government under the Crown and limited the role of the household in favour of 'national' administration. But 'his' Privy Council differed from that of 1540. Its membership had been revised as early as 1537 and remained fluid until Cromwell's

fall.[40] Nor did Cromwell give the Privy Council organized
bureaucracy after the defeat of the Pilgrimage. He reasserted
instead his own ministerial control over official business and
thereby prevented the Council from exercising its corporate
authority until his fall.[41] (This was hardly surprising when his
enemies were so powerfully represented at the board.) Only after
his execution was it resolved to give the Privy Council its own
official registers and a professional secretariat.[42] For, just as
Cromwell stood for 'edification' in government, so his opponents
stood for his 'destruction'.[43] In the verdict of posterity Cromwell
is amply vindicated, but the 'permanent' Privy Council was
'created' less because he lived than because he died.[44]

Tudor government extended beyond the Court and Privy
Council. To complete the picture we need to examine the
relationship between Court and country. It has been said that
the question of the Court's standing in the counties 'barely arises'
under the Tudors. But this view is incomplete.[45] The politics
and institutions of Henrician government cannot adequately be
assessed without reference to the counties. 'Court' and 'country'
were interdependent in early modern England, relying on each
other for mutual support.[46] Henry VIII 'was far from
omnipotent, and the real measure of his power was his ability
to have his decisions executed at the level of the county and
village'.[47] It goes too far to suggest that power accruing to the
centre through the consent of the counties overshadowed
the personality of the king, the functions of his institutions, and
the centralizing role of royal patronage and the judicial system.
But the point stands that central administration was effective
only when it enjoyed the support of the local governors. Of
course, in a patriarchal society, the king had an in-built
advantage. His authority bolstered that of heads of households
in general, and it was unthinkable for landowners to distinguish
between the Crown's authority and their own. Henry's anti-papal
propaganda was also successful. His subjects were taught to
regard him as a 'patriot king': the anniversary of his death would
be marked by solemn mourning until the 1560s. It is a platitude
that the Crown had neither a standing army nor a salaried local
bureaucracy in the sixteenth century. Yet stability was preserved
until Henry VIII's death despite the Pilgrimage of Grace, the

revival of war and taxation in the 1540s, the increase of population, and the beginning of volatile movements in food prices.

The technique that Henry used to build bridges between his Court and the counties can be described in a sentence. He followed late-medieval Crown policy by constructing an affinity in the country. Beginning with Richard II during his last years, the Crown had attempted to split entrenched noble and gentry affinities and to create networks of royal power instead. Some three hundred to four hundred knights and esquires were invited to Court for reasons which were not chiefly military, conciliar, diplomatic, or domestic—but local. They were not given salaried Court appointments, but often received annuities and robes. (In a sense, they were like private retainers who had no household or estate functions but who were bound to a lord by means of gifts and wore his livery.) Richard II first realized that he needed to cultivate these men in order to widen his power-base and win the support of their own retainers and followers too. For, as Fortescue observed in *The Governance of England*, 'the people will go with him that best may sustain and reward him'.[48] So political security was the key to Richard's plan, which failed because he was vindictive to persons he suspected, and because he moved too quickly and ended up by dividing the counties. But the essential step was taken: the value to the Crown of a governing élite more broadly based than in the past was recognized.[49]

In this matter Henry IV followed Richard's example. In 1400 his Council advised him 'that in each county of the kingdom a certain number of the more sufficient men of good fame should be retained . . . and charged also carefully and diligently to save the estate of the king and his people in their localities'.[50] Again, Edward IV selected his household men so as to link the Court to the country, especially the outlying counties. In a very real sense he tried to create a system of interlocking territorial lordship centred on the Court and the Yorkist dynasty. It was a form of political control that reinforced his more concrete policies of resumption, attainder, and the 'land revenue' experiment.[51] As an observer remarked, 'the names and circumstances of almost all men, scattered over the counties of the kingdom, were known to him just as if they were daily within his sight'.[52] Certainly

Edward's methods owed everything to personality, not bureaucracy. The idea of a Crown-controlled magistracy was as yet indistinct. But only the events of 1483–5 shattered Edward's political networks, which in any case Henry VII had largely rebuilt by 1503.

Royal patronage was obviously crucial to establishing political control. After dissolving the monasteries, Henry VIII possessed between 1,000 and 1,200 paid offices worthy of a gentleman's standing, a supply of booty both adequate and comparable to the resources of Francis I who had roughly 4,000 offices at his disposal in a country three times as large. (The multiplication of offices in France to 46,000 by 1665 had not yet begun.)[53] Since, however, not every local landowner or JP could expect to be invited to Court or to win salaried office, a further mechanism for Court–country stability was necessary. In France the axial institution was the Council, which was unequivocally subsumed within the Court. The term *conseiller du roi* did not designate a 'privy councillor' at all; it applied to everyone nominated to a royal institution, and meant that the *conseiller* was numbered among the king's affinity. The striking fact is that almost half the senior provincial élite in France were *conseillers*. The ten largest provinces also provided some fifty working members of the institutional King's Council.[54]

For purposes of analysis, the governmental system in both Henrician England and Valois France should be seen as a series of concentric circles with the king as the focus. Writing *La Monarchie de France*, which he presented to Francis I in 1515, Claude de Seyssel advised the king how to deploy his *conseillers*. At the centre he placed the *conseil secret*, the smallest circle — perhaps three or four intimate councillors. The next council, radiating outwards, was the *conseil ordinaire*, which should sit three times a week, or every day if pressure of business demanded. Some ten or twelve members were needed, and lawyers and financial experts who were not members would be required as advisers. But the largest council — the outer circle — was the *conseil général*, or *l'assemblée casuelle des notables*. The king, Seyssel argued, should always consult the estates on matters affecting the whole realm. So, whenever important national business was on the agenda, the presidents of the *parlements*, the provincial prelates, and other local leaders should be summoned as well as the nobility, great officers of state, and other leading councillors.[55]

It was the Valois technique of designating provincial leaders as *conseillers* that Cromwell considered in 1534. He wrote in his memoranda: 'to appoint the most assured and most substantial of all gentlemen within every shire of this realm to be sworn of the King's Council, and they to have commandment to explore and ensearch to know who shall preach, teach and speak anything to the advancement of the pope's authority.'[56] The idea was abandoned, but the underlying theory remained. Henry VIII's intimate circle comprised the great officers of state, privy councillors, gentlemen of the privy chamber, king's confessors and clerks of the Chapel Royal, and favoured nobles. The second circle numbered between four hundred and seven hundred members of the royal household and government bound to the king by ties of service and wages. The third circle, which Cromwell considered extending to include the country gentry, embraced the knights and esquires, gentlemen ushers, grooms, and pages who attended the king at Court but who remained supernumerary — i.e. the 'local' men the Crown attempted to make its own at minimum cost.[57]

Between his accession and 1539–40 Henry VIII appointed 493 chamber officials at Court, including 120 knights and esquires of the body.[58] These knights and esquires had soon surrendered their duties as the king's intimate body servants to the gentlemen of the privy chamber. But their posts were not abolished, and several incumbents were later preferred to the privy chamber or the Council.[59] Yet, despite the rise of the privy chamber by 1518, Henry and Wolsey continued to recruit supernumeraries from the counties. In 1519 Wolsey made a 'privy remembrance' for Henry 'to put himself in strength with his most trusty servants in every shire for the surety of his royal person and succession' — Edward IV's policy by another name.[60] Soon a special book recorded the names 'of the king's servants of the shires of England sworn to the king', listing knights, esquires, carvers, cupbearers, sewers, and gentlemen ushers in order of their counties.[61] By 1525 over two hundred county landowners or their sons were recorded as in attendance at Court. There was a certain fiction here: supernumeraries did not receive free food and accommodation, therefore their attendance at Court was probably occasional. But their 'service'

was assured once they were 'sworn' and their names entered
in the register. By 1535 the number of supernumeraries from
important landowning families had risen to 263, the list being
headed by 182 knights and esquires of the body.[62] Lastly,
organization of these lists by counties meant that the Crown could
estimate at a glance the size of its affinity in particular regions.

When, therefore, Henry VIII attempted to build networks
of power in the counties, he had three main objectives in mind.
He sought personal connections among the 'men of power and
worship' upon whose acquiescence his government ultimately
depended. He wished to increase his following in county
government, especially among JPs and local officials. Last but
not least, he needed soldiers for his armies: he aimed to recruit
to his affinity territorial leaders whose *own* servants and
dependents could be transformed into the nucleus of a battle
army.[63] Of course, these objectives overlapped and imitated the
Crown's use of its salaried patronage, as Cromwell demonstrated
in 1539. In Tudor speech the vassals or dependents whom a
landowner had the right to muster in time of war were called
the 'manred', and their service lay at the heart of the quasi-feudal
military 'system' of Henry VIII's reign.[64] When Cromwell
conceived 'Articles for the ordering of the manred of this the
King's realm and for the good advancement of justice,
preservation, and maintenance of the common weal of the same',
he therefore planned three things. First, to make all paid royal
officials in the counties responsible for the mustering of specified
numbers of troops for the king's army as well as for the
performance of their normal duties; second, to swear all the
important landowners in every county to be members of the
king's affinity; and, third, to select five or six 'head
commissioners' in every county who were to direct both police
and military functions in their localities under the Crown.[65]

Yet Henry VIII's policy was bilateral. In addition to bringing
prominent local landowners within the orbit of the Court, he
'exported' leading privy councillors and members of the privy
chamber to the counties by naming them to offices and
commissions.[66] In fact, Cromwell's enforcement policy centred
on the co-ordinated use of nobles, assize judges, privy councillors,
courtiers, bishops, JPs, and mayors and aldermen of towns in
the service of the Crown. Where necessary, lists of JPs were

vetted and the nobility ordered to reside in their counties. Following Wolsey's lead, Cromwell systematically developed the notion of a Crown-controlled magistracy, writing letters to county leaders transmitting Crown orders, and ensuring that sheriffs, JPs, and others understood their task to be exemplary. As well as detecting and quelling resistance to the Reformation, they were to 'speak at their boards, and also teach their servants to declare, that he, that calleth himself Pope, is but the Bishop of Rome, and under the obedience of the General Council'.[67]

At the level of county administration, the ancient offices were those of sheriff, coroner, escheator, and constable or bailiff. Until the fourteenth century the sheriff had enjoyed primacy; there were twenty-eight shrievalties covering thirty-eight English counties, and the king made appointments annually from lists of names submitted by the judges in the Council's presence. Since resident sheriffs were preferred, Henry VIII chose prominent county landowners, but sometimes appointed a councillor or gentleman of the privy chamber to the post. In practice the sheriff employed a deputy or undersheriff, who was invariably a qualified lawyer, and one or more clerks. Legal expertise was necessary because the principal duties of the sheriff were to serve royal writs, summon juries, arrange the sittings of the royal courts and the execution of sentences, and collect fines. But the sheriff retained a political function, since he was authorized to raise 'the power of the county' (*posse comitatus*). This meant that, when faced with civil commotion or contempt of royal authority, he was allowed to raise armed men within the county to restore order.[68]

Unlike sheriffs, coroners and escheators were professionals. Chosen locally under the sheriff's supervision, coroners performed a range of duties linked to criminal proceedings such as homicides, suicides, and outlawries. In addition, they inquired into escapes of murderers, treasure troves, and (in coastal counties) shipwrecks. Between four and six coroners served in each county, and appointments were held for a number of years. By contrast, escheators were appointed annually by the lord treasurer to administer the Crown's rights in feudal land in each county. Lastly, constables and bailiffs operated at hundred and parish level. Charged to help detect crime and keep the peace, they assisted sheriffs and JPs; they organized 'watches' for

criminals and vagrants at village level; and they raised the 'hue
and cry' along the highway and from village to village in pursuit
of offenders who had committed felony or robbery in their
districts.[69]

Edward I and his successors had increasingly commissioned
county landowners to perform administrative tasks instead of
sheriffs and coroners. The result was the rise of new officials —
the JPs, whose role as keepers of the peace was confirmed by
Parliament in 1328. Six or more knights and gentry in each shire
would be commissioned to inquire into felonies and trespasses,
and to arrest criminals. Thereafter, their duties mushroomed.
After 1361 they were empowered to try felonies and trespasses
done in the county, as well as to detect suspects. During the Black
Death they were charged with supervising local markets,
regulating weights and measures, fixing prices and wages, and
coping with the disastrous effects of plague mortality. Initially
JPs had to be resident in their counties, and by 1439 it was settled
that they had to hold freehold land worth £20 per annum. The
senior JP was appointed keeper of the records, and those with
legal training were specified as members of the *quorum*, an inner
group of justices in each county of whom one or more had to
be present for particular business. Lastly, JPs were expected to
attend quarterly sessions in their counties in order to perform
their judicial and administrative functions. Although the records
are defective before Elizabeth's reign, it appears that no more
than half the bench of justices in any county was active at quarter
sessions by Henry VIII's reign. Often business was done in
sessions lasting a single day with perhaps half a dozen JPs present,
although this fact should not be misinterpreted: county
government involved 'policing the parishes nearest one's seat,
rather than assiduous attendance at sessions'. Probably even
before the break with Rome, JPs had begun to act as much 'out
of sessions' as 'in' them.[70]

By 1500 numbers of JPs had risen to between twenty and
thirty-five in each county, of whom six or seven would usually
be non-resident king's councillors. New commissions were issued
by the lord chancellor whenever the composition of a bench
changed; nominations were in the gift of the Council on the
recommendation of the assize judges or of individual councillors
or courtiers. Once appointed, however, a JP would normally

remain on the bench until his death or retirement. Most JPs sat for at least five to ten years, and several for twenty or thirty years. Both Wolsey and Cromwell cast a viligant eye over appointments, but political purges of the county benches were rare. Although the Crown's ultimate objective was control, it realized that excessive interventionism would prove counter-productive.

County commissions were also used for special purposes, for example to assess and collect taxation and muster soldiers in time of war. Those appointed as subsidy or muster commissioners would normally be JPs wearing other hats. They were appointed by the Council and were held accountable at the Council board and in star chamber. In coastal counties commissioners were named to supervise coastal defences and maintain the beacons which warned of the danger of possible invasion. In Lincolnshire and the Fens they were expected to deal with drainage and flooding. Also special commissioners were appointed to manage food supplies in times of scarcity; to prevent exports of grain; to fix prices of essential consumables; to punish speculators or racketeers in foodstuffs; to apprehend vagabonds; and generally to enforce law and order. In issuing commissions for wider purposes of social control during the dearth of 1527–9, Wolsey set a benchmark for the rest of the century. Imitating French practice, he charged commissioners in every county to search the barns and stores of everyone suspected of having more grain than was necessary to feed their households, and to compel anyone with surplus food to sell it at a fair price in local markets. Registers of speculators and black marketeers were to be compiled, and their stocks compulsorily liquidated at reasonable prices. Next, the commissioners were to assess the likely availability of foodstocks in relation to estimated parish population totals. Lastly thieves, coiners, vagrants, and criminals were to be imprisoned, pilloried, or reported to the centre.[71]

The dynamic change in Henrician England was the pace at which Wolsey and Cromwell centralized government. In fact, Wolsey turned his attention to local government as soon as his law-enforcement plan was announced in May 1516. Within a month he attacked Sir John Savage, whose family had held the shrievalty of Worcestershire since 1487. Savage was sent to the Tower for corruption, indicted in king's bench, and dismissed in favour of Sir William Compton. Next, Wolsey issued revised instructions for use at the annual swearing-in of sheriffs (November 1519). These explained in detail how sheriffs were to exercise their offices. In particular, they were to prevent their subordinates from embezzling royal writs and perverting the Crown's instructions. Juries were to be composed of honest and impartial residents of the county 'most near to the place where the matter or cause is alleged'. Sheriffs were not to accept money or favours for naming a corrupt jury or otherwise obstructing the course of justice. And they were to demand the highest standards of conduct from their undersheriffs and clerks, who were to be sworn in. The oath taken annually by sheriffs in star chamber was likewise tightened and printed alongside the new instructions.[72]

Wolsey also insisted that as many JPs as possible attend annually in star chamber to be 'new sworn' in a ceremony held immediately before the swearing-in of the sheriffs. Although not everyone could be expected to be present, JPs who absented themselves were later sworn in their counties by special commissioners led by the assize judges. At the new star-chamber ceremonies a homily was read by Wolsey on the duties of JPs. But he chiefly used such opportunities to emphasize the bilateral relationship between the centre and localities. For instance, in July 1526 as many JPs and subsidy commissioners as could be crammed into star chamber were summoned to hear a speech from Wolsey, and were then ordered to fill out written answers to a twenty-one-section questionnaire on the state of law enforcement in their counties.[73]

In 1521–2 Wolsey purged the commissions of the peace for Kent and Gloucestershire, possibly for political reasons but more probably because he thought they had become cumbersome. Between 1513 and 1525 he used his power to appoint JPs in the north who were prepared to implement Crown policy at the expense of local vested interests. In the West Riding of Yorkshire the number of local gentry in the commissions of the peace was reduced from a dominant twenty-nine to fifteen, and the number of JPs who were 'outsiders' was correspondingly increased. Also the number of clerical JPs was increased from one to six. Although some former JPs had died, the exclusion of leading Yorkshire gentry like Sir Richard Tempest of Bolling and Sir

William Gascoigne of Gawthorpe from Wolsey's commissions can only have been the result of deliberate planning. In particular, several of the new JPs were Wolsey's own servants, for instance Sir William Gascoigne of Cardington (Bedfordshire), the treasurer of his household.[74]

In addition to indicting Sir John Savage, Wolsey taught some two dozen delinquent sheriffs and JPs the 'new law of the star chamber'. Some offenders were officially prosecuted while others appeared as defendants in private suits, for Wolsey urged litigants vexed by corruption in their counties to travel to star chamber where they 'shall not dread to show the truth of their grief'.[75] Wolsey maintained his interest in northern affairs, too, despite not entering his diocese of York until after his fall. For example, the bailiffs of Beverley and Hexham were threatened for failing to report riots to the nearest JPs; the mayor of York was deposed for various alleged offences; and Wolsey kept a list in star chamber of 'misdemeanours, enormities, injuries and wrongs' committed in Yorkshire which remained as yet 'unreformed'. In July 1524 he named special commissioners to reform 'enormities' in Yorkshire and Northumberland. The duke of Norfolk, sent to the northern marches as lieutenant-general for the second time in two years, was chief commissioner, sitting at York and Newcastle upon Tyne. And on the duke's recommendation, Wolsey tried the border magnate, Lord Dacre, in star chamber for maladministration and corruption of justice in 1525.[76]

The crucial decade was the 1530s. In Wales, the north, and in private lordships or 'liberties' where legal jurisdiction was still exercised by bishops, abbots, or territorial magnates rather than the Crown, the need to enforce the break with Rome led to the reconstruction of local government. By Edward I's Statute of Rhuddlan (1284) Wales had been 'annexed and united' to the English Crown. But Welsh jurisdiction was a labyrinth before 1536. The lands of the principality, customarily granted to the Prince of Wales, were situated in Anglesey, Caernarvon, Merioneth, Flint, Carmarthen, and Cardigan; they belonged to the English Crown. Some other Welsh estates were part of the duchy of Lancaster or had reverted to the Crown by forfeiture or inheritance. However, marcher estates distinct from these were held by feudal lords in chief of the Crown. So conflicts of jurisdiction enabled criminals to escape trial by fleeing from one lordship to another; Welsh and English litigants both complained that Wales was lawless, since, where the king's writ did not run, the remedies of common law were unavailable.

Edward IV and Henry VII had bound the marcher lords in 'indentures of the marches'. These obliged them to exercise control over their officers and servants, who in turn were bound by recognizances to good behaviour. For instance, the duke of Buckingham was bound to ensure that, 'if any person for dread to be punished in his own country flee from thence into the lordships of the said duke', then the duke's officers would arrest the criminal and send him back. Also Edward IV and Henry VII appointed councils in Wales and the marches to administer the estates of the Prince of Wales and govern his household. Although the council's first duty was to administer the prince's estates, it also attempted to co-ordinate justice and maintain law and order.[77] In 1525 Wolsey reconstituted this body as Princess Mary's Council, but its leading members were inexperienced, and the initiative failed. Wolsey's ordinances 'for the better preservation of order on the Welsh Marches' were likewise ignored.

After the Act of Appeals Cromwell started planning a major reform.[78] His position was strong, since recent attainders of Edward Stafford, duke of Buckingham, and Rhys ap Gruffydd had returned substantial Welsh estates to the Crown by escheat. In 1534 he dispatched Rowland Lee to Ludlow as lord president of the Council. But the real work was tackled by Thomas Englefield, a talented judge with local experience. Under his supervision, crime was attacked and legislation steered through Parliament to reform Welsh legal procedure. This culminated in the so-called Act of Union of 1536, reinforced by further massive legislation in 1543, whereby the principality and marcher lordships were amalgamated into twelve shires of Wales, English laws and methods of administration were introduced, and the new counties and county towns were allocated twenty-four seats in the House of Commons. Welsh JPs, sheriffs, escheators, coroners, and constables were appointed in the same manner as for England, and when lords-lieutenant and deputy lieutenants were later appointed they appeared in both England and Wales.

To introduce common law into Wales, the act of 1543 established courts of great sessions. These were county sessions held twice yearly, the equivalent of English assizes, since the Welsh counties were grouped into four circuits: the Chester Circuit, the North Wales Circuit, the Brecon Circuit, and the Carmarthen Circuit. There was no appeal in criminal cases, though certain categories of civil action could be taken on appeal to the Council in the Marches of Wales or to king's bench. Lastly, the Council in the Marches was reorganized. Its post-Cromwellian history is elusive, but by the 1550s it had changed from being the household and council of a member of the royal family into an institution of government and law enforcement that survived until 1689. Combining the functions of a Welsh privy council and court of star chamber, the Council enforced English law throughout Wales and the borderlands: Celtic law and customs of tenure and inheritance were phased out.[79]

The Welsh union begun in 1536 implemented Cromwell's vision of the unitary state: his policy was broadly conceived. When he remodelled the Council of the North in 1537, his instructions likewise included wide powers derived from commissions of the peace and of *oyer et terminer* which enabled members to proceed without delay in all cases of treason, murder, and felony. The Council was freed from its former responsibility for managing Crown estates and became the chief executive authority north of the River Trent. It was through this Council that royal proclamations were made and orders transmitted to sheriffs and JPs in the north. The Council also undertook an enforcement campaign after the Pilgrimage of Grace: forty-one alleged traitors were denounced to Cromwell, twenty-three of whom were executed. Overt opposition was crushed: the Council was largely successful in enforcing the break with Rome and restraining recusancy under Elizabeth. Throughout the sixteenth century, therefore, it exercised a supervisory jurisdiction over northern administration comparable to that undertaken for southern England by the Privy Council and star chamber. Councillors had responsibility for nominating and controlling JPs, overseeing food supplies, regulating trade, and organizing musters. Lastly, the Council determined private suits arising locally, work which took up much of its time.[80]

In 1539 Cromwell created a short-lived Council in the West to fill the power vacuum caused by the attainder of the marquis of Exeter. The Council exercised jurisdiction over the counties of Devon, Cornwall, Somerset, and Dorset, and Cromwell's instructions required its eighteen members to supervise the administration of civil and criminal law as well as enforce the break with Rome. Sir John Russell, a privy councillor and gentleman of the privy chamber, was ennobled and appointed lord president of the Council and granted a large portion of the estates of the dissolved Tavistock Abbey to maintain his household. Indeed, when further granted the high stewardship of the duchy of Cornwall and lord wardenship of the stannaries, Russell became the political arbiter of the south-west. But he was reluctant to spend much time there, and after Cromwell's death the Council disintegrated. Nor was it revived after the 1549 revolts, although Russell was then appointed lord-lieutenant in the western counties and performed functions reminiscent of his former presidency of the Council.[81]

Cromwell completed his reform of county government by attacking the territorial franchises or 'liberties' that had survived the inroads made into feudal jurisdiction by his predecessors, and which thwarted the full operation of royal justice. At the time of the planned confiscation of the smaller monasteries, he scribbled in his memoranda: 'For the dissolution of all franchises and liberties throughout this realm, and specially the franchises of spirituality.'[82] The result was the Act for Recontinuing of Certain Liberties and Franchises (1536), which drastically curtailed local jurisdictional anomalies. No longer could feudal or ecclesiastical officials prevent the assize judges, sheriffs, or JPs from performing their legal duties within their jurisdictions.[83]

Yet, if Cromwell's achievements strengthened royal institutions at the expense of the church and the old 'feudal' nobility, they barely impinged on mainstream local concerns. Despite the size of Henry VIII's affinity and the expanding role of privy councillors and gentlemen of the privy chamber in the provinces, the balance of power at county level remained with the landowners who served as sheriffs and JPs. A plethora of local networks bisected central ones, and the limited extent to which Wolsey and Cromwell might purge commissions of the peace exemplified this fact. Only active opponents of the regime were purged by Cromwell. Passive opponents were left in the commissions, and critics of the regime remained as supernumeraries at Court. On the one hand, both sides perceived the need to maintain communications between Court and country and avert clashes. On the other, county landowners were so jealous of their positions in local government that they saw them as proprietary interests. True, the defeat of the Pilgrimage of Grace meant that 'overmighty subjects' never again frustrated Tudor policy, but the Crown still walked a tightrope. The gentry believed 'that they had a right to a share of the king's authority'.[84] In this respect, the Henrician 'revolution' in government changed nothing.

POLITICS, RELIGION, WAR

CROMWELL was arrested at the Council board on 10 June 1540 because he had advanced the Reformation beyond the point Henry VIII had decided was expedient. The truth of this charge must be examined. Did Cromwell use his position as the king's vicegerent in spirituals to promote nascent Protestantism more energetically than Archbishop Cranmer? To label Cromwell a 'Protestant' *tout court* is too bold, especially before the Council of Trent (1545–63) when rigid definitions of 'Catholicism' and 'Protestantism' did not exist. In any case, Cromwell did not deny the real presence in the Eucharist or teach the doctrine of 'justification by faith alone'—the two most compelling tests of 'heresy' while he was alive. But his emphasis on faith, the primacy of the Bible, and the value of preaching put him firmly in the 'reformed' camp; it is significant that Protestant contemporaries saw him as the 'hammer of the monks' and a 'valiant soldier and captain of Christ'.[1]

Cromwell showed an increasingly 'reformed' outlook after Wolsey's fall, and may have decided that England was best served by a form of Protestantism after the Act of Appeals.[2] As vicegerent he possessed the power to issue injunctions to all the bishops and clergy, and to enforce them at visitations. So his First Injunctions (1536) ordered clergy to defend the royal supremacy in sermons; to teach children the Lord's Prayer, Ten Commandments, and other articles of faith out of Scripture; to abandon pilgrimages; to keep chancels in good repair; and to give money for educational purposes. His Second Injunctions (1538) went further by encouraging iconoclasm and by reviling rituals and beliefs not justified by Scripture. Cromwell ordered images that were objects of pilgrimage or superstitious veneration to be stripped from the churches on grounds of 'idolatry'; prohibited the burning of candles for saints and the dead; recognized the Bible as the chief authority for faith and required an English translation to be placed in every church for parishioners to read; and instituted registers to record baptisms, marriages, and burials in every parish in order to reduce disputes over descent and inheritance.[3]

The effect of Cromwell's attack on cults of saints, pilgrimages, 'lights', and (by implication) the Catholic doctrine of purgatory is best seen at local level. In southern counties the enforcement of change was uneven but relatively unopposed; even the remote south-west offered little resistance. Obviously Cromwell did not crush ancient rites overnight; many images and relics were spared and in Exeter groups of women upbraided the iconoclasts. Yet in many areas of the south-east compromise was the norm. It was in Lincolnshire, the north, and to some extent the City of London where resentment flared into violence. The scene depicting the martyrdom of St Thomas Becket in the east window of Gray's Inn chapel was smashed without exciting trouble, but some images were removed from London churches at night to reduce the risk of rioting. Although devotion to images continued until Henry VIII's death, the grosser superstitions were dropped. The ground was prepared for the Crown's subsequent attacks on chantries and prayers for the dead.[4]

The two formularies of faith issued during Cromwell's vice-gerency, the Ten Articles (1536) and *Institution of a Christian Man* (1537), were also 'reformed' in slant. (Strictly the formularies were Convocation's work, but Cromwell as vicegerent stood behind them.) A companion to the First Injunctions, the Ten Articles sought unity 'by ambiguity and silence'. The Bible and the Apostles', Nicene, and Athanasian Creeds were seen as the foundations of Christian belief; baptism, penance, and the Eucharist were stated to be sacraments; the real presence was affirmed; lastly, auricular confession was said to be expedient and necessary. As in the Lutheran Confession of Augsburg, therefore, no mention was made of four of the seven sacraments: matrimony, confirmation, ordination, and extreme unction; since Cromwell instructed his client Richard Taverner to translate the Confession of Augsburg for publication, the question of Lutheran influence is relevant.[5]

Yet the majority of bishops (and probably Cranmer) adhered to the seven sacraments in 1536. The Ten Articles sparked a heated debate on the nature and number of the sacraments. Throughout, Cromwell was in control; in particular he convened a meeting at the House of Lords in 1537 to resolve whether sacraments could exist in the absence of Scriptural authority and whether 'unwritten verities' (i.e. traditional Catholic doctrines not founded on Scripture) were valid. He opened the proceedings with a stern warning that Henry VIII would not 'suffer the Scripture to be wrested and defaced by any glosses, any papistical laws, or by any authority of doctors or councils'. He would not 'admit any articles or doctrine not contained in the Scripture, but approved only by continuance of time and old custom'. Whether in fact Cromwell spoke for Henry VIII or himself on this occasion is arguable. But, either way, the heterodoxy of his stand was the idea that Scripture stood in opposition to traditional Catholic teaching. The crux of the Reformation, in Henrician England as much as in Europe, was the division between the church and the Bible which the reformers regarded as the basis for their attack on Catholicism.[6]

So, while he enjoyed Henry VIII's confidence, Cromwell manipulated the bishops. The *Institution of a Christian Man* (called the 'Bishops' Book' because it was issued under the bishops' authority not the king's) expounded the Creed, the seven sacraments, the Ten Commandments, and the Lord's Prayer. It admitted that the four disputed sacraments were valid, but claimed they were inferior to baptism, penance, and the Eucharist as only the last three were instituted by Christ as 'necessary for salvation'. A draft was sent to the supreme head for his approval, but, since Henry was preoccupied with Prince Edward's imminent birth, he told Cranmer that he lacked 'time convenient' to read it. He agreed that it could be printed as the bishops' work, but sanctioned only its interim use. It was not long before he was altering it and haggling over his amendments with Cranmer, who in turn reported to Cromwell.[7]

Cranmer's role in the Reformation was, of course, essential. As co-compiler of the *Collectanea satis copiosa*, he was one of the 'think tank' responsible for the ideology of the royal supremacy. Like Cromwell, too, he was a 'reformer' in Henry VIII's reign, but not a full-blooded 'Protestant'. (It was in Edward's reign that he underwent a 'conversion' to a more or less Zwinglian view of the Eucharist, drafting the Second Book of Common Prayer and revising the articles of faith.) But he admitted privately that he doubted the doctrine of transubstantiation and was afforded unusual latitude by Henry VIII. When his enemies later produced evidence of alleged heresy, the king rebuked them with the words, 'I would you should well understand that I account my lord of Canterbury as faithful a man towards me as ever was prelate in this realm, and one to whom I am many ways beholden.' He lent Cranmer substantial sums of money and took a remarkably tolerant view of his marriage to a niece of the Lutheran reformer Andreas Osiander. (Luther's marriage to Katherine von Bora had turned clerical celibacy into a shibboleth.) True, Henry was ignorant of Cranmer's married state when he made him archbishop of Canterbury, but Cranmer had confessed everything by 1543. In 1539 he had sent his wife to the safety of her family in Germany, but four years later she returned with Henry's tacit permission.[8]

More important is that Cranmer had different priorities from Cromwell. By nature he was a private man not a politician. He had only been recruited to royal service after a chance meeting with Edward Foxe and Stephen Gardiner in 1529. Until then he had been a divinity scholar at Cambridge — unlike Gardiner, he did not seek preferment either in the university or at Court. After the Act of Supremacy he obeyed Cromwell's directives; he also granted dispensations and consecrated new bishops as authorized by Parliament. But he played little part in organizing the king's propaganda campaign or in dissolving the monasteries. Despite Catholic allegations that he spearheaded a campaign of iconoclasm, his destructive urge was largely confined to the demolition of Becket's shrine at Canterbury. When More and Fisher offered to swear an oath to the body of the First Act of Succession but not to the preamble, he urged unsuccessfully that this compromise be accepted. In brief, his temperament was scholarly; his twin concerns were the pastoral care of his diocese and the propagation of sound biblical scholarship; and it was his unassuming manner as much as his belief that Scripture justified the royal supremacy that assured his special relationship with Henry VIII.[9]

Cromwell was therefore the driving force behind the Reformation in the 1530s. He used his influence over episcopal appointments to ensure that reformers were preferred; he made London the centre of a major preaching campaign during the period of the attack on images; and he intervened in the mayoral elections in London in 1535–7 in order to support candidates with Protestant leanings. Above all he orchestrated mass circulation of the English Bible, a step which Henry VIII in principle endorsed but conservative bishops opposed on the grounds that they believed it would foment heresy. In fact, when Cranmer had tried to promote an official translation by the bishops, he had been rebuffed. Yet Tyndale's *New Testament* was still proscribed. And, though Cromwell's client Miles Coverdale made a translation derived from the Vulgate and Luther (1535), and the Marian martyr John Rogers revised Tyndale's translations for an edition of 1,500 copies which, according to its title-page, was the work of one 'Thomas Mathew' (1537), the number of Bibles on sale could not approach the demand created by Cromwell's injunction of 1538 that a Bible should be placed in every parish church.[10]

So Cromwell turned print broker; he lent £400 of his own money, as well as exerting considerable pressure, to publish a new edition that was essentially a revision by Coverdale of Tyndale's translations. Begun at Paris where printing technology was ahead of London, but finished in England owing to the intervention of the French Inquisitor General, some 3,000 Bibles were printed in November 1539. By then Cromwell had obtained royal letters patent giving him exclusive power to license new Scriptural translations and enabling him to grant the printers of his 'Great Bible' a monopoly of the market for five years. He then reduced the suggested retail price from 13s. 4d. per copy to 10s. Finally, he printed another 3,000 Bibles at London in March–April 1540 and negotiated the return of 2,500 more from the Inquisitor in Paris. By the time of his execution, he had therefore matched supply to potential demand, as there were 8,445 parishes in England. True, few rural parishes had purchased the Bible by 1540, but most had acquired it within five years. Although his plan to create a Scripturally-literate society was visionary, Cromwell did more than any other Englishman to put the Bible into the hands of ordinary people.[11]

The Pilgrimage of Grace, however, showed the dangers of Cromwell's Reformation. Tension accumulated at Court as his enemies argued that he would spark social revolt. Yet the matter is more complex. Whereas Henry VIII is correctly characterized as 'conservative', it is also true that he flirted with Protestantism.

His religious pluralism was most conspicuous in his diplomacy. In 1529 he told Chapuys that Luther was right on several points, and he continued by endorsing the Lollard view that, if a priest could have two benefices, a layman could commit bigamy. In 1540 two Saxon ambassadors informed the Protestant diet of Schmalkalden that, during a personal interview, Henry had expressed desire for a religious and political understanding with the League. In 1546 the king suggested to the French ambassador that France and England should abolish the mass and replace it with a Protestant communion service. Lastly, Henry kept strange friends: Sir Francis Bryan, Sir Anthony Denny, and William Butts were among his trusted intimates who held reformed views. So it is a possibility—no more—that Henry might have turned Protestant but for the fact that, like John of Gaunt when entreated by Wyclif, he refused to imperil the stability of the realm.[12]

The French Affair of the Placards may be the clue to the direction of Henry's mind. In October 1534 posters went up in Paris and several provincial towns that revealed the existence in France of organized networks of sacramentarians (i.e. Protestants who denied the real presence in the Eucharist). The effect was shattering; hysteria swept through France as rumours spread that Protestants were about to sack the Louvre, burn down churches, and massacre Catholics. Francis I had immediately to change his religious policy and persecute religious dissidents: in the ensuing decade any reformer risked the stake. Also in 1534 the Münster Anabaptist experiment started: private property was abolished, books except the Bible burned, polygamy encouraged, and 'unbelievers' killed. It seemed that Protestantism and social anarchy were one and the same.[13]

European politics started to veer against Cromwell's Reformation when a *rapprochement* was reached between France and Spain which led to the peace of Nice in June 1538.[14] In London several Protestant activists went too far, and the turning-point for Henry VIII was the case of John Lambert. A protégé at Cambridge of Bilney, Lambert had been several times suspected of heresy. Most recently he had confuted a sermon by Dr Taylor, the rector of St Peter's, Cornhill, and was charged with denying the real presence in the Eucharist. In a show trial at Whitehall over which Henry VIII presided as supreme head, flanked by his bishops, nobles, and gentlemen of the privy chamber, the king asked the accused whether the Eucharist was Christ's body (16 November 1538). When Lambert denied it, the king expostulated: 'Mark well! for now thou shalt be condemned even by Christ's own words, "Hoc est corpus meum." '[15] He at once issued a proclamation against sacramentarians, unlicensed books, and married priests. Cromwell was then pushed seriously on to the defensive as Pope Paul III pronounced the long-delayed sentence of excommunication against Henry, and Charles V and Francis I agreed not to ally with England save by mutual consent (treaty of Toledo, January 1539). In December 1538 the pope sent the exiled Reginald Pole to persuade Francis and Charles to lead a crusade against England. His mission failed because both sovereigns decided that the elimination of Henry would work to the advantage of the other, but the scare was real. When France and Spain recalled their London ambassadors at the beginning of 1539, a concerted Catholic invasion of England on the scale of Philip II's Armada of 1588 was feared.

In 1539 musters were held, men and armour assembled, and ships fitted out. A general survey of coastal defences was undertaken—the most thorough since Edward I's reign. And a national network of fortifications was built which was the largest before the Napoleonic Wars. The cost, including works at Calais, was £376,477. Since Henry VIII was also skimming cash from the monastic land sales to rebuild his numerous houses—some £170,000 was spent chiefly at Hampton Court, Whitehall, and Nonsuch—over half a million pounds were disbursed on building operations between 1539 and the king's death.[16]

Yet the invasion never came, and Cromwell turned to diplomacy. Jane Seymour had only survived the birth of her son by twelve days, since when Henry had entered into parallel negotiations aimed at marriage with the duchess of Milan or a French princess. So, when the treaty of Toledo curtailed these discussions, Cromwell persuaded a reluctant king to seek marriage with a German noblewoman in order to negotiate an alliance with the Protestant League of Schmalkalden. The result was a treaty, signed at Hampton Court in October 1539, between Henry VIII and Duke William of Cleves. Yet Henry married Anne of Cleves under protest (6 January 1540); Cromwell's career lay in the balance. His enemies in the Privy Council were the duke of Norfolk, Bishop Tunstall, Sir William Fitzwilliam, Lord Sandes, and Sir Anthony Browne. Gardiner was temporarily in disgrace and Cromwell managed to exclude him from the Privy Council in 1539. But Gardiner continued to attack Cromwell's religious policy, and his absence from the Privy Council was offset when Lambert was condemned to the stake. For, when the king's 'conservatism' was publicized, loyalists on the Council like the earl of Sussex, Sir John Russell, Sir Thomas Cheyney, and Sir William Kingston swung round. Cromwell and Cranmer became isolated. From the beginning of 1539 Henry planned a religious settlement of his own choosing, and, when he summoned Parliament to meet on 28 April 1539, the stage was set.[17]

On 5 May Henry asked the House of Lords for a committee to prepare for what, in effect, was an act of uniformity. This committee was evenly divided between conservatives and reformers but, although appointed chairman, Cromwell could not oppose the king's will. He attempted to distract Henry by seeking another peacetime subsidy, but, when he failed, the duke of Norfolk pressed ahead. Parliament debated six questions: (1) whether the Eucharist could be the body of Christ except by transubstantiation; (2) whether the laity might receive communion in both kinds; (3) whether vows of chastity were immutable; (4) whether private masses should continue; (5) whether priests might marry; and (6) whether auricular confession was necessary. Since the king had already endorsed the answers of traditional theology, they were carried in both Parliament and Convocation. The entire thrust of Cromwell's vicegerential policy was reversed. Next, severe penal clauses were drafted to enforce the Act of Six Articles, which quickly became law. Denial of transubstantiation became punishable by *automatic* burning—even the pre-1534 heresy law had permitted one recantation. And the remaining doctrines were supported by the penalties of *praemunire* or felony. Protestants called this 'the whip with six strings' because the act was enforced: commissions were directed to bishops, JPs, mayors, and bailiffs in every county; dozens of Protestants were imprisoned or burned.[18]

Cromwell's position may have deteriorated when, in the same session of Parliament, an Act of Precedence advanced him personally but reasserted his opponents' wider political authority.[19] No one except the king's children was to sit by the cloth of estate in the House of Lords: this was really a posthumous strike against Wolsey, who had so presumed in 1523. The meat of the act, however, granted the great officers of state precedence in Parliament, the Privy Council, star chamber, and elsewhere. Although notionally about seating arrangements, the act had political implications. As vicegerent in spirituals, Cromwell exercised the king's delegated authority over the church and took precedence over other peers. Lord Chancellor Audley, ennobled in 1538, was elevated too. The act listed the great offices of state in order of precedence: the lord chancellor, lord treasurer, lord president of the Council, and lord privy seal were to sit above all dukes except those of the royal blood. And the lord great chamberlain, constable, earl marshal, admiral, great master of the king's household, and king's chamberlain were to sit in that order above others of their own degree. Yet the majority of these offices were linked to the nobility, and some were hereditary. Although Cromwell and Audley superficially gained from the new order of precedence, the catch was that the office-holders named by the act were to have precedence in the Privy Council too. The Act of Precedence 'pinpointed' the offices that carried membership of the Privy Council. Whether intentionally or not, the act forced Cromwell to concede *ex officio* membership to his adversaries.[20]

Cromwell fought back at Court. He first assumed the titular headship of the privy chamber, then persuaded the king to invest him with the earldom of Essex and appoint him lord great chamberlain, the highest Court office (April 1540). Next he resumed what was begun by his *putsch* in 1536: he packed the privy chamber with his own men to balance his disadvantage in the Privy Council.[21] He planned to control the household of Anne of Cleves. He then continued his recovery in the session of Parliament that opened on 12 April 1540 by obtaining peacetime taxation worth £214,065 over four years. (His client Richard Moryson, for whom he obtained a Commons' seat, advocated this grant.) From his position in the House of Lords, Cromwell himself appealed for religious unity. The king had demanded revisions to the Bishops' Book, and committees were appointed to examine this formulary and to investigate rites and ceremonies. Attempting to salvage what he could of his religious policy, Cromwell condemned both the 'rashness' of the radicals and the 'superstition' of the traditionalists. The king, he said, wanted Christ and His Gospel — the truth alone — to prevail.

For three reasons it was too late. First, the duke of Norfolk had travelled in person to the French Court in February 1540, where he not only drove the first wedge between Francis and Charles V, but actually discussed Cromwell's overthrow. He persuaded the French that they would be in a better bargaining position if Cromwell was ousted. By April the widening breach between France and Spain confirmed that the treaty with Cleves was not essential to Henry's safety.[22] Second, Cromwell had exaggerated the beauty of Anne of Cleves; Henry was complaining, 'I liked her before not well, but now I like her much worse.' He called her 'the Flanders mare' and resolved to be rid of her. Since the marriage was unconsummated, divorce was in theory easy. But Henry's choice for his fifth queen was Catherine Howard, the duke of Norfolk's niece. Cromwell knew that to arrange the Cleves divorce would be to put his enemy in the seat of power, so he hesitated. Third, Norfolk had discovered in the spring of 1539 that Cromwell was protecting Protestants officially denounced as heretics by Lord Lisle, the deputy of Calais. Over sixty sacramentarians were discovered to be among the Calais retinue and the king ordered a full inquiry. Reporting on 5 April 1540, the commissioners confirmed that there were sacramentarians at Calais and hinted at Cromwell's refusal to enforce the Act of Six Articles.[23]

Everything therefore conspired against Cromwell. So dire was the minister's position that he invited Gardiner to dinner and attempted a reconciliation.[24] (Gardiner was about this time readmitted to the Privy Council.)[25] News then broke of the Botolf conspiracy: Sir Gregory Botolf, one of Lord Lisle's chaplains, had defected to Rome, where he had offered to betray Calais. This gave Cromwell a lever, enabling him to 'frame' his Calais accusers as actors in the Botolf conspiracy, so that, far from Lord Lisle being a witness against the sacramentarians, they testified against him! In the most audacious move of his career, Cromwell shifted the attack against Norfolk.[26]

He might even have succeeded had not the Cleves marriage tipped the scales. Sir Thomas Wriothesley, Cromwell's former secretary whom he had placed on the Privy Council in an attempt to buttress his position, later explained:

He asked lord Cromwell to devise some way for the relief of the King, for if he remained in this grief and trouble, they should all one day smart for it. To which lord Cromwell answered that it was true, but that it was a great matter. 'Marry,' said Sir T[homas], 'I grant, but let the remedy be searched for.' 'Well,' said lord Cromwell, and then brake off from him.[27]

The king's 'great matter' was Cromwell's too. The irony resounds, for Thomas More had quipped that Henry's first 'great matter' was also his. In June 1540 Cromwell was stymied. At 3 o'clock on the 10th the captain of the guard entered the Council chamber to arrest him. Cromwell threw his bonnet to the floor, turned to Norfolk, and demanded whether this was the reward for all his service. In reply, the duke snatched the badge of St George from Cromwell's neck while Fitzwilliam unclasped the Garter. By nightfall the minister's goods and papers had been seized—the fatal sign. He was executed on 28 July after providing from the Tower the evidence needed for the Cleves divorce.

Sir Thomas Wyatt, Cromwell's client who witnessed his beheading, wrote his obituary:

> The pillar perished is whereto I leant,
> The strongest stay of mine unquiet mind;
> The like of it no man again can find.[28]

Like Empson, Dudley, and Wolsey, Henry VIII's second chief minister had been thrown to the wolves. He had steered the Reformation beyond the point the king decided was expedient; had married Henry to the wrong wife; and, when the Franco-imperial accord dissolved, his pro-Lutheran foreign policy became more a liability than an asset.[29] Also in his later diplomacy and in the matter of the Calais sacramentarians, Cromwell had allowed personal religious commitment to cloud his political judgement. In this sense, he was as much a martyr to his faith as More and Fisher were to theirs.

Yet he died unmourned. Henry VIII instantly married Catherine Howard, and the Norfolk–Gardiner hegemony tested its strength. Anne of Cleves received her divorce without demur; she actually thanked Henry for his 'goodness, favour and liberality' and a month later was enjoying an annual income of £4,000, the manors of Richmond and Bletchingley, and precedence over all ladies in England after the new queen and royal children. Norfolk's Privy Council then declared its hand, appointing a permanent secretary and ordering records to be kept of all future Council business in contrast to Cromwell's 'personal' style of government (10 August). Lastly, Cromwell's most loyal dependents were purged: Sir Ralph Sadler and Wyatt were arrested and sent to the Tower in manacles (January 1541); Richard Moryson was expelled from the privy chamber; and William Gray was interrogated as a suspected traitor — the 'evidence' was that he had scrawled Melanchthon's name in the margin of a book.[30]

It is often argued that the Privy Council contained no one of Cromwell's talent in 1541–7, therefore Henry VIII consciously decided upon 'personal rule'. This is misleading. Cromwell's fall marked the triumph of adversaries who justified his overthrow as a victory for 'conciliarist' over 'ministerial' government.[31] It is clear from the Privy Council's own registers that nine privy councillors best described as loyal 'Henricians' or *politiques* ran the country (and the wars) until the king's death.[32] Although Henry intervened, he did so spasmodically and in matters that had always concerned him: diplomacy, military strategy, theology, and his wives. The irony is that the duke of Norfolk was not among the nine councillors, nor was his niece crowned queen. In November 1541 Henry received evidence that Catherine Howard had committed adultery. He called for a sword to slay her, then pitifully lamented 'his ill-luck in meeting with such ill-conditioned wives'. More significantly, he blamed the Privy Council for his misfortune, and he deputed Cranmer, Audley, and Sadler — the fallen Cromwell's allies — to investigate the charges against the queen. The entire Howard connection was threatened with destruction, and the duke only extricated himself by admitting 'the abominable deeds' and 'repeated treasons' of his family. The queen and her alleged accomplices were soon executed, and the dowager duchess of Norfolk, her son Lord William Howard, her daughter, and her daughter-in-law were imprisoned and their property seized.

With his ego in this fragile state, Henry resolved to restore his 'honour' in war against France. With the amity between France and Spain dead in the summer of 1541, both sides courted England's support, and by 1542 an understanding was reached with Charles V that resulted in a formal treaty the following year. Charles and Henry agreed to invade France in person in the summer of 1544, each with thirty-five thousand foot and seven thousand horse. The target was ostensibly Paris—the emperor was to march through Champagne and Henry through Picardy—though Henry had reservations about this strategy after the duke of Suffolk's experience in 1523. But his first priority was Scotland, where the regime was dominated by the French faction headed by Cardinal Beaton. In October 1542 an army led by the duke of Norfolk crossed the border. Initially little was achieved, but a Scottish counterstroke proved a worse disaster than Flodden. At Solway Moss some three thousand English triumphed over ten thousand Scots (24 November 1542)—the news of the disgrace killed James V within a month. Scotland was left hostage to the fortune of Mary Stuart, a baby born six days before James's death.

Henry used the prisoners taken at Solway Moss as the nucleus of an 'anglophile' party in Scottish politics. He forced on the Scots the treaties of Greenwich (July 1543), which projected union of the crowns in the form of a future marriage between Prince Edward and Mary Stuart. But this interventionism miscarried; the treaties were built on sand. The Scots preferred 'to suffer extremity than be subject to England', as Henry's agent reported. When Beaton escaped from prison, the 'anglophile' party collapsed and surrendered its castles. In quick succession Beaton returned to power, Mary Stuart was crowned, and the Scottish Parliament reaffirmed the French alliance. Henry retaliated first with pensions, and then by sending the earl of Hertford north. Hertford was Prince Edward's uncle, and the rising star at Court after Catherine Howard's fall. His orders were to destroy the palace and abbey of Holyrood and every house and village within 7 miles of Edinburgh. But Henry's 'rough wooing' backfired: the French faction remained ascendant.

On 14 July 1544 Henry turned to France. Despite bad health and swollen legs, he followed his army to Calais and himself took charge of strategy. He cancelled the projected march on Paris; instead his forces were put under the separate commands of the dukes of Norfolk and Suffolk, who then besieged Boulogne, which yielded, and Montreuil, which held out. If he suspected duplicity on the part of his ally, his instinct was sound. For Charles V jilted Henry on the very day he entered Boulogne, by making a separate peace. So Henry dug in, encircling Boulogne with fortifications which the French answered with rival defences designed to make the English positions untenable.

Of course, Henry was fighting on two fronts. In an attempt to buttress the 'anglophile' party in Scotland, he had married his niece, Lady Margaret Douglas, to the earl of Lennox before sailing for France. He promised to appoint Lennox governor of Scotland when the kingdom should fall into his hands (June 1544). But Lennox was ineffective. And when Henry's border captain Sir Ralph Evers was defeated at the battle of Ancrum Moor (27 February 1545), the Scottish Privy Council decided to invade England with the aid of French troops. By August Hertford had learned that this army was approaching the border but was short of victuals. So he waited until September when the English harvest was in and the Scottish corn cut. He then unleashed a counter-invasion which devastated the Scottish side of the border: 16 castles, 7 monasteries, 5 towns, and 243 villages were burned. Eight months later Beaton was assassinated with Henry VIII's connivance, but the French faction remained in power at Edinburgh.

More serious for Henry was the French naval raid on Portsmouth and the Isle of Wight in July 1545. Over two hundred French ships entered the Solent: when the wind dropped, four oared galleys took the English fleet by surprise. Before the king's own eyes his ship the *Mary Rose* heeled in the confusion and sank with the vice-admiral Sir George Carew and five hundred men on board. A French landing on the Isle of Wight was then repulsed. Faced with the costs and dangers of the war, however, the Privy Council urged Henry to make peace. Still directing strategy, Henry opened parallel sets of negotiations with France and Spain through different privy councillors whom he kept in ignorance of each other's commissions![33] But by the treaty of Camp (near Ardres), England made peace with France on condition that Henry retained Boulogne until 1554, when France

would buy it back for £600,000 complete with its new
fortifications (June 1546). French pensions totalling £35,000 per
annum were to be restored to Henry—Francis I had stopped
earlier payments in 1534. Lastly, if the Scots refused to approve
the treaty, the French would coerce them.[34]

These terms were less attractive than they seemed. Boulogne
was expensive to garrison and the proposed compensation
for its return bore little relation to the charges of the wars. The
siege of Boulogne cost £586,718, the garrisoning of it £426,306,
the Scottish campaigns £350,243, the navy £265,024. The total
bill (including fortifications) was £2,134,784. On the other side
of the ledger, £656,245 was raised by taxation (including
Cromwell's last peacetime subsidy); £270,000 had accrued from
forced loans; £799,310 was obtained from sales of ex-religious
lands; and £100,000 was borrowed on the Antwerp money
market.[35] To cover the deficit Henry reorganized the mint and
debased the coinage: the profit from debasements in 1544–6 was
£363,000. Also legislation was obtained in December 1545 to
permit the dissolution of chantries and colleges of priests which
earlier confiscations of church property had left untouched,
though this act was not invoked during Henry VIII's lifetime.

Despite sales of the bulk of the ex-religious lands in the 1540s,
the Crown could not balance its books. If Henry VIII's
wars satisfied his 'honour' and exercised his manhood, they were
still wasteful and ineffective.[36] But a positive development
was that new ideas resulted from the invasion scares and
war expenditure of his last years. The principle was established that coastal defence was the responsibility of royal
government rather than a piecemeal exercise of co-operation
between the Crown, territorial magnates, and local self-help.[37]
The draftsmen of the subsidy acts of 1540, 1543, and (later)
1553 argued that defence was submerged within royal government: the king defended the realm, therefore taxation was
appropriate for the preservation of his royal estate; the Crown
was 'the saviour and sole defender of the nation', therefore what
contributed to royal preservation also defended the realm.[38] Of
course, to associate normal government with defence equated
the latter with the maintenance of the Crown. The outcome was
the thesis that royal need *alone* was sufficient to justify
parliamentary taxation.

Debating this question in 1549, Edward VI's privy councillor Sir Thomas Smith wrote: 'So long as the subjects have it [i.e. money], so it is meet the King should have as long as they have it.' And he added, 'What King can maintain his estate with his yearly revenues only growing of his lands?'[39] In the fiscal climate of the 1540s, therefore, theories of taxation started to abandon Fortescue's distinction between 'ordinary' and 'extraordinary' expenditure. Whereas *The Governance of England* had argued that it was only defence expenditure *above the average* that was properly met by taxation, Smith saw grants of taxation as the duty of the citizen. 'Necessity' was seen to bisect 'ordinary' and 'extraordinary' categorization and render it outmoded. This lack of distinction had also appeared in practice: the king's coffers, to which a quarter of a million pounds were transferred in 1542–7, contained cash skimmed from the courts of augmentations and first fruits and tenths, as well as revenues obtained from taxation and the Crown lands. Disbursements, too, muddled sums for royal building works, the household, and the wars.[40]

Although highly conservative, religious policy in 1541–7 was also far more positive than is often thought — less a 'conservative reaction' than an attempt at 'conservative reform'.[41] The objective was a programme of education designed to thwart Protestant advance and defend the royal supremacy. Doctrine was that of the Act of Six Articles, but 'reformed' instruments such as vernacular statements of faith, an English Litany, and an English Primer were used to transmit it. At the height of the so-called 'conservative reaction', Henry VIII continued to urge that children be taught the Creed, Lord's Prayer, and Ten Commandments in English as vigorously as had Thomas Cromwell.[42] But he insisted that 'reform' be consistent with the Six Articles and the royal supremacy; especially that the institutional structure of 'his' church should not be touched.[43]

In May 1543 a formulary to replace the Bishops' Book, *A Necessary Doctrine and Erudition for any Christian Man*, or King's Book, was 'read in the Council Chamber before the nobility of the realm'.[44] Officially licensed by the supreme head, the King's Book revised its predecessor by expounding the Creed, seven sacraments, Ten Commandments, and Lord's Prayer according to the Act of Six Articles. The bishops were blamed by Protestants for the 'damnable doctrine' of the work, but the politics of the revision are clearly shown by the handwritten instruction on the inside cover of Henry's thickly amended copy of the Bishops' Book: 'not [to] be had out of the privy chamber.' Henry VIII penned the King's Book himself.[45]

But the Privy Council sought to quell social revolt as much as to enforce the Six Articles. When Parliament debated an Act for the Advancement of True Religion, the main emphasis was on limiting access to Scriptural and theological writings on the basis of social rank. Both Henry VIII and Convocation had objected to the translation of ninety-nine passages in Cromwell's Great Bible, and the king had referred the matter to the universities.[46] It was still intended that the Bible should be read at services in parish churches on Sundays and that Scripture should be expounded in sermons. But Parliament enacted that 'no women nor artificers, [ap]prentices, journeymen, serving men of the degrees of yeomen or under, husbandmen nor labourers' were to read the English Bible under penalty of a month's imprisonment. The reason was that subjects 'of the lower sort' had 'increased in divers naughty and erroneous opinions, and by occasion thereof fallen into great division and dissension among themselves'. Exceptions were made for women of noble or 'gentle' status, who might read the English Bible privately, but otherwise it was to be read only by upper-class males.[47]

On the other hand, the act tempered the Act of Six Articles by allowing offenders to recant or abjure their heresies twice. Only 'obstinate' heretics or third-time offenders would now be burned. Next, common lawyers in the House of Commons spearheaded an attack on *ex officio* heresy trials in church courts similar to that launched in 1534, and they won legal safeguards which in practice considerably impeded heresy trial procedure (January 1544). For in future an accused was not to be tried under the Act of Six Articles except after indictment by a grand jury; presentments were to be made within a year of alleged offences; no one was to be arrested or imprisoned before indictment, etc.[48]

Cranmer, meanwhile, continued to promote the Reformation in his diocese. Several of his officials and chaplains were reformers, and he protected the radical party in Kent after

Cromwell's fall.[49] He also liked to experiment, nominating preachers of both the 'new learning' and the 'old' at Canterbury Cathedral in order to 'try out the truth of doctrine'.[50] The resulting sparks flew far beyond the cathedral precinct, but the plot engineered against Cranmer in the spring of 1543 reveals a fundamental tension in late-Henrician religious policy. Withholding evidence collected from some prebendaries of Canterbury Cathedral until the Anglo-imperial alliance and King's Book were finalized, Gardiner then attacked Cranmer in the Privy Council. But when the charges were shown to Henry VIII, he handed them over to Cranmer and told him to conduct the investigation himself![51] Perhaps on this occasion, too, Henry gave Cranmer a ring which he produced when brought before the Privy Council. The councillors went to the king, who rebuked them and exonerated Cranmer. (Shakespeare knew this story and staged it in his play of Henry VIII.)

So why did Henry protect Cranmer? Was it simply out of personal affection, or did he mean to issue a warning to both 'reformers' and 'conservatives' to avoid undue factionalism and disunity? The latter is more likely. But it is equally possible that Henry was being pragmatic at a moment in his reign when war with Scotland had begun and war against France was imminent. The grass-roots Reformation had made considerable strides in the south-east by 1543, in Kent especially, where by Cromwell's fall it was too well entrenched among local gentry to be overthrown.[52] In the final analysis, his reaction to the so-called Prebendaries' plot suggests that Henry acknowledged under pressure that he presided, as supreme head, over contradictory religious movements he did not fully control: 'conservative' reform from above, and grass-roots Protestant evangelism from below.[53]

The reformed cause revived at Court when Henry married his sixth wife, Catherine Parr (12 July 1543). The editor of *Prayers Stirring the Mind unto Heavenly Meditation* (1545) and patron of the English translation of Erasmus's *Paraphrases on the New Testament*, Catherine used her influence to mitigate the Act of Six Articles in several cases. Her intimate circle was centred on the royal nursery, where John Cheke, Richard Cox, Anthony Cooke, and other 'reforming' humanists were appointed tutors to Prince Edward and Princess Elizabeth. She kept in continual contact with Cranmer; she appointed a reformer, Walter Bucler, as her secretary; and she patronized radical preachers such as Coverdale and Latimer.[54] (If an explanation of Edward VI's Protestant *credo* is sought, it may lie in the influence of Catherine's circle.)

Yet the discovery of a Protestant cell at Windsor Castle which included the king's organist John Marbecke emphasized the difficulty of containing Protestantism in the counties when it was plainly visible at Court.[55] Soon Catherine Parr was herself threatened by 'conservative' denunciations. But the sequel to the trial of the Lincolnshire gentlewoman Anne Askew is ambiguous. Askew's trouble began when she relapsed after recanting a Protestant view of the Eucharist. She was examined by the Privy Council, racked in the Tower, and burned for heresy in July 1546. Under torture she was found to have Court connections, as was her teacher Dr Edward Crome, a prominent London reformer, who was also interrogated. The trail led first to the wives of six of Henry's courtiers and then to Catherine Parr herself. The king suspected sacramentarianism, and signed a warrant for a full investigation. Then in a well-publicized (and possibly staged) interview Catherine 'submitted' to her husband's direction in religion, whereupon Henry called off the inquiry. As told in Foxe's *Acts and Monuments*, however, the story is *ben trovato*. Since Henry nominated Cheke and Cox to the investigating committee as well as Bishops Gardiner and Bonner, it is likely that he was again signalling courtiers to avoid factionalism.[56]

Factionalism, nevertheless, was encouraged by the hottest political issue of the king's last years — the succession. Henry's crossing with his army to France in 1544 raised the spectre of what would happen should he die before 1555, the year of Prince Edward's majority.[57] A Third Act of Succession was obtained in Parliament, which restored Mary and Elizabeth to the succession after Edward (thereby tacitly recognizing their legitimacy), and vested power during Edward's minority in a regency Council to be nominated by Henry in his last will and testament. So the question of whom the king would appoint to this Council inevitably fired ambitions at Court. Gardiner, Norfolk (aged over seventy), and his reckless and haughty son, the poet Henry Howard, earl of Surrey, led one faction. Thwarted by Catherine Howard's adultery in 1541, they wished to secure the offices of protector of the realm and governor of Edward's person during his expected minority. But in opposition to them emerged a far more powerful coalition of Hertford–Lisle and Parr–Herbert interests.

Edward Seymour, earl of Hertford (later Protector Somerset), and John Dudley, Viscount Lisle (later earl of Warwick and duke of Northumberland), had risen at Court through successes in war that brought them close to the king and rendered the Howards expendable. Hertford was Prince Edward's uncle and brother of Thomas Seymour (Henry VIII's rival for the hand of Catherine Parr who married her after the king's death). He wielded immense territorial and political power, not least because he administered the royal household as lord great chamberlain. A man of consuming ambition, he forged an alliance with Lisle, a privy councillor and member of the privy chamber, whom Henry had appointed lord admiral in 1543 and who commanded the fleet in battle against the French. The son of Henry VII's councillor Edmund Dudley, Lisle was briefly rusticated in November 1546 for striking Gardiner in the Privy Council.

Linked to Hertford and Lisle were the Parr and Herbert families, both tied by blood to the queen and Court. Although William Parr, earl of Essex (later marquis of Northampton), held no significant office beyond membership of the Privy Council, he was the queen's brother. Sir William Herbert (later earl of Pembroke) was her brother-in-law, the steward of her lands, and a chief gentleman of the privy chamber. Both men possessed followings in Parliament and the country, and both supported Hertford. Also Hertford won the confidence of two key officials at Court: Sir William Paget, the king's secretary and most trusted adviser, and Sir Anthony Denny, the second chief gentleman of the privy chamber.

So the defeat of Norfolk and Gardiner became inevitable. They were outflanked in the Privy Council by *politiques* and members of Hertford's axis, while in the privy apartments Lisle, Herbert, Denny, Paget, and Thomas Seymour surrounded the king.[58] With the connivance of Paget and Denny, Hertford obtained control both of the king's signet seal and of his signature itself. For in his last years Henry VIII refused to sign state papers himself, instead delegating the task to his intimates, who were given the use of a secret 'dry stamp'.[59] Application of this stamp was directed by Denny, whose brother-in-law John Gates held the box containing it. The office routine was performed by William Clerk, who affixed the stamp and kept registers of documents 'signed'. An impression of Henry's signature was first made by the stamp 'without blackening' (i.e. use of ink), and afterwards Clerk, Denny, or Gates 'shall blacken the same' — that is, ink in the signature. The result was a perfect facsimile — political dynamite.[60]

In July 1546 the Hertford–Lisle coalition was joined by the earl of Arundel, one of the wealthiest and most respected nobles in England. Hertford's coup was staged five months later. First, Gardiner was excluded from the Privy Council; then Norfolk and Surrey were arrested and sent to the Tower (12 December). Surrey was executed on 21 January 1547 and, if the king had not died during the night, Norfolk would have followed on the 28th.

Yet the key document is Henry VIII's will. When the two extant versions of this are compared, it is clear that Hertford's coup was approved by a king who 'very much knew to whom he wished to bequeath the government of his son and kingdom'.[61] The day after the Howards' arrests Henry altered his will so as to oust Gardiner and Norfolk from the regency Council.[62] Then on 26 December, when 'very sick and in some peril', he summoned Hertford, Lisle, Paget, and Denny to his bedside and made further revisions. He left the Crown to Edward, Mary, and Elizabeth in that order and nominated a regency Council of sixteen members to govern until Edward was eighteen years old.[63] The Council's members were to implement the will by majority decision, and no provision was made at this stage for the appointment of a Protector. But when the king lapsed into unconsciousness in the early hours of 28 January, the will was not signed. So it was signed by stamp under the supervision of Hertford, Paget, Herbert, and Denny.[64] The will, as stamped, provided the basis for the new regime. First, Paget drafted a clause giving the regency Council 'full power and authority' to undertake *any action* necessary for the government of the realm during Edward's minority, as if Henry VIII himself had given them a commission under the great seal of England. Next, an 'unfulfilled gifts clause' was added or rewritten that empowered the regency Council to award posthumously whatever Henry had 'granted, made, accorded, or promised' but failed legally to convey during his lifetime.

Paget later denied that anything was done in Edward's reign that Henry VIII had not authorized, but it is possible that the king's will was 'doctored' in his dying hours to enable Hertford to assume the title of Lord Protector; to enable him to reward his followers with the confiscated Howard lands; and to permit him to buy off his opponents.[65] Hertford's son certainly admitted that his father was 'his own carver', and the posthumous patronage of Henry VIII is undisputed: four promotions within the peerage, four new peerages, and a shower of Crown lands worth £27,053 per annum granted by Hertford's men to reward themselves and their friends.

The news of Henry VIII's death was kept secret for three days: Edward VI's succession was not proclaimed and Parliament was left in session until Hertford was secure. He fetched Edward (nine years old) and brought him to the Tower; he seized the remaining assets of Henry VIII stored in the secret jewel houses; and he debated with the Council whether to execute Norfolk—in the end he was kept in prison. These manœuvres were unconstitutional. The legality of government derived from royal authority which terminated with the king's death, as did sessions of Parliament.

On 31 January the regency Council heard Henry VIII's will read and then named Hertford Protector and governor of Edward's person. In exchange Hertford and Paget implemented the 'unfulfilled gifts clause' of the will. Hertford became duke of Somerset, Essex (William Parr) became marquis of Northampton, Lisle became earl of Warwick, Wriothesley became earl of Southampton, and Thomas Seymour became a baron. But on 6 March Somerset purged Wriothesley, who was charged with illegal acts as lord chancellor, deprived of his office, and fined £4,000. Wriothesley had resisted the creation of the Protectorate—and his judgement was sound.[66] Six days later Somerset overthrew the will: he obtained letters patent granting him near-sovereign powers as Protector and enabling him to appoint anyone he chose to the Council. Somerset's style of government was, however, so personal that the Council's role was steadily undermined. He often settled state business in his own household, where he relied on what contemporaries called his 'new council': men like Sir Thomas Smith, Sir Michael Stanhope, William Cecil, Edward Wolf, Sir John Thynne, and William Gray. None except Smith, whom he appointed the king's secretary, was a privy councillor. Stanhope was his brother-in-law, Cecil his personal secretary, Thynne his steward, and Wolf an ex-naval captain. Although Somerset's behaviour was not illegal, his arrogance and incivility aroused resentment. Memoranda addressed to him equated the king's business with his personal affairs. For instance, Paget wrote to him of 'your proceedings in Parliament', 'your foreign affairs', 'your debt', 'your navy', 'your order for religion', etc. Councillors complained that letters had not been 'so princely written' by a subject since Wolsey's time.

But Somerset achieved what Wolsey could not manage: he ruled at Court as well as at Westminster. He made Stanhope his man at Court by promoting him chief gentleman of the privy chamber and groom of the stool. Hence Stanhope replaced Denny as administrator of the king's coffers. He also kept the 'dry stamp' of Edward's signature—the new stamp enabled Somerset to warrant financial business and raise troops. Indeed, with the king's signature at his disposal, the Protector took possession of the royal will; he became quasi-king.[67] But the Council was alerted when he commanded that nothing was to pass under Edward's true signature without his counter-signature, and when he had partially blank warrants stamped. When he raised troops by the stamp against Kett's rebels, his opponents viewed his action as the first step towards 'protection' of the king against them. His autocracy—as much as his policies—provoked Warwick's counter-coup.

Factionalism also soured the atmosphere. Within days of Henry VIII's death Warwick had persuaded Thomas Seymour, the Protector's brother, who was severely disappointed at not being named to the regency Council, to claim the governorship of Edward's person from the Protector on the grounds that he, too, was the prince's uncle. First Warwick trapped Seymour into asserting his claim, then told Somerset, 'Did I not tell you ever that he would . . . envy your state . . . he will never rest till he do out-throw you again.'[68] So Somerset conceded his brother a place ón the Council and appointed him lord admiral, but a wedge was driven between them. This suited Warwick's new political game: he knew that he had to split the two brothers to advance his own career. His ends were served after Catherine Parr's death, when Thomas Seymour schemed to marry Princess Elizabeth. By Christmas 1548 gossip was rife that she was pregnant by the admiral, who did nothing to quash these rumours; he even encouraged them. He also courted Wriothesley's support for a plot against his brother, insinuating that this would enable the ousted lord chancellor to recover his post.[69] But Wriothesley was a much sharper and more experienced politician. Far from joining Thomas Seymour, he denounced him, a service for which Protector Somerset readmitted him to the Council! So Seymour was arrested on 17 January 1549 and charged with thirty-three articles of high treason. This smacked of overkill, but the Protector saw the danger: that his opponents would strike at him via his brother. Seymour was therefore attainted in Parliament without trial; his execution followed on 20 March.

The key to Somerset's policy was his personality. He was vacillating but self-willed, highminded yet prone to *idées fixes*. Seeking to appear virtuous and to be held in wide esteem, he courted mass popularity while sugar-coating his natural severity with talk of clemency and justice. This partly reflected Renaissance self-fashioning and partly his wish to set a tone for the reign. Yet altruism was absent: more than any Tudor politician except Elizabeth's last favourite, the second earl of Essex, Somerset equated his ambition with the public good. He sponsored enclosure commissions and a tax on sheep in a purported attempt to champion the poor against the rich, but his true opinions were always those of his time: aristocratic, acquisitive, authoritarian.[70] Those who mistakenly believed that English social structure was on the agenda of political action were declared rebels. If Somerset was slow to respond to revolt, this stemmed not from charity but from irresolution and his urge not to be distracted from his consuming obsession: the conquest of Scotland.

Scotland was crucial. Whereas her affairs were for Henry VIII a sideshow of his French campaigns, for Somerset the reverse was true. He meant to win the war begun by Henry VIII and

impose on Scotland the treaties of Greenwich; to assert Edward
I's ancient claim of suzerainty; to unite the crowns; and to enforce
the marriage between Edward VI and the infant Mary Stuart.
Of course, he appreciated that England could not afford to invade
Scotland constantly in order to enforce the treaties. Therefore
his military strategy was to build and maintain permanent
garrisons in Scotland manned by Englishmen or foreign
mercenaries.

Invading Scotland in September 1547, he first won the battle
of Pinkie and then built and garrisoned forts that were largely
concentrated on the border with England and the East Coast.
But the castles of Dunbar and Edinburgh were not taken, and
doubts may be expressed about the location of Somerset's
garrisons: in particular, although the major fortress at
Haddington was only 18 miles from Edinburgh, it was awkward
to victual. The whole purpose of permanent garrisons was
defeated if armies had annually to march into Scotland in order
to relieve them. Here Somerset's poor sense of topography and
haste to build new forts were to blame. Also he neglected to
enforce the naval blockade of the Firth of Forth, and
miscalculated the strength of the Franco-Scottish amity.

Before June 1548 French aid to Scotland was meagre, but on
19 June some six thousand crack troops with artillery for
siegework landed at Leith. The French settled their own garrisons
at places the English coveted, and captured some English
positions. Somerset's naval incapacity now cost him dear, and
his military reprisals backfired. When he sent armies into
Scotland in August 1548 and January and July 1549, the French
shipped Mary Stuart to the safety of France, thereby depriving
the Protector of his principal *raison d'être* in waging the war. As
a result his policy became defensive: many garrisons were
abandoned and those that remained had to be protected even
though they no longer served a valid purpose.[71]

Military expenditure in Edward VI's reign was £1,386,687
(including the navy and fortifications). Somerset spent £580,393
against Scotland, a staggering £351,521 on troops alone.
England's recruiting system, surveyed but neglected by Wolsey,
could not provide sufficient men for regular service, therefore
the Protector hired 7,434 mercenaries—Italians, Spaniards,
Germans, Hungarians, Albanians, and Irishmen. (As conditions

worsened, even mercenaries refused to serve in Scotland; manpower problems contributed to the collapse of the garrisons.) Compared to Henry VIII, Somerset spent half as much again on Scotland in half the time. He shirked open hostilities with France; nevertheless Henry II declared war on 8 August 1549. Somerset offered to return Boulogne immediately instead of waiting until 1554, but negotiations collapsed when Henry demanded Calais as well. Additional fortifications were erected at Boulogne and Calais; an attack on Boulogne was repulsed. Yet when Mary Stuart was betrothed to the Dauphin, the futility of Somerset's policy was reiterated.

Coinage debasements mostly paid for the war; the government's profit in 1547–51 was £537,000. More money was raised when the dissolution of the chantries and colleges was re-authorized by Parliament in December 1547. Receipts had totalled £110,486 by Michaelmas 1548, and sales of confiscated land in 1549–50 realized £139,981. Parliamentary taxation yielded £335,988 in Edward's reign but only £189,802 of this money went towards the costs of war and defence. The balance was met by sales of Crown lands and borrowing.[72]

The Protector's religious policy was to move towards Protestantism. Although Somerset had conformed to the Act of Six Articles under Henry VIII, he now took Protestants such as John Hooper, Thomas Becon, and William Turner into his household: they had fled to Strasburg and Zurich to escape the Act. All were prolific writers whose books Somerset sanctioned along with others by Luther, Tyndale, Wyclif, Barnes, Bullinger, and Frith — reformers proscribed by Henry VIII. No fewer than 159 out of 394 new books printed during the Protectorate were by Protestant reformers.[73]

Somerset's shift is partly explicable in Henrician terms: the young Edward VI was Protestant, therefore *cuius regio eius religio* — orthodoxy was obedience to the supreme head's will. Matters were more complex than this: Edward was a minor and the supremacy was exercised by the regency Council of Henry VIII's will, which functioned by majority voting. However, the Crown was not the only driving force. Moderate concessions to Protestants were essential if unity was to be preserved — the repeal of the Act of Six Articles was the minimum requirement.

Henry VIII's death had provoked spontaneous responses.
Radical London clergy dispensed with the mass and conducted
services in the vernacular before the Act of Uniformity; surviving
images were stripped from the city's churches before their final
proscription by the Council; and thirty-one tracts attacking the
mass were printed during 1548 alone. Public controversies,
ballads, sermons, and stage plays exposing and ridiculing the
mass had to be prohibited on grounds of public order. And by
August 1549 the Council was obliged to reinstate official
censorship.[74]

Although accurate figures are lacking, roughly one-fifth
of Londoners were Protestant by 1547. In Kent, Sussex,
Essex, London, and Bristol, Protestants were an entrenched
minority, but elsewhere Protestantism had barely progressed.
Yet London activists had disproportionate influence on
official policy; they were a vocal lobby — the 'storm centre'
for the nation's beliefs. Secret cells of 'Christian brethren'
existed to spread the Word; links were forged with Lollard
congregations; the Protestant book trade was established; the
example of the 'martyrs' to the Six Articles gave inspiration;
and refuges were provided for European exiles after Charles V
destroyed the Schmalkaldic League at Mühlberg (24 April
1547).[75] Since so many of Somerset's supporters were radical,
he had an incentive to assimilate the supremacy to their interests.
The danger was that religious opinion would polarize and lead
to civil discord; uniformity was the linchpin of order.

Scottish policy was an opposing influence; Somerset was
obliged to appease Charles V in the interests of the war.
Paget urged that reforms be presented 'as God be pleased and
the world little offended'. For this reason Princess Mary's
Catholicism was tolerated — the only nonconformity Somerset
sanctioned save that of foreign immigrants. And the policy
worked in so far as Charles closed his ports to French
shipping engaged in the Scottish war, prevented the French
from raising troops in his dominions, and permitted the
English to do so. Yet the price was a 'stop–go' religious policy.
Only under Northumberland, when the emperor was distracted
by wars with the German princes, the French, and the
Ottoman Turks, could the regime declare itself unequivocally
Protestant.[76]

The paradox is that Somerset demolished Catholic rites while circumventing doctrinal change. He reissued Cromwell's injunctions in July 1547, then divided the realm into six circuits for enforcement purposes. He appointed Protestant activists or reliable servants to these commissions; four to six visitors were selected for each circuit — those for London were led by Anthony Cooke. Enforcement was strict; the visitors themselves shattered images at Hull. When Parliament met on 4 November, a single repeal act (1 Edward VI, c. 12) revoked the Act of Six Articles, the Act for the Advancement of True Religion, the heresy laws, Cromwell's treason laws, and several other statutes. Both Lords and Commons amended the government's bill; stronger pressure was brought against the Henrician settlement than the Council had expected. Nevertheless, denial of royal supremacy and infringements of the Third Act of Succession remained high treason. Also the clergy were deprived of their traditional benefit for major crimes, but the peerage were granted the privilege even if they could not read!

Another act censured persons reviling the mass, but approved communion in both kinds 'except necessity otherwise require'. The legislation dissolving the chantries was approved: confraternities, guilds, free chapels, 'lights', and obits were appropriated as well as chantries and colleges of priests on the grounds that purgatory and prayers for the dead were superstitious. Although promises that resources would be re-allocated were broken, hospitals were exempted from the act and chapels and colleges were spared if they met pastoral needs. Some schools were lost but the majority were protected. Schoolmasters and inmates of almshouses were given pensions; existing poor relief was maintained. Yet the Crown did not refound schools unbidden. Re-endowment was normally achieved through the efforts of local citizens who repurchased property from the court of augmentations. Very few outright gifts came from the Crown.[77]

Elimination of chantry chapels from the side aisles and precincts of churches was one of the biggest architectural changes of the sixteenth century. And further iconoclasm was countenanced. Although the injunctions specified destruction of images idolatrously abused, the Council ruled that images which had not been cult objects could be shattered if the priest, churchwardens, or the visitors so decided. In February 1548 radical demand was propitiated: stating as a reason that 'almost in every place [there] is contention for images', the Council commanded demolition of all images and depictions of saints in stained-glass windows, as well as the liming of churches to obliterate wall pictures. Since four of the most important ceremonies were forbidden the previous month — Candlemas candles, Ash Wednesday ashes, Palm Sunday palms, and Good Friday creeping to the cross — the visual symbolism of English religion was devastated.[78]

The order to remove images was obeyed: all were cleared by the end of 1549; altars too were jettisoned in at least fourteen parishes.[79] Private masses were also abolished and instructions printed for the administration of communion in both kinds (March 1548). Drafted by an assembly of divines convened at Windsor, these provided for public confessions by intending communicants but retained the option of private or 'auricular' confession to a priest. The 'sentences' read at the distribution of the Eucharist defended the real presence while also permitting belief in transubstantiation. Yet this meant that Somerset's initiatives on ritual and theology contradicted each other; as Foxe observed, 'there did arise a marvellous schism, and variety of fashions'.[80] Gardiner protested and was imprisoned (September 1547 to January 1548), then confined to London, and finally sent to the Tower (July 1548). Edmund Bonner, bishop of London, recoiled from innovation but complied until the Uniformity Act was implemented. Throughout 1548 the Council tried to avert discord. Unlicensed preaching was banned (24 April), then *all* preaching (23 September); clergy were instead to recite twelve official homilies from the pulpit. But Somerset's homilies attacked images, purgatory, and good works, and advocated salvation by faith alone — so they upset traditionalists.

This situation was explosive; therefore decision-making was attempted in the next session of Parliament (24 November 1548 to 14 March 1549). The Council prepared the way by authorizing Cranmer and the divines to draft 'one convenient and meet order, rite, and fashion of Common Prayer' for use in England, Wales, and Calais. They produced the first Book of Common Prayer in English and submitted it to Parliament for discussion. Full-scale debate ensued: Somerset began in the House of Lords with the question, 'Whether the bread be in the sacrament after the consecration or not?' To Bonner's defence of transubstantiation, he replied that 'there is bread still' — so he denied transubstantiation but was ambiguous on the real presence.[81] Already Cranmer and Nicholas Ridley, bishop of Rochester, had become converted to a Protestant view of the Eucharist. But Parliament eschewed radical theology; the final wording of the first Prayer Book reiterated the existing communion order. Nothing new resulted except that the Prayer Book was enforced by the First Act of Uniformity — it was printed as a schedule to the act and thus rested on parliamentary authority. However, it failed because it was ambiguous: neither Catholics nor Protestants accepted it, and its ambiguity stemmed from Somerset's fear of offending Charles V. Of course, the Protector's task was difficult: the disputation in Parliament exposed an unbridgeable gulf between traditionalists and the reformers. Eight bishops voted against the Prayer Book (six had opposed the Chantries Act and five communion in both kinds); since there were also conservative lords temporal, defeat was not impossible for the Council. When the Act of Uniformity was followed by legislation relaxing the prohibition of clerical marriage, eight bishops dissented.[82] Bonner had to be deprived of his bishopric and imprisoned in October 1549 for thwarting the Council. Yet Somerset had created his own obstacles: his religious policy was chaotic by 1549 because of his opposing stance on rites and doctrine.

Somerset's economic policy was his worst. Although population growth was the underlying cause of the price rise, currency debasements accelerated inflation and Sir Thomas Smith advised restoration of the coinage — the necessary solution. But recoinage was impossible if the Scottish garrisons were to be built; Somerset therefore refused to listen. He delegated policy-making to John Hales, who sponsored bills in the 1548–9 session of Parliament to maintain tillage, to punish regraters of foodstuffs, and to improve meat, milk, butter, and cheese supplies by making sheep farmers keep two cows and rear one calf for every 100 sheep they owned over 120. Hales also attacked purveyance (i.e. compulsory purchase by the Crown of food supplies at fixed prices). His bills failed, but a tax on sheep and woollen cloth was approved—the intention was to raise money for the Scottish war while discouraging sheep farming and thus enclosures.[83]

Hales also resumed Wolsey's work. Enclosure commissioners were appointed on 1 June 1548. Their task was to collect evidence, as under Wolsey. But the only commission to proceed was that for the Midlands—Hales himself was a member. The exercise failed; Hales claimed that the commissioners were frustrated by enclosing landlords who packed the juries with their servants. Somerset therefore intervened. On 11 April 1549 he proclaimed that landlords would be coerced. He shifted the emphasis to direct action: parts of the forfeited estates of the duke of Norfolk and Thomas Seymour were ploughed up, as was a park of the earl of Warwick. Commissioners were named for the Midlands, Cambridgeshire, Kent, Sussex, and the West Country, with instructions that forbidden enclosures 'should be reformed'. Yet this action was illegal; the sole authority was the previous year's commission for gathering information. So Somerset exceeded his powers.

In May revolts broke out in Somerset, Wiltshire, Hampshire, Kent, Sussex, and Essex, and the commissions helped to spark them. Hales's charge to the commissioners was that there was a conspiracy of landlords whose greed had obstructed enforcement of the enclosure legislation. People took the law into their own hands, tearing down hedges and filling ditches. Somerset threatened force against the rioters—but it was too late. Devon and Cornwall rebelled in June; Norfolk, Suffolk, Cambridgeshire, Hertfordshire, Northamptonshire, Bedfordshire, Buckinghamshire, Oxfordshire, and Yorkshire erupted in July; and there were disturbances in Leicestershire and Rutland during August. The nobility and gentry restored order in the south, the Midlands, Cambridgeshire, Essex, and Yorkshire. Troops meant for Scotland neutralized the rebels in Oxfordshire, Buckinghamshire, and Suffolk. The Western Rising and Kett's Norfolk rebels, however, required musters, Italian and German mercenaries, and set-piece battles. Expeditionary forces led by Lord Russell, Sir William Herbert, and Warwick restored order. But there was considerable slaughter: 2,500 westerners were slain; Kett lost 3,000 men.[84]

The 1549 revolts were the closest thing Tudor England saw to a class war. No single cause was responsible: agrarian, fiscal,

1. Henry VII by Michel Sittow, 1505.

2. Cardinal Wolsey (unknown artist).

3. Henry VIII in his early thirties (unknown artist).

4. Anne Boleyn (unknown artist)

5. Cartoon of Henry VII with Henry VIII, by Hans Holbein the Younger. For the left-hand section of the dynastic wall-painting in the privy chamber of Whitehall palace, 1537.

6. Thomas Cranmer by Gerlach Flicke, 1546.

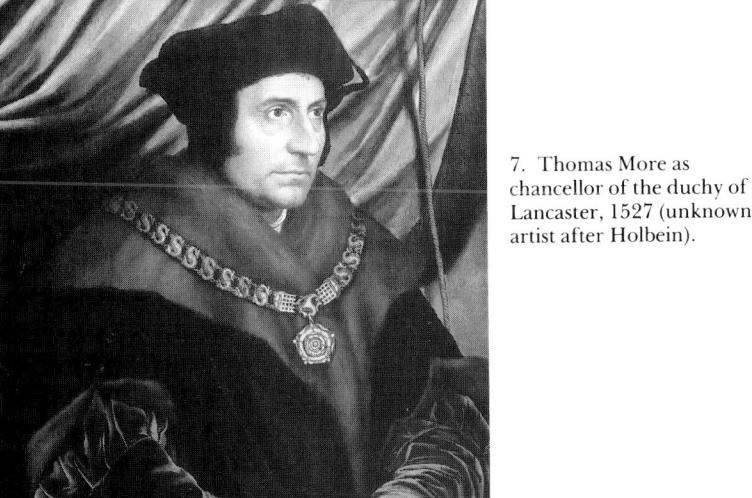

7. Thomas More as chancellor of the duchy of Lancaster, 1527 (unknown artist after Holbein).

8. Thomas Cromwell (unknown artist after Holbein). He was created earl of Essex in April 1540.

9. A sermon at St Paul's Cross, London, the 'official' government pulpit in the churchyard of St Paul's Cathedral. Although painted by John Gipkym in 1616 and depicting a sermon attended by James I and Anne of Denmark, the octagonal roofed pulpit and the cathedral retain their sixteenth-century appearance.

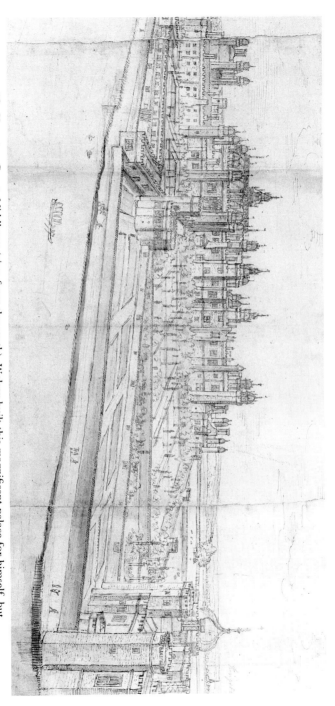

10. Hampton Court, Middlesex (view from the south). Wolsey built this magnificent palace for himself, but prudently presented it to Henry VIII in 1525. Drawing by Anthony Van Wyngaerde, c.1558.

11. The French attack on Portsmouth harbour which caused the loss of the *Mary Rose*, 19 July 1545 (detail from an eighteenth-century entraving of a Tudor wall-painting). Two masts of the sunken ship protrude above the water (right-hand side).

12. Edward VI and the pope: an allegory of the Reformation painted shortly after the Privy Council ordered the final destruction of images (February 1548). From his death-bed Henry VIII points to his successor, seated enthroned beneath a cloth of estate. To the right of Edward stands Protector Somerset. The first three figures around the table (facing front) from left to right are: John Dudley (duke of Northumberland), Archbishop Cranmer, and John Russell (earl of Bedford).

13. Edward Seymour, earl of Hertford and duke of Somerset (unknown artist).

14. Cardinal Pole (unknown artist).

15. Edward VI as Prince of Wales (unknown artist).

16. Lady Jane Grey, attributed to Master John, *c*.1545.

17. Philip II of Spain, *c*.1580 (unknown artist).

18. Queen Mary by Antonio Mor, 1554.

religious, and social grievances fused. It was a hot summer and
the crops failed; prices rose and the Protector compounded
the problem by fixing maximum prices at terrifyingly high
metropolitan levels. The Devon rebels condemned the sheep tax
which, if efficiently assessed, would have hit them hard; they
misunderstood the Prayer Book, thinking that children could
be baptized only on Sundays and that the Eucharist 'should not
differ from other common bread'; and they disputed that
confirmation should be delayed until children reached the age
of discretion. Both Devonians and Cornishmen disliked the
service in English; they claimed to prefer Latin or Cornish. Yet
Somerset knew they 'hath conceived a wonderful hate against
the gentlemen and taketh them all as their enemies'.[85] The
Cornishmen's slogan was: 'Kill the gentlemen and we will have
the Six Articles up again and ceremonies as they were in King
Henry VIII's time.'[86] After the Devon and Cornish rebels
united, they refused to treat with any gentleman accompanied
by his servants on the grounds that 'serving man trusts
gentleman'. Although this shows that the people were divided,
it confirms that the rebels distrusted the gentry. When the rebels
besieged Exeter, they lacked recognized gentry leadership. Also
their demand that half of the former monastic lands be restored
implies that persons who had acquired the land were not
involved. But the leaders came from just outside the governing
class: Arundell was a 'mere' gentleman; Underhill and Segar
were from yeoman backgrounds; and Maunder was a
tradesman.[87]

The East Anglian revolt was of the 'camping' variety: the
rebels did not march anywhere but 'camped' throughout Norfolk
and Suffolk — at Norwich, Ipswich, Bury St Edmunds, and
King's Lynn. Again their leaders were just outside the magisterial
orbit: Kett was a yeoman freeholder; Levet was a butcher; Brand
was a chamberlain of Ipswich; and Harbottle — a leader of the
1525 revolt against Wolsey's Amicable Grant — was a lesser
merchant and chamberlain. Although their articles emphasized
their antagonism to the governing class, they wanted 'alternative'
government not mob rule. They sought to exclude the gentry
and clergy from their world; to recapture an imaginary past in
which landlords paid certain rents and dues, kept their beasts
off the commons, made fishing rights freely available, etc. They

wanted feudal taxes restricted to the gentry; priests barred as
landowners or officers of the gentry; lords of manors prevented
from serving as bailiffs to other lords; and royal officials to avoid
other men's service. Violence was to be eschewed. When
Norwich was captured, private property was respected: 'justice'
and 'good governance' were Kett's slogans. His programme also
reflected the power vacuum created in East Anglia by the duke
of Norfolk's attainder: the Howards had been harsh landlords
who retained villeinage on their estates. By rejecting the Howard
yoke, Kett's rebels showed their sense of social grievance. Since,
however, they managed their affairs responsibly, it is well said:
'the frightening lesson of 1549' for the gentry was 'that those
outside the magisterial class could get on very well without them
until confronted with brute force'.[88]

Somerset mishandled the revolts. He vacillated in the spring
of 1549, not wishing to disrupt his Scottish campaign. He relied
on pardons and proclamations and was criticized by Paget,
Russell, and Smith for ignoring the Council's advice. In July
he ordered military reprisals without scruple and cancelled his
Scottish project, but the charge of procrastination levelled against
him turned into an accusation of unwarranted leniency, even
sympathy with the rebels. Soon it was falsely murmured that
the Protector had 'some greater enterprise in [his] head that
lean so much to the multitude'. The gentry were 'in jealousy
of my lord's friendship, yea, and to be plain, think my lord grace
rather to will the decay of the gentlemen than otherwise'.[89] The
gentry's extreme conception of rebellion quickly branded the
Protector a revolutionary. His overthrow became inevitable.

Paget drove the nails into Somerset's coffin. He reminded him:

Society in a realm doth consist and is maintained by mean of religion
and law. And these two or one wanting, farewell all just society,
farewell king, government, justice and all other virtue. . . . Look well
whether you have either law or religion at home and I fear you shall
find neither. The use of the old religion is forbidden by a law, and
the use of the new is not yet printed in the stomachs of the eleven of
twelve parts in the realm, what countenance so ever men make
outwardly to please them in whom they see this power resteth.

The cause of the revolts was 'your softness, your opinion to be
good to the poor. The opinion of such as saith to your grace:
''O Sir, there was never man that had the hearts of the poor

as you have!'' ' Such vanity turned the world upside down. The people 'is become a king, appointing conditions and laws to the governors, saying grant this and that, and we will go home'. Somerset's vacillation gave rebels both occasion and boldness to strike. He had thus betrayed the governing class: 'Take pity', Paget urged, 'of the king, of your wife and your children, and of the conservation and state of the realm.'

Paget then delivered the *coup de grâce*: 'And put no more so many irons in the fire at once as you have had within this twelvemonth — war with Scotland, with France . . . commissions out for that matter, new laws for this, proclamation for another, one in another's neck.' He would seek to resign if Somerset did not reform. And he discreetly threatened him:

Remember what you promised me in the gallery at Westminster before the breath was out of the body of the king that dead is. Remember what you promised immediately after, devising with me concerning the place which you now occupy . . . and that was to follow mine advice in all your proceedings more than any other man's. Which promise I wish your grace had kept.[90]

Whatever happened beside Henry VIII's deathbed, the consequences reverberated down the corridors of power.

REFORMATION
AND COUNTER-REFORMATION

THE earl of Warwick's *putsch* was Byzantine but unplanned. Begun in October 1549 when he conspired against the Protectorate, took possession of Edward's person, arrested Somerset, and captured the privy chamber with Cranmer's help, it did not end until February 1550 when he trumped his fellow-conspirators in favour of the Protestant Reformation. That Warwick denied Mary's claim to serve as regent once Somerset was overthrown also has significance. The *putsch* was itself threatened in December 1549 by plotters attempting to oust both Somerset *and* Warwick in favour of a return to Catholicism. This threat against his life may have persuaded Warwick that Mary should thereafter be excluded from the succession.

Warwick's principal allies were Wriothesley (earl of Southampton), the earl of Arundel, Sir Edward Peckham (Wriothesley's brother-in-law), and Sir Richard Southwell. Arundel, Peckham, and Southwell were Catholics who supported Mary's regency; Warwick and Wriothesley were *politiques* who opposed Somerset's autocracy. Warwick stood 'neither on the one side nor on the other' in religion; his *credo* was obedience to the supreme head's will.[1] He apparently accepted the idea of Mary's regency if she would support Somerset's overthrow — he was thus prepared to dissemble in religion until Edward's minority ended — but, when she refused to implicate herself, he turned to Cranmer, whose influence over Edward gave him power at Court.

Acting on orders from the Council, Cranmer and Paget banished Somerset's men: Stanhope, Smith, Thynne, Wolf, and Gray were sent to the Tower. When Edward expressed surprise, Cranmer did the talking. New attendants were placed in the privy chamber and the captain of the guard 'severed the Lord Protector from [Edward's] person and caused the Guard to watch him till the Lords coming'. Warwick and five other peers immediately took lodgings close to Edward 'to give order for the good government of his most royal person'.[2] The Protectorate was thereby dissolved (13 October); Somerset was incarcerated in the Tower.

Yet none of the conspirators could effect a claim to be governor of Edward's person: Somerset's removal began a Court battle which Warwick won with Cranmer's help—but not before Wriothesley and Arundel had invoked Mary's assistance against him. So Warwick backed Protestantism. He admitted Henry, marquis of Dorset (father of Lady Jane Grey), and Thomas Goodrich (bishop of Ely) to the Privy Council. He then allied with Paget, who took a peerage, and Cranmer, who assisted a godly cause. Wriothesley, however, proposed Somerset's execution and linked Warwick's fate to this. So Warwick had to reprieve Somerset, who signed thirty-one articles of submission but was not attainted. St John and Russell then joined Warwick in exchange for earldoms; Parliament ratified Somerset's submission (14 January 1550); and Warwick reorganized the Council. Wriothesley and Arundel were exiled from Court and Warwick was appointed lord president of the Council and great master of the king's household. When Somerset was released from the Tower, Warwick augmented the Council to strengthen his own faction. When he allowed Somerset back to Court, he surrounded the privy chamber with guardsmen.[3]

Since this was the fiercest struggle for power since the fifteenth century, it is necessary to ask why it did not provoke civil war. The answer is that Somerset alone pursued the fight outside the Court. He charged the mayor of London in Edward's name to send him a thousand armed men, but the order (leaked by Paget?) was countermanded by the Council. The threat of war evaporated, but not before one alert Londoner drew the parallel with the baronial coup of 1258.[4] By contrast Warwick, Wriothesley, and Arundel never attempted to raise forces. Warwick did not turn the army that defeated Kett's rebels against Somerset; Wriothesley and his clients had restored calm in Winchester and Hampshire when Catholic dissidents linked their cause to the Western Rising; the earl of Arundel—far from raising his tenantry for political ends—had sat in the great hall of Arundel Castle dispensing justice to the people.[5] Although the nobility were still the Crown's agents for the recruitment and organization of armies, centralization since 1485 had diminished the importance of the regions as centres of political power. Attainders, star chamber's enforcement function, and the reconstruction of provincial councils during the 1530s were weakening the territorial magnates: the Crown was acquiring the monopoly of violence. The 'new' nobility of Tudor England were courtiers or privy councillors. Also Renaissance theory of 'gentility' undermined medieval ideas of lordship and lineage. Under Henry VIII the Court became the arena of national politics, the source of patronage, and the social centre of the elite: political magnetism and conspicuous consumption concentrated power about the king. Yet the dangers of religious strife were stark during Edward's minority. In fact, new 'commotions' were expected in February 1550 which, if not on the scale of those of 1549, nevertheless demanded the united presence of the nobility and JPs in their counties. This Wriothesley knew. He could not bring himself to rebel and died in July 1550 amid rumours of suicide.

Having seized power, Warwick governed at first through the Privy Council. He accepted a blueprint, written by Paget, that re-established the Council's executive, administrative, and quasi-judicial functions: letters and state papers were to be signed by six or more members at the board; documents under Edward's signature were to be countersigned by six councillors. Warwick, however, presided over Council meetings and controlled the privy chamber. Sir Andrew Dudley (his brother), Sir John Gates (who again held the king's stamp as under Henry VIII), and Sir Thomas Darcy were his Court agents. Darcy and Gates were appointed privy councillors when they successively became captain of the guard with instructions to police the precincts of the Court and report comings and goings. John Cheke, Edward's tutor, spoke for Warwick to the king, as did Henry Sidney (royal cupbearer and Warwick's son-in-law). William Cecil became Warwick's man and was named a secretary of state and privy councillor in September 1550: he prepared agendas and letters for the Council but Warwick dictated their contents. Cecil served alongside Sir William Petre and together they educated Edward in the business of government, assisted by Cheke. Yet their methods were distinctive: they 'persuaded the boy of the wisdom of decisions already taken, as if they were recommendations the

King himself should propose'. Edward became 'an articulate puppet'; Warwick began to usurp the dynastic element in politics.[6]

Yet Somerset's re-admission to the Council provoked clashes and, inevitably, a plot. From the moment of his release he challenged Warwick's authority, undermining his ability to govern. Somerset twice met the earl of Arundel to discuss the chances of 'apprehending' Warwick. He admitted that he sought revenge and, if 'contemplation' was not treason, Warwick saw the danger — that, like Cromwell, he might be arrested and then attainted in Parliament.[7] He therefore cemented alliances and destroyed Somerset. On 11 October 1551 the marquis of Dorset was promoted duke of Suffolk; the earl of Wiltshire (St John) was elevated marquis of Winchester; and Sir William Herbert was made earl of Pembroke. Warwick also advanced himself duke of Northumberland. The strike, as so often, was presaged by theatre: Somerset was invited to an elaborate dinner, being seated below Northumberland and Suffolk at the opposite side of the table. Five days later he was arrested. Tried by his peers (1 December), he was acquitted of treason but found guilty of felony under the terms of an act (3 & 4 Edward VI, c. 5) steered through Parliament by Northumberland in response to Wriothesley's attempted counter-coup. He was beheaded on 22 January 1552.

Northumberland next purged the Council. Tunstall, the conservative bishop of Durham, was sent to the Tower; Paget was committed to the Fleet prison; and Rich felt obliged to resign the chancellorship in favour of Bishop Goodrich. Northumberland silenced Paget as the prelude to his personal rule: with Somerset dead, the 'dry stamp' in the hands of his agent Gates, and Edward in his confidence, the duke claimed it was 'some derogation to his Majesty's honour and royal authority' for the Council to countersign royal letters.[8] The procedure was therefore dropped; instead summaries of documents stamped were kept as witness to the stamp's application. Gates alone was authorized to seal warrants to the privy seal. Hence Northumberland obtained unhindered power to command in Edward's name: like Somerset he became quasi-king; the difference was that he managed the bureaucracy on the pretence that Edward had assumed full sovereignty whereas Somerset had asserted the right to near-sovereignty as Protector.

And military backing was provided. In February 1551 Northumberland created a new mounted guard of 850 cavalry — the 'gendarmes' — organized in twelve trained bands and paid for by the king. Since ten bands were captained by councillors loyal to himself, the duke took the first step towards the formation of a standing army in England that might be used to deter events other than invasions or rebellions. In fact, it is easy to see the special troops as Northumberland's palace guard.[9]

The duke's prime administrative task was to restore the Crown's finances. Opinion favoured retrenchment and reconstruction, therefore Sir Walter Mildmay (since 1547 one of the general surveyors in the court of augmentations) and Cecil, who acted as Northumberland's public and private secretary, were asked to find ways and means. Their fiscal aims were revenue enhancement, debt collection, stricter accounting, and the rebuilding of cash reserves; their structural goal was to replace, if possible, the autonomous revenue institutions of Henry VIII's last years — augmentations, exchequer, duchy of Lancaster, first fruits and tenths, and wards and liveries — with a single agency of finance corporately managed by the Privy Council. This single financial institution was likely to be an upgraded exchequer, as it was recognized that the 'chamber system' of Edward IV and Henry VII had collapsed and that the multiple separate revenue departments of Henry VIII had outlived their usefulness. Reorganization had in fact begun in 1545, when commissioners were first appointed to assess Crown income and revenue administration, culminating in the merger of general surveyors and augmentations to form the second court of augmentations (January 1547). Mildmay had been prominent in this work. He realized that integrated administration was needed to maximize the benefits of retrenchment; to reflect the shift from a financial system under the direct personal control of the monarch to one governed largely by the Privy Council; to encourage responsibility and accountability for the overall management of Crown finance instead of only for receipts and disbursements within separate departments; and to neutralize the role of the privy chamber by placing cash deposits under conciliar control.[10]

Northumberland summarized his financial policy in June 1551: regular income should match regular expenditure and the king's debts be liquidated. Insolvency had ruined Protector Somerset. Northumberland, therefore, raised revenue through selling Crown lands and confiscated lead, coining bullion melted down from church plate, seizing various episcopal lands, and securing taxation. Crown debts were collected and government expenses pruned: it is ironic that in October 1552 the duke had to sacrifice his gendarmes to save money — they might have excluded Mary from the throne. Borrowing was initially extended but — partly thanks to manipulation of the foreign exchanges by Sir Thomas Gresham — £132,372 in Flanders and £108,800 in England were repaid by 1553. Yet the greatest liability was the debased currency. Northumberland authorized recoinage in April 1551 upon Cecil's persuasion but, first, could not resist the profits of another debasement. £114,500 was netted before remedial action started the following October. Finally, regular audits were ordered to limit embezzlement. Peter Osborne became the link between the exchequer and Court: he was appointed clerk to the principal gentlemen of the privy chamber and lord treasurer's remembrancer in the exchequer. Between January 1552 and May 1553, £39,948 passed through his hands, spent under conciliar supervision upon 'special affairs' (i.e. fortifications, the repayment of loans, household expenses, etc.). Further lump sums were channelled through him to the treasurer of the chamber, who disbursed them in smaller amounts by warrant of the Council.[11]

Northumberland's deflationary policy was successful: the price of victuals was driven down. However, restoration of gold and silver coinage drained the treasuries of bullion. The Crown was bankrupt in the summer of 1552: certain payments were suspended for the dubious reason that, since Edward was on progress, he would not 'be troubled with payments until his return'.[12] No fewer than twenty financial commissions were named in 1552-3, the most important being that 'for the Survey and examination of the state of all his Majesty's Courts of Revenue' (23 March 1552). Nine members were appointed but, of those six who assembled, Mildmay was the only technical expert. They undertook their inquiry between May and September 1552, reporting to Edward and the Council on

10 December. Their working conclusions were in three parts: the first and longest provided an account of normal income and expenditure for the financial year ending at Michaelmas 1551; the second cited specific instances of abuses and corruption in each department; and the third proposed three methods of avoiding them, either through the reduction of excessive salaries and superfluous offices in the existing system, or through the amalgamation of the main revenue institutions into one or two streamlined bodies.

The report stated Crown income to be £271,912 and expenditure £235,398 per annum, but these figures were incomplete, misleading, and inaccurate. The commissioners investigated only the main revenue courts, the chamber, and Calais, and did so, chiefly, as an aspect of Northumberland's attack on Crown debtors. They ignored departments that dealt in 'extraordinary' revenue, for instance the mint, minor household offices, and independent casual treasurers; they ignored taxation, land sales, the navy, ordnance, and Ireland; and they took an optimistic view of Crown income. The reforming third part of their report, moreover, was not submitted to the Council. Written by Mildmay — or so it appears — this section was considered too radical for the incumbent lord treasurer, the marquis of Winchester. Conservative retrenchment not innovative reform was the overriding objective; Mildmay and Cecil were in a minority in 1552. Moreover, two months before the commissioners actually reported, a different scheme was being discussed to amalgamate augmentations and first fruits with the exchequer, while the duchy of Lancaster and court of wards and liveries remained independent institutions. Work began in the last Parliament of the reign (1–31 March 1553): an Act for the Dissolving, Uniting, or Annexing of Certain Courts authorized the necessary mergers. But the Council was unable to implement any changes before Edward's death. Since the statutory powers died with him, it was left to Mary's regime to accomplish this scheme.[13]

In fact, the success of Northumberland's retrenchment depended on ending Somerset's wars. Negotiations between England and France offered advantages to both sides: to the English the salvage of some prestige plus (inadequate) indemnity for Henry VIII's investment in Boulogne; for the French the freedom to unleash new war against the emperor. Final agreement was delayed by haggling over terms for the English evacuation of Scotland and the exact quantity of artillery to be left at Boulogne. However, the treaty of Boulogne (24 March 1550) was not entirely dictated by the French, who obtained the town for 400,000 crowns (£133,333)—more than Henry II wanted to pay. Northumberland's military commitments were thereafter limited to the defence of Calais, which itself cost £25,000 per annum to garrison above the rents of the town and wool customs. A year later the *rapprochement* culminated in a marriage alliance with France and a treaty with Scotland. Although Edward's proposed marriage to a daughter of Henry II never took place, the arrangement compensated for Mary Stuart's betrothal to the Dauphin Francis upon her removal to France in 1548.[14]

Why Northumberland promulgated undiluted Protestantism is an enigma: something perhaps motivated him beyond political advantage and obedience to Edward's will. The constraint of diplomacy was removed by the treaty of Boulogne, but this was a circumstance not a reason. In fact, the duke lacked theological learning and his comments during the real presence debate of 1548 revealed his distaste for fine distinctions. The mass, however, was not celebrated at his house after Henry VIII's death; he appointed the radical John Hooper to the see of Gloucester; and he permitted John Knox to preach at Court and offered him the bishopric of Rochester (October 1552). When Knox, who refused, questioned his faith, the duke grumbled to Cecil: 'I have for twenty years stand to one kind of religion.'[15] Although his meaning is opaque, no evidence exists that he was unspiritual. Trained as a soldier not a scholar, he may have been swayed by the zeal of Protestant activists.

But it is possible that public order considerations were relevant. Population had climbed, harvests were bad, prices high, and 'the sweat' killed thousands in 1551. Distress was immense; Protestants interpreted it as a providential scourge for delay of the Reformation (Catholics took the opposite view but were shouted down). As when harsh economic conditions had prevailed in the late thirteenth and early fourteenth centuries —likewise during the 1590s—the response of landowners was to take control of the poor by imposing strict moral codes.[16] The suppression of both promiscuity and alehouse keeping was common: brewing ale and selling it was the commonest resort of the poor in times of economic stress; all people needed was a bench and some ale. Parliament therefore enacted in 1552 that alehouses had to be licensed by JPs. Moreover, Somerset's visitation commissioners had suppressed folk rituals alongside Catholic ceremonies without any official instructions: church ales, 'Plough Monday' gatherings, maypoles, 'hocking', and 'hognels' (various methods of raising money for parish funds) were put down as 'superstition'. In other words, an alliance between the Protestant Reformation and the regulation of folk recreations in the name of public order was forged. In *A Discourse of Superstition*, dedicated to Henry VIII, Cheke's imagery of superstition was that of drunkenness, sexual lust, venereal disease, and witchcraft.[17] The link between 'godly discipline' and social control has often been overstated: it goes too far to suggest that Northumberland saw Protestantism as a weapon of government. Yet the association of ale, sex, and superstition is resonant. Whatever the religious sentiments of local magistrates, they began to realize that Protestantism posed no social threat provided it was legally enforced.

Religious reformers were constructive too. Welfare schemes distinct from the charitable functions of the church were discussed by St German in 1531, Cromwell and his coterie of advisers in 1535–6, then Northumberland and Cecil. Cromwell had attempted statutory price controls (they failed), and the parliamentary drafts of St German and William Marshall advocated special taxation to fund poor relief and public employment on the assumption that work should be provided by the state for those unemployed who could not find it. Parliament did not accept the idea of compulsory poor rates until 1572, but in 1536 civic officials and churchwardens were mandated to organize voluntary funds. Open begging was forbidden, while vagrants caught idle more than once were to suffer whipping and ear-cropping.[18]

A private attempt at a Vagrancy Act (1547) was a total failure: its harsh proposal that vagrants be bound as slaves for two years was impractical. In 1552, however, another step was taken towards poor relief: the bill introduced into the Lords was entitled 'for Taxes and Assessment for the relief of poor and impotent persons'. Given a mixed reception, it was replaced by legislation (5 & 6 Edward VI, c. 2) that authorized weekly parish collections with the stipulation that unwilling contributors should be 'induced' by the priest and, if he was unsuccessful, the bishop. Bishops Hooper and Coverdale were involved with the act, which was rushed through all its parliamentary stages at the end of the session. So it had Northumberland's support. At the same time Edward and the Privy Council co-operated with a group of London aldermen founding hospitals to ameliorate poverty and disease in the capital.[19]

Theology was nevertheless paramount, the Swiss and Rhineland exiles especially influential. Hitherto the English Reformation had exhibited many facets: Lollardy; criticism of the cults of saints and veneration of images; Erasmianism; justification by faith alone; and sacramentarianism. Various combinations were possible but Somerset's synthesis was doctrinally incoherent: the exiles remedied this by winning Edwardians to their view of Eucharistic theology and doctrine of divine grace, thereby establishing the central tenets of the Reformation as it was officially re-established by Elizabeth and Cecil in 1559.

The Swiss and Rhineland group of reformers included Zwingli, Hausschein, Bucer, Bullinger, and some who were born elsewhere: Peter Martyr (Italy), John Calvin (France), and later Theodore Beza (France). The theology of Bucer and Peter Martyr, who came to England, was in two parts: believers perceived Christ's presence in the Eucharist through faith; and salvation was a free gift of God to believers. But salvation in the Swiss–Rhineland scheme was predestinarian. God knew his 'elect', who progressed in an 'order of salvation' from predestination to vocation, justification, sanctification, and finally glorification. Many later Elizabethan divines were students during Edward's reign or in exile during Mary's. The doctrine of predestination became a pillar of English Protestant theology at this time.[20] Bucer was appointed regius professor of divinity at Cambridge where his impact was electric. His lectures were packed and two future archbishops of Canterbury became his protégés: Matthew Parker and Edmund Grindal. He wrote a critique of the First Book of Common Prayer before he died

(March 1551) that influenced the contents of the Second Book. Peter Martyr held the regius chair at Oxford, returning to Strasburg on Mary's accession.

During Northumberland's ascendancy the output of the printing presses remained high: many of the 113 titles that appeared on average each year were Protestant polemics.[21] When Parliament reassembled on 4 November 1549, three religious bills passed. They ordered the destruction of missals, antiphonaries, and other books superseded by the Book of Common Prayer, and the shattering of images removed from parish churches; authorized commissioners to revise canon law, resuming where attempts of 1534, 1536, and 1544 had failed; and approved a commission to reform ordinations. Six bishops and five lay peers opposed the bill on books and images; five bishops the commission on ordinations; and ten bishops (including Cranmer) the canon-law commission since it included laity.[22] Although privy councillors skilfully managed the Houses, no margin existed for complacency. Of the conservative bishops, Bonner had been deprived by Somerset, and Rugge resigned during the 1549–50 session. Gardiner was deprived in February 1551; Vesey resigned the following August; Heath and Day were deprived in October 1551; and Tunstall in October 1552. All were replaced by Protestants.

Events moved quickly during 1550. In March Cranmer's new *Ordinal* took the place of the old Catholic *Pontificale* and abolished the minor orders of sub-deacon, acolyte, etc. Bucer's treatise *On Lawful Ordination* guided him: priests were ordained 'to preach the Word of God and to minister the holy Sacraments'—a Protestant perspective.[23] Next, Nicholas Ridley, Bonner's successor as bishop of London, ordered altars to be taken out of churches in his diocese and communion tables installed. His reason was that 'a table shall more move the simple from the superstitious opinions of the popish mass, unto the right use of the Lord's Supper' (i.e. communion was not a Roman sacrifice but a memorial of Christ's passion).[24] This change had been enforced throughout Ridley's diocese and in other places too by the end of the year. When on 23 November the Council told the bishops that most altars had been taken down and that the remainder should be removed to avoid 'inconvenience', they were barely exaggerating.[25] Catholics began to go into exile abroad; some who stayed behind noted down the names of radicals demolishing altars and rood-lofts spared when images were eliminated — reprisals were exacted via the church courts during Mary's reign.[26] In East Anglia and Lancashire some clergy and JPs took fright at what was done: Catholicism was under attack while little or no effort was being made to substitute a new faith for the old. Bucer astutely observed that the English Reformation was too negative; it was imposed 'by means of ordinances which the majority obey very grudgingly, and by the removal of the instruments of the ancient superstition'.[27] Catholic resistance has been overstated: historians have relied too much on the records of the church courts and too little on churchwardens' accounts and wills.[28] Yet Bucer's point stands. Decatholicization and looting were not valid substitutes for missionary work. Anti-papalism became the norm and the Catholic attitude to saints was abrogated; secularization triumphed in the dissolution of the religious houses and chantries; the ancient rites were vilified. However, rural areas and small towns had little contact with reformed preaching: outside London, the south-east, and the universities there were few Protestant 'conversions'. Despite Cromwell's and Somerset's injunctions requiring children to be taught the rudiments of Scripture, Protestantism could not be spread by literate means alone because access to literature and schooling in the provinces was limited. Lastly, respect for the clergy diminished as the 'miracle' of the Eucharist was lost and the clergy were stripped of many of their lands.

Popular feeling may have been strongest where parish churches were concerned. Since English piety had been so materialistic, church goods formed a final source of spoil, as the Privy Council noted in 1547 when it required parish inventories to be made. In 1549 sheriffs and JPs were instructed to take fresh inventories and to prosecute persons who had embezzled goods. At last the Council decreed (3 March 1551) that church plate should be confiscated 'forasmuch as the King's Majesty had need presently of a mass of money'.[29] Nothing was done until April 1552, when commissioners were again appointed to check and inventory goods, but in January 1553 new commissioners were ordered to seize everything except linen, chalices, and bells. Plate, cash, and jewels were sent to London whilst vestments and base metals were sold locally and the proceeds forwarded. Although the commissioners were strict, Edward was dead before the trawl was completed.

More insidious attacks came via parochial amalgamations and 'exchanges' of episcopal lands. Somerset had allowed parishes to be united in York (1547), Lincolnshire, and Essex (1548-9). Northumberland suppressed the newly founded diocese of Westminster, sharing its lands between the Crown and the bishopric of London (March 1550). He also obtained legislation to partition the vacant see of Durham (March 1553).[30]

Yet Northumberland's major advance was the Second Act of Uniformity. New Eucharistic debates had preceded the deprivations of Bonner and Gardiner, while Bucerian debates at Cambridge were linked to the Court through a group of 'Athenians' — the party of Cheke and Sir Thomas Smith that rejected the corrupt pronunciation of Greek used by the sixteenth century in favour of the pronunciation of classical antiquity.[31] Cecil was an 'Athenian' and he took the lead in organizing London debates on the Eucharist in October and November 1551 at his home and that of Richard Moryson. Leading courtiers listened while Cheke, Cecil, Edmund Grindal, Robert Horne, and David Whitehead confuted transubstantiation and other disputants defended it.[32] The double significance of the London debates was that they paved the way for the Second Book of Common Prayer (1552) while this Book was itself promoted in 1559 by Elizabeth and Cecil. Also in 1559 Grindal was appointed bishop of London, Horne became bishop of Winchester, and Whitehead was rumoured to have had first refusal of Canterbury. All owed their positions to Cecil's patronage. So the foundations of the Elizabethan settlement were laid in Cecil's house under Northumberland: the plan of 1559, it can be argued, was that of 1551-2 dusted down.

Parliament sat from 23 January to 15 April 1552. Acts passed regulated holy days and fasts, legitimized the children of married clergy, and clarified their right to inherit property. Another Treason Act brought back the legislation that Somerset had repealed. However, the crucial statute was the Second Act of Uniformity.[33] This required 'every person' living in England, Wales, and Calais to attend church on Sundays; replaced the First Book of Common Prayer with the Second; and instructed the assize judges and JPs to enforce its use under penalty of life imprisonment for third-time offenders. The Prayer Book was opposed in the Lords by two bishops and three lay peers only, since traditionalists like Lord Morley declined to meet the Council head-on.[34] It was nevertheless radical. Rites and doctrine were reconciled in its terms: matins and evensong were retitled 'morning prayer' and 'evening prayer'; the Eucharist was named 'the Lord's Supper or Holy Communion'; and the 1549 phrase 'commonly called the Mass' was excised. The term 'offertory' was avoided, and 'table' and 'Lord's table' were substituted for 'altar'. Whereas the 1549 liturgy had closely resembled the Sarum rite of the Catholic mass in English translation, the 1552 service bore no relation to it. In particular, the communion 'sentences' were memorialist: Christ's presence was apprehended by believers but transubstantiation was overthrown. Vestments were abolished apart from the rochet and surplice; singing was discouraged except in the epistle, gospel, and Gloria. Finally, a rubric on kneeling—called the 'black rubric' because on Knox's recommendation it was overprinted after sheets of the book had been prepared—denied that kneeling at the communion implied adoration.[35]

The last Edwardian steps towards Reformation were taken when Cranmer drafted articles of faith and the canon-law commission—headed by Cranmer, Bishop Goodrich, Peter Martyr, and Dr Richard Cox—reported. Cranmer's draft of forty-five articles was submitted to Cheke and Cecil, who referred it to the Council. On 20 November 1552 the Council passed back suggested amendments, which led to a revised draft.[36] Cranmer returned forty-two articles with a request that they be authorized for subscription by the clergy. Since permission was not obtained before Edward's terminal illness, it was too late to impose them, but they formed the basis of the Elizabethan Thirty-nine Articles. By contrast, the projected reform of canon law was defeated in the Lords in 1553. It failed because peers who could barely tolerate the reform of rites and doctrine would not also accept the reformation of discipline. So the report remained in manuscript until 1571, when it was printed under the title *Reformatio legum ecclesiasticarum*—only to be laid aside again.[37]

Edward's health collapsed in the spring of 1553: his pulmonary tuberculosis was incurable—he was given nine months to live at the most. If, however, Northumberland had little choice but to usurp power, Edward himself wished to exclude his sister Princess Mary from the throne. The councillors who plotted against her therefore implemented the royal will. Various drafts of a 'Device for the Succession' were prepared to thwart the terms of Henry VIII's Third Act of Succession. Sir John Gates communicated them to Edward at Court and the boy wrote them out. He first projected the succession of a male Protestant from the Suffolk line—that is, the descendants of Henry VIII's younger sister Mary—but neither Frances, duchess of Suffolk, nor her three daughters had borne sons. So he named as his successor her eldest daughter, Jane Grey, who married Northumberland's eldest son in May 1553. On 21 June letters patent bastardized Princesses Mary and Elizabeth. Writs were then ordered to summon Parliament to give legislative force to the 'Device'. When Edward died on 6 July, however, Northumberland was unprepared. He waited three days before proclaiming Queen Jane, during which time Mary fled to Kenninghall in Norfolk. She mustered forces at Framlingham Castle and marched south to a groundswell of popular support. For several reasons the people flocked to her: they respected her legitimism; they hated Northumberland for his treatment of Kett's 'camps'; and they took revenge on the gentry for their role in the events of 1549. Religious motivation was absent at this stage: Catholic reaction was not on the agenda until Mary arrived at London. If anything, her East Anglian followers believed that she would maintain the religion of Edward VI. Of course, Mary most needed gentry leadership but she obtained this too. The conservative gentry rallied to her at Kenninghall; then they persuaded uncommitted and Protestant gentry that she was a serious contender for the throne. Northumberland marched north with Gates and the guard, but changed sides when he reached Cambridge on 20 July. By the time Mary entered London on 3 August, the duke and his associates were in the Tower.[38]

Despite the efforts of modern historiography to boost her reputation, Mary I will never appear creative. This has little to do with her campaign of persecution: in a European context her 'inquisition' was small scale; we must beware of the bias of John Foxe and other Protestants writing in Elizabeth's reign who prefer us to believe that Mary did nothing but persecute. It has more to do with her financial and governmental 'reforms', which, although recently thought to have 'revitalized' exchequer and common law in innovative style, were in fact inspired by near-ideological conservatism. Even her reunion with Rome, it can be argued, lacked the fire of true Counter-Reformation. Although the Council of Trent (1545–63) had so far produced only draft decrees that were not binding, the spirit of papal counter-attack was alien to Marian church leaders, who eschewed excitement of the sort the Edwardian Protestants had provided. Compared to Tridentine rigour, this peaceable approach is more attractive to historians, but it lacked the necessary missionary zeal at the time. Unlike the Jesuit colleges on the Continent, Mary's church forgot that it was fighting a battle for personal convictions.

In fact, the atmosphere of Mary's reign owed something to her character. By the summer of 1553 she was thirty-seven; tested and toughened by her experiences, pious, yet amiable and generous, she was politically self-deceived. Her piety and unmarried state gave her the intensity of a nun. Early betrothals were diplomatic pledges, not serious intentions of matrimony; later she had been bastardized, which had slimmed her prospects of marriage. She had contemplated taking the veil during the 1530s; remote not from politics but from the art of the possible, she had a highly developed sense of her royal standing but lacked the resources to take a firm line. She therefore seemed limited, conventional, and stubborn. Seeking a husband to manage affairs of state, she took the advice of her cousin, Charles V, to marry his sole heir Philip without critical review of the political costs at home. Like Cardinal Pole, she saw the future in terms of the past. This underpinned both her Spanish marriage and the persecution of heresy, as well as the attempt to restore Catholicism. A more experienced politician would have paid attention to the anti-papal and anti-Spanish xenophobia that Henry VIII's propaganda had made part of England's culture, and to the aspirations of youth. Although the reconciliation with Rome was accomplished, the secular interests of the ruling élite dictated the terms. Then Philip II's quarrel with the pope sabotaged Pole's position. When his legatine commission was revoked and his jurisdiction fell into abeyance, full 'restoration' of Catholicism became impossible: the English church temporarily reverted into two decentralized backwaters of Paul IV's hostile Rome. Mary's involvement in the French war, the loss of Calais, and demographic calamity then fuelled impressions that her reign was 'ill starred' — this bolstered Protestant rather than Catholic polemic. Finally, the queen's health was poor. She suffered from anxiety, depression, and neuralgia; her phantom pregnancies, which the courts of Europe ridiculed, may be explained as symptoms of severe physical and emotional stress in the face of crucial political decisions.[39]

At Court Mary was the first Tudor to surround herself with devotees in preference to experienced advisers. A woman ruler required female attendants, but Mary named to the privy chamber her existing servants. All six ladies and thirteen gentlewomen belonged to her former affinity, a recipe for insularity, if not friction. Only in one respect was factionalism diminished, since, despite commissioning a 'dry stamp', Mary does not appear to have used it, signing state papers with her own hand until the day of her death.

Yet all Mary's intimates urged the Spanish marriage except the marchioness of Exeter, mother of Edward Courtenay, Philip's rival for the queen's hand — she was evicted from her lodgings at Court. The male courtiers were also Mary's devotees; all of Edward VI's principal officers except Sir Thomas Cheyney were ousted. The earl of Arundel became great master of the household and lord steward; the earl of Oxford became lord great chamberlain; Robert Rochester was named comptroller of the household; Edward Waldegrave was appointed keeper of the wardrobe; Sir Henry Jerningham replaced Gates as vice-chamberlain and captain of the guard. In effect, Court offices were monopolized by Mary's Kenninghall faction and those who joined her *en route* for Framlingham and London. The Kenninghall loyalists comprised her first Privy Council, which was her 'council of war'. Quickly displaced from administration by those Edwardian privy councillors — the 'men of business' — who abandoned Northumberland and declared for Queen Mary as she approached London, the Kenninghall–Framlingham group nevertheless retained ascendancy at Court, where Mary was distanced from public opinion unless she attended the Privy Council, which she did infrequently. So, while she attempted to build a 'consensus' government from which radical Protestants and Northumberland's close adherents alone were excluded, her Court was dominated by a reactionary caucus reinforced by omnipresent imperial envoys.

In fact, leaving aside the strategic Habsburg role in securing Pole's dispensation to ex-religious property owners, Mary had to dictate to her Privy Council the three major policies of her reign: her marriage, the reunion with Rome, and the declaration of war with France. Her weakness lay in the making of decisions, not their implementation. Yet positions conventionally attributed to Mary's 'obstinacy' may, in fact, have been fomented at Court. Since no adequate study of the Marian Court yet exists, the matter remains elusive.[40]

Mary appointed fifty privy councillors during her reign, thirty during July 1553 before she entered London. Her Kenninghall 'council' comprised eighteen members; twelve men were sworn on the road to London; another twelve were sworn in August 1553; three more by January 1554; and five thereafter. Seventeen had numbered among Henry VIII's or Edward VI's privy councillors: prominent were Paget (lord privy seal), Gardiner (released from the Tower, promoted lord chancellor), the marquis of Winchester (lord treasurer), the earls of Shrewsbury and Pembroke, Sir John Gage, Sir Thomas Cheyney, and Sir John Baker. The veteran duke of Norfolk and Tunstall were rehabilitated — neither was a political asset but Mary's sense of justice prevailed. By contrast, Northumberland and his fellow-conspirators were put on trial. The duke and Gates went to the block; Guildford Dudley, Jane Grey, and her father followed after Wyatt's rebellion. Cranmer was attainted but Mary believed heresy to be the main charge against him — he was burned in 1556. Lastly, Cecil, who enjoyed Paget's protection, was briefly imprisoned, while Darcy was placed under house arrest.

Paget quickly organized the Privy Council on late-Henrician lines. The large board was reduced to its core of working councillors. In any case, Mary's devotees were no match for Gardiner, Winchester, Paget, and Sir William Petre. Only nineteen councillors attended over 20 per cent of the meetings during their term of office. Thirteen attended over 40 per cent, eight over 50 per cent, and only four took part in over 60 per cent of them. An average attendance at meetings in 1555 was twelve. Attendances in the court of star chamber were slightly higher: in 1557–8 the bench numbered twenty-two or so persons—between sixteen and eighteen privy councillors plus four or so expert judges.[41]

Of Mary's nineteen working councillors, twelve joined her government on or after 20 July 1553, when Northumberland's cause collapsed. And eight of the twelve had previously been privy councillors. So there was striking continuity; the experience of the eight 'was bound to influence the conduct of the queen's business'.[42] In fact, Norfolk, Gardiner, and Gage had more in common with Winchester, Arundel, Pembroke, Paget, and Petre than has usually been thought. At worst traditionalists (Norfolk, Gardiner, Arundel, Gage) were bedded down with *politiques*, but this is to say no more than that the lines of the 1540s were redrawn. There were, however, differences between Paget and Gardiner: the latter's clericalism was obnoxious to his colleagues, while Paget articulated the standpoint of peers who had purchased ex-religious property. In this respect, Gardiner's views were closer to Mary's but it was an uphill struggle to turn them into policy.

Yet the dynamic 'conflict' of Mary's reign remained that between her councillors and courtiers as groups. The 'men of business' in her Privy Council believed that they collectively were the ones who should decide policy; this marked a change. Policy since Wolsey's fall had emerged from Privy Council and Court in combination. Factionalism, where it existed, had bisected both institutions, since competing politicians held offices in both. The potential for conflict within Mary's regime must not be exaggerated. Yet, whereas the recent tendency had been for the institutions of Court and state to merge towards national government, the character of Mary's rule was dynastic. Had she possessed the resources to create a Counter-Reformation nobility to bolster her territorial power, then dynastic ambitions might have sufficed. As things stood, whether her strict Catholicism was compatible with the secular priorities of the existing purchasers of the ex-religious property was itself an open question.

Its debates upon Mary's marriage are not evidence of a fundamental split in the Privy Council. Courtenay's candidature was advocated by all her working councillors apart from Paget, who saw the potential of the situation and made Philip's claim his own. His motive was to outflank Gardiner by becoming Philip's chief minister in England. Hence Gardiner was temporarily wrong-footed. He found himself in opposition to Mary, who never contemplated marrying Courtenay, even before his ambition and dissolute behaviour became objectionable. When this fact became known, the working councillors swung round; Arundel and Pembroke were first to respond. Yet their initial reaction was correct. Philip sought the marriage to accomplish the smooth transition of Hispano-Burgundian power from his father to himself. A widower with one son, he had ruled Spain as regent since 1551 and hoped soon to acquire the Netherlands and northern Italy. He therefore wished to resurrect the Anglo-Burgundian–Spanish alliance epitomized by Catherine of Aragon. But he intended neither to govern England nor to deal much with domestic issues beyond the preparedness of the navy and defence of the borders. And Elizabeth continued heir to the throne under the marriage treaties. Philip's rights ended if Mary died childless, so he lacked incentive to take a long-term view.[43]

Popular opposition to Philip sprang from anti-papal xenophobia linked, via English commercial connections, to German and Flemish fears of 'Spanish tyranny'. The marriage was ill-regarded in Spain too, but Mary was adamant; the draft treaties were approved on 7 December 1553. They favoured English interests, since, while Philip was titled king during Mary's lifetime, he was not to drag England into the Franco-Habsburg war, appoint aliens to English offices, exercise independent rights of patronage, nor take Mary or their children abroad without consent. In fact, Philip saw these terms as so insulting that he repudiated them in a secret declaration; and he was never crowned, since his opponents linked that question to fears of involvement in the war. The treaties were ratified by Parliament in April 1554 and the marriage celebrated on 25 July—but not before it had precipitated revolt.

A rebellion was planned in November 1553 by former adherents of Somerset and Northumberland. Four concerted risings were timed for the following March: one in Devon to be led either by Courtenay or Sir Peter Carew; one in Leicestershire led by the duke of Suffolk; one in Kent led by Sir Thomas Wyatt; and one on the Welsh borders led by Sir James Croft. But when news of the plan leaked in January, the rebels were forced into premature action. Only Kent succeeded in putting a force into the field: Wyatt, a military expert who had proposed to Somerset the idea of a standing army prepared against 'all sudden attempts, either at home or abroad', raised three thousand men. London wavered but, partly through Mary's resolve, partly because of his own delays, and partly because the citizens feared a sack, Wyatt failed. The revolt collapsed after Wyatt found Ludgate shut against him (7 February). Some forty of his men were killed and ninety executed, including nearly twenty of the gentry leaders. Yet 480 persons had been convicted — 350 from Kent, 76 from London, 37 from Southwark, and 17 from elsewhere. Also 285 rebels were pardoned before conviction. At first Mary had looked set to exact reprisals, but she then switched to a policy of leniency. She did not allow so many opponents to escape later when the heresy laws were re-enacted, but she believed that criticism of her marriage was exaggerated — a misapprehension. When Wyatt was executed on 11 April, the people dipped their handkerchiefs in his blood, regarding him as something of a martyr.[44]

Wyatt's rebellion endangered Elizabeth, whom Mary mistrusted. Although Wyatt claimed he sought 'no harm to the Queen, but better counsel and Councillors' (an allusion to her Court intimates?), had the revolt succeeded the beneficiary would have been Elizabeth.[45] So Paget's proposal that she be married to Courtenay and recognized as heir in default of Mary's issue was instantly vetoed. Gardiner, who recovered lost ground by attributing a religious motive to the rebels, then engineered Elizabeth's arrest (9 February). But the evidence of her complicity was circumstantial, and she survived. In fact, Gardiner's hands were tied by his wish to save Courtenay, who was plainly implicated. So Paget continued to protect Elizabeth. He also thwarted Gardiner several times in Parliament during April 1554, for which Mary rusticated him to his estates, but he was too valuable to be kept long away from the Council board.

Mary's reconciliation with Rome was, meanwhile, stymied. Only when his son's marriage was celebrated would Charles V allow Julius III's legate, Reginald Pole, to cross to England, despite Mary's belief that submission to the Holy See was her first and unavoidable duty. Even then Spain wanted the pope to amend Pole's brief. Although Philip, after his arrival on 20 July 1554, gave reconciliation top priority to enhance his honour, he distrusted Pole's discretion. The key issue was the status of the ex-religious property: until that was resolved, Pole languished in the Low Countries and Mary's religious policy marked time.

The Edwardian legislation could nevertheless be dismantled, Catholic bishops restored, Protestant exiles who had settled in London and Glastonbury expelled, and Protestant preachers arrested. It is perhaps too bold to say that Mary cheated by concealing the extent of her Catholicism until she was enthroned at Westminster; her initial tolerance rested on her innocent assumption that coercion would be unnecessary—that, when the 'heretics' were exposed to the liberated forces of truth, they would reconvert to Rome. When, however, Cranmer threw down the gauntlet by offering to defend in disputation the orthodoxy of Edwardian doctrine, Mary attacked. With the exception of Gardiner, the Privy Council was alarmed to discover her attitude; her allies were Rochester, Waldegrave, and others at Court. Yet she had to use Parliament and royal supremacy as weapons, to her distaste. Although the judges ruled that her supremacy was only an 'addition' to her royal style, she nevertheless could not divest herself of 'schismatic' powers she regarded as void without using Parliament. This itself strengthened Parliament in the long term. By accepting statutory repeals in her Parliaments, Mary admitted the validity in law of the former Acts of Appeals, Supremacy, and Uniformity, while her repeals themselves necessitated Elizabeth's use of Parliament in 1559 to repeat the break with Rome. This process achieved Cromwell's posthumous victory over Henry VIII's 'imperial' view of his supremacy: the religious settlement was placed on a statutory footing—Henry's assumption that Parliament had not 'made' his supremacy but simply 'declared' divine truth became implausible.

Mary's first Parliament (5 October to 6 December 1553) repealed Northumberland's treason law and cut back definitions of treason to those prevailing during the fifteenth century, while new felonies and crimes of *praemunire* introduced since Henry VII's death were abolished. In fact, Mary was forced to bring back treason by words in January 1555 when the law was extended to cover Philip, but at first the clock was turned back. Next, the Edwardian Reformation statutes were repealed: the Acts of Uniformity, the acts permitting clerical marriage and proscribing images and missals, the act enabling the monarch to appoint bishops, that approving communion in both kinds, and that altering the forms of consecration and ordination. Instead the rites and ceremonies of Henry VIII's last year were to be used. Yet opposition was voiced in the Commons to the treasons bill, which some MPs thought was intended to restore papal authority; this raised the question of the future of the ex-religious property. The Commons' voting figures for repealing the Reformation legislation — roughly 270 to 80 — and the length of debate — five days — indicate stiff resistance. The repeal act had an immediate impact: in the dioceses of London and Norwich over a quarter of parochial incumbents were deprived for taking wives; in the north, where fewer clergy had married, the figure was nearer 10 per cent. Unbeneficed clergy were purged too. Counter-Reformation polemicists from Thomas More onwards linked 'heresy' with sexual misconduct, though Protestants were baffled as to why the canon law punished clerical marriage more severely than fornication. Since parishes still needed clergy, the bishops had to readmit many incumbents after they had performed penance. However, many clergy later reappeared before consistory courts for 'frequenting' the women they had married.[46]

Although Mary abandoned the title of supreme head at the end of 1553, it was not until November 1554 that Pole landed in England and absolved the realm from sin. Under Habsburg pressure, Julius instructed a reluctant Pole to give a general dispensation to the owners of the ex-religious property, whereupon Charles V allowed the legate to leave Brussels. Addressing Parliament, Pole said: 'My commission is not to pull down but to build; to reconcile, not to censure; to invite but without compulsion.' Yet his approach was visionary. Pole would restore discipline and worship by re-creating a harmonious unity. The church militant was unknown to this eirenic theologian, who urged doctrinal *rapprochement*, had been associated with the reforming Oratory of Divine Love, and got into serious difficulties over the doctrine of justification by faith. Few understood him, for he was unwilling to be known. Born in Worcestershire of Plantagenet blood, he studied at Oxford and Padua, and in Italy underwent the conversion that led him to play an important role in the Catholic reform movement. He fled from England in 1532, enraged Henry VIII by attacking his first divorce in print, and was the target of several assassination attempts ordered by the king and organized by Cromwell. He was appointed a cardinal by the pope, and later named one of three legates commissioned to open the Council of Trent. In a conclave after Paul III's death he missed election to the papacy by only one vote (December 1549). Typically he had declined to lobby, for he was self-conscious of his nobility, was patronizing to those of inferior social status, and was no diplomat. By 1554 he was a spent force, not least because his views on justification were rejected at Trent, where he was even suspected of heresy. Also his approach to reconciliation was too personal: he sought to be an 'indulgent loving father', who relieved people of choices he thought they could not make for themselves. Since 'peace' was his objective, he was unprepared for heresy on the Marian scale. Dubbing himself the 'Pole Star', he thought his mere presence could guide lost souls. Yet in this he deluded both Mary and himself.[47]

The third Parliament of the reign (12 November 1554 to 16 January 1555) reversed the break with Rome, re-enacted the heresy laws of Richard II, Henry IV, and Henry V, and nullified the attainders of Pole, William Peto, and other Catholic exiles. Consent was purchased by the incorporation of Pole's dispensation to landowners within the act repealing the Henrician settlement (1 & 2 Philip and Mary, c. 8), which also insisted that titles to secularized church lands were valid, and that disputes concerning them were triable by common law. But attempts were made by the Marian bishops to recover their lost property. Also Pole refused to concede the validity of the new owners' titles: his dispensation was a 'charitable permission' from the pope that did not *in principle* permit Parliament to transfer church property to the Crown and laity. In 1557 Pole preached a sermon in which he argued that, although the church had behaved as an indulgent

mother who allows her child to keep an apple even though it
will make him ill to eat it, God the father would take a much
sterner line. So the spectre of possible reconfiscation stalked
Parliament. The common lawyers were adamant that the ex-
religious lands were under the sole jurisdiction of English law,
and Philip overruled Mary in their favour to secure a pragmatic
outcome that gave the credit to Habsburg tact. Yet the matter
was not finally settled. No English statute could be made binding
on the pope or his successors — that was a matter of papal
conscience. So, when Julius III died in March 1555, the fate
of the church lands crept back on the agenda. Of course, the
Catholic bishops based their claims to recovery on conscience,
not common law. Once the royal supremacy was repealed, there
was nothing to stop them — this issue returned with a vengeance
in 1559.

As legate Pole concentrated on behaviour rather than belief.
He saw people not as individuals but as a multitude: discipline
came before preaching — obedience to Rome, to the priesthood
and canon law, to the habit of the mass. His legatine synod
during the winter of 1555–6 should have been a blueprint for
Catholic regeneration: since Mary appointed him archbishop
of Canterbury when the synod met, he had the advantage over
Wolsey in 1519. However, the synod dealt with obedience to
Rome, the restoration of respect for canon and papal law, the
revival of Catholic ceremonies, non-residence of bishops, and
preaching — in that order. Pole rejected offers of help from Loyola
and the Jesuits. He also insisted on collecting definitive
information — on parochial impropriations, non-residence,
pluralism, etc. — before taking any action. This testified to his
seriousness, but wasted time. He took charge of church finances,
but resources were insufficient even though the queen renounced
her right to first fruits and tenths, and remitted outstanding
arrears of taxation. Mary restored important episcopal estates,
returned Crown advowsons to the bishops for the benefit of the
parishes, and refounded religious houses at Westminster,
Greenwich, Sheen, and elsewhere. The Order of St John of
Jerusalem was re-established together with some colleges, chapels,
hospitals, guilds, and 'lights'. Yet with very few exceptions the
laity were deaf to her example. This was damaging, since
improving clerical standards depended on raising resources.[48]

Although Pole revived the whole gamut of Catholic
sacramental ritual, he fostered the attitude he had advocated in
Italy — that ceremonies were chiefly an aid to worship not an
end in themselves. Nevertheless, the emphasis was on order:
metropolitan, episcopal, and archidiaconal visitations and royal
commissions enforced the ancient rites. Altars and rood-lofts
were rebuilt, images returned, vestments and copes worn, the
utensils and ornaments of the mass restored, and the necessary
missals, antiphonaries, breviaries, etc. obtained. Equipment
was variously brought out of hiding, recovered from expropri-
ators, salvaged, or repurchased. But expenditure was kept to
a minimum. If old rood-lofts could not be reused, cheap
replacements were ordered. A wooden crucifix appeared at first
in many parishes, to be replaced with a silver or gilded one later.
Restoration of images was also slow and was sometimes greeted
with contempt, though the usual cause was impiety rather than
Protestantism.

But Marian Catholicism was incomplete. Although the
liturgical rites returned and religious art and drama enjoyed a
partial renaissance, the cults of saints, pilgrimages, and belief
in purgatory were casualties of Henry VIII's and Edward's
propaganda. Few shrines and relics reappeared, while miracles
aroused scepticism. The oral tradition that Catholics held to
be equivalent to Scripture had largely evaporated, and the
dissolution of the chantries made Catholic re-education difficult
at a popular level. A minority of guilds and fraternities were
re-established but without obvious intercessory functions. Lastly,
the size of church attendances is doubtful. Congregations declined
when the Edwardian Prayer Books were introduced, but it is
unclear that they recovered under Mary. So, even if she had
lived longer, the religion of her realm would have been neither
that of Wolsey's church nor that of the Counter-Reformation.[49]

Pole also found 'peace' an inadequate platform. Protestant
activists craved war; Latimer had quipped, 'Where there is
quietness, there is not the truth.' Although Marian Protestantism
was largely unorganized, underground groups met in London,
Essex, Kent, Sussex, Hertfordshire, and Suffolk. Bristol radicals
stood their ground in the church courts, while the mayor and
aldermen resisted Catholicism until ordered by the Privy Council
to conform. So Pole had to use force. Only two extremists had

been burned during Edward VI's reign: George van Parris, a Flemish surgeon who denied Christ's divinity, and Joan Bocher, an ex-Lollard turned anabaptist. A minimum of 287 people were, however, burned between February 1555 and November 1558, while others died in prison. Some 85 per cent of burnings took place in London, the south-east, and East Anglia; there was only one execution in the north, five in the south-west, and three in Wales. Protestant preachers were first silenced, then put on trial for heresy: the fortitude with which Hooper, Latimer, Ridley, Cranmer, John Rogers, John Bradford, and others met their deaths was a propaganda victory that helped Protestantism prove its credentials. Many martyrs, too, were young. Three-quarters of those whose ages can be discovered had reached the age of spiritual discretion—fourteen years—after the break with Rome, therefore they were not strictly apostate since, if they had not known Catholicism, they could not have renounced it. Their stand vindicated the Protestant cause in the eyes of believers. John Foxe quoted the Bible: 'Out of the mouth of babes and sucklings hast thou ordained strength because of thine enemies'! And the martyrs had local supporters; sometimes three hundred gathered at Smithfield. In January 1556 the Privy Council first forbade householders to allow servants and apprentices out when burnings were planned, then barred all 'young folk' from attending.[50]

Socially the majority of martyrs were wage-labourers, though clergy formed a significant minority. Protestants who were gentry or merchants, by contrast, sought refuge abroad, along with clergy and theological students, while some yeomen and husbandmen moved within the realm. Beginning in January 1554, about eight hundred persons fled to Switzerland, Germany, Italy, and France. They proved an embarrassment as well as a threat to the regime, for, apart from plots hatched in France and Venice, the exile community printed effective propaganda—ninety-eight titles have been identified. Although the penalty for possession of any heretical or treasonable book became death by martial law, the Crown was unable to suppress these tracts. Furthermore, a handful of exiles embraced resistance theory: John Ponet's *Short Treatise of Politic Power* (1556), Christopher Goodman's *How Superior Powers ought to be Obeyed* (1558), and John Knox's *First Blast of the Trumpet* (1558) ventilated arguments not heard again in England until the 1640s. Catholic propaganda therefore appeared in reply—sixty-four titles between January 1554 and November 1558. As in Edward VI's reign, few vernacular works were officially commissioned, but, since Philip cared about his European standing, some continental printers enjoyed Habsburg and Tudor sponsorship. Otherwise, the government believed that printing could do little to further its cause at home—the exception was Bishop Bonner, who imitated Cromwell's patronage of printed aids to preaching and catechizing. Historians have said that Mary's regime failed to understand the importance of printing, but press activity inevitably declined during her reign because many foreign Protestant printers resident under Edward VI returned home— the number of London stationers dropped from eighty to forty-one.[51]

Mary's pregnancy, rumoured for over a year, was disproved by late 1555. But the greatest irony of her reign is that her interests as queen of England were sacrificed to those of her husband and the papacy when events in Europe required it. In quick succession negotiations between France and the empire collapsed; Mary's failure to produce an heir cost Philip his ace; then a diplomatic *renversement* occurred at Rome. Although Marcellus II was elected Julius III's successor, he shortly became ill and died (1 May 1555), whereupon Philip's opponent Gian Pietro Carafa was elected Paul IV. Again a papal candidate, Pole lacked Philip's support and failed by two votes. When European diplomacy then veered towards France, Philip left England for Brussels (29 August). There he decided to abandon his claim to the imperial succession, and Charles V acknowledged his failure in Germany by accepting the religious peace of Augsburg. Then over a period of six months, starting in October, Charles abdicated his sovereignty over Spain, the Netherlands, and his lands in the New World and Italy to his son. Although Mary daily awaited her husband's return, England was a remote square on Philip's chessboard. Moreover, after the duke of Alva invaded the papal states in September 1556, Paul IV had his own battles to fight. He therefore revoked Pole's legatine commission (9 April 1557). True, Pole remained archbishop of Canterbury, but the loss of his legatine jurisdiction was a catastrophe: his national authority collapsed, and his London synod lost its vital second session in which the information accumulated during the previous two years was to be presented and plans finalized for seminaries in cathedral churches to educate future priests, for a Catholic translation of the Bible, and for a vernacular prayer book to counter accusations that Marian Catholicism was 'foreign'.[52]

Lastly, Pole was reported to the papal Inquisition as a suspected Lutheran and formally recalled to Rome. When, however, a nuncio reached Calais in July 1557 with letters naming the octogenarian Peto in Pole's place, Mary denied him entry to the realm. Although conceding that, if Pole were guilty of heresy, she would condemn him, she demanded that as an Englishman he be tried in England. This created a breach in Anglo-papal relations that outlasted Philip's quarrel with Paul IV. So Mary and the papacy were in dispute! The pope refused to sign documents relating to England. By January 1559 Elizabeth had nine sees either vacant or held by unconsecrated nominees, Canterbury among them, since Pole died within hours of Mary (17 November 1558).[53]

In government too Mary's achievements were equivocal. Northumberland's policy of retrenchment was continued: an inherited debt of £185,000 swelled to £300,000 owing to involvement in the French war, but this increase was modest. Crown lands (including Irish estates) worth £5,000 per annum were sold in 1554; £8,000 accrued from sales in 1557–8; and Mary's munificence to the church sliced £29,000 from her annual income. Also her decision to remit the unpaid portion of the subsidy granted by Edward VI's last Parliament cost £50,000. Although attainders yielded lands worth £20,000 per annum and at least £18,000 in cash and plate, lands worth £9,835 per annum were restored to the Howards, Courtenays, Nevilles, and Percies, while additional grants and annuities cost £14,750 annually. For instance, Pole received a personal estate for his lifetime valued at £1,252 per annum. Expenditure at Court rose steeply at first but was then curtailed; regular revenues in the exchequer were overspent in 1553–4 but remained in modest surplus in 1554–5 and 1556–7; defence spending was pruned and the costs of fortifications appraised. Yet government could no longer function adequately without new sources of revenue or periodic resort to taxation to meet the costs of normal administration.[54]

Taxation in 1555 and 1558 raised £349,000. In addition, two fifteenths and tenths granted in March 1553 and not remitted by Mary yielded £59,000. Government attempts to vary the rates of taxation and provide realistic valuations of taxpayers' wealth were resisted. Forced loans in 1556 and 1557 were unpopular too, but they grossed £42,100 and £109,269 respectively. And the 1555 subsidy act was another step towards regular peacetime taxation. Whereas the acts of 1540, 1543, and 1553 had claimed that defence was submerged within royal government, the 1555 act first praised 'the great and sundry benefits' of Tudor rule, then acknowledged 'the great debts wherewith the Imperial Crown of this realm was charged' and 'the great intolerable charges wherewith her Majesty hath been many ways burdened'. This amounted to recognition of beneficial rule and necessity *tout court*, since defence was not mentioned. In fact, the House of Commons struck at the crucial point, that it was improper to relieve royal necessity by taxation when 'ordinary' income might be augmented by normal methods. Unwilling taxpayers saw that taxation was becoming a first not a last resort. Following patterns established since 1485, Mary used tax receipts to defray the current costs of normal government and to discharge Crown debts as well as to meet the expenses of the navy, ordnance, and fortifications. Even the war tax of 1558 was partly applied to maintain the regular services of the royal household.[55]

To increase 'ordinary' income, royal debtors were attacked, the Crown lands revalued, concealments of land investigated, and tight controls applied to leasing policy. To stabilize prices, Northumberland's reformed coinage was protected by continued minting of fine coin. Yet Mary could not resist debasement, turning £54,900 of base English money into coinage for use in Ireland—the government's profit was £58,000. Since forgery of coinage was a major problem—with the mint producing high quality coin, the temptation to melt it down to counterfeit the base Henrician and Edwardian issues still in circulation was irresistible—a general recoinage was first projected in 1556, but was postponed until 1560–1. The customs were, however, reformed. Since the book of rates had not been revised since 1507, receipts had fallen in real terms. So a new book was introduced on 28 May 1558 that raised rates on average by 100 per cent and placed a new duty on cloth exports. A few weeks before, the Privy Council had imposed duties upon imports of French wine and 'dry goods', and upon exported beer. Customs revenues rose from £25,900 in 1550–1 and £29,315 in 1556–7 to £82,797 in 1558–9. Elizabeth therefore reaped the advantage.[56]

Financial administration continued the corporate approach adopted after Cromwell's fall. In this respect comparison with France is instructive. At the assembly of Rouen (1596–7) Pomponne de Bellièvre proposed a *conseil de bon ordre* to manage 16 million *livres* independently of the Crown. He planned to break the patronage system in an attempt to balance the budget. Next, the Paris *parlement* suggested that a 'council of twelve' should separately govern branches of finance. Like mid-Tudor projects, these were designed to achieve more efficient administration. Yet the marquis of Winchester's treasurership (1550–72) was conservative. When he supervised the final financial reorganization in 1553–4 whereby the courts of augmentations and first fruits were united with the exchequer, the letters patent called not only for retrenchment but also for return to the 'ancient course' — the procedures established in the twelfth century and set down in the Black Book of the Exchequer! According to this all Crown properties in England should account through the sheriffs and those in Wales through the chamberlain; the advanced accounting methods of augmentations would be discarded; and the roles of exchequer officials would be limited to those specified in the Dialogue of the Exchequer.[57]

Although this reactionary interpretation was not sustained, Winchester supported it for three reasons. First, the policy mistakenly assumed that, if revenue administration reverted to the 'ancient course', the queen might 'live of her own'. Second, stricter accounting might have stemmed embezzlement thereby obviating the need for further sales of Crown lands, which Winchester in principle disliked. Third, Winchester's authority was under threat; Northumberland had formulated his own financial policy, turning for advice to Cecil, Mildmay, and Gresham and using Peter Osborne as his link man at the exchequer. Then Mary was cool towards Winchester, forcing him to surrender the mastership of the wards to a courtier, Sir Francis Englefield. It was even rumoured that Waldegrave would replace him as lord treasurer, so he fought back but with muted success. When his case impressed the exchequer judges, Mary intervened to send him a general commission of lieutenancy that kept him in the provinces and away from Privy Council meetings.

This is not to deny that anything positive resulted. Crown finance had hitherto been managed in terms of its constituent parts, but the reorganization of 1553–4 brought a massive influx of cash into the exchequer which concentrated minds upon it. In Edward VI's reign less than one-third of centrally administered income had been accounted there but, by 1555–6, the exchequer tellers were handling three-quarters of Crown income — £265,000 per annum. Furthermore, these receipts were mainly in cash, in contrast to the decentralized debit finance of the fifteenth-century exchequer. Since Mary lacked cash surpluses, her exchequer was not a national deposit treasury. She herself did not think in such terms since her approach to finance was dynastic. From the early months of 1555 she employed as her personal 'treasurer' Nicholas Brigham, a teller of the exchequer who had no previous connection with the Court. He managed large accounts for her own use, for instance £290,000 in 1557–8 when acting as extraordinary treasurer for the French war, receiving and issuing 70 per cent of cash paid into the exchequer by 1558. Soon privy councillors had to write to him personally for information about cashflow. Yet categorization is elusive. Like Denny, when he served as chief gentleman of the privy chamber and keeper of the palace of Whitehall and its deposit treasury, Brigham served a bureaucracy that was autonomous and formal, yet versatile and intimate. He epitomized at once both the shift towards 'national' finance and the flexible methods of personal rule.[58]

Mary's five Parliaments realized 104 acts in six sessions. Since Edward's two Parliaments passed 164 in five sessions, and the four sessions of Elizabeth's first three Parliaments added 122, this was not an especially productive record. The matter is complex but the Marian House of Lords looks to have been less effective at legislative leadership than that of Edward VI: whereas two-thirds of the acts passed in Edward's reign originated in the Lords, only one-third of Mary's acts began there. Edwardian privy councillors and non-conciliar courtiers could take the initiative because they worked together to dominate the upper house. When a minority of conservative bishops and peers consistently opposed Northumberland's Reformation, the unanimity of councillors and courtiers ensured the passage of important bills. By contrast the Marian Parliaments were characterized by briefer sessions, inferior standards of record-keeping, and increasing absenteeism, some of it politically motivated. In particular, the Lords was scarred by fissures that marked the regime's internal disarray. Since Mary sought 'tractable' Parliaments by remodelling the bench of bishops, intervening in elections, creating four new peerages and nineteen new Commons' seats, as well as by dispensing Habsburg patronage to her supporters, her failure to obtain constructive, unified leadership is the more striking.[59]

Opposition to Crown policy was nevertheless exceptional. Relations were most soured over issues of property: the restoration of the bishopric of Durham in April 1554 was carried in the Commons by 201 to 120 votes; the return of first fruits and tenths to the church was accomplished in December 1555 by 193 to 126 votes; and the Crown's bill to seize the lands of the Protestant exiles was rejected the same month. If a balance sheet is required, Parliament's main success during the reign was to limit Philip's power and protect Elizabeth's claim to the throne; its failure was to prevent English involvement in the French war. Once the fight to safeguard ex-religious property rights was won, Parliament was relatively compliant in religious policy, though there was conspicuous absenteeism in both Houses during the reconciliation with Rome. Yet mid-Tudor Parliaments were less battlefields than shareholders' meetings: the interests of Crown and members were usually the same, while relationships were based on mutual need and the fear of social revolution in the wake of the risings of 1549.[60]

Of the Marian acts, 27 dealt with attainders, restitutions in blood, and the security of the regime; 19 continued or repealed existing statutes; 30 related to private interests; 7 modified legal procedure in criminal cases; 8 concerned social discipline and poor relief; and 13 were miscellaneous. In general, acts were uninspired: they rarely addressed immediate social problems, they willingly defended vested economic interests, and they expressed constant anxiety about sedition and public order. Yet a minority broke new ground. Two tackled criminal procedure in the localities, where private individuals still filed 'appeals' of felony. Although grand juries and JPs had prosecutorial duties which Henry VII's legislation had cemented, enforcement was patchy, because some JPs failed to react. So acts of 1554 and 1555 reiterated the principle of prosecution by JPs.[61]

Equally important were acts passed during the first session of 1558 to reorganize the militia. Neither Wolsey nor Cromwell had reformed the army; the problem was that the quasi-feudal 'system' of territorial recruitment was collapsing with the decline of the old nobility, the dissolution of the monasteries, and the reduction in the size of gentry households resulting from inflation. Somerset and Northumberland hired mercenaries to bridge the gap, but what was needed was a 'national' system of musters. The 1558 acts therefore built upon pre-feudal obligations as revived by Henry II's assize of arms and defined by the Statute of Winchester in 1285. An Act for the Taking of Musters obliged every section of society to contribute men, horses, and equipment to the shire levies. The system of musters was tightened, and penalties imposed for absence and for giving or accepting bribes. A statute of Edward VI making desertion of soldiers a felony was also revived. Next, an Act for Horse Armour and Weapons laid down what equipment was needed according to a graded hierarchy of wealth, making provision for modern weapons as well as supervision of parish armouries. While a landmark in English military organization, however, these acts did not emanate from the Council's advance planning but from the experience of the nobility and gentry during the musters of 1557–8. And both measures encountered some resistance: the act for musters had five readings in the Lords while that for weapons met misgivings in the Commons over its cost to individuals and local communities.[62]

In parallel with the shift from quasi-feudal to 'national' methods of recruitment went Mary's decision to divide the country into ten lieutenancies. Originally temporary posts intended to subordinate the shire levies to a single official, the lieutenancies were first given expanded functions after the 1549 rebellions. Northumberland's lieutenants performed both police and military duties and he contemplated making their posts permanent. Mary, however, made appointments at irregular intervals, and, when the threat of French invasion waned in 1558, most lieutenancies were terminated. Yet this was one stage in a longer process of development. During Elizabeth's war years appointments were used to match military needs to aristocratic traditions. In 1585 the country was divided into settled districts under lords-lieutenant who had deputies to assist them in the recruitment of the 'national' militia. Later non-military duties were added, for instance the management of food supplies during war or famine, and the collection of forced loans. A permanent hierarchy of command was thereby created: the lord-lieutenant was normally the senior resident nobleman or privy councillor in a county with minor peers or leading gentry acting as deputies.[63]

With Philip's encouragement, Mary also refurbished the English navy. Of Henry VIII's fifty ships, all but one had survived Somerset's campaigns, but twenty-one were defective. So fourteen were scrapped, six new ships built, and others repaired. At the outbreak of the French war twenty-one men-of-war were available, with others nearing completion or repair. An annual peacetime appropriation of £14,000 was also provided: naval finance was supervised by Lord Treasurer Winchester, who relied on Benjamin Gonson as naval treasurer. As a result, the navy by 1557 was better organized and managed than before.[64]

Another domestic topic claims attention. Under Northumberland and Mary alike the common lawyers lobbied to restrict the hearing of lawsuits upon titles to land to the common-law courts. Their attitude deserves to be better known because it epitomizes the conservatism that pervaded the 1550s. Speaking for the Privy Council in October 1551, Winchester agreed that pleas 'to the derogation of the common law' should no longer be taken in star chamber, in chancery, or in the court of requests.[65] In fact, the change took a decade to enforce. At first the lawyers' professional self-interest was the key: the older benches had lost customers to Wolsey's chancery and star chamber, so much so that king's bench fought back by developing bill procedures modelled on chancery that allowed plaintiffs to begin their suits without writs and to have defendants arrested at the outset. Yet the campaign became near-ideological under Mary, when clerical lord chancellors (Gardiner, 1553-5; Archbishop Heath, 1556-8) were in a position to try titles to land (ex-religious lands?) by rules other than those of common law. While the link is conjectural, this fits neatly with Winchester's demand that exchequer be administered according to the 'ancient course'. That would have obliged exchequer universally to follow common-law accounting methods, in contrast to those of augmentations which stemmed from the Yorkist–Tudor 'land revenue' experiment the lawyers had challenged in 1509.

The last months of Mary's reign were tense. Severe dearth in 1555–7 caused malnutrition and some starvation. Resistance to disease was lowered and the death-rate soared during the influenza epidemic of 1556–60. The population dropped by about 200,000, which Protestants interpreted as God's verdict on the regime, and Catholics as punishment for 'rebellious murmuring against our regal rulers appointed of God'. Rumours of sedition and incipient rebellion were commonplace: alleged assassination attempts, claims that Edward VI was still alive, an obscure rising at Cambridge, and another at Yaxley in Suffolk. A substitution plot was even bruited. Alice Perwick of London was indicted for saying, 'The Queen's Grace is not with child, and another lady should be with child and that lady's child when she is brought in bed should be named the Queen's child.' The imperial envoy compared the 'opposition' to a Hydra constantly sprouting fresh heads. Philip, who consulted astrologers, was advised that a major rising was expected in England. And the conspiracy planned in Elizabeth's favour by Sir Henry Dudley (March 1556) was menacing: key officials such as the captain of Yarmouth Castle were implicated, as were some Protestant gentry, while the conspirators' attempt to finance themselves by robbing the exchequer came within a whisker of success.[66]

Foreign policy was, however, crucial. Although the Habsburg–Valois negotiators of the truce of Vaucelles (6 February 1556), while spurning English mediation, obtained a breathing space, the European conflict resumed when Alva invaded the papal states. Philip therefore returned to England in March 1557 to seek Mary's intervention in the war. In fact, the importance of England's help overtook the value of her fighting capacity, partly because Philip's honour was at stake and partly because Spain was bankrupt: revenues were committed three years ahead and loans cost 54 per cent. But Philip's most consistent supporter, Gardiner, had died in November 1555. With the exception of Paget and, probably, Arundel and Pembroke, the Privy Council resisted entry into the war, which only became justifiable at the end of April 1557, when the Protestant exile Thomas Stafford 'invaded' England with two ships and at most a hundred men. He landed at Scarborough, took the castle, and proclaimed himself 'protector of the realm'. Although crushed on the 28th by the earl of Westmorland, Stafford was supposedly backed by Henry II of France. So, when Mary had interviewed her privy councillors individually, war was declared on 7 June. Yet the chief argument in its favour—that the threat of an external enemy might reunite a divided ruling elite—was a gamble. It is true that some prominent exiles and opponents of the regime commanded English contingents, among them the three surviving sons of Northumberland—Harry (killed at St Quentin), Ambrose, and Robert (later earl of Leicester). In the event, however, the war led to Mary's humiliation.[67]

It nevertheless began well. Embarking on 5 July, Philip took with him 7,221 troops under the earl of Pembroke. But English involvement was in four theatres: the navy cleared French shipping out of the Channel thereby protecting Philip's supply lines to the Low Countries; Pembroke's troops played a minor role at the siege of St Quentin; a Scottish invasion of England was mooted but flopped owing to divisions in Scotland; and 1,600 men were stationed at the three English strongholds of the Pale of Calais during the winter of 1557–8. On New Year's Day 27,000 French troops attacked Calais. The marshes were frozen, which enabled them to capture Rysbank, the fortress between the harbour and the sea-coast. As soon as they controlled the harbour, the French bombarded Calais Castle, which its defenders abandoned. (Their plan was to let the French in, then detonate a mine—but it failed to explode.) All three Calais garrisons had surrendered by the end of the month: without immediate reinforcements, they had no alternative.[68]

Mary began 1558 by announcing her pregnancy. No one, however, took this seriously. Charles de Guise unkindly quipped that she would not have long to wait, 'this being the end of the eighth month since her husband left her'. But Calais cast the longest shadow: it symbolized Edward III's victory at Crécy and

Henry V's at Agincourt; its loss was more than bad luck. Yet the Privy Council refused to recover it on grounds of cost and feasibility. The Scottish situation was steadily deteriorating: the projected marriage between the Dauphin and Mary Stuart was celebrated in April 1558, while seven months later the Scottish Parliament offered him the 'crown matrimonial'. Scotland was a threat throughout the summer, requiring nine thousand English troops to be kept on alert as well as the reconstruction of Berwick, which was fitted with new walls to resist artillery. Also the navy remained on active service. In June it helped to repulse an attack on Gravelines, then joined the Flemish fleet in a badly planned attack on Brest. Since, however, Henry II was financially exhausted as well as Philip, peace negotiations had begun at which Philip increasingly regarded Calais as dispensable. The Privy Council was therefore persuaded to yield it — then Mary died. In 1559 Elizabeth reluctantly sacrificed the town in exchange for a face-saving formula and peace with Scotland.[69]

The South East Essex College of Arts & Technology

ELIZABETH I:
THE ENGLISH DEBORAH?

MARY's regime, like that of Oliver Cromwell a century later, lacked the undivided support of the gentry needed to secure stability. Her death (17 November 1558) was not accompanied by spontaneous public mourning such as had dignified the passing of Henry VIII. On the contrary, the popular mood switched immediately to optimism, though this was partly the result of a propaganda exercise. Elizabeth was adopted by the City of London as a Protestant saviour, or as Deborah, 'the judge and restorer of Israel'.[1] Her coronation pageants combined the themes of Tudor stability, epitomized by Henry VII's marriage to Elizabeth of York, and religious harmony in place of confessional strife. 'Concord' was the slogan: the twenty-five-year-old queen was fêted as a peacemaker. At one pageant the throne was garnished with red and white roses, beneath which was written, 'The uniting of the two houses of York and Lancaster'. And the child–narrator intoned:

> Therefore as civil war and shed of blood did cease;
> When these two Houses were united into one:
> So now, that jar shall stint and quietness increase,
> We trust, O noble Queen! thou wilt be cause alone!

Another pageant placed the queen, clad in parliament robes and holding a sceptre, above her nobility, clergy, and people. The legend read, 'Deborah, with her estates, consulting for the good government of Israel'. A palm tree, an emblem of victory, overshadowed the stage. And again a child recited:

> Jabin, of Canaan King, had long, by force of arms,
> Oppressed the Israelites; which for God's people went:
> But God minding, at last, for to redress their harms;
> The worthy Deborah, as judge among them sent.

All this was quite unsubtle: as an official pamphlet remarked, it was to put the queen 'in remembrance' to employ wise counsel and thereby emulate Deborah, who ruled unchallenged for forty years.[2] In this respect London proved prophetic: Elizabeth survived until the forty-fifth year of her reign. Yet undoubtedly she was being 'packaged' by image-makers. For instance, she was presented with an English Bible by a child clad as Truth, while treated to a dumb show in which Pure Religion trampled Ignorance and Superstition underfoot.[3] Superficially she was impressed, watching each scene attentively rather than rushing past; but a basic tension prevailed because the City's radicals did not represent the opinions of all Englishmen, neither was Elizabeth unequivocally Protestant. She was, however, the Protestants' hope. By adopting her as their sponsor they aimed to attach her to their cause; by presenting her with the Gospel they urged her to propagate it at home and abroad. The question was, how would she respond?

As a ruler Elizabeth controlled her own policy more than any other Tudor. She was talented, engaging, and hard-working, yet cautious, conservative, imperious, and petulant in the face of change. A moderately tall, attractive woman with bright eyes and auburn hair, she was described by Henry III of France as 'la plus fine femme du monde'. Like her mother, Anne Boleyn, whose memory she protected, she was intelligent and accomplished, speaking French, Italian, and Spanish as well as reading Latin, playing the virginals, dancing, and hunting with unusual skill. At Windsor in 1593 she translated Boethius' *On the Consolation of Philosophy* in less than a month for fun. But her vanity was notorious, her tongue sharp, and, despite her declared intention to 'live and die a virgin', sexual jealousy soured many of her personal relationships. Those who knew her said: 'When she smiled it was pure sunshine that everyone did choose to bask in if they could; but anon came a storm from a sudden gathering of clouds and the thunder fell in wondrous manner on all alike.'[4] Like her father and sister she particularly stressed her royal prerogative, erecting rigid barriers that created problems for her councillors as well as her Parliaments. Sir Robert Naunton (1563–1635) wrote: 'Though very capable of counsel, she was absolute enough in her own resolution, which was apparent even to her last.'[5] She knew her mind; her instinct to power was infallible. Councillors attempted to manipulate her on sensitive issues either individually or in concert, but were rarely successful; she would lose her temper, whereupon the matter would rest in abeyance.

Although her religious beliefs cannot be pinned down, Elizabeth was a moderate, if secular-minded, reformer who rejected 'popery' but kept the crucifix and candles on the altar of the Chapel Royal. She also continued to employ Catholics such as Thomas Tallis, William Byrd, and John Bull as chapel organists on the grounds that she enjoyed their music. She was not dogmatic, and showed no objection to what Bucer and John à Lasco condemned as 'parliamentary theology'. But she disapproved of clerical marriage, partly on principle and partly because it was held that the bishops and clergy would marry the daughters of the nobility and gentry, thereby claiming higher social status.

Elizabeth's weakness was that she vacillated when faced by important decisions: unless panicked, she could delay for years. This, combined with her haughtiness, drove her councillors to distraction. But her attitude had political merit, as William Cecil acknowledged at the end of his career. The majority of English people were not Protestant 'converts' in 1558, therefore caution was essential. Since England in alliance with Philip II's Spain was negotiating peace with France and Scotland, conservatism and delay were prudent. Elizabeth's policy also has to be judged in the light of her financial position and the conservatism of her subjects before the outbreak of war with Spain. Perhaps her greatest asset was her *lack* of preconceptions; she was not a conviction-politician like Walsingham or Leicester, though her taste for *realpolitik* went beyond Cecil's. Apart from her concern to recover Calais, or a French port in lieu, as revealed by the Le Havre adventure, she ignored conventional royal ambitions. Her father's expansionist dreams were absent; her sister's ideological passions were eschewed; and, despite constant diplomacy conducted on the question until 1582, a dynastic marriage was avoided. Perhaps better than any other European ruler, Elizabeth mastered the political game. True, the second half of the sixteenth century saw the polarization of international politics upon religious grounds. But the queen knew better than some of her councillors that England did not possess sufficient

resources to wage open war until the 1580s. A passive stance
that responded to events, while shunning obvious initiatives, was
a more astute strategy than a Protestant crusade.[6]

The political climate of 1558–9 was largely shaped by the return
of the 'Athenians' and their friends to government. Sir John
Cheke, around whom the group had coalesced, was dead.
Kidnapped by Philip's agents in May 1556 *en route* between
Antwerp and Brussels, he was imprisoned at the Tower. Forced
by Mary and Pole to recant, he died of shame in September 1557.
Sir Thomas Smith, their other leader, was kept in the background
before the Le Havre expedition, having alienated many by his
arrogant conduct. But Sir William Cecil, Sir Nicholas Bacon,
Francis Russell (second earl of Bedford), Sir Francis Knollys,
and Sir Ambrose Cave were named to Elizabeth's Privy Council.
So too were William Parr (restored as marquis of Northampton),
Sir Thomas Parry (Cecil's kinsman and Elizabeth's cofferer since
1548), and Sir Edward Rogers (*quondam* principal gentleman of
Edward VI's privy chamber and Cranmer's brother-in-law). The
change of regime is therefore obvious, even though twelve
(reduced to ten by 1559) Marians remained in harness as privy
councillors for reasons of rank and service, including Lord
Treasurer Winchester and the earls of Arundel, Derby,
Pembroke, and Shrewsbury. Furthermore, Cecil, whom
Elizabeth had trusted for years and whom she had appointed
surveyor of her estates in 1550, did not need to wait until he
was officially named secretary of state before functioning in this
capacity. His relationship to Elizabeth was deep-rooted, perhaps
emotionally based. Already at the centre of affairs a week before
Mary's death, he was in December 1558 described by the Spanish
ambassador as 'the man who does everything'.[7]

In fact, Cecil secured for himself from the start a clear working
majority in the Privy Council. Paget, who was implicated in
Cheke's kidnapping as well as being too closely associated with
Philip II, was ousted. For, unlike Wolsey, Thomas Cromwell,
and Protector Somerset, who neglected to cultivate personal
followings in the Council, and who paid the price, Cecil could
immediately count on Bacon, Knollys, Parry, Cave, Parr,
Pembroke, Bedford, Rogers, and the Marian Sir Richard
Sackville, who was Elizabeth's cousin by marriage. This was

itself a bare working majority, yet Derby, Shrewsbury, and
Arundel were neutral, while Lord Howard of Effingham was
a Protestant devoted to Elizabeth's interests, and Sir William
Petre and Sir John Mason were loyal officials and friends of Cecil.
Since Sir Walter Mildmay (chancellor of the exchequer), Sir
Nicholas Throckmorton (ambassador to Paris), and other
prominent 'Athenians' obtained administrative posts or
appointments at Court or at least on its fringe, Cecil's power-
base was narrow but secure. Of the chief contenders for power
in 1558–9, only the Dudley circle was excluded: Lord Robert
Dudley (created earl of Leicester, 1564) was named master of
the horse but had to wait until October 1562 for admission to
the Privy Council; his older brother Sir Ambrose (created earl
of Warwick, 1561) was master of the ordnance but excluded from
the Council until 1573; and Sir Henry Sidney was lord president
of the Council in the Marches of Wales but not a privy councillor
until 1575.

Naunton said of Elizabeth: 'She ruled much by factions and
parties, which she herself both made, upheld and weakened, as
her own great judgement advised.'[8] Accepted as truth for
generations, this oracular proposition is a travesty of Elizabethan
politics. There was little, if any, Elizabethan factionalism before
the outbreak of war with Spain of the type that had prevailed
under Henry VIII, even if personal rivalries pervaded the Court
circle.[9] Feuding erupted between Cecil and Leicester over the
latter's wooing of the queen, his early (but short-lived) pro-
Spanish diplomacy, his pushy attempts to seat Throckmorton
on the Privy Council in 1564–5, and his conspiratorial
endorsement of an anti-Cecil coalition in 1569. Several times
during the 1560s the Privy Council disputed whom Elizabeth
should marry, an issue which caused Leicester to collide with
Cecil and the third earl of Sussex. Cecil largely favoured a
dynastic match, perhaps with the Archduke Charles of Austria,
who would have proved a moderating influence at Court and
bolstered England against France. But Leicester first schemed
to marry Elizabeth himself, and then supported the claim of the
Catholic Mary, Queen of Scots, to the succession. A decade later
Leicester and Sussex sharply disagreed over intervention in the
Netherlands and the linked question of Elizabeth's proposed
marriage to the brother and heir of Henry III of France.

Following a series of intemperate rows, the queen disciplined both men.[10] But only when Leicester and Walsingham continued to lobby for English military intervention against Spain in the Netherlands did opinion begin to polarize. For Cecil (following Elizabeth) did not share the enthusiasm of Leicester and Walsingham for a European Protestant coalition, and refused to commit England to unnecessary war with Spain against overwhelming odds.[11]

Yet the assumption of traditional historiography that the Elizabethan establishment was permanently split into opposing factions — 'moderates' led by Cecil, and 'Protestant ideologues' led by Leicester — is misleading. The truth is that the Privy Council was agreed in the 1560s upon the need to settle the succession, and in the 1570s and 1580s upon the broad aims of a Protestant foreign policy. Nor were Elizabethan institutions organized in a way conducive to factionalism, as becomes clear when Cecil's technique is seen in the context of political practice since 1518. Under Wolsey and Cromwell friction had several times arisen between the Council and privy chamber. The dukes of Somerset and Northumberland therefore merged the memberships of these institutions and enforced religious uniformity in both. But their regimes were unrepresentative; they amounted to 'single-party' government. So Mary attempted consensus politics but failed; conflicts between councillors and courtiers resumed with adverse consequences for the management of Parliament. Cecil in 1558–9 therefore adopted less strident, more effective methods. Elizabeth's government relied upon men who were at once major political figures and leading Court officials, and her privy chamber upon gentlewomen who were either her former servants or the wives and daughters of these same politicians. For example, Parry, Knollys, Rogers, Sir Thomas Heneage, Sir Christopher Hatton, Sir James Croft, and Sir John Stanhope held key Court offices, yet all were busy privy councillors and executives. The wives of Parry, Cecil, Knollys, Heneage, Rogers, Sackville, Mason, Cave, the marquis of Northampton, the earl of Warwick, Lord Clinton, and Sir Henry Sidney were among those who attended the queen between 1559 and 1585. Of the nobility in the Privy Council, Arundel, Leicester, Sussex, Howard of Effingham, Lord Hunsdon, and the fourth earl of Derby held significant

Court positions. Until 1572, when he succeeded Winchester as lord treasurer, Cecil worked within the household as secretary, presenting himself as the 'humble servant' and mouthpiece of the queen, rather than her chief minister. He sought to mollify the nobility who, like Winchester and Pembroke, were his seniors in age and experience as well as rank. Son of a page of Henry VIII's chamber who had risen through the royal household and profited from the dissolution, Cecil, aged thirty-eight in 1558, was the youngest Tudor minister and second youngest Elizabethan councillor after the earl of Bedford.[12]

Furthermore deliberate schemes to resolve political tension were afoot, one being a draft dated 16 May 1559 'for redress of the state of the Realm'.[13] Its author hoped that Elizabeth would 'have no officers of the household and chamber, but such as be able to serve in the privy council'. Officials listed were the lord steward, lord chamberlain, treasurer and comptroller of the household, master of the horse, vice-chamberlain, captain of the guard, secretary, dean of the chapel, and royal almoner. They were to combine membership of the Privy Council with these positions and, the steward and chamberlain excepted, were to reside at Court. In addition, the lord chancellor, lord treasurer, lord privy seal, lord great chamberlain, and admiral were to be councillors normally absent from Court. So the demands of the great offices of state were recognized, while the fusion of Court and state functions was, meanwhile, resumed. But the process was to be gradual, since six gentlemen of the privy chamber and two gentlemen ushers were to be appointed who were not councillors. They were, however, 'to be chosen of the wisest and honestest sort of gentlemen in the Realm' in order that they might fill vacant posts in Court and Privy Council as they arose; a career structure was thus envisaged.

Probably this was an Edwardian blueprint recycled in 1559, but its inspiration was Cecil's policy, for the keynote of the Elizabethan system was homogeneity.[14] Not only were privy councillors and leading courtiers the same people, but the staff of the privy chamber were not allowed to take independent political initiatives. Although they controlled access to Elizabeth's presence, they barely influenced patronage, and policy not at all. True, Robert Beale in his 'Treatise of the Office of a Councillor' (1592) urged the prudent secretary about to approach the queen to ascertain her disposition through contacts in the privy chamber, 'with whom you must keep credit, for that will stand you in much stead'. But he warned of the gentlewomen's importunity for suits, which itself implies that they could not secure favour unaided. Sir Walter Ralegh said of them, 'like witches they could do hurt but could do no good'. They did not have a stamp of the queen's signature. Although Elizabeth possessed one, she kept it under lock and key. (Cecil had to obtain a special warrant in order to use it to levy troops against the Northern Rising.)[15] Though Catherine Ashley, the queen's former governess and closest confidante, was punished for forwarding the marriage suit of Eric XIV of Sweden in 1561–2, the episode is unique. Catherine was married to John Ashley, Elizabeth's cousin, whom she appointed master of the jewels. Indeed, Elizabethan homogeneity owed much to kinship relationships, since the queen's kindred via the Boleyns included Lord Hunsdon, Knollys, Sackville, and John Fortescue (master of the wardrobe), while connections via the Parrs included the marquis of Northampton and earl of Pembroke. Lastly, Matthew Parker, consecrated archbishop of Canterbury in December 1559, had been Anne Boleyn's chaplain, whom she had charged with her daughter's spiritual welfare.

Other circumstances reinforced political stability. Apart from their 'Athenian' links, Cecil and Nicholas Bacon were both sons-in-law of Sir Anthony Cooke, the Edwardian Protestant activist and gentleman of the privy chamber. Even when the remaining followers of Somerset and Northumberland reached the fringes of the Court, there was no resumption of the Dudley–Seymour rivalry, because Somerset's son, whom Elizabeth had restored to the earldom of Hertford, ruined his career by secretly marrying Lady Catherine Grey, heiress presumptive to the Crown through the Suffolk line by Henry VIII's will. When Hertford's fall left his clients without a patron in 1561, they gravitated towards Leicester.[16] His affinity had already afforded him political weight and a role, despite Cecil's resistance, as potential consort to Elizabeth. Indeed, as master of the horse Leicester rode immediately behind the queen on progress as well as being third officer of the royal household after the lord steward and lord chamberlain. When he was admitted to the Privy Council, the balance of power was fixed until his death in 1588. Despite their rivalry and rows, Cecil and Leicester were not political opponents: specific collisions aside, they co-operated widely until the debates over intervention in the Netherlands polarized opinion. Each had something the other needed: Cecil, before 1571, lacked noble rank and networks in the localities, which the Dudleys enjoyed; in turn, Cecil's power came from the queen's trust and his position at the centre of government, which Leicester coveted. In religion both men acted as patrons to conviction-Protestants, and in foreign policy they achieved the Anglo-French *entente* of the 1570s. Leicester naturally resented Cecil's monopolistic tendencies, while his attempt to define his own role as that of 'honest broker' is unconvincing. What matters, however, is the place of both at the centre of policy-making.[17]

In 1558–9 the main issue was the religious settlement. Even before the London authorities signalled their rejection of Catholicism, iconoclastic riots and anti-Roman demonstrations disturbed the city, and Protestant congregations came out of hiding to meet in private houses. But the vital indicator came from the Court: the dancers at the Twelfth Night masque depicted crows disguised as cardinals, asses as bishops, and wolves as abbots. In December 1558 heresy trials were stopped, prosecutions since 1555 were investigated, and surviving prisoners released. Under the cover of general musters, commissioners were appointed by the Privy Council to report stocks of armour and weapons held by the bishops.[18] Lastly, the pulpits were silenced by proclamation to prevent disorder, while everyone was commanded to observe Marian rites and ceremonies 'until consultation may be had by Parliament' (27 December). Exceptions were only that the vernacular Litany printed for Henry VIII in 1545 might be used, and the Lord's Prayer and Creed said in English. But Parliament was summoned to meet on 25 January 1559.

Although Elizabeth's own intentions cannot be reconstructed, she heard the Litany in her chapel, refused at mass to offer the sacrificial elements, and forbade the celebrant to elevate the Host. Also the words of consecration were spoken in English. So she repudiated transubstantiation but concealed her wider purpose.[19] By contrast, Cecil's immediate plan to reintroduce both royal supremacy and the 1552 Prayer Book may be inferred from the advice he sought. The most comprehensive paper was a 'Device for the Alteration of Religion', written by an unknown but important official before Christmas 1558. It recommended a return to Edwardian forms as soon as possible, suggested how this might be done, weighed the demands of domestic enforcement, and calculated the likely effect upon European diplomacy. Religious uniformity based on the 1552 Book of Common Prayer was the keynote. The Prayer Book should first be revised by a committee of learned men, then approved by the queen, and enacted by Parliament. Names suggested for the committee were a handpicked group of 'Athenians', Cecilians, and former participants in the Edwardian Eucharistic debates, whose support for the 1552 Book was guaranteed. Although there is no evidence that they met to draft the religious settlement, provision was made for their accommodation, food, and fuel.[20]

The 'Device' advised caution until the Prayer Book was approved by Parliament: it would be risky to permit un-licensed forms of worship. Also the bishops and former Marian officials should be watched. Ex-councillors and JPs should be attacked if they opposed the settlement. Younger and lesser gentry should be appointed JPs to replace Catholics in the shires, while the bishops and clergy should be coerced by penal laws or *praemunire* actions. The author then warned Cecil against Protestant zealots, remembering the disputes under Edward VI as well as among the Marian exiles at Frankfort which had divided the Coxians, who supported the 1552 Prayer Book, and the Knoxians, who wanted 'pure' Genevan worship. Since the Marian exiles returned late to England, they played no direct role in the settlement. But the 'Device' acknowledged that many would be upset to discover that 'some old ceremonies shall be left still, or that their doctrine which they embrace is not allowed and . . . all other abolished'. They would call the settlement 'a cloaked papistry or a mingle-mangle'. Yet 'better it were that they did suffer than her highness and commonwealth should shake or be in danger; and to this they must well take heed that draw the [Prayer] Book'. So, whereas the author validated the autonomy of the Church of England in relation to Rome, he left the question of its relationship to the Calvinist reformed church unresolved.[21]

This was partly because royal supremacy was the hallmark of Anglicanism, and partly because Elizabeth had to persuade the Catholic powers that she was acceptable. The 'Device' listed the dangers: the pope would excommunicate her; the French might revive the war; and the Scots might consequently invade. Rome's censures, however, were regarded as bluster, while Scotland was certain to follow France into peace providing existing negotiations could be completed. Since Henry II was bankrupt, there were grounds for optimism. Nothing was said about Spain, but this reflected reality. For, despite Philip II's mistrust of Elizabeth, he was obliged to protect her, since, if England succumbed to a Franco-Scottish onslaught, the Netherlands could be cut off from Spain by sea. In fact, Philip sought to marry Elizabeth and thereby to retain England as an ally, though he found the field full of candidates. Naturally she did not refuse him until the *rapprochement* with France was safe. But even when she declined his offer and the terms of the religious settlement were published, Philip's concern for his sea route ensured cordial relations with Elizabeth for a decade and delayed her excommunication by the pope.[22]

When Parliament assembled, Cecil quickly introduced bills to re-establish royal supremacy and Protestant worship based on the 1552 Prayer Book. These were integrated into a single bill by 21 February, but it was wrecked. Although the Commons approved it after a stormy debate, the Lords forced its committal to opponents of the supremacy. So the bill was emasculated: the committee's version retained the mass, though it conceded that Elizabeth might take the supremacy if she wanted it. True, papal authority was abrogated and communion in both kinds permitted, but the Marian heresy laws were untouched. Since everyone expected Parliament to be dissolved in time for Easter (26 March), the Commons rushed through a bill that 'no persons shall be punished for using the religion used in King Edward's last year' (18 March). By repealing the heresy laws, this bill attempted to secure religious toleration; but it was lost in the Lords. At Easter 1559, therefore, the Protestants were in agony: the Marian bishops and conservative peers had outvoted Cecil's scheme.[23]

So at the last minute Parliament was ordered to reconvene on 3 April. A disputation was begun on 31 March at Westminster

Abbey too; its purpose was to undermine the bishops. Organized by Cecil and Bacon, it baited a trap for Catholics, since the set questions repudiated the 'oral tradition' and restricted discussion to what was justified by Scripture alone. So the Catholics walked out, which gave the Privy Council a propaganda victory. Not only were the leading Catholic disputants, Bishops White of Winchester and Watson of Lincoln, sent to the Tower for contempt, but their houses were also searched by Cave and Sackville for evidence of a plot to excommunicate Elizabeth. On Easter Day, meanwhile, the order of service in the queen's chapel was framed to resemble the Edwardian communion rite.[24]

As Parliament's second session began, separate bills for supremacy and uniformity were drafted. The supremacy bill replaced the title of 'Supreme Head' with that of 'Supreme Governor of the Church'; authorized communion in both kinds; repealed the heresy laws; and reinstated the Henrician act for consecrating bishops. These matters were lumped together because royal supremacy was less controversial than Protestant uniformity: if the uniformity bill failed, the Supremacy Act would permit limited religious toleration by itself. And the words 'Supreme Governor' satisfied some objections that Christ alone is 'Head' of the church, though they did not, in Elizabeth's opinion, affect her jurisdiction. More controversially, the uniformity bill, in its final form, reimposed the Prayer Book of 1552 with minor revisions. In particular, the ornaments of the church and dress of the clergy were reserved to Elizabeth's decision. Also the communion sentences of 1549 and 1552 were amalgamated. The words spoken at the delivery of the consecrated bread were: 'The body of our Lord Jesus Christ which was given for thee, preserve thy body and soul into everlasting life: and take and eat this, in remembrance that Christ died for thee, and feed on him in thy heart by faith, with thanksgiving.' Denying transubstantiation, this Scriptural formula assured Christ's real presence in the Eucharist to those who fed on him in faith. It mollified conservatives without incensing the more radical Protestants. But, whereas the 'ornaments' section may have been intended to establish a legal norm that would pre-empt haggling over 'things indifferent' (i.e. 'externals not necessary to salvation'), it backfired when the queen later imposed conformity on her clergy. When the 1559

Prayer Book appeared, it stipulated that the clergy should wear the mass vestments used during 1548; in practice this meant surplices over which copes were sometimes worn. This clash with the Prayer Book's Protestant theology sprang from Elizabeth's conservatism: like Henry VIII, she held ornaments, rites, and ceremonies to be her business. In fact, she never altered the rubric for vestments, while she also declined to legitimize clerical marriage by statute. That reform had to wait until 1604, despite the grudging toleration extended to clergy wives by the 1559 royal injunctions. Also Cranmer's *Ordinal* was dropped, together with the 'black rubric' of 1552 which had denied that kneeling implied adoration.[25]

The new supremacy bill passed the Commons in four days (10–13 April) but was committed in the Lords. Although Cecil this time ensured that Catholics were in a minority on the committee, they still managed to amend the bill: the main change was that the High Commission could not judge Catholicism to be heresy. When this point was settled, the bill passed its third reading (26 April). Not one bishop supported it, and neither did Viscount Montague. The Commons then expedited the uniformity bill, and quickly conceded the Lords' amendments to the supremacy bill.

When the uniformity bill reached the Lords (26–8 April), several lay peers defended the mass, but Bishops White and Watson were in prison, Abbot Feckenham of Westminster missed the vote, and Bishop Goldwell of St Asaph was absent. So the bill succeeded: nine spiritual and nine temporal peers, including Lord Treasurer Winchester, the earl of Shrewsbury, and Lords Morley and Rich, voted against it and twenty-one temporal peers in favour. The Acts of Supremacy and Uniformity therefore imposed religious change without a single churchman's consent, making constitutional history. Whereas many bishops had supported the Crown during the 1530s, the Elizabethan settlement was enacted by laity alone. The cry of 'foul' was taken up by Catholic apologists, who accused Cecil and Bacon of coercion 'partly by violence and partly by fear'. And if 'secularization' was less obvious in 1559 than under Henry VIII and Edward VI, it was only because less church property remained to plunder.[26]

The outcome was probably inevitable. Even if Elizabeth had accepted her supremacy under the terms of the emasculated bill of 21 February, she could have changed her bishops. Practical politics pushed her and Cecil towards the Protestant goal: the demands of finance, private property, greed, and intransigent legalism on the part of individuals bisected the religious issues. For instance, the Crown urgently needed to recover first fruits and tenths along with Mary's other gifts to the church, and to dissolve those monasteries and chantries that had reappeared. This was done in March and April 1559. And Cecil steered another bill through Parliament. Like Northumberland, he mistrusted powerful bishops, so he resolved to put their wealth to better use. The Crown was authorized, during episcopal vacancies, to exchange the lands, castles, manors, and other temporal property of the sees for impropriated rectories, tithes, and tenths of equivalent value in the Crown's possession; also the length of leases which incumbent bishops could make was limited to twenty-one years or three lives, except when the lessee was the Crown. Although superficially fair, the bishops lost money by these terms. The bill stirred anxiety in the Commons, where it passed by 134 votes to 90. (The Lords approved it, the bishops dissenting.)[27]

The most vexed property debates, however, concerned *private* claimants to episcopal property restored in Mary's reign at the expense of lay Edwardian grantees. At stake was an important legal issue: the claimants sought to recover lands surrendered to the Crown by Edwardian bishops, and sold or regranted to new beneficiaries by royal letters patent, when those lands had been returned to Catholic bishops under Mary without compensation. Although Mary had not expressly revoked exchanges of land made between the Edwardian bishops and the Crown, she had issued a warrant to Bishop White, permitting him to cancel enrolments and deeds in Edward VI's favour by his predecessor. The claims of the Edwardian patentees were opposed by the bishops in 1559. If the bishops won the argument, however, Edward VI's grants of ex-religious property by letters patent would be invalid. The bishops had started a property scare.

In addition, the spectre of future reconfiscation of the secularized church property still stalked Parliament. Mary had reunited England to Rome upon the assurance of Pole's dispensation, as reluctantly approved by Julius III, that possession of the ex-religious lands remained unchanged. But Pole's dispensation was not absolute or a precedent: it could not bind the conscience of Paul IV, whom Pole had persuaded in 1555 to make allowance for the English situation, but who denounced the alienation of church property in principle. Although Pole's dispensation had been enshrined in legislation which insisted that common-law titles to secularized lands were valid, Bishop Bonner took his stand in 1559 upon conscience, not common law.[28]

It follows that Thomas More's trial had not ended juris-prudential debate in England by asserting the omnicompetence of parliamentary statute and the supremacy of common law over other species of law. For statute was the superior human law only in the context of royal supremacy. Papal law was as valid in England as common law under Mary: the question was what would happen next? So, if the Protestants got their settlement in 1559, it was partly thanks to the property scare. Indeed, just as Paget had resisted Mary until ex-religious property rights were secured, so Lord Rich in 1559 supported the supremacy bill because it protected his estates while voting against the uniformity bill because the mass protected his soul. Not everyone took this line; for example, Winchester and Lord North opposed the Edwardian patentees as well as the uniformity bill.[29] Yet, when landowners wanted security, Protestantism had more to offer than the pope.

By the time Parliament was dissolved (8 May), the peace of Cateau-Cambrésis had concluded the French war. The first treaty (2 April) provided Elizabeth's face-saving formula: France retained Calais for eight years, after which the town would be restored providing England kept the peace, otherwise an indemnity of 500,000 crowns would be payable by France in default of its return; and France undertook to pacify the Scottish border. The second treaty (3 April) between France and Spain gave Philip II control of Italy, while Henry II kept Metz, Toul, and Verdun. But the peace was tested when Henry II was fatally wounded in a jousting accident (30 June), for his son, Francis II, was married to Mary Stuart, queen-regnant of Scotland, queen-consort of France, and Catholic claimant of England. The Guise faction, which gained power in Paris as well as Edinburgh, sought to make Scotland an instrument of French foreign policy, despite the unpopularity of Mary of Guise, mother of Mary Stuart, who had ousted the earl of Arran from the regency of Scotland in 1554. When French troops were used to garrison Scottish fortresses, there were outbreaks of political resistance that culminated in full-blooded Protestant revolution in 1559-60. John Knox returned from exile in Geneva to preach a sermon at Perth (11 May 1559) that sparked iconoclasm and looting; the lords of the congregation began military operations; and by 21 October the insurgents felt strong enough to 'suspend' the regent. Against regular French troops, however, Protestant volunteers were ineffective: English assistance was needed. Cecil immediately saw the dangers and the opportunity. He wrote: 'It is double the danger . . . to venture battle upon the frontiers of England to a battle upon the frontiers of Calais or Boulogne.'[30] Yet at a stroke the Scottish Reformation could be made the vehicle for French expulsion from the British Isles, Scotland's position as an English satellite cemented, and Mary's claim to the English throne weakened.

While the Scottish campaign of 1559-60 gave Cecil a diplomatic prize, it taught him the extent of Elizabeth's conservatism. She refused to allow Protestant ideology to dictate her policy; indeed she loathed Knox, whose *First Blast of the Trumpet* asserted that 'nothing can be more manifest' than God's denial that 'a woman should be exalted to reign above men'. Knox's targets were Mary I and Mary of Guise, but his book appeared in 1558!

Although Elizabeth consented to clandestine aid of money and munitions for the Scots in August 1559, the question of military intervention was still unresolved at Christmas. At a Privy Council meeting in mid-December Bacon reiterated the objections: to send an army was 'to join with the subject against the sovereign' and 'to be the first breaker of a League'. He acknowledged that invasion could be presented as self-defence, and that the peace was first broken by the French royal couple, who had sported the arms of England 'in open triumph'. But he advised 'succouring the Scots by all ways and means secretly' until the French could be routed.[31] Winchester, Petre, and Mason supported this opinion and Arundel opposed any direct aid to Scotland, but they were in a minority. Elizabeth, nevertheless, procrastinated and Cecil, exasperated, drafted a letter that hinted at his resignation.

Elizabeth did, however, yield. She dispatched the navy to the Firth of Forth to prevent the arrival of French reinforcements, and mustered an army in March 1560 to join in blockading Leith, where the main French force was concentrated. Although these tactics tried to avoid Protector Somerset's mistakes, the siege failed. But the loss of the French fleet in a storm, the Huguenot Tumult of Amboise (15 March), and the death of Mary of Guise (11 June) crippled France, enabling Cecil to negotiate the treaty of Edinburgh (6 July). This guaranteed the evacuation of foreign troops from Scotland: the lords of the congregation became a provisional government. As for the Queen of Scots, when her husband died the following December, she was elbowed aside by the new regent of France, Catherine de Medici. By August 1561 she had little choice but to return to Scotland, where she was obliged to recognize the Reformation.

Elizabeth's attitude to this Scottish campaign showed that she meant to control her own policy. For the remainder of the reign, diplomacy and sensitive issues such as dynastic marriage negotiations and the succession to the throne were *arcana imperii* (i.e. 'mysteries of state'): matters reserved by Elizabeth for her own decision — or more often indecision — and then hammered out with her inner circle at Court before being presented for wider discussion in the Privy Council. Of course, the Privy Council and leading nobility continued to be involved in policy-making, and it would be false to conclude that the consultative process suddenly narrowed. But there is a parallel with Henry VIII's first divorce campaign when the king and his selected 'political' councillors set the pace at Court. In the 1560s Elizabeth's 'inner ring' comprised Cecil, Parry (d. December 1560), Leicester, Winchester, Pembroke, and Bacon.[32] Other politicians were not expressly excluded, but Cecil followed the queen's own preference when he decided that the Elizabethan establishment should close ranks. True, politics were not yet ideological, but already several radical Protestants were urging the regime to give priority to religious goals. Some Edwardians like Sir Peter Carew and Sir William Pickering had to be kept out of political office. Cecil was further alerted by the career of the idealist Throckmorton, who as ambassador to France worked openly with political revolutionaries among the Huguenots and became so great a liability that he had to be replaced by Sir Thomas Smith.[33]

Yet, backed by Lord Robert Dudley, Throckmorton managed to persuade Elizabeth in 1562 to intervene in the first French War of Religion. The episode caused the queen to burn her fingers, though it served Dudley's purpose by enabling him to make his political début. For, when his whirlwind affair of 1559–60 with the queen stabilized and the scandal had subsided, he adopted Throckmorton as his protégé and tried to trump Cecil's Scottish ace. The massacre of a Huguenot congregation at Vassy by the duke of Guise caused the French Protestants to turn for help to England, which gave Dudley his opportunity (March 1562). Elizabeth's 'fame is great here', Henry Killigrew, a Dudley client and Cecil's future brother-in-law, wrote from a Huguenot stronghold at Le Havre. 'It lies in her hands to banish idolatry out of France.'[34] But Elizabeth's own objective was far more mundane, since she sought to recover Calais, or a French port in lieu, and when she gained possession of Le Havre, the aid she gave the Huguenots was minimal.

By the treaty of Hampton Court Elizabeth promised the Huguenot leader, the Prince of Condé, six thousand troops and a loan of £30,000, in return for which she would hold Le Havre and Dieppe as pledges until Calais was restored (20 September). Robert Dudley was admitted to the Privy Council, and his brother Ambrose, earl of Warwick, was named commander of the army. Cecil, meanwhile, concocted a *pièce justificative* which attempted to put the best possible light on Elizabeth's interventionism. He argued that she sought: (1) to defend the peace of Christendom; (2) to defend England against the consequences of a religious war that would spread throughout Europe if it were not stopped; (3) to defend the people of France against the 'tyranny' of the Catholic Guise faction; and (4) to defend Calais against a Guise plan to prevent its restoration to England under the terms of the treaty of Cateau-Cambrésis.[35]

But the Huguenot field army was routed at Dreux and Condé captured. Next, the duke of Guise was assassinated, and both sides therefore accepted the peace of Amboise which ended the civil war and enabled all Frenchmen to reunite in recovering

Le Havre from the English (19 March 1563). Himself badly
wounded and with his army encircled and stricken by plague,
Warwick agreed to surrender on 28 July. Dudley's attempt to
fuse the backward-looking policy of recovering Calais with the
new-fashioned goal of the Protestant cause had failed.[36]
Although the treaty of Troyes (11 April 1564) ostensibly did little
but end the fighting, Elizabeth lost Calais and forfeited the
indemnity promised by the treaty of Cateau-Cambrésis. Also
her claims for the ransom of four French hostages were halved.
So her aversion to military adventures increased. Meanwhile
Spain sounded a warning that sponsorship of international
Protestantism was unacceptable: Cardinal Granvelle, chief
minister of Philip II's regent in the Netherlands, Margaret of
Parma, closed Flemish ports to English commercial traffic under
the pretext of an outbreak of plague in England; trading was
not resumed until 1565. Despite the threat to English exports,
however, the embargo hurt Antwerp more than London. It even
had a positive result, since cloth-exporters started to develop
alternative markets in Germany and the Baltic region, which
provided a base when Elizabeth's 'cold war' with Spain opened
in December 1568.

Domestic politics in the 1560s centred on the succession to the
throne, Elizabeth's matrimonial intentions, and the Scottish
question. Raised as early as the first week of the 1559 Parliament,
the succession issue became critically urgent several times: in
October 1562 when the queen contracted smallpox; in December
1564 when she was 'sore sick of the flux'; in October 1572 when
she succumbed to fever; and in the autumn of 1584 after William
of Orange was assassinated. Mary, Queen of Scots, was the
strongest claimant on dynastic grounds as grand-daughter of
Margaret Tudor and James IV of Scotland, the next in line being
the Countess of Lennox, child of Margaret's second marriage.
But, under the terms of the Third Act of Succession (1544) and
Henry VIII's last will and testament, Lady Catherine Grey
(younger sister of Jane Grey) had precedence. Moreover, since
Mary remained a Catholic, it followed that Catherine was backed
by the Protestants. So Elizabeth, who was anxious in the light
of mid-Tudor experience not to do anything which would create
a focus for political disaffection, refused to recognize any claim.

She even sent Catherine Grey to the Tower after the latter's clandestine marriage to Hertford, ordering that the union be legally annulled and its offspring bastardized. (Catherine died while under house arrest in January 1568.)

If, however, the Privy Council was united in its wish to see the succession settled, members were divided in their choice of candidate. It was widely acknowledged that an accommodation with Mary was desirable, but the Scottish queen was overconfident, and refused to treat with Elizabeth or to ratify the treaty of Edinburgh unless she was 'by Parliament established heir apparent, or adopted daughter of the queen's majesty'. One scheme mooted in 1563–4 was that Mary should marry Robert Dudley; Elizabeth herself advocated it when Dudley's clients stirred up debate in Parliament about her own marriage (12 January to 10 April 1563).[37] Since Dudley's aim was to marry Elizabeth himself, the manœuvre stopped him in his tracks until September 1564, when Elizabeth created him earl of Leicester. Yet Anglo-Scottish diplomacy remained stalemated, and in July 1565 Mary took unilateral action by marrying her cousin, Henry Darnley, son of the Countess of Lennox. At a stroke she merged the two Scottish claims to the English throne, and bolstered her own claim since Darnley had been born in England, owned land in Yorkshire, and therefore had an unquestionable legal entitlement to inherit property in England. Elizabeth vented her rage on Leicester and attempted to limit the damage, but had been outmanœuvred.

But Mary's star shortly waned: the birth of her son, the future James VI and I, on 19 June 1566, did not prevent this. Until 1565 her Scottish reign achieved real, if uneasy, consensus; her opportunism and self-interested tolerance gave both radicals and conservatives a sufficient sense of security. Inconsistent and indecisive, however, Mary sowed mistrust. She also kept her distance, while her marriage awakened Lennox–Hamilton dynastic rivalry in Scotland. Furthermore, when Darnley was murdered, she married his alleged assassin, the earl of Bothwell, who divorced his wife. So the Scottish nobility formed a confederacy pledged to set Mary 'at liberty'; this sparked civil war, since 'liberty' meant abdication in favour of James, who could be manipulated during a long minority. In so far as Mary had a party by 1567, it was a coalition of Hamiltons, their

affinity, and the opponents of the 'confederacy'. And still Mary
made mistakes. When she escaped from the confederate lords,
she threw her forces into battle at Langside (13 May 1568)—
and lost. She fled across the Solway to seek Elizabeth's aid against
her rebellious subjects.[38]

Against this background the Privy Council and, in 1563 and
1566, Parliament, pressed Elizabeth to settle the succession or
to marry. In perhaps his shrewdest political diagnosis since the
religious settlement, Cecil wrote privately before the session of
1566: 'To require both marriage and stablishing of succession
is the uttermost that can be desired. . . . To require marriage
is most natural, most easy, most plausible to the Queen's
Majesty. To require certainty of succession is most plausible
to all the people' but 'is hardest to be obtained both for the
difficulty to discuss the right and for the loathsomeness in the
Queen's Majesty to consent thereto . . . Corollary: the mean
betwixt these is to determine effectually to marry, and if it succeed
not, then proceed to discussion of the right of the successor.'[39]
And these were the Privy Council's broad tactics in the 1560s:
to petition Elizabeth to marry, and, if she refused, then to use
Parliament as a platform from which to ventilate public fears
over the succession in defiance of the queen's insistence that these
were 'mysteries of state'.

In 1563 Dudley's men persuaded both Houses of Parliament
to petition the queen, but Elizabeth deflected these manœuvres
by saying that she was not vowed to remaining unmarried, and
by promising to settle the succession at the appropriate time.
Among privy councillors in Parliament, Bacon helped to forward
the succession debates, and from another angle Cecil promoted
an unsuccessful bill to perpetuate the Privy Council as a council
of regency should Elizabeth die without naming her successor.
According to an unfinished draft written in his own hand, the
existing Privy Council would be augmented by any additional
councillors named by the queen in her will, and would lawfully
stay in office as a 'Council of State' until a new monarch had
been proclaimed by authority of Parliament.[40]

Nothing was, however, achieved by the petitioning of 1563,
and in the next parliamentary session (30 September 1566 to
2 January 1567) tempers rose sufficiently to threaten a political
crisis. It is not true, as is sometimes argued, that MPs

campaigned from the outset to trade progress on the Crown's subsidy bill for a settlement of the succession. Only a few members tried to tie the two issues together; the Privy Council's efforts were directed until the last minute into *avoiding* rows over taxation which would inhibit 'planted' petitioning manœuvres. But, in the sense that the Council was soon forced to allow that, if the money bill was to succeed, the question of Elizabeth's marriage would have to be allocated parliamentary time, it acknowledged the strength of public opinion. Thereafter, councillors could not fully control debate, partly because they were themselves divided over their choice of candidate for the succession. Elizabeth reacted violently. She berated a parliamentary delegation for insolence; dropped hints that she would imitate Henry VIII's response to opposition; and threw tantrums—in a spectacular scene at Court she banished Leicester and Pembroke from the Presence Chamber (27 October). She called the fourth duke of Norfolk a traitor and embarrassed Northampton by probing how he managed to remarry while his first wife was still alive. Lastly, she harangued the Privy Council, accusing everyone except Lord Treasurer Winchester of thwarting her. Cecil only escaped dismissal because he took care to work through a client of Sir Ambrose Cave when making a desperate final bid *really* to link the money bill to a settlement of the succession.[41]

Yet Elizabeth would not be ruled by her subjects. She also spotted (and exploited) the fact that the demand that she should settle the succession was made by petitioners who could not themselves agree on a candidate: 'They would have twelve or thirteen limited in succession, and the more the better'! True, in 1566 she virtually promised to marry, thereby restoring outward harmony. But she hit out in her dissolution speech, warning Parliament to 'beware how ever you move your prince's patience as you have now done mine'. So, as Cecil observed in his end-of-session 'memorial', no more was gained than in 1563: 'The succession not answered, the marriage not followed.' Although the Archduke's suit dragged on, and Charles IX of France was briefly considered, neither marriage project matured. Almost certainly Elizabeth had nailed her true colours to the mast in 1559, when she told Parliament that 'this shall be for me sufficient that a marble stone shall declare that a Queen, having reigned such a time, lived and died a virgin'.[42]

If, however, the succession was left unsettled, the security of the regime was enhanced in the 1560s by the success of the Court circle in extending its power in the counties. Privy councillors who built up their estates and sat as JPs included Cecil in Lincolnshire and Northamptonshire; Bedford in Devon and Cornwall; Knollys in Oxfordshire; Cave in Leicestershire; Pembroke in Wiltshire and South Wales; and Rogers in Somerset. When the Le Havre expedition was at its climax, Lord Robert Dudley was granted Kenilworth Castle together with vast estates in Wales and the marches, including the lordships of Mortimer and Denbigh. Next, when ennobled earl of Leicester, he replaced the earl of Derby as chamberlain of the palatinate of Chester. His power in the provinces was indeed remarkable. He was a JP in several counties, and became high recorder of Maldon (1565), high steward of Cambridge University (1563), chancellor of Oxford University (1564), and high steward of seven important towns all by 1572. But his role was not unique, only its scale was unusual. The change seems to have been that, whereas under Henry VIII local patronage was exercised by a number of interests, under Elizabeth courtiers gained a monopoly.

The Court's hegemony was, nevertheless, confined to the southern and midland counties. In the north adherence to the 1559 religious settlement, and even perhaps to the regime, was qualified. Mary, Queen of Scots, made no secret of her belief that she could win to her cause all the magnates north of the Trent, since they were 'of the old religion'. In 1564 dioceses most hostile to Elizabeth were Carlisle, Durham, and York. In Cumberland and Westmorland the Catholic mass was openly retained; York diocese was said to be more 'tractable' save that 'the nobility remain in their wonted blindness'. So Elizabeth and Cecil had no choice but to complete Henry VIII's policy of displacing the Percies, Nevilles, and Dacres from offices of military or political importance in the far north. Thomas Percy, earl of Northumberland, was deprived of the wardenship of the Middle March; the southerner Lord Hunsdon was put in charge of Berwick; and Lord Grey of Wilton and the earl of Bedford were named wardens of East March in succession. Next, Northumberland's enemy, Sir John Forster, was given the Middle March; and Lord Scrope was appointed warden of West

March on the death of the fourth Lord Dacre. But this sweep made the earls of Northumberland and Westmorland a destabilizing force: in 1569 they attached their hopes to a *putsch* linked to the succession of the Queen of Scots.[43]

The Northern Rising followed the disintegration of a powerful aristocratic and semi-Catholic lobby at Court that wished Cecil ousted for his seizure of Philip II's treasure-ships in December 1568, and aimed to rescue the fortunes of Mary, Queen of Scots, with minimum harm to Elizabeth. The immediate objective was advocacy of a proposal to marry Mary to the duke of Norfolk, England's premier peer, who would use his influence to settle the succession to the throne and to secure the interests of the nobility and a *rapprochement* with Philip II at a swoop by replacing Cecil as chief minister. Norfolk was prominent in this conspiracy, and his most consistent Court supporters were Arundel, Pembroke, and Lord Lumley. They regarded Mary as the 'second person' of the realm and wished to protect her claim to the throne both as an end in itself, and as the route to overthrowing the Cecil regime. An allied party led by Leicester and Throckmorton, whose co-operation they secured, was also important, because it believed that Mary, if restored to the Scottish throne, would quickly pledge herself to a Protestant and anglophile policy. Here crossed wires existed, because Norfolk was nominally Protestant but really semi-Catholic, and it is far from clear that Mary would have done what Leicester hoped as the duke's wife. Leicester perhaps wished to discomfort Cecil, but it is unlikely that he was among those who sought to topple him.

Yet the crucial connection, as events turned out, was the northern one. Norfolk's Court party was backed by the earls of Northumberland and Westmorland. They were not the duke's most influential supporters, but they were staunch. Charles Neville, earl of Westmorland, was involved as Norfolk's brother-in-law, while Northumberland was motivated by religion as well as by thwarted ambition: he stood for ultra-Catholicism, having reconverted to Rome in 1567. Honour dictated that these peers should help their southern counterparts. But Norfolk's objectives were designed to appeal to the northern nobility in the broadest sense: preferment of 'new men' by Henry VIII and Elizabeth had eroded the traditional definition of 'nobility' based on land

and lineage. In this respect, however, it is significant that Lord Scrope was willing to condone an internal Court coup but refused to join the Northern Rising and was active in its suppression; although he, too, was Norfolk's brother-in-law, he valued his lineage connection less than his Crown appointment as warden of West March.[44]

When Elizabeth learned of Norfolk's proposed marriage, she angrily vetoed it and the Court campaign collapsed. The Northern Rising was sparked when the earls of Northumberland and Westmorland were abandoned by their southern allies and left to fend for themselves. Norfolk, Arundel, Pembroke, Lumley, and Throckmorton submitted to the queen; Leicester contrived to emerge unscathed 'considering he hath revealed all that he saith he knoweth of himself'. When, however, these leaders withdrew, their link with the northerners ceased. The northern nobility itself split after Norfolk sent them a message forbidding a rising; if one was unleashed, his head was forfeit — this left Northumberland and Westmorland isolated.

Still revolt was not inevitable until Norfolk was sent to the Tower and the two militant earls themselves received Elizabeth's summons. They feared to comply, for they had discussed the succession and sought Spanish and papal aid. Westmorland cursed Norfolk, saying 'he was the undoing of them for by that message [i.e. not to rise] . . . their friends fell from them and gave them over'.[45] But they had taken their cause beyond the limits of acceptable political action and their sense of fear and isolation drove them into revolt. They therefore fell back on the old baronial argument that the queen was misled by evil councillors and mustered their forces after some delay. They marched to Durham, and restored the Catholic mass in the cathedral (14 November). Ripon and Hartlepool were then taken; in a procession at Ripon the banner of the Five Wounds of Christ (the emblem of the Pilgrimage of Grace) was raised alongside the standards of Percy and Neville. But there was no mass resort to arms, and, before the earls could challenge York, their support collapsed. Perhaps their one chance of success depended on rescuing Mary, Queen of Scots, by a raid on Tutbury where she was confined, but she was hastily moved out of range by her custodian, the earl of Shrewsbury. Fleeing into Scotland, Westmorland escaped to the Netherlands, his estates confiscated by the Crown; Northumberland was executed after the Scots sold him to Elizabeth for £2,000 in 1572.[46]

It is misleading to see the Northern Rising as a 'neo-feudal' revolt. Its inspiration came from events at Court, and the rebels numbered 5,700 at most, of whom only 140 to 180 were members of Percy or Neville affinities. But the result was that the earls were as outmanœuvred regionally as Norfolk had been at Court. Elizabeth and Cecil therefore seized their opportunity to subdue the north and enforce compliance, acting with a degree of severity that reflected their sense of insecurity in the region. First, Elizabeth ordered the summary hanging of seven hundred of the rebels. Examples were to be made in every village represented in the Rising, though commanders on the spot moderated the queen's instructions; in Darlington, where exact figures are known, only twenty-four persons suffered out of forty-one 'appointed' to be hung. These reprisals were followed by raids into Scotland by the earl of Sussex and Lord Hunsdon that burned three hundred villages, razed fifty castles, and weakened the party of Mary, Queen of Scots, in the civil war.[47]

Next, Cecil planned a comprehensive redistribution of northern patronage: lands and offices forfeited by attainted nobles and rebels were to be given only to members of the Elizabethan establishment; loyal local gentry were to be 'commended and noticed'; and forfeited castles were to be handed only to the Crown's wardens and officials. Lastly, the Council of the North was reconstituted in 1572 under a new president, the puritan third earl of Huntingdon, Elizabeth's cousin. Whereas previously the Council had been directed by local magnates or men with northern kin, Huntingdon was an outsider with no local ties who relied entirely on his Crown appointment and the backing of the Privy Council. Despite this disadvantage, however, he attacked Catholic recusancy and noble retaining with unprecedented vigour; he issued instructions to the northern JPs urging enforcement of the penal laws, the removal of illegal enclosures, and the relief of the poor. In particular, he ensured that sound Protestants were appointed as preachers in the market towns of the north, thereby promoting the Reformation. He was even willing to shield radical puritans in the dioceses of York and Durham on the grounds that they were the scourge of recusancy.[48]

The defeat of the Rising silenced criticism of Cecil's foreign policy. But why had he ended cordial relations with Spain by advising Elizabeth to 'borrow' the Genoese bullion which Philip II's ships were transporting to the Netherlands to pay the duke of Alva's troops? When the small Spanish vessels took refuge at Plymouth and Southampton to escape a gale and privateers, coffers containing £85,000 in cash were seized and brought to London (December 1568). Alva retaliated by arresting English merchants and by placing an embargo on English property in the Netherlands, which led in return to similar measures against Spaniards in England and consequent disruption of trade. Superficially Cecil urged this brinkmanship after the English ambassador to Spain had been declared *persona non grata* for calling the pope 'a canting little monk', and after skirmishes in the Atlantic in which John Hawkins was said to have plundered goods worth a quarter of a million ducats. But more dangerous concerns motivated Cecil, who for two years had suspected that Catherine de Medici and Philip II were planning a Catholic coalition, a suspicion reinforced when the Wars of Religion resumed in France. But the balloon went up in northern Europe in August 1567, when Alva marched into the Netherlands at the head of the main field army of Spain: eight thousand veteran infantry reinforced by German, Italian, and Walloon levies to the number of forty thousand. Quite apart from the threat to the Dutch Calvinists, Philip II had lodged a potential Catholic invasion force less than 200 miles from London.[49]

The importance of Alva's arrival cannot be overestimated. As the 'revolt of the Netherlands' slowly unfolded, so did the biggest European crisis of the second half of the sixteenth century. True, the Calvinists were largely confined to the northern coastal provinces of Holland and Zeeland, but elsewhere in the Netherlands Catholics resented their Spanish 'colonial' status, rejected the Inquisition, and saw Philip II as an alien bureaucrat. Exacerbated by high food prices, famine, and unemployment, spontaneous iconoclasm erupted in 1566, which was why Alva's troops were sent to restore order. But the Spanish *tercios* alternately won victories, then abandoned their posts and mutinied for lack of pay. So Alva and his successor, Don Luis de Requesens, could neither subdue nor conciliate the Dutch, and England faced a dilemma when the capture of Brielle and Flushing by William of Orange and the Sea Beggars signalled open but confused revolt (April 1572). For without English aid the Dutch rebels were likely to turn to France against Spain, which raised the spectre of Valois domination of the entire Channel and North Sea. So the fate of the Dutch became a matter of political as well as religious concern to England. On the one hand, the Privy Council feared for the safety of the Dutch Calvinists and that of Antwerp as a mercantile centre. On the other, the fact that Philip's crack troops were so close proved terrifying, since it was obvious that any concerted Catholic effort to extirpate European Protestantism must first attempt the reduction of England.

The slide towards ideological confrontation in the 1570s accelerated when Pope Pius V proclaimed Elizabeth's excommunication and deposition in the bull *Regnans in excelsis* (February 1570). Although the bull arrived too late to assist the leaders of the Northern Rising, it created an inexorable logic for Elizabeth: that Protestants were loyalists and Catholics traitors. When Parliament next met (2 April to 29 May 1571), every member had to take the oath of supremacy. Thereafter, the Privy Council steered through severe penal legislation which included a new Treason Act to protect Elizabeth's title to the throne; an Act against Bulls from the See of Rome which made it treason for English subjects to obtain, publish, or receive papal documents; an Act against Fugitives to confiscate the goods, chattels, and landed income of Catholic exiles; and an act confirming the attainders of the northern rebels.[50]

Anti-Catholic fears multiplied when Cecil detected the Ridolfi plot, the object of which was to land six thousand Spaniards at Harwich in order to depose Elizabeth and enthrone Mary, Queen of Scots. Despite being imprisoned after her flight to England, Mary had become a focal point for conspiracies. A spin-off from the Northern Rising, the Ridolfi plot linked Mary, the duke of Norfolk, Lord Lumley, Guerau de Spes (the Spanish ambassador in London), the Florentine banker Roberti di Ridolfi, Philip II, and the pope. Norfolk, who had been released from the Tower in August 1570, was rearrested, tried, and convicted of treason (16 January 1572). But Elizabeth dithered over his execution and the limits to which she would go against Mary. So the Privy

Council demanded an emergency session of Parliament which opened on 8 May, whereupon councillors and their 'men of business' staged a concerted drive to persuade Elizabeth to execute Norfolk and attaint Mary. But they succeeded only to the extent that Norfolk was sacrificed (2 June). When shown a bill that Mary 'be attainted and disabled to take any dignity of this realm upon her', Elizabeth insisted that it be dropped. Instead she opted for a lesser bill that the Scottish queen be 'unable to enjoy the Crown of this realm'—but then vetoed it! Despite the Privy Council's endorsement of the first bill, Elizabeth would not be 'bounced' into a course of action she preferred not to take. As Cecil wrote to Walsingham, then in France: 'All that we have laboured for and had with full consent brought to fashion—I mean a law to make the Scottish Queen unable and unworthy of succession to the crown—was by her Majesty neither assented to nor rejected, but deferred.'[51]

Walsingham had been sent as ambassador to France in 1570 when Anglo-Spanish tension was high. Soon his commission was to negotiate an Anglo-French *entente*: the bait was a proposal of marriage between Elizabeth and the duke of Anjou, second son of Catherine de Medici, and brother of Charles IX. A defensive league with France as a counterweight against Spain was envisaged, though, when this was achieved by the treaty of Blois (19 April 1572), the marriage decoy was forgotten. Had not the Massacre of St Bartholomew followed, the treaty would have been a landmark, since by its terms Mary, Queen of Scots, was effectively abandoned by France. As Sir Thomas Smith told Elizabeth, 'if Spain will now threaten . . . it will be afraid hereafter, seeing such a wall adjoined'.[52]

Yet the treaty was eclipsed by tragedy. Beginning with their leader Coligny, some three thousand Huguenots were slaughtered in Paris (24–30 August), and ten thousand more were killed in provincial France over a period of three weeks. To Protestants the Massacre was clear proof of a Catholic conspiracy between the French royal family, Philip II, and the papacy; premeditated crime was assumed. Since official French accounts of events conflicted, the Protestants' hysteria seemed justified. All England was on fire with the news. Bishop Sandes of London advised Cecil: 'Forthwith to cut off the Scottish Queen's head.'[53] In a panic Elizabeth, Cecil, and Leicester sent

Killigrew to Scotland on an abortive mission to persuade the Protestant earl of Mar (regent, 1571–2) to accept Mary for trial in Scotland 'so as neither that realm nor this should be endangered by her hereafter'. Cecil told Walsingham:

I see the Devil is suffered by the Almighty God for our sins to be strong in following the persecution of Christ's members. And therefore we are not only to be vigilant of our own defence against such traitorous attempts as lately have been put in use there in France, but also to call ourselves to repentance.[54]

So Cecil saw the Massacre as a providential scourge. God spoke through events to warn men of the consequences of their transgressions. Thereafter, Elizabethan politics oscillated between *realpolitik* and religion, though this was a wider European development. For, whereas dynastic, chivalric, commercial, and personal ambitions had hitherto chiefly dominated the Renaissance stage, the polarization of rival religious creeds after the closing session of the Council of Trent meant that politicians increasingly saw themselves as combatants engaged in a cosmic confrontation between right and wrong. The concept of the 'true church' that Catholics and Protestants promulgated in their diametrically opposed ways was pervasive; it ensured that pragmatism was overtaken by dogmatism, haggling by perpetual struggle, and compromise by persecution.[55]

Within the Elizabethan establishment itself, committed Protestants steadily replaced the older generation of privy councillors in the 1570s. New appointments included Sir Walter Mildmay, Sir Ralph Sadler (perhaps an absentee councillor since the beginning of the reign), the earl of Warwick, Sir Thomas Smith, Sir Francis Walsingham, and Sir Henry Sidney (lord president of Wales and lord deputy of Ireland). True, there were exceptions to the rule: the earl of Sussex was a pragmatist, while Sir James Croft was semi-Catholic—he owed his appointment to Elizabeth's habit of balancing points of view. In addition, the queen's second favourite, Christopher Hatton, who replaced Knollys at Court as captain of the guard, and was knighted and sworn of the Privy Council in 1577, was anti-puritan enough to become the target of an assassination attempt in 1573. But the overwhelming balance of power in the Privy Council after

1572 was Protestant; even Hatton's position was equivocal. His anti-puritan bark was worse than his bite and partly reflected his client status. Originally a gentleman pensioner at Court who 'danced his way' into office and who constantly owed Elizabeth money, he acquired a special obligation to attack religious nonconformity.[56]

The 'inner ring' at Court in the 1570s and early 1580s centred on Cecil, Leicester, Sussex (d. 1583), Bedford, and Mildmay, who were joined by Walsingham, Hatton, and Sir Thomas Bromley (lord chancellor, 1579-87).[57] Walsingham was the most single-minded ideologue in this group, an avowed 'political puritan' who at every opportunity championed the Protestant cause. Leicester, Bedford, and Mildmay were less strident but equally militant; Leicester's goal was to lead an English expeditionary force in support of the Dutch revolt, something which in 1576-7 was tantalizingly close until Elizabeth changed her mind. By contrast, Cecil became cautious in the 1570s. First, Elizabeth raised him to the peerage as baron of Burghley (February 1571) and admitted him to the Order of the Garter (June 1572). Next, when the marquis of Winchester died, she appointed him lord treasurer (July 1572). Thereafter, he avoided taking risks, though his reasons are elusive. It was said that his personal ambition came to overshadow his public ambition, whereas the opposite was true of Leicester.[58] But to accuse him of complacency is unfair. He knew almost as well as Elizabeth that *realpolitik* required England to respond to external events after the Massacre of St Bartholomew. He also knew that Walsingham's emphasis on a Protestant coalition sprang as much from the latter's urge to see the Anglican Church transformed into a Calvinist reformed church than from objective military calculations.[59]

Burghley nevertheless allowed Walsingham after 1572 to assume the dynamic role he himself had played earlier. (He had known the younger man since Cambridge days, had employed him on minor Court business, and ensured his election to the House of Commons in 1559 and 1563.) When he vacated the secretaryship of state, Burghley first suggested his 'Athenian' mentor Sir Thomas Smith for the post, and then placed Walsingham alongside him (December 1573). After Smith's death, Thomas Wilson served as second secretary until 1581;

thereafter Walsingham served alone until his death (April 1590), except for an interlude in 1586–7 when William Davison was second secretary. (Although Davison drew his salary until 1608, he was disgraced for his part in dispatching Elizabeth's signed warrant for the execution of Mary, Queen of Scots.)[60]

To some extent Burghley stepped back from the limelight because he was overworked. His expertise was largely in the fields of financial, religious, and socio-economic policy, whereas Walsingham specialized in diplomacy and espionage. As lord treasurer Burghley co-ordinated the Privy Council, managed Parliament, presided over the exchequer and court of wards, sat as a JP in five counties, and kept a vigilant eye on recusants and English Catholic exiles abroad. Perhaps consciously after 1572 he turned elder statesman. But if so, he also believed that Walsingham was the ablest man for the secretaryship in the 1570s. At the very least the latter's ideological standpoint was in tune with the changed European order. Certainly there was no sign that the crisis caused by the revolt of the Netherlands admitted an easy solution. On the contrary, Holland and Zeeland managed barely to hold out until Philip II went bankrupt again (September 1575). Thereafter, both Philip's Walloon and Spanish armies mutinied (July and November 1576): the brutal pillaging of the towns of Aalst and Antwerp provoked a new wave of hispanophobia in the Netherlands.

Elizabeth's preferred diplomatic tactic in the 1570s was defensive neutrality: she adopted it whenever possible. She denied that links existed between the Anglican Church and the Calvinist reformed church. More than Cecil and the Privy Council, too, she appreciated the tenacity of Habsburg–Valois rivalry: an *entente* with France could be used to counter the threat of Spanish hegemony. But her prevarication became a matter of passionate concern to many committed Protestants. When a planned Huguenot campaign to relieve the Dutch rebels was frustrated by the Massacre of St Bartholomew, private initiatives were taken to compensate for the queen's inertia. Several thousand volunteer soldiers, led by a Welshman, Thomas Morgan, crossed to Holland and Zeeland; more followed under Sir Humphrey Gilbert. Yet Gilbert was given official instructions to keep the French out of Flushing. As Cecil later noted: 'Necessary for England that the State of the Low Countries should continue in their ancient government, without either subduing it to the Spanish nation or joining it to the Crown of France.'[61]

So the six principles of English diplomacy from the Massacre of St Bartholomew until 1585 were gradually formulated: (1) England would not directly intervene in the Netherlands; (2) volunteers might assist the Dutch upon conditions; (3) a defensive Anglo-French *entente* would be deployed against Spain; (4) France would be encouraged to support the Dutch revolt, but a French conquest of the Netherlands must at all costs be prevented; (5) Spain should be persuaded to return the Netherlands to the semi-autonomous position they had enjoyed under Charles V; and (6) the *entente* should be couched so as to exclude French influence permanently from Scotland.

The Massacre of St Bartholomew caused an estrangement in Anglo-French relations. Walsingham, who as ambassador in Paris allowed his house to become a sanctuary for Protestants, said of the perpetrators: 'I think less peril to live with them as enemies than as friends.'[62] But moral outrage was tempered by *realpolitik*. Elizabeth authorized the sending of munitions to assist the Huguenots and allowed the count of Montgomery to muster ships in England for the relief of La Rochelle. Yet simultaneously she agreed to stand as godmother to Charles IX's daughter, and entertained a fresh round of dynastic marriage negotiations — this time the candidate was Francis, duke of Alençon, brother of Charles IX and of the duke of Anjou, and the youngest of Catherine de Medici's brood.[63] Catherine pushed this match to the extent of offering Leicester a royal bride, so she was in earnest. Furthermore, the negotiations proved to be Elizabeth's winning card for a decade: Alençon was deployed whenever an English reaction was required abroad. He was used to bind England with France against Spain; to protect the Huguenots and *politiques* against the French Catholic League; to fight Elizabeth's battles in the Netherlands; and even in a short-lived final attempt to recover Calais. He was manipulated to curtail Guise intrigue in France, Scotland, and England; and to persuade Philip II to compromise with the Dutch. France, too, was attracted to a scheme that dignified the duke while withdrawing him from the domestic arena where he provided a focus for disaffection. So Alençon visited England in August

1579 and October 1581 to forward his marriage suit, on the latter occasion staying for three months. During his first visit Elizabeth seriously contemplated marrying him; but she shook off sentiment for diplomatic dividends — at his second departure she privately rejoiced to see him leave.

On these matters the Privy Council was split. But divisions were not pro- and anti-Spanish but between *realpolitik* and religion. With few exceptions, councillors were united against Spain and committed to the European Protestant cause. The difference was that Sussex and Burghley opposed unnecessary expenditure and risks; Walsingham and Leicester, by contrast, advocated military intervention in the Netherlands. The whole Court was drawn into the debate, because Leicester mobilized the Dudley clientage, which joined forces with Walsingham's circle of government officials. Yet Elizabeth remained unmoved. Her policy — if the defensive expediency of 1572–85 can be dignified with that term — attempted to reconcile conflicting strategic, commercial, and religious interests at minimum cost. When Charles IX died in May 1574, she renewed the treaty of Blois with Henry III but sent money to the Protestant John Casimir of the Palatinate to muster aid for the Huguenots. Only after Philip II's bankruptcy was she briefly prepared to consider mediation or intervention in the Netherlands. In 1576–7 the Privy Council debated terms for an Anglo-Netherlands *entente* and urged William of Orange to restrain Dutch privateers, whom the queen habitually used as an excuse for inaction. The Council was possibly even unanimous in its support for the Dutch *entente*. But when all the diplomatic work was done, Elizabeth refused to budge. When faced with taking the final decision she threw tantrums and reverted to a policy of pseudo-mediation between Philip II and his subjects.[64]

In the autumn of 1577 Spanish finances again permitted a resumption of limited offensives in the Netherlands under the command of the new governor-general, Don John of Austria. Some five or six thousand more English and Scottish volunteers therefore joined the Dutch; Elizabeth sent Casimir £40,000 to recruit mercenaries; and she lent the States General £20,000 while guaranteeing further loans totalling £28,757. Since Elizabeth refused direct intervention, however, William of Orange turned to France, and, shortly before Don John died (October 1578),

Alençon accepted the title of 'Defender of the Liberties of the Low Countries'. But the Dutch revolt became too extreme for the Catholic southern (Walloon) provinces; they cut their ties with Calvinism, formed the Union of Arras, and made peace with Spain (January 1579). The Calvinist United Provinces were left to fight on alone, though Spanish operations were virtually abandoned in 1580–1 while Philip II annexed Portugal and the Azores, which added Brazil, parts of Africa and India, and the Moluccas to his empire. Elizabeth reacted to this extended Spanish hegemony by subsidizing Alençon as leader of the Dutch revolt and by unsuccessfully attempting to negotiate a full offensive and defensive alliance with France. Alençon even accepted the hereditary sovereignty of the United Provinces and sailed to Flushing to lead an invading Huguenot army (February 1582). But, despite an English subsidy of £70,000 towards his costs of 2.7 million *livres*, his enterprise collapsed through arrogance and incompetence. He abdicated in disgrace and returned to France, where he died (10 June 1584).

The new governor-general of the Netherlands was Philip's nephew, the celebrated prince of Parma, who recalled the Spanish *tercios* to fight the Dutch in 1582. But Elizabeth's diplomacy fell apart less because of Alençon's defeat than because her luck ran out. True, the Privy Council's efforts to obtain a full Anglo-French alliance failed largely because of her vanity. She could not bring herself to marry Alençon, yet insisted on a treaty at the cheapest possible price and on terms that left her the widest latitude.[65] But a full alliance would have dissolved on Alençon's death, and it is more correct to say that Elizabeth's diplomacy was overwhelmed by events. In 1578 James VI (aged twelve) listened to the enemies of the Protestant regent in Scotland, the earl of Morton, whereupon Esmé Stuart, Lord of Aubigny, heir to the Lennox interest in the succession, sailed from France and captivated James, who created him duke of Lennox (August 1581). A conspiracy to reimpose Catholicism on Scotland and to conquer England with Spanish and papal aid then took shape: Lennox, the Guises, Mary, Queen of Scots, Bernardino de Mendoza (the Spanish ambassador in London), the Jesuits, the pope, and a sceptical Philip II were involved. Lennox was ousted after a palace coup by the Protestant lords (August 1582); he fled to France, where he died. Yet further plots were spawned.

In November 1583 the Privy Council tortured Francis Throckmorton, who implicated the Queen of Scots, Mendoza, and some disaffected Catholic nobility in a Guise plan to invade England.

Next, the militant pope Gregory XIII (1572–85) financed an invasion of Ireland by Thomas Stukeley (1578). Always a gambler, Stukeley shifted his attention at the last minute to Morocco, where he died at the battle of Alcazar. But in 1579 James Fitzmaurice Fitzgerald, cousin of the earl of Desmond, and Nicholas Sander, Counter-Reformation polemicist and papal legate, sailed to Ireland with Philip's covert aid. Although the invaders were only sixty in number, with reinforcements of six hundred sent the following year, their arrival sparked a revolt in Munster that cost Elizabeth £254,960 to extinguish.

Lastly, Alençon's demise reopened the French civil wars. Henry III lacked issue, therefore the succession, when he died, would pass to his nearest male relative, the Protestant Henry of Navarre (later Henry IV), whom the Guises aimed to exclude with Spanish help (secret treaty of Joinville, December 1584). When Navarre was debarred from the succession and excommunicated, fighting resumed. So the succession struggle neutralized France just as Philip II came under pressure to protect his Atlantic economy from English plunder. For Sir Francis Drake's expedition of 1577–80 — which achieved the circumnavigation of the globe — pillaged Spanish property under Elizabeth's direct commission, the 'interventionist' party at Court having persuaded her of the profits of 'underhand' warfare on the Spanish Main. In 1578 Hawkins was appointed treasurer of the navy: he undertook privateering voyages against Spain using his own and Elizabeth's ships, while lesser men resorted to straightforward piracy. Yet Philip II was strong at sea; the size of his fleets (300,000 tons) exceeded that of the Netherlands (232,000 tons) and England (42,000 tons) combined. In fact, his naval strength inspired the marquis of Santa Cruz, Spain's premier admiral, to propose the 'Enterprise of England' — an armada to overthrow Elizabeth. The Spanish mercantile community was enthusiastic; Parma approved, too, provided the Netherlands were subdued first, and a surprise attack by thirty-four thousand troops across the Straits of Dover launched afterwards. (Spanish debate centred on whether the Netherlands or England should be targeted first.)[66]

The pivotal incident, however, was the assassination of William of Orange (10 July 1584). This created panic among English politicians who feared that Elizabeth, too, might fall victim to the bullet or knife. When news of the treaty of Joinville reached Walsingham in the spring of 1585, the Catholic–Habsburg domination of Europe was apparent. Then Philip II seized all English ships in Spanish ports on the pretext that he needed shipping for a fleet assembling at Lisbon (May 1585). Englishmen feared this was the Armada, though it was not. These events coincided with Parma's masterful assaults upon the rebel towns of Flanders and Brabant, which fell like ninepins before his encircling blockades. Between 1583 and 1585 Philip II devoted all his resources to Parma's reconquest, using bribes as well as arms: the Dutch lamented his 'golden bullets' that pierced men's hearts better than Catholic gunnery.[67]

The Privy Council's debates thus reached their climax. Since Henry III had become the puppet of the Catholic League, should Elizabeth rescue the United Provinces? In answering this question the 'interventionists' sought to demonstrate that outright war was unavoidable, while the 'neutralists' reasoned that coastal defences, the Scottish border, and the navy should be strengthened, but intervention in Europe avoided. 'So would England become impregnable and she on every side be secure at home and a terror to her enemies.'[68] Of course, Elizabeth disliked Calvinists; she regarded the Dutch as rebels against their lawful monarch; she wanted peace rather than war; and she preferred moderate Spanish to alternative rule in the Netherlands — a 'Fortress England' policy appealed to her.

Yet the split between 'interventionists' and 'Fortress English' can be exaggerated. With few exceptions, all were Protestants who believed that, if Parma subjugated the Netherlands, Philip II would invade England; and with France divided and the ports and shipping of Holland and Zeeland in Spain's possession, England would succumb. As Burghley warned Elizabeth in the autumn of 1584: 'Your strength abroad, it must be in joining in good confederacy, or at least intelligence with those that would willingly embrace the same.'[69] He suggested alliances with the

Turks, Morocco, Florence, Venice, and Ferrara; but especially pleaded for relief for the United Provinces. So there was no factional dimension to the Privy Council's debates in 1584–5, only the difference of emphasis concerning military overextension that had existed since the Le Havre expedition.

On 7 July 1585 the 'interventionists' handed Elizabeth a synopsis of their case: its theme was 'protection from Spain'. It elucidated Philip's military aims and leadership of the Catholic cause; the machinations of the papacy; the prospect of a Hispano-Guise Catholic crusade in Europe; the weakness of Elizabeth's land forces; and the value of England as booty. It urged the creation of a Protestant coalition in Europe; the mustering of an English citizen-militia modelled on that of ancient Rome; and the improvement of the navy. While hinting that Elizabeth should accept the sovereignty of the United Provinces, it did attempt to debate both sides of the question. Finally, it claimed that, if Philip triumphed, France must 'in policy' join him in partitioning England to avert her own encirclement by Spain.[70]

Elizabeth resolutely rejected the Dutch offer of sovereignty in 1576 and 1585. Escalating costs of warfare and her refusal to allow the Crown to assume unlimited liability for European adventures rendered the attitudes of Edward III, Henry V, and Henry VIII anachronistic. She was, however, persuaded that, if the Dutch revolt failed, Philip II would launch the 'Enterprise of England'. She therefore signed a preliminary treaty of alliance with the States General on 10 August 1585 at Nonsuch, offering 6,400 infantry and 1,000 cavalry, together with £126,000 per annum for their maintenance — roughly a quarter of the cost of the war. As security for reimbursement, she was to garrison Brielle and Flushing — the two 'cautionary' towns; and she promised to appoint a nobleman to command her forces who, with two colleagues, would serve as political advisers to the States. Lastly, Drake was unleashed with a mixed squadron of private and naval ships, with orders to free seized English vessels and crews from Spanish ports, and afterwards to lead a privateering expedition against Philip's silver fleet.[71]

In the last week of August 1585 the professional soldier and English 'volunteer' captain since 1577, Colonel John Norris, landed two thousand infantry at Middleburg. In September Leicester obtained command, but did not arrive at Flushing until

10 December. His nephew, Sir Philip Sidney, and Burghley's son, Thomas, were put in charge of the 'cautionary' towns — this signalled political compromise. Also Sir Henry Killigrew was named one of the English members of the Dutch Council of State. So had Elizabeth espoused the Protestant cause? Was she the English Deborah, as the London radicals had hoped in 1559?

The truth is that, six weeks after backing the 'interventionists', the queen fell victim to doubts. If *realpolitik* at last dictated that she follow religion, instinct urged caution and reserve. In effect, she insulated herself from the implications of the treaty: Leicester was given instructions that restricted him to defensive rather than offensive operations; Norris was rebuked for engaging Parma's army; and Burghley began to reopen negotiations with Spain. Leicester's aims thus contradicted Elizabeth's from the moment he reached The Hague. He attempted to establish a firm base in the Netherlands and to forge a Protestant coalition; his supporters depicted him as Moses, the 'protector' of the 'true' (i.e. Calvinist reformed) church. Yet his orders required him to avoid the 'hazard of a battle', to 'govern' the United Provinces politically — acting as something more than an ambassador but less than a viceroy — and to embargo Dutch trade with Spain. Elizabeth, meanwhile, neutralized James VI with a pension (July 1585). Also she lent Navarre £38,937 in a last-ditch attempt to prevent France from falling into Guise hands (1586–7). But she shunned a Protestant coalition: Navarre's subsidy was paid through Horatio Palavicino to Duke Casimir, who was to supply German *secours*. (It was regrettable that Navarre's bonds for the repayment of his loan were lost by the exchequer!) If rationalized, Elizabeth's objective in 1585–8 was to restore Dutch morale in order to induce a compromise with Spain. All this frustrated Walsingham and Leicester, who advocated a 'godly league' uniting England, Holland, the Huguenots, German princes, and James VI. When Elizabeth delayed a portion of Navarre's subsidy, even Burghley grumbled: 'Thus you see how her Majesty can find means at small holes to stop her own light.' And Walsingham observed: 'The whole course of her Majesty's proceedings showeth that she hath no power to do things in season as may work her security and therefore we must prepare ourselves for the cross.'[72]

Ralegh quipped of Elizabeth's foreign policy, 'Her Majesty did all by halves.' However, her attitude must be placed in context. While the fate of the Dutch captured the hearts and minds of Europeans, and was of vital significance to international politics, it was not the sole concern of England, Spain, France, and Germany. Was England to withdraw from Ireland in order to safeguard the Protestant cause? Was Spain to abandon the Mediterranean in order to reconquer the Netherlands? It is well said, 'These were real choices, for no European state in the early modern period possessed sufficient resources to fight effectively in the Netherlands and also attain its political objectives elsewhere.'[73] So 'Deborah' and 'Moses' symbolized unattainable aspirations. Ideological politics were not omnipotent: the New Jerusalem was a mirage. Yet the stakes were never higher, nor the dangers greater. When the Armada sailed past the Lizard in July 1588, Elizabeth was isolated. In the last analysis, Protestant England's deliverance was a matter of luck.

ELIZABETHAN RELIGION

It is a paradox that, at the time the Elizabethan religious settlement was made, it settled little. The royal supremacy was restored; the Act of Uniformity came into effect on the feast of the Nativity of St John the Baptist 1559 (24 June); and the secularized church lands were to remain in the hands of the laity—a vital principle unchallenged until the ascendancy of Archbishop Laud. The Uniformity Act required that every cathedral and parish 'minister'—a significant word, for 'priest' now smacked of 'popery'—should 'say and use the Matins, Evensong, celebration of the Lord's Supper and administration of each of the sacraments' according to the revised Prayer Book,[1] but, while this meant that England suddenly became Protestant in the eyes of central government, a huge missionary effort to win the hearts and minds of parishioners (especially those in remoter counties and borderlands) lay ahead. For outside London, the south-east, parts of East Anglia, and towns such as Bristol, Coventry, Colchester, and Ipswich, Catholicism predominated at Elizabeth's accession; the bishops and most parochial incumbents were Marians or traditionalists, whilst fully committed Protestants were few. Whereas Elizabeth and Cecil inherited all the negative and destructive elements of Henrician anti-papalism and Edwardian Protestantism, they had inadequate resources to build the Anglican Church, though it is false to see their task purely in confessional terms. By this stage inertia was strong among those who had come to regard the church as a rich corporation to be asset-stripped, or as a socio-political nexus whose leaders were local governors and whose festivals characterized the communal year. In addition, Protestantism, with its emphasis on 'godly' preaching and Bible study, was an academic creed, unattractive to villagers steeped in the oral traditions and symbolic ritualism of medieval England.

Since all but one of the Marian bishops refused to take the oath of supremacy, they were deprived and replaced by

Protestants. Cecil made the new selections, choosing with three exceptions Cambridge men: university professionals linked to the 'Athenian' group who had in most cases been exiles under Mary. Those who had not gone abroad, like Matthew Parker, archbishop of Canterbury (1559–1575), had lived privately or in hiding, except for William Downham, who had served as Elizabeth's chaplain.[2] Yet the Protestantism of most of these men contradicted the queen's conservative views. While Elizabeth's church government was largely one of delegated control interrupted by occasional but decisive interventions, leading bishops such as Edmund Grindal of London (later of York and Canterbury), Thomas Bentham of Coventry and Lichfield (a contributor to the Geneva Bible), Robert Horne of Winchester, John Parkhurst of Norwich, James Pilkington of Durham, Edwin Sandes of Worcester, and Edmund Scambler of Peterborough supported the returned exiles' desire for reformation beyond the terms of the Act of Uniformity. While these bishops rarely declined to implement royal policy—Grindal as archbishop of Canterbury was alone willing to tell Elizabeth he was subject to a higher power—they were scarcely satisfied with the political *via media* that the 1559 settlement represented. Men of Calvinist convictions, they saw the settlement as flawed, though it is too bold to say that the Elizabethan church was hijacked by an émigré government at odds with the supreme governor's intentions.[3]

The Acts of Supremacy and Uniformity were supported by royal injunctions and commissions for a visitation to enforce them.[4] Drafted by Cecil and his men in June 1559, the injunctions imitated Protector Somerset's that, in turn, reissued those of Thomas Cromwell, though there were changes and additions. Clergy were ordered to observe the royal supremacy and preach against superstition and papal usurpation; images, relics, and miracles were attacked (but surprisingly not forbidden); the Bible and *Paraphrases* of Erasmus were to be placed in churches; unlicensed preaching was outlawed; recusants were to be denounced to the Privy Council or local JPs; the Litany was to be substituted for processions except at Rogationtide; and a pulpit and alms chest were to be obtained by every church. Clergy might marry only with the permission of their bishop and two JPs. Also they were to dress properly—though here the stated norm was the vestments of 1552–3; interruptions of preachers were forbidden; and due reverence (i.e. kneeling during prayers, and bowing at the name of Jesus) was to be observed at services. Altars were not compulsorily to be removed from churches, though communion tables might replace them if the minister and churchwardens or the visitors so decided. Lastly, all printing was to be licensed.[5]

Yet the apparent moderation of the injunctions concerning images, remaining relics, and altars is illusory. Although Elizabeth wished to avoid the iconoclasm of her brother's reign, the visitors of 1559 were abrasively Protestant. Whereas on paper 125 commissioners were shared between six circuits, in practice the real work was performed in each area by a small number of clerics and lawyers of whom the former were led by Marian exiles, and the latter by their sympathizers. The visitations took place during the late summer and autumn: the visitors claimed compliance mingled with a certain amount of 'inveterate obstinacy'; surviving churchwardens' accounts show that this inquiry was as exacting as any Henrician or Edwardian precursor.[6] The arrival of the visitors was promptly followed by the removal of altars and images; bonfires consumed roods, statues, banners, ornaments, and sometimes even vestments. On the northern circuit, Edwin Sandes praised Elizabeth for destroying 'the vessels that were made for Baal' along with altars and roods 'builded for idolatry'.[7] In most parishes the ancient cults and rites were eliminated with a speed that confirms the partial nature of the Marian restorations, though the campaign of iconoclasm was not relaxed until 1570, and isolated examples of 'popish' survivals remained in Wales and the north until 1595.[8] While Protestantism never totally erased the memory of the saints, the decline of cults was irreversible and many saints were forgotten. Yet Protestant substitutes—chiefly preaching and Bible-reading—received a mixed welcome. Moreover, the vestry meetings of the Elizabethan parishes never adequately discharged the social functions of the late-medieval guilds and religious confraternities, and there may have been a significant rise in impiety among ordinary people.[9]

The visitors were also empowered to investigate the clergy and punish those who 'obstinately and peremptorily refused to subscribe' to a summary oath to Elizabeth's supremacy, the Book of Common Prayer, and the injunctions. So this was the cue for the deprivation of (especially higher) clergy who rejected the new order. Although nearly half the clergy absented themselves from the 1559 visitation, courts of High Commission erected in the same year for the two provinces of Canterbury and York under the authority of the Act of Supremacy dealt with those who refused to acknowledge the settlement. (The High Commissions combined judicial and visitatorial functions and survived until 1641.) Some four hundred Marian clergy were deprived or resigned between November 1559 and November 1564, but some dismissals were for offences unconnected with either royal supremacy or Prayer Book, and the number apparently deprived for Catholicism was about two hundred.[10]

That piety declined in proportion to the extirpation of Catholic rites is suggested by the condition of parish churches and behaviour of the laity. Only nineteen churches or chapels were built or rebuilt during Elizabeth's reign, and church fabric was neglected. 'Damp green walls, rotting earth floors, and gaping windows' were occasionally reported, though more frequently inside walls were limed, the Ten Commandments and royal arms prominently displayed, and straw or rushes placed on the floor. Pews and pulpits, which had begun to appear in the later Middle Ages, continued to be installed, though the reason for the development of the 'box pew' was probably the functional one of enabling the occupants to avoid draughts. Church attendances did not improve, and probably declined. Indeed, some parishioners found the Prayer Book services tedious: they laughed, talked, slept, and refused to stand up for the Creed or the gospel, or to bow at the name of Jesus. In Suffolk William Hills 'used in time of divine service open and loud speeches to the disturbance of the minister', while Mary Knights brought fierce dogs to church and Jane Buckenham called the minister a 'black sooty-mouthed knave'. Irreverent behaviour and brawling in church, the refusal of church members to serve as churchwardens, and depressed levels of parish income were not untypical.[11] Indeed, visitation instructions of 1565 for the diocese of Coventry and Lichfield required churchwardens to choose four to eight 'bouncers' in each parish who would take an oath to maintain order during services.[12]

Attitudes to parish clergy and Protestant preachers sometimes divided on confessional lines, but anticlericalism was sparked by financial and jurisdictional grievances especially tithes disputes. In fact, when lay–clerical relations are examined in terms of litigation, clerical recruitment, and religious benefactions, it becomes clear that anticlericalism was a consequence, rather than a cause, of the English Reformation. Tithes disputes accelerated after the 1540s as inflation reduced the value of commuted cash payments, and as clergy and lay impropriators alike sought to overthrow customary settlements, while tithe payers struggled on the opposite side to increase commutation at less than market prices and retain customary settlements. In the dioceses of Norwich and Winchester the annual number of tithes cases before church courts doubled between the 1540s and 1560s, a typical pattern.[13] In the diocese of York the alienation of over half the church's property in the form of tithe, first to the Crown and then, by virtue of sales, to the laity, caused acrimony, not simply between parochial clergy and their lay masters, but between gentry impropriators and tithe-paying parishioners.[14] Also lay hostility to ecclesiastical discipline burgeoned, especially among the gentry, despite the increasing appointment of laymen as church-court officials. Lastly, concern for a 'reformation of manners' increased the prosecution of sexual offenders in church courts and therefore the number of resentful victims.

When clerical recruitment and benefactions are considered, it is clear that the Reformation was accompanied by a decline in the reputation of the clergy; in consequence, fewer candidates for the ministry presented themselves, while bequests to the church peaked in the 1510s and fell rapidly thereafter.[15] Allowing for inflation, religious benefactions plummeted from a total of £81,836 in 1501–10 to £26,598 in 1531–40, £5,354 in 1551–60, £2,534 in 1571–80, and £1,790 by 1591–1600.[16] The Prayer Book had repudiated the 'miracle' of the mass: no longer did priests possess quasi-magical powers; their role was that of preachers of the Word, though most non-graduate clergy were incapable of preaching a sermon and the majority of graduates were skilled in the writings of Aristotle, not theology or moral philosophy. The south-west was typical in suffering a dearth of licensed preachers, only twenty-one in Devon and eight in Cornwall by 1561. Despite Protestant efforts, pulpit instruction was largely confined to recitation of official homilies (i.e.

pre-packaged sermons printed for public reading in church) and injunctions in the face of popular disinterest.[17] Whereas in the diocese of Worcester the proportion of graduates among ministers rose from 19 per cent in 1560 and 23 per cent in 1580 to 52 per cent by 1620, the fact remains that barely half the beneficed clergy (including graduates) had licences to preach by 1603. In London almost all clergy were graduates by 1603, and elsewhere in southern counties the proportion of graduates was rising. But in the north the position remained critical owing to the poverty of the parishes — in the dioceses of York and Chester, for instance, fewer than one-third of clergy were graduates as late as 1592–3. Indeed, Archbishop Whitgift estimated in 1584 that barely six hundred parishes nationally yielded an income sufficient to attract a minister with academic qualifications.[18] Yet ministers who urged Bible-reading upon predominantly illiterate congregations, or who replaced ancient rites and communal ceremonies or recreations with sermons while denigrating traditional feasts and Rogationtide 'magic', could be as unpopular as 'dumb dogs'. Zealous incumbents were as likely as the idle or incompetent to be accused of maladministration of communion, imperfect manners, or sexual misdemeanours — familiar pre-Reformation charges.

So there was popular irreligion as well as religion in the later sixteenth century, something Italian Counter-Reformation writers also noticed. That churches were empty while places of amusement were packed was a commonplace. Bear-baiting, gaming, piping, dancing, archery, and football were among the sports that attracted young Elizabethans. Dancing was thought especially subversive: it drew 'youth together in time of preaching and prayer, whereby they continue in ignorance'. Hunting, bowls, and football distracted men of all ages; footballers at Great Baddow (Essex) so annoyed the minister in 1598 that he confiscated their ball.[19] Indeed, Nicholas Bacon asked Parliament in 1563: 'How commeth it to pass that the common people in the country universally come so seldom to common prayer and divine service . . .? And yet to the help of this there was . . . a law made, but hitherto no man, no, no man — or very few — hath seen it executed.'[20] He referred to the penalties of the Act of Uniformity which required church attendance on Sundays and holy days. Delinquents were to suffer the 'censures'

of the church and pay a fine of one shilling to the use of the poor
for each offence.[21]

The prevalence of absenteeism is undisputed. Whereas
between 80 and 85 per cent of the population may have made
their traditional Easter communion, at other times slackness was
rife.[22] Absenteeism rose as rapidly as the population. For
ordinary folk the alehouse 'increasingly constituted a rival pole
to the respectable, establishment meeting place of the church'.
Bishop Pilkington wrote: 'For come into a church on the sabbath
day, and ye shall see but few, though there be a sermon; but
the alehouse is ever full.'[23] Even where the progress of
Protestantism was advanced, as in Kent, a fifth of the population
regularly stayed away from church, and the task of checking
attendances was complicated by the fact that household
servants—one of the largest occupational groups—could be
required (as in Canterbury) to be absent every other Sunday
by their conditions of employment. In Restoration England
absenteeism, it has been argued, could reflect religiosity as much
as irreligion, because villagers valued the Eucharist so highly
that they were unwilling to risk taking it unworthily. This anxiety
was derived from the Prayer Book rubric which warned that
unworthy reception of the sacrament would lead to divine
retribution.[24] But there does not appear to be an Elizabethan
parallel. In fact, during periods of crisis, church attendance was
used as a test of political rather than religious loyalty. In April
1585, for example, the Privy Council ordered JPs to strip
absentees of their armour and weapons until they came to
church.[25]

Indeed, the official requirement of outward conformity
was not equivalent to one of conscientious assent. Even after
Pius V's bull *Regnans in excelsis*, Francis Bacon's aphorism that
Elizabeth did not 'make windows into men's hearts and secret
thoughts' accurately reflected the scope of her religious policy.
But 'godly discipline' and the perceived need by social superiors
to control both the rural poor and urban immigrants bisected
the issue of conformity. Bishops, JPs, mayors, and aldermen
alike sought to strip away the last vestiges of viable communal
life in order to enhance law and order in the name of 'godliness'.
They suppressed church ales, May games, morris dances,
Hocktide gatherings, hognel or hoggler collections, rush-bearings,

and Plough Monday festivities, though with mixed success. For some reason popular pastimes did not succumb to Elizabeth's Reformation as quickly as to Edward's.[26] Thus Bishop Cooper, on his translation from Lincoln to Winchester in 1584, deplored the durability of 'heathenish and ungodly customs' such as morris dances. He sent a strongly worded letter to all ministers and influential laity in his diocese attacking recreations that filled young people's heads with profane thoughts, and kept them away from church. The circular reverberated with the ethical radicalism normally associated with Sabbatarianism. But Cooper's demand that the laity generally should assist the church by tracking down offenders for punishment was too extreme to be generally acceptable; indeed such techniques may have been counterproductive.[27]

So, it is rightly asked, how was the church to detect absentees?[28] The 1559 injunctions required three or four 'discreet men' to be charged in every parish with supervising church attendances and ensuring that everyone stayed 'the whole time of the godly service'. Those 'slack or negligent in resorting to the church' were to be visited and admonished. And 'if they amend not', the bishop was to be informed.[29] But these regulations were barely regarded; very few presentments in the ecclesiastical courts were for absence from church. At Cranbrook in Kent only 2 per cent of Elizabethan cases were for absenteeism; in the deanery of Doncaster (Yorkshire) 31 out of 286 cases related to absenteeism in 1590; and in the deanery of Sudbury (Suffolk) there were 154 presentments in 1593 but none was for skipping church. From Black Notley (Essex) came complaints of 'a great many of the parishioners upon the sabbath days absent from evening prayer, and the churchwardens and questmen sometimes themselves, and not presented'.[30] In any case, the decline of new church building meant that the ability, in particular of towns, to meet potential demand for places at services fell in relation to the increasing population. Strikingly true of London where many churches stood in the City but few in the mushrooming suburbs, inadequacy of church accommodation also affected smaller provincial towns like Exeter and Sheffield.[31] So an absentee's excuse that 'he could not get into the church by reason of the crowd of people', whatever its superficial plausibility, is not evidence of popular piety.

If, however, the authorities could afford to turn a blind eye to absenteeism, it was because the laws against Catholic recusants were fortified in line with political dangers. Both the Privy Council and the majority in Parliament saw penal laws as a necessary aspect of state security. But lay Catholics were rarely threatened unless they professed papal allegiance: Anglicanism had to be fashioned out of the groundswell of opinion prevailing in 1559 — the Elizabethan church was for nearly two decades a 'camel' in which perhaps 40 per cent of its ministers had been ordained before 1559.[32] It was, therefore, obedience to Rome, as well as devotion to the sacraments and old liturgy to which the Anglican Church also laid claim in limited degree, that gave recusancy its character.[33] In practice, the vast majority of Catholic gentry were sincere in their protestations of loyalty to the Crown; but the flight of Mary, Queen of Scots, the Northern Rising, *Regnans in excelsis*, and the arrival after 1574 of Catholic missionary priests recruited from the English exile community upset the political equilibrium.

Although the penal clauses of the Act of Uniformity had been strengthened in 1563 by legislation that made it *praemunire* and, ultimately, treason either to refuse the oath of supremacy or to defend papal authority, it was not until 1571 that coercive measures outran the scope of those formerly devised by Henry VIII. A new Treason Act modelled largely on Cromwell's act of 1534 (including treason by words) was passed, together with an act making it treason either to obtain bulls from Rome or to implement them in Elizabeth's dominions.[34] Within another decade, papal invasion of Ireland, Philip II's annexation of Portugal, and the start of the Jesuit mission to England ensured that anti-Catholic opinion which Elizabeth had previously overruled was unleashed. But she would not allow legislation to compel the receiving of communion. Perhaps she agreed with Edward Aglionby, MP for Warwick, who argued in 1571 that church attendance was a public matter, something of 'outward show' that was 'tolerable and convenient' to demand, whereas 'the conscience of man is internal, invisible and not in the power of the greatest monarch in the world'?[35] Her secular-mindedness and dislike of zeal evidently made compulsory communion abhorrent to her. She was also pragmatic enough to see no need to threaten traditionalists in conscience when the chief political issue was allegiance. Burghley and the bishops took a different view, but Elizabeth had the veto.

The Act to Retain the Queen's Majesty's Subjects in their Due Obedience therefore attacked those who were or became Catholics. Finally approved in March 1581, it extended the treason law to cover anyone who withdrew subjects from their obedience either to the queen or to the Church of England, or who converted them 'for that intent' to Roman Catholicism. Those who willingly allowed themselves to be so withdrawn or converted were to be adjudged traitors. Anyone saying mass was to be fined 200 marks (£133) and imprisoned for a year, while anyone hearing it was to pay half that fine but suffer the same detention. Fines for non-attendance at church were raised to £20 per month; anyone absent for a year was to be bound over in the sum of £200; and any person or corporation employing a recusant schoolmaster was to pay £10 per month.[36] Less draconian than most privy councillors and MPs wished, these penalties would have proved devastating if enforced. That they would be applied selectively was, however, inevitable given the high level of fines and the intimacy of Elizabethan kinship relationships, though the severity of the Privy Council's intentions is illustrated by its establishment of state prisons for recusants.

Catholic apologists from Nicholas Sander and Edward Rishton onwards cited official persecution as the reason for the reduction of Catholicism to minority status by 1603. But most lay Catholics were not seriously threatened: persistent persecution was reserved for notorious malcontents and otherwise attempted only during the crisis years immediately before and after the Armada, when political plots were interwoven with religion.[37] In fact, the habit of 'occasional conformity' made it impossible for Catholicism to be destroyed by anti-recusancy laws. Although by mid-1564 the Holy Office at Rome had declared that English Catholics might not attend the services of the Anglican Church, a ruling which Pius V later confirmed, in practice many Catholic heads of households made infrequent visits to their parish churches to maintain their political credibility. Furthermore, the manuals of casuistry used to instruct missionary priests in the seminaries at Douai, Rheims, and Rome explicitly allowed a measure of co-operation with heretics and schismatics and acknowledged that occasional church attendance must be permitted if the loyalty and power of leading lay Catholics were to be protected.[38]

Instead, the decline of Catholicism in the parishes during Elizabeth's reign was due partly to its own internal changes and partly to the success of committed Protestants in marketing a rival evangelical product. Although the Council of Trent (1545–63) had denounced Protestant theology and reaffirmed the traditional role of priests and true veneration of saints, its reforming decrees castigated the superstitions of popular piety and several of the rituals practised in England, as elsewhere. In fact, Counter-Reformation Catholicism was as anxious as Protestantism to purge itself of ecclesiastical magic. So the proliferation of masses for special occasions was limited; the availability of cheap religious books was restricted; religious confraternities were regulated; fertility rites were suppressed; prophecies and judicial astrology were condemned; and horse-play at weddings, noisy music during Holy Week to ward off evil spirits, and excessive mourning practices were prohibited. All this meant that post-Tridentine Catholicism became less relevant to villagers, many of whom did not break with quasi-paganism until the Industrial Revolution.

Yet the dynamic change sprang from mortality. For the post-Reformation English Catholic community owed everything to Henrician and Marian survivalism, and relatively little to the missions of seminary priests and Jesuits after 1570.[39] Although apologists have claimed that the recusant tradition was forged by missionary priests in the face of widespread Catholic inertia before their arrival, the truth is that the essential concept of a separated Catholic church existed before the seminarians and Jesuits landed; there was already a recusant priesthood providing sacraments for lay people who regarded themselves as Catholics; and it was the ex-Marian clergy who nurtured lay recusant Catholicism and established it before the missionaries could have had any significant effect.[40] Over 225 Marian priests who saw themselves as Roman Catholics and who had separated from the Anglican Church were active in Yorkshire and Lancashire before 1571, supported by a fifth-column within the official church that remained willing to proselytize for Rome. These were remote counties fairly free from central government interference, but recusant clergy have also been traced before the Northern Rising and *Regnans in excelsis* in the dioceses of Hereford, Lichfield, Peterborough, Worcester, and Winchester.[41]

By 1590 perhaps a quarter of the Marian clergy were still alive, but no more than a dozen by 1603. If Catholicism were to endure within a separate community, the sacraments had to be administered by Catholic priests whose ordinations were valid: pastoral ministry was crucial to survivalism. In gentry households the problem was reduced, since recusant clergy might safely settle there, while the attendance of gentry families and their servants at private chapels attached to country houses was recognized as satisfying the conditions of conformity laid down by the Act of Uniformity. In fact, Catholicism had finally withdrawn from the parish church to the gentry household by 1603, thereby creating the seigneurial minority pattern that existed until Catholic Emancipation in 1829. Indeed, the gentry arrogated to themselves a disproportionate share of the clerical resources of post-Reformation Catholicism. If they ensured thereby the long-term survival of the faith, it was at the expense of everyone else.[42]

The erosion of parish Catholicism was largely complete by the end of the 1590s. It was a slow process, but one that the seminarians and Jesuits could not have prevented. It has been said that their mission was a success only 'in the sense that it created the seigneurially structured form of Catholicism which was to survive'.[43] In fact, their efforts marked a heroic failure. Also the number of seminary priests sent from the Continent to England was smaller than has sometimes been claimed: not all were ordained, not everyone went to England, and some were not active there until the reign of James I. Of 804 seminarians, perhaps only 471 were active in England under Elizabeth, and more than a quarter of these were executed.[44] It is important not to forget the conditions in which the missionaries had to work: they were very much on their own, ill-informed about pastoral needs.[45] In the Parliament of 1584–5 the Act for the Queen's Safety was buttressed by savage legislation against Jesuits and seminarians. If it could be shown that a priest had been ordained by papal authority since 1559, no additional proof was needed to convict him of treason. Furthermore, 123 of the 146 priests executed between the passing of this act and Elizabeth's death were indicted under its terms, and not under those of earlier treason laws.[46]

It was, however, the challenge of Anglicanism, rather than the threat of persecution, that succeeded by the 1590s in forcing Catholicism into minority status. The term 'Anglicanism' is here used to mean adherence to the Prayer Book and national church erected by the settlement of 1559, rather than 'godly' zeal, since sermons, psalm-singing, and catechetical exercises were often resented, justification by faith and Calvinist predestinarianism had restricted appeal, and only the literate minority could properly ground their faith upon Bible-reading.[47] Yet positive, if uneven, steps towards evangelism were sanctioned by Protestant bishops supported by Burghley, Leicester, and the Council, in turn assisted by a few hundred puritan preachers and divines as well as by the active minority of Protestant JPs. Also the drift towards ideological polarization on religious grounds in Europe that pushed Elizabeth's diplomacy into the Protestant camp during the 1570s and 1580s did much to forge the link between Protestantism and national identity.

Of course, all Elizabeth sought to enforce was Anglicanism. Paradoxically, it was the majority of conservative parochial clergy, who implemented the Prayer Book after 1559 in order to preserve some of their traditional ceremonies, who first 'legitimized' it.[48] Thereafter, both the Prayer Book and official homilies had the power, it has been said, to 'distil and drop into the mind, almost by an osmotic process' in order to lay the foundations of an Anglican mentality.[49] While 'godly' zeal — especially Calvinist theology of grace and liturgical nonconformity — proved repellent to many churchgoers, the Prayer Book symbolized the Anglican ideal summarized by John Jewel, bishop of Salisbury, in *An Apology of the Church of England* (1562). His argument (not dissimilar to that of Edward Foxe and Cranmer under Henry VIII) was that the English had left the Roman obedience justly, because the post-Hildebrandine papacy had abandoned the Apostles, the Scriptures, and the Fathers of the church. Elizabeth and Parliament had duly *returned* to the 'true Catholic church' founded by Apostles and Fathers and justified by Scripture. Jewel claimed England to have renounced 'that church wherein we could neither have the word of God sincerely taught, nor the sacraments rightly administered, nor the name of God duly called upon'. Elizabeth had 'departed from that church which these men call [Roman] catholic . . . and we are come, as near as we possibly could, to the church of the apostles and of the old catholic bishops and fathers'.[50]

This *raison d'être* of Anglicanism was reinforced by the Thirty-nine Articles (1563), the doctrinal statement to which, after 1571, clergy were required to subscribe as the standard of the church's public teaching.[51] Also the *Acts and Monuments* of John Foxe (1563 and innumerable later editions; earlier continental versions had appeared in 1554 and 1559) reiterated the view that true religion had reached England directly via the Apostles when St Joseph of Arimathea came to England about AD 63 with the Holy Grail and built the first church in the country at Glastonbury. Foxe's volumes, the culmination of a lifetime's effort, were based on hugely impressive (if unashamedly Protestant) scholarship. They provided a history and martyrology of the church from the earliest Roman persecutions to the death of Mary I, a data bank for the justification of Elizabethan 'godly' reformation. Yet Foxe's basic message was that the Anglican Church was a 'true' historical church guided by the spirit of God: this was the key to his assimilation of traditional and reformed ideas.[52]

The Geneva Bible (1560; the New Testament alone appeared in 1557), begun by the Marian exiles in that city and completed after Elizabeth's accession, went further. In addition to an accurate English translation, it provided 'arguments', marginal glosses, headings, and 'explanatory' notes that urged Calvinist theology and prompted Archbishop Parker to commission a rival Bishops' Bible (1568). But the Geneva version retained its popularity until the Restoration, went through more than 130 editions, and became the standard text for household use.[53] Moreover, although Bible study was confined to the literate elite, catechisms and cheap religious tracts poured from the presses, especially after 1570. About a hundred catechisms were published in Elizabeth's reign, the best known being by Alexander Nowell, John More, Eusebius Paget, and Edward Dering; the idea was to teach Protestantism, especially to children, by process of question and answer. Many catechisms were too long. An observer in 1588 thought only one household in a hundred used them. But Paget claimed he could teach his version to a whole household, including servants, in four months.[54] In addition, uneducated people had access to twopenny tracts and ballads, the latter published on single sheets, sometimes with a woodcut at their head and the name of a popular tune to which they could be sung. Written in vehemently anti-papal and xenophobic verse, ballads were theologically negligible. But they identified the Anglican Church with patriotism, depicting Englishmen as God's chosen people.

The most potent component of Anglican and Protestant evangelism was preaching, though the 'hotter sort' of Calvinist predestinarian preaching encountered consumer resistance. Four phases of development have been identified, not all reached at the same time in each diocese or county: first, the 'apostolic' or primitive stage, when itinerant preachers travelled the country-side; second, the formative phase, when the people came to the preacher on market days or at 'prophesyings', 'combination lectures', 'exercises', or puritan 'fasts'; third, the intermediate stage, when a settled preaching ministry was established in many market towns and rural parishes as well as in urban centres; and lastly the fully developed stage (not attained everywhere before the 1620s), when sermons were common. Yet the striking thing is that Elizabeth's personal views and lack of resources precluded a full government programme for the propagation of Protestant preaching. So what was achieved was largely due to the voluntary efforts of a minority, even though many of their activities were unlicensed or 'extra-legal'. Whereas under Henry VIII and Edward VI the impetus for the Reformation had come largely from above, under Elizabeth, by contrast, the 'primary thrust' of Protestant evangelism came from below.[55]

The wider assumption of conventional historiography that mainstream puritanism was potentially anarchical, and therefore external to the Anglican Church, is misguided. Few puritans had 'revolutionary' plans; the vast majority firmly disavowed separation. Rather than puritanism being an external threat, the internalization of Protestantism within the Anglican Church was largely due to 'puritan' preachers and pulpit lecturers, as well as to the infectious enthusiasm of those who 'gadded' to sermons. 'Godly' preachers and lecturers, though socially isolated by virtue of their minority status, compensated for the inadequate provision of official Protestant teaching and did much to shift parish Anglicanism decisively towards the reformed faith by 1603. Whereas, too, it is often thought that the Elizabethan church was a rigid institution with a limited capacity to absorb autonomous movements, this fails to do justice to the value 'puritan' evangelism had in validating the national church in the eyes of committed Protestants.[56] In fact, it was far from inevitable before Laud's ascendancy that mainstream puritanism would challenge the national and parochial church.

A term of abuse, 'puritan' was used to index the nature and extent of opinions of which opponents disapproved. It could be defined in a religious sense—i.e. a puritan is a 'church rebel' or 'hotter sort' of Protestant; in a moral sense—i.e. a puritan is 'censorious' or narrow-minded; or in a social sense—i.e. no gentleman, none but 'mean persons' are puritans. At the level of straightforward vituperation, the insult is meaningless; Ben Jonson's definition—'hypocrite and heretic'—epitomizes this cul-de-sac. The puritan role in evangelism and education, and the *value* to government of 'puritan' publicists as anti-papal propagandists after *Regnans in excelsis*, testify to the pervasive ambiguities. The basic division was between the 'godly' and the 'ungodly': those who used the term 'puritan' to attack the 'godly' were regarded as having condemned themselves out of their own mouths.[57]

The core of the puritan position lay in the capacity of 'godly' Protestants to recognize each other within a corrupt and unregenerate world.[58] What counted was their trust in the transformative effect of God's Word. A believer's spiritual progress was achieved through a combination of 'godly fellowship' and the puritan spiritual dynamic that forced men and women to internalize their struggle for salvation. Believers followed a Calvinist *ordo salutis*: election, vocation, justification, sanctification, glorification. This was the psychological pattern which all the 'saints' were supposed to have exemplified, and which everyone who desired to be saved hoped to emulate. So 'puritans', by intense introspection, followed the workings of the law of predestination within their own souls, and then gave witness to the grace that had befallen them through a campaign of works directed against Antichrist, the flesh, sin, and the world.[59] Their evangelical impulse was therefore more than the convention of their art; it was the essence of their outlook. Their various assaults on the Prayer Book and episcopacy were the visible and external signs of their drive towards 'further reformation'.

That 'puritan' or 'precisionist' elements would criticize the Elizabethan settlement as 'but halfly reformed' had been expected by the author of the 'Device for the Alteration of Religion', who warned that Anglicanism could be seen as 'a cloaked papistry or a mingle-mangle'.[60] The main concern in 1559 had been to establish the autonomy of the Anglican Church in relation to Rome, not to define its position as a reformed church. So zealous puritans sought to extirpate corruption and 'popish rituals' from the church (the cross in baptism, kneeling at the communion, wearing of copes and surplices, the use of organs, etc.) in order to build a church wherein beliefs and ceremonies were consistent with Scripture. They insisted upon God's promise of a living, regenerative faith to those destined by grace to number among his 'elect'. A small vanguard wished to take over the Anglican shell and construct within it a 'true' church along presbyterian lines. But the presbyterian impulse was attacked and crushed after Grindal's suspension as archbishop of Canterbury by Elizabeth for refusing to suppress 'prophesyings' (June 1577). After John Whitgift's appointment as his successor (September 1583), a tiny handful of puritans cut the Gordian knot and became separatists. But separatists were quickly disowned and persecuted by a polity that consensually supported a national church structure. So a semi-sect based at Plumbers' Hall in London was broken up in 1567; the 'Family of Love' in Surrey and Southampton was suppressed in 1580–1; the Norwich sect known as the 'Brownists' was forced into exile in 1581; and the separatists Henry Barrow, John Greenwood, and John Penry were tried and executed in 1593.

Elizabeth, therefore, refused to adjust the religious settlement even in detail. The most she was prepared to do was to refer petitions of which she approved to the bishops, whereupon it was the business of Convocation to enact appropriate canons.[61] Indeed, when points were tested by critics of the settlement, strict conformity was purposefully required. Thus Archbishop Parker's *Advertisements* (1566), issued in response to disputes over clerical dress and ceremonies, enforced the rubrics of the Prayer Book;

assent to the Thirty-nine Articles was next demanded of beneficed clergy, despite puritan howls of anguish; and Whitgift, who invoked the weapons of High Commission and, sometimes, star chamber, required all clergy to subscribe to the royal supremacy, Prayer Book, and Thirty-nine Articles, or else be deprived.

If, however, the Vestiarian Controversy and its sequels ended in victory for the official church, attention was focused on episcopal discipline. Puritan clergy doubted that bishops could dictate what others must do in conscience; so the institution of episcopacy began to be challenged. After 1569 the presbyterians, led by John Field, Thomas Wilcox, and Thomas Cartwright, concerted their strike in Parliament, pulpit, and press. Two outspoken *Admonitions to the Parliament* (1572) signalled the tone. But their radicalism was counterproductive, their support in Parliament limited, and Elizabeth could always outflank political moves by wielding familiar weapons: expressing her displeasure, or commanding that no more bills for religion should be read in Parliament unless they had first been discussed with the bishops and their permission had been obtained. This proved sufficient. Elizabeth succeeded to a remarkable extent in preserving a firm separation of church and state. Yet she had powers in reserve, for she could veto bills and prorogue or dissolve Parliament. Although the assimilation of puritanism to Anglicanism was attempted by Grindal during his brief tenure as metropolitan, his suspension by Elizabeth was the turning-point — for Whitgift, though a Calvinist, shared Elizabeth's abhorrence for innovation in religion. Within ten years the Elizabethan puritan 'movement' was dead, the collapse in 1586–7 of a final presbyterian attempt to abolish bishops and replace the Prayer Book with a Genevan-style *Book of Discipline* epitomizing the defeat.[62]

Yet, if the Elizabethan 'puritan movement' was dead, the evangelical impulse which had given Reformation from below its momentum since Lollard, Edwardian, and Marian-exile days was flourishing. It can be argued that the removal of presbyterianism from the agenda encouraged puritan divines to give their undivided attention to their main mission as preachers and pastors.[63] In addition, the acerbity of Whitgift's drive against puritan ministers led to gentry protests and petitions from all over southern England. In counties like Suffolk it sparked the puritan–politicization of the country gentry, who in their various roles as deputy lieutenants, muster commissioners, JPs, and assistants to the assize judges wielded local power.[64] True, the 1590s saw religion fading as a major divisive issue, but, when Richard Bancroft preached a sermon at Paul's Cross in February 1589 which argued that episcopacy was divinely appointed, he signalled the advent of a new series of debates that finally culminated in the Arminianism of the Laudians and transmuted puritanism from the pietistic core of the Elizabethan and early Jacobean era into the Root-and-Branch sentiment of 1640–1.

PRIVY COUNCIL
AND PARLIAMENTS

'OUR part is to counsel.' So Burghley reminded his fellow-privy councillor Sir Ralph Sadler on the eve of the Northern Rising. The Privy Council was the foremost (and permanent) instrument of Tudor government; its primary function was to assist the monarch in the formulation of foreign and domestic policy. 'The queen's majesty hath no surety but as she hath been counselled', Burghley told Leicester in August 1572. Although the extant registers of the Privy Council minute formal decisions and not the discussions that preceded them, it is clear that collectively Elizabeth's councillors offered the best advice they could. They tendered their opinion to the queen, who then accepted or rejected it. Often she vacillated, and on some issues she went her own way, notably in the matters of her marriage, the succession, and the fate of Mary, Queen of Scots. Burghley complained in 1575, 'My doings have been interpreted as diminutions of her majesty's prerogative.' But in the ordinary affairs of government Elizabeth accepted advice, and she consulted her councillors even on sensitive matters. For instance, when the Queen of Scots signalled her intention to marry Darnley in 1565, Elizabeth immediately involved the Privy Council. True, she could moderate the counsel of one adviser with that of another. Sometimes she interviewed councillors individually as well as receiving their corporate advice. Her appointments show that she liked to balance points of view in the Privy Council. But, unlike Philip II, she did not deliberately choose as councillors men of such divergent temperaments that they could rarely agree and therefore had to couch their advice in the form of multiple choices. On the contrary, Elizabeth expected to have one decision to make at a time. Somewhat less reasonably, though, she expected the Privy Council to assume responsibility for her own independent decisions as well as those she took on their recommendation.[1]

Yet especially under a woman ruler the Privy Council was more than an advisory body. Whereas under Henry VIII the gentlemen of the privy chamber had worked alongside ministers and councillors as impromptu advisers and administrators, under Elizabeth the privy chamber was neutralized politically leaving the Privy Council as the unrivalled executive board. Of course, at the highest level of policy-making the Elizabethan Privy Council was subsumed within the Court. For three decades after the Scottish intervention of 1559–60, Elizabeth took most of her advice from an 'inner ring' of trusted 'political' councillors, and it was also her habit to consult the nobility at Court at times of crisis. But the bulk of the Privy Council's work was administrative and quasi-judicial, not advisory. It was, after all, largely due to the need to enforce the break with Rome and suppress the Pilgrimage of Grace that the principle of a small working Council had been sustained during the 1530s. The same view had been taken in France, where Francis I resorted to a *conseil des affaires* after 1526.[2]

The size of the Council narrowed under the Tudors from 227 during Henry VII's reign and 120 during Wolsey's ascendancy, to 19 members in 1536–7, 19 in 1540, 22 in 1548, 31 in 1552, 50 under Mary (though only 19 were working councillors), 19 in 1559, 19 in 1586, 11 in 1597, and 13 in 1601. The tempo of government considerably quickened during the same period, and privy councillors were forced to work progressively harder. During the 1520s, 1540s, 1550s, and 1560s the Council usually met three or four times a week, but by the 1590s it was meeting nearly every day, sometimes in both mornings and afternoons.[3]

Since the fall of Wolsey in 1529 the executive Privy Council had been a 'Court' Council. It met at Court in the house or palace where the monarch was living at the time. As Sir Julius Caesar, one of James I's councillors, explained, the Privy Council 'had always . . . a fair chamber in every standing house, where the king's majesty's abode is, where they keep the Council table, with a little room thereto adjoining, where the clerks of the said Council and their servants sit and write'. At least three clerks were needed 'to enact their orders, and write such letters, or answers as their Lordships shall command them'.[4] Most Elizabethan Council meetings were held at Greenwich, Hampton Court, or Whitehall, but when Elizabeth was travelling the country on progress, or when plague raged in London, meetings would be held at each place where she stopped. Owing to duties elsewhere, not every member could therefore attend every meeting. The average rate of attendance was between six and nine privy councillors per meeting. The most regular attenders before the outbreak of war with Spain were Burghley, Leicester, Sir Francis Knollys, Walsingham, Sir Thomas Smith, the third earl of Sussex, Lord Howard of Effingham, and Sir James Croft.[5]

In general the post-1540 Privy Council comprised the great officers of state and of the royal household. Disputes over policy occasionally erupted between councillors and courtiers under Elizabeth, as in 1570 when Thomas Heneage, then a gentleman of the privy chamber and treasurer of the chamber, was forced to assure Burghley that 'mine own conscience cannot accuse me that I ever gave her majesty advice in a corner against the determination of her Council, or ever opened my mouth to her highness in matter concerning the public estate or government, except it pleased her to ask mine opinion'.[6] But such clashes were few; the stability of the Elizabethan political system sprang from its homogeneity, and major policies were invariably discussed and approved by the whole Privy Council before they were implemented, even if they originated from the inner Court circle. Several critics, for instance Sir Thomas Elyot in Henry VIII's reign, complained that the consultative process narrowed in the sixteenth century. The Elizabethan 'inner ring' certainly mirrored the select councils of the 1530s and 1540s. But precisely because so much of the Privy Council's time was spent on administration, the advantages of a small executive board outweighed the political disadvantages.

Throughout Elizabeth's reign the Privy Council's methods were simple but effective. It implemented and enforced its decisions chiefly by means of state papers: that is, by dispatching official letters signed by seven or eight councillors ordering things to be done. Letters might be sent alone or in support of related royal proclamations, commissions, or writs. Councillors wrote to lords-lieutenant and their deputies, JPs, subsidy commissioners, sheriffs, and escheators. They instructed commissioners for recusancy, muster commissioners, and (in coastal counties) commissioners for piracy. The matters dealt with included crime prevention, socio-economic regulation, religious conformity, training of the militia, coastal defence and harbour repairs, taxation, distribution of food supplies, poor relief, and the game laws. The Council frequently issued orders to JPs, for instance to investigate riots and crimes, to enforce the statutes against vagrancy and illegal games, to maintain tillage and dismantle illegal enclosures, to regulate alehouses, and to collect any information central government needed from the counties. In socio-economic matters the Privy Council issued proclamations on behalf of the Crown which were then enforced in the exchequer and star chamber. Councillors also signed warrants authorizing the issue of judicial commissions or writs, or commanding action by officials of the exchequer, chancery, or other courts.

Among the Privy Council's most significant tasks was its corporate management of 'national' finance. Under the Yorkists and Henry VII the king had been involved personally in the minutiae of revenue-raising and cash disbursement, while under Wolsey and Cromwell the initiative largely passed to their informal control. But during the 1540s and 1550s privy councillors assumed collective responsibility for 'national' financial administration. The rise of the executive Privy Council was accompanied by a decline in the personal interest and control of the monarch over the majority of financial decisions. True, the Council worked *ad hoc* and was obliged to co-operate with the queen, lord treasurer, chancellor of the exchequer, and other officials. But by the middle of Elizabeth's reign clear lines of demarcation were settled: the queen decided how in principle her revenue should be managed, and the lord treasurer and his subordinate officials supervised the technical aspects of fiscal administration. The Privy Council kept itself informed about cashflow, prepared summary accounts, and took steps to ensure that income and expenditure were kept in balance. Fiscal policy was frequently debated at Council meetings, and councillors were responsible for authorizing cash expenditure. The task of signing warrants for payment must have taken up a fair amount of councillors' time, since cash was disbursed by the exchequer only after the issuing officials had received specific authorization by warrant from the queen or Privy Council.[7]

Warrants for payment signed by groups of councillors survive from the 1540s onwards, while by the 1590s they were marked as 'allowed by the lords and others of the Privy Council . . . signed W. Burghley'. Large payments might require a double authorization, though there was no strict rule. A privy seal warrant would be sent to the exchequer authorizing payments of £1,000 or more upon subsequent warrants signed by a stipulated number of privy councillors (usually six or seven). Letters from the Privy Council were also used to authorize cash disbursements. For example, in 1574, when he wanted £3,000 for military expenses in Ireland, Burghley wrote to Robert Petre, auditor of the receipt of the exchequer, 'you shall herewith receive a letter from the lords of the Council to me, which letter I pray you keep, and observe the contents thereof'.[8]

Councillors sometimes even had money paid to themselves before officially disbursing it. Walsingham drew £8,000 in cash at the receipt of the exchequer in October 1581, while in January 1574 the Council instructed Burghley to appoint someone to receive and disburse cash to its specific instructions.[9] The Privy Council's powers of fiscal control were thus fluid, but essentially bureaucratic. Councillors stood between the queen and her financial ministers. After the queen's, their authority was decisive. Although Lord Treasurer Winchester was the financial minister most sensitive to the privileges of his official rank, he told the tellers of the receipt in 1568 that when he was absent in the country they were to do whatever the Privy Council wanted. This reformed structure, though far from perfect, provided a stable framework for central finance until Elizabeth's death.[10]

Corporate development was also pronounced in the later years of Elizabeth's reign, when the Privy Council assumed a degree of control over grants under the great seal that would have seemed alien to Henry VII. For Lord Keepers Puckering and Egerton both received 'restraints' on their powers that forbade them to allow even routine commissions or pardons to pass the seal on the authority of the queen's signature alone unless the warrant in question was also signed by three privy councillors.[11] Henry VII had ensured that his signature on a document took precedence over the seals of established constitutional practice, while under Wolsey and Cromwell efficiency and speed had taken priority over the letter of the law.[12] (Cromwell may have wished to tighten up the system, but his fall intervened.) True, the procedures of the 1540s and 1550s require further research, while the status of 'immediate warrants' (as they were called) during the early years of Elizabeth's reign is obscure. But it is clear that the war with Spain and patronage log-jam at Court inspired tighter working practices than those found at the beginning of the century. Henry VII and the mature Henry VIII would certainly not have allowed their councillors to vet their decisions. So, as in fiscal administration, privy councillors assumed new duties that enhanced their wider authority.

The Privy Council's most urgent task after 1559 was to enforce the Elizabethan religious settlement in the counties. In particular, the detection and, if necessary, punishment of Catholic recusants was its responsibility. To this end, a census of JPs and other county and municipal officials was ordered in October 1564. The bishops were asked to rank the leaders of provincial society according to their attitudes to the settlement; they were to recommend names of persons fit to be put into office, and identify officials who should be removed; and they were to consult the known gentry supporters of the settlement in their dioceses, and with their advice suggest measures for the repression of recusancy and promotion of Protestantism. In consequence the Council collected a wealth of information that enabled it to monitor appointments in town and country. The ultimate effect on the counties may not have been great, since, of JPs covered by the surviving returns, 431 were ranked favourable to the settlement, 264 neutral or 'indifferent', and only 157 hinderers or adversaries. But, as population pressure and migration of landless labourers to towns increased, the Privy Council used its discretionary powers to ensure that opponents of the settlement were excluded from civic office in the interests of order and conformity.[13]

The Privy Council also maintained lists of Catholic recusants at home and fugitives in exile abroad. According to a statute of 1381, no one was supposed to enter or leave the realm unless he was a fisherman or merchant, or had a royal licence or passport, provisions which the Council started seriously to enforce. In March 1583 Walsingham scribbled in his day-book under the heading 'Cowncell': 'Proclamation on ports'; 'A view of strangers'; and 'Recusants, Jesuits [and] . . . divers obstinate blaspheming papists'. At times of crisis the Council made a show of strength by 'interning' or fining prominent recusants in the shires as well as seizing their armour and weapons, while referring lesser men to the supervision of local Protestant clergy or JPs. After the Northern Rising and the bull *Regnans in excelsis*, JPs and diocesan bishops were regularly asked to provide the Privy Council with lists of people who refused to attend the Anglican Church. During the war with Spain, the Privy Council was understandably obsessed by the problem of recusancy. It started to enforce the penal laws against recusant gentry who were thought to be a threat to state security, while recusants deemed loyal to Elizabeth were bound over to keep the peace or to remain within 3 miles of their houses, and not to consort with other recusants.[14]

At the top of the Privy Council's agenda was national defence and fortifications. Before 1585 its authority over national musters was derived from commissions issued by the Crown under the great seal. Privy councillors supervised the workings of the Marian Act for the Taking of Musters and Act for Horse Armour and Weapons; muster commissioners were named for each county, who were ordered to implement the Council's instructions. Since the lord keeper was authorized by royal letters patent 'to alter or renew' muster commissions—which he did only on the Council's resolution—the Privy Council again exercised corporate control.[15] After 1569 the names and parishes of residence of men mustered were to be registered locally, while after 1573 the need to train adequately at least some of those liable for military service was emphasized. When war with Spain threatened, comprehensive reports were prepared of the local militias, of ships and seamen, of coastal forts and castles, of the numbers of men appointed in each county to serve in the trained bands, and of current stocks of guns and munitions.[16] Thereafter, the Privy Council directed the war effort under Elizabeth's authority, planning military and naval logistics and issuing warrants for conscription, impressment, and the strengthening of coastal fortifications.

Yet the most significant innovation was the lieutenancy system made permanent in 1585. Whereas earlier lieutenancy appointments had been temporary, designed to subordinate the shire levies to a single official, the outbreak of war with Spain prompted a new departure. Lieutenancy commissions were issued for nearly all the English and Welsh counties, and the length of the war meant that in many cases the appointees continued in post for life. The lord-lieutenant was usually either the senior resident nobleman or the senior resident privy councillor in a district.[17] According to his commission, he was to put his district into the best possible state of defence, to which end he was authorized to muster everyone eligible for service overseas or in the trained bands, arm them, drill them, and if necessary discipline them by invoking martial law. If martial law were needed, a provost marshal was to be appointed to execute it. Lastly, all other local officials were to obey and assist lieutenants and their deputies.[18]

Although the Crown's policy was *ad hoc* and reflected military and political needs, the appointments assisted stability for two reasons. First, the Privy Council enjoyed direct lines of communication to the lieutenants; second, the appointments matched military needs to aristocratic traditions. The defence of the realm against the Crown's enemies was the ancient role of the nobility, satisfying their honour and justifying their privileges. But, whereas under Henry VIII's military system the nobility mustered their feudal retinues as quasi-independent territorial magnates, Elizabeth's lieutenants were agents of the Crown who could be dismissed or summoned to answer for their conduct in star chamber.

The majority of privy councillors also served as lords-lieutenant after 1587. In many cases the top officials in central and local government were the same people! Since so many lieutenants were privy councillors, they responded more readily to central government initiatives than did JPs. They sent a steady flow of information from the localities back to the Privy Council, forging a bilateral chain of communication between central and local government. Relays of messengers travelled to and from the Court bearing instructions and returning with replies. Special posts were often laid on to speed the correspondence. True, lieutenants or their deputies sometimes complained that the Crown's demands were too ambitious. But the pace and scale of local administration visibly increased; better records were kept, ordnance depots were established, new transport facilities were provided, members of the trained bands began to be recruited for overseas service alongside the forced levies, while elaborate arrangements were made for one county to send its men to defend another.[19]

The Privy Council's constant concern was to enforce law and order and regulate economic affairs. The two aims were linked, since rising population, prices, and rural unemployment nurtured the seeds of potential revolt. So the Privy Council fixed prices and wages in London, advised JPs on wages elsewhere, controlled exports of grain in an attempt to keep prices down and maintain supplies, supervised poor relief, and invoked the law against speculators in foodstuffs and other basic commodities. It enforced the penal laws and regulated internal trade. One of Burghley's special interests was the fishing industry. In the Parliament of 1563 he promoted an act making Wednesday a compulsory fish day as well as every day in Lent. He argued that the decline of fishing could be checked by restoring demand to the level customary before the dissolution of the monasteries! The Privy Council regularly issued orders forbidding the killing and eating of meat during Lent and requiring JPs to ensure that butchers, innkeepers, and victuallers did not sell meat on fish days.[20]

In the general field of law and order individual privy councillors and JPs were expected to assume responsibility without specific mandate. Typical was the reaction of the Leicestershire JP who told Walsingham in April 1582 that 'at our last assizes . . . a fellow suspiciously wandering about our county was taken. . . . I find him so subtle that my advice was that the lords of her majesty's Privy Council should be advertised.'[21] Such spontaneous initiative in the counties was partly the result of Cromwell's tactics during the 1530s. Cromwell had fostered an impression of eternal governmental vigilance, which his successors inherited and exploited. But fears of vagrancy and recusancy kept councillors, JPs, and village constables on their toes under Elizabeth. In particular, the political conspiracies of the 1570s and 1580s encouraged intensive security measures designed to thwart sedition and rebellion. When the Jesuit John Gerard arrived in England, he avoided the roads as much as possible until he had acquired a horse, since 'people travelling on foot . . . [were] often taken for vagrants and liable to arrest'.[22] He had barely ridden 2 miles when he encountered a 'watch' for 'licentious persons' on the outskirts of a village. He persuaded the local constable that he was an 'honest fellow', though he was eventually captured and tortured under Privy Council supervision.

The dark side of Elizabethan enforcement was, of course, that torture *was* used. True, official Council warrants first had to be obtained, which specified the names of the victims and listed their alleged offences. But the reign of Elizabeth was the period when torture was most used in England. Of the eighty-one documented cases between 1540 and 1640, fifty-three (65 per cent) were Elizabethan. Before 1589 torture was undertaken at the Tower, and between 1589 and 1603 at Bridewell in London, where special equipment was available. The majority of victims were Catholic conspirators, Jesuit priests, and recusants. Only in a quarter of cases were victims ordinary criminals, for torture was rarely used to obtain the evidence necessary to secure courtroom convictions, but to discover the 'truth' about accomplices in cases of threatened sedition. Many Elizabethan victims would have been vulnerable to state security measures by the standards of later governments. A few were, however, victims of official hysteria. For example, the pathetic 'prophet' William Hacket, who in 1591 mounted a cart in the main thoroughfare of London and proclaimed himself to be Jesus Christ, was tortured, convicted, and executed.[23]

In the minds of Tudor councillors and JPs the boundary between administration and justice was blurred. So, following patterns established by Wolsey and Cromwell, Elizabeth's Privy Council used the assize judges as extra-legal supervisors of the local magistracy. The judges were lectured in star chamber before they left to ride their twice-yearly circuits, and they were expected to assess the workings of justice and efficiency of JPs in their areas and report back to Burghley and the Council. This arrangement was especially valuable to the Privy Council in the decades before the lieutenancy system became permanent. In addition to enforcing the criminal law in their official capacities, the assize judges acted as unofficial agents of the Crown, checking how far Council policies were being implemented and law and order maintained at quarter sessions.[24]

Lastly, the Privy Council itself acted as a quasi-judicial body. Since the bifurcation of Henry VIII's Council into its component parts in the 1530s—the Privy Council and the court of star chamber—it was no longer a court of law, but as the superior administrative body it continued to investigate sedition and treason as well as to exercise other functions appropriate to its standing. Of course, it was continually swamped with unwanted petitions and private suits which, for the most part, it strictly referred to the ordinary courts of law. Nevertheless, cases involving the security of the regime, major economic offences, international law, or civil commotion were investigated at the board, though formal trials would be held elsewhere. Also officials reported for abusing their positions or persons charged with perverting the course of justice would be brought to answer before either the Privy Council or the court of star chamber.[25]

Unlike the Privy Council, Parliament was an intermittent institution. Elizabeth's ten meetings had thirteen sessions lasting a total of 126 weeks out of forty-four years of her reign.[26] Indeed, twenty-six separate calendar years elapsed without a session.[27] Expressed in another way, Parliament sat for an average of only three weeks for every year of the reign or just 5.5 per cent of the time. Moreover, Elizabeth prided herself on this. Lord Keeper Puckering informed Lords and Commons in 1593: 'Her majesty hath evermore been most loth to call for the assembly of her people in Parliament, and hath done the same but rarely and only upon most just, weighty and great occasions.' The inconvenience of travelling to London and Westminster being what it was, this view was popular. As Sir Thomas Smith explained, 'What can a commonwealth desire more than peace, liberty, quietness, little taking of base money, few parliaments . . .?'[28]

Writing his *De republica anglorum* in France during 1565, Smith listed Parliament's functions.

The Parliament abrogateth old laws, maketh new, giveth orders for things past, and for things hereafter to be followed, changeth rights, and possessions of private men, legitimateth bastards, establisheth forms of religion, altereth weights and measures, giveth forms of succession to the Crown, defineth of doubtful rights, whereof is no law already made, appointeth subsidies, *tailles*, taxes, and impositions, giveth most free pardons and absolutions, restoreth in blood and name as the highest court, condemneth or absolveth them whom the Prince will put to that trial . . .[29]

Public and private legislation, taxation, attainders and their reversal, and other legislative business such as statutory pardons were the main functions of Parliament. While Smith referred to 'consultation' meaning deliberation and debate, he did so only in the context of legislative procedure—the discussion, if necessary amendment, and approval of bills in both Houses before their presentation to the sovereign for the royal assent.

By contrast, some historians have argued that Parliament became politicized under Elizabeth; ordinary MPs, especially 'puritans' and common lawyers, according to this view, ventilated their 'opposition' to her conservatism. But this interpretation endows the House of Commons with a preconceived status and fails to recognize the influence of the Lords in an aristocratic age. It also falsely presupposes that 'adversary politics' prevailed in the sixteenth century. True, royal needs and pressure from below ensured that the size of the Commons climbed from 296 members under Henry VII, to 302 by 1512, 349 by 1545, 389 by 1553, 402 by 1559, 438 by 1571, and 462 by 1586.[30] The Elizabethan House of Lords fluctuated between 75 and 88 members (exceptionally 90 in 1572). But size alone did not determine political weight; those who have posited the 'rise' of the Commons have studied Tudor Parliaments from the perspective of a determinist interpretation of the 'origins' of the Civil War and Interregnum. By seeking the origins of Stuart conflict in the so-called 'apprenticeship to future greatness' of the Elizabethan House of Commons, the leading exponent of this interpretation was driven to manufacture a 'puritan choir' supposedly operating within Elizabeth's early Parliaments; to posit non-existent links between parliamentary development and the presbyterian movement; to argue that policy differences were thrashed out in Commons' debates rather than at Court and in the Privy Council; and to misrepresent Thomas Norton, William Fleetwood, and Peter Wentworth as the forerunners of Sir John Eliot and John Pym.[31]

If, however, the official Journals of both Houses are studied as well as unofficial reports of debates, and when Parliament's business is analysed in conjunction with the preoccupations of Burghley and the Privy Council, a different picture emerges. First, it is quite clear that queen, Lords, and Commons were co-equal partners in the legislative process, though the queen retained executive power and the Lords enjoyed social superiority over the Commons; second, the Journals indicate that the chief functions of Parliaments were indeed to enact laws and vote taxes, as Smith supposed; and third, Parliaments were co-operative ventures in which unity, harmony, and the sovereign's honour were the norms and conflict and opposition exceptional. While Tudor Parliaments did see isolated instances of dissension, these usually marked failures of conciliar management or the spilling over of Court factionalism into Parliament. In any case, political debates in Parliament, especially under Elizabeth, served little, if any, purpose when the monarch chose to ignore them.[32]

It would, of course, be perverse to claim that Parliament had no 'political' or 'representative' role when it had historically asserted one on particular occasions. In the fourteenth century Parliament served as a political 'ventilation shaft': the Lords Ordainers in 1311 held that the great affairs of the kingdom should be decided there — war, the king's absence from the land, the nomination of a regent, grants from the royal estates, the appointment of ministers of the Crown, and the enactment of reforms and inquiries into breaches of the Ordinances.[33] The parliamentary propagandists of 1641–2 took a similar view, though Parliament's essential (and defining) function was always legislative. As Henry III noted, justice was administered there to all and sundry and, with the king's consent, existing law could be changed and new law enacted.[34] The author of *Fleta*, writing at the end of the thirteenth century, described Parliament in terms similar to those of Smith: 'In his parliaments the king in council holds his court. . . . There judicial doubts are determined, new remedies are devised for wrongs newly brought to light, and justice is dispensed to everyone according to his deserts.'[35] But when the authors of the Provisions of Oxford (1258) provided for both regular Parliaments and baronial representation therein, their stated objective was 'to survey the state of the realm and to discuss the common interests of the king and the kingdom'.[36] From the age of Simon de Montfort onwards, ideas of consent or 'common counsel' flourished, chiefly when exasperated barons were strong and the Crown weak. In this respect a dissident baronage, acting politically, could turn the king's instrument against him. As a result of medieval upheaval, however,

Parliament became a significant point of contact between the Crown and the counties.[37]

Also until the reign of Henry VII, on occasions when legislation or taxation were not expressly required (though these might be discussed in principle), the Crown summoned Great Councils, non-parliamentary assemblies otherwise called 'colloquies' or 'treaties', *'magna consilia'* or *'grands conseils'*. With their composition often restricted to nobles and councillors but sometimes identical to that of Parliament (i.e. including burgesses), Great Councils were afforced meetings of the King's Council for political, financial, diplomatic, and ceremonial business.[38] During the sixteenth century the Great Council was eclipsed as the Privy Council assumed the leading executive and consultative role and as the Court became the focus of politics. Yet ideas of 'counsel' survived, as did the notion that magnates should be consulted on key political issues 'in' or 'out of Parliament'. It is interesting that Elizabethan writs of summons to the House of Lords called peers specifically to counsel the queen on religion and defence of the realm.[39] Though this theory of 'counsel' was barely developed, Parliament *was* sometimes used politically under Elizabeth. While she repudiated the demands of Paul and Peter Wentworth for full freedom of speech, meaning the right of the Commons to serve as a council of the realm—her view was shared by the majority—the distinction is between counsel as a right and as a duty. Even in the Privy Council counselling was a duty not a right; no one disputed that Parliament was an appropriate place to discuss high policy. The House of Lords provided a deliberative forum for the nobility and leaders of the church, while the peers' voting system (though rarely used before 1542) enabled them to signal assent or dissent to bills individually, and to register their dissent in the Journal. Always weightier than the Commons before 1832, the House of Lords offered an alternative route to political participation after the establishment of the select Privy Council, though it remained a 'secondary instrument' for use by men whose real power lay elsewhere.[40]

So-called 'government *versus* opposition' clashes during Elizabeth's Parliaments usually amounted to debates orchestrated by privy councillors and their clients in attempts to 'bounce' the queen into decisions she refused to take. Only the monopolies debates of 1597 and 1601 signalled more serious rumblings, and then the issue was exacerbated by divisions of opinion within officialdom itself.[41] The classic examples of 'orchestrated' debates are those of 1563 and 1566 on the succession; of 1571 on religion; of 1572 and 1586–7 on the fate of Mary, Queen of Scots; and of 1584–5 on the Bond of Association and Act for the Queen's Safety. In the course of these debates Elizabeth's inflexibility on important political issues was contested, but this was the stance not of a small 'opposition' clique but of a majority of the Privy Council, bishops, peers, and Commons' members who represented the political nation.

Yet the queen's response was negative. She evaded any direct answer in 1563, and in 1566 sought to halt debate. In 1571 a significant alignment of bishops, privy councillors, and their 'men of business' favoured six bills enforcing the Thirty-nine Articles, improving the condition of the church and standards of the clergy, and enacting the long-delayed code of canon law prepared in Edward VI's reign entitled *Reformatio legum ecclesiasticarum*. Burghley himself supported most of these reforms, but the campaign came unstuck when the radical William Strickland produced a bill for a revised version of the Book of Common Prayer. The queen intervened and only two bills passed, one enforcing clerical assent to the Articles and the other prohibiting corrupt leases of benefices.[42] Employing similar tactics in 1572 when offered two bills against Mary, Queen of Scots, Elizabeth opted for the lesser and then vetoed it with the excuse that she needed further advice in the matter.[43] On this occasion parliamentary pressure paid off to the extent that she was obliged to commit the duke of Norfolk to the scaffold. But in 1584–5 she stopped Burghley's attempt to provide by statute for an ordered succession should she be assassinated, and she safeguarded James VI's rights unless he were 'privy' to a crime against her. Lastly, she made 'answer answerless' in November 1586 to Parliament's petition that sentence against the Queen of Scots be executed. True, Elizabeth herself used Parliament as a propaganda tool—for, if parliamentary petitioning was largely unwelcome to her and a waste of members' time, its spin-off was to mobilize hostile public opinion against Mary in the 1570s and drive her into conspiracy, as well as to furnish some justification for her death in February 1587.[44] Yet the special

Parliament roll containing a formal account of the 1586 action against Mary was not placed with the records of Parliament at the end of the session.[45] Perhaps this was an oversight, but it is hard not to conclude that the queen forbade so pungent a memorial to Parliament's political role to be so preserved for posterity. In 1571 and 1593, moreover, Elizabeth insisted that 'matters of state' could not be discussed at all in Parliament unless introduced on her behalf and with her permission — a novel doctrine that made her the first Tudor successfully to restrain freedom of debate on foreign policy.[46]

A particular irony is that Norton and Fleetwood, whom the theorists of conflict in Parliament single out as the forerunners of Eliot and Pym, numbered in reality among Burghley's own parliamentary managers or 'men of business', working in the Commons to further the Privy Council's ends, especially after 1571 when Burghley was elevated to the Lords. Some relevant techniques had been developed in the 1530s by Thomas Cromwell, who first saw management of Parliament as an essential aspect of ministerial power. Methods could be formal and institutional: for example, advance preparation of business by privy councillors who then sat as members in Parliament and steered debates; use of the Speaker to guide the House of Commons and determine the order in which bills were read; nomination of committees to draft or amend bills; setting the length of the session to suit the government's purpose; exercise of royal patronage; and in the last resort the royal veto. But equally important were informal kinship networks, patron–client relationships, political and religious connections, and local and economic interests.

In the informal arena moved the 'men of business', members linked to privy councillors who served as their advisers, informants, spokesmen, and public relations officers.[47] Thomas Norton and William Fleetwood were the best of them. Norton was a London lawyer and moderate puritan with a virulent anti-Catholic streak; his links ran to Mildmay, Hatton, and Walsingham as well as to Burghley. 'Man of business' *par excellence* between 1563 and 1581, Norton was an inexhaustible committee man, a prolific parliamentary draftsman, and a popular Commons' man. Fleetwood was also a London lawyer, who served the City as recorder between 1571 and 1592 and was active in the Commons for over thirty years. Like Thomas Digges (client of the earl of Leicester), Thomas Dannett (Burghley's cousin), James Dalton (linked to Burghley), William Fitzwilliam (Mildmay's son-in-law), and more than a dozen others, he aimed to ease the passage of parliamentary business by working in concert with the Privy Council. As Norton declared, 'All that I have done I did by commandment of the House, and specially of the Queen's Council there, and my chiefest care was in all things to be directed by the Council.'[48] So the 'men of business' were invaluable: they were the Council's eyes, ears, and hands in the lower house. One even recommended that the subsidy bill should be 'ready written both in paper and parchment' before a session of Parliament began, significant advice since it implies that even the Commons' exclusive power to initiate lay taxation may have been reduced to a formality by the Privy Council.[49]

If, however, Elizabethan Parliaments were well managed, it was because legislative business was properly directed, for, although Elizabeth insisted upon short sessions of Parliament, an unprecedented number of bills competed for attention. Whereas in Edward VI's reign an average of 93 bills had been proposed in each session, and 48 per session under Mary, the average was 126 bills per session under Elizabeth.[50] Even this figure may not be complete: in 1581 Norton told his dinner companions that he had written 'many a bill of articles that the House did not see'.[51] So the main task of management was neither 'orchestrating' nor reporting debates but coping with the inundation of bills, many of which concerned personal, local, or sectional interests. Priorities had to be determined that gave preference to public measures. The productivity of the Elizabethan Parliaments is the measure of their success. They generated 272 public acts and 166 private acts, an average of 33 acts per session. Averages mislead since they conceal the legislative slump of 1586–7 and 1589 when only 11 and 24 acts respectively resulted. There were also more private acts in 1559, 1563, and 1584–5 than in other sessions.[52] But the wider picture is clear. Also taxation was granted in every session except that of 1572, when none was requested.

Of the public acts, the most important after the religious settlement and anti-recusancy laws concerned social policy and the criminal law. Moves towards welfare provisions more enlightened than whipping and licensed begging had first been made in 1536 and 1552, and in 1563 an Act for the Relief of the Poor authorized the collection of near-compulsory donations for parish relief administered by churchwardens supervised by JPs and diocesan officers.[53] Refusal to contribute could lead to imprisonment, but donations could be as small as an individual chose. When the act expired, Parliament returned to the subject and approved in 1572 a bill for the punishment of vagrants and relief of the poor. Repealing earlier legislation since 1531, the act combined severity with positive thought. Adult vagrants were to be whipped and bored through the right ear for a first offence, condemned as felons for a second offence, and hanged without benefit of clergy for a third. Yet the act also instituted a scheme of compulsory local rates to relieve the aged and dependent poor: JPs were to list the poor in each parish, assess rates for their maintenance, and appoint overseers to administer the welfare system, deploying surplus funds to provide houses of correction for vagrants.[54] Also in 1576 an act implemented ideas first mooted during the 1530s by ordering the purchase of raw materials such as wool, flax, hemp, or iron, upon which the able-bodied unemployed could be set to work at parochial level.[55]

Of course, these measures contained nothing that had not already been put into practice in the more enlightened towns. In Parliament they began as private initiatives before they were taken over by the Privy Council. Yet they formed the beginnings of a realistic national code completed in 1598 and 1601 when further Acts for the Relief of the Poor improved and extended previous legislation and streamlined its implementation. In particular, the duties of overseers of the poor and JPs were defined; authority was given for the imprisonment or distraint of unwilling ratepayers; and provision was made in a related Act for the Relief of Soldiers and Mariners for the payment of pensions to wounded ex-servicemen.[56] Acts for the erection of hospitals and houses of correction and for the supervision of charitable trusts were also passed in 1598 and 1601.[57] Finally, the penalties of ear-boring and death for vagrants were removed in 1593, but the codifying Vagabonds Act of 1598 ordered dangerous rogues to be banished or sent to the galleys and other vagrants to be whipped and sent to houses of correction.[58]

Implicit throughout this legislation was the idea that the balance between agricultural and urban communities should be held static and everyone forced into employment. The fear of vagrancy in Tudor England was largely due to the perceived threat that unemployed people posed to private property when they took to the roads.[59] Yet labour reform was already overdue when Elizabeth ascended the throne. Earlier legislation had been overtaken by inflation, and the influenza epidemic of 1556–60 had caused turmoil. Strikes in many towns meant that labourers had to be paid higher wages than those authorized by statute. So central government and local magistrates alike wished to regulate labour afresh.[60]

The Parliament of 1559 provided a stage for action. The Privy Council's programme included two bills, one 'for servants of husbandry and artificers and their wages' and one 'for taking and having apprentices and journeymen'.[61] Although both were lost owing to lack of parliamentary time, they were reintroduced in 1563, when they were amalgamated into a single bill. The result was the Statute of Artificers that settled the legal framework of English labour for two centuries.[62] It transferred responsibility for fixing wages from Parliament to local JPs so that there was no longer a statutory wage ceiling. But it became an offence either to demand or to pay more than the locally assessed wage. Also labour mobility was restricted through compulsory seven-year apprenticeships, while property qualifications for admission to urban apprenticeships were increased to inhibit migration of population into towns. The act's attempt to outlaw mobility by forbidding workers to change their employers or place of employment without first obtaining written certificates was clearly unenforceable. But, though the act did little to reduce unemployment, as soon as it became law JPs began fixing wages and publishing lists of them. They set higher wages than the old maxima, but did not compensate for losses since the 1530s; and real wages fell again after 1585.[63]

Criminal law reform chiefly concerned forgery, fraud, perjury, and benefit of clergy. Despite some earlier amendment, the Tudor criminal law was imperfect. Precise on felonies, it was vague and outdated on misdemeanours, for criminal law had been settled in an age of force rather than of cunning.[64] It was underdeveloped in cases of fraud, forgery, perjury, the rules of evidence, perversion of the course of justice, and conspiracy. Acts of covin or oppression, especially false or pretended claims of title to land, and multiple or vexatious pursuit of lawsuits designed to get an opponent to sell his land cheaply, were more significant offences in Tudor society than the old crimes of disseisin, forcible entry, and trespass. In the 1530s Cromwell had attempted reform in this field, but had been frustrated by vested interests and the conservatism of lawyers in the House of Commons.[65] By Elizabeth's reign attitudes were changing, especially in the court of star chamber, which after 1560 made cases of misdemeanour its speciality.[66] Yet the Tudor and Stuart mind tended to attribute abuses to individual greed rather than to flaws in the system. The result was that the Privy Council continued to suppose that remedy lay in moral persuasion rather than legal reform.

Three acts of 1563 against embezzlement by servants, witchcraft, and sodomy restored felonies first identified in Henry VIII's reign but subsequently repealed.[67] In the same session forgery and perjury were attacked.[68] Forgery was defined as 'willingly, subtlely and falsely' forging and showing in evidence false title deeds or other legal documents; offenders were liable to double damages, corporal punishment, imprisonment, and (for a second offence) hanging. Covering a huge field, the forgery act required judicial interpretation, which was given in star chamber. That court also punished perjury and subornation of perjury, which another act of 1563 deemed a misdemeanour when committed in cases concerning lands, goods, debts, or damages in any court of record.[69] Something of a legal landmark, the act enforced higher standards not only in the central courts, but also locally at assizes and quarter sessions, as well as in the ecclesiastical courts. Also acts of 1571 and 1584–5 punished fraudulent collusion intended to defraud creditors and purchasers.[70] Lastly, benefit of clergy was abolished for cutpurses working in groups as well as for rapists and burglars.[71] The privilege was finally curtailed in 1576 when it was decided that, although genuine clergy and literate laymen might read the 'neck-verse' once in their lifetime to escape punishment as criminals, they should nevertheless suffer twelve months' imprisonment at the discretion of the secular judges. So the act severed benefit of clergy from the church and indicated that its role in the post-Reformation era would be as a mitigating agent in criminal sentencing.[72]

Yet two-fifths of Elizabethan acts dealt with private business. It is argued that the importance of private-act legislation to Tudor government was that it formed a stabilizing dimension in society lacking, by contrast, in Scotland and Ireland.[73] The Crown had earlier shown how Parliament could be exploited for private business, in particular to reorganize its own landed estates. Private or sectional interests followed suit, though the Crown itself largely abandoned the method after 1546. The average number of private acts per parliamentary session in Henry VII's reign was 18.7 (an untypical figure inflated by restitutions in blood and resumptions of lands confiscated by attainder); in Henry VIII's reign 8.3; under Edward VI 9.2; under Mary 4.3; and under Elizabeth 13.4.[74] But these were only the bills that passed; as the century progressed, abortive bills considerably outnumbered successful ones.

Neither were 'private' parliamentary initiatives restricted to personal or local concerns. Urban corporations attempted to promote legislation affecting national as well as sectional interests, and so did JPs. The Tudor division of bills and acts into 'public' and 'private' categories is misleading, since classification was not determined by criteria of scope and content; the tests were whether fees were paid to the clerks during the passage of a bill and whether the Crown decided to print the act in full in the sessional statute or simply listed its title in a table of private acts. The difference was that a 'public' act was published by the Crown and could be pleaded generally in litigation, whereas the contents of the 'private' acts were not published.[75] Therefore, if needed in court, private acts were pleaded in the form of either parchment copies certified by the clerk of the Parliaments or 'exemplifications' under the great seal.

Of some 283 private bills introduced during the first seven sessions of the Elizabethan parliaments, 22 became public acts, 98 became private acts, and 163 bills failed. In total some 885 bills, public or private, were introduced during this period, 146 of which resulted in public acts and 106 in private.[76] So, whereas 24 per cent of public bills were enacted, 8 per cent of private bills became public acts too, which means that 'public' measures could very definitely be promoted by private members.

Indeed, many Elizabethan bills for the commonwealth were in the nature of cut-and-paste jobs, redactions of different drafts on the same subject by several hands, assimilated inside Parliament by committees or outside by privy councillors and their 'men of business'. A grey area existed between many official bills and those of private origin. Since, therefore, more public acts than before originated in whole or part with ordinary members, there was probably less need than formerly for the Council to survey the whole field of general legislation in order to ensure that the needs of the commonwealth were met.[77] It is barely an exaggeration to say that, while for the Crown Parliament largely meant taxation, for members it meant legislation.[78] So Parliament in this sense afforded opportunities for 'bottom-up' policy-making that complemented the 'top-down' model centred on the Privy Council. Moreover, this analysis could be enriched by a fuller study of the use of Court connections by local interests throughout the sixteenth century, but this question has as yet barely begun to be explored by historians.

THE WAR WITH SPAIN

THE events of 1583–5 racked the regime: Hispano-Guise conspiracy, the success of Parma's reconquest in the Netherlands, John Somerville's plan to fire a pistol at Elizabeth, and William of Orange's assassination prompted panic measures. The earls of Northumberland and Arundel were imprisoned as abettors of Throckmorton, while in October 1584 Burghley and Walsingham drafted the Bond of Association. Modelled on instruments fairly common in more turbulent Scotland (by a bond of 1568 the party of Mary, Queen of Scots, swore to restore her to the throne), the Association committed itself to defend Elizabeth's life and 'pursue as well by force of arms as by all other means of revenge all manner of persons of what estate so ever they shall be . . . that shall attempt . . . the harm of Her Majesty's royal person'. Also members swore 'never [to] desist from all manner of forcible pursuit against such persons to the uttermost extermination of them', while no 'pretended successor by whom *or for whom* any such detestable act shall be attempted or committed', would be tolerated.[1] This, of course, meant that, should Elizabeth's life be threatened, the Queen of Scots was to be killed, whether guilty or not. Moreover, though the wording was ambiguous, the implication was that, if James VI claimed the throne, he should be destroyed too.

In effect, the Association was a political vigilante group; thousands joined it. Formal methods and legal process were abandoned: members were recruited by the nobility and gentry acting not as public officials but as social leaders; the object was revenge *tout court*; and retribution was to be immediate. When the scare of 1584 subsided, privy councillors, Parliament, lords-lieutenant, and JPs camouflaged these points. Elizabeth herself claimed to have been ignorant of the Bond until she saw copies with members' seals attached. Yet the weakness of the Tudor state, momentarily, had been exposed. If martial law had been declared during previous crises (for instance in 1487, 1495,

1536–7, 1549, and 1569–70), that was entirely constitutional: the Crown's 'emergency' powers rested on royal prerogative, which was itself granted by English law. By contrast, the Association was lynch law. The episode, however, was not unique. 'Binding the nation' had been considered in 1569, and was repeated in 1696, when a second Association was formed to thwart a Jacobite assassination plot.[2]

When Parliament assembled on 23 November 1584, legislation for the queen's safety and against Jesuits and Catholic priests predominated. The first bill for Elizabeth's safety closely resembled the Bond of Association, but some MPs criticized its dubious legality and danger to James if he were innocent of any crime. Elizabeth strongly shared these reservations, though they posed the problem that persons who had sworn the original Association were exposed to perjury if different terms were enacted. But the queen had her way; the issue was resolved after Christmas, when a new bill was accepted overriding the existing Association and exempting James from the penalties of the act unless he were 'privy' to a crime. The second act of the session required Jesuits, seminary priests, and others who had entered the Catholic priesthood since 1559 to depart the realm within forty days; prohibited their return on pain of treason; and made it felony for anyone knowingly to receive or aid Jesuits or priests. In addition, Englishmen abroad at Catholic seminaries were to return within six months, the penalty being treason if they otherwise entered the realm.[3]

Yet a spectre stalked the debate on the Association. What would happen if Elizabeth were suddenly murdered? How would the succession be decided? These questions became urgent when news of the Parry plot broke, for, whether William Parry, MP for Queenborough, was a traitor or *agent provocateur*, the revelation that he had schemed to assassinate Elizabeth provoked hysteria. When Elizabeth had succumbed to smallpox in 1562–3, Burghley had proposed that, should she die, a council of regency comprising privy councillors and persons named by Elizabeth in her will should govern until Parliament resolved the succession. Drafts of a bill for the succession upon which he worked with Attorney-General Popham during January 1585 mooted a similar scheme. In the event of the queen's death, the Privy Council would within ten days summon as many lords spiritual and temporal of Parliament as possible, select 'so many as with the Privy Council aforesaid may make up the number of thirty persons at the least', and they together with the chief justices 'shall for the time aforesaid be the Great Council of the Realm'. The Great Council should investigate Elizabeth's death and 'shall by all means to the uttermost of their power . . . pursue the prosecution, punishment, and execution of the offenders of what estate so ever they be in that behalf'. Meanwhile, a Parliament consisting of 'those persons which were of the Parliament then next before' should be summoned. Lastly, Parliament was to determine claims to the succession, choosing the person who had 'best right . . . in blood by the royal laws of the Realm', announcing its decision in the form of an act of Parliament.[4]

So, like Thomas Cromwell, Burghley in the last resort regarded Parliament as an omnicompetent instrument of government in a revolutionary situation. By stifling his bill at birth, Elizabeth indicated rigid disapproval, though whether she or Burghley was the better judge of the situation is elusive. To reject contingency plans calculated to minimize the risk of anarchy was irresponsible. On the other hand, a Parliament held posthumously was invalid since its authority lapsed on the sovereign's death. As Sackville and Norton advised in *Gorboduc* (1562), the succession was better settled while the sovereign was still alive:

> Alas, in Parliament what hope can be,
> When is of Parliament no hope at all,
> Which, though it be assembled by consent,
> Yet is not likely with consent to end?
>
> (*Gorboduc*, v. ii. 253–6)

An accurate verdict on the Parliaments of Oliver Cromwell, these lines did not apply to Elizabeth only because she was lucky enough to survive until 1603.

Mary, Queen of Scots, nevertheless, looked unlikely to succeed. Opinion in 1584–5 echoed that of 1572, despite Elizabeth's negotiations for Mary's return to Scotland to share the throne with her son under safeguards. In fact, this diplomacy was out of touch with reality, since the issue of Mary *versus* her son evaporated as James VI approached the age when he would become the unquestioned ruler of Scotland. So Elizabeth,

Burghley, and Hunsdon proposed an *entente* with Scotland. In July 1585 James accepted £4,000 down and a pension of £4,000 annually to support a defensive alliance which implicitly kept Mary in captivity; these terms were confirmed by a formal league a year later. Of course, the Scottish amity owed everything to the Hispano-Guise threat and nothing to Walsingham and Davison, who distrusted James and pressed for action against Mary. Burghley had doubts too, but Leicester wished to placate James in order to marry his son to Arabella Stuart. James was himself swayed by a letter from Elizabeth promising that she would allow nothing to be done that imperilled his title to the English Crown. Thereafter, his grudging co-operation was bought by subsidies and enhanced prospects of that glittering prize. (In any case, he had no illusions about winning French or Spanish support.)

Yet the Throckmorton and Parry plots created the atmosphere in which Walsingham thrived. Mary was first moved from the earl of Shrewsbury's custody to that of Sir Amyas Paulet, a radical puritan who isolated her from the outside world. Next Walsingham, with Paulet's aid and that of a defecting Catholic refugee, Gilbert Gifford, established a monitored channel of communication between Mary and the French ambassador in London, using a watertight box which was slipped through the bung-hole of a beer cask. By the time that Anthony Babington's plot to assassinate Elizabeth was spawned, Walsingham's network was complete. He wrote to Leicester, 'If the matter be well handled, it will break the neck of all dangerous practices during her Majesty's reign.'[5] When Mary endorsed the planned murder in a dictated letter (17 July 1586), she was trapped. The Babington conspirators were tried and hanged, but Elizabeth agonized even more over Mary's execution than she had over Norfolk's after the Ridolfi plot.

Since the Tower was considered insufficiently secure and too close to London, Mary was sent to Fotheringhay Castle, where her trial formally began on 14 October 1586. Her judges were a committee of nobles, privy councillors, and leading justices appointed under the terms of the Act for the Queen's Safety. Although Mary objected that she was a queen and thus not subject to English common law, she was persuaded that she damaged her reputation by refusing to defend herself. She denied any complicity in attempted assassination but, by virtue of her letter to Babington, was plainly guilty. Indeed, if sentence had not been stayed by Elizabeth's command, the court's verdict would have been published immediately. On the other hand, Mary's demand that her guilt be established by her own words or her own handwriting was not met.

So Elizabeth vacillated. Amply fulfilled was Davison's prediction that she would not take her rival's life unless 'extreme fear compel her'.[6] Although she allowed the commissioners to sentence Mary on 25 October, the Privy Council failed in its attempt to use Parliament to force Elizabeth to proceed further. As Burghley wrote to Walsingham, 'We stick upon Parliament, which her Majesty mislikes to have, but we all persist, to make the burden better borne and the world abroad better satisfied.'[7] Persuaded to summon the Houses for 20 October, Elizabeth was loyally petitioned to execute Mary. Her gnomic response was given on 24 November: 'If I should say, I would not do what you request, it might peradventure be more than I thought; and to say I would do it, might perhaps breed peril of that you labour to preserve.'[8] She herself called this an 'answer answerless', though there were reasons for delaying. Not only was it important to verify that James would not avenge his mother in battle, but it was also necessary to check that Henry III saw Mary's offer to transfer her presumptive right in the matter of the English succession to Philip II as cutting her links with France. But the main reason was that Mary was a sovereign ruler, subject to no earthly power 'because absolute princes ought not to be accountable for their actions to any other than to God alone'.[9] Therefore, Elizabeth had to exhaust every alternative to executing sentence upon her. In fact, she went as far as to suggest that others might relieve her of the burden. At her request, a letter was written to Paulet asking him to do away with his prisoner without warrant according to the Bond of Association. But Paulet refused: 'God forbid', he replied, 'that I should make so foul a shipwreck of my conscience.' Doubtless he foresaw Davison's fate, though Elizabeth stormed at his 'daintiness'. And she spoke of 'one Wingfield' who with others might perform the murder.[10]

In desperation the Privy Council took independent action. Sentence against Mary had been proclaimed on 4 December but its implementation was 'utterly repugnant' to Elizabeth. Although Burghley prepared a death warrant in late December, she could not bring herself to sign it, wavering only on 1 February 1587 when panicked by rumours sweeping the country that Spanish troops had landed in Wales and Mary had escaped from prison. She ordered Davison to bring the document. She called for pen and ink, and signed. Yet Davison next received contradictory verbal commands — first to get the warrant sealed, then not to have it sealed until further ordered. In fact, he had it sealed at once, and, at a crisis meeting of eleven councillors, including Burghley, Leicester, Hatton, Davison, and the second Lord Howard of Effingham, it was decided to despatch the warrant and not to inform the queen 'before the execution were past'. The necessary instructions were issued, and Walsingham's signature was obtained at his house (he lay ill in bed).[11]

Elizabeth's hand was thus forced, though the option of murder was kept open. When the warrant arrived at Fotheringhay, the precedents of the deaths of Edward II and Richard II were pondered but 'it was not thought convenient or safe to proceed covertly, but openly according to the statute' of 1585.[12] So Mary was beheaded on 8 February. (As of her grandson, Charles I, it was said that nothing in her life so well became her as the leaving of it.)

As Shrewsbury's son rode to London with the news, bonfires blazed and bells rang, but Elizabeth flew into an uncontrollable rage. The sacrilege of executing an anointed queen broke her nerve; she was distraught and grief-stricken. She refused to see Burghley for a month and declined his letters. She even took legal advice to see whether Davison might be hanged by royal prerogative for allowing the warrant to leave his possession — for three weeks Burghley feared that her wrath would usurp the rule of law. Normal relations with the Privy Council were not restored for four months. Finally, Davison was sent to the Tower, tried in star chamber, fined 10,000 marks, and imprisoned at the queen's pleasure. After eighteen months he was released and his fine remitted. He continued to draw his secretary's salary until his death, but he never recovered royal favour. In short, he was the scapegoat for political necessity.

After Mary's execution, war with Spain was certain. Elizabeth therefore conserved her resources, refusing increased subsidies to James VI, the Huguenots, and the Dutch. Leicester's expedition to the Netherlands had failed. From the moment he arrived, tensions existed between his aims and Elizabeth's, and between his supporters among the officers (Sir Philip Sidney, governor of Flushing; the earl of Essex, general of the horse; and Thomas Digges, muster-master general) and Sir John Norris, colonel-general of the foot. In fact, Leicester proved incompetent both as a soldier and an administrator. He quarrelled with Maurice of Nassau, with Norris, with the treasurer at war Richard Huddleston (Norris's uncle), and with his own civilian counsellor, Thomas Wilkes. Not only did he raise his officers' pay when he arrived, but he probably also paid eight thousand English volunteers with money intended for the main expeditionary force. Lacking financial discipline, he could not keep within his allotted annual budget of £126,000.[13]

Yet the political imbroglio exceeded the financial one. In January 1586 Leicester accepted the office of governor-general from the States without consulting Elizabeth. His assumption of the title and authority that Philip II's representative had formerly held was a flagrant defiance of her instructions: it implied that Elizabeth had accepted the sovereignty of the United Provinces which he was exercising as viceroy. Although Leicester tried to play off the Privy Council against the queen over the matter, he lost, not least because Elizabeth reacted strongly against suggestions that he was establishing a rival Court at The Hague. It took six months for her fury to abate, by which time the Council's composition had veered against Leicester's interest. In February 1586 Archbishop Whitgift, Lord Buckhurst (son of the former privy councillor, Sir Richard Sackville), and Lord Cobham were appointed instead of Leicester's candidates, the earls of Pembroke and Huntingdon, Arthur Lord Grey, and Henry Grey, earl of Kent. While, therefore, Leicester's objectives —a firm base in the Netherlands; a Protestant coalition; the erosion of French influence among the Orangists; and a counterbalance to Elizabeth's reopened negotiations with Parma—are comprehensible, his means of their pursuit were counterproductive.[14]

Recalled in November 1586 to attend Parliament and to assist in the sentence of Mary, Queen of Scots, Leicester found his conduct of the expedition subject to misrepresentation. Returning to the Netherlands in June 1587, he failed to relieve the siege of Sluys (the stepping stone to Flushing). Already Deventer and the fort dominating Zutphen had been lost owing to the treason of their English captains, Sir William Stanley and Rowland Yorke (lacking pay they surrendered to Parma's 'golden bullets'). Also Leicester's final efforts to assert his authority over the States backfired, bringing the Provinces to the brink of civil war. By September 1587 the earl was desperate: he decided to resign, returning to England in early December. When Lord Willoughby de Eresby was installed as commander of the English forces — with strict orders not to meddle in politics — the myth that Leicester's intervention would redeem the Dutch was exposed for what it was: Protestant chivalric romance.[15] While the image of Sir Philip Sidney dying at Zutphen after sharing his last water bottle with a poor soldier captured later imaginations, it was mere tinsel. Sidney died at Arnhem four weeks after being wounded at Zutphen, and the famous story of the water bottle came from Fulke Greville, who was not present and wrote over twenty years later. In any case, the Dutch needed statesmanship, leadership, money, and military organization to match that of the Spanish Habsburgs. When Leicester could not provide these, his spirit broke and health failed — he died in September 1588. Writing his obituary, Edmund Spenser intoned:

> He now is dead, and all his glory gone,
> And all his greatness vapourèd to naught,
> That as a glass upon the water shone,
> Which vanished quite, so soon as it was sought.[16]

> (*The Ruins of Time*, 218–21)

English intervention in the Netherlands, however, was seen by Spain as an act of war. As early as 1583 Philip II had considered the idea of an Armada; on 29 December 1585 he began gathering plans, maps, and intelligence. His informants were optimistic as to Catholic support for an invasion: reports suggested that only twelve English counties were Protestant; that the old nobility and gentry would rally to the cause, if given the opportunity; and that the supporters of Mary, Queen of Scots, would be friendly to Spain or neutral. More accurate were claims that English forces were weak and unprepared; that no town could withstand a three-day siege with artillery; and that the invasion could partly be financed by plunder. Lastly, Philip's advisers noted that France was divided by civil war, that the Turks were unlikely to break their truce with Spain, and that he would be backed by the pope.[17]

The objective of the Armada was the conquest of England, which would itself assure the reconquest of the Netherlands. The Armada was to proceed to the 'Cape of Margate' and 'join hands' with Parma to ensure the safe passage of his army from Flanders to England. If he landed unscathed, his orders were to march through Kent, then to capture London and await Catholic risings in the border regions and Ireland. Should he land but fail to win a decisive victory, he was to make terms with Elizabeth on the basis of her abandoning aid for the Portuguese claimant, Dom Antonio, and for the Dutch revolt, while tolerating Catholicism in England and perhaps paying a war indemnity.

From the beginning of 1586, therefore, the marquis of Santa Cruz was mustering ships and men. Intended for 1587, the Armada was delayed until 1588 by a raid by Drake on Cadiz: in April 1587 he destroyed between two and three dozen Spanish ships before making for Cape St Vincent, where he intercepted the barrel staves intended for the Armada's water casks. He sailed next to the Azores, where he captured a Portuguese East Indiaman worth £140,000 and obliged Santa Cruz to leave port to protect the returning silver fleet. When the marquis returned to Lisbon, it was too late to launch the 'Enterprise of England' that year. Furthermore, Santa Cruz died in February 1588 and his replacement, the duke of Medina Sidonia, was sceptical about his mission, on the grounds that supplies of stores, ammunition, and guns were inadequate.

Since Philip II intended the invasion to be carried out by his crack troops, an assault force of 4,000 Spaniards, 3,000 Italians, 1,000 Burgundians, 1,000 English Catholic exiles, and 8,000 Germans and Walloons was assembled in the ports of Flanders to await the arrival of 131 vessels, themselves manned by 7,000 seamen and 17,000 troops. Medina Sidonia hoped to defeat the English fleet in battle so that Parma could transport his army unimpeded to England in barges and flyboats; how the two forces were to join is not clear, but 6,000 troops of the Armada were to reinforce Parma once he had established a bridgehead.[18]

Although English preparations against the Armada did not begin in earnest until 1587, foreign mercenaries were no longer needed for home defence as under Somerset and Northumberland. A coherent attempt had been made to capitalize upon the Marian militia statutes: the 1560s had seen some training of the militia, which culminated in more vigorous action prompted by the Northern Rising. Of the European states, however, only Spain had the resources to maintain an efficient army that was properly supplied, and which provided medical care, marriage allowances, and welfare services. English soldiers lacked adequate facilities until the rise of the New Model Army in the 1640s, while the late-seventeenth-century reforms of Michel le Tellier and Louvois changed the picture in France.[19] But in 1573 Elizabeth decided to organize better training for roughly one-tenth of the militia. Since 250,000 able-bodied men aged between sixteen and sixty were theoretically liable for service, it was impossible to do more. So 'trained bands' were selected; out of a total of 182,929 men registered in national musters by 1575, 11,881 received special training and weapons, 62,462 were equipped but untrained, 12,563 were neither trained nor provided with weapons, and 2,835 were cavalry.[20] Costs of militia recruitment and training were met by the localities. But the charges of an 'army royal' levied by the Crown for service abroad, in Ireland, or in England, as in 1588, were partly paid by the exchequer. When the Armada sailed up the Channel, troops were stationed in four locations: the men of Yorkshire and the northern counties watched Scotland and the east coast north of Harwich; mobile units placed along the south coast shadowed the Armada's progress—their combined strength was 27,000 infantry and 2,500 cavalry; an army of 16,500 was assembled at Tilbury under Leicester, though the earl was under a cloud and took little part in the preparations; and the nobility, privy councillors, and bishops raised 16,000 men from their private followings for Elizabeth's personal bodyguard. Yet many of these troops were raw recruits, and their number was modest by Habsburg standards.[21]

Elizabeth's navy in 1559–60 comprised twenty-seven ships, plus seven which were in dry dock awaiting rebuilding or repairs.

At the same date seven merchant vessels were in royal service too.[22] The Privy Council continued the Marian naval programme until 1564, by which time thirteen new ships had been added to the fleet in addition to rebuilt vessels, but older ships were taken out of service, leaving a total force of twenty-four ships. In 1575 the navy mustered twenty-three men-of-war, though the Council estimated that 135 merchant ships above 100 tons and 656 between 40 tons and 100 tons could be requisitioned in a crisis.[23] When William of Orange was assassinated and war loomed in 1584, four new ships were initially commissioned, then another fourteen, then nineteen in the 1590s. By 1603 Elizabeth had forty-two ships, though this compared barely favourably with the navy of Henry V, who had owned thirty-seven ships.[24]

On 19 July 1588 the Armada was sighted off the Scilly Isles. It entered the Channel in a crescent formation, the wings protecting transports and supply vessels: the objective was to intimidate and destroy English ships *en route* so that there would only be the main fleet left to engage. The English, however, contrived a two-pronged assault organized in squadrons: ninety ships including most of the royal navy vessels under the lord admiral, Charles, second Lord Howard of Effingham, with Drake as vice-admiral, formed the western contingent off Plymouth, while Lord Henry Seymour commanded some fifty barques and pinnaces guarding the Downs and the mouth of the Thames. In fact, more English ships were encountered than Medina Sidonia had expected; they poured shot into the Spaniards' wings, 'plucking their feathers' as Howard expressed it. Yet only two Spanish vessels were captured before Howard and Drake joined Seymour off Dover to form an undamaged fleet better gunned than the Armada. Thereafter, the key to the battle was artillery. The Armada carried only nineteen or twenty full cannon and its 173 medium-heavy and medium guns were ineffective — some exploded on use, which suggests that the products of the Lisbon and Malaga foundries had not been fully tested; and, whereas the Armada had only twenty-one culverins (long-range iron guns), the English fleet had 153; whereas the Spaniards had 151 demi-culverins, the English had 344.[25]

The junction of the undamaged English fleets trapped Medina Sidonia in the Calais roadstead. Since English guns prevented close engagement in which seventeen thousand Spanish soldiers might have triumphed, he anchored the Armada off Calais on the 27th. At this point he expected Parma to break cover and attempt the Channel crossing, but Dutch flyboats controlled the banks and shoals of the Flemish coast and frustrated three attempts at embarkation. When the English sent fire-ships against the Armada at Calais on the evening of the 28th, Medina Sidonia thought they were bomb-ships, which were deadly. He ordered his ships to move by cutting cables if necessary, the loss of 120 anchors causing problems later. On the 29th the main battle began off Gravelines on the Flemish coast, the action swaying north and south with the tides. The English used their artillery to advantage: many enemy ships were holed and crew killed, though only one galleon sank and two made for the Netherlands in distress. A change of wind cut the fighting short and enabled Medina Sidonia to flee to the north-west, gathering his scattered transports and supply ships as he went. The English pursuit could only be nominal, since ammunition and stores were exhausted. Sir Thomas Heneage complained that Lord Howard was reduced to eating beans and his men to drinking their own urine. More English seamen reputedly died from hardship than from Spanish weaponry, which caused bitter recriminations afterwards. So, once the Armada had passed the Firth of Forth, it was shadowed by a couple of English ships only. After it rounded the Orkneys on 10 August, Atlantic gales and loss of anchors wreaked havoc. Only half the battered ships trailed back to Spain past the west coast of Ireland; Spanish casualties in the region of 5,500 were estimated.[26]

The English fleet therefore outsailed and outgunned its opponents, and Parma's invasion was thwarted. He could only embark his troops at high tide, when the weather was fair, and when the Dutch blockade had been raised by superior naval forces—conditions no longer applicable. However, the defeat of the Armada marked only the beginning of the war, which lasted until 1604. By the 1620s it was said that Elizabeth had defeated Spain at minimum cost by avoiding foreign alliances and relying chiefly on the royal navy and part-time privateers who preyed on enemy shipping. Indeed, it is true that Elizabeth's navy extended her control over the coastline of the British Isles and waters of north-west Europe; true, too, that English counter-strategy advocated a self-financing war in which privateering raids on the coast of Spain and across the Atlantic met the expenses of the European land war, though the war never, in practice, became self-financing.[27]

Yet the supremacy of naval over land warfare is a myth. The war at sea was only part of a struggle that gripped the whole of western Europe. Resistance to Hispano-Guise aggression centred on the French civil war. Hence northern France and the Netherlands were England's main military theatres in 1589–95. For, if Philip II and his subsidized ally the Catholic League triumphed over Henry of Navarre, both England and the United Provinces would collapse in turn: Philip's Army of Flanders would crush the Dutch without fear of French intervention. And after the death of the Cardinal of Bourbon, the League's 'Charles X' (May 1590), the temptation for Philip would be to claim the French throne for himself or his daughter Isabella, in which case English naval power would be quite inadequate to cover all possible invasion routes from an enemy coastline that might stretch from Brest to Emden. Since Elizabeth lacked the land forces, money, and manpower to rival Spain, she was obliged to help Navarre and the Dutch. The Catholic League was strongest in Picardy, Normandy, and Brittany; these regions and the Netherlands formed what amounted to a continuous war zone. In 1589–95 Elizabeth sent twenty thousand troops to France and eight thousand to the Netherlands, while aid to Navarre totalled at least £300,000 and to the Dutch £750,000 in these six years. By contrast, English naval operations in this period were side-shows: a mismanaged expedition in 1589 to destroy the remnants of the Armada cost the queen £49,000, whilst £172,259 was invested in 'voyages by adventurers'.[28]

In October 1587 Navarre led the Huguenots to victory over Henry III's army at the battle of Coutras, but the following month a German mercenary force *en route* to join him was routed by the duke of Guise. In Paris an extremist wing of the League planned to unleash popular revolt — their purpose was to bind Henry III irrevocably to the League. The king's attempted counter-coup then sparked the 'Day of the Barricades': Guise and the Paris League had to rescue Henry from the mob (11 May 1588). He fled and at first capitulated to the League's demands. But, seeking revenge, he had Guise and his brother, the Cardinal of Guise, murdered at Blois, and leading members of the League arrested (December 1588). When the Catholic towns immediately revolted, Henry allied with Navarre against the League (April 1589), but was himself assassinated on 22 July. However, he had recognized Navarre as his successor before he died.

These events intensified the French civil war, since Philip II was prepared to intervene openly against the Protestant Henry IV. On 2 September 1589 the Spanish Council of State resolved upon full military support for the League, and five days later Parma was ordered to move all available forces in the Netherlands down to the French frontier. Spain subsidized the League to the tune of 15 million florins by 1595; 3,500 Spanish troops were sent to Brittany in 1590; Languedoc was invaded in 1591; and four major campaigns were launched in northern France by the Army of Flanders (1590, 1592, 1594, 1596). Also Philip's client the duke of Savoy occupied part of Provence, while the pope sent ten thousand men in 1591–2 to fight for the League.[29] So, far from eschewing foreign alliances after the Armada, Elizabeth ended her diplomatic isolation. In response to Henry IV's pleas for aid, she lent him £35,000 in 1589, plus £2,350 worth of powder and shot; and £10,000 in September 1590 to raise German *secours*. She sent 4,000 troops under Lord Willoughby as far as the Loire in October–December 1589; 3,000 to Brittany to fight the Spaniards in 1591; 3,000 under the earl of Essex the same year to besiege Rouen; 1,600 to face Parma and reinforce the siege in February 1592; 4,000 to strengthen the Brittany campaign later that year; another 1,200 to Brittany in February 1593; 600 to defend the Channel Islands the same year; and 2,000 more to Brittany in 1594 for the relief of Brest. To equip Willoughby's men alone cost the queen £6,000; operations in Brittany consumed £191,878; and expenses of £97,461 were incurred in Normandy and Picardy. (These figures are minima.)[30]

Despite their number, Elizabeth's forces were auxiliaries to Henry IV's own troops and those of the Dutch and German Protestants. (In addition to sending Henry 300,000 florins in 1588–91, the Dutch provided expeditionary forces in 1592, 1594, 1596, and 1597.)[31] Yet the aims of Henry IV and his allies diverged. In particular, Elizabeth complained that Henry was

slow to take the initiative against League strongholds in
Normandy. She knew that, if the League overran Normandy,
the Spaniards occupying Brittany would be able to link up with
the Army of Flanders. Also Brittany was in danger of being
completely overrun by Spanish troops from their base at Blavet
while Henry campaigned in central France. Of course, Elizabeth
sought to keep the northern and western coasts and ports out
of Spanish control without assuming the role of a principal in
the civil war. Self-interest was her overriding motivation, which
is why she tolerated Henry's broken promises and continued to
support him after his not unexpected conversion to Catholicism
in July 1593. *Realpolitik* guided her actions. Although Henry's
conversion was accompanied by a truce with the Catholic League
and an agreement that all foreign troops should leave the country
or at least be quartered in garrisons, this suited Elizabeth. A
Catholic and united France would restore the balance of power
in Europe, while Henry IV's debts ensured the continuation
in the medium term of Anglo-French collaboration as a
counterweight to Spain — the policy successfully pursued in the
1570s.[32]

When the last English troops left France in February 1595,
Henry IV was firmly seated on the throne. The Catholic League
was destroyed apart from a handful of nobles; the Jesuits were
expelled in the autumn of 1594; and in January 1595 Henry
appealed to French national sentiment by declaring war on Spain.
Faced with internal anarchy, the propertied classes preferred
Bourbon autocracy to social revolt. Like the English gentry in
1689, they patched up their factional and religious divisions in
order to create an *ancien régime*. And the French war with Spain
was largely a national affair, closer in type to earlier contests
between Habsburg and Valois. Elizabeth did, however, intervene
when Spaniards captured Cambrai and, in April 1596, forced
the surrender of Calais. She sent two thousand troops under Sir
Thomas Baskerville to defend Boulogne and Montreuil and to
fight under Henry in Picardy. She even overcame her objections
to a triple alliance between France, England, and the Dutch —
a significant step since she thereby at last recognized the United
Provinces as a sovereign state. Despite this eleventh-hour
coalition, however, Henry IV made a separate peace with Spain
by the treaty of Vervins (2 May 1598), which restored the

territorial position agreed forty years before at Cateau-Cambrésis. Elizabeth sent Robert Cecil and Thomas Wilkes to negotiate an English position and insist that the Dutch must be a party to any treaty, but to no avail. Henry's concession to the Huguenots of limited toleration under the law — the Edict of Nantes was proclaimed two days before the peace of Vervins — meant that he no longer needed a foreign war to distract his subjects from domestic matters.[33]

In the Netherlands the momentum of Spanish reconquest was lost after 1586. When the Dutch imposed their naval blockade, victualling the areas recovered by Parma became impossible. The harvest failed in 1587–9, and without Baltic grain the Netherlands suffered the worst famine of the century: the population was decimated along with the troops assembled for the invasion of England. In October 1588 an English victory at Bergen-op-Zoom (north of Antwerp) thwarted Parma's main army; and a year later Sir Francis Vere routed three thousand Spaniards and Italians. These successes were qualified by the loss of St Geertruidenburg, a key town on the lower Maas, which its garrison sold to Parma (31 March 1589). Next, Spanish troops overran the island of Bommel, but their advance was checked by a mutiny. In fact, divisions of Philip's army mutinied every year between 1589 and 1602. He had diverted his resources to France, which limited his capability against the Dutch, and he was fighting on two fronts, because he had rejected Parma's proposal that Calvinist worship should be tolerated in the rebel provinces during the French intervention.[34]

While Parma was away in France in 1590, Maurice of Nassau captured the strategic town of Breda. Appointed captain-general of the United Provinces in 1588, Maurice reorganized the Dutch forces on the lines of classical antiquity. He stormed Breda after eighty picked men had infiltrated the town hidden in peat barges. Emerging at midnight from their Dutch 'Trojan Horse', this commando force seized the castle, then alerted Maurice, who was waiting outside with 1,700 men (600 were Vere's Englishmen). Next, Maurice and Vere took towns on the lower Maas and around Breda. Parma warned Philip that they were embarked upon a serious campaign, but was told that the French war had priority; so Parma disobeyed his orders to return to France in 1591. (Philip was distracted by a revolt in Aragon in

1591–2.) Maurice and Vere then mustered 10,000 infantry and 1,800 cavalry (May 1591). Moving north-eastwards they recaptured Zutphen and Deventer in three weeks, while Nijmegen fell in October. Philip recalled his nephew for delaying the French campaign, but his decision did not need to be implemented since Parma was hit by a bullet, and died at Arras (6 December 1592). Before his replacement arrived at Brussels, army mutinies had again signalled Spanish military over-extension.[35]

From Elizabeth's viewpoint, the benefit was that, thereafter, it became militarily (if not diplomatically) feasible to employ Vere's companies as a mobile strategic reserve for use in both the Netherlands and northern France. She aimed to limit her costs either by persuading the States General to assume responsibility for paying her troops, or by withdrawing them. So *realpolitik* continued to dictate her policy. She spent £144,786 on France in 1589–91; charges in the Netherlands were £100,000 per annum; the Channel guard of seven frigates and four pinnaces cost £1,000 per month; and the expenses of additional summer garrisons in Ireland climbed to £5,000 per month. If, however, expenditure was high in cash terms, manpower costs were exorbitant. The drain on the supply of seamen for service in the navy and aboard privateers was severe, while on land 11,000 English soldiers were killed in France in less than three years, though only 1,100 fell in battle. The remainder died from plague, insanitary conditions, and shortages of supplies and transport. Moreover, when the survivors reached home, they spoke 'most slanderous speeches of those Her Highness's service and entertainment'. (The military 'hardship' scenes in Shakespeare's history plays are a reflection of public opinion.)[36]

In 1591–4 Maurice of Nassau reconquered all the Spanish outposts north of the Maas: St Geertruidenberg surrendered in June 1593; Groningen fell a year later. Although Vere's forces attended both sieges, 1,500 of his men had been transferred to the pay of the States, and Elizabeth refused to supply the additional 3,000 infantry requested by the Dutch. In fact, the States' massive debts became a sensitive issue. By 1596 Burghley estimated that the exchequer had sent £1.1 million to the Netherlands, though during the 1590s Spain spent practically as much there every year. An Anglo-Dutch agreement of 1598 finally recognized a debt of £800,000.[37]

The turning-point of the Dutch revolt came in the years 1593–4. With the fall of Groningen, Spain lost its hold upon the vital north-east provinces. At last the Dutch occupied most of the territory up to the German border and controlled the great rivers from there to the sea. So, by campaigning in France and the Netherlands at once, Philip II failed in both. In November 1596 he declared bankruptcy for the third time. Although he still managed to remit American silver to the Netherlands, his position in 1598 was worse than in 1589. When he died, at the age of seventy-one, on 13 September 1598, English intervention was no longer vital to the survival of the United Provinces. Even Philip III's renewed offensives could not be sustained.[38]

Whereas the costs of land warfare were prohibitive, the war at sea attracted private investors, though (in Elizabeth's words) naval commanders 'went to places more for profit than for service'.[39] This was certainly true of the Drake–Norris expedition of 1589 to which Elizabeth contributed £49,000. The mission had three aims: to destroy the battered half of the Armada at Santander and San Sebastian; to proceed to Lisbon to provoke a revolt which would enthrone Dom Antonio, the Portuguese claimant; and to sail to the Azores 'thereby to intercept the convoys of the treasure that doth yearly pass that way to and from the West and East Indies'. Drake and Norris took 150 vessels, including six royal navy ships, sixty Dutch transports, and other ships of less than 200 tons; and mustered 19,000 soldiers, 290 pioneers, and 4,000 seamen. Since this huge force must have been intended to invade Portugal, not to burn Spanish ships at anchor, the expedition to some extent had incompatible objectives, a flaw Elizabeth compounded by breaking her promise to supply siege-artillery. (Perhaps she wished to guard against military overextension? Her orders forbade Drake and Norris to besiege Lisbon unless 'the party Dom Antonio hath there is great'.) Yet the earl of Essex joined, unauthorized, at the last minute, and what Drake and Norris themselves intended is obvious. They sailed straight to Corunna, then made an unsuccessful attack on Lisbon, but when the Portuguese did not revolt and Norris retreated with the loss of two thousand men, they ignored the Biscay ports in defiance of the queen and sailed for the Azores. In other words, the commanders first attempted a coup in Portugal, and, when that failed, they tried to recoup their investments by privateering raids. The strategic goal of destroying Philip's fleet was not on their agenda. However, a southerly gale prevented them from capturing either the Azores or Philip's treasure-fleet. By the time the expedition returned to Plymouth, eleven thousand men had been killed or died of sickness.[40]

The Privy Council brought Drake and Norris to account. A unique opportunity had been missed, enabling Philip II to rebuild his navy. So the lesson was plain: 'this army was levied by merchants; whereas in matters of this kind, princes only ought to have employed themselves.'[41] Yet there was no remedy. Elizabeth lacked the resources to create a professional navy of sufficient size. But the 'joint-stock' nature of existing English naval enterprise meant that, the minute her commanders were over the horizon, they set their eyes on booty rather than the strategic war effort.

In so far as 'plunder' itself had a rationale, it was the concept of a 'silver blockade' devised by Hawkins. But while 236 English privateering vessels took 300 prizes worth £400,000 in 1589–91, they worked as individuals not as a team. No systematic plan of interception existed: the earl of Cumberland, Sir Martin Frobisher, Hawkins, and Sir Walter Ralegh oscillated between the Spanish and Portuguese coasts and the Azores. Patrolling the Atlantic in 1591, Lord Thomas Howard and Sir Richard Grenville encountered a Spanish fleet. Disobeying an order to withdraw, Grenville, in the *Revenge*, engaged it alone for fifteen hours. His bravado was legendary, but defied logic and epitomized the strategically valueless commerce-raiding of the war. In any case, a partial blockade was virtually useless. In 1590 two fast-sailing treasure-frigates and all the East India carracks except one reached Spain safely. Thereafter, New World silver arrived in record quantities as Philip built sufficient warships to protect his convoys. Some gratifying Spanish prizes were taken, notably the *Madre de Dios* in 1592. Yet this carrack's capture occasioned a saturnalia of plunder: the English officers and men ransacked jewels, plate, silk, and perfume worth £100,000 before returning to Dartmouth. What remained on board was valued at £141,120, of which only £80,000 reached the exchequer.[42]

By 1595 Philip's navy was rebuilt: a mere squadron of English warships could not hold the Azores station against his reconstructed fleet. Thereafter, Spain and England struck at each other by sea. Invasion scares gripped England and Ireland, and Elizabeth commissioned Drake and Hawkins to attempt a hit-and-run raid on Panama. This proved a disaster from which neither man returned. By contrast, an expedition against Cadiz in June 1596 financed jointly by Elizabeth, Howard, and Essex was successful. The Dutch were induced to join; Vere was summoned from the Netherlands; and the command was divided between Essex and Howard, with Ralegh as their principal lieutenant. Ten thousand men and 150 vessels were mustered: eighteen royal navy ships, eighteen Dutch warships, and twelve London merchantmen. Initially delayed, the force was well organized and achieved a surprise attack. Two of Philip's galleons were destroyed and two captured, while Cadiz was stormed. Essex wished to retain the town as a base, but it was pillaged for two weeks and then set on fire. More spoil was obtained at Faro in southern Portugal on the return voyage: Essex plundered the bishop's library, now in the Bodleian at Oxford. Yet the outgoing Indies fleet was given time to destroy itself; no attempt was made on Lisbon where Philip's main fleet lay at anchor; nor was the incoming treasure-fleet intercepted, while much of the loot of Cadiz was embezzled at the expense of the expedition's investors. If the lessons of 1589 and 1592 had been learned, Elizabeth could not profit from them. For in 'joint-stock' warfare, every vessel raced for home as soon as sufficient booty was aboard.[43]

Philip II retaliated by dispatching from Lisbon an Armada as large as that of 1588, but it fell victim to a storm off Finisterre (October 1596). In 1597 a projected attack by Essex on Ferrol that was comparable in scale to the Cadiz expedition was driven back to Plymouth by bad weather. When Essex sailed again with reduced forces for the Azores, he missed the Spanish treasure-fleet by a few hours but avoided battle with a third Armada intended for Ireland. This sailed from Ferrol only to be scattered by a north-east wind. When a final Armada was diverted to the Azores in 1599, it seemed that Spanish efforts were in vain as long as bad weather prevailed. Neither was any decisive victory likely as long as Elizabeth refused to throw her whole fleet into battle. The queen never again committed her entire resources at once after 1588, thus ensuring that no English enterprise was a complete success and several were failures. On the other hand, the risk of total defeat was reduced.

In 1586–8 Thomas Cavendish emulated Drake's Pacific voyage, returning with a great haul of loot and a report on Manila and the China trade. In 1593–4 Richard Hawkins burnt Valparaiso, but was defeated and captured by a Spanish force off Peru. In 1598 the earl of Cumberland sacked Puerto Rico. During this 'war of reprisal' English privateers captured over a thousand Spanish and Portuguese prizes, thereby undermining the Iberian economy. Indeed, before his death, Philip II recognized that sooner or later Spain would have to grant the English some share in the traffic of the New World. The privateers were, in effect, pursuing commerce by other means in order to obtain luxury imports. They accumulated the wealth, shipping, and expertise that launched the East India Company (1600), the Virginia Company (1606), and the Newfoundland Company (1610); financed the Caribbean contraband trade; sponsored the short-lived Wiapoco colony in Guiana (1604); and expanded the existing Levant, Barbary, and Muscovy trades. The capital available to investors in the seventeenth century was considerably greater than under Elizabeth, owing to the rise of money markets linked to government borrowing. But the British and Dutch colonial empires were founded on the profits of the privateering war against Spain. On the other hand, the contribution of the privateers to overseas expansion was neither planned nor deliberate. Although eulogized as naval commanders, strategists, and imperial pioneers, the Elizabethan 'sea dogs' were motivated by greed not altruism. If a parallel is sought, they were linked in spirit to the plunderers of religious houses in Henry VIII's reign.[44]

THE MAKING
OF THE TUDOR STATE

IT is striking that, whereas in 1500 the word 'state' had possessed no political meaning in English beyond the 'state or condition' of the prince or the kingdom, by the second half of Elizabeth's reign it was used to signify the 'state' in the modern sense. In the reigns of Henry VII and Henry VIII politicians had spoken only of 'country', 'people', 'kingdom', and 'realm', but by the 1590s they began to conceptualize the 'state'.[1] Even the Act of Appeals, which unequivocally ventilated an idea of the unitary state, had proclaimed in 1533 that 'this *realm* of England is an empire'. If, however, the shift from 'realm' to 'state' is among the more interesting developments in English history, it was the product of an amalgam — an unstable mixture — of various ideas which did not easily cohere with one another. The concept of the 'state' identified England as (1) a defined territory; (2) a monarchical society organized for civil rule; and (3) a sovereign government which recognized no superior in political, ecclesiastical, and legal matters. Also important were three underlying beliefs: (1) that humanity was divided into races or nations; (2) that the purity of the English nation would be sullied by foreign admixtures; and (3) that English language, law, and customs (including dress) were the badges of nationality. In this chapter I shall explore these ideas in an attempt to show that language, ethnography, territory, law, theories of sovereignty, Protestantism, and Tudor Irish policy were components of the amalgam.

No single event such as war, trade, population growth, or the Reformation uniquely shaped the Tudor state. Many issues were involved, including ethnographic ones. In the fifteenth century there was no conception of England as a unitary state: *regnum* and *sacerdotium* owed allegiance to king and pope respectively, though a sense of 'Englishness' was beginning to evolve. Whereas

Venetian observers categorized Welshmen and Cornishmen as separate races or nations, *The Commodities of England* (1451) defined English national identity as one 'land' but 'three diverse languages' (English, Welsh, and Cornish).[2] Late-medieval and Tudor speech often defined 'nation' in ethnic terms, as when Shylock says of Antonio, 'He hates our sacred nation',[3] or the Irishman MacMorris asks the Welshman Fluellen, 'What ish my nation?'[4] But this usage had started to become dated in Shakespeare's lifetime. By the 1590s English 'nationhood' was most widely perceived in terms of English culture and law. The nobility and gentry throughout Elizabeth's territories spoke English and considered themselves Englishmen, even in Ireland where Tudor policy had increasingly alienated the Old English. (When the Old English complained that Shakespeare's English was newfangled, and that they alone spoke 'old ancient Chaucer English', they had something more than speech patterns in mind.)[5]

It was Tudor policy increasingly to ignore minority culture and languages: the use of English was made compulsory for legal business if not for church services. When Welsh parliamentary lobbying managed to obtain an act for a Welsh translation of the Bible and Prayer Book in 1563, a proviso ordered that the English version should be placed in churches alongside the Welsh so that people comparing the two would learn English.[6] Furthermore, the indigenous communities of Wales and Ireland were granted the rights of freeborn Englishmen only if they adopted English customs, language, and law. Neither Celtic nor Gaelic culture was tolerated at national level. The legal status of Gaelic Irishmen in Tudor society actually remained that of serfs: their deaths were no felony; they could not litigate as demandants or plaintiffs in the royal courts; their wills were invalid; and their widows were not entitled to dower.[7] Probably the Tudors sought to create a dominant English culture rather than to kill native customs outright; many inhabitants of Wales and Cornwall became bilingual. But the scales were loaded against ethnic minorities. Advocating a plan for the conquest of Ireland in 1565, Sir Thomas Smith summarized official policy in a simple phrase: 'To augment our tongue, our laws, and our religion in that Isle, which three be the true bands of the commonwealth whereby the Romans conquered and kept long time a great part of the world.'[8]

At another important level, the break with Rome and Protestant Reformation, Henry VIII's 'imperial' theory of kingship, and anti-Catholic xenophobia sharpened the definition of 'Englishness'. The cumulative impact of Henrician and Edwardian religious propaganda was revealed by the spontaneous opposition after 1553 to Queen Mary's 'Spanish' marriage and wish to crown King Philip, as well as by the polemics of the Protestant exiles during her reign. Next, Elizabethan anti-Catholicism merged with attacks on the 'tyrannical' conduct of Spain in the New World. The classic account by Bartolomé de las Casas of the American Indians' sufferings, published at Seville in 1552, was translated as *The Spanish Colonie* (1583). The rise of the Spanish and Roman Inquisitions, and extension by Philip II of the inquisition to the New World, reinforced the Protestant idea of England as an 'elect nation' under a godly queen. It was predictable that John Foxe should provide gruesome reports of Catholic inquisitors in Spain, Italy, and France who whipped, tortured, and even murdered men, women, and children.[9] In brief, developments in English culture and language, Protestant polemic, and Elizabethan seapower united to transform the old fifteenth-century emphasis on 'abuttals' into new patriotic visions of England as a 'scepter'd isle' and 'other Eden'.

> This fortress built by Nature for herself
> Against infection and the hand of war,
> This happy breed of men, this little world,
> This precious stone set in the silver sea.
>
> (*Richard II*, II. i. 43–6)

The concept of *patria* was capturing English sentiment by 1603: travellers had tested foreign lands but found them wanting. Advising Robert Cecil, Burghley urged: 'And suffer not thy sons to pass the Alps, for they shall learn nothing there but pride, blasphemy and atheism.'[10]

The image of England as a 'scepter'd isle' probably reflected insecurity as much as self-confidence during Elizabeth's war with Spain. But the Tudor state remained cohesive despite war and the Reformation, partly because the Crown did not attempt to

rule all its territory direct from Westminster.[11] Henry VII and
Henry VIII both practised decentralized administration: Wales
and the north, and briefly (1539–40) the south-western counties,
were administered by councils acting as regional governing
boards. In addition, Elizabeth created councils for Connaught
and Munster answerable to the Irish Privy Council. Doubtless
it is too bold to say that Henry VIII and Elizabeth saw their
borderlands as 'strategic buffer zones' designed to protect their
more populous and advanced southern counties. But the
jurisdiction of the Council in the Marches of Wales extended
into Shropshire, Worcestershire, Herefordshire, Gloucestershire,
and, until 1569, Cheshire. In general, Crown policy was 'to
maintain a provincial council in any region in which the
government felt that its control was inadequate'.[12]

Some further distinction should be made for territory north
of the River Tyne. In the far north the Crown's consolidation
of its power could not match its success elsewhere on the
mainland. After the Pilgrimage of Grace and Northern Rising,
the Council of the North was reconstructed to bring not only
Yorkshire, but also Durham, Northumberland, Cumberland,
and Westmorland within its jurisdiction. In peacetime the Crown
was restricted to promoting to wardenships of the Scottish
marches resident landowners of lesser rank than the Percies,
Nevilles, Cliffords, and Dacres who traditionally had dominated
the area. Rarely except in time of war or revolt was the
appointment of southern nobles a feasible option. A policy of
ruling the border in peacetime through 'new men' whose service
to the Crown raised them to a place beside the 'old' territorial
magnates they displaced was more realistic. But Elizabeth was
able to appoint three southerners to northern office in the 1560s,
while her cousin, the earl of Huntingdon, was named president
of the Council of the North in 1572. Southern nobles were also
made lords-lieutenant of Durham: the earl of Bedford after 1569,
and earl of Huntingdon in 1587. This was possible because
Elizabeth could build on half a century of co-operation with the
bishop of Durham since Wolsey's ascendancy.[13]

It would be misleading to classify the Tudor borderlands
generally as pluralist societies. Some jurisdictional anomalies
persisted in England despite Cromwell's attack on franchises and
liberties in the 1530s: the duchies of Lancaster and Cornwall

were administered independently from the national system, while the palatinates of Durham, Chester, and Lancaster retained their special courts. But each of these mainland jurisdictions enforced common law under the Crown's direction.[14] The exception was Ireland, which was divided between English and Gaelic civilizations. Although the Normans had colonized the low-lying areas of Munster and Leinster and laid claim to the whole island, by 1461 English rule was limited to the Pale. Running from Dundalk to Dublin along the coast and extending inland for some 20–40 miles, this region was the heart of the medieval English lordship with Dublin as its seat of power. The region contiguous to the Pale, if partially anglicized, was by comparison less amenable to English control. Otherwise only the towns of Waterford, Cork, Limerick, and Galway, and the royal fortress of Carrickfergus, were considered loyal. So Gaelic Ireland possessed the lion's share of Irish territory, ruled by independent chiefs highly adept at exploiting the terrain. Yet areas of influence were rarely defined clearly in Ireland. During much of the Yorkist and early Tudor period Crown administration was delegated to the Fitzgeralds of Kildare, the greatest dynastic family of the medieval colony, whose connections straddled both English and Gaelic cultures.[15]

In the reign of Henry VI, Richard, duke of York, had been so preoccupied with English politics as lieutenant of Ireland that he achieved little. But there was no real threat from the Gaelic clans, and in the lordship the Crown had wide support. Thereafter, Edward IV, Henry VII, and Wolsey were successful largely because they applied methods adopted on the mainland. The Pale was kept loyal by delegating government mainly to trusted nobles, an approach sustained until the Kildare rebellion of 1534. In addition, Henry VII's Irish legislation included provisions that certain English statutes should also apply to Ireland, and that the Irish Parliament could only meet with the king of England's prior consent.

Gerald Fitzgerald, eighth earl of Kildare, and his son Gerald, ninth earl, were the leading Crown deputies between 1478 and 1534. Despite such lapses as the crowning of Lambert Simnel in May 1487 and intermittent clashes with Henry VIII and Wolsey, the Fitzgeralds broadly advanced Crown interests alongside their own. In fact, the ambiguity of their position was the key to their success, for they managed Gaelic lords in accordance with native customs, but maintained their own English identities as partners of the Crown. Hence, far from the lordship being an embattled colony swamped by Gaelic incursions before the Reformation, it was a stable society governed by institutions modelled on those of England. True, the Dublin administration was less sophisticated than that of Westminster, though Wolsey established an executive Privy Council in Ireland that anticipated the English version by fifteen years. But the lordship's needs were met and the way paved for interventionism after 1534. The defect of Henry VIII's policy, which moved by fits and starts, was that Irish government remained at the level of competing local interests: frequent changes of deputy and consequent disruption were matched by falling revenues. Also various royal experiments marginally weakened English power: Henry was reluctant to spend money on Ireland in the 1520s, and too prone to use Irish offices as rewards for English courtiers. Lastly, he was less tolerant of the ninth earl of Kildare than Henry VII had been of the eighth. Henry VIII had his own ideas about Ireland, and Kildare's lack of interest may have given the impression that he opposed reforms on principle.[16]

A crisis erupted in 1533 when Kildare was summoned to England. Irish politics had begun to merge with those of the king's divorce and break with Rome, and Kildare looked to the duke of Norfolk and earl of Wiltshire for support as his rivals turned to Cromwell. Even Chapuys took an interest in Kildare since Charles V saw Ireland as a potential lever against Henry VIII. When Kildare appeared in London he was interrogated about his conduct. By May 1534 'manifold enormities' were proved and he was forbidden to return to Ireland. His son and heir, Thomas Lord Offaly ('Silken Thomas'), was then summoned to Court, but Kildare warned him to stay away. Offaly marched to Dublin with a thousand men to denounce Henry VIII. At first he did not plan outright revolt, but when Kildare was sent to the Tower rebellion was unleashed (July 1534).[17] Taken by surprise, Henry VIII could only parley with the rebels until a relief army under Sir William Skeffington was organized, though without Charles V's support the rebels were unlikely to succeed. But they held most of the Pale and surrounding districts. They gained considerable clerical support which they exploited to create the impression that the revolt was sparked by Henry VIII's divorce and attacks on the church. Lastly, Skeffington's arrival threw the young earl of Kildare (the ninth earl died in the Tower in September 1534) into the arms of the Gaelic chiefs, and the revolt turned into something approaching a Gaelic war of independence.[18]

Kildare's surrender in August 1535 was followed by a major change of Tudor policy: aristocratic delegation was replaced by direct rule. Cromwell's aim was to assimilate Ireland into the unitary realm of England under the control of an English-born deputy. But when Kildare and his supporters were attainted, this policy required the backing of a standing army controlled from Westminster. The creation of a resident garrison was not a deliberate policy: it was the only available option. Yet English garrisons threatened Gaelic Ireland. Also relations started to polarize when the Crown attempted to manage directly networks previously managed by Kildare. Consensus was being replaced by confrontation.[19]

After his appointment in July 1540 the English deputy Sir Anthony St Leger attempted to reconcile the chiefs to the Crown by a policy designed to incorporate the Gaelic lordships by consent into a fully anglicized kingdom of Ireland. He asked the chiefs to recognize Henry VIII as their liege lord, to apply for Crown grants of their lands and peerages, to repudiate papal jurisdiction, and to attend the Irish Parliament. In turn, he vainly urged Henry VIII to limit his ambitions, abandoning what could not be enforced in exchange for stability and the prospect of peace.[20]

Although this conciliatory policy might gradually have reduced Gaelic Ireland to English ways at minimal cost, it was suspended in 1543. A major obstacle blocked the way to conciliation — Henry VIII radically altered his constitutional position when he amended his royal style from 'lord' to 'king' of Ireland (June 1541). His assumption of the kingship was justified on the grounds that 'for lack of naming' of sovereignty the Irish had not been as obedient 'as they of right and according to their allegiance and bounden duties ought to have been'. His timing was, however, the key. It had been argued in Ireland that the 'regal estate' rested in the papacy: the 'dominion' enjoyed by the king of England was 'but a governance under the obedience of the same'. So the decision of 1541 followed from the break with Rome. A more constructive pretext was to enable the Gaelic population to be 'accepted as subjects, where before they were taken as Irish enemies'. Instead of Ireland being partitioned into English and Gaelic zones, a 'kingdom of Ireland' was to embrace the whole island and its people, who would speak English and be governed by English law. In addition, the Gaelic population would receive the same rights under the Crown as the Old English.[21]

This position had been implicit in legislation of 1537 declaring that diversity of language, dress, and manners caused the inhabitants of Ireland to appear 'as it were of sundry sorts, or rather of sundry countries, where indeed they be wholly together one body'. The act ordered both Gaelic Irish and Old English to speak English and wear English clothes. Indeed some progress was made in persuading the chiefs to see that English dress was worn, to adopt English agricultural methods, and to build houses of similar design to those in England.[22]

Yet Henry VIII's assumption of Irish kingship committed England to a possible full-scale conquest of Ireland, should the chiefs rebel, or should the Irish Reformation, begun by Cromwell, fail. It even militated *against* the idea of a unitary state, for a subordinate superstructure had been created for Ireland: the later Tudors ruled technically two separate kingdoms, each with its own bureaucracy. In future ideological terms, it became possible to conceive of Anglo-Irish nationalism, as opposed to English or Gaelic civilization. Lastly, despite the confiscation of Kildare's estates and the dissolution by Henry VIII of half the Irish monasteries, the Irish revenues were insufficient to maintain either the Crown's new royal status or its standing army. Since the army could not be withdrawn, the case for the conquest of Ireland was reinforced.

It was therefore predictable, given his Scottish policy, that Protector Somerset would cease to regard Ireland as a borderland requiring techniques of government similar to those of Wales and the north, in favour of a military solution. Just as Somerset tried to hold down Scotland by installing permanent English garrisons there, so too in Ireland he reinforced the army and put garrisons in key marches, also taking tentative steps towards the plantation of Leix and Offaly. In short, conquest and colonization reached the political agenda. Whereas the Protector's Scottish strategy collapsed, he discovered that in Ireland a larger army gave the government greater freedom of manœuvre in managing both Gaelic and Old English communities—Crown attention was focused on the planned reduction of Gaelic Ireland. A garrison of 500 men was augmented to 2,600 by 1551, and, despite temporary reductions under Mary, it rarely dropped below 1,500 thereafter. A background of administrative inadequacy likewise encouraged politicians to think of anglicization by force, since the Irish bureaucracy could not be increased to match the Crown's interventionism for financial reasons. In particular, the absence of JPs and lords-lieutenant in Ireland left local government overdependent on the sheriff.[23]

By 1558, therefore, the Crown was committed to an 'interventionist' strategy which was unjustifiable by the normal tests of Elizabethan policy-making, even if conquest and colonization were not yet being pursued consistently. Whereas *realpolitik* and anxiety about military overextension dictated Elizabeth's attitude to European policy, in Ireland everyone wanted quick results. At length a full-scale conquest became necessary. Attempts to extend English influence and promote colonies in the vicinities of garrisons either failed or were frustrated by revolt. English standing was damaged when Irish offices became competitive prizes to be divided among the clients of courtiers. Also factionalism was more pronounced in Ireland than in England, since deficit financing and the presence of a standing army turned the colonial service from an area of honourable exile into a breeding ground for fortune-hunters and aristocratic swordsmen. Aims constantly outstripped resources, while arbitrary taxation (to pay garrisoning costs), frequent resort to martial law, the suspension of Parliament during the last seventeen years of Elizabeth's reign, and a 'get rich quick' attitude among the colonists soured relations with Old English and Gaelic communities alike.[24]

In particular, frequent challenges to Crown authority and resurgent feuding among the Gaelic chiefs tested the steel of successive deputies. Beginning in 1558, the third earl of Sussex competed with Shane O'Neill to control Ulster. Shane sought to be O'Neill, lord of Tyrone, and king, in the Gaelic sense, of Ulster. His quarrels with his family over the disputed succession and feuds with the O'Donnells of Tyrconnell, O'Reillys of East Breifne, and Maguires of Fermanagh were legendary. But Sussex failed either to defeat or to poison him; Elizabeth therefore summoned Shane to Court. Since he seemed willing to compromise, she confirmed him as 'captain' of Tyrone in exchange for acknowledging the Crown's overlordship. When he returned to Ireland, however, he instantly took up arms to recover what he claimed as his rights.

In 1565 Sussex was replaced by Sir Henry Sidney, whose arrival saw the evolution of a 'programme for the conquest of Ireland'. The essence was conquest and colonization backed by garrisons and regional councils under effective presidents, though Sidney's particular contribution was his advocacy of privately financed colonies, which he thought a valid alternative to more costly Crown projects. In fact, most of Sidney's ideas were modelled on a plan prepared by Sussex in 1562. But a novel aspect was that, to justify the subjugation of Gaelic Ireland, he equated the 'wild Irish' with barbarians. He told Elizabeth in 1567:

There was never people that lived in more misery than they do, nor as it should seem of worse minds, for matrimony among them is no more regarded in effect than conjunction between unreasonable beasts. Perjury, robbery, and murder [are] counted allowable. . . . I cannot find that they make any conscience of sin, and I doubt whether they christen their children or no.[25]

Writing to the earl of Leicester, Sidney denounced Shane, who had intrigued with Mary, Queen of Scots, and attempted to obtain six thousand reinforcements from Charles IX of France in April 1566.[26] He launched a major offensive against him and restored the power of the O'Donnells in Tyrconnell. In the end it was Hugh O'Donnell who defeated Shane in battle (8 May 1567). The vanquished O'Neill fled and threw himself on the mercy of Scots settlers at Cushenden (Co. Antrim), only to be hacked to pieces. His head was obtained by the Carrickfergus English, and was sent pickled in a barrel to Dublin.[27]

Sidney's attention was next directed to Munster, where fighting between the Fitzgerald earls of Desmond and Butler earls of Ormond laid waste large tracts of Limerick, Tipperary, and Kilkenny. In what proved to be the last private war between Tudor noblemen, Gerald, fourteenth earl of Desmond, routed Thomas Butler, eleventh earl of Ormond, at Affane, near the River Blackwater below Lismore (February 1565). Summoned to Court, the two earls submitted to Elizabeth, but Desmond defaulted and was arrested by Sidney in the spring of 1567. He was sent back to London and incarcerated in the Tower. But his removal created a power vacuum. Also the arrival in Munster of English adventurers who claimed to be heirs of the Norman invaders of Ireland was seen to threaten Irish property rights. So the earl of Desmond's cousin, the unscrupulous James Fitzmaurice Fitzgerald, engineered election as 'captain' of Desmond, appealed for Catholic and foreign aid, and raised south-west Ireland in revolt (June 1569). The revolt was quickly subdued, though Fitzmaurice did not surrender until January 1572. The earl of Desmond was then permitted to return to Ireland. Provocatively he wore Irish dress, and he fortified the castles in his territory, but Burghley called his bluff. His castle of Derrinlaur was taken and its defenders executed (August 1574).[28]

Elizabeth, meanwhile, had established provincial councils in Connaught and Munster in 1569 and 1571, modelled on the Council of the North and Council in the Marches of Wales, but answerable to the Irish Privy Council. When, however, their presidents launched direct attacks against local magnates and their retainers, and enforced English law at the expense of Gaelic institutions, they provoked a backlash so strong that the councils had temporarily to be suspended. An atmosphere was created in which loyal subjects appeared to be treated as Irish 'enemies' — the cost to Crown–community relations was high. Then, after Pius V's bull *Regnans in excelsis*, Irish opposition appealed to Catholicism. This led first to Thomas Stukeley's projected invasion of Ireland financed by Pope Gregory XIII (1578), and then to an expedition organized jointly by Fitzmaurice and Nicholas Sander, an exiled English recusant leader who secured appointment as papal nuncio. Landing at Smerwick, the curiously matched pair set up the papal standard, built a fortified camp, and recruited the earl of Desmond, whose financial straits drove him finally to treason (July 1579). This caused the biggest crisis since Kildare's rebellion, because Elizabeth had not yet replaced Sidney, whom she had recalled, having lost confidence in his interventionism. First Munster and then Leinster took up arms, and there were secondary upheavals in Ulster and Connaught. Defeating the rebels and their Italian and Spanish reinforcements fell initially to Sir Nicholas Malby and Sir William Pelham, and later to the new lord deputy, Lord Grey of Wilton.[29]

Since Grey's field army numbered 6,500 men, he could barely have failed to defeat the rebels. His attitude was, however, shaped by his belief in widespread Catholic conspiracy. Exceptional severity was everywhere applied: an entire garrison was massacred despite having surrendered; leaders of the Old English as well as the Gaelic community were executed; the harvest of 1580 was burned; and cattle slaughtered. By the time of Grey's recall in August 1582, famine raged even in the Pale. The Munster population was decimated, and the poet Edmund Spenser (Grey's secretary) wrote: 'In short space there were none almost left and a most populous and plentiful country suddenly left void of man or beast.' Indeed, when Elizabeth (to reduce military costs) decided to pardon all but the chief rebels, Grey complained that this would mean leaving the Irish 'to tumble to their own sensual government'. (He meant that everyone would demand protection, while reserving the right to be a traitor.) So he largely thwarted the amnesty.[30]

Yet the effect of Grey's policy was to overcome opposition in Munster and Connaught to Sidney's 'programme for the conquest of Ireland'. Grey's 'pacification' was not equivalent to a conquest, but it paved the way for systematic colonization. Despite the fact that projects of the 1570s for the plantation of parts of Ulster had proved a disaster, colonization was seen as the way to challenge Old English power and erode the independence of the Gaelic territory. The Ulster projects of Sir Thomas Smith and his son, and Walter Devereux, first earl of Essex, were ill conceived and incompetently executed: they precipitated a further deterioration in Anglo-Gaelic relations as well as costing Elizabeth £87,000 within three years. On the other hand, the Munster settlement begun in 1586 upon land forfeited by the attainted earl of Desmond was relatively successful. It was a going concern by 1589, though there were only 775 English tenants by 1592 instead of the 1,720 envisaged. Also they were swamped by Gaelic Irish despite original conditions that stipulated only tenants of English birth.

By contrast the Connaught settlement by 'composition' was a complete success. In the summer of 1585 commissioners travelled through the province to register landowners, who were then obliged to 'indent' with the president of the Council of Connaught to pay a yearly rent of 10*s*. per *c*.120 acres of inhabited land. This rent replaced all arbitrary exactions and garrison charges; Gaelic jurisdictions and the system of land and stock allocation that was part of them were also abolished. So the end result was to create vested interests which worked to consolidate English control. In addition, the system raised sufficient revenue to enable Connaught to pay for itself until north Connaught joined Tyrone's rebellion.[31]

The outbreak of war with Spain in 1585 little affected Ireland. On the contrary, the Munster and Connaught settlements raised the possibility that Tudor rule might be consolidated without new revolts. True, the English presence was barely more than a military occupation, but the resident troops had adjusted to the terrain so that, barring Spanish invasion or the loss of military superiority, the reduction of the entire west coast of Ireland and its hinterland seemed feasible. Indeed, inroads were being made into Ulster from the south-east and south-west when the earl of Tyrone's rebellion turned the tables.

Hugh O'Neill had been created second earl of Tyrone in 1585. His dual position as a Gaelic dynast and English earl afforded him enviable latitude, though he was at best a speculative investment for Elizabeth—when he felt his position as arbiter of Ulster was threatened he broke with the Crown. Initially his conduct was ambivalent: he helped both sides in 1593 when Hugh Maguire, his son-in-law, campaigned against English incursions. In February 1595 he sent his brother Art to destroy Blackwater Fort, on the River Blackwater. Soon he commanded 1,000 pikemen, 4,000 musketeers, and 1,000 cavalry. He invested the garrisoned post at Monaghan and mauled an English army at Clontibret. The O'Donnells of Tyrconnell then rose, capturing

Sligo and north Connaught. Tyrone was proclaimed a traitor (June 1595), and Elizabeth raised an army augmented by 1,600 veterans from Brittany under Sir John Norris. Yet she wished to avoid the costs of a major battle; therefore she made a truce with the earl and his confederates which, by creating a breathing space, enabled them to seek Spanish aid. The crown of Ireland was offered to Cardinal Archduke Albert, Philip II's nephew and governor of the Netherlands. So the Armada of 1596 included a contingent for Ireland, but it was scattered off Finisterre.[32]

The rebel leaders championed Catholicism too. They petitioned the pope to grant them patronage of Irish benefices, and called on 'the gentlemen of Munster' to join the confederacy and to 'make war with us'. The Munster settlement was attacked, and the O'Byrnes of Wicklow joined the rebels. In May 1597 Elizabeth appointed Thomas, Lord Burgh, as deputy. He built and garrisoned a new Blackwater Fort, but Tyrone besieged it. Then Burgh contracted typhus and died (13 October).

In late October an Armada for Ireland failed to arrive, so Tyrone offered a truce. When it expired, however, he routed Sir Henry Bagenal at the battle of the Yellow Ford (14 August 1598). This was the worst disaster in Ireland during Elizabeth's reign. Some 830 troops were killed, 400 wounded, and 300 Irish deserted to Tyrone. Bagenal was killed and barely half his men returned. Also Blackwater Fort surrendered. Next, O'Donnell gained almost total control of Connaught; the O'Mores attacked the Leix–Offaly settlement; the entire Munster plantation was destroyed in a few days; and rebel chiefs were set up in Connaught and Leinster as well as in Munster to supersede loyalists. Thereafter, English problems in Ireland looked uncomfortably like Spanish ones in the Netherlands. While almost thirty-five thousand English and Welsh levies were sent to Ireland between 1595 and 1601, Tyrone commanded a remarkable degree of unity and support for an independent Catholic Ireland, gaining credibility as the leader of a spontaneous nationalist uprising.[33]

By the beginning of 1599 Elizabeth had accepted the unpalatable fact that conquest of Ireland was essential. On 15 April her waning favourite, Robert Devereux, earl of Essex, landed at Dublin to take up office as queen's lieutenant. Most of his troops were raw recruits, but he had 16,000 infantry and 1,300 cavalry. Yet his boast, 'By God, I will beat Tyrone in the field,' proved empty. He wasted the summer on what looked suspiciously like a royal 'progress' into Leinster and Munster; and, when ordered by an exasperated Elizabeth to head northwards, he made a truce with Tyrone (8 September). In fact, Tyrone may have tricked his opponent by inciting him to 'stand for himself', promising that, if he did so, 'he would join with him' — an allusion to the earl's continuing feud with Robert Cecil. But whether or not this is true, Essex's failure in Ireland surpassed Leicester's in the Netherlands. After twenty-one ineffectual weeks, he defied his orders and deserted his post in a last-ditch attempt to salvage his career at Court by personal magnetism.[34]

When the truce expired, Tyrone marched south, burned the lands of loyalists, and camped near Kinsale on the Cork coast. In February 1600 Charles Blount, Lord Mountjoy, replaced Essex, assisted by Sir George Carew, who was appointed president of Munster. Mountjoy commanded 13,200 men, though the nucleus of his force was the demoralized remnant bequeathed by Essex. Yet Carew secured Cork and steadily subordinated Munster, while Mountjoy settled the Pale and nudged Tyrone back to Ulster. Then the greatest combined operation of the century in Ireland was accomplished when four thousand men under Sir Henry Docwra landed in Lough Foyle (May 1600), coupled with a movement northward of a second force intended to distract Tyrone's attention from the landing. Mountjoy marched from the south into Ulster. Although he did not pass beyond Newry, he brought fire and the sword in an attempt to starve the rebels into submission. A new Blackwater Fort was built near Dungannon linked to garrisons further south. Tyrone was deprived of food and supplies, and cut off from Munster. In fact, Mountjoy's severity was compared unfavourably to Grey's. His secretary, Fynes Moryson, wrote: 'the common sort of the rebels were driven to unspeakable extremities, beyond the record of most histories that ever I did read.' Tyrone held out, but the rebels' last hope was *deus ex machina*.

Their prayers were answered. Philip III landed 3,400 crack troops and a battery of siege-guns at Kinsale in September 1601. The war with Spain had finally spread to Ireland. Philip reasoned that to assist the Irish was an appropriate retaliation for Elizabeth's intervention in the Netherlands. Also a toe-hold in Ireland might establish an Atlantic base comparable to that which his father had held at Blavet in Brittany.

Mountjoy's reaction was immediate. Since an adequate field army could only be mustered at the expense of stripping the garrisons, he hastened to Cork, determined to expel the invaders before Tyrone could join them. By late October he was besieging Kinsale with seven thousand troops, but his move freed Tyrone and O'Donnell, who arrived in Munster in early December, O'Donnell via Connaught and Tyrone via Leinster. When the rebel army approached Kinsale on the 21st, it numbered 6,500. So Tyrone risked a formal battle. Disease had depleted the English, who were also caught between the Spaniards and rebels. Tyrone's plan was to attack Mountjoy while the Spaniards sallied out. But the attempt failed. Mountjoy rushed the enemy as it was deploying its divisions and scattered it with heavy losses (24 December). This battle ended the war. O'Donnell fled to Spain, Tyrone retreated to Ulster, and the Spanish garrison surrendered (2 January 1602). Carew then completed the pacification of Munster, while Mountjoy and Docwra harried Ulster.

But Tyrone went underground: his guerrilla tactics forestalled plans for settling Ulster. He finally submitted on 30 March 1603 in exchange for a generous pardon. This was six days after Elizabeth's death, and the circumstances were murky. Tyrone did not know of the queen's death, so it can be argued that Mountjoy gambled on getting the best available deal before his opponent learned that James I reigned. But Mountjoy was among Robert Cecil's critics and wanted to return to London to greet the new king. He certainly offered vital concessions that recognized Tyrone as chief lord of Ulster under the Crown and sole owner of his lordship—terms almost identical to those Tyrone had demanded in 1594. So the settlement, paradoxically, increased rather than decreased the local power of Tyrone and of Rory, brother of the late O'Donnell, who was created earl of Tyrconnell in September 1603. It also committed James I to a policy of delegating Ulster government to 'trusted' nobles— the approach abandoned as unsatisfactory in 1534.[35]

If, therefore, Ireland was controlled, it was not pacified. The late-Elizabethan campaigns cost England £2 million, while the cost to Ireland was even greater, as Ulster was devastated, Munster west of Cork almost uninhabited, trade disrupted, towns ruined, and the population stricken by famine. By the manner of its execution and subsequent settlement, Mountjoy's conquest caused great bitterness and alienation of the Gaelic and Old English communities from royal government. Elizabeth had never seriously challenged the assumption that Gaelic Ireland could be reduced despite inadequate resources and without long-term commitments. In consequence, the prospect of peaceful assimilation of Ireland within the unitary realm of England was greatly diminished.

Equally serious from the English viewpoint, the Irish Reformation put down only the shallowest of roots. Although political opposition to Henry VIII's and Elizabeth's assertions of royal supremacy was limited, the necessary Protestant missionary effort was lacking. It was difficult to attract preachers to Ireland, the official requirement to provide an English Bible had to be waived owing to problems of supply and the prevalence of Gaelic, and even a Gaelic New Testament was not printed until 1603. Realistically, the government might have expected gradually to erode popular religious culture, beginning in the Pale and royal towns and radiating outwards. But vigorous enforcement of the Elizabethan settlement was beyond the regime's resources and probably counterproductive anyway, since Catholic clergy remained in post, half the Irish religious houses outside the Pale still functioned, and the church's administration was weak. In Gaelic Ireland Tudor religious policy quickly became identified with conquest and colonization; in the Pale the conservatism of the Old English community was entrenched, and the gentry perpetuated the Roman mass by appointing private chaplains. Some proselytizing efforts were made, but the poverty of Irish bishoprics and parochial livings was an insuperable constraint; there was no printing press in Ireland until 1551; and, despite attempts to improve education, Trinity College, Dublin, was not founded until 1592. Lastly, it was not compulsory for Irish officials to swear an oath acknowledging royal supremacy.[36]

The Irish Reformation was not totally unsuccessful. Despite *Regnans in excelsis*, most Catholics were prepared to acknowledge Elizabeth as queen, if not as head of the Irish church. But the

19. Protestants brought from Colchester (Essex) to London for interrogation by Bishop Bonner in 1556. On the advice of Cardinal Pole, they were finally released after re-affirming their belief in Christ's real presence in the Eucharist.

20. Elizabeth I, attributed to Nicholas Hilliard, *c.*1575.

21. Mary, Queen of Scots (unknown artist after Hilliard).

22. Robert Dudley, earl of Leicester, by Nicholas Hilliard, 1576.

23. Sir Christopher Hatton by Nicholas Hilliard, after 1588.

24. Thomas Radcliffe, third earl of Sussex (unknown artist).

25. Sir Francis Walsingham, probably by John de Critz the Elder.

26. Sir Philip Sidney, *c*.1576 (unknown artist).

27. Sir Walter Raleigh by Nicholas Hilliard, *c*.1585.

28. A detail from Vischer's panorama of London, showing Southwark Gate with traitors' heads on poles (1616).

29. The Spanish Armada in the roads of Dover, 29 July 1588, showing Medina Sidonia's flagship, the *San Martin*, being attacked to port by the English *Rainbow* and astern by the Dutch *Gouden Leeuw*. By Aert Anthonisz.

30. William Cecil, Lord Burghley, on a mule, clasping a pink and honeysuckle (artist unknown).

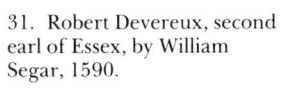

31. Robert Devereux, second earl of Essex, by William Segar, 1590.

32. Elizabeth I attended in procession by her gentlemen pensioners, attributed to Robert Peake the Elder.

33. The outer front ot Longleat House, Wiltshire, by Robert Smythson.

34. The Somerset House Conference, 1604 (unknown artist), which ended Elizabeth's war with Spain. On the left is the Hispano-Flemish delegation. On the right are (from the window end) Thomas Sackville, earl of Dorset (formerly Lord Buckhurst); Charles Howard, earl of Nottingham; Charles Blount, earl of Devonshire (formerly Lord Mountjoy); Henry Howard, earl of Northampton; Robert Cecil, Viscount Cranborne.

failure of Protestantism was crucial. On the one hand, a sense of the Irish as irreconcilably 'papist' contributed to the hardening of English attitudes. On the other, its self-conscious Catholicism heightened the Old English community's sense of isolation and autonomy. When James I planted a new Protestant elite in Ireland to insure the Crown against the Catholic Irish, he played with fire. Neither was Stuart government of Ireland constitutional by English standards. True, the Irish parliament was summoned in 1613, 1634, and 1640, but abrasive management was needed if legislation inimical to the Catholic majority was to be achieved. In 1613 the House of Commons was blatantly packed with Protestants. Yet the crunch came in 1641 when the expropriated Gaelic Ulstermen spontaneously attacked the Protestant planters in a fury that precipitated national revolt in Ireland and contributed to the outbreak of Civil War in England.

In terms of sovereignty the shift from 'realm' to 'state' was most obviously underpinned by the Reformation. Cromwell had quipped to Henry VIII that the English prelates were only 'half the king's subjects' before the break with Rome. And the Reformation transformed England into a unitary state in the abstract sense that the king-in-Parliament could make laws that bound church and state equally. This amounted to a revolution in jurisdiction, for, as Robert Aske, a leader of the Pilgrimage of Grace, noted, the old custom was that:

spiritual matters should always be referred to the Convocation house and not discussed in Parliament, and that . . . the first thing they always communed of after the Mass of the Holy Ghost was to affirm the first chapter of Magna Carta touching the rights and liberties of the Church, and it was not so now.[37]

The Reformation statutes repudiated Magna Carta because the 'liberty' of the church from secular jurisdiction had been abrogated. No pre-Tudor Parliament enjoyed the jurisdictional competence that underpinned the Acts of Appeals and Six Articles or the Uniformity Acts of 1549, 1552, and 1559.[38] The Elizabethan Acts of Supremacy and Uniformity even went beyond Henrician practice, passing into law without a single churchman's consent and despite Convocation's formal protest.

If legislative competence widened, however, royal supremacy was not equivalent to parliamentary sovereignty. On the contrary, it was modelled on Constantine's government of the Roman Empire after his conversion to Christianity: the Crown assumed full responsibility for the ordering of the church. In addition, Henry VIII claimed the right to define the articles of faith. So both his 'supreme headship' and Elizabeth's 'governorship' were 'imperial', despite being enacted by Parliament. True, Marian repeals and Elizabethan re-enactments of Reformation statutes assured Parliament's role as a legislative instrument. But in 1534 and 1559 the supremacy was announced as inherent in the monarch alone: Parliament simply recognized that pre-existent fact. According to Tudor theory, royal supremacy had actually been established in Anglo-Saxon times. (When Matthew Parker studied the Anglo-Saxon manuscripts he had salvaged from ex-monastic libraries, he sought to verify the constitution of the English, not the Celtic church.) The thesis was that royal supremacy was divine not human; it was enforced but not created by Parliament since it was ordained by God not men. Royal power was justified by Scripture and those authorities cited in the *Collectanea satis copiosa*. Many of these texts were included by Edward Foxe, Stephen Gardiner, Richard Sampson, and others in propagandist treatises, and John Foxe discussed several, including the supposed letter of Pope Eleutherius to Lucius I, in his *Acts and Monuments*.

Since royal supremacy was ordained by God, it followed that Parliament's authority in the matter was either irrelevant or additional. When Elizabeth expounded her position in *A Declaration of the Queen's Proceedings*, prepared during the Northern Rising, she said her power came from 'the laws of God and this realm always annexed to the Crown of this realm and due to our progenitors'. She was 'bound in duty to God to provide that all estates, being subject to us, should live in the faith and the obedience and observance of Christian religion'. Whereas Christian princes had 'care' of their subjects' souls, pagan rulers 'take only a worldly care of their subjects' bodies'. This had been Henry VIII's opinion. Yet Elizabeth differed from her father when she denied herself power 'to define, decide or determine any article or point of the Christian faith and religion'. That function she thought belonged to Convocation; therefore, as a matter of principle as much as to sidestep the presbyterian parliamentary lobby, she upheld the separation of church and state in practice, ruling both but through different channels of administration.[39]

Yet the 'royalist' interpretation of the supremacy was contentious. Even Thomas Cromwell disputed that 'imperial' kingship meant the Crown's absolute right to govern the church without the consent of Parliament.[40] His drafts in 1532 proposed a submission of the clergy to the king-in-Parliament, not to Henry VIII alone.[41] Cromwell even *deleted* a reference to England as an 'empire' when correcting a draft of the Commons' Supplication against the Ordinaries,[42] and as vicegerent in spirituals he succeeded in neutralizing Henry VIII's absolutism in practice. So the Act of Appeals contained a dramatic internal contradiction between Henry's and Cromwell's ideas. It illustrated the extension of Parliament's jurisdictional competence; but it also signalled that the king was henceforward to manage the English church and clergy as an absolute ruler, in which case Parliament was no more sovereign than it had been when the English church owed allegiance to Rome and the papacy.

Veiled hints were even dropped that absolutist theory might infiltrate the civil side of government. One of the most important treatises of the Middle Ages was Bracton's *On the Laws and Customs of England*, which stated that the king of England was 'under God and the law, because the law makes the king'.[43] But in the *Collectanea satis copiosa* Foxe and Cranmer claimed the king was 'under God but not the law, because the king makes the law'![44] Such a proposition might barely be justifiable in terms of Bracton's distinction between *jurisdictio* and *gubernatio*. When acting as 'vicar of God', the monarch was not answerable to anyone and could exercise all the power deputed to him by God, but, when acting as a feudal king, he was bound by law.[45] Only if Henry VIII could have completely replaced feudal ideas of kingship with 'imperial' ones, assimilating English law to the *lex regia* in Roman law which enshrined the principle 'What pleases the prince has the force of law', might the *Collectanea*'s dream have come true. There was a rumour that Stephen Gardiner, Cromwell's rival, insinuated the idea to Henry VIII. But he was rebuffed by the common lawyers. Lord Chancellor

Audley told Gardiner during a parliamentary debate that the Act of Supremacy restrained the king's unlimited power to spiritual causes. ' "And [if] this were not," quoth he, "you bishops would enter in with the king, and, by means of his supremacy, order the laity as ye listed. But we will provide . . . that the *praemunire* shall ever hang over your heads; and so we laymen shall be sure to enjoy our inheritance by the common laws, and acts of Parliament." '[46]

Yet ideas of 'imperial' kingship flourished after the Act of Appeals. A new edition of the *Debate of the Heralds* appeared in Edward VI's reign, which argued that the king was emperor in his realm and 'holdeth of no man', that he was supreme head of the churches of England and Ireland, wore an imperial diadem, held in his left hand an orb representing his empire, and in his right hand carried a sword to minister and defend justice. In this version the English protagonist cited national history, which turned out to be the familiar material of the *Collectanea satis copiosa*, including the letter of Pope Eleutherius. The herald then claimed that Constantine was the son of an Englishwoman, and had been king of England as well as emperor of Rome. Also King Arthur had conquered an empire extending to Ireland, Denmark, Norway, France, Germany, Spain, the Netherlands, Italy, and beyond.[47]

Next, the dedication to Elizabeth I in the 1563 and 1570 editions of Foxe's *Acts and Monuments* apostrophized her as Constantine's heir. The first English editions were embellished by a portrait of the enthroned queen holding the sword of justice and the orb of *imperium*. On her right stood three figures representing the estates of the realm, while under her feet lay the pope, wearing the papal tiara and holding broken keys. Thereafter, Elizabethan literature was crammed with identifications of the queen as empress of the world, defender of religion and justice, guardian of virtue, and restorer of peace. Astraea, the last goddess of the golden age to leave the earth, represented in the heavens as the constellation Virgo, was a common image: innumerable verses exhorted gods and men to visit her 'imperial' court. The play *Histriomastix* (1589?) hailed her with a Roman triumph, and she mounted the throne to a eulogy:

> Mount, Empress, whose praise for peace shall mount,
> Whose glory, which thy solid virtues won,
> Shall honour Europe whilst there shines a sun![48]

In Spenser's epic poem *The Faerie Queene* Astraea's role as the 'imperial' Virgin is the lynch-pin of the action. In Book III the prophecy of Merlin foretells that from Britomart and Artegal (Chastity and Justice) will stem an 'imperial' dynasty of kings and 'sacred emperors' culminating in the royal Virgin Elizabeth. Later the queen's 'divine right' is defined:

> Dread sovereign goddess, that dost highest sit
> In seat of judgment, in th' Almighty's stead,
> And with magnific might and wondrous wit
> Dost to thy people righteous doom aread,
> That furthest nations fills with awful dread.
>
> (*Faerie Queene*, Bk. V, intro., xi. 1–5)

Tudor emphasis on 'imperial' ideology did not, however, greatly disturb existing concepts of 'feudal' kingship. The Crown needed to maximize its revenue from feudal incidents, in particular the wardship of heirs during their minorities. So Cromwell created a new court of wards in 1540, and Henry VIII re-asserted his right to feudal taxes by the Statute of Uses (1536). True, protests and evasion obliged him to accept a compromise in 1540 whereby property owners were at last allowed to devise feudal land by will. Yet 'feudal' dues were not abolished until the reign of Charles II. Also Henry VIII continued to define his 'rights' in Ireland and *vis-à-vis* Scotland in feudal terms. He was adamant that his new style as 'king of Ireland' should be couched so as to include 'our old inheritance and title to the said land'.[49] When he issued *A Declaration Concerning the Just Causes and Considerations of this Present War with the Scots* on the eve of the 1542 invasion, his key argument was likewise feudal: 'the kings of Scots have always acknowledged the kings of England superior lords of the realm of Scotland, and have done homage and fealty for the same.'[50]

Perhaps in purely secular affairs there was no serious clash between 'feudal' and 'imperial' concepts of kingship. Medieval orthodoxy held that the rights of the Crown were inalienable. The king's private person was separate from his public responsibility: the king was mortal, but the Crown's rights were perpetual. What the king did as an individual was separate from his role as custodian of the Crown, and the king's inalienable rights were the 'rights of the imperial Crown'. Indeed, English kings sometimes wore an arched or 'imperial' crown in validation of this point. Yet Yorkist and Tudor theorists defined statecraft in terms of 'absolute' or 'constitutional' rule: Fortescue's *The Governance of England* spoke of 'regal' monarchy as in Louis XI's France, as against 'mixed' monarchy (*regnum politicum et regale*) in England.

Hence the implications of 'imperial' kingship deeply disturbed some common lawyers, notably Christopher St German, who was the first English writer to publish a virtually complete theory of parliamentary sovereignty.[51] In *New Additions* (1531) he claimed that the king-in-Parliament was 'the high sovereign over the people, which hath not only charge on the bodies, but also on the souls of his subjects'.[52] In *An Answer to a Letter* (1535) he argued that *all* law, whether ecclesiastical or civil, was properly made by king, Lords, and Commons in Parliament assembled, 'for the Parliament so gathered together representeth the estate of all the people within this realm, that is to say of the whole catholic church thereof'.[53] St German extended the theory of 'mixed' monarchy to the church: Henry VIII was not to be an autocrat in his ecclesiastical polity. In fact, since St German saw a need to withhold from the king the right as supreme head to expound Scripture, he reasoned that Parliament should perform this vital role since 'the whole catholic church' came together in Parliament, an equating of the 'church' with Parliament that found echoes in the work of William Marshall, Cromwell's client, who translated *The Defender of Peace* by Marsiglio of Padua (*c.*1275–1342).[54]

So St German saw Parliament as the rightful body to govern both church and state, and held that the royal supremacy should be shared with Parliament. It is unclear whether his goal was national sovereignty in the modern sense. He believed that parliamentary statutes were omnicompetent in so far as they bound church and state equally, and he allowed Convocation jurisdiction only over the church's sacramental life and ceremonies. Sometimes his argument was crudely empirical. Who apart from Thomas More, John Fisher, and the London Carthusians would deny that Parliament could do what it had done? But his intellectual mentors were Fortescue and the Parisian Jean Gerson (1363–1429). His thought was thus rooted in late-medieval conciliarism, the essence of which was that the pope was an officer of the church charged with specific duties and therefore responsible to the whole Christian people through their representative general council. Amalgamating this with Fortescue's theory of 'mixed' monarchy, it followed logically that Henry VIII should exercise the royal supremacy in co-operation with Parliament and that both secular and ecclesiastical law-making required the assent of the 'people' in Parliament.

It is, of course, astonishing that *both* St German *and* Edward Foxe acted as Henry VIII's propagandists. Foxe was joint-compiler of the *Collectanea satis copiosa* and author of *On the True Difference between Royal and Ecclesiastical Power* (1534). In the *True Difference* he argued the case for Henry VIII's caesaropapism. But St German defended his view of parliamentary sovereignty in *A Treatise Concerning the Power of the Clergy and the Laws of the Realm* (1535), *A Treatise Concerning Divers of the Constitutions Provincial and Legantines* (1535), and *An Answer to a Letter*. The outlooks and conclusions of the two men were so fundamentally different that they could not both be right. Henry VIII left a deeply ambiguous legacy in the government of the church.[55] Yet Foxe's theory was muzzled by Elizabeth's Privy Council. Faced with Catholic conspiracy and the claim to the throne of Mary, Queen of Scots, leading Protestant politicians such as Burghley, Lord Keeper Bacon, Leicester, Walsingham, and the earls of Bedford and Pembroke preferred the option of *limiting* the powers of the Crown if the worst happened. Their independent initiatives in 'orchestrating' debates in Parliament 'were almost certainly predicated on a view of England as a mixed polity very similar to that held by Thomas Cartwright himself'.[56] Even Archbishop Whitgift partially endorsed St German during the Admonition controversy. His *Defence of the Answer* (1574) explained: 'I perceive no such distinction of the commonwealth and the church that they should be counted, as it were, two several bodies, governed with divers laws and divers magistrates.' The religious settlement had been enacted by the queen-in-Parliament; therefore, bishops and clergy were 'ordained and chosen' according to Parliament's 'order and rule'.[57] At a quite different level, however, straightforward practicalities advanced St German's argument, because the Reformation statutes were drafted and enforced by judges and common lawyers who increasingly shared his views. Treason, not heresy, was the penalty for denying royal supremacy and, in Elizabeth's reign, for Catholic priests or laymen who withdrew Englishmen from their allegiance either to the queen or to the Church of England. By 1600 it was hard to envisage that any future king of England could seek to govern after the fashion of a late-Roman emperor.

Richard Hooker's *Of the Laws of Ecclesiastical Polity* cemented the Tudor compromise. (Even the title of his work implied a denial of theocratic kingship.) Books I–V were published in 1594–7 and Books VI–VIII were left in draft when Hooker died in 1600.[58] His main objective was to refute puritan criticism of the Anglican Church and defend its 'national' structure, but in the process he erected a systematic political theory. And the centrepiece of this was his agreement with St German and the common lawyers that membership of church and state was co-extensive: ecclesiastical laws in a Christian commonwealth must have the consent of the prince and of the clergy in Convocation, and 'the consent as well of the laity' in Parliament.

The parliament of England together with the convocation annexed thereunto, is that whereupon the very essence of all government within this kingdom doth depend; it is even the body of the whole realm; it consisteth of the king, and of all that within the land are subject unto him: for they all are there present, either in person or by such as they voluntarily have derived their very personal right unto.[59]

If church and commonwealth be one, Parliament must represent the church. All laws (including ecclesiastical ones) 'do take originally their essence from the power of the whole realm and church of England' — here Hooker echoed St German's *An Answer to a Letter*. The supremacy of kings in making laws 'resteth principally in the strength of a negative voice; which not to give them, were to deny them that without which they were but kings by mere title'.[60] Hooker arrived at this position by utilizing the 'ascending' thesis of government and law that Marsiglio of Padua and Bartolus of Sassoferrato (d. 1352) had pioneered. He argued that 'imperial' power was 'derived' to the ruler by 'consent of the people', correctly adding that the *original* purpose of the *lex regia* had been to explain how the Roman people had at first possessed all public power, but had transferred it to the emperor. He then maintained that 'imperial' dignity in the church from the time of Constantine onwards had been used for the whole church's benefit, while in matters touching the sacraments princes were bound to obey the bishops — here Henry VIII would have disagreed.[61]

So Hooker's *Polity* raised many questions. He accepted that rulers and magistrates were 'God's lieutenants' and so ruled by 'divine right', but only because they were circumscribed by law. 'The axioms of our regal government are these: "Lex facit regem"' — 'law makes the king'![62] When, however, Hooker turned Bracton against the 'vicar of God', he adduced not proof but a point of view. Also his concern to give the Anglican Church as broad a base as possible led him to repudiate Calvinist doctrine of a church defined by groups of 'elect' believers in favour of a church whose membership was equivalent to that of the civil state, including (presumably) papists. His emphasis on the sacraments as the true source of God's grace, instead of predestination and sermons, was especially controversial.

It followed that Hooker's attempt to legitimize in religious terms the Anglican Church that was the political legacy of Henry VIII and Elizabeth opened a fresh series of debates that culminated when Charles I revived the caesaropapist interpretation of Henry VIII's royal supremacy. Despite his father's rejection of their case, Charles backed 'Arminian' bishops, who emphasized worship and the sacraments, rejected predestination, and defined the Protestant church in terms of its Catholic antecedents. He even attempted to impose his view of the church by proclamation. In Calvinist eyes this was idolatry: it arrogated to the Crown and clergy the power to dictate the terms and pace of reform within the church.[63] Yet Charles's ministers merged this policy with their conviction that executive action in both civil and ecclesiastial government defined sovereignty. In star chamber Laud quoted Scripture in support of the proposition that he would 'make a proclamation as available as an act of Parliament'. Then Strafford told the Irish that 'the King's little finger would be heavier than the lines of the law' and that they 'must expect laws as from a conqueror, and an act of state should be as binding as an act of Parliament'.

In short, a royal prerogative based on the 'public good' and on 'reason of state' as determined by the Crown was asserted.[64]

So this was 'imperial' kingship with a vengeance. Little room remained for the sovereignty of the king-in-Parliament and for the 'mixed' monarchy theory of Fortescue, St German, and the common lawyers. Charles I challenged established consensus on the question of political obedience at a time when a high proportion of the nobility and gentry educated their sons at the inns of court. One cannot therefore but ask, was it merely a coincidence that a majority both of common lawyers and legally educated gentry as well as 'puritans' sided with Parliament during the Great Civil War?

14

ELIZABETHAN GOVERNMENT

EVALUATION of Elizabethan government has provoked extensive debate. From the perspective of Charles I's reign, Bishop Goodman commented: 'The people were very generally weary of an old woman's government.'[1] When an Oxford divine published a sermon celebrating the queen's Accession Day in 1601, he felt it necessary to include 'An Apologetical Discourse' justifying his opinion. The question is whether, during the long war with Spain, Tudor government finally succumbed to a mixture of external pressure and internal structural decay. Criticism centres on the inadequacy of Elizabethan finance, local government, and military recruitment; an alleged 'slide to disaster' in the counties caused by alienation of less exalted 'country' gentlemen from the Court; the rise of 'corruption' in the central administrative and judicial systems; the abuse of purveyance and of royal prerogative to grant lucrative 'monopolies' or licences in favour of courtiers and their clients, who might also enforce certain statutes for profit; and the claim that the benefits of the Poor Laws were negligible in relation to the rise in population and scale of economic distress in the 1590s.

The strategy of a self-financing war proving entirely misconceived, Elizabeth resorted to taxation, sales of Crown lands, borrowing, and other expedients to meet the costs of defence, augmented between 1585 and 1588 by cash reserves accumulated in the exchequer. Before 1585 Elizabethan financial policy had been a success story. The policy of retrenchment and reconstruction initiated by the duke of Northumberland and resumed by Mary had been continued. Revenue enhancement, debt collection, stricter accounting, and the rebuilding of reserves were the objectives. In particular, the recoinage projected in 1556 was successfully achieved in 1560–1. Starting in December 1560, £670,000 of base money was withdrawn from circulation and converted into new fine coin. Despite its scale and complexity, the operation was completed within a year, and by careful management the Crown even made a small profit. The benefits were assured, too, for there was only one further exploitation of the English coinage before 1603. This was a scheme of the mid-1580s whereby foreign gold was purchased at prices slightly above those on the open market and shipped to London, where it was recoined and exported again for use at the artificially high rates prevailing in the Netherlands. But the Irish coinage was debased by Elizabeth in 1558–9 and 1601–3.[2]

Although their approach differed, the aims of Lord Treasurers Winchester and Burghley were the same: to balance the budget by whatever means were necessary. So Crown debtors were pursued, attempts made to raise income, economy urged in royal patronage and expenditure at Court, and Crown lands sold. Sales between 1560 and 1574 realized £267,827, and between 1589 and 1601 £608,505. Winchester had improved the management of royal estates in Mary's reign; there was little scope for raising income, though rents were increased to match inflation. Whereas net income from the Crown lands at the start of Elizabeth's reign was £66,448 per annum, it was £88,767 per annum at the end. Customs revenues ranged from between £60,000 and £85,000 per annum thanks to Mary's revision of the book of rates. But there was disagreement as to how profits could be maximized. Whereas Winchester sought to extend the system of general surveyors used for Crown lands to customs administration, Burghley preferred to secure fixed annual returns through leasing (or 'farming') the collection of duties to private interests for a fixed rent. So the duties on wines and beer were farmed on an experimental basis in 1568, while the farming of customs on imports into London and duties of import and export elsewhere started two years later.[3]

At Court salaries were held back. To keep household expenses within the limit of £40,000 per annum, Burghley enforced economies, abridging menus and abolishing breakfasts for lesser officials and servants. Although Elizabeth was not ungenerous with her friends, especially during the 1560s, she gave little land away. Only her favourites—Leicester, Hatton, and Essex—received special treatment; Leicester was given two former monasteries in Yorkshire and a house at Kew, the lordship and castle of Kenilworth, the vast lordship and castle of Denbigh, plus lesser estates in more than twenty counties. Few gifts of money were made, even to favourites. Also Elizabeth restricted herself to less than a tenth of her father's expenditure on buildings. The budget for the surveyor of the works was modest: in years such as 1583 and 1585 he was assigned £5,000, but normal spending was less than £4,000 per annum. The Crown even divested itself of seven superfluous palaces by sale or gift, though Elizabeth recovered Nonsuch palace, which Mary had granted to the earl of Arundel in 1556.[4]

Lay taxation was granted during each session of the Elizabethan Parliaments save in 1572, when none was requested. It is estimated that combined receipts of taxes granted by the laity between 1559 and 1571 totalled £690,000; taxes granted between 1576 and 1587 yielded £660,000; and those between 1589 and 1601 yielded £1.1 million.[5] In addition, the clergy offered taxation whenever the laity provided it, except in 1559 when Mary's last clerical subsidy was remitted. Unlike lay subsidies, clerical taxation increased in value, especially after 1594.[6] By 1598 annual receipts of clerical taxation, including first fruits and tenths, averaged £35,000. Total aggregate yields of lay and clerical taxation reached £115,500 per annum during the last years of the reign.[7]

Supply continued to be justified on the grounds that defence was submerged within royal government, but, despite the innovative theory of 1534, 1540, 1543, 1553, and 1555, Elizabeth and the Privy Council did not seek to make beneficial rule and necessity alone sufficient causes for taxation. Elizabethan theory was ambiguous in tone, since emphasis on good government and payment of Crown debts in the period before 1585 was linked to the fact or threat of war and costs of coastal fortifications and Ireland. The logic of mid-Tudor tax doctrine that the nation should assume responsibility for a national budget indexed to match population, inflation, the costs of warfare, and expanding bureaucracy was not developed.[8] But the extent of Elizabeth's regression in tax theory must not be exaggerated. Lord Keeper Bacon told Parliament in 1571: 'For like as the "ordinary" charge hath been always born by ordinary Revenues, so the "extraordinary" charge hath always been sustained by an extraordinary relief.'[9] This statement was far less equivocal than Fortescue's in *The Governance of England*, where he argued that only 'extraordinary' expenditure *above the usual average* was chargeable to taxation. In Fortescue's theory, the costs of repairing castles, harbours, and fortifications and garrisoning Berwick were to be met from normal Crown income.[10]

If, therefore, the theory of Tudor taxation approached a breakthrough by 1555 but then withdrew, the wider case for 'national' finance was sustained by Elizabeth's assumption that 'extraordinary' charges *however incurred* should be met by taxation. Since a quarter of her 'ordinary' expenses were in fact being paid out of tax receipts by 1572, her fiscal practice was more advanced than her theory.[11] True, the earlier momentum was lost, but the real regression came in the 1620s when antiquarian lawyers and opponents of the duke of Buckingham recast the entire debate in medieval terms.

Short-term deficits were met by borrowing, but foreign debt was eschewed after 1574. Burghley made concern for cash surpluses central to his strategy as lord treasurer. Cash in hand was £270,000 on the eve of Leicester's expedition to the Netherlands.[12] This was a considerable achievement, since Mary's accumulated deficit had been £300,000. Also the cost of military operations in Scotland and France in 1559–60 and 1563 had totalled £750,000 (including the navy, ordnance, and fortifications at Berwick).[13]

Between 1559 and 1574 Elizabeth borrowed £1 million abroad. Thereafter she borrowed only at home. The Corporation of London lent £30,000 in 1575–6, and £63,000 in 1588–9. Forced loans levied in 1569, 1588, 1590, 1597, and 1601 raised a total of £330,600. Lastly, £90,000 was borrowed from London between 1598 and 1601. All but £85,000 of these domestic loans were raised without payment of interest. Forced loans and Corporation loans therefore amounted in effect to an exercise of royal prerogative. Like Henry VII and Wolsey, Elizabeth knew that such methods also heightened her control over the sources she chose to tap, though they were cumbersome and unpopular.[14]

Yet Elizabeth and Burghley allowed the lay taxation system to decline. Not only did the value of parliamentary subsidies fail to increase in line with inflation despite soaring levels of government expenditure, but net receipts also dropped in cash terms owing to static tax assessments and widespread evasion.

Whereas Wolsey had rejected stereotyped rates of tax and static assessments of taxpayers' wealth in favour of a flexible approach designed to maximize receipts, both rates and assessments became inflexible under Elizabeth. First, rates became fixed at 4*s.* in the £ of the annual value of land, or 2*s.* 8*d.* in the £ of the value of goods. Second, while valuations were required upon oath down to 1563, thereafter the basis of assessment became the taxpayer's unsworn declaration. As Burghley noted, conceding the principle of unsworn assessments reduced receipts. Subsidy commissioners and assessors also allowed assessments to become stereotyped so that variations in wealth were inadequately noted, names of new taxpayers were not added promptly to the records, and receipts fell again if existing taxpayers died or 'decayed'. Lastly, whereas Wolsey had attempted to tax wage-earners as well as substantial property owners, Mary and Elizabeth largely abandoned the effort.[15]

Although the yield of a subsidy was £140,000 at the beginning of Elizabeth's reign, it was only £80,000 at the end and continued to fall to £70,000 by 1621 and £55,000 by 1628. In Sussex the average tax assessment of seventy leading families fell from £61 in the 1540s to £14 in the 1620s; and some potential taxpayers escaped altogether. In Suffolk 17,000 taxpayers were assessed for the subsidy of 1523 but only 7,700 for that of 1566. In London, whereas 7,123 paid the subsidy of 1563, of whom 323 were valued as worth at least £100, by contrast 4,968 paid that of 1606, of whom only 29 were valued at £100 or above. In 1576 the Privy Council ordered subsidy commissioners to ensure that assessments were made impartially and 'answerable to the meaning of Parliament' and 'not so underfoot as heretofore hath been used'. They were to set a good example by 'just taxation' of themselves, which would induce others to admit more realistic valuations. In 1594 it was ordered that, if any in the commission of the peace assessed themselves at less than £20 per annum, 'they must look to receive the disgrace to be put out of the commission'.[16]

But Burghley evaded tax himself, despite holding office as lord treasurer after 1572. He grumbled hypocritically in Parliament about tax cheating, but kept his own assessment of income static at £133 6*s.* 8*d.* — his real income was approximately £4,000 per annum. Roger, Lord North, admitted that few taxpayers were assessed at more than one-sixth or one-tenth of their true wealth, 'and many be 20 times, some 30, and some much more worth than they be set at, which the commissioner cannot without oath help'. Again, a Sussex JP complained that 'the rich were often rated . . . much too low, at not a fortieth part of their wealth'. When arguing in Parliament for exemption of lesser taxpayers in 1601, Ralegh suggested that, while the wealth of a person valued in the subsidy books at £3 per annum was close to his true worth, 'our estates that be £30 or £40 in the Queen's books are not the hundredth part of our wealth'.[17] Lastly, William Lambarde, the Kentish lawyer and antiquary, went so far as to suggest that dishonest assessors should be prosecuted under the medieval statutes against maintenance.[18]

The initiative had to come from the Crown. The striking feature of Elizabeth's strategy is that, while elsewhere European rulers were inventing new taxes under the pressure of war or threat of invasion, Elizabeth stuck to precedent. During the Nine Years War, William III would introduce a land tax and a tax on houses, the latter assessed by the number of windows; also duties became payable on servants, horses, and carriages. During the Napoleonic Wars, new taxes were imposed on personal incomes at the rate of 2s. in the £. By contrast, Elizabeth resisted fiscal innovation. It is estimated that she extracted some 3 per cent of England's national income for the war, whereas Philip II appropriated 10 per cent of Castile's.[19] True, she exacted multiple subsidies and fifteenths and tenths in and after 1589. In that year two subsidies and four fifteenths and tenths were voted; in 1593 and 1597 three subsidies and six fifteenths and tenths were required; and in 1601 four subsidies and eight fifteenths and tenths were granted. Yet to be seen to 'multiply' subsidies at a time when subsidy receipts were actually declining was bad public relations. Also multiple subsidies were subject to the law of diminishing returns: the same few taxpayers were assessed using the same stereotyped valuations, though no taxpayer was charged at modern rates of income tax.

If, however, her failure to maintain the yield of the subsidy exposed a source of weakness in the Tudor state, Elizabeth's crowning achievement was to leave to her successor an accumulated debt totalling only £365,254.[20] Since Mary had left a debt of £300,000, the comparison (allowing for inflation) is entirely creditable. By 1609 James I had paid all but £133,500 of this debt, though his own deficits dwarfed anything envisaged by Elizabeth.[21] On the other hand, she bridged the gap between receipts and expenditure during her war years by selling Crown land. This prejudiced the Crown's future interests, since it left the Stuarts with diminished regular income and deprived the king of security against loans. Yet how many sixteenth-century rulers took a long-term view, particularly in wartime? On the contrary, Elizabeth was not accountable to an electorate, a fact which opinion tends to underrate.

Another qualification is that local taxation escalated under Elizabeth, especially for poor relief, road and bridge repairs, and militia expenditure, all of which compensated for the inadequacy of national taxation. Although this subject is relatively unexplored, it is clear that the recruitment and training of the militia were very expensive and burdened the country with additional rates which were authorized by JPs and collected by hundred and parish constables.[22] Training cost considerable sums by the 1580s; the counties were responsible, too, for providing stocks of parish arms and armour; for paying muster-masters; for repairing coastal forts and building beacons; and for issuing troops mustered for the foreign service with weapons and uniforms, as well as conveying them to the required port of embarkation. In Kent the cost of military preparations borne by the county between 1585 and 1603 exceeded £10,000. True, a proportion of 'coat-and-conduct' money required to equip and transport troops was recoverable from the exchequer, but in practice the counties met roughly three-quarters of the cost. Also, whereas merchant ships (except customarily fishing vessels) had traditionally been requisitioned from coastal towns and counties to augment the royal navy in time of war, the Crown in the 1590s started demanding money as well as ships, and impressed fishermen for service in the royal navy and aboard privateers to the detriment of the local economy. When the ship money rate was then extended to inland areas such as the West Riding of Yorkshire, it aroused opposition to the point where the Crown's right to impose it was questioned.[23]

While, however, the needs and agencies of defence, military recruitment, and finance assumed prominence in Elizabethan local government, the backbone of the system was the civil magistracy. The key officials remained unsalaried JPs, whose numbers steadily increased during the century. Whereas under Wolsey twenty-five JPs on average served for each county, by the middle of Elizabeth's reign the average was forty or fifty, and by 1603 the number of justices in a county ranged from forty to ninety. But the rise was not simply due to heavier workloads, since by mid-century a seat on the bench had become the recognized social prerequisite for a gentleman keen to advance himself in county affairs. In fact, the prestige of the office and ambition of the gentry to 'bear rule' precipitated an invasion of the benches. Burghley wanted select benches working with 'herculean courage'. So he tightened up the nomination system and collected information, plotting the seats of the principal nobility and gentry on a series of county maps. Yet, despite at least seven major purges, his policy of exclusion was difficult to sustain: the assize judges, whose task it was to supply detailed assessments to the Privy Council after their twice-yearly circuits, could be lobbied or misinformed by sitting JPs. Reports were often coloured by local factionalism, and purges could actually deprive benches of their most talented members. Moreover, since the demands of patron–client relationships were significant in making appointments, the pressure from below to increase the numbers of JPs could prove irresistible.[24]

Only half the JPs in most counties tended to be active, meaning that they regularly enforced law and order on the bench at quarter sessions, arbitrated in local disputes, and undertook administrative functions. Their duties derived from two sources: statutes and the commission of the peace. The workload in the law-and-order field was heavy: Tudor statutes had created several new felonies concerning riots, damage to property, clipping coins, witchcraft, hunting and game rights, and recusancy. By 1603 no fewer than 309 statutes imposed responsibilities on JPs, and of these 176 had been enacted since 1485. True, the duty to hear and determine felonies was finally transferred to the assize judges by 1590. But this apparent reduction in trial work was more than offset by the creation of new statutory misdemeanours: for instance, abduction of heiresses, damage to crops, fence-breaking, swearing, profanation of the Sabbath, alehouse nuisances, drunkenness, perjury, and malfeasance by officials.

In addition, the administrative role of the justices was considerably expanded in the fields of religion, economic regulation, the Poor Law, control of vagrancy, upkeep of roads and bridges, and arbitration of lawsuits in response to requests from the courts of chancery and star chamber.[25]

Of course, county government was markedly strengthened by the lieutenancy system made permanent in 1585.[26] But the appointees, especially when they were also privy councillors or the presidents of the Councils of Wales and the North, could rarely fulfil the full range of local tasks in person. Accordingly two or three deputies were assigned to each district, assisted by captains of companies and muster-masters. Deputy lieutenants were usually minor peers or leading JPs who assumed responsibility for militia training and recruitment. They supervised the levying of militia rates, and civilian duties were added in the 1590s, for instance management of food supplies, collection of forced loans, detection of recusants, and enforcement of economic regulations.[27]

Yet the strain of a war economy was cumulative: 105,810 men were impressed for service in the Netherlands, France, Portugal, and Ireland during the last eighteen years of the reign. Attempts to send men overseas from the trained bands to join expeditionary forces or to replace losses through death and desertion were resisted by 1592. Although members of the trained bands seemed obvious recruits for active combat on grounds of their training and experience, they were the backbone of national defence and thus considered exempt from foreign service. In general, too, the trained bands were recruited from among servants of the gentry and the ranks of yeomen, greater husbandmen, and more prosperous artisans. When the Essex deputy lieutenants admitted that they had substituted persons of lower rank to replace men originally selected from the trained bands for service abroad, the implication is that the bands contained men of sufficient social standing to avoid being impressed as conscripted soldiers. In consequence the overseas armies largely comprised the labouring poor, criminals, and vagrants, and armies for Ireland had a core of forced levies from Wales and the marches.[28]

During the 1590s levies of men and equipment for overseas service were costing each county up to £2,000 per annum. In Sussex and north and west Norfolk many people refused to pay

and were bound over to appear before the Privy Council. Sussex
also begrudged the cost of provost marshals, and was allowed
to appoint unpaid local gentlemen to exercise the office. In
London objections to ship money became overt in 1596, while
many residents resisted payment of militia rates for the Middlesex
musters. In Hampshire only three-quarters of the men from the
trained bands selected to reinforce the Isle of Wight in case of
an invasion were equipped with any kind of weapon. In Suffolk
the Privy Council's request for money for equipping cavalry for
Ireland fell on deaf ears. In March 1592 thirteen counties were
found to have failed to return certificates of their forces as
demanded by the Privy Council eighteen months earlier, while
six more counties had omitted to report their stocks of
ammunition. The pressure was greatest on the coastal counties,
and in Kent the lord-lieutenant bemoaned 'how unwilling the
country seems (I will not say unable) to supply the losses of
armour and furniture'. Yet it was conscription for Ireland after
1595 that aroused the greatest resentment. In 1600 there was
a near mutiny of Kentish cavalry at Chester during the summer
as they travelled to Ulster. The drain of manpower was relentless;
between 1591 and 1602 about 6,000 Kentish men were impressed
at a time when the county's total population was no more than
130,000.[29]

So the strain on the counties led to administrative breakdowns
and opposition to central government's demands. However,
obstinate traditionalism among the gentry and even a smattering
of constitutional idealism were to be expected given the corrosive
length of the war, disruption of trade, outbreaks of plague (much
of it imported by soldiers returning from abroad), ruined harvests
of 1596 and 1597, and acute economic depression. Yet the idea of
a 'slide to disaster' in the counties caused by the alienation of
'country' gentlemen from the Court, coupled with a slow
disintegration of traditional socio-political networks, remains
unproven. On the basis of analogies with the Personal Rule of
Charles I and Bishops' Wars, it is sometimes claimed that by
the late-1590s unpaid county governors were aware of a
discrepancy between the trouble and expense, and diminishing
rewards, of continuing to act on the central government's behalf.
In these circumstances, local magistrates might either become
involved in Court factionalism as a means of securing the

patronage and rewards they required—thereby forsaking
their county roots; or they might eschew the Court for the
'pure' country (i.e. adopt a negative 'localist' attitude)—in which
case they would cease to be of further use to the regime. But
when applied to Elizabeth's reign, this model is anachronistic.
In the 1590s tension between 'Court' and 'country' was neither
as ideological as was the opposition to Charles I, nor in
most cases were deputy lieutenants and JPs expressing more
than war-weariness and dislike of fiscal burdens. In 1639–40
sheriffs, JPs, and parish constables refused actively to administer
ship money and other expedients, while deputy lieutenants
failed to muster troops on a scale that suggests a groundswell
of popular hostility to Charles's regime. By contrast, in
1598–1601 local resistance to central demands remained
largely passive, though exceptions might arise in coastal counties
such as Norfolk.[30]

The homogeneity of Tudor government also militated against
a 'slide to disaster'. From the 1540s to the end of Elizabeth's
reign between 60 and 90 per cent of courtiers who were knights
or gentlemen of the royal household served simultaneously as
MPs in Parliament or as JPs in their counties. The overlap is
so striking that it is useful to regard 'Court' and 'country' as
the same people at different times of year.[31] Meanwhile the
Privy Council remained a tightly organized body: its members
dominated the Elizabethan lieutenancy system, which structured
Court–country relations on the basis of consultation. When a
lieutenant received his commission, he assembled the local
magistrates and gentry to consider how to keep the district 'both
in quiet from dangers of mutinies and rebellion, and also from
offence of enemies'. The objectives were home defence and
musters for service abroad. Yet the keynote was shared
responsibility—the obligation of everyone to work for the good
of the community.[32] By 1596, when the Privy Council was
attempting to levy ship money to finance vessels for the Cadiz
expedition, the idea of collective obligation had worn thin. But
earlier the approach helped to limit conflict and avert the
excessive imposition of martial law. In this respect, the contrast
with late-Elizabethan Ireland, where consultation was negligible
and martial law the norm, is obvious.

So resistance to Crown demands was concentrated in the coastal shires of eastern and southern England which carried the heaviest burdens of musters and local rates. In Norfolk tension arose between JPs and the lieutenancy over the extensive and ill-defined powers of deputy lieutenants. A flashpoint was the Crown's instruction of 1589 empowering lieutenants in every district to nominate provost marshals to discipline disbanded soldiers, deserters, and vagabonds. Provost marshals administered martial law, and therefore encroached on the civilian jurisdiction of JPs in quarter sessions. Norfolk justices also became alarmed at the Crown's use of administrative patents as an alternative form of local control which bypassed them. By letters patent under the great seal, the Crown delegated certain categories of administration to private individuals who levied rates for road or pier repairs, or who undertook the inquiries needed to prove that certain lands were ex-religious property wrongfully concealed from the Crown—in return for a share of the profits. The activities of patentees were resented: JPs believed their public authority had been weakened by prerogative devices which enabled others to decide whether a rate should be levied, and how much it should be. Magistrates felt 'robbed' of their local autonomy, and so cultivated the posture of 'guardians of the county' against 'exploitation' by courtiers.[33]

If some counties experienced conflict, however, 'country' resistance to 'Court' demands was exceptional. The whole idea that conflict necessarily arose in wartime between loyalty to the nation and loyalty to the local community ignores the complex relationship between local and central concerns.[34] The gentry sought friends at Court in order to secure office and privilege, military commands, or election to Parliament. In turn, the standing of a courtier or Crown official was enhanced if he commanded local standing. Particularist disputes at local level only took on a broader dimension if the participants appealed to the centre, which regularly happened in the 1590s when Essex–Cecil rivalry permeated the entire administration. Symbolic was the feud at the Tower where the lieutenant and master of the ordnance were not on speaking terms![35]

It is clear that gentry factionalism in Norfolk itself sparked combustion. Duelling and personal squabbles overshadowed disagreements over the government of the shire; alignments within the county were modelled on the Essex–Cecil conflict, which enabled the Privy Council to divide and rule.[36] But elsewhere conflict was muted before 1598. Lords-lieutenant and their deputies had dual responsibilities. As well as being privy councillors and courtiers, a majority of lieutenants and virtually all deputies were also JPs. Thus 'opposition' to the Council's levies of ship money and soldiers in Suffolk was led by the deputy lieutenants and muster-masters themselves. In Wiltshire the lord-lieutenant was opposed by an alliance of his own deputies and the JPs. Although the gentry leaders of Suffolk were summoned before the Privy Council and threatened with dismissal, there is no evidence of this threat being implemented. Against such men the Council had no real sanctions: the real limitation of Elizabethan local government by 1598 was that a united magistracy could decline to co-operate with either the Privy Council or its lord-lieutenant, while invoking Court connections to escape punishment.[37]

At the level of central government the rise of 'corruption' signalled the drift towards venality. In particular, the shortage of available patronage during the long war and log-jam in promotion prospects encouraged a traffic in offices. Contrary to received opinion, however, corruption was not inevitable. When Sir James Croft informed Burghley in 1583 that 'Inferior servants and ministers are driven for necessity to make spoil of as much as they can embezzle,' having 'only the bare wages of ancient time allowed', he was offering an excuse rather than an explanation. Not only had official salaries been raised generously by Henry VIII, but also improved methods of provisioning and the possibility of taking subsistence allowances in either cash or kind compensated to an extent for the rising cost of living. It follows that 'corruption' sprang less from poverty than from increased tolerance of dishonesty by the 1590s. On the other hand, the patronage log-jam was genuine enough. Whereas the Crown possessed 1,200 or so offices worthy of a gentleman's standing in Elizabeth's reign, Henry VIII had enjoyed similar patronage at a time when aspiring gentry were fewer and official pluralism less pronounced. Also the Reformation had ended the system whereby many of the Crown's bureaucrats were rewarded by preferment as non-resident clergy.[38]

By her constant vigilance, Elizabeth staved off the worst abuses of the patronage system during her reign.[39] She or Burghley vetted candidates for office, while she contrived to ensure that her discretion was not undermined by collusion between suitors and courtiers. If she suspected deceit, she would invoke her talent for procrastination. In August 1593 she refused to sign a bill sponsored by Robert Cecil on the grounds that 'she would make no continuance of inheritance in any [of] her offices, meaning that she would not jointly in one book bestow it upon the father and the son'.[40] Yet the force of competition at Court to exploit political advantage especially during the war years created a 'black market' in which influence was increasingly bought and sold.[41] This meant that offices were overtly traded, but, unlike Henry VII's sales, the Crown was rarely the financial beneficiary. From the 1560s onwards payments were made instead to privy councillors and courtiers to influence the queen's choice: any fiscal benefit to the Crown was incidental, being restricted to the increase in New Year's gifts Elizabeth received when appointments were pending. Otherwise, individuals scooped the profits. The diplomatist Armigail Waad reminded Burghley:

You told me that this buying and selling of offices was not to be suffered, and that it was not likely that the buyer of an office would behave himself well in it, especially having bought it at an unreasonable price. This is true, and I wish that the laws of the realm against such offices being bought and sold might be put in execution. I am sorry too that in this time, wherein there is a general expectation that things should go well forward, the same fault, as it is said, is winked at, and the mart kept within the Court.[42]

The law to which Waad referred was the Act against Buying and Selling of Offices passed in 1552.[43] If, however, this forbade direct sales by administrators in whose gift a particular Crown office lay, it did not cover abuses of influence by courtiers when they advised the queen—in any case something almost impossible to prove. Also the act was unable to prevent officials from bargaining to surrender their patents of offices to purchasers, who then lobbied to secure their own appointment. So for a minor post £200 or so would be offered, while competitive bids of £1,000 to £4,000 were taken for such lucrative offices as the receivership of the court of wards or treasurership at war.

There was even a queue for an Irish office worth £300 that Burghley wished to suppress to save money: hard cash was offered 'in the Chamber and elsewhere'. As Spenser quipped:

> For nothing there is done without a fee:
> The Courtier needs must recompensèd be.
> *(Mother Hubberd's Tale*, 515–16)[44]

And bids were undoubtedly investments, since, if an appointment resulted, the new incumbent would so exercise his office as to recoup his outlay plus interest, for which reason the system was corrupt by Tudor as well as modern standards because the public interest was sacrificed to private gain.[45]

The exchequer and court of wards were particularly prone to scandals. For instance, Lord Treasurer Winchester dealt on a direct but informal basis with one of the four tellers of the receipt, Richard Stonley. Between Michaelmas 1558 and Michaelmas 1566 £1,171,050 was channelled through Stonley's hands—52 per cent of all cash paid into the exchequer—and not all this money was handled with strict propriety. Winchester borrowed funds for his own use and bypassed formal procedures whenever it suited his purposes.[46] True, corporate management of 'national' finance by the Privy Council created the system within which he had to work. But the tellers, whenever possible, resisted the Council's efforts to remit cash surpluses to the deposit treasury. In April 1562 a signet letter from Elizabeth addressed to Winchester, Sackville, and Mildmay forbade the tellers to store the Crown's money at their private houses to prevent losses and embezzlement.[47] But the instruction was ignored. The tellers continued to work mainly from home, the reason being that cash surpluses accumulating in their coffers were a source of personal profit: the crunch came in 1571 when all but one of the tellers in office since 1567 defaulted on their accounts at a cost to the Crown of £44,000. Stonley had 'borrowed' £6,100 to buy lands; William Patten, Richard Candler, and Richard Smythe had taken a total of £16,700; and Thomas Gardiner had lost £21,600 attempting to farm the duties on French wines.[48]

The ensuing scandal rocked the exchequer. Not only were two of Winchester's servants implicated, but the treasurer himself owed £11,500. When he died in March 1572, his debts exceeded £46,000.[49] An Act for Tellers and Receivers (1571) therefore made officials liable for their arrears and empowered the Crown to confiscate and sell the lands of defaulters.[50] But the wording of the act was imperfect.[51]

Winchester was succeeded as lord treasurer by Burghley himself. Working with Sir Walter Mildmay and Sir William Cordell, he did much to restore confidence in the central financial system. But even Burghley failed to prevent the tellers from accumulating 'private' cash surpluses.[52] Unauthorized 'borrowing' to purchase lands or make loans at interest continued unabated: the bubble burst in 1585 when Leicester was sent to the Netherlands. Steadily the Crown drew upon its cash and the credit structure of the tellers started to collapse. Within three years two out of four tellers were bankrupt; when the Armada sailed up the Channel, there was nothing left in the deposit treasury but £3,000 and a pile of obligations.[53]

The episode is revealing. The worse bankrupt was Stonley, who had been allowed to remain in office when Burghley assumed the treasurership; his diaries illuminate the range and extent of his dealings.[54] First, he was intimate with the governors of the City of London, doubtless as a moneylender as much as through family connections. Next, he did business with the peerage, and even sold property to Burghley.[55] So the issues are muddled; the efficiency of exchequer officials could be subordinated to private financial interests. Moreover, few thought this wrong *in principle*. An investigation only began in 1578, when Stonley was £19,000 in debt to the Crown.[56] Since his arrears were thought to be balanced by his assets, Burghley did not even dismiss him at first. The crash came in 1586 when Robert Petre, writer of the tallies and auditor of the receipt of the exchequer, told the treasurer that 'Mr. Stoneley being unable to make up his accounts by £16,000, he has been forced to lay the burthen on the other three tellers'.[57] One of these was Robert Taylor, who had also 'borrowed' the Crown's money. He too defaulted and was ruined, though he claimed that his servant had embezzled £7,500.[58]

Yet there is more to this story. It was not until December 1588 that Burghley forbade Stonley and Taylor to handle any more cash.[59] In fact, Stonley was not dismissed until 1597. Burghley and Mildmay first concealed the truth from Elizabeth and then minimized its seriousness.[60] Indeed, if Stonley's diary is credible, Burghley feared damage to his own career.[61] He kept the lid on the affair, while quietly chasing Stonley through the courts and promoting legislation reinforcing the Act for Tellers and Receivers.[62] After an eleven-year legal battle, Stonley's assets were finally recovered, though the teller died in 1600 still in considerable debt.[63]

Likewise George Goring, receiver-general of the court of wards from 1584 to 1594, died owing the Crown £19,777. Gossip had it that there was £12,000 in cash in his house a few days before he died; and that he 'bought land in other men's names and he secretly conveyed away his lands to defeat her majesty'. He certainly owned several Sussex manors, and had a house built of brick at a cost of £4,000 and another of stone costing £2,000. Since his official salary was £66 per annum plus £70 diet and allowance, the figures speak for themselves! On Goring's death there were many candidates for his post: the mere whisper of the vacancy started a Gadarene scramble. One suitor offered Burghley and Robert Cecil £1,000; another suggested £1,000 for Cecil plus £100 for his wife. Goring's son cheekily entered a bid, offering another £1,000 if the size of his inherited debt could be written down.[64]

A list of Burghley's income as master of the wards during the last two and a half years of his life shows that he accepted £3,301 from private suitors as 'arrangement fees' for eleven grants of wardship at a time when his official annual salary as master was £133. His profit tripled that of the Crown, which gained a mere £906 from these transactions. Of course, it was only the Crown's receipts that were entered in the official records; Burghley's profits were listed in a paper endorsed: 'This note to be burned.' Yet Burghley was unscrupulous only in his desire to advance Robert Cecil as his successor. There is no sign that he ever allowed his advice or political judgement to be deflected by the prospect of gain, and he refused to tolerate outright bribery. True, gifts of plate to privy councillors and judges were frequent and the value of Burghley's collection approached £15,000 at his death. But his contemporaries thought this sum modest in relation to his opportunities.[65]

By contrast, it was said of Sir Thomas Heneage in 1592, 'I think your best friend unto him will be your £1,000.' It was notorious that he accepted £60 as chancellor of the duchy for subscribing a bill for a minor official. When Sir John Carey learned that Elizabeth had criticized his wife for selling minor offices in the garrison at Berwick, he complained, 'If her Majesty would search into takers so narrowly . . . she might find takers of another kind nearer hand, such as take more in one day than she [Lady Carey] hath done in all her life.' Again, when Sir Thomas Shirley, treasurer at war, was accused in 1593 of misappropriating £30,000 per annum of the funds allocated for campaigns in the Netherlands, the charges were that he had 'infinitely bribed' Burghley's clerk to secure his ends; speculated with the soldiers' pay; sold concessions to army victuallers; and operated as a moneylender. His income ranged between £3,000 and £16,000 per annum, though his official salary was £365.[66] Lastly, it was said of Robert Cecil, 'You may boldly write for his favour. . . . You paid well for it'! A friendly source probably underestimated his income in 1598 as £10,000 per annum. Between 1608 and 1612 his profits from political office alone exceeded £6,860. Also an approach to the Spanish ambassador resulted in a cash gift of £12,000 — a sum considerably greater than Wolsey's pension from Francis I. In these circumstances, the theory that there was a deterioration of public morality in the 1590s and 1600s bears examination. Whereas it took Burghley fifty years in public office to build three houses and acquire a landholding appropriate to a peer, his son accumulated larger estates and built five houses in under sixteen years, even though Burghley received more land in the form of free gifts from the Crown.[67]

Yet corruption in the judicial system was small scale. It is true that the conduct of Sir Roger Manwood was scandalous, while Sir Edmund Anderson was the judge who, on the death of an official of the court of common pleas, 'had given the place and sworn an officer before eight o'clock the next morning; and within an hour after, came the Queen's letters for another, which by that means were frustrate'.[68] But clerkships in the courts of law had traditionally been regarded as in the gift of the judges: when John More (Sir Thomas's father) sat in king's bench, almost the entire clerical establishment was in the hands of his extended family. Manwood's first offence was probably to sell a clerkship at an extortionate price rather than simply to bargain for it. He then wrote a bilious letter to the Privy Council when told that

his conduct in an exchequer case set 'a very foul example
. . . to the rest of your calling'. When he almost immediately
asked for the office of chief justice of queen's bench, offering
Burghley a bribe of 500 marks (£333), his letter was too blatant.
Numerous charges of bribery, corruption, and oppression had
been levelled against him as chief baron of the exchequer. Not
all may have been true, but the complaints were so many and
so consistent that Manwood was suspended in 1592.[69]

But Manwood *was* suspended; Burghley did all he could to
keep him out of the offices he tried to buy; and contemporary
comment suggests that the judge's behaviour was exceptional,
if not unique. True, the courts of chancery and star chamber
became more expensive than ever in the later years of Elizabeth.
Sinecurism first reared its head in star chamber with Bacon's
nomination to the reversion of the clerkship; and complaints that
officials in chancery sold writs of subpoena for money were not
without foundation. On the other hand, the courts of common
law became cheaper as fees were pegged in an age of inflation.
Litigants from the ranks of the gentry and above were heavily
outnumbered by lesser men. Popular opinion that attorneys
cheated their clients and incited them to engage in superfluous
litigation, or that 'as a man is friended, so the law is ended',
were misplaced. The Elizabethan legal system worked as well
as the majority of litigants wished. In particular, the rise of star
chamber as a central criminal court after 1560 ensured that
Wolsey's emphasis on law enforcement and impartial justice,
first announced in 1516, was consolidated into an effective
supervisory jurisdiction that punished perjury, corruption, and
malfeasance throughout the legal system.[70]

Elizabethan government aroused more vocal dissent in the matters
of purveyance and monopolies. Purveyance was the Crown's
long-established right to purchase provisions for the royal
household at between half and one-third of the market price.
It sparked friction in the country, offered opportunities for
corruption, and earned criticism in Parliament. Although by the
end of Mary's reign the more obnoxious practices of purveyors
had been curbed by legislation, the flow of complaints continued.
If, however, Elizabeth could not afford to surrender a benefit
worth perhaps £37,000 per annum, she attempted to smooth

relations with the country. Instead of purveyors compulsorily purchasing provisions direct from local suppliers, counties were permitted to supply the Court with fixed annual quantities of foodstuffs at agreed prices, whereupon purveyors were withdrawn from their areas. A gap remained between the market price at which local authorities purchased food from farmers and the 'royal' price at which they resold it. But JPs were authorized to recoup this deficit by levying county rates.[71]

Although this procedure should have allayed the worst drawbacks of the old methods, only fifteen counties had entered into the new 'compositions' by 1580. First, the contracts the Crown demanded were not linked to a county's wealth or agricultural surpluses, but were based upon distance from London. Kent and Essex were effectively rated at £3,000 per annum; Norfolk at £1,000; and Yorkshire at £495. Second, property owners repudiated the Privy Council's demands that the new rates should be levied largely on justices, gentry, and wealthier persons, rather than the poor. Third, a number of JPs argued that the new system nullified the statutory limitations already imposed on purveyors, who were supplanted by 'compounders' and their 'undertakers'—often purveyors in another guise. Persons in dispute with the new 'compounders' had no redress in the common-law courts, but had to appear before the Board of Green Cloth—the court of the lord steward's department, which enforced the Crown's prerogative. In Norfolk some JPs said outright that 'it was better to have the former course when the purveyors were prescribed to take by a course of law though it had been harder for the subject, than to endure this course of composition which is without the compass of the law'.[72]

A parliamentary bill of 1589 against the abuses of purveyance included a section to 'prevent any purveyor, regardless of the service in which he was employed, from summoning persons before the Board of Green Cloth, except upon certificate obtained from two JPs'. Elizabeth saw the bill as an attack on her prerogative and ordered that it be dropped. But she recognized the strength of opinion when she undertook to reform purveyance herself and permitted four MPs to confer with privy councillors and household officials about new regulations for purveyors. So, as in her last two Parliaments when the grievances of monopolies were debated, Elizabeth defused the attack without conceding that her prerogative was touched. By 1591 she had appointed a committee of privy councillors led by Burghley — 'the commission for household causes' — to restructure purveyance. True, when this body reported, the new system of 'compounding' ceased to be voluntary. In fact, the commissioners instructed twenty-six counties to send delegates to Court by October 1592 in order to conclude comprehensive 'composition' agreements for all provisions supplied to the royal household. But, although the constitutional objection stood that purveyance by 'composition' rested exclusively on the prerogative, Burghley's tactful handling of the negotiations ensured that objections were muted, except in Norfolk, where a majority of the JPs refused to co-operate. By 1597 almost all other counties had compounded for purveyance and there was no further parliamentary agitation on the subject until the reign of James I.[73]

The clashes over monopolies in 1597 and 1601 were, by contrast, the ugliest in Parliament during the Tudor period, signalling unequivocal resentment of abuses promoted by courtiers and government officials. True, some monopolies or licences were genuine patents or copyrights, while others established trading companies with overseas bases which also provided valuable consular services for merchants abroad. But a number of monopolies were designed simply to corner the market in commodities for the patentees, or to grant them exclusive rights which enabled them to extort payments from tradesmen for carrying out their normal businesses. Beginning with new manufactures, monopolies were extended to old ones, while courtiers also obtained licences to export goods prohibited from export by statute or to dispense (at a profit) with the requirements of the penal laws (i.e. those regulating agriculture and trade). Such grants could not be revoked by the courts without royal assent. All patents rested on royal prerogative, so the courts lacked jurisdiction at common law. On the other hand, patentees enjoyed the support of the Privy Council and star chamber in defending and enforcing their privileges.[74]

Criticism of this method of rewarding courtiers was not new. Thomas Starkey had grumbled in the 1530s, 'there be few laws and statutes in parliaments ordained but by placards [i.e. letters patent] and licence obtained of the prince they are broken and abrogate'.[75] In 1559 a bill for abolition of licences *non obstante* (i.e. those dispensing with penal statutes) passed the Commons only to vanish from sight.[76] Indignation was next vented in Parliament in 1571 by a Norfolk lawyer, Robert Bell, one of the Privy Council's men of business, who obviously departed from his instructions and was forced to withdraw by recommending no more than a humble suit to Elizabeth for reform.[77] Lastly, an unofficial reform programme drafted between 1572 and 1576 recommended that 'Licences exempting from the penal laws should be revoked and the laws themselves be reviewed in Parliament, to distinguish the necessary from the superfluous.'[78]

It was, however, the late-Elizabethan mushrooming of monopolies and licences that provoked the backlash of 1597 and 1601. Ralegh, for example, enjoyed monopolies for tin, playing-cards, and the licensing of taverns. He blushed when his cards were mentioned, but defended his tin patent on the grounds that it enabled him to pay the miners 4*s.* a week instead of 2*s.* (20 November 1601). Yet monopolies had doubled the price of steel; tripled that of starch; caused that of imported glasses to rise fourfold; and that of salt elevenfold. Richard Martin, MP for Barnstaple, who had first impugned Ralegh, claimed to speak 'for a town that grieves and pines, and for a country that groans under the burden' of monopolists whom he dubbed 'bloodsuckers of the commonwealth'.[79] When Sir Robert Wroth listed next day the monopolies created since the previous Parliament, the young lawyer, William Hakewill, interjected:

'Is not bread there?' 'Bread?', quoth one. 'Bread?', quoth another . . . 'This voice seems strange', quoth a third. 'No', quoth Mr. Hakewill, 'If order be not taken for these, bread will be there before the next Parliament'.[80]

When faced by pungent criticism and demands for a committee of investigation in November and December 1597, Elizabeth had neutralized the attack by promising to scrutinize existing monopolies and not to allow prerogative machinery to prevent dishonest patentees from being sued in the common-law courts. While this marked a significant concession and cannot have been palatable to the queen, it defused a threatening situation and left her prerogative intact. But the promised reforms failed to materialize. After Parliament was dissolved in February 1598, more new monopolies were granted than old ones rescinded. True, shortly before Elizabeth's last Parliament assembled (27 October to 19 December 1601), Lord Treasurer Buckhurst and Cecil had investigated monopolies in an effort to tackle them before it was too late. But the commission of privy councillors appointed to consider the problem did nothing, and in October 1601 at least 157 MPs were returned who had also sat in 1597–8, while 253 members were either barristers or gentry educated at the inns of court (the biggest legal contingent of any Tudor Parliament). So the continuing inability of subjects to obtain redress against patentees in the law courts would have been fully understood.[81]

The 1601 Parliament was the most fractious of the reign. Privilege cases abounded, elections were challenged on various grounds, and there were heated exchanges between members, as well as criticisms of the Speaker and rejection of his choice of bills to be read. Robert Cecil's management was partly to blame: the Crown wanted only subsidies, and the Privy Council served notice via the lord keeper's speech 'that this Parliament should be a short Parliament'. Cecil hoped that there would be 'no new laws made', and warned against 'fantastic speeches or idle bills'. But members of the Commons wished to promote unofficial bills on matters of local concern. Robert Wingfield, a leader of the attack on monopolies, dared to suggest 'that seeing the subsidy was granted, and they yet had done nothing, it would please her Majesty not to dissolve the Parliament until some Acts were passed'. As a parliamentary manager, it seems that Cecil lacked his father's wisdom. Despite having no serious rival after Essex's fall, he was 'tetchy, censorious, even tactless'. He hectored MPs and swiped at 'men that have desired to be popular without the House for speaking against monopolies [who] also labour to be private within'. He lost control of the Commons several times, and was forced to apologize for his discourtesy and mistakes.[82]

If, however, the Commons' protest against monopolies in 1601 partly expressed wider frustrations, its explosive potential derived from popular indignation at the scale of abuses, as well as from MPs' realization that the petitioning of 1597–8 'had no successful effect'. Robert Wingfield reminded members that Elizabeth had promised 'That she would take care of these monopolies and our griefs should be redressed. If not, she would give us free liberty to proceed in making a law the next Parliament.' And hotheads urged that Parliament should invoke bill procedure without attempting further to petition the queen, even though Cecil brusquely indicated that any attempt to pursue legislation against the prerogative would be blocked. As therefore in the early debates on the Petition of Right (1628), when MPs likewise wielded a royal 'promise' in an attempt to initiate similarly unwelcome legislation, the outcome was a minor constitutional crisis.

Cecil's most impassioned outburst occurred when 'a multitude of people . . . who said they were Commonwealth men' crowded the Parliament lobby and stairs, demonstrating in order that Parliament might 'take compassion of their griefs, they being spoiled, imprisoned and robbed by monopolists'. He rose in a rage, demanding an immediate explanation. For to vent popular opinion in Tudor political affairs was *lèse-majesté*. Cecil later cautioned, 'Whatsoever is subject to a public exposition cannot be good. Why, Parliament matters are ordinarily talked of in the streets! I have heard myself, being in my coach, these words spoken aloud: "God prosper those that further the overthrow of these monopolies!" ' Of members who discussed Parliament's debates outside the House, he added: 'I think those persons would be glad that all sovereignty were converted into popularity.'[83]

Yet Elizabeth stooped to conquer. Determined that the subsidy bill should complete its parliamentary stages as quickly as possible, she sent a message via the Speaker that some monopolies 'should be presently repealed, some suspended, and none put in execution but such as should first have a trial according to the law for the good of her people' (25 November). The crisis was thus averted at the expense of the patentees: three days later a proclamation annulled twelve monopolies condemned in Parliament; authorized subjects grieved by other patents to seek redress in the courts of common law; and rescinded all letters of assistance from the Privy Council in support of patentees.[84] But whether the queen's concession promised more than it achieved is a matter for further research. In June 1602 the Privy Council upheld Edward Darcy's plea for enforcement of his monopoly of selling playing-cards, ordering his opponents to be imprisoned.[85] Also patents and monopolies were the source of major clashes under the early Stuarts, culminating in mass revocations during the summer of 1639 that denoted the collapse of Charles I's Personal Rule.[86]

The final criticism levelled against Elizabethan government is that the benefits of the Poor Laws were crushed by the rise of Tudor population and the economic distress of the 1590s. Although this question raises problems, a Malthusian diagnosis can be eliminated. The Elizabethan state profited from a steadily rising birth-rate that coincided with increased life expectancy. In particular, the mortality emergencies of 1586–7 and 1594–8 were not national in geographical extent. It has been argued that mortality caused by harvest failure was concentrated in upland regions where crops were grown under marginal conditions or where grains had to be purchased, while these same regions were usually spared plague owing to their relative isolation. By contrast, starvation was averted in London, the south-east, and East Anglia, which had local food supplies and convenient access to imported grain from the Baltic region, although London and the larger towns, the mixed farming lowlands, and other areas with well-developed communications were especially vulnerable to plague.[87]

An innovation was the printing of Books of Orders to be circulated to all JPs specifying the measures they should take to minimize the effects of plague and famine. For instance, plague orders first printed in 1587 and reissued in 1592 and 1593 required infected houses to be quarantined, watchmen to be appointed to ensure that the sick and their families were isolated, and special rates to be levied in support of infected persons. Likewise dearth orders first published in 1586, and reprinted in 1594 and 1595, formalized the methods of official searches for grain and compulsory sale of surpluses to needy householders in local markets that Wolsey had pioneered in 1527 and which had been repeated in 1550 and 1556. It is true that these orders rested solely on royal prerogative, so that some JPs questioned their validity. Since, however, they were implemented only during emergencies, they sparked no obvious resistance. Unlike the Books of Orders promulgated by Charles I's regime, they did not attempt to impose new standards of central inter-ventionism.[88]

Yet the Elizabethan Books of Orders were experiments and cannot be seen as the basis of a coherent social policy. In any case, the size of the 1594–8 crisis meant that the Privy Council could do little beyond maximizing grain imports, forbidding exports, and supervising the transfer of food supplies from areas of relative surplus to those of immediate need. The death-rate jumped by 21 per cent in 1596–7, and by a further 5 per cent in 1597–8. True, fewer parishes experienced crisis mortality than during the influenza epidemic of 1555–9, and later economic depressions in 1625–6 and 1638–9 were more severe. But average agricultural prices climbed higher in real terms in 1594–8 than at any time before 1615, while real wages plunged lower in 1597 than at any time between 1260 and 1950.[89] Perhaps two-fifths of the population fell below the margin of subsistence. Malnutrition reached the point of starvation in the uplands of Cumbria; disease spread unchecked; reported crimes against property increased; and thousands of families were thrown on to parish relief. That whole families as well as individuals sought relief by 1598 indicates the scale of distress.[90]

So in a material sense the Poor Laws must have been inadequate. The estimated cash yield of endowed charities for poor relief by 1600 totalled £11,776 per annum—0.25 per cent of national income. Yet the estimated amount raised by poor rates was smaller. If these figures are correct, what was audible was not a bang but a whimper.[91] On the other hand, food and enclosure riots were markedly fewer than might be expected. At a different level the Poor Laws operated as a placebo: the 'labouring poor' were persuaded that their social superiors shared their view of the social order and denounced the same 'caterpillars of the commonwealth'—chiefly middlemen.[92]

An important reason for the decline of rebellion and popular protest in Tudor England was the steady polarization of rich and poor that led prosperous farmers and tradesmen (i.e. property owners) to side with the gentry against their social inferiors. Potential class conflict after 1580 disposed property owners to assume local office, to settle their disputes in the law courts, and to identify with the gentry as magistrates. Richer husbandmen, too, declined to resort to violence, especially if literate.[93] Moreover, the 'reformation of manners', also prominent during the adverse economic conditions of the 1550s, reinforced the Poor

Laws. Prosecutions escalated in both secular and church courts against poaching, pilfering, sexual offences, popular recreations, inns and alehouses, drunkenness, profanation of the Sabbath, and swearing. These cases were not initiated from above by the Privy Council, but from below by jurors and informers. They reflected a growing divergence between the values of established members of the community on the one hand, and those of the mass of 'labouring poor', household servants, transient workers, and urban immigrants on the other.[94]

In the spring and summer of 1586 food riots in the cloth-making areas of Gloucestershire, Wiltshire, and Somerset were sparked by a severe but short-lived trade recession, exacerbated by food shortages created by speculators hoarding grain in anticipation of the expected bad harvest. An abortive rising in Hampshire in June the same year resulted equally from food shortages and the trade recession. In the 1590s the Privy Council's fear was that the 'camping' rebellions of 1549 would be repeated. In 1595 food riots erupted spasmodically in London, the south-east, and the south-west. Two riots in the capital involved up to 1,800 apprentices, disbanded soldiers, and masterless men. Although they were suppressed, some apprentices tried to seize armour in order to free their imprisoned fellows and then 'play the Irish trick' on the mayor — in other words, cut off his head (16 June). In Kent the possibility of staging a 'camp' to settle scores with farmers and grain speculators was mooted (February 1596). In Norfolk it was said that there should again be 'such as Kett's camp was and there men should fight for corn'. In 1596–7 there were food riots in East Anglia, the south-west, and on the Kent and Sussex border.[95]

Given this volatile background, the so-called 'Oxfordshire Rising' of November 1596 created panic. Yet the irony is that fear was in the eye of the beholder. 'Fact dissolved into fantasy' as the latent possibility of popular revolt gnawed at the minds of privy councillors and JPs. True, the leaders of the 'Rising' had planned to attack the nearby house of the lord-lieutenant, Lord Norris, seize his arms and artillery, and march 'with all speed towards London' to reinforce the City's apprentices. But, despite careful preparation by the leaders, only four rebels assembled at the appointed time and place: they waited for two

hours before disbanding, and were quickly arrested! Still the
Privy Council wrote repeatedly to Norris demanding additional
arrests and examinations. The ringleaders were to be brought
to London under strong guard, 'their hands pinnioned and their
legs bound'. They were not to 'have conference one with the
other in the way hither'. Lastly, Norris was to prepare to counter
the threat of new revolts in any part of the county.[96]

The 'rebels' and their associates were examined by a powerful
committee of the Privy Council headed by Attorney-General
Coke. This committee was empowered to use torture 'for the
better bolting forth of the truth'; it was so obsessed by its own
sinister version of events that, in attempting to 'discover' non-
existent gentry backers of the revolt, it may have tortured two
men to death.[97] Coke then had the 'rebels' tried and executed
as traitors for levying war against the queen—a controversial
interpretation of the law, since no violence had been used. Yet
the interrogations had a positive result too. The Privy Council
perceived itself 'forced' in the light of the 'revolt' to mitigate
grievances against enclosures which the Oxfordshire men were
found to have voiced during their village recruiting drive. So
the assizes at which the ringleaders were indicted heard a special
'charge' concerning the evils of enclosure; members of the 1597–8
Parliament were allowed to tackle poor relief on a sustained basis
as well as to enact anti-enclosure statutes; and JPs were constantly
chided to ensure that the poor received adequate relief.[98]

The papers of Coke's committee establish that the Oxfordshire
'rebels' were young and unmarried artisans and servants with
nothing to lose. Only one was a husbandman, and no women
supported them. As a group they lacked the social influence to
translate their discontent into political action. Despite the Privy
Council's fears, no gentleman or yeoman backed the revolt, while
the 'middling sort' who had been the backbone of the 1549
rebellions were conspicuous by their absence. In a sense, the
episode offered a parable. Although Elizabethan government
worked well until 1595, thereafter the strains of war, taxation,
and economic distress proved corrosive. In 1596 the Privy
Council fell victim to moral panic, 'their own anxieties seemingly
confirmed by the fantasies blown into their ears'.[99] On the other
hand, the governing class stood more united than ever before
when faced by the mass of 'labouring poor', servants, and

vagrants. Indeed, more meaningful than notions of a declining taxation system, 'corruption' in central government, and an alleged 'slide to disaster' in the country is the idea of an expanding early modern state in which the powers of 'established authority' were growing at the expense of the population as a whole. True, the relationship between rulers and ruled was becoming fragile. But the solidarity of propertied society ensured that the putrefying effects of war and Court factionalism were muted before 1603.

POLITICAL CULTURE

MIDWAY through an audience with the Kentish antiquary
William Lambarde, six months after the earl of Essex's rebellion,
Elizabeth I suddenly became agitated. She seized upon references
to Richard II in a manuscript Lambarde had presented to her,
saying 'I am Richard II, know ye not that?' For Essex's
sponsorship in the City of London of plays of Richard II shortly
before his revolt still rankled. The historical allusion could not
have been more blatant: that the Essexians saw their leader as
Bolingbroke, and that, had their rising succeeded, they would
have deposed Elizabeth as Bolingbroke had deposed Richard.[1]
Yet this is only the most obvious illustration of the link between
Tudor politics and literature, which was crammed with political
statements and advice. For example, when Thomas More set
his *Dialogue of Comfort against Tribulation* in Hungary on the eve
of a Turkish invasion, he established a metaphoric analogy that
enabled readers to assimilate the enemy without to the enemy
within: Turk became Protestant and infidel heretic, while the
'Great Turk' stood at one level of meaning for 'tribulation' in
general, and at another level for Henry VIII. Even More's
devotional works, for instance his *Treatise on the Passion*, were
littered with analogies, the most striking of which linked the
council of Caiaphas and the Jews to debates in Henry VIII's
Council and Reformation Parliament.[2]

In More's *Utopia* the fictional traveller Raphael Hythlodaeus
knew that a method of advising princes in the Renaissance was
to write books of 'counsel'. This mirrored the humanistic
convention that political debate, in so far as it was permitted,
was conducted in advice books, histories, interludes, dramas,
and literary 'dialogues' (i.e. works cast in partially dramatized
form). Advice and courtesy books included *Utopia* itself, Sir
Thomas Elyot's *The Book Named the Governor*, and Sir Thomas
Hoby's translation of Castiglione's *The Book of the Courtier*.
Dialogues apart from *Utopia* were More's *Dialogue Concerning*

Heresies, Elyot's *Pasquil the Playne*, St German's *Salem and Bizance*, Thomas Starkey's *Dialogue between Reginald Pole and Thomas Lupset*, and Sir Thomas Smith's *Discourse of the Commonweal of this Realm of England*. Among the best histories and dramas were More's *Richard III*, John Bale's *King John*, Sackville and Norton's *Gorboduc*, Christopher Marlowe's *Edward II*, and Shakespeare's Roman and English history plays.

Poetry, too, became politicized in the hands of Skelton, Sir Thomas Wyatt, and Henry Howard, earl of Surrey. When Wyatt translated Petrarch, the result was a poetry of protest. Sir Philip Sidney in his *Apology for Poetry* (written in 1581) defended poetry partly on account of its political utility: 'Is the poor pipe disdained, which . . . can show the misery of people, under hard lords, and ravening soldiers? And again . . . what blessedness is derived, to them that lie lowest, from the goodness of them that sit highest?'[3] The earl of Essex was himself a minor poet, whose 'common way' was 'to evaporate his thoughts in a Sonnet . . . to be sung before the Queen'. A poem written after his clash with Elizabeth in July 1598 clearly signalled his mood of bitterness and frustration.[4] And Sidney's *Arcadia*, a prose pastoral romance designed to 'represent the growth, state, and declination of Princes . . . with all other errors, or alterations in public affairs', was interspersed with poems. For instance, an eclogue argued that the nobility were the natural protectors of the people against tyranny. The poem described how order was maintained in the golden age by the greater beasts, but how, when the lesser beasts asked Jove to give them a king, man was created, and man quickly established a despotism by fomenting factions: he set the 'weaker sort' against the 'nobler beasts', and, when he had destroyed the nobler ones, he enslaved the weaker and killed them for his sport. As in Starkey's *Dialogue between Pole and Lupset*, the implication was that a monarchy limited by a strong nobility would insure the state against tyranny.[5]

Less allusive was Spenser's *Mother Hubberd's Tale*, written about 1580, which impugned the planned marriage between Elizabeth and Francis, duke of Alençon. The work exploited the well-known fact that Elizabeth addressed her courtiers by animal nicknames: Alençon was the frog, his agent Simier the ape, Burghley the fox, Hatton the sheep, and so on. At one level *Mother Hubberd's Tale* was, therefore, a poetic allegory against ambition modelled upon Aesop's fables. But the coded message was clear that collusion between Burghley and the French threatened to subvert the Elizabethan regime. If the marriage went ahead, the 'fox' would rule through a weak king–consort to the point where Elizabeth's sovereignty was extinguished — this view reflected the anxieties of Leicester's circle. In *The Shepherd's Calendar* Spenser again echoed debates over the proposed match, dramatizing Leicester's feared eclipse and that of the Protestant cause. As in *The Faerie Queene*, allegory was not employed as a disguise to allow the author to cloak his meaning, but as a veil through which he might reveal what would otherwise be *lèse-majesté*.[6]

So literature was the prevailing medium of élite political discourse, one which Renaissance convention recognized as a valid means of counselling the prince. True, Hythlodaeus conceded that few princes in practice acknowledged this fact. But ambition was mightier than observation: courtiers who picked up their pens in defeat or out of office included Skelton, More, Elyot, Starkey, Smith, Sidney, Spenser, Ralegh, and Francis Bacon. As Petrarch had written in 1350: 'I was conceived in exile and born in exile.' Although he meant that he felt exiled from the achievements of the classical past, the disappointments of later counsellors gave his words added poignancy.

If, however, debate centred on 'counsel', it was conducted within humanist–classical terms of reference. Authors drew freely upon classical Greek and Roman, as well as Italian Renaissance sources. Crucial to this tradition was the antithesis between 'action' and 'contemplation', and the respective weight to be accorded to the ideas of Plato, Aristotle, and Cicero. Plato had argued in his *Republic* that the ideal state should be governed by philosophers; under any less perfect system the active life would corrupt the intellectual. By contrast, Aristotle in his *Politics* and *Ethics* had urged virtuous men to be active. Just as at the Olympic Games the winning athletes came only from those who chose to compete, so in political affairs honour belonged to those who put their virtue into practice. Virtue was the qualification for citizenship, and the good citizen was the man who would dutifully accept political, legal, or administrative office.[7] True, Plato's visit to Sicily to counsel Dionysius II of Syracuse had ended in disaster: he had been forced to return to Athens. So

Aristotle allowed that 'contemplation' might be preferable to 'action' in conditions where vice and corruption overwhelmed virtue. But the ideal was that the good man should become the good citizen.

Following Aristotle, Cicero crystallized this debate in the form transmitted to the Renaissance in *De officiis*. Starting from the premise that intellectuals preferred 'contemplation' to 'action', he argued that it was still their duty to participate in public life: the *vita activa* yielded the highest fulfilment; those who retreated to the ivory tower merely abandoned others whom they ought to defend. In fact, just as actors choose plays best suited to their talents, so wise men should select their part in life: 'if at some time necessity shall thrust upon us roles which we do not in the least feel to be suitable, we must devote to them all possible thought, practice, and pains, performing them, if not decorously, at least as indecorously as possible.'[8]

The intellectual challenge to Cicero came from the later Platonists whose writings were popularized during the 1480s. Colet encountered their arguments in Italy, and Erasmus urged Christian Platonist values when he advised him:

I'd like to see you withdrawn to as great a distance as possible from the world's affairs: not because I fear this world may entangle you . . . but because I'd rather see your distinguished talents, eloquence and learning wholly devised for Christ. But if you can't completely get clear, still beware of sinking daily deeper in that bog. Perhaps defeat would be better than victory at such a cost; for the greatest of all blessings is peace of mind.[9]

The classic discussion ensued in Book I of More's *Utopia*. In a central passage Hythlodaeus, a self-confessed Platonist, debated with a fictional 'Thomas More' the merits of the *vita activa*. Hythlodaeus wished to speak the truth and not succumb to flattery: 'If I proposed beneficial measures to some king and tried to uproot from his soul the seeds of evil and corruption, do you not suppose that I should be forthwith banished or treated with ridicule?' He reiterated Plato's view that, if kings did not turn to philosophy, 'they would never approve of the advice of real philosophers because they have been from their youth saturated and infected with wrong ideas'.[10] 'More' advocated in reply 'another philosophy, more practical for statesmen, which knows its stage, adapts itself to the play in hand, and performs its role neatly and appropriately'. 'Whatever play is being performed, perform it as best you can.' This was a metaphor for statecraft:

If you cannot pluck up wrongheaded opinions by the root, if you cannot cure according to your heart's desire vices of long standing, yet you must not on that account desert the commonwealth. You must not abandon the ship in a storm because you cannot control the winds. On the other hand, you must not force upon people new and strange ideas which you realize will carry no weight with persons of opposite conviction. On the contrary, by the indirect approach you must seek and strive to the best of your power to handle matters tactfully. What you cannot turn to good you must at least make as little bad as you can.[11]

Although Hythlodaeus deemed this akin to madness, he failed to refute it. And this is the nub. For the rebuff to the 'Platonist' position was More's intention. The fictional 'Thomas More' stood firm in *Utopia* because his real-life counterpart decided that he should; and his 'Ciceronian' values held the field in Tudor England. In 1529 Starkey opened his *Dialogue between Pole and Lupset* by remarking that, if anyone 'by his own quietness and pleasure moved, leaveth the care of the common weal and policy, he doth manifest wrong to his country and friends'. Such a person 'regardeth not his office and duty'. Elyot, though otherwise a genuine Platonist, solicited preferment from Wolsey and Thomas Cromwell. His *Book Named the Governor* (1531) attempted to compromise by urging persons 'called' to office to retreat to 'a secret oratory' in order to 'contemplate' virtue. Again, Smith's *Discourse of the Commonweal*, written in 1549 but not printed until 1581, incorporated the essence of Cicero's defence of the active life. Lastly, Roger Ascham, author of *The Schoolmaster* (1570), supplemented Bible study with reading of Plato, Aristotle, and Cicero, 'which is a veritable handmaid and attendant'.[12]

So Henry VIII, Edward VI, and Elizabeth attracted the best minds of their generations to Court without the slightest difficulty. It was said of Burghley, 'he would always carry Tully's [i.e. Cicero's] *Offices* about him, either in his bosom or his pocket', and Archbishop Whitgift ordered copies for his students while master of Trinity College, Cambridge.[13] The inevitable corollary was a revival of Aristotelianism, since Cicero's teaching had always been founded on Aristotle's. Not only were the *Ethics*,

Politics, and *Rhetoric* the starting-point for Elizabethan discussions of the nature and conduct of government, but Aristotle's methods of empirical analysis were also regarded as vital equipment for administrators. Councillors and their clients from Thomas Cromwell onwards drew their techniques from the *Politics* as well as from Aristotle's treatises on animals and natural philosophy. Such methods had a discernible effect upon statecraft: the books of Starkey, Moryson, Smith, John Ponet, Lawrence Humphrey, and Ralegh signalled this shift of emphasis. In fact, Smith's *Discourse of the Commonweal* was the most advanced statement of economic thought in Tudor England. Whereas his predecessors had tackled economic issues by way of allegories and moral *exempla*, assuming a static conception of society, the *Discourse* diagnosed problems, debated solutions, and proposed remedies within a dynamic conception of society that recognized legitimate self-interest as an instrument which councillors could harness for the public good.[14]

It can be argued that Platonism reappeared in the work of Sir Philip Sidney. He followed Aristotle when he declared in his *Apology for Poetry* that 'the best of the historian is subject to the poet, for whatsoever action or faction, whatsoever counsel, policy, or war stratagem, the historian is bound to recite, that may the poet if he list with his imitation make his own'. Yet Sidney also believed that man rose above his fallen self through poetry in the quest for perfection. Like many puritans seeking to emphasize the purity, internality, and directness of the individual's path to divine truth, he was attracted to Platonism.[15] True, Reformation religious controversies sparked little fresh examination of theories of knowledge and belief. Renaissance self-expression, textual rigour, and disapproval of 'scholastic' methods of disputation rendered ontological debates divisive rather than innovative. It was partly for lack of substitutes that Aristotle's books remained standard. But it was also because the 'new' Aristotle was studied from Greek texts with humanistic and classical commentaries. The 'old' scholastic apparatus was banished in favour of a tradition that was by no means reactionary, and was used to support and accommodate new currents of thought.[16]

True, Aristotle was challenged in some university circles by adherents of the Parisian Peter Ramus (1515–72), but Ramists

were a small minority much criticized at Oxford. Their slogan
was that 'everything said by Aristotle is false'! Ramus's *Institutions
of Dialectic* and *Animadversions on Aristotle* had begun a search for
'true reason' and 'true religion' that interested several lawyers
and puritans, Lord Keeper Egerton among them. Converts
argued that each man was a microcosm of the world: true
learning was 'naturally' based on an individual's speech and
language. In practice this meant a critical study of sources,
mastery of all relevant facts and points of view, use of dichotomies
in organizing facts and propositions, and scrutiny of meaning
through appropriation of words and phrases. When, however,
Gabriel Harvey's *De restitutione logica* appeared in 1583, it was
ridiculed.[17]

No link existed between Ramism and secularism. There were
Elizabethan sceptics like Reginald Scot, whose *Discovery of
Witchcraft* (1584) denied that God could ever have allowed witches
to exercise supernatural power, or have intended to persecute
them for allegedly doing so. There were the counterparts and
imitators of French *libertins érudits*, though sceptics argued less
that the 'supernatural' did not exist than that it had no biblical
justification. On the other hand, Florio's translation of
Montaigne's *Essays* (1603) was read as much for its exotic style
and vocabulary as for its contents. Also Jones's translation of
Justus Lipsius' controversial *Six Books of Politics* (1594) was
probably read for its view that princes should only allow a single
form of worship within their territories. Yet the dramatist
Marlowe (1564–93) claimed that the New Testament was 'filthily
written', that Jesus was a bastard and perhaps a homosexual,
and that the apostles were 'base fellows'. He argued that 'the
first beginning of religion was only to keep men in awe' — the
Machiavellian view of religion. Furthermore, he was linked to
Ralegh's circle, which had supposedly denied the immortality
of the soul. Lesser persons, too, were accused of denying Christ's
divinity, the Resurrection, and even God's existence, though
it is doubtful whether anything approaching 'atheism' in the
modern sense can be identified before the eighteenth century.[18]

Yet a rationalized historiography was stimulated by
translations of the works of Tacitus: the *Histories* and *Life of
Agricola* (1591), and the *Annals* and *Description of Germany* (1598).
True, the *Annals* had been known to More and Elyot, supplying

deficiencies in their knowledge of imperial Rome in the first century and influencing More's characterization of Richard III. But during the 1590s Tacitus was read as the historian who thought the past too complex and recalcitrant to be reduced to straightforward moral lessons. Empathy with his approach was felt by disillusioned courtiers and critics of late-Elizabethan venality and 'corruption'. Hence writers dissatisfied with the literature of 'counsel' sought to create a 'Tacitean' alternative. Their goal was to discover how great men attained their ends within a framework freed from the providentialist bias of popular histories such as John Lydgate's *Fall of Princes* and William Baldwin's *Mirror for Magistrates*. Moral *exempla* and divine intervention received short shrift from this approach. Instead history became 'a field for the play of the heroic energy of the autonomous politic will, seeking to dominate events by its command of the politic arts'.[19]

The earl of Essex, in particular, was a Tacitean patron: Francis Bacon, Sir Henry Savile, and Henry Cuffe were among his clients. Savile, who was warden of Merton College, Oxford, and later provost of Eton, had translated the *Histories* and *Life of Agricola*. Cuffe, who was regius professor of Greek at Oxford before joining Essex's revolt, proclaimed from the scaffold that 'learning and valour should have the pre-eminence yet'. His complaint was that 'scholars and martialists . . . in England must die like dogs and be hanged'. The view of Essex's circle was that aristocratic honour would be revived through its alliance with letters. George Chapman hailed Essex as 'most true Achilles, whom by sacred prophecy Homer did but prefigure'. Whether the earl's political failure discouraged or fed Tacitean imaginations is elusive. Ben Jonson's *Sejanus* (1603) and *Cataline* (1611) were too academic, and failed in performance despite Shakespeare's presence among the actors. But the effects of Tacitean revulsion against courts, and despair of the humanist idea of 'counsel', were evident by 1642.[20]

Political debate was, however, constrained under the Tudors. First, few publications apart from the Bible, Foxe's *Acts and Monuments*, and other religious works were intended to engage their readers, rather than entertain them. Humanist–classical issues were rarely addressed outside the circles of Court and

government, universities, and inns of court. Humanist authors
seeking to attract a wider audience assimilated their material
to the chivalric traditions of Chaucer, Malory, and the *Roman
de la rose*. In schools and gentry households Erasmus's New
Testament, *Paraphrases*, *Colloquies*, and *Adages* remained favourite
reading, supplemented by Sir Thomas North's edition of
Plutarch's *Lives of the Noble Grecians and Romans*, Elyot's *The Book
Named the Governor*, and Hoby's translation of *The Courtier*. At
a more popular level Caxton's *The Golden Legend*, Baldwin's *Mirror
for Magistrates*, sensational stories and pamphlets, printed
sermons, chronicles, travel books, almanacs, herbals, and
medical works were devoured. At the lowest level of literacy,
ballads disseminating 'hot news' were bought for a penny and
handed from person to person: they told of 'moving accidents',
murders, robberies, and battles.

Next, the Privy Council surveyed the printing presses with
a watchful eye. In Elizabeth's reign 2,760 books were published
between 1558 and 1579, and 4,370 between 1580 and 1603.
Assuming that the size of an average print run had climbed to
roughly 1,250 copies, this represents an average of just two books
per head for a population of 4¼ million over a generation and
a half. True, book-owners always formed a small minority of
the population. But the printed word was potentially explosive,
especially at a time when inflation qualified a whole new range
of modest property owners for jury service, parochial and civic
office, and even the parliamentary franchise. Elizabeth therefore
retained Mary's censorship measures in full. The Stationers'
Company policed the fifty or so London presses, subject to
instructions from the Crown and Privy Council. From 1586
licences to print individual titles had to be obtained from the
archbishop of Canterbury or bishop of London, who deputed
twelve 'preachers and others' to examine submitted works. The
only authorized presses outside London were those of the
universities of Oxford and Cambridge. In fact, few privy
councillors or magistrates would have disagreed with the
pamphleteer of 1653 who claimed that printing was 'a pestilent
midwife to those accursed brats, Error in the Church and Sedition
in the State. . . . there should be such a circumspect care of
prevention, and such painful pursuance of misdemeanours as
would be required against the most dangerous crimes'.[21]

Yet the crucial determinant was literacy. John Rastell observed that, since Henry VII's reign, 'the universal people of this realm had great pleasure and gave themself greatly to the reading of the vulgar English tongue'. There is no doubt that the vernacular triumphed over Latin and French after 1485: the writings and translations of More, Elyot, Starkey, Ascham, and Florio — particularly Elyot's Latin–English *Dictionary* — virtually doubled the size of Tudor vocabulary by creating English equivalents of foreign nouns and compounds. Tyndale's *New Testament*, official translations modelled upon it, and Cranmer's Prayer Book then shaped the syntax recognized as 'Bible' English. Lastly, the primacy of the vernacular was cemented by its near-exclusive adoption by the departments of Crown administration save in the records of the courts of exchequer, king's bench, and common pleas. The language of Shakespeare's age was enriched by these developments. Indeed, Shakespeare is said to have learned 750 new words from studying Florio's translation of Montaigne's *Essays*.[22]

On the other hand, the issue of the extent of literacy has divided historians. In his *Apology* (1533) More estimated that 'far more than four parts of all the whole divided into ten, could never read English yet, and many [are] now too old to begin to go to school' — he therefore thought roughly half the population literate. In late-Elizabethan Cambridgeshire an interest in education permeated some whole villages, and the extent of lay puritan Bible study suggests that basic reading skills were prevalent.[23] The difficulty is how to generalize, since it has been argued that the only measurable indicator of literacy at this time is the ability to sign one's name. On this basis 80 per cent of Elizabethan men and 95 per cent of women have been classified 'illiterate', while by 1642 the figures are said to be 70 per cent and 90 per cent respectively. It has even been claimed that ordinary people could cope with illiteracy and have no sense of it being a handicap, since the inherited oral culture still sustained a satisfactory alternative.[24]

But a significant difference exists between reading and writing proficiency. All Tudor theorists concurred that reading was properly taught before writing; writing was a subordinate part of the elementary school curriculum. Since most children's attendance at school fluctuated according to economic needs and the dictates of the agricultural seasons, many must have learned to read but not write. Furthermore, writing of personal names was discouraged in Tudor schools, because the irregular forms of names thwarted the strict rules of spelling that teachers were trying to instil. Another blind spot of the 'signature-counting' technique is that innumerable gradations of reading ability, and reading material, existed. True, most people would have been unable to master either More's *Dialogue Concerning Heresies* or Sidney's *Arcadia*. But it is entirely probable that spelling out the Ten Commandments from a version painted on the wall of a parish church, or extracting the gist of a printed ballad or broadsheet, was within the competence of half the population as More thought. Progress in literacy was demonstrated by 'sounding and saying' words or phrases letter for letter: each word was 'written' out loud, not set down for inspection on paper. It is also relevant that ordinary men and women found the 'black letter' gothic-style typography of the period far easier to decipher than the roman and italic fonts favoured by educated readers. Finally, there was a sudden growth in the number of books published for women in the 1570s, which would be inexplicable if 95 per cent had been illiterate.[25]

Variations in literacy skills can, however, be inferred from measuring people's ability to sign their names. Few women apart from gentlewomen were able to write in the sixteenth century; those who could used a more rounded hand and more relaxed spelling and layout than men. Literacy was standard among the gentry save in the north-east, where 36 per cent could not sign documents. Again, writing ability among tradesmen and craftsmen was more commonly found in the south-east than in the Durham region, but a majority everywhere could not sign their names at the beginning of Elizabeth's reign. Yet half of this group nationally had learned to write by 1600, while between one-half and two-thirds of Elizabethan yeomen did so too. On the other hand, a plateau in attainment levels among these groups was reached during the 1580s, followed by a drop in writing ability in outlying regions. Finally, husbandmen and labourers remained largely illiterate before the eighteenth century.[26]

Qualification must be made for London, where literacy rates were higher than in the provinces. In fact, the foundations were laid in the capital under Elizabeth for the rise of political consciousness in the seventeenth century. Literacy rates among tradesmen and craftsmen, servants, apprentices, and women were between 5 and 15 per cent higher in the City and its suburbs than elsewhere. Proximity to the presses encouraged people to learn to read, and those remaining illiterate could listen to others reading aloud. Also ballads and political prints transmitted their message to the semi-literate. By 1640-2 London experienced political lobbying and mass petitioning, while the Interregnum period saw political matters regularly debated in meeting houses and parish churches, ward-clubs, and in taverns and coffee-houses.[27]

Whether a direct causal relationship existed between the Reformation, printing, and literacy is arguable. The invention of printing would by itself have stimulated increasing numbers of people to learn to read. In this respect, Renaissance technology was a catalyst of the Reformation. Yet religious propagandists who exploited the press provided printers with the 'bread-and-butter' business needed to develop their trade. And a generation of editor–printer–publishers in France and England fostered the nascent Reformation: for example Robert Estienne, Robert Redman, William Marshall, and John Byddell. When he ordered clergy to teach children the Lord's Prayer, Ten Commandments, and articles of faith in English, Cromwell himself sought to lay the foundations of a literate society:

And to the intent this may be the more easily done, the said Curates shall in their sermons deliberately and plainly recite one clause of the said pater noster, articles or commandments one day, and another another day, till the whole be taught and learned by little and little. And shall deliver the same in writing or show where printed books containing the same be to be sold.[28]

Catholics and Protestants, however, relied equally on the printing press in the sixteenth century. Also Cromwell's injunctions merely updated techniques Colet had already recommended in sermons.[29] So improved literacy was not a product of the Reformation specifically, but was possible because the new technology and triumph of the vernacular coincided with a movement that involved the rediscovery of old books and the writing of new ones for mass markets.

The issue of educational opportunity is more complex. The number of endowed grammar schools by 1530 had reached 124, supplemented by hundreds of alphabet or parish schools where elementary reading, writing, and arithmetic were taught. Schools were often held in church porches or chantries until 1548, or in the master's house. This tradition of 'petty' schools was well established: an illuminated fourteenth-century manuscript shows a teacher at his desk, three pupils sitting on a bench, and a white-haired figure with writing implements. But in Henry VIII's reign monastic schools were vulnerable to dissolution, and the endowed secular schools were threatened by a slump in educational philanthropy. True, 'king's schools' were attached to several newly established cathedrals. Moreover, the flow of private educational benefactions resumed in the 1540s and 1550s: whereas thirteen schools had been founded in the 1520s and only eight in the 1530s, thirty-nine were founded in the 1540s and forty-seven in the 1550s. But these figures can mislead. Several schools were dissolved in the 1530s, for example at Bury, Tewkesbury, Bridgewater, and Cirencester. Also a number of Edwardian foundations simply re-endowed schools lost during Protector Somerset's dissolution of chantries and colleges.[30]

Fewer schools were founded per decade in Elizabeth's reign than in the 1550s, but confidence in education remained high until the 1580s. Some forty-two schools were endowed in the 1560s, and thirty in the 1570s. Charitable giving to education declined somewhat in real terms, but the effects were not immediately felt. Demand for schooling also increased from families below the ranks of the privileged elite; established schools in both town and country offered instruction for classes of 'petties', who were taught either by the usher or the older pupils. Likewise 'dame' schools flourished, though their efficiency was suspect. The 'dames' put in charge of poor children in early seventeenth-century Norwich were child-minders by another name. In 1579 it was said of Elizabeth Snell, of Watford, Hertfordshire, that 'she teacheth scholars to read and she herself cannot read'. In this extraordinary case Snell was tested in the court of the archdeacon of St Albans; the judge 'did openly make trial whether she could read or not, and laying before her the book of common prayer in a very fair and broad print, she could read nothing'.[31]

Educational provision contracted in the decades from 1580 to 1610 as inflation combined with the economic depressions of 1586–7 and 1594–8 discouraged charitable giving and undercut the real value of existing endowments. Only twenty schools were founded in the 1580s and twenty-four in the 1590s, while the number of licensed schoolmasters dropped by between 15 and 45 per cent. Possibly the heightened emphasis on pedagogy in late-Elizabethan elementary schools narrowed their intake, but it is more likely that the costs of schooling discouraged families hit by high food prices, for, although some schooling was free, more often quarterly fees were charged. In fact, the majority of 'free' schools charged for candles, coal, and educational materials. In places where no formally endowed or organized institution existed, informal schools kept by the clergy or village tradesmen or craftsmen probably disappeared at times of crisis. Beyond the circle of the élite—whose children were usually tutored at home—we should probably think in terms of a shifting tide of children whose access to schooling varied according to their domestic and economic circumstances. If this is correct, a decline in both attendances and literacy rates would be expected during the 1590s.[32]

Higher education was largely restricted to persons entering the two universities and four inns of court, though inns of chancery provided initial instruction for those seeking entry to the legal profession.[33] In Elizabeth's reign the inns of court were known as the third university, since increasing numbers of young gentry finished their education there. Charles I's Privy Council described them as 'Seminaries and Nurseries wherein the Gentry of the Kingdom and such as serve his Majesty in the Common Wealth are bred and trained up'. Indeed, the number of legally educated MPs rose from 140 in 1563, to 253 in 1601, and 306 in 1640. How much law the gentry learned in London is arguable, but the system of 'readings' and learning exercises developed in the late-fifteenth century suffered no apparent decline. Between 1560 and 1640 the inns were regarded as both professional law schools and fashionable academies. Members became acquainted with the legal processes they would invoke as property owners, while dabbling in anatomy, astronomy, geography, history, mathematics, theology, and foreign languages in their spare time.[34]

In *The Third University of England* (1612) Sir George Buck extended the term 'third university' to all forms of learning in London. Instruction was available in science, medicine, cosmography, hydrography, navigation, music, painting, poetry, languages, and dancing, as well as law. Teachers charged fees, though various free public lectures had been endowed. At Gresham College, opened in 1596, lectures were delivered on astronomy, geometry, music, medicine, divinity, geography, and navigation, while the College of Physicians sponsored lectures in medicine. Sports such as vaulting, tumbling, rope-climbing, and swimming were taught. Riding was practised by the Gentlemen of the Stable Royal at Charing Cross, and also on Clerkenwell Green and at Mile End. Shooting with ordnance could be learned in the Artillery Yard, while experts on fencing and martial arts offered private lessons.[35]

If, however, the established universities were Oxford and Cambridge, the contrast should not be overdrawn. Many students attended lectures and tutorials at university without taking a formal degree. Prominent among them were the sons of the gentry; their overall numbers among the student population rose during the sixteenth century, but by how much has been contested. The evidence points to an expansion of higher education across the board. It is possible that the sons of poorer gentry were actually losing ground to those of the more opulent, but even this is speculative. In both universities matriculants ranged from the sons of the nobility and gentry to those of husbandmen and college cooks. Indeed, attempts to plot the social origins of matriculants have proved inconclusive. Very roughly, the proportion of university students during Elizabeth's reign who came from noble and gentry families was between one-third and two-fifths. This figure may have increased marginally during the sixteenth century, but the sources are defective.[36]

The scale of the expansion of the universities is also disputed. Although admissions figures suggest that freshmen numbers soared from an average of 317 per annum in the 1550s to an average of 721 per annum in the 1590s, this is *trompe-l'œil*: whereas in Henry VIII's reign it was possible to be a student without leaving any trace in either university or college records, Elizabethan matriculation statutes enforced the registration of all students, including those not taking degrees. It is obvious that the creation of new university registers resulted in increased numbers of students being recorded as present in the universities. Also the expansion of colleges and halls at both universities during the sixteenth century marked a change from earlier practice, when Oxford and Cambridge were not essentially collegiate universities. As the century progressed, town-dwelling and loosely attached students were resettled and registered at undergraduate colleges where teaching was increasingly concentrated.[37]

William Wentworth advised his son the future earl of Strafford in 1604: 'Be directed in your studies by some learned judicial man of the university, methinks logic, philosophy, cosmography and especially histories yield excellent matter of instruction and judgement.'[38] The late-Elizabethan universities were renowned for their vitality and breadth of learning, since, if a student did not seek a degree, he might devise his own course of study as long as his tutor approved. But if intellectual curiosity was the crowning achievement of the Renaissance, the Reformation had devastated libraries. Protestant academics were not responsible for the loss of the monastic libraries in Henry VIII's reign, but they pillaged the university libraries in Edward's reign. At Oxford the manuscripts from Duke Humphrey's library were dispersed and the furniture sold. At Cambridge the main library was turned into a lecture room, and the illuminated manuscripts 'very sore cut and mangled for the limned letters and pictures'. The energy and generosity of Andrew Perne, master of Peterhouse, and Archbishop Parker ensured that 435 volumes were restored by 1574. Sir Thomas Bodley had also donated 2,500 volumes to Oxford by 1602. Yet the vandalism of the mid-Tudor decades was irreversible: the burning of Duke Humphrey's books testifies to a pervasive religious intolerance.[39]

The Court culture inherited by the Tudors fell within the Franco-Burgundian chivalric tradition. Although in England its potency waned during the fifteenth century, it remained the dominant influence in Europe. Decline in Lancastrian spectacle was largely the result of Henry VI's incapacity. Chivalric challenges, martial exploits, and dramatic displays were focused on the king as initiator and leader. If he lost control, their purpose was undermined. In the fourteenth century jousts and tournaments had been romanticized to make the fighting appear to follow an allegorical story: the element of real combat was sacrificed to the demands of display and 'disguising' (i.e. dressing the combatants in exotic costumes). Edward III's mistress, Alice Perrers, had appeared in 1374 as 'Lady of the Sun', while lords led ladies' horses by decorative bridles to the accompaniment of minstrelsy. But this fashion declined until revived by Edward IV, when the tournament effectively became a heroic costume drama. In the fullest sense, Edward IV reinstated the Burgundian cultural connection, an emphasis reinforced by his sister's marriage to Charles the Bold. In the jousts for Prince Edward in January 1477 two knights entered the lists aboard mobile pageants modelled upon those of France and Burgundy, and such allegorical pageant car entries were to become the cornerstone of the Elizabethan Court masque and Accession Day tilts.[40]

The indoor entertainments of Edward IV and Henry VII were known to contemporaries as 'disguisings': mimed costume dances performed without audience participation. They evolved out of medieval mummers' plays, but the one devised for the nuptials of Prince Arthur and Catherine of Aragon in November 1501 broke with tradition. It involved pageant cars in the shape of ships, arbours, lanterns, castles, mountains, and two-storey thrones, designed to carry up to twenty-four dancers. Thereafter scenic devices were applied to 'disguisings' and tournaments equally, transforming each into an enacted emblem. Henry VII and especially Henry VIII gave their plays and sporting events allegorical and dramatic significance. Their objectives were chiefly propagandist: Court displays provided a method of transmitting political, diplomatic, and religious messages as well as of glorifying the Tudor dynasty. Yet cultural genres developed in the process. In particular, 'disguisings' acquired new momentum as first speeches, and then 'communing' and dancing between masked actors and members of the audience, were added to the singing, dancing, and mechanical effects. By contrast, the dramatic development of the tournament was complete by 1500. Costumed combatants appeared in lists adorned with trees, ships, mountains, and heraldic beasts. Romanticized allegory became *de rigueur*. Yet tournaments and diplomatic triumphs could be staged to make statements about the monarch, as when Henry VIII appeared in the role of Hercules at the Field of Cloth of

Gold. They also emphasized the social order, since the most powerful subjects of the Crown performed feats of arms before their king.

Such spectacle was indeed vital in an age which valued visual symbols as a means of communication. Richard Moryson reminded Henry VIII that, 'Into the common people things sooner enter by the eyes, than by the ears: remembering more better that they see than that they hear.' His opponent Bishop Gardiner agreed: 'the pursuivant carrieth not on his breast the King's names written in such letters as a few can spell, but such as all can read, be they never so rude, being great known letters in images of three lions and three fleurs-de-lys, and other beasts holding those arms.' Both men were trying to justify their own rival versions of religious iconography, but their words applied equally to Court displays. Although 'disguisings' were private events which only invited persons might attend in addition to members of the Court, no restrictions were placed upon spectators at tournaments: everyone could watch provided they did not enter the lists or take seats reserved for their superiors. Also the Tudors stamped their dynastic symbols everywhere. Henry VII's stonemasons, carpenters, glaziers, painters, tapissiers, and book illustrators systematically propagated the Tudor 'cult'. The king commissioned a dynastic sequence from his tapissier, built a magnificent chapel at Westminster to house his tomb and that of Elizabeth of York, and adorned royal buildings with red roses, portcullises, dragons, leopards and other Tudor badges. Yet it was Henry VIII who first harnessed visual propaganda to the cause of advancing policy: anti-papal allegories were painted on the walls of his palaces and a mock battle staged on the Thames between 'royal' and 'papal' barges — the actors playing the 'pope' and 'cardinals' were severely ducked.[41]

A revival of tournaments organized by private individuals suggests that the chivalric tradition was re-established by the end of Henry VII's reign. The first Tudor king aimed to stimulate sufficient spectacle to augment his reputation at home and abroad. Whether he did so at minimum cost is arguable; by comparison, the young Henry VIII spared no expense: he swamped his Court with 'disguisings', 'maskings', interludes, dances, tournaments, and other sports at the main festivals — Christmas, New Year, Shrovetide, Easter, May Day, and

Midsummer. Despite a serious accident in the lists, he fought as chief challenger or chief answerer in every major tournament until 1527. Unlike his father, he participated to the full in 'disguisings', leading the procession of dancers and revellers. Huge pageant cars were built for indoor and outdoor use, and an entire temporary palace, banqueting house, tiltyard, and circular theatre were transported across the Channel for the meeting with Francis I.[42]

The celebrations for Anne Boleyn's coronation marked a minor watershed. After 1533 Henry jettisoned the glittering displays of his earlier career in favour of the anti-papal campaign. Although Court festivals were not abandoned, they became relatively tawdry affairs. True, the shift was partly due to Henry's increasing corpulence as well as to changes of personnel in the revels department. But the crucial reason was his new understanding of kingship gained from *Collectanea satis copiosa* and the Acts of Appeals and Supremacy. In 1533–4 the 'Renaissance prince' was transformed into the 'Reformation patriarch' — a new 'image' was therefore required. Hans Holbein's depictions of Henry as King Solomon and 'Imperial' Caesar set the required standard. Also the output of the printing press to an extent superseded public spectacle. The frontispiece to Cromwell's Great Bible of 1539 showed Henry distributing the word of God to his subjects, who loyally cried 'Vivat rex' and 'God save the King'. Throughout, the press campaign was masterminded by Cromwell. But the most original proposals came from Moryson, who suggested official sponsorship of plays setting forth 'the abomination and wickedness of the bishop of Rome, monks, friars, nuns, and such like', and argued the case for an annual public triumph to commemorate England's delivery from 'bondage' complete with bonfires, processions, feasts, and special prayers.[43]

In the reigns of Edward VI and Philip and Mary innumerable Court masques, plays, and 'pastimes' were staged — this despite the Crown's near-bankruptcy. True, costumes and scenery were kept to a minimum by Mary, who ordered materials to be retained and recycled. But the vast temporary banqueting houses built by the duke of Northumberland in Hyde Park and Marylebone for the entertainment of visiting French ambassadors evoked memories of Henry VIII's grandest follies. The sheer vitality of the Edwardian revels would indeed surprise, were it not abundantly clear that their purpose was to boost morale both within and outside the Court. On the other hand, full-scale tournaments were avoided by Edward's councillors: a disastrous experiment in May 1551 had left the king bewildered and his supporters badly mauled. Mary, too, eschewed tournaments. Probably this was because her husband declined to participate, though martial exercises were regularly practised at Court by both Englishmen and Spaniards.[44]

The Court displays of the first two decades of Elizabeth's reign were largely indoor entertainments. Anti-papal shows in January 1559 and January 1560 signalled the nature of the religious settlement. Otherwise, masques and 'disguisings' embellished topics such as Turks, Moors, Amazons, conquerors, fishermen, mariners, astronomers, barbarians, and Irishmen. Since the first Florentine masque had been on the theme of 'sellers of sweetmeats', Elizabeth's productions were consistent with tradition. Examples for which texts have survived were allegorical interludes or morality plays diversified with dumb shows and extended dancing. But none was printed; the Elizabethan masques were even more ephemeral than their Jacobean and Caroline counterparts. On the other hand, Court masques heightened interest in drama, since many were staged during the queen's summer progresses. It was Elizabeth's habit to take her entire Court on summer visits to the country houses of leading nobility and gentry. She visited Hampshire in 1560 and 1569, Huntingdonshire and Leicestershire in 1564, Oxford University in 1566, the Midlands in 1572, Bristol in 1574, Kenilworth in 1575, the southern counties in 1577, and East Anglia in 1578. On these occasions the host's house and grounds became allegorical terrain abounding in gods, nymphs, and wild-men, who eulogized the queen in prose or verse.[45]

It is well known that the sixteenth century saw major advances in vernacular dramatic art. Sidney was scathing in his *Apology for Poetry*, saying that the plays were 'neither right tragedies, nor right comedies, mingling kings and clowns'. If, however, Shakespeare must thereby be condemned, the matter is contentious. In fact, the great merit of Tudor drama was its variety and accessibility: common speech mingled freely with 'purer' medieval and Renaissance forms. In many towns the medieval morality cycles flourished as late as 1575. In the universities, classical drama was continuously performed from Henry VIII's reign onwards: the first meeting of the later privy councillors Stephen Gardiner, Thomas Wriothesley, and William Paget was as Cambridge students acting Plautus' *Miles gloriosus*. Also professional actors played in the banquet halls of Crown, nobility, and gentry. Lastly, choristers of the Chapel Royal and St Paul's Cathedral assumed leading roles in Elizabethan Court plays. Their popularity may have encouraged the formation of professional companies of actors, though it also brought drama under puritan scrutiny on grounds of paganism, idolatry, and moral corruption. Plays were criticized for drawing apprentices away from their regular employment, for being staged at Court (though not elsewhere) on Sundays as well as weekdays, and for casting boys in female roles. Critics saw no difference between stage plays, bear-baiting, bowling alleys, and prostitution. Yet it was the queen's patronage of choristers that caused particular offence to puritan consciences. 'Plays', griped one pamphleteer, 'will never be suppressed, while her majesty's unfledged minions flaunt it in silks and satins.'[46]

The most important Elizabethan companies of actors were those patronized by members of the Court. The earls of Leicester, Warwick, Sussex, Pembroke, Oxford, Essex, and Worcester had their own players, and Leicester's were the first to receive the royal licence in 1574. In 1585 he took them to the Netherlands, and on his return they went on tour. Elizabeth herself formed a company by poaching the stars of established troupes. An observer reported:

Comedians and stage-players of former time were very poor and ignorant in respect of these of this time: but being now grown very skilful and exquisite actors for all matters, they were entertained into the service of divers great lords: out of which companies there were twelve of the best chosen, and, at the request of Sir Francis Walsingham, they were sworn the queen's servants and were allowed wages and liveries as grooms of the chamber.[47]

Queen Elizabeth's Men performed at Court from Christmas 1583, and travelled the country on tour: the same plays given at Court were accessible to anyone within walking distance of the larger towns who could afford the admission price of a penny.

Next, Lord Admiral Howard formed a company led by the virtuoso Edward Alleyn and financed by Alleyn's stepfather, Philip Henslowe. Ben Jonson said of Alleyn, he 'gave so many Poets life'. His legendary renditions of the title roles of Marlowe's *Jew of Malta*, *Tamburlaine*, and *Dr Faustus* secured the dramatist's reputation. Yet the laurels were taken by the 'Lord Chamberlain's Men', a company reorganized by the first Lord Hunsdon in 1594. Acquiring the services of William Kemp, Richard Burbage, and William Shakespeare, Hunsdon formed a troupe which later passed under James I's patronage. Among Shakespeare's plays written and performed before 1603 were *Titus Andronicus*, *The Taming of the Shrew*, *Love's Labour's Lost*, *Romeo and Juliet*, *Two Gentlemen of Verona*, *Merchant of Venice*, *Richard II*, *Henry IV*, *Henry V*, *Hamlet*, and *Twelfth Night*. Elizabeth attended a performance of *A Comedy of Errors* with Essex, and is said to have been guest of honour at the first production of *A Midsummer Night's Dream* staged for the earl of Derby's marriage to Burghley's granddaughter, Lady Elizabeth Vere. When Lord Hunsdon died, the company passed to his son George (July 1596), by which time it was so successful it had little incentive to travel on tour.[48]

The real breakthrough was the establishment of permanent theatres in London. Despite puritan attacks and other opposition on grounds of nuisance, overcrowding, the alleged link between plays and petty crime, and fear of contagion of plague, the London authorities were persuaded to license 'game' or 'play' houses that doubled as amphitheatres for playgoing and bull- or bear-baiting. The first was named the 'Theatre' and was built in 1577. Thereafter, at least six more opened with four regular companies of players giving daily performances save on Sundays, in Lent, and during plague epidemics. In particular, Burbage and his partners built the first Globe Theatre on the Bankside in Southwark (1599). This was the first playhouse erected in England by professional actors, and designed for their own exclusive use. Described by Jonson as 'the glory of the Bank', it was a major advance on the multipurpose gamehouses. Shakespeare partly owned this theatre, and its destruction by fire in June 1613 after a stage cannon exploded during a performance of *Henry VIII* effectively ended his career.[49]

The development of drama was paralleled by the revival of the tournament, for Elizabethan Court culture entered a highly intense phase in the 1570s. The context was the ideological polarization of European politics that threatened war and Elizabeth's security. The crucial political issue became that of national unity, and the queen's Accession Day, 17 November, was recognized as a festival for the whole country, with bell-ringing, bonfires, firing of guns, martial sports, and prayers. In a sense Moryson's proposal to Henry VIII was accepted: the themes blended by the Accession Day festivities were loyalty, patriotism, and anti-Catholicism. Yet a group of courtiers took this process a stage further, particularly Sir Henry Lee (master of the armoury from 1580), who invented for himself the office of queen's champion of the tilts. He revitalized and transmuted the tradition of Burgundian chivalry reinstated by Edward IV, Henry VII, and Henry VIII, delving into the mists of Arthurian romance to 'discover' a variety of chivalry with a militant Protestant face. To graft this Protestant chivalric ethic on to the 'cult' of Elizabeth as Gloriana and Astraea was thereafter straightforward, and the allegorical model that resulted formed the basis of the Accession Day tilts.[50]

By 1581 Lee had turned these tilts into a dazzling annual spectacle that eclipsed even Henry VIII's Court festivals. The evidence is patchy, but the general pattern was described by a visiting German, Lupold von Wedel, who attended in 1584. According to his account, Elizabeth and her gentlewomen took their seats in the tilt gallery at Whitehall at twelve noon promptly. The event was open to the public, and large stands adjacent to the lists accommodated several thousand spectators — men, women, and children. When the queen was seated, the costumed 'knights' entered the lists in pairs inside pageant cars or on horseback. Their servants and horses wore 'disguises' appropriate to the theme of the entry — equipment for the tournament was said to have cost each competitor several hundred pounds. As each knight approached the barrier (i.e. the rail running down the centre of the lists), he halted beneath the tilt gallery while his squire explained to the queen his allegorical identity in prose or verse. Thereafter, the squire in the name of his lord presented the queen with a pageant shield painted with the knight's *impresa* (i.e. the device he bore for the tournament). These formalities completed, the tournament commenced, the proceedings lasting until dusk.[51]

The jousts themselves were the least important part of the spectacle. Francis Bacon wrote:

the glories [of jousts and tournaments] are chiefly in the chariots, wherein the challengers make their entry, especially if they be drawn with strange beasts, as lions, bears, camels, and the like; or, in the devices of their entrance, or in bravery [i.e. show] of their liveries, or in the goodly furniture of their horses and armour.[52]

Some pageant entries were so elaborate that they required complicated stage-management as well as the services of scholars, actors, and musicians to compose and perform the necessary speeches. It even became customary to provide spectators with programmes containing copies of the verses and devices. Yet displays were meant to be amusing as well as instructive. An autobiographical allusion was mandatory, though this required careful handling. Essex only irritated Elizabeth in 1595 with his high-flown discourse on the merits of serving the queen. She tartly remarked 'that if she had thought there had been so much said of her, she would not have been there that night; and so went to bed'. The earl also failed dismally in his attempt to use an entry as an 'Unknown Knight' in 1600 as a means to recover royal favour.[53]

The Protestant ethos of the Accession Day tilts is documented by surviving devices and speeches. They adapted chivalric tradition to create the legend of Elizabeth as the Vestal Virgin of the Reformed Religion, worshipped by her knights on the occasion of a new 'quasi-religious' festival. A speech of the 'Hermit of Woodstock' suggested that advance notice of the Accession Day tilts was given by ministers from the pulpits of parish churches. Certainly preachers claimed that 17 November was a holiday 'which passed all the Pope's holidays'. Literary scholars likewise link Accession Day to the Protestant chivalric romance of Spenser's *The Faerie Queene* and Sidney's *Arcadia*. Thus Spenser's Sir Guyon said of Gloriana:

> An yearly solemn feast she wonts to make,
> The day that first doth lead the year around,
> To which all knights of worth and courage bold,
> Resort, to hear of strange adventures to be told.
>
> (*Faerie Queene*, Bk. II, canto 2, xlii. 6–9)

In Sidney's *Arcadia* the ceremonial jousts were held annually on the anniversary of the marriage day of the Iberian queen. When, therefore, the 'Message of the Damsel of the Queen of the Fairies' was first delivered on behalf of an 'Enchanted Knight' in the tiltyard one Accession Day, fact and fantasy merged. The myth of the Fairy Queen was born, for the 'Damsel' announced that many knights were gathered 'not far from hence' to show their prowess in the Virgin's honour.[54]

Political symbolism was also central to Elizabethan painting. As European opinion polarized during the 1570s, images of the Virgin Queen multiplied in the shape of engravings, woodcuts, medals, and badges. The 'cult' of Elizabeth was particularly propagated after 1586, when the queen distributed portrait miniatures of herself, so that recipients might wear her image as a badge of loyalty or cherish it as a sign of a special favour. Henry VIII had similarly exploited the royal image. Hans Holbein had created a vast dynastic wall-painting for the privy chamber at Whitehall that was said to make men tremble long after the king's death. Miniatures were commissioned, too, from artists trained in the manuscript workshops of Ghent and Bruges, chiefly members of the Hornebolte and Benninck families. (It was Lucas Hornebolte who had taught Holbein the 'secret art' of the miniature.) After Hornebolte's death Mary and Elizabeth patronized Levina Teerlinc (*née* Benninck), who served at Court as an artist and gentlewoman of the privy chamber. Her skill in execution could not match her flair and inventiveness in design, but she was responsible for the first example of an allegorical miniature and taught the craft to Nicholas Hilliard (1547–1619), who became the leading Elizabethan miniaturist.[55]

Despite Henry VIII's commissions, the miniature originally belonged to the closet: it recorded what Hilliard in his *Treatise Concerning the Art of Limning* called the 'lovely graces, witty smilings, and these stolen glances which suddenly like lightning pass and another countenance taketh place'. Intimacy was the key to the style, combined with a wealth of emblematic allusion that added depth to the mirror-like image. Hilliard's work was technically ravishing: he used gold as a metal, burnishing it 'with a pretty little tooth of some ferret or stoat or other wild little beast'. Likewise his method of simulating jewels was utterly convincing. In every respect he was a perfectionist, even insisting on wearing silk clothes for painting, in order to avoid the slightest impregnation of dust.[56]

Elizabeth kept her own collection of miniatures wrapped in paper in a cabinet in her bedchamber. Sir James Melville was shown them during a private interview in 1564. He reported: 'Upon the first that she took up was written, "My Lord's picture". I held the candle, and pressed to see the picture so named. She seemed loath to let me see it; yet my importunity prevailed for a sight thereof, and found it to be the Earl of Leicester's picture.' Whereas, however, Teerlinc's miniatures of the 1560s were tokens of love or courtly dalliance, by 1590 Hilliard and his studio were mass-manufacturing political icons. Following Elizabeth's disastrous encounter with the brilliant French immigrant artist Isaac Oliver (c.1560–1617), whose mistake as a miniaturist was to paint the queen as he saw her, Hilliard created an idealized image of Elizabeth as a young woman which won official approval. This so-called 'Mask of Youth' bore no relationship to the ageing queen's true likeness, but, when set against an allegorical overlay, made the perfect image for propaganda purposes.[57]

So during her final decade it became part of the 'cult' of Gloriana for courtiers to 'venerate' the queen's image, almost as pre-Reformation Catholics had venerated the Virgin Mary. Lord Zouche told Robert Cecil in 1598 that he held the 'Mask of Youth' to be the fairest picture in Europe. Some recipients wore their miniatures pinned to their dress in 'picture boxes', while others had them set in lockets or jewels. A locket adorned with rubies and diamonds celebrating Elizabeth as the 'Star of Britain' has survived. By contrast the famous Heneage or 'Armada' Jewel unfolded in layers. Made of enamelled gold set with diamonds and rubies, the front exterior depicted Elizabeth as queen and 'empress' by means of a Roman imperial profile which was also struck as a medal, and the back adopted a Noah's Ark device to illustrate her as supreme governor of the church and 'Defender of the Faith'. When opened the locket displayed the 'Mask of Youth' image, while on the reverse of the lid was a red rose, badge of the Tudor dynasty and emblem of Venus, goddess of love and beauty.[58]

Sidney wrote in his *Apology for Poetry* that poetry is 'a speaking picture'. Poetry and painting were closely linked, but, following Aristotle's *Poetics*, painting was held to be an inferior art in Tudor England since it dealt only with outward appearances.[59] True, Elyot devoted a chapter of *The Book Named the Governor* to the proposition 'that it is commendable in a gentleman to paint and carve exactly, if nature thereto doth induce him'. But he assured his readers, 'I intend not, by these examples, to make of a prince or nobleman's son a common painter or carver.' In particular, a gentleman should paint or carve 'but as a secret pastime'. Once attained these arts should 'be never much exercised'.[60] Whether or not this snobbish attitude explains the paucity of easel paintings, Henrician taste ranked tapestries above paintings in its scale of values: the patronage of Holbein by Thomas More, Thomas Cromwell, and Henry VIII was exceptional. Moreover, Elizabethan taste rejected the assumptions and accomplishments of European art: the Mannerist experiments of Isaac Oliver were disliked before 1603. There was no market, in any case, for anything but portraits, and the majority of surviving full-length examples were mass-produced images designed to hang in Elizabethan and Jacobean long galleries.[61]

Architecture was the field where Gloriana's impact was least conspicuous. Between Henry VIII's death and 1603, not a single new palace was constructed or acquired. Some alterations and redecorations were undertaken: Elizabeth erected banqueting houses at Greenwich and on the terraces at Whitehall and Windsor, but otherwise few changes were made. Speaking through the mouth of Lord Keeper Bacon, she told Parliament in 1571 that she did not require 'gorgeous sumptuous superfluous buildings'. Also her annual progresses shifted the responsibility for housing the Court during the summer on to her subjects. In the wider sense that courtiers therefore rivalled each other to build magnificent houses for her entertainment, she exercised residual influence on architecture. But the aesthetic initiative passed to the nobility and gentry: the finest examples of Elizabethan style were Burghley's house at Theobalds, Leicester's at Kenilworth Castle, Hatton's at Holdenby, Sir John Thynne's at Longleat, Sir Francis Willoughby's at Wollaton, and the Countess of Shrewsbury's at Hardwick.[62]

Size and symmetry were especially valued in Elizabethan and Jacobean architecture. Great houses were seen as 'lanterns': light inside, glittering outside. Hardwick Hall, which Robert Smythson built in 1591–7, was universally praised for these qualities, as well as for its square towers and neo-Gothic staircases. When Burghley visited Holdenby, he admired its symmetry and the 'stately ascent' from the great hall to the well-lit apartments above. Again, light and space were emphasized by the observer of Kenilworth Castle:

Every room so spacious, so well belighted, and so high roofed within; so seemly to sight by due proportion without; in day time, on every side so glittering by glass; at nights, by continual brightness of candle, fire and torchlight, transparent through the lightsome windows, as it were the Egyptian Pharaohs relucent unto all the Alexandrian coast; or else . . . thus radiant as though Phoebus for his ease would rest him in the Castle, and not every night so travel down unto the Antipodes.[63]

Equally important were rising standards of comfort. Before the Reformation property owners had endowed their churches; afterwards they improved their houses. Probate inventories suggest that, whereas in Henry VIII's reign the average size of the Tudor house was three rooms, between 1570 and 1603 it became four or five. In the latter part of Elizabeth's reign, yeomen might have six, seven, or eight rooms, while husbandmen might aspire to two or three, rather than the one-room cottages usual in 1500. Richer farmers would build a chamber above the hall, replacing the open hearth with a fireplace and chimney. Poorer people favoured ground-floor extensions, adding a kitchen or second bedchamber to their cottages. Kitchens were often separate buildings to reduce the risk of fire: a typical late-Elizabethan farmhouse was described as 'one dwelling house of three bays, one barn of three bays, one kitchen of one bay'. Brick chimneys became a familiar feature of Elizabethan mansions, signalling the arrival of kitchen and service quarters within the main house, either in a wing or semi-basement. By 1600 basement services were frequently found in town houses built on restricted sites. Lastly, provision of water supplies and improved sanitary arrangements reflected the Renaissance concern with private and public health. In the case of town houses, owners would go to considerable lengths to solve drainage problems, often paying a cash composition to the civic authorities, but sometimes performing some service for the town at Court or at Westminster in return for unlimited water or drainage.[64]

More than medieval castles and manor houses, Elizabethan mansions were designed with privacy in mind. The great hall was not abandoned, but the family used it as an eating place only on rare occasions. Instead they withdrew to the parlour and great chamber, while their servants lived in turrets or attics and continued to eat in the hall. The distinction between parlour and great chamber was that the former was for domestic use and the latter for entertaining. Parlours were situated on the ground floor: the family lived and relaxed there, and took informal meals in a dining parlour. The formal or 'state' rooms were on the first floor, usually comprising a great chamber, a withdrawing-chamber, one or more bedchambers, and a long gallery. This was the standard arrangement of rooms by 1560, though the 'long gallery' was an architectural novelty. Intended for exercise, recreation, and private conversation, Elizabethan examples were modelled on earlier royal ones. The first galleries had been added by Henry VII to his palaces of Westminster, Richmond, and Windsor, and Henry VIII had installed them at New Hall and Bridewell by 1522. But the most significant influence came from Wolsey. The galleries he built at Hampton Court and Whitehall 'were fair, both large and long, to walk in them when that it liked [him] best'. In fact, Thomas More told Cromwell in a letter that it was when walking privately in the Hampton Court gallery with Henry VIII that he had first learned of the plan to divorce Catherine of Aragon. By 1540 the gallery had been imitated at leading courtiers' houses. By the middle of Elizabeth's reign it was considered a matter of social prestige to possess one, though a number had reverted to being linen stores or 'junk rooms' by the 1630s.[65]

THE TUDOR *FIN DE SIÈCLE*

THE death of Leicester in September 1588 was the first of several events that steadily transformed the membership and profile of the Elizabethan establishment, giving it a feeling of downhill. Mildmay died in 1589, Walsingham and the earl of Warwick in 1590, and Hatton in 1591. Sir Walter Ralegh seemed likely to become Elizabeth's third favourite: despite her jest that 'she had rather see him hanged than equal him with [Hatton] or that the world should think she did so', he was granted most of the offices in the south-west vacated by the death of the second earl of Bedford, as well as lucrative monopolies and estates in the east Midlands and Ireland. As captain of the guard, he had regular access to Elizabeth, gaining influence to the point where more experienced courtiers felt threatened. But she barred him entry to the Privy Council, and he was eclipsed when she discovered that he had secretly married Elizabeth Throckmorton, one of her maids of honour. True, he hoped to avoid disgrace by success in a privateering voyage to the Azores, but he was recalled and sent to the Tower (July 1592). Although released when his fleet captured the *Madre de Dios*, he remained under a cloud. The Virgin Queen held herself to be *in loco parentis* to her maids, but her sexual jealousy was widely suspected.[1]

Burghley meanwhile dominated the Privy Council. He exploited his position to ensure that the former advocates of an 'interventionist' foreign policy (Leicester, Walsingham, Warwick) were replaced by more cautious strategists, and thereby continued the policy he had begun when persuading the queen to prefer John Whitgift, Lord Cobham, and Lord Buckhurst to Leicester's nominees in 1586.[2] So Sir Thomas Heneage, John Fortescue, Robert Cecil, and Sir John Puckering (lord keeper of the great seal) were chosen as new privy councillors. Yet it was Elizabeth's loyalty to her old servants and desire to restrict membership of the 'inner ring' to a select group of Court intimates that brought Heneage and Fortescue to the fore.

Heneage (d. 1595) was successively gentleman of the privy chamber, treasurer of the chamber, vice-chamberlain, and chancellor of the duchy of Lancaster: it took him twenty-six years to win a place in the 'inner ring' as an adviser on intelligence and diplomatic affairs.[3] By comparison, Fortescue's career began earlier but took even longer to reach fruition. A member of Elizabeth's household by 1555, he was appointed keeper of the wardrobe in 1559, but had to wait until Mildmay's death to secure office as chancellor of the exchequer and under-treasurer.[4]

Although Elizabeth favoured Burghley's younger son, Robert Cecil, for his talent and support for her defensive war strategy, she advanced him out of respect for his father, who lobbied her vigorously. She knighted him when she visited Burghley's house at Theobalds in Hertfordshire (May 1591).[5] The following August he was admitted to the Privy Council at the age of twenty-eight, making him the second youngest entrant of the reign.[6] He joined a board of office-holders while holding no office; he had sat as an MP only since 1584. Of course, he hoped for Walsingham's secretaryship. Elizabeth, however, tended to leave important posts vacant for a time, usually to emphasize her prerogative, but in the last years of her reign as much to avoid choosing between the protégés of competing factions. (By 1597 membership of the Privy Council had shrunk to eleven, rising only slightly by the end of 1601 to thirteen.) So the secretaryship remained unfilled, and was contested between the Cecils and Robert Devereux, second earl of Essex, who wanted Davison reinstated. Burghley technically resumed the duties he had himself performed until 1572, but in practice he delegated them to his son. This way both exercised power while Robert made himself indispensable; Thomas Wilkes was essentially correct when he claimed that Cecil's privy councillorship 'will be a bar to the choice of any secretary during the life of his father'.[7] In fact, Cecil finally secured the coveted post after Essex had sailed on his Cadiz expedition in 1596, when Burghley's legs and hands were almost crippled and he could write only with the utmost difficulty.

Inevitably Burghley's monopolistic tendencies provoked resentment. It can be argued that the Cecils in the 1590s surrounded themselves with second-rate men on whom they could rely, and on whom they bestowed office so that no rival

might challenge their ascendancy. Most of their officials were
'pen-clerks': contemporaries regarded their system as corrupt,
because it sacrificed the public to the private interest. Burghley
may perhaps be excused on grounds of age, but few would claim
that Robert Cecil was a man of integrity. He enjoyed intrigue
as well as wealth and power; he liked secrecy, and preferred to
join rather than restrain the scramble for profits;[8] and the father
was reviled for the ambition of his son. Spenser (who believed
that Walsingham alone could have secured him Court patronage
in the face of Burghley's opposition) published an attack on him
as thinly veiled as anything written against Wolsey by John
Skelton:

> O grief of griefs, O gall of all good hearts,
> To see that virtue should despisèd be
> Of him, that first was raised for virtuous parts,
> And now broad spreading like an agèd tree,
> Lets none shoot up, that nigh him planted be.[9]
>
> (*The Ruins of Time*, 449–53)

Since Plato, Aristotle, and Cicero had all argued that ministers
should be the most virtuous men, to say that Burghley despised
virtue was defamatory. If John Weever can be believed, he was
angry enough to have the poem censored.[10]

It was, however, the dazzling but paranoid Essex, Elizabeth's
third and last favourite, who self-consciously rivalled the Cecils
for patronage and power. By the late 1590s their feud had
escalated into a factional battle to control her policy. The
atmosphere at Court deteriorated; for the first time in her reign
the queen was on the sidelines. Always indecisive, she
increasingly brooded as her mind and body aged, though she
remained as vain as ever. Ambassadors noticed her extravagant
attire and low-cut dresses, yet she could barely ride, she wore
a wig, her teeth were bad, and she placed a perfumed silk
handkerchief in her mouth before receiving visitors. In her Privy
Council a gouty, irritable eminence and his physically puny son
locked horns with an arrogant Adonis—for, whereas Robert
Cecil suffered from a deformed spine and diminutive height—
Elizabeth called him her 'little elf'—Essex was tall and well-
proportioned. His lofty bearing and aristocratic disposition were
legendary: he was as long on lineage as he was short of cash.

But his temperament was mercurial: 'full of humours', impatient, capricious, hotheaded, impulsive, baroque. Francis Bacon described him as 'a man of nature not to be ruled'. He was 'of an estate not grounded to his greatness; of a popular reputation; of a military dependence'. The last two were undesirable: Essex took the chivalric model of Sir Philip Sidney to excess, fighting duels, cultivating a military clientele, and posturing as a hero. He overstepped the mark when he deliberately courted public opinion—a fatal trait that fed his ambition, as well as his illusions and the queen's mistrust.[11]

Yet it was an unequal contest. When Elizabeth realized that her favourite sought to rule her Court, she granted Robert Cecil an authority not previously allowed to any other councillor. Cecil had the queen's ear throughout, while from July 1598 Essex was forbidden the royal presence.[12] Indeed, Essex's brashness and presumption consistently won him enemies: when disgraced, he had only himself to blame. The battle for control was, however, fought as single-mindedly as anything since the Court struggle after Wolsey's fall. The reason was that Essex pursued ideology as much as patronage. He assumed the militant Protestant mantle of Leicester, Walsingham, and the Sidneys. His mother was the daughter of Sir Francis Knollys, who had married Leicester as her second husband, while he himself married Walsingham's daughter, Frances, who was Philip Sidney's widow. Essex's marriage was frowned on by Elizabeth: the earl risked his career. But when he consented that his wife should live 'very retired in her mother's house', he recovered royal favour. In 1587 he had succeeded Leicester as master of the horse and was said in 1591 to be 'like enough, if he had a few more years, to carry Leicester's credit and sway'.[13] When admitted to the Privy Council in 1593, he championed an offensive strategy, urging land campaigns in Europe. He also resumed Leicester's secret correspondence with James VI of Scotland in an effort to sponsor a Protestant coalition. But he lacked Leicester's private patronage, as well as failing to win royal patronage for his followers, the real test of a faction leader's credibility. His supporters increasingly complained that he could get anything for himself but nothing for his friends, though Essex's own view in the darkening weeks before his departure for Ireland was that he could do neither.[14]

The Essex and Cecil factions dominated the political scene until Essex's rebellion and execution in February 1601. Thereafter, Sir Walter Ralegh and Henry Brooke, eighth Lord Cobham, formed the Durham House set which led them finally into conspiracy against the succession of James I. At Court Burghley's prominent allies included Charles, second Lord Howard of Effingham (created earl of Nottingham, 1597); Lord Buckhurst, Leicester's former enemy; and Sir John Stanhope (treasurer of the chamber, 1596–1618; vice-chamberlain, 1601–16). When Burghley died in August 1598, these heavyweights transferred their support to Robert Cecil. Stanhope was admitted to the Privy Council after the overthrow of Essex. The anti-Essex coalition was led by Cecil, Nottingham, Cobham (Cecil's brother-in-law), and Ralegh, who were united upon a primarily maritime war strategy as well as by personal enmity to Essex. The appointment of Thomas Cecil (second Lord Burghley, Robert's half-brother) as president of the Council of the North was significant, because it strengthened the group's military potential (August 1599). Lastly, three leading privy councillors and courtiers — Sir Thomas Heneage, John Fortescue, and George, second Lord Hunsdon (admitted to the Privy Council, 1597; lord chamberlain, 1597–1603) — gravitated towards Cecil.[15]

Of Essex's faction, the Sidney circle formed the coherent core: Sir Robert Sidney (younger brother of Sir Philip); Penelope, Lady Rich (Essex's sister and the 'Stella' of Sir Philip's sonnets); Roger Manners, earl of Rutland (Sir Philip's son-in-law); and Sir Edward Dyer. Admirers who joined the rebellion included Henry Wriothesley, earl of Southampton; Edward Russell, earl of Bedford; William, Lord Sandes; William Parker, Lord Monteagle; Edward, Lord Cromwell; Sir Charles Danvers; and Sir Christopher Blount. More tenuously linked to Essex were Whitgift; Sir Thomas Egerton; Robert Radcliffe, fifth earl of Sussex; Charles Blount, Lord Mountjoy; Lord Henry Howard; and John, Lord Lumley. But Lord Mountjoy, Robert Sidney, and Lord Henry Howard, particularly, kept lines open to Cecil, and each of these highly influential figures refused to countenance overt revolt. When pushed to a choice, their loyalty to the Crown threw the divided counsels and moral disarray of Essex's faction into sharp focus. Essex had support at the Council board only from his uncle Sir William Knollys (comptroller of the household, 1596–1602; treasurer of the household, 1602–16), and from the gallant Roger, Lord North—both were military men admitted to the Privy Council in August 1596. But even Knollys was a somewhat equivocal ally, who was spared a final conflict of loyalties by being taken hostage by Essex when sent to parley with him at the start of the revolt.[16]

Shortly after Robert Cecil was admitted to the Privy Council, Essex drew into his circle the Bacon brothers, Francis and Anthony, Burghley's nephews. Anthony (b. 1558) had recently returned from thirteen years' service abroad in Walsingham's intelligence corps. Francis (b. 1561) was among the most gifted scholars of the Renaissance, a bencher of Gray's Inn who made little effort to practise law and may not have pleaded in court before 1594, but who was a member of every Elizabethan House of Commons after 1584. He had acted as Robert Cecil's private secretary, and Burghley had secured for him the appointment in reversion of the lucrative clerkship of the court of star chamber (1589). But neither brother regarded this as adequate. It was Francis who first turned to Essex; he later wrote: 'I held at that time my lord [Essex] to be the fittest instrument to do good to the state; and therefore I applied myself to him in a manner which I think happeneth rarely among men.' Then Francis introduced his brother to the earl: Anthony was soon among the most committed Essexians.[17]

Anthony was a valuable asset because his connections, especially in France, enabled him to organize an intelligence service for Essex which kept him as well informed of developments abroad as the Cecils. He recruited Thomas Phillips, formerly Walsingham's chief clerk and spymaster, who under cover of his post as a London customs official supplied Essex with news. In fact, the Bacons were canny; their ploy was that Essex (using his position as master of the horse) should feed the intelligence gleaned from Phillips direct to Elizabeth at Court, thereby validating the earl's claim to succeed to Walsingham's secretaryship. It was a subtle attack on the Cecils at the heart of their power, and it worked to the extent that Elizabeth did admit Essex to the Privy Council, though her decision may have owed as much to her habit of balancing points of view.[18]

Yet Essex rejected Francis Bacon's shrewd advice to exchange his military affiliation for a civilian one in tune with majority opinion in the Privy Council. While his struggle with the Cecils largely centred on rivalry for control of patronage and policy, a vital dimension was Essex's innate preference for military action, as against that of the Cecils for peaceful (and legal) civilian rule. In fact, the earl would confidently have extended to England during Elizabeth's war years — and perhaps longer — methods of government more readily adopted in Ireland: a direct (i.e. violent) approach to administration through resort to martial law, arbitrary taxation, and military rather than civil patronage. The contrast should not be overdrawn. Essex moved on both military and civilian fronts at once, persuading Elizabeth's last two keepers of the great seal, Puckering (1592–6) and Egerton (1596–1603), to include his clients in the commission of the peace and seeking their advancement in the order of precedence prevailing in the commission. But he believed that a war should be administered by generals not civilians, and he equated Bacon's opinion with legal guile, telling him it was his 'robe' and not his mind that spoke. In fact, Essex saw himself as a 'man of arms', bound by the nobility's code of honour and rules of chivalry, which were alien to common law. He thought common law stood by comparison for ease, pleasure, profit, and pedantry.[19]

So Essex ventilated the French antithesis between *noblesse d'épée* and *noblesse de robe*. Whereas in France it was the military nobility who dominated the royal council and ruled the provinces as governors, in England it was the civil magistracy. But it was the French Crown which held the balance between 'sword' and 'gown', and it is not too bold to say that Essex's ultimate objective in his contest with the Cecils was to change the balance in England. Hence his frequent allusions to his rights under the 'law of nature', by which he meant his belief in the nobility's right to use violence in defence of honour and pursuit of 'legitimate' political ends. In this respect the introduction on a permanent basis of the lieutenancy system in 1585 helped the earl, who succeeded in recruiting over twelve deputy lieutenants from counties as far apart as Staffordshire, Sussex, and Worcestershire to his cause. In addition, he enjoyed the support of colonels, captains, and other officers of the military and naval expeditions in which he had held commands. Lastly, he was admired by economically declining families of ancient lineage who saw their long-established place in provincial hierarchies being challenged by *parvenu* families rising on the profits of careers in the law, as courtiers, or in the City of London.[20]

If, however, the validity of the 'law of nature' was admitted by the European civil law, it was unknown to English common law. Since the late fifteenth century councillors had eschewed the 'politics of violence' except in Ireland. But if Essex's rebellion had succeeded, things might have been very different. The crucial issues of Crown–subject relations — the legality of forced loans, arbitrary taxation, billeting, and martial law — could have been decided unequivocally in favour of the Crown. A successful Essex might have raised an army in 1601 to purge his opponents from the counties as well as from the Court. In fact, he asked his successor in the government of Ireland, Lord Mountjoy, to divert half his army towards an invasion of England beginning with a landing in Wales. Mountjoy replied that, while he was willing to help enforce the premature succession of James VI of Scotland, he would not satisfy Essex's 'private ambition'.[21] Moreover, though Essex failed and the succession of James I was peaceful, the key debate during his son's reign still became the relationship of politics and property to law and the sword. Indeed, if Charles I's favourite, the duke of Buckingham, is seen as the heir of Essex, the 'pettifogging' behaviour of parliamentary lawyers which seemed almost purposefully designed to prevent Charles from fighting a successful war in the 1620s becomes comprehensible.

Essex, however, could not consolidate his power by conventional means, failing to obtain either the post of attorney-general or that of solicitor-general for Francis Bacon. True, he increased his personal hold on Elizabeth in 1594 by detecting the alleged plot of her Portuguese physician, Dr Roderigo Lopez, to poison her. But, as with the Parry plot of 1585, the issue turned on whether an *agent provocateur* had turned traitor in the end, for Lopez had long been used by Walsingham and Burghley to communicate with Spanish spies. In fact, his real offence may only have been to make money out of Philip II, in which case Essex merely manipulated him to discredit Burghley's intelligence machine and exalt his own. Since the Lopez 'plot' also lacks corroboration from Spanish sources, its long-term importance may have been to awaken Robert Cecil to the value of detecting 'conspiracy' at the crucial political moment—a technique he arguably applied to the Gunpowder plot of 1605.[22]

By October 1596 Francis Bacon was urging Essex to ingratiate himself with the queen; to shun military ambition; to avoid giving the impression that he was self-opinionated; to seek the highest civilian offices of state; to conceal his true emotions; and to play the courtier by the existing rules. He made some effort to comply, and six months later was on relatively good terms with the Cecils and Ralegh. When, however, Lord Howard of Effingham was promoted earl of Nottingham at Burghley's suggestion in October 1597, Essex claimed that he was 'dishonoured'—he meant that, by virtue of Henry VIII's Act of Precedence, Howard as lord admiral and a baron had formerly sat in the Privy Council and House of Lords below Essex, but now as lord admiral and an earl ranked above him. To satisfy his 'honour', Essex challenged Nottingham or any of his sons to a duel. And Elizabeth, who had not intended to snub Essex, somewhat grudgingly took his side in the dispute. So, when secret attempts to induce Nottingham to forego his due precedence failed, she created Essex earl marshal (December 1597), an office which by the Act of Precedence had seniority over the admiral and which had fallen vacant seven years before upon the death of the earl of Shrewsbury.[23]

Yet Essex's sexual conquests at Court soon attracted gossip and Elizabeth's frigid rebuke. Next, disputes in the Privy Council over whether England should negotiate to end the war following the Franco-Spanish treaty of Vervins or continue to support the Dutch revolt found Essex and the Cecilians on opposite sides. Burghley confronted the earl with a text from the Psalms, 'The bloodthirsty and deceitful men shall not live out half their days.'[24] When Essex then appealed to public opinion outside the Council chamber, he touched the queen on her most sensitive nerve. But the crunch came in July 1598 during discussion of the appointment of a successor to Lord Burgh as lord deputy in Ireland. Elizabeth proposed Sir William Knollys, but Essex countered by recommending that a Cecilian, Sir George Carew, be sent. In a furious exchange, Essex turned his back on the queen, who immediately recalled him and hit him across the face, telling him to 'go and be hanged'. By striking him before witnesses, Elizabeth subjected Essex to the unbearable dishonour that by convention a woman's blow entailed.[25] He replied by clasping his sword, said he had been done 'an intolerable wrong', and used other offensive words until compelled to withdraw by other councillors who interposed themselves between the combatants.

Thereafter, Sir William Knollys and Sir Thomas Egerton urged Essex to abandon his 'careless humour', for the political context was fluid. In the same month as Elizabeth and the earl quarrelled, the queen sat at Burghley's bedside and fed him with a spoon. The veteran minister's final illness had begun; he died on 4 August and was accorded a state funeral. At the ceremony held in Westminster Abbey, Essex showed 'the heaviest countenance of the company'. But the Cecil–Essex rivalry had reached its climax at just the moment when Essex was forbidden to enter the queen's presence on account of his behaviour, which was fatal to his role as a faction leader. Egerton told him: 'In this course you hold, if you had enemies, you do that for them which they could never do for themselves.' He further warned him that obedience to his sovereign was 'a duty not imposed upon you by nature and policy only, but by religious and sacred bonds: wherein the divine majesty of Almighty God hath by the rule of Christianity obliged you'.[26] Essex replied that obedience could not be demanded beyond the bounds of honour. He repudiated unconditional religious obligation with the challenging words, 'What, cannot princes err? Cannot subjects receive wrong? Is an earthly power infinite?'[27] Yet Egerton's hint was well-founded. Essex had given his opponents the chance of levelling the charge of atheism against him by his allusions to his rights under the 'law of nature', his emphasis on his 'honour', and his obsession with secular political ends. It could be made to appear that he denied the divine authority of kingship and quasi-sacerdotal role of Elizabeth as supreme governor of the church.

When Essex apologized to the queen in October, a fragile reconciliation was effected. But the earl was humbled as much by his debts as his loyalty. When he sought, and finally obtained, appointment as queen's lieutenant in Ireland, he knew that he wagered his future on success (25 March 1599). His mission was the talk of London: *The Fortunate Farewell* by Thomas Churchyard compared him to Publius Cornelius Scipio, whose military genius

defeated Hannibal at the battle of Zama.[28] While he was gone,
the Essexians sought to capitalize on their leader's heroic image,
a propaganda effort reflected in Shakespeare's *Henry V*, where
the chorus to the fifth act promised Essex a 'Roman' triumph
on his return like that given to Henry V after Agincourt:

> Were now the general of our gracious empress,
> As in good time he may, from Ireland coming,
> Bringing rebellion broached on his sword,
> How many would the peaceful city quit
> To welcome him!

Essex's failure in Ireland therefore sealed his fate. When in
September 1599 he deserted his post, hastened to Court to justify
himself, and burst unannounced into Elizabeth's bedchamber
at ten o'clock in the morning, his career was over. Elizabeth
was initially gracious, but her sunshine quickly turned to storms.
It was the last time Essex saw the queen. She sent him to answer
before the Council, where he was kept standing and placed in
the custody of Egerton. On 29 November he was charged in star
chamber with maladministration and abandoning his command
against the queen's express orders.[29] Although his appeal in a
personal letter persuaded Elizabeth at the eleventh hour to
substitute for a star-chamber trial a private hearing before a
special committee of eighteen councillors, nobles, and judges,
Essex was suspended from his membership of the Privy Council
and offices of earl marshal and master of the ordnance, and put
under house arrest. He was allowed to retain the mastership of
the horse, but was to stay secluded at Essex House during the
queen's pleasure (5 June 1600).[30]

On 26 August Essex's sentence was relaxed subject to his
continued banishment from Court. But a new investigation had
begun into the circumstances of publication of John Hayward's
The First Part of the Life and Reign of King Henry IV (1599), a work
dedicated to Essex and printed just before his departure for
Ireland. The subject-matter was the overthrow of Richard II,
so the implications were obvious. Hayward's interpretation,
wrote Attorney-General Coke, was 'that of a King who is taxed
for misgovernment, and his council for corrupt and covetous
dealings for private ends'. The king was censured for his use
of patronage, the nobles became discontented, and the commons

'groan under continual taxation', whereupon Richard was deposed, and finally murdered.[31] Particularly relevant to the official inquiry was that Hayward had used underhand methods to get his book past the censor, and the dedication to Essex had been inserted after the book had been approved. Yet Elizabeth's most serious objection to the work was its popularity among the Londoners, which she took to imply her own unpopularity. When asked about sales, the printer replied, 'No book ever sold better'! Six hundred copies of the first edition had been purchased before the dedicatory epistle had been excised, and a similar number afterwards. When a second edition was suppressed, people clamoured to obtain the book.[32]

Hayward's interrogation by the Privy Council was the cue for a charge of treason against Essex in the summer of 1600. The alleged grounds were that he had conspired with Spain and the pope to obtain the crown of England. He had connived with Tyrone to 'let him [Tyrone] rule under the Pope in Ireland, until the Earl was fully confirmed to the Crown and reconciled to the Pope', when 'by the Pope's command' Tyrone would submit to Essex under the pope. Essex had supposedly also agreed to restore the Netherlands to Spain, and to defend Spanish interests in the New World![33] While these putative charges were absurd, they signalled the state of political play. Although Cecil decided to stay his hand on this occasion, Essex was increasingly vulnerable. For he *had* flirted with treason in his secret correspondence with James VI of Scotland, as well as having considered using two or three thousand troops from his Irish forces in 1599 to oust Cecil and his collaborators from the Privy Council.

So the earl desperately turned his mind to a coup in the autumn of 1600. When Elizabeth refused to renew his patent of sweet wines in September, his credit structure collapsed. She had effectively condemned him to a life of poverty, nor would she answer his appeal for an audience. Lacking the means to raise further loans from the wine merchants, he reckoned his debts at £16,000; creditors were pressing for payment and starting to arrest his servants who had stood surety for him. Yet Essex's motivation went beyond this. A faction leader who was denied access to the monarch was in an untenable position: the earl saw himself compelled to act because his Court opponents had exploited their 'corrupt' monopoly of power. He particularly thought himself 'called' by his lineage and rank to rehabilitate the nobility as natural political leaders. After his disgrace, his urge to oust the Cecilian 'upstarts'—the 'caterpillars of the commonwealth'—became obsessional. As in the case of Northumberland's strike against Protector Somerset, theatre presaged the action: Essex sponsored and applauded the performance in the London streets of a play of Richard II. And the very night before the revolt, his followers paid for and attended a performance of Shakespeare's *Richard II* at the Globe Theatre.[34]

Since Essex lacked adequate estates and territorial connections, a regional revolt was not a reasonable proposition. In fact, the whole idea of a successful 'neo-feudal' rebellion was anachronistic by the end of the sixteenth century. The apparatus of 'bastard feudalism' had been superseded by the rise of the Tudor 'national' state. Patronage and politics were centred on the Court and Privy Council, while the lieutenancy system ensured that the militia was firmly controlled by the Crown. True, there were deputy lieutenants among the Essexians, but not a single lord-lieutenant in their ranks apart from Essex himself; and, without a warrant from the lieutenant, the county regiments could not be mobilized without obvious treasonable intent.[35]

Essex therefore had two options: a Court revolt or a rising in London, where he hoped his image as a Protestant hero and his systematic patronage of puritan clergy since his return from Ireland would ensure spontaneous support. Shortly before Christmas he mooted a Court *putsch*: an armed appeal to the queen against the misrepresentations and plottings of his enemies. The plan as later formulated was that élite swordsmen should seize and hold the palace of Whitehall. Some were to take the gatehouse and the hall, while others penetrated the guard chamber and presence chamber, permitting Essex and his bodyguards to enter the privy chamber where he would find Elizabeth. The Tower was also to be stormed, so that Essex would have a military base in the likely event that his *putsch* aroused resistance in London. Lastly, a Parliament was to be called, the Privy Council purged, and the succession assured to James VI.[36]

At the beginning of February 1601, however, Essex learned that his intentions were suspected, and a leading conspirator, Sir Ferdinando Gorges, claimed that the queen's guard had been doubled. A new plan was therefore devised to stage a demonstration in London. Yet the confusion is obvious. While the plan to raise the City was an extension of the earlier project to storm the Tower, the rationale of the first plan already admitted that popular support for a *putsch* was unlikely to be forthcoming. Of course, the reason was that many of Essex's clients were getting cold feet, and the advantage of an entry into London was that, superficially, it was not treasonable unless conducted forcibly. Also the idea of using the City as a base from which to negotiate with the Court was not entirely implausible.[37]

Yet the events of Sunday, 8 February, were a fiasco. Some three hundred people assembled at Essex House early in the morning, and at ten o'clock four privy councillors, Lord Keeper Egerton, Lord Chief Justice Popham, the earl of Worcester, and Sir William Knollys, arrived bearing a conciliatory message from the queen. They assured Essex that his grievances would be heard. He retorted, however, that Sir Walter Ralegh and Lord Cobham had conspired against his life and that he had been perfidiously treated. When Egerton then ordered everyone to disperse in the name of the queen, an Essexian shouted 'Kill them!', whereupon Essex brought the councillors indoors for their 'protection' — in effect, he took them hostage. Having reached the point of no return, he then marched his company out of Essex House into the Strand. He walked in front accompanied by six noblemen — three earls and three barons; behind followed over a hundred gentlemen and their servants. Onlookers were spellbound: would Essex turn left to the palace of Whitehall, or right to the City? In the event he marched to the house of Sheriff Smythe who lived in Gracechurch Street in the City, for the previous night he had received a verbal message via Sir Henry Bromley that Smythe would lend him a thousand soldiers.

But Essex was deceived. Smythe had sent no message; he commanded only a hundred pikemen and two hundred musketeers; and he flatly refused to join the revolt. He offered the earl and his men refreshments, then slipped away to join the mayor and aldermen in raising London's defences. At

Whitehall, meanwhile, the Court was seized by panic: an improvised barricade was thrown up, and reinforcements mustered. Lastly, heralds were sent to proclaim Essex a traitor. Soon the earl found himself virtually encircled by the City's trained bands, while many of his company melted away. Four hours after entering the City he attempted to force his way back to Essex House. But Ludgate was shut against him, a fight broke out, and the Essexians were repulsed with casualties. So they retreated through Bow churchyard and Bow Lane to the river at Queenhithe, where as many as were able to find boats returned by water to Essex House. Sir Ferdinando Gorges had, however, preceded them and released the hostages. Essex therefore prepared to resist the siege of Essex House, which began at dusk.

When heavy artillery was fetched from the Tower, the Essexians surrendered on condition that they might have honourable treatment and a fair trial — the revolt had lasted almost exactly twelve hours. The leaders were sent to the Tower; the rank and file split among several prisons. Convicted of high treason, Essex mounted the scaffold on 25 February. Although Elizabeth showed characteristic reluctance to sign his death warrant, his execution went ahead. While her private grief for her lost favourite was genuine, she made clear in a letter to James VI that she thought his sentence just. Yet leniency was extended to many of the earl's followers, a prudent policy since the Essex faction disintegrated after its leader's fall. True, the earl's personal servants and intimate adherents were executed, but the earls of Southampton, Rutland, and Bedford were spared. Southampton was incarcerated until Elizabeth's death; Rutland, Bedford, and thirty-six lesser Essexians were released on payment of fines.[38]

The historian William Camden, an eyewitness of the revolt, wrote: 'to this day there are but few that ever thought it a capital crime.' Likewise the earl of Lincoln deemed it to be a riot not a rebellion. But, if Essex's action was non-treasonable in the narrow sense that he did not intend to use violence but simply to excite the Londoners through a dazzling display of chivalry, the fact remains that a dissident nobleman who appealed to the London crowd had overstepped the bounds of legitimate political action. Moreover, when his slogan 'For the queen, for the queen; there is a plot against my life' had proved ineffective, he had added the false allegation that England was sold by Cecil and Ralegh to the Infanta of Spain. Lastly, he had invited the citizens to bear arms in support of his cause.[39]

Essex's demise assured Robert Cecil's triumph. A satirist quipped:

> Little Cecil tripping up and down,
> He rules both Court and Crown,
> With his brother Burghley clown,
> In his great fox-furred gown;
> With the long proclamation
> He swore he saved the town.[40]

The 'long proclamation' had denounced Essex as author of treasons extending back to 1599. But Cecil's charges—that Essex had sought the Crown, had intended to lay violent hands on Elizabeth, had plotted to kill the judges, had engaged in Catholic conspiracy, and had agreed with Tyrone that the latter should land an army of eight thousand men to overthrow the queen— were fabricated.[41] If, however, Cecil was unscrupulous in the matter, his purpose was to create the atmosphere in which he could engineer the smooth succession of James VI and himself remain chief minister, despite Burghley's role in the execution of Mary, Queen of Scots.

Cecil thus opened a secret correspondence with James in order to establish mutual trust, instruct the future king in the tasks that would await him in London, and make himself indispensable in the process.[42] Letters were first exchanged between March and June 1601, and the correspondence was undertaken on negotiated principles. The first was that every respect should be accorded to Elizabeth, and that James should abandon any attempt to obtain power before his time or to seek a parliamentary recognition of his title. The second was that the arrangement should be clandestine, for, as Cecil said, 'if Her Majesty had known all I did . . . her age and orbity, joined to the jealousy of her sex, might have moved her to think ill of that which helped to preserve her'.[43]

Elizabeth's last illness overtook her at Richmond in February 1603. 'I am not sick, I feel no pain,' she said, 'and yet I pine away.' Insomnia, loss of appetite, and physical frailty were the symptoms. For twenty days she barely slept, refusing the attention of her physicians. Cecil enforced total secrecy for twelve days, but during March began implementing the final transition. The earl of Northumberland, whom he consulted, told James VI of Scotland on the 17th: 'This accident hath made all the whole nation look about them. Men talk freely of your Majesty's right, and all in general give you a great allowance.' The earl believed opinion to be squarely behind James, 'though some are silent and say nothing'. And he reported the steps taken by the Privy Council to assure the succession: 'they have called to them some of the nobility . . . hereafter a greater number will be summoned.' The London watches were reinforced and instructions sent to the presidents of the regional councils and lords-lieutenant in the shires. The Privy Council saw the nobility's role as especially important 'both in advice and other ways, for the good of the state, and depression of such as would move insurrections'.[44]

About 20 March Cecil sent James a draft of the intended proclamation of his succession, a document which 'sounded so sweetly' in his ears 'that he can alter no notes in so agreeable a harmony'.[45] Following a brief remission, Elizabeth had become feverish, and by the 21st she wanted to die. On the evening of the 23rd she fell unconscious, waking in the early hours of the morning. She died shortly before 3 a.m. on the 24th, attended by privy councillors and bishops led by Archbishop Whitgift. The councillors immediately posted to Whitehall. At 6 a.m. the text of the proclamation of James's accession was approved. A few hours later it was read at Whitehall Gate, and then repeated in a stage-managed ceremony at the Cross in Cheapside, London. Four earls, four non-conciliar barons, the whole Privy Council, the judges, and the mayor and aldermen processed through the City in their robes, led by trumpeters, heralds, and Garter King of Arms. Cecil himself proclaimed 'James I, King of England, France and Ireland, Defender of the Faith, etc.' The proclamation was then printed for distribution to the counties.[46]

Throughout, discussion of rival dynastic claims to the throne was avoided. It is sometimes said that Elizabeth named James as her heir on her deathbed, but firm support is lacking for this view. On the contrary, James I succeeded because Cecil and

Lord Henry Howard had paved the way, because he was the most realistic alternative, and because fifteen nobles and councillors signed the warrant that ordered proclamation of his style. In fact, his peaceful accession showed that the centralization of politics and triumph of the Court circle were complete, though whether the Court's ascendancy in national politics could long be sustained was a different question.

Between the battle of Bosworth and Elizabeth's death massive changes occurred. The population doubled; the religious houses and chantries were dissolved; and the church was subordinated to the Crown and laity. National identity was sharpened by Henry VIII's anti-papal campaign and the Elizabethan war with Spain: 'nationhood' became defined in terms of English culture and law. The claims of the unitary state and common law were asserted and enforced; the Anglican Church put down roots in the parishes; the north and Wales were subordinated to regional councils; and Ireland was conquered. Concepts of 'neo-feudal' dissent disappeared: the power of the 'old' nobility was usurped by the 'new' generation of courtiers. Although political power was more widely diffused in 1600 than in 1480, this positively enhanced stability. The gentry sat in Parliament and played a crucial role in local government as deputy lieutenants and JPs. Indeed, as local rates became a significant part of civilian and military administration, lesser officials such as constables, churchwardens, and overseers of the poor became important too. Yet whereas Henry VII had governed in partnership with territorial magnates and their dependent affinities, Elizabeth ruled through her courtiers, their servants, and clients. Lastly, a rudimentary print culture was in process of formation following technological and linguistic innovation and increasing literacy at yeoman level and above.

Particularly important in comparison with France, the 1559 religious settlement was implemented without resort to arms. The near-unanimous support of the purchasers of ex-religious property for the return of royal supremacy was crucial, but violence was less endemic in Tudor society than in the fifteenth century. Disputes were settled by litigation or arbitration rather than by the sword, especially after the revolts of 1549. On the one hand, the Tudors enforced respect for statute and common law, while on the other the rise in numbers of 'labouring poor' encouraged property owners to close ranks. In sixteenth-century France the walls and moats of fortified towns were maintained, but in England they collapsed or were dismantled. Despite threats of Catholic invasion and possible civil strife, Henry VIII and Elizabeth never assigned their castles and defences a domestic police function. Only in the northern garrisons of Berwick and Carlisle was there a citadel within the town. The neo-Gothic courtyards, gatehouses, moats, parapets, towers, and turrets of Tudor 'prodigy' houses were ornamental, not utilitarian.

It is true that late-fifteenth century attempts to 'refound' the English monarchy by financial re-endowment failed. Especially significant is that Henry VIII dissipated the lion's share of the proceeds of the ex-religious lands in the 1540s, while Elizabeth and Burghley declined to invent new taxes or maximize customs revenue by revising the book of rates to match inflation. Yet the rise of the corporate Privy Council as the agent of 'national' financial administration was more than adequate compensation. The essential shift was made from undifferentiated household administration of Crown revenue under Henry VII, to diversified management by means of multiple revenue departments under Henry VIII and Cromwell, and finally to co-ordinated exchequer-based fiscal control under Mary and Elizabeth. Whereas in the 1490s accounting was done partly by word of mouth in the king's chamber, by the 1550s it was achieved corporately by the Privy Council. Despite Elizabeth's failure to develop the innovative fiscal theory of 1534, 1540, 1543, 1553, and 1555, the case for 'national' finance was adequately sustained by her concurrence that 'extraordinary' charges, however incurred, should be met from the proceeds of taxation.

I have argued in this book that the strength of the state and of corporate government were linked. Whereas bouts of intense factionalism had divided courtiers and councillors under Henry VIII with inevitable disruption to careers and government alike, the homogeneity of Court and Privy Council under Elizabeth was a major source of stability. It has often been claimed that late-Elizabethan government was inherently weak, and that 'corruption sapped the system's vitality' until 'it collapsed'.[47] But there was no high road to the Civil War. If the breakdown of 1640–2 had a number of long-term causes, the vital dynamic was always Charles I's conduct and policies. Clarendon began his *History of the Rebellion and Civil Wars* by observing: 'I am not so sharp-sighted as those, who have discerned this rebellion contriving from (if not before) the death of Queen Elizabeth.'[48] He knew that, if we read history backwards, Elizabeth's inertia and immobility in the 1590s, combined with the rise of 'venality' at Court, could be said to have established a pattern that precluded comprehensive reform. Of course, no one would deny that Elizabeth's last years were tainted by the cumulative strain of a war economy, Irish affairs, Essex's revolt, and the harvest failures of 1594–7. It is also clear that by the 1620s England was unable to engage in warfare without engendering domestic political friction, and that the 'live' issues of the 1620s were strikingly similar to those of the 1590s.

Yet history is properly read forwards. When this is done, it is clear that a 'slide to disaster' was inconceivable in the sixteenth century. Elizabeth controlled her own policy; the Privy Council was a tightly organized body; communications with the localities were good; a Protestant consensus had emerged. True, financial administration was not free from scandals, but Elizabeth left her successor a relatively small debt. The militia and local government were reorganized, and they satisfied the demands placed on them before 1603. In particular, the dual role of privy councillors as central executives and local lieutenants was a positive asset as long as workloads did not exceed the tolerance limits of an individual.

Tudor success was in the last resort a matter of political acumen. Each successive regime with the possible exception of Mary's sought the support and co-operation of wider ruling élites. If the Privy Council remained a small board, the consultative process did not narrow. Sir Thomas Elyot in *The Book Named the Governor* expressed fears on this question: he urged that 'no good counsellor be omitted or passed over'.[49] But, despite the small size of the reconstituted Privy Council, the voices of magnates and senior gentry had not, and would not, be ignored by the Tudor establishment. Henry VII's title to the throne, the break with Rome, the Henrician Acts of Succession, the First and Second Acts of Uniformity, and the Elizabethan settlement and anti-recusancy laws were all approved by Parliament. Mary knew she could not attempt Philip's coronation without parliamentary approval. And the career of Mary, Queen of Scots, received parliamentary attention that may have been unwelcome to Elizabeth, but was engineered in part by loyal privy councillors. Also Henry VII summoned five Great Councils to take advice, as well as to authorize in principle the levying of taxation and the making of war. Henry VIII, when Parliament stood adjourned in 1530, summoned the nobility to Windsor in June to debate and sign a letter to the pope asking him to grant his divorce from Catherine of Aragon as a matter of national policy; this meeting was, in effect if not in fact, a Great Council. Again, Henry discussed the Nun of Kent affair with his noblemen in November 1533, another meeting was expected in January 1534, and there was talk early in 1537 of an assembly of peers or a Great Council to consider the state of the north after the Pilgrimage of Grace.[50] Fifty years later, amid the crisis of 1584, it was the nobility and senior gentry who were called upon to recruit members for the so-called 'Association' to defend Elizabeth's life and, if their protection should fail, to hunt down her murderers and resist the succession of the Queen of Scots. Lastly, the nobility were enlisted in support of the Privy Council's proclamation of James I as Elizabeth's successor.

By contrast, the Jacobean Privy Council grew in size, but its consultative base actually narrowed. Whereas Henry VIII's Privy Council had nineteen members and Elizabeth's between eleven and nineteen, James's had twenty-three, and its efficiency was dubious. It muddled along with little sense of its corporate identity or control over its flow of business. So miscellaneous was its business, much of which concerned unsolicited petitions from individuals and institutions, that it failed to maintain its role as a policy-making body. Decisions were taken at random, and without cross-referencing. Correspondence with the counties lacked attention to detail and even contradicted itself. Lastly, letters were dispatched weeks after they were dated.[51]

Early Stuart central government has not yet received sufficient attention from historians, but it appears to have lacked Tudor finesse. When the Great Contract collapsed to renewed demands that the king should 'live of his own', parliamentary business was brought to a standstill. Thereafter confidence started to falter. Robert Cecil called Parliaments 'the plagues of Job', and

Ralegh's *Dialogue between a Councillor and a Justice of the Peace*, written from his cell in the Tower, spoke in reply of Magna Carta, parliamentary appropriation of taxation, and ministerial accountability.[52] Ralegh cited Machiavelli's advice that evil councillors should be delivered to the people: he argued that ambitious politicians subverted the monarchical state. Of course, identical arguments had been adduced by malcontents as diverse as Simon de Montfort, Richard, duke of York, the Pilgrims of Grace, and the earl of Essex. Yet we find ourselves entering a changed political world. Whereas Tudor governments got things done, Stuart politicians fumbled. James I and Cecil ended the war with Spain in 1604, but the failure of the Great Contract was symbolic. In the last resort, whether Elizabethan government is judged 'brittle' or 'durable' is a matter for legitimate debate. The simple fact is: while Elizabeth lived, it worked.

NOTES

CHAPTER 1. THE ADVENT OF THE TUDORS

1. K. B. McFarlane, *England in the Fifteenth Century: Collected Essays* (London, 1981), 231–61; A. Goodman, *The Wars of the Roses: Military Activity and English Society, 1452–1497* (London, 1981); J. Gillingham, *The Wars of the Roses* (London, 1981); J. R. Lander, *The Wars of the Roses* (London, 1965); R. A. Griffiths, *The Reign of King Henry VI: The Exercise of Royal Authority, 1422–1461* (London, 1981); C. D. Ross, *Edward IV* (London, 1974); his *Richard III* (London, 1981).
2. *The Governance of England*, ed. C. Plummer (Oxford, 1885; 2nd edn., 1926), 348–53.
3. Ibid. 109–57.
4. B. P. Wolffe, *The Royal Demesne in English History: The Crown Estate in the Governance of the Realm from the Conquest to 1509* (London, 1971), 112–23; *EHD* iv. *1327–1485*, ed. A. R. Myers (London, 1969), 516–22; Griffiths, *Henry VI*, pp. 107–22.
5. D. A. L. Morgan, 'The House of Policy: The Political Role of the Late Plantagenet Household, 1422–1485', in D. R. Starkey (ed.), *The English Court: From the Wars of the Roses to the Civil War* (London, 1987), 55–6; B. P. Wolffe, *The Crown Lands, 1461–1536* (London, 1970), 33–41, 52–4, 67–70, 84–5; his *Royal Demesne*, pp. 79–84, 113–16, 124–58, 196–201.
6. J. R. Lander, *Crown and Nobility, 1450–1509* (London, 1976), 127–58, 307–8; M. Hicks, 'Attainder, Resumption and Coercion, 1461–1529', *Parliamentary History*, 3 (1984), 15–31; W. R. Stacy, 'Richard Roose and the Use of Parliamentary Attainder in the Reign of Henry VIII', *Historical Journal*, 29 (1986), 1–15.
7. Lander, *Crown and Nobility*, pp. 127–58, 307–8; Ross, *Edward IV*, pp. 66–70; S. B. Chrimes, *Henry VII* (London, 1972; repr. 1977), 207, 328–9.
8. Wolffe, *Crown Lands*, pp. 51–75; his *Royal Demesne*, pp. 158–212; Ross, *Edward IV*, pp. 373–7.
9. Wolffe, *Royal Demesne*, pp. 212–25; his *Crown Lands*, pp. 66–86; Ross, *Edward IV*, pp. 371–87; Chrimes, *Henry VII*, pp. 194–218.
10. Lander, *Crown and Nobility*, pp. 171–219, 309–20; C. G. Bayne and W. H. Dunham (eds.), *Select Cases in the Council of Henry VII* (Selden Society, London, 1958), pp. xix–xli; Chrimes, *Henry VII*, pp. 97–114; J. A. Guy, *The Cardinal's Court: The Impact of Thomas Wolsey in Star Chamber* (Hassocks, 1977), 9–10.
11. G. R. Elton, *The Tudor Constitution* (Cambridge, 1960; 2nd edn., 1982), 102.
12. *Governance*, ed. Plummer, pp. 145–9, 349–50.
13. Guy, 'The King's Council and Political Participation', in A. G. Fox and J. A. Guy, *Reassessing the Henrician Age: Humanism, Politics, and Reform, 1500–1550* (Oxford, 1986), 121–47; *Sir John Fortescue: De Laudibus Legum*

Anglie, ed. S. B. Chrimes (Cambridge, 1949), 86; S. E. Lehmberg, *The Later Parliaments of Henry VIII, 1536–1547* (Cambridge, 1977), 170.

14. *The Monarchy of France*, ed. D. R. Kelley, J. H. Hexter, *et al.* (New Haven, Conn., 1981), 41.

15. D. R. Starkey, 'After the Revolution', in C. Coleman and Starkey (eds.), *Revolution Reassessed: Revisions in the History of Tudor Government and Administration* (Oxford, 1986), 199–208; R. J. Knecht, *Francis I* (Cambridge, 1982), 128–31; Starkey (ed.), *The English Court*, pp. 71–118. See pp. 312–13.

16. G. R. Elton, *Studies in Tudor and Stuart Politics and Government* (3 vols.; Cambridge, 1974–83), iii. 216–33; J. D. Alsop, 'The Theory and Practice of Tudor Taxation', *English Historical Review*, 97 (1982), 1–30; his 'Innovation in Tudor Taxation', ibid. 99 (1984), 83–93; G. L. Harriss, 'Thomas Cromwell's "New Principle" of Taxation', ibid. 93 (1978), 721–38; his 'Theory and Practice in Royal Taxation: Some Observations', ibid. 97 (1982), 811–19.

17. J. K. McConica, *English Humanists and Reformation Politics* (Oxford, 1965; repr. 1968), 13–149; R. Weiss, *Humanism in England during the Fifteenth Century* (Oxford, 1941; 2nd edn., 1957), 39–70.

18. Weiss, pp. 84–140, 160–78.

19. W. Nelson (ed.), *A Fifteenth Century School Book* (Oxford, 1956), pp. vii–xxix; J. H. Lupton, *A Life of John Colet* (London, 1887; 2nd edn., 1909), 271–84.

20. Lupton, *Colet*, pp. 45–87.

21. J. A. Froude, *Life and Letters of Erasmus* (London, 1895), 43–4.

22. E. W. Ives, *The Common Lawyers of Pre-Reformation England* (Cambridge, 1983), 36–59; his 'The Common Lawyers' in *Profession, Vocation, and Culture in Later Medieval England* (Liverpool, 1982), 181–217; *The Reports of Sir John Spelman*, ed. J. H. Baker (2 vols.; Selden Society, London, 1977–8), ii. *28–46, 123–42*; D. R. Kelley, *Foundations of Modern Historical Scholarship* (New York, 1970), 19–148.

23. Ives, *Common Lawyers*, pp. 37–53.

24. *De Laudibus Legum Anglie*, ed. Chrimes, pp. 116–20; *The Book Named the Governor*, ed. S. E. Lehmberg (London, 1962), 51–6.

25. *Reports*, ed. Baker, ii. *193–298*; M. Blatcher, *The Court of King's Bench, 1450–1550* (London, 1978), 90–137; J. A. Guy, *The Public Career of Sir Thomas More* (Brighton, 1980), 37–79.

26. J. Rhodes, 'Private Devotion in England on the Eve of the Reformation', unpublished Durham Ph.D. dissertation (1974), fos. 73–196.

27. J. J. Scarisbrick, *The Reformation and the English People* (Oxford, 1984), 3–39.

28. P. Heath, *The English Parish Clergy on the Eve of the Reformation* (London, 1969), 93–103.

29. Ibid. 81–92; M. Bowker, *The Secular Clergy in the Diocese of Lincoln* (Cambridge, 1968), 44–5.

30. *Piers the Ploughman*, ed. J. F. Goodridge (London, 1959; 2nd edn., 1966; repr. 1968), 72–4.

31. G. R. Owst, *Literature and Pulpit in Medieval England* (Cambridge, 1933), 278–9.

32. Bowker, *Secular Clergy*, pp. 110–54; Heath, *English Parish Clergy*, pp. 104–134.

33. Heath, *English Parish Clergy*, pp. 187-96.

34. J. A. F. Thomson, *The Later Lollards, 1414-1520* (Oxford, 1965), 4-15; M. Aston, 'Lollardy and Sedition, 1381-1431', *Past and Present*, no. 17 (1960), 1-44; K. B. McFarlane, *Lancastrian Kings and Lollard Knights* (Oxford, 1972).

35. J. A. Guy, 'The Legal Context of the Controversy: The Law of Heresy', in *CW* x. *The Debellation of Salem and Bizance*, ed. Guy, R. Keen, and C. H. Miller (New Haven, Conn., 1987), pp. xlvii-lxvii.

36. Ibid.

37. Thomson, *Later Lollards*; C. Cross, *Church and People, 1450-1660* (Fontana edn., 1976), 31-52.

38. J. F. Davis, *Heresy and Reformation in the South-East of England, 1520-1559* (London, 1983), 5.

39. M. Wilks, '*Reformatio Regni*: Wyclif and Hus as Leaders of Religious Protest Movements', in D. Baker (ed.), *Schism, Heresy and Religious Protest* (Cambridge, 1972), 109-30.

40. *Political Poems and Songs Relating to English History*, ed. T. Wright (2 vols.; London, 1859-61), ii. 202.

41. *The Works of Sir John Fortescue, Knight, Chief Justice of England and Lord Chancellor to King Henry the Sixth*, ed. T. Fortescue [Lord Clermont] (2 vols.; London, 1869), i. 549-54.

42. S. B. Chrimes, *English Constitutional Ideas in the Fifteenth Century* (Cambridge, 1936), 300-24; Elton, *Studies*, ii. 28-9.

43. Wilks, '*Reformatio Regni*', p. 123.

CHAPTER 2. THE CONDITION OF ENGLAND

1. E. A. Wrigley and R. S. Schofield, *The Population History of England, 1541-1871: A Reconstruction* (London, 1981), 645-85; D. M. Palliser, 'Tawney's Century: Brave New World or Malthusian Trap', *Economic History Review*, 2nd ser. 35 (1982), 339-53; J. Thirsk (ed.), *The Agrarian History of England and Wales*, iv. *1500-1640* (Cambridge, 1967); W. G. Hoskins, 'Harvest Fluctuations and English Economic History, 1480-1619', *Agricultural History Review*, 12 (1964), 28-46; C. J. Harrison, 'Grain Price Analysis and Harvest Qualities, 1465-1634', ibid. 19 (1971), 135-55.

2. Wrigley and Schofield, *Population History*, pp. 174-9, 207-10, 234, 531, 645-85; J. Hatcher, *Plague, Population and the English Economy, 1348-1530* (London, 1977); J. Cornwall, 'English Population in the Early Sixteenth Century', *Economic History Review*, 2nd ser. 23 (1970), 32-44; A. B. Appleby, *Famine in Tudor and Stuart England* (Liverpool, 1978); his 'Disease or Famine? Mortality in Cumberland and Westmorland, 1580-1640', *Economic History Review*, 2nd ser. 26 (1973), 403-32; F. J. Fisher, 'Influenza and Inflation in Tudor England', ibid. 18 (1965), 120-9; P. Slack, 'Mortality Crises and Epidemic Disease in England, 1485-1610', in C. Webster (ed.), *Health, Medicine and Mortality in the Sixteenth Century* (Cambridge, 1979), 9-59; his *The Impact of Plague in Tudor and Stuart England* (London, 1985); D. M. Palliser, 'Dearth and Disease in Staffordshire, 1540-1670', in C. W. Chalklin and M. A. Havinden (eds.), *Rural Change*

and Urban Growth, 1500–1800: Essays in English Regional History in Honour of W. G. Hoskins (London, 1974), 54–75.

3. C. G. A. Clay, *Economic Expansion and Social Change: England, 1500–1700* (2 vols.; Cambridge, 1984), i. 13.

4. Wrigley and Schofield, *Population History*, pp. 234, 528.

5. A. R. Bridbury, 'Sixteenth-century Farming', *Economic History Review*, 2nd ser. 27 (1974), 538–56.

6. e.g. Norfolk Record Office, Norwich Mayor's Court Book 1510–32, pp. 201–2, 207, 227, 269 ff.; King's Lynn Assembly Book, 1497–1544 (KL/C7/5), fo. 197ᵛ.

7. D. M. Palliser, *The Age of Elizabeth: England under the Later Tudors, 1547–1603* (London, 1983), 135–50.

8. The idea of the preventative check was introduced in the 1803 edition of the *Essay*. The edition of 1816 was the last revised by Malthus, supplying the final text from which it has since been reprinted.

9. Wrigley and Schofield, *Population History*, pp. 356–401.

10. K. Wrightson, *English Society, 1580–1680* (London, 1982), 130–42.

11. *The Description of England*, ed. G. Edelen (Folger Books, Ithaca, NY, 1968), 200–3.

12. Wrightson, *English Society*, pp. 125–30; J. O. Appleby, *Economic Thought and Ideology in Seventeenth-century England* (Princeton, NJ, 1978), 129–57.

13. D. S. Berkowitz (ed.), *Humanist Scholarship and Public Order* (Folger Books, Washington DC, 1983), 136–7.

14. R. M. Kingdon, 'Social Welfare in Calvin's Geneva', *American Historical Review*, 76 (1971), 50–69; N. Z. Davis, 'Poor Relief, Humanism and Heresy: The Case of Lyon', *Studies in Medieval and Renaissance History*, 5 (1968), 217–75; H. J. Grimm, 'Luther's Contributions to Sixteenth-century Organization of Poor Relief', *Archiv für Reformationsgeschichte*, 61 (1970), 222–34; H. Heller, 'Famine, Revolt and Heresy at Meaux, 1521–25', *Archiv für Reformationsgeschichte*, 68 (1977), 133–56; B. Pullan, *Rich and Poor in Renaissance Venice* (Oxford, 1971), 239–91; P. A. Fideler, *Discussions of Poverty in Sixteenth-century England* (Brandeis University, Ph.D. dissertation; published University Microfilms, Ann Arbor, 1971).

15. E. M. Leonard, *The Early History of English Poor Relief* (Cambridge, 1900), 25–40; J. Webb (ed.), *Poor Relief in Elizabethan Ipswich* (Suffolk Records Society, Ipswich, 1966), 11–20; J. Pound, 'An Elizabethan Census of the Poor: The Treatment of Vagrancy in Norwich, 1570–1580', *University of Birmingham Historical Journal*, 8 (1962), 135–61; his *Poverty and Vagrancy in Tudor England* (London, 1971; repr. 1978); A. L. Beier, 'The Social Problems of an Elizabethan County Town: Warwick, 1580–90', in P. Clark (ed.), *Country Towns in Pre-industrial England* (Leicester, 1981), 46–85.

16. *Description of England*, pp. 180–6.

17. P. Clark and P. Slack (eds.), *Crisis and Order in English Towns, 1500–1700* (London, 1972); P. Clark (ed.), *The Early Modern Town* (London, 1976); D. M. Palliser, *Tudor York* (Oxford, 1979); W. T. MacCaffrey, *Exeter, 1540–1640* (Cambridge, Mass., 1958; 2nd edn., 1975).

18. The following paragraphs are informed by J. P. Cooper, *Land, Men and Beliefs: Studies in Early Modern History* (London, 1983); L. Stone, *The Crisis of the Aristocracy, 1558–1641* (Oxford, 1965); H. Miller, *Henry VIII and*

the English Nobility (Oxford, 1986); Thirsk (ed.), *Agrarian History*, iv. 276–306; M. A. R. Graves, *The Tudor Parliaments: Crown, Lords, and Commons, 1485–1603* (London, 1985).

19. *Description of England*, pp. 113–14.
20. Cooper, *Land, Men and Beliefs*, pp. 25–6.
21. Palliser, *Age of Elizabeth*, p. 86.
22. Clay, *Economic Expansion and Social Change*, i. 143.
23. Ibid. i. 158.
24. Palliser, *Age of Elizabeth*, p. 70; cf. Cooper, *Land, Men and Beliefs*, pp. 43–77.
25. Clay, *Economic Expansion and Social Change*, ii. 6.
26. Ibid. ii. 36–7.

CHAPTER 3. HENRY VII

1. Cf. K. Pickthorn, *Early Tudor Government: Henry VII* (Cambridge, 1934), 141 n. 1.
2. D. R. Starkey, 'Court and Government', in C. Coleman and Starkey (eds.), *Revolution Reassessed: Revisions in the History of Tudor Government and Administration* (Oxford, 1986), 48.
3. See pp. 74–7.
4. J. R. Lander, *Crown and Nobility, 1450–1509* (London, 1976), 209–10, 219.
5. Derby did not serve continuously as constable; the Tudors kept this office vacant whenever possible.
6. M. M. Condon, 'Ruling Elites in the Reign of Henry VII', in C. Ross (ed.), *Patronage, Pedigree and Power* (Gloucester, 1979), 113–14.
7. J. A. Guy, *The Cardinal's Court: The Impact of Thomas Wolsey in Star Chamber* (Hassocks, 1977), 19.
8. See p. 3.
9. Condon, 'Ruling Elites', p. 113.
10. C. L. Kingsford (ed.), *Chronicles of London* (Oxford, 1905), 213–16.
11. S. B. Chrimes, *Henry VII* (London, 1972; repr. 1977), 135.
12. P. J. Holmes, 'The Great Council in the Reign of Henry VII', *English Historical Review*, 101 (1986), 840–62; R. A. Griffiths and J. Sherborne (eds.), *Kings and Nobles in the Later Middle Ages* (Gloucester, 1986), 242–3, 275–6; *The Monarchy of France*, eds. D. R. Kelley, J. H. Hexter, *et al.* (New Haven, Conn., 1981), 73–4.
13. R. S. Schofield, 'Parliamentary Lay Taxation, 1485–1547', unpublished Cambridge Ph.D. dissertation (1963), fos. 61–4, 156–9, table 40 (facing fo. 416).
14. Ibid., fos. 160–98, table 40.
15. Roper claimed that Henry VII had been told that 'a beardless boy had disappointed all his purpose', but there is no evidence that More was even elected to the 1504 Parliament. R. S. Sylvester and D. P. Harding (eds.), *Two Early Tudor Lives* (New Haven, Conn., 1962; repr. 1969), p. 199.
16. *Bacon's Works* (Chandos edn.), 423, 425.
17. Chrimes, *Henry VII*, p. 177.
18. 3 Henry VII, c. 1; C. G. Bayne and W. H. Dunham (eds.), *Select Cases in the Council of Henry VII* (Selden Society, London, 1958), pp. xlix–lxiv; Guy, *The Cardinal's Court*, p. 20.

19. 11 Henry VII, c. 25; Bayne and Dunham (eds.), *Select Cases*, pp. lxii–lxiii; Guy, *The Cardinal's Court*, p. 20 and n. 173.

20. *Political Poems and Songs Relating to English History*, ed. T. Wright (2 vols.; London, 1859–61), ii. 252.

21. Chrimes, *Henry VII*, p. 185.

22. Condon, 'Ruling Elites', pp. 115, 121, 125; P. Clark, *English Provincial Society from the Reformation to the Revolution: Religion, Politics and Society in Kent, 1500–1640* (Hassocks, 1977), 17–20; G. R. Elton, *Policy and Police: The Enforcement of the Reformation in the Age of Thomas Cromwell* (Cambridge, 1972), 293–400.

23. 4 Henry VII, c. 13.

24. *The Reports of Sir John Spelman*, ed. J. H. Baker (2 vols.; Selden Society, London, 1977–8), ii. *329–30*.

25. I am grateful to Miss Margaret Condon for numerous discussions of Henry VII's system of bonds.

26. Dudley's petition, addressed in 1509 to Fox and Lovell, is printed by C. J. Harrison, 'The Petition of Edmund Dudley', *English Historical Review*, 87 (1972), 82–99.

27. Chrimes, *Henry VII*, p. 213 and n. 1.

28. Ibid. 212.

29. Condon, 'Ruling Elites', p. 122.

30. *The Anglica Historia of Polydore Vergil*, ed. D. Hay (Camden Society, 3rd ser. 74; London, 1950), 127–9.

31. Lander, *Crown and Nobility*, p. 292.

32. Condon, 'Ruling Elites', p. 122.

33. *Anglica Historia*, ed. Hay, p. 127.

34. G. R. Elton, *Studies in Tudor and Stuart Politics and Government* (3 vols.; Cambridge, 1974–83), i. 45–99; cf. J. P. Cooper, 'Henry VII's Last Years Reconsidered', *Historical Journal*, 2 (1959), 103–29.

35. R. Somerville, 'Henry VII's "Council Learned in the Law" ', *English Historical Review*, 54 (1939), 427–42; Condon, 'Ruling Elites', pp. 133–4.

36. Condon, 'Ruling Elites', p. 134.

37. Lander, *Crown and Nobility*, p. 293.

38. Harrison, 'Petition of Edmund Dudley', p. 87.

39. Elton, *Studies*, i. 73–6.

40. Condon, 'Ruling Elites', pp. 127–8.

41. Ibid.; E. W. Ives, *The Common Lawyers of Pre-Reformation England* (Cambridge, 1983), 85–6. In December 1503 Shaa and the recorder of London offered up to £7,500 if the king would annul the Merchant Tailors' charter and confirm that of the City of London. He partially complied for 5,000 marks, which the City tried to recoup on Henry VIII's accession. Corporation of London RO, Repertories of the Court of Aldermen 1, fo. 149; 2, fos. 27, 75^v.

42. D. R. Starkey, 'After the Revolution', in Coleman and Starkey (eds.), *Revolution Reassessed*, p. 203.

43. C. S. L. Davies, 'Bishop John Morton, the Holy See, and the Accession of Henry VII', *English Historical Review*, 102 (1987), 2–30.

44. *Reports*, ed. Baker, ii. *65*.

45. Davies, 'Bishop John Morton', pp. 18, 22; S. B. Chrimes, *English Constitutional Ideas in the Fifteenth Century* (Cambridge, 1936), 379–80.
46. Davies, 'Bishop John Morton', pp. 16–19; *Reports*, ed. Baker, ii. *334–46.*
47. Davies, 'Bishop John Morton', p. 17; R. L. Storey, *Diocesan Administration in Fifteenth-century England* (Borthwick Institute, York, 1959; 2nd edn., 1972), 29.
48. Henry E. Huntington Library, Ellesmere MS 2652, fo. 6.
49. Storey, *Diocesan Administration*, p. 31.
50. 35 Edward I, st. 1; 25 Edward III, st. 5, c. 22; and st. 6, c. 2; 27 Edward III, st. 1, c. 1; 38 Edward III, st. 1, c. 4; and st. 2, cc. 1–4; 3 Richard II, c. 3; 7 Richard II, c. 12; 12 Richard II, c. 15; 13 Richard II, st. 2, cc. 2–3; 16 Richard II, c. 5; 2 Henry IV, cc. 3–4; 6 Henry IV, c. 1; 7 Henry IV, c. 8; 9 Henry IV, c. 8; 3 Henry V, c. 4.
51. Storey, *Diocesan Administration*, pp. 30–1; Harrison, 'Petition of Edmund Dudley', pp. 87–90.
52. *Reports*, ed. Baker, ii. *66–8.*
53. Condon, 'Ruling Elites', pp. 110–11.
54. Ibid. 111 and n. 9.
55. Ibid. 112.
56. This account of foreign policy follows R. B. Wernham, *Before the Armada: The Emergence of the English Nation, 1485–1588* (New York, 1966; repr. 1972), 27–76; Chrimes, *Henry VII*, pp. 272–97.
57. This large sum was provided in cash, plate, and jewels, for the use of Maximilian, Philip, or his son Charles. It shows that Henry VII was in earnest, since it was equivalent to three years' revenue. The chief attraction was probably Henry's proposed marriage to Margaret of Savoy, but she declined the suit in 1508.
58. G. Kipling, 'Henry VII and the Origins of Tudor Patronage', in G. F. Lytle and S. Orgel (eds.), *Patronage in the Renaissance* (Princeton, NJ, 1981), 117–64.
59. E. G. Duff, *The Printers, Stationers and Bookbinders of Westminster and London from 1476 to 1535* (Cambridge, 1906; repr. New York, 1971), 133–4, 169.
60. J. Foxe (ed.), *The Whole Workes of W. Tyndall, John Frith, and Doct. Barnes* (London, 1573 [1572]), sig. A2.
61. H. S. Bennett, *English Books and Readers, 1475 to 1557* (Cambridge, 1952), 194.
62. D. R. Starkey, 'From Feud to Faction: English Politics *c.*1450–1550', *History Today*, 32 (Nov. 1982), 16–18.

CHAPTER 4. WOLSEY'S ASCENDANCY

1. B. P. Wolffe, *The Crown Lands, 1461–1536* (London, 1970), 76–88, 162–3.
2. Henry E. Huntington Library, Ellesmere MS 2655, fo. 8.
3. *LP* I (2nd edn.), i, no. 448 (4).
4. E. W. Ives, *Anne Boleyn* (Oxford, 1986), 75.
5. *The Acts and Monuments of John Foxe*, ed. G. Townsend (8 vols.; London, 1843–9), v. 605–6.

6. V. M. Murphy, 'The Debate over Henry VIII's First Divorce: An Analysis of the Contemporary Treatises', unpublished Cambridge Ph.D. dissertation (1984), fo. 261.

7. Cf. G. W. Bernard, *War, Taxation and Rebellion in Early Tudor England: Henry VIII, Wolsey and the Amicable Grant of 1525* (Brighton, 1986); W. E. Wilkie, *The Cardinal Protectors of England: Rome and the Tudors before the Reformation* (Cambridge, 1974); G. Walker, *John Skelton and the Politics of the 1520s* (Cambridge, 1988). Similar ideas have been independently argued by Mr P. J. Gwyn in two unpublished papers.

8. R. S. Sylvester and D. P. Harding (eds.), *Two Early Tudor Lives* (New Haven, Conn., 1962; repr. 1969), 14.

9. Ibid. 13.

10. *The Complete English Poems*, ed. J. Scattergood (London, 1983), 289.

11. Walker, *John Skelton and the Politics of the 1520s*.

12. Bernard, *War, Taxation and Rebellion*, p. 155.

13. G. Mattingly (ed.), *Further Supplement to Letters, Despatches and State Papers Relating to the Negotiations between England and Spain* (London, 1940), p. xv; cf. Bernard, *War, Taxation and Rebellion*, pp. 60–3.

14. J. J. Scarisbrick, *Henry VIII* (London, 1968), 90–2; Mattingly (ed.), *Supplement*, p. xvi.

15. *LP* I. ii, nos. 3139–40.

16. *LP* II. i, no. 967.

17. *LP* II. i, no. 894.

18. *LP* IV. iii, no. 5750 (p. 2559).

19. *St Thomas More: Selected Letters*, ed. E. F. Rogers (New Haven, 1961; repr. 1967), 68.

20. J. A. Guy, *The Cardinal's Court: The Impact of Thomas Wolsey in Star Chamber* (Hassocks, 1977); his 'Thomas More as Successor to Wolsey', *Thought: Fordham University Quarterly*, 52 (1977), 275–92; F. Metzger, 'Das Englische Kanzleigericht Unter Kardinal Wolsey 1515–1529', unpublished Erlangen Ph.D. dissertation (1976).

21. *St. Pap.* iv. 155.

22. J. A. Guy, *The Court of Star Chamber and its Records to the Reign of Elizabeth I* (London, 1985), 6–17.

23. J. J. Scarisbrick, 'Cardinal Wolsey and the Common Weal', in E. W. Ives, R. J. Knecht, and Scarisbrick (eds.), *Wealth and Power in Tudor England* (London, 1978), 45–67.

24. J. A. Guy, 'Wolsey and the Parliament of 1523', in D. Loades *et al.* (eds.), *Law and Government under the Tudors* (Cambridge, 1988), 1–18.

25. *LP* IV. ii, no. 4796. Cf. *LP* III. ii, app. no. 21.

26. *A Discourse of the Commonweal of this Realm of England*, ed. M. Dewar (Charlottesville, Va., 1969), 50.

27. PRO STAC 2/15/188–90.

28. P. L. Hughes and J. F. Larkin (eds.), *Tudor Royal Proclamations*, i. *The Early Tudors* (New Haven, Conn., 1964), nos. 118, 121, 125, 127.

29. Henry E. Huntington Library, Ellesmere MS 2655, fo. 16.

30. PRO STAC 2/26/103; 2/32/bundle of unlisted fragments (Roger Barbor's case); Guy, *Cardinal's Court*, pp. 70–1.

31. PRO SP 1/232, Pt. 1, fos. 58–69 (*LP Add.* I, no. 206).
32. *LP* III. i, no. 365.
33. BL Cotton MS Titus B.I, fos. 178–84 (*LP* III. i, no. 576).
34. *LP* IV. iii, no. 5750 (p. 2562).
35. D. R. Starkey, 'Court and Government', in C. Coleman and Starkey (eds.), *Revolution Reassessed: Revisions in the History of Tudor Government and Administration* (Oxford, 1986), 30–46; D. R. Starkey (ed.), *The English Court: From the Wars of the Roses to the Civil War* (London, 1987), 71–118; and his 'Representation through Intimacy: A Study in the Symbolism of Monarchy and Court Office in Early Modern England', in I. Lewis (ed.), *Symbols and Sentiments: Cross-cultural Studies in Symbolism* (London, 1977), 187–224.
36. S. G. Ellis, 'Tudor Policy and the Kildare Ascendancy in the Lordship of Ireland, 1496–1534', *Irish Historical Studies*, 20 (1977), 239.
37. *LP* II. i, no. 1959; H. Miller, *Henry VIII and the English Nobility* (Oxford, 1986), 108–9. Cf. G. W. Bernard, *The Power of the Early Tudor Nobility: A Study of the Fourth and Fifth Earls of Shrewsbury* (Brighton, 1985), 11–26.
38. BL Cotton MS Titus B.I, fo. 94 (*LP* XXI. ii, no. 554); F. R. Grace, 'The Life and Career of Thomas Howard, Third Duke of Norfolk', unpublished Nottingham MA dissertation (1961).
39. Miller, *Henry VIII*, pp. 108–9.
40. B. J. Harris, *Edward Stafford, Third Duke of Buckingham, 1478–1521* (Stanford, Ca., 1986).
41. Miller, *Henry VIII*, pp. 50–1, 166–7.
42. *LP* III. i, no. 1 (misdated).
43. Harris, *Edward Stafford*; Miller, *Henry VIII*, pp. 50–1; A. G. Fox, *Thomas More: History and Providence* (Oxford, 1982), 101–4.
44. J. J. Goring, 'The General Proscription of 1522', *English Historical Review*, 86 (1971), 681–705.
45. Bernard, *War, Taxation and Rebellion*, pp. 119–20.
46. *LP* III. ii, no. 2484; BL Cotton MS Cleopatra F.VI, fos. 316–20.
47. PRO SP 1/25, fo. 55 (*LP* III. ii, no. 2393).
48. R. S. Schofield, 'Parliamentary Lay Taxation, 1485–1547', unpublished Cambridge Ph.D. dissertation (1963) fos. 198–215.
49. Ibid. table 40 (facing fo. 416); M. J. Kelly, 'Canterbury Jurisdiction and Influence during the Episcopate of William Warham, 1503–1532', unpublished Cambridge Ph.D. dissertation (1963), fos. 301, 316–17.
50. F. C. Dietz, *English Public Finance, 1485–1641* (2 vols.; Urbana, Ill., 1921; 2nd edn., London, 1964), i. 90–102; Wolffe, *Crown Lands*, pp. 84–5.
51. C. Whibley (ed.), *Henry VIII* [an edition of Hall's Chronicle] (2 vols., London, 1904), i. 286–7; *The Anglica Historia of Polydore Vergil*, ed. D. Hay (Camden Society, 3rd ser. 74; London, 1950), 306; Sylvester and Harding (eds.), *Two Early Tudor Lives*, p. 206; H. Ellis (ed.), *Original Letters Illustrative of English History*, 1st ser. (3 vols.; 2nd edn., London, 1825), i. 221; *LP* III. ii, no. 2484; BL Cotton MS Cleopatra F.VI, fos. 316–20; Goring, 'The General Proscription of 1522', p. 700.
52. Bernard, *War, Taxation and Rebellion*, pp. 110–30; Guy, 'Wolsey and the Parliament of 1523'.

53. Ellis, 1st ser. i. 221.
54. Bernard, *War, Taxation and Rebellion*, pp. 115–17.
55. Whibley (ed.), *Henry VIII*, i. 287; Ellis, 1st ser. i. 221.
56. Whibley (ed.), *Henry VIII*, i. 287–8; Guy, 'Wolsey and the Parliament of 1523'.
57. Schofield, 'Parliamentary Lay Taxation', table 40 (facing fo. 416).
58. Guy, 'Wolsey and the Parliament of 1523'.
59. Henry E. Huntington Library, Ellesmere MS 2472; PRO E 159/303, *communia* Mich. rot. 1; PRO C 193/3, fos. 24–5; *LP* III. ii, no. 3504.
60. Schofield, 'Parliamentary Lay Taxation', table 41 (facing fo. 432); Bernard, *War, Taxation and Rebellion*, pp. 118, 122–3.
61. Bernard, *War, Taxation and Rebellion*, pp. 53–72.
62. Whibley (ed.), *Henry VIII*, ii. 37; Bernard, *War, Taxation and Rebellion*, p. 154.
63. Whibley (ed.), *Henry VIII*, ii. 36; Bernard, *War, Taxation and Rebellion*, p. 154.
64. D. MacCulloch, *Suffolk and the Tudors: Politics and Religion in an English County, 1500–1600* (Oxford, 1986), 290–3; Bernard, *War, Taxation and Rebellion*, pp. 136–48.
65. MacCulloch, *Suffolk and the Tudors*, p. 293.
66. Bernard, *War, Taxation and Rebellion*, pp. 56–60; MacCulloch, *Suffolk and the Tudors*, p. 293.
67. *LP* IV. ii, nos. 3318, 3360; Starkey (ed.), *The English Court*, pp. 105–7; his 'Privy Secrets: Henry VIII and the Lords of the Council', *History Today*, 37 (Aug. 1987), 27–8.
68. Bodleian Library MS Laud. Misc. 597, fos. 24–31.
69. A. F. Pollard's view (*Wolsey* (London, 1929), 121–2, 161–4, 330–2) has been challenged by D. S. Chambers, 'Cardinal Wolsey and the Papal Tiara', *Bulletin of the Institute of Historical Research*, 38 (1965), 20–30, and by Scarisbrick, *Henry VIII*, pp. 46–8, 107–10. The matter is not quite settled, though it is agreed that Pollard considerably overstated Wolsey's personal ambition to become pope; Wilkie, *Cardinal Protectors*, pp. 125–41.
70. *LP* III. ii, no. 1960.
71. J. W. McKenna, 'How God Became an Englishman', in D. J. Guth and McKenna (eds.), *Tudor Rule and Revolution* (Cambridge, 1982), 25–43.
72. Ellis, 1st ser. i. 136 (*LP* II. ii, no. 2911). For further evidence of the origins of Henry VIII's 'imperial' sovereignty, see W. Ullmann, ' "This Realm of England is an Empire" ', *Journal of Ecclesiastical History*, 30 (1979), 175–203.
73. J. J. Scarisbrick's argument (*Henry VIII*, pp. 49–162) that 'Wolsey's policy was a peace policy and for about fifteen years he struggled to make it work' has been successfully challenged by P. J. Gwyn, 'Wolsey's Foreign Policy: The Conferences at Calais and Bruges Reconsidered', *Historical Journal*, 23 (1980), 755–72, to which this account stands indebted. See also Bernard, *War, Taxation and Rebellion*, pp. 3–45.
74. Gwyn, 'Wolsey's Foreign Policy'.
75. *St. Pap.* i. 51.
76. *LP* III. ii, no. 2755.

77. *LP* III. ii, nos. 2948, 2952, 2966–7, 2984, 2996, 2998, 3071–2, 3107, 3114–16, 3118, 3123, 3134, 3138, 3149, 3153–4, 3194, 3203, 3207, 3215, 3220–5, 3232–3, 3268, 3271–3, 3281, 3291, 3307; PRO SP 1/27, fos. 189–204 (*LP* III. ii, no. 2958); Guy, 'Wolsey and the Parliament of 1523'.

78. *LP* III. ii, nos. 2476, 2728.

79. *Complete English Poems*, ed. Scattergood, p. 287.

80. *St. Pap.* i. 143; Bernard, *War, Taxation and Rebellion*, pp. 44–5.

81. S. J. Gunn, 'The Duke of Suffolk's March on Paris in 1523', *English Historical Review*, 101 (1986), 596–634.

82. Scarisbrick, *Henry VIII*, p. 136.

83. Bernard, *War, Taxation and Rebellion*, pp. 30–1.

84. Henry E. Huntington Library, Ellesmere MS 6109; *LP* II. i, no. 1313; J. A. Guy, 'Henry VIII and the *Praemunire* Manœuvres of 1530–1531', *English Historical Review*, 97 (1982), 495–8.

85. For discussion of the contradictions between 'common-law' and 'caesaro-papist' theory of royal supremacy, see A. G. Fox and J. A. Guy, *Reassessing the Henrician Age: Humanism, Politics, and Reform, 1500–1550* (Oxford, 1986), 164–73.

86. Kelly, 'Canterbury Jurisdiction and Influence', fos. 148–206; Pollard, *Wolsey*, pp. 165–216; D. Knowles, *The Religious Orders in England*, iii. *The Tudor Age* (Cambridge, 1959; repr. 1971), 157–64.

87. *LP* III. i, no. 1122 (misdated).

88. Wilkie, *Cardinal Protectors*, p. 158.

89. *LP* III. i, nos. 77, 693; *LP* IV. i, nos. 80, 953; *LP* IV. ii, no. 4900; *LP* IV. iii, nos. 5607–8, 5638–9; R. M. Woolley (ed.), *The York Provinciale* (London, 1931); Knowles, *Religious Orders*, iii. 159–60; P. Heath, *The English Parish Clergy on the Eve of the Reformation* (London, 1969), 189–90; S. B. House, 'Sir Thomas More and Holy Orders: More's Views of the English Clergy, both Secular and Regular', unpublished University of St Andrews Ph.D. dissertation (1987), fo. 105.

90. Heath, *English Parish Clergy*, pp. 124–5.

91. J. K. McConica (ed.), *The History of the University of Oxford*, iii. *The Collegiate University* (Oxford, 1986), 26–32, 337–41; E. L. Taunton, *Thomas Wolsey, Legate and Reformer* (London, 1902), 111.

92. Sylvester and Harding (eds.), *Two Tudor Lives*, p. 24.

93. Ibid. 24, 62.

94. Kelly, 'Canterbury Jurisdiction and Influence', fos. 164–73.

95. Wilkie, *Cardinal Protectors*, pp. 157–8; A. F. Pollard, *Henry VIII* (London, 1902; new edn., 1951, repr. 1963), 190. A similar thesis has been argued by Mr P. J. Gwyn in two unpublished papers which I am grateful to have heard read.

96. Sylvester and Harding (eds.), *Two Tudor Lives*, p. 183.

CHAPTER 5. THE BREAK WITH ROME

1. 'If a man shall take his brother's wife, it is an impurity. He hath uncovered his brother's nakedness; they shall be childless' (Levit. 20: 21).

2. 'When brethren dwell together, and one of them dieth without children, the wife of the deceased shall not marry to another; but his brother shall take her, and raise up seed for his brother' (Deut. 25: 5).

3. V. M. Murphy, 'The Debate over Henry VIII's First Divorce: An Analysis of the Contemporary Treatises', unpublished Cambridge Ph.D. dissertation (1984).

4. J. H. Lupton, *A Life of John Colet* (London, 1887; 2nd edn., 1909), 299.

5. J. F. Davis, *Heresy and Reformation in the South-East of England, 1520–1559* (London, 1983).

6. M. Aston, 'Lollardy and the Reformation: Survival or Revival?', *History*, 49 (1964), 149–70.

7. D. D. Wallace, *Puritans and Predestination: Grace in English Protestant Theology, 1525–1695* (Chapel Hill, NC, 1982), 1–15; H. Davies, *Worship and Theology in England from Cranmer to Hooker, 1534–1603* (Princeton, NJ, 1970), 95–103; Davis, *Heresy and Reformation*, pp. 26–65.

8. Wallace, *Puritans and Predestination*, pp. 12–13.

9. I am indebted to an unpublished Folger Institute seminar paper by Professor Richard Marius for a better understanding of Tyndale's political thought.

10. H. Walter (ed.), *Doctrinal Treatises and Introductions to Different Portions of the Holy Scriptures by William Tyndale* (Parker Society, Cambridge, 1848), 177.

11. J. A. Guy, *Christopher St German on Chancery and Statute* (Selden Society, London, 1985), 19–55.

12. J. A. Guy, 'The Legal Context of the Controversy: The Law of Heresy', in *CW* x. *The Debellation of Salem and Bizance*, ed. Guy, R. Keen, and C. H. Miller (New Haven, Conn., 1987), pp. xlvii–lxvii.

13. PRO SP 6/2, pp. 110–11.

14. J. B. Trapp (ed.), *CW* ix. *The Apology* (New Haven, Conn., 1979), pp. lvi–vii.

15. *The Correspondence of Sir Thomas More*, ed. E. F. Rogers (Princeton, NJ, 1947), 496.

16. G. R. Elton, *Reform and Reformation: England, 1509–1558* (London, 1977), 130–56; J. A. Guy, *The Public Career of Sir Thomas More* (Brighton, 1980), 113–74.

17. R. Marius, *Thomas More* (New York, 1984), 397–401; Guy, *Public Career*, pp. 167–71.

18. R. S. Sylvester and D. P. Harding (eds.), *Two Early Tudor Lives* (New Haven, Conn., 1962; repr. 1969), 228.

19. *LP* XVI, no. 101.

20. T. F. T. Plucknett and J. L. Barton (eds.), *Doctor and Student* (Selden Society, London, 1974), 327.

21. Ibid. 317.

22. J. A. Guy, 'Henry VIII and the *Praemunire* Manoeuvres of 1530–1531', *English Historical Review*, 97 (1982), 481–503; G. W. Bernard, 'The Pardon of the Clergy Reconsidered', *Journal of Ecclesiastical History*, 37 (1986), 258–82.

23. The *Collectanea* is BL Cotton MS Cleopatra E.VI, fos. 16–135, discovered and analysed by G. D. Nicholson, 'The Nature and Function of Historical

Argument in the Henrician Reformation', unpublished Cambridge Ph.D. dissertation (1977); A. G. Fox and J. A. Guy, *Reassessing the Henrician Age: Humanism, Politics, and Reform, 1500–1550* (Oxford, 1986), 151–78.

24. C. Whibley (ed.), *Henry VIII* [an edition of Hall's *Chronicle*] (2 vols.; London, 1904), ii. 185.

25. *LP* v, no. 171; *Sir Thomas More: Neue Briefe*, ed. H. Schulte Herbrüggen (Münster, 1966), 97.

26. Guy, *Public Career*, app. 2 (pp. 207–12).

27. E. W. Ives, *Anne Boleyn* (Oxford, 1986), 195–214.

28. G. R. Elton, *Studies in Tudor and Stuart Politics and Government* (3 vols.; Cambridge, 1974–83), ii. 82–106.

29. Fox and Guy, *Reassessing the Henrician Age*, pp. 162–3.

30. S. T. Bindoff (ed.), *The House of Commons, 1509–1558* (3 vols.; London, 1982), i. 10–11.

31. Ibid.

32. G. R. Elton, *The Tudor Constitution* (Cambridge, 1960; 2nd edn., 1982), 364–5.

33. J. J. Scarisbrick, 'Clerical Taxation in England, 1485 to 1547', *Journal of Ecclesiastical History*, 11 (1960), 41–54.

34. G. R. Elton, *Policy and Police: The Enforcement of the Reformation in the Age of Thomas Cromwell* (Cambridge, 1972), 171–216.

35. Ibid. 231–43; A. S. Bevan, 'The Role of the Judiciary in Tudor Government, 1509–1547', unpublished Cambridge Ph.D. dissertation (1985), chs. 7–8.

36. Elton, *Policy and Police*, pp. 217–62.

37. C. Haigh, *Reformation and Resistance in Tudor Lancashire* (Cambridge, 1975), 113; M. Bowker, *The Henrician Reformation: The Diocese of Lincoln under John Langland, 1521–1547* (Cambridge, 1981), 137–9.

38. H. Miller, *Henry VIII and the English Nobility* (Oxford, 1986), 68.

39. Bindoff (ed.), *House of Commons, 1509–1558*, i. 12–13.

40. R. W. Chambers, *Thomas More* (London, 1935; repr. 1957), 320; *LP* VIII, no. 856 (p. 326).

41. Fox and Guy, *Reassessing the Henrician Age*, p. 164.

42. *Correspondence*, p. 498.

43. *CW* ix. *De Tristitia Christi*, ed. C. H. Miller (2 vols.; New Haven, Conn., 1976), ii. 1073; *Correspondence*, p. 498.

44. In 1537 Wilson took the oath and was pardoned; *LP* XII. i, no. 1330 (64).

45. Sylvester and Harding (eds.), *Two Early Tudor Lives*, p. 250.

46. Guy, *Public Career*, pp. 75–7.

47. R. M. Warnicke, 'Sexual Heresy at the Court of Henry VIII', *Historical Journal*, 30 (1987), 247–68; Ives, *Anne Boleyn*, pp. 343–408.

48. M. L. Robertson, 'Thomas Cromwell's Servants: The Ministerial Household in Early Tudor Government and Society', unpublished UCLA Ph.D. dissertation (1975), fo. 316; D. R. Starkey (ed.), *The English Court: From the Wars of the Roses to the Civil War* (London, 1987), 110–15.

49. *Sir Thomas Wyatt: The Complete Poems*, ed. R. A. Rebholz (London, 1978), 155.

50. Elton, *Policy and Police*, pp. 383–400.

51. P. de Gayangos (ed.), *Calendar of Letters, Despatches, and State Papers Relating to the Negotiations between England and Spain*, iv, pt. ii (London, 1882), 623.

52. J. Youings, *The Dissolution of the Monasteries* (London, 1971), 145.

53. G. R. Elton, *The Tudor Revolution in Government* (Cambridge, 1953), 198; R. S. Schofield, 'Parliamentary Lay Taxation, 1485–1547', unpublished Cambridge Ph.D. dissertation (1963), table 40 (facing fo. 416); M. Kelly, 'Canterbury Jurisdiction and Influence during the Episcopate of William Warham, 1503–1532', unpublished Cambridge Ph.D. dissertation (1963), fos. 312–13.

54. Elton, *Studies*, iii. 216–33; J. D. Alsop, 'The Theory and Practice of Tudor Taxation', *English Historical Review*, 97 (1982), 5–7.

55. F. C. Dietz, *English Public Finance, 1485–1641* (2 vols., Urbana, Ill., 1921; 2nd edn., London, 1964), i. 137–49; D. Knowles, *The Religious Orders in England*, iii. *The Tudor Age* (Cambridge, 1959; repr. 1971), 393–401; Youings, *Dissolution of the Monasteries*, pp. 117–31; H. A. L. Fisher, *The History of England from the Accession of Henry VII to the Death of Henry VIII* (2nd edn., London, 1913), app. 2 (p. 499).

56. D. Starkey, 'Court and Government' in C. Coleman and Starkey (eds.), *Revolution Reassessed: Revisions in the History of Tudor Government and Administration* (Oxford, 1986), 45–6; Starkey (ed.), *The English Court*, pp. 96–8.

57. Elton, *Tudor Constitution*, pp. 143–4; Starkey (ed.), *The English Court*, pp. 97–8.

58. *LP* XVII, no. 267; Starkey, 'Court and Government', p. 45; Alsop, 'Theory and Practice of Tudor Taxation', p. 19; Starkey (ed.), *The English Court*, pp. 97–8.

59. Dietz, i. 130.

60. F. A. Gasquet, *Henry VIII and the English Monasteries* (London, 1906), table at p. 360 n. 1. For some reason Waltham's surrender was delayed; the great sweep really ended in Jan. 1540.

61. Knowles, *Religious Orders*, iii. 389–92, 402–17; T. H. Swales, 'The Redistribution of the Monastic Lands in Norfolk at the Dissolution', *Norfolk Archaeology*, 34/1 (1966), 14–44.

62. M. H. and R. Dodds, *The Pilgrimage of Grace, 1536–1537, and the Exeter Conspiracy, 1538* (2 vols.; Cambridge, 1915); C. S. L. Davies, 'The Pilgrimage of Grace Reconsidered', *Past and Present*, no. 41 (1968), 54–76; his 'Popular Religion and the Pilgrimage of Grace', in A. Fletcher and J. Stevenson (eds.), *Order and Disorder in Early Modern England* (Cambridge, 1985), 58–91; M. E. James, 'Obedience and Dissent in Henrician England: The Lincolnshire Rebellion 1536', *Past and Present*, no. 48 (1970), 3–78; C. Haigh, *The Last Days of the Lancashire Monasteries and the Pilgrimage of Grace* (Chetham Society, 3rd ser. 17; 1969); his *Reformation and Resistance*, pp. 118–38; R. B. Smith, *Land and Politics in the England of Henry VIII: The West Riding of Yorkshire, 1530–46* (Oxford, 1970), 165–212; S. M. Harrison, *The Pilgrimage of Grace in the Lake Counties, 1536–7* (London, 1981).

63. A. Fletcher, *Tudor Rebellions* (London, 1968; 2nd edn., 1973), 124.

64. Davies, 'Popular Religion and the Pilgrimage of Grace', pp. 68–72.

65. Ibid. 75–8.
66. Elton, *Studies*, iii. 183–215; James, 'Obedience and Dissent', pp. 51–68; Smith, *Land and Politics*, p. 208; Davies, 'Popular Religion and the Pilgrimage of Grace', pp. 89–91.
67. *LP* VII, no. 1206.
68. Davies, 'Popular Religion and the Pilgrimage of Grace', p. 90; James, 'Obedience and Dissent', pp. 57–68.
69. James, 'Obedience and Dissent', pp. 62–3; Smith, *Land and Politics*, pp. 171–6.
70. Dodds, *Pilgrimage of Grace*, ii. 297–327; Elton, *Reform and Reformation*, pp. 279–81. The countess was condemned by act of attainder in May 1539.
71. All Souls College, Oxford, MS 258, fo. 64; J. S. Block, 'Religious Nonconformity and Social Conflict: Philip Gammon's Star Chamber Story', *Albion*, 13 (1981), 331–46; cf. Guy, *Christopher St German*, pp. 27–8, 131.

CHAPTER 6. HENRICIAN GOVERNMENT

1. R. B. Merriman, *Life and Letters of Thomas Cromwell* (2 vols.; Oxford, 1902), ii. 129. This account of Cromwell's early career is based on ibid. i. 1–55; G. R. Elton, *Studies in Tudor and Stuart Politics and Government* (3 vols.; 1974–83), ii. 215–35, iii. 373–90; his *Reform and Renewal: Thomas Cromwell and the Common Weal* (Cambridge, 1973); A. J. Slavin, 'The Gutenberg Galaxy and the Tudor Revolution', in G. P. Tyson and S. S. Wagonheim (eds.), *Print and Culture in the Renaissance: Essays on the Advent of Printing in Europe* (Newark, NJ, 1986), 90–109.
2. *The Acts and Monuments of John Foxe*, ed. G. Townsend (8 vols.; London, 1843–9), v. 362–403.
3. J. G. A. Pocock, *The Machiavellian Moment* (Princeton, NJ, 1975), p. 277.
4. A. G. Fox and J. A. Guy, *Reassessing the Henrician Age: Humanism, Politics, and Reform, 1500–1550* (Oxford, 1986), 143–4; G. Burnet, *History of the Reformation of the Church of England* (3 vols. in 6 parts; Oxford, 1820), I. ii. 278–9; D. R. Starkey, 'Privy Secrets: Henry VIII and the Lords of the Council', *History Today*, 37 (Aug. 1987), 30.
5. The principal writings are G. R. Elton, *The Tudor Revolution in Government* (Cambridge, 1953); his *Reform and Reformation: England 1509–1558* (London, 1977); his *Studies*, i. 173–88, iii. 373–90; his 'The Tudor Revolution: A Reply', *Past and Present*, no. 29 (1974), 26–49; his 'A New Age of Reform?', *Historical Journal*, 30 (1987), 709–16; C. Coleman and D. R. Starkey (eds.), *Revolution Reassessed: Revisions in the History of Tudor Government and Administration* (Oxford, 1986); Fox and Guy, *Reassessing the Henrician Age*; D. E. Hoak, 'The Secret History of the Tudor Court: The King's Coffers and the King's Purse, 1542–1553', *Journal of British Studies*, 26 (1987), 208–31; P. Williams and G. L. Harriss, 'A Revolution in Tudor History?', *Past and Present*, no. 25 (1963), 3–58; their 'A Revolution in Tudor History?', ibid., no. 31 (1965), 87–96; D. R. Starkey

(ed.), *The English Court: From the Wars of the Roses to the Civil War* (London, 1987).

6. Elton, *Tudor Revolution*, esp. pp. 415–16, 420, 426–7.

7. Starkey (ed.), *The English Court*, *passim*.

8. J. D. Alsop, 'The Structure of Early Tudor Finance', *c*.1509–1558', in Coleman and Starkey (eds.), *Revolution Reassessed*, pp. 135–62; Hoak, 'Secret History of the Tudor Court', esp. pp. 215–31; Elton, 'A New Age of Reform?', pp. 714–15.

9. Elton, *Tudor Revolution*, p. 416.

10. *Oxford English Dictionary*, s.v. 'revolution'.

11. *Bacon's Works* (Chandos edn.), 102; quoted by Starkey (ed.), *The English Court*, p. 21.

12. Starkey (ed.), *The English Court*, p. 21.

13. N. Z. Davis, 'Poor Relief, Humanism and Heresy: The Case of Lyon', *Studies in Medieval and Renaissance History*, 5 (1968), 217–75; H. J. Grimm, 'Luther's Contributions to Sixteenth-century Organization of Poor Relief', *Archiv für Reformationsgeschichte*, 61 (1970), 222–34; H. Heller, 'Famine, Revolt and Heresy at Meaux, 1521–25', ibid. 68 (1977), 133–56; R. M. Kingdon, 'Social Welfare in Calvin's Geneva', *American Historical Review*, 76 (1971), 50–69; B. Pullan, *Rich and Poor in Renaissance Venice* (Oxford, 1971), 239–91; F. R. Salter (ed.), *Some Early Tracts on Poor Relief* (London, 1926).

14. *De la vicissitude ou variété des choses en l'univers* (Paris, 1579); N. Z. Davis, 'A New Montaigne', *The New York Review of Books* (19 Nov. 1987), 53.

15. J. A. Guy, *Christopher St German on Chancery and Statute* (Selden Society, London, 1985), 25–33, 127–35; his 'The Tudor Commonwealth: Revising Thomas Cromwell', *Historical Journal*, 23 (1980), 681–7; G. R. Elton, *Reform and Renewal*, pp. 66–157; his 'English Law in the Sixteenth Century: Reform in an Age of Change', in *Studies*, iii. 274–88; his 'A New Age of Reform?', p. 716. Although St German was not a Lutheran, many of his ideas on the church and poor relief were anticipated in Luther's pamphlet *The Address to the German Nobility* (1520). See A. J. Slavin, 'Upstairs, Downstairs: Or the Roots of Reformation', *Huntington Library Quarterly* (1986), 243–60; Grimm, 'Luther's Contributions to Sixteenth-century Organization of Poor Relief', pp. 225–33.

16. Elton, *Tudor Revolution*, pp. 316–52; his *Studies*, iii. 21–38.

17. S. G. Ellis, *Reform and Revival: English Government in Ireland, 1470–1534* (London, 1986), 31–48; *A Collection of Ordinances and Regulations for the Government of the Royal Household* (London, 1790), 159–60; J. A. Guy, 'The Privy Council: Revolution or Evolution?', in Coleman and Starkey (eds.), *Revolution Reassessed*, pp. 67–8; Fox and Guy, *Reassessing the Henrician Age*, pp. 135–6.

18. PRO SP 1/59, fo. 77; SP 1/235, fo. 37; *LP* IV. iii, app. 67; *LP Add.* I, no. 481.

19. 27 Henry VIII, c. 63. Sir William Fitzwilliam (later earl of Southampton) was the inspiration behind the act. See Starkey, 'Privy Secrets', p. 31.

20. *LP Add.* I, no. 944.

21. *LP* VI, no. 551.
22. Starkey (ed.), *The English Court*, pp. 16-20.
23. *LP* VI, no. 1071.
24. Guy, 'Privy Council', pp. 68-75. Cf. Starkey, 'Privy Secrets', pp. 29-31.
25. *LP* XIII. i, no. 1 (wrongly dated by *LP* to 1538); from internal evidence the document was compiled shortly after the Pilgrimage was suppressed. Guy, 'Privy Council', pp. 74-85; his *The Court of Star Chamber and its Records to the Reign of Elizabeth I* (London, 1985), 6-8.
26. Elton, *Studies*, iii. 27-8.
27. G. R. Elton, 'Revisionism Reassessed: The Tudor Revolution a Generation Later', *Encounter* (issue for July/Aug. 1986), 38, where Cromwell is said to have created the Privy Council 'before ever rebellion broke out in Lincolnshire, as the exclusion of the Lord Mayor of London, hitherto always sworn of the Council, indicates'.
28. BL Lansdowne MS 160, fo. 312; *St. Pap.* i. 384-5; *LP Add.* I, no. 1053.
29. BL Lansdowne MS 160, fo. 312; *St. Pap.* i. 384-5; *LP Add.* I, no. 1053; Elton, *Studies*, iii. 27 n. 55 (where the stated reference to *LP* VII, no. 1060, does not refer to the mayor); John Stow, *Survey of London*, ed. H. B. Wheatley (London, 1912; rev. edn. 1956, repr. 1970), 469.
30. *LP Add.* I, no. 1053, cited by Elton, *Studies*, iii. 27-8. The fact is that Warren simply disappears from the record, as do the other lesser councillors and judges. But, given the paucity of the sources, and the fact that these various disappearances occur at quite different times, no light is thrown one way or the other on the question of the date of exclusion.
31. Guy, 'Privy Council', pp. 76-80; Fox and Guy, *Reassessing the Henrician Age*, pp. 121-47.
32. Guy, 'Privy Council', pp. 78-9; Starkey, 'Privy Secrets', pp. 29-31; Elton, *Studies*, i. 190-200. Important new light is thrown on this question by T. F. Mayer, *Thomas Starkey and the Commonweal: Humanist Politics and Religion in the Reign of Henry VIII* (Cambridge, 1988). The ideological input is stressed more strongly still by D. R. Starkey, 'The Lords of the Council: Aristocracy, Ideology, and the Formation of the Tudor Privy Council', unpublished paper read to the 101st Annual Meeting of the American Historical Association, 27-30 Dec. 1986. I am much indebted to Dr Starkey for sending me a copy of his paper in advance of publication.
33. Elton, *Tudor Revolution*, pp. 330, 337; Guy, 'Privy Council', pp. 77-80.
34. Elton, *Tudor Revolution*, pp. 331, 338-9; Guy, 'Privy Council', pp. 77-9.
35. Elton, *Tudor Revolution*, pp. 331, 338.
36. *St. Pap.* i. 508.
37. Elton, *Tudor Revolution*, p. 338; Guy, 'Privy Council', p. 77.
38. Repr. in D. S. Berkowitz (ed.), *Humanist Scholarship and Public Order* (Folger Books, Washington DC, 1984), 181-2.
39. Guy, 'Privy Council', pp. 78-80.
40. *LP* XIII. i, no. 1. By 1540 seven members of the 1536-7 body had been removed; Guy, 'Privy Council', p. 79.
41. On this question, I think Dr Starkey's critique of my 'Privy Council' is convincing; see his 'The Lords of the Council', and his 'Privy Secrets', pp. 30-1.

42. PRO PC 2/1, p. 1; Guy, 'Privy Council', p. 74.

43. See pp. 185-8.

44. Here I argue against my 'Privy Council', p. 85, accepting Dr Starkey's criticism that I was too vague as to when the 'emergency Council' of 1536-7 became the mature Privy Council of 1540. See his 'The Lords of the Council', and his 'Privy Secrets', pp. 30-1.

45. Starkey (ed.), *The English Court*, p. 21.

46. See especially D. Hirst, 'Court, Country, and Politics before 1629' in K. Sharpe (ed.), *Faction and Parliament: Essays on Early Stuart History* (Oxford, 1978), 105-37.

47. R. B. Smith, *Land and Politics in the England of Henry VIII: The West Riding of Yorkshire, 1530-46* (Oxford, 1970), 123; P. Williams, *The Tudor Regime* (Oxford, 1979).

48. *The Governance of England*, ed. C. Plummer (Oxford, 1885; 2nd edn., 1926), 129.

49. C. Given-Wilson, *The Royal Household and the King's Affinity: Service, Politics and Finance in England, 1360-1413* (New Haven, Conn., 1986), 203-57.

50. Quoted in ibid. 219.

51. D. A. L. Morgan, 'The House of Policy: The Political Role of the Late-Plantagenet Household, 1422-1485', in Starkey (ed.), *The English Court*, pp. 64-7.

52. Ibid. 66.

53. R. Mousnier, *Le Conseil du Roi de Louis XII à la Révolution* (Travaux du Centre de Recherches sur la Civilisation de l'Europe Moderne, 6; Paris, 1970), 5-20.

54. M. Harsgor, *Recherches sur le personnel du Conseil du Roi sous Charles VIII et Louis XII* (4 vols.; Lille, 1980); F. Decrue, *De consilio regis Francisci I* (Paris, 1885); J. A. Guy, 'The French King's Council, 1483-1526', in R. A. Griffiths and J. Sherborne (eds.), *Kings and Nobles in the Later Middle Ages: A Tribute to Charles Ross* (Gloucester, 1986), 274-94.

55. La Monarchie de France, ed. J. Poujol (Paris, 1961), esp. pp. 135-42; *The Monarchy of France*, ed. D. R. Kelley, J. H. Hexter, *et al.* (New Haven, Conn., 1981), esp. pp. 73-81.

56. BL Cotton MS Titus B.I, fo. 466 (*LP* VII, no. 420).

57. For this policy in the later Middle Ages, see Given-Wilson, *Royal Household and the King's Affinity*, pp. 203-17.

58. The breakdown is 50 knights for the body, 70 esquires for the body, 69 gentlemen ushers, 65 yeomen ushers, 82 sewers of the chamber, 39 yeomen of the chamber, 68 grooms of the chamber, and 50 pages of the chamber. These figures are provisional, and derive from my current research.

59. Among them the duke of Suffolk, Sir Thomas Cheyney, Sir William Sandes, Sir William Parr, Sir Thomas Boleyn, Sir William Fitzwilliam, Sir Anthony Browne, Sir John Russell, and Sir Edward Seymour.

60. BL Cotton MS Titus B.I, fo. 184 (*LP* III. i, no. 576 (3)).

61. *LP* III. i, no. 578; H. Miller, *Henry VIII and the English Nobility* (Oxford, 1986), 83-4.

62. *LP* II. i, no. 2735 (wrongly dated to 1516; the correct date is *c.*1535); *LP* IV. i, no. 1939 (8).

63. For this process in action before the Boulogne campaign of 1544, see *LP* XIX. i, nos. 273–6.

64. *OED* s.v. 'manred'.

65. *LP* XIV. i. 643.

66. For some examples, see Starkey (ed.), *The English Court*, pp. 90–1.

67. *St. Pap.* i. 411–15, 545–7.

68. G. Jacob, *Law Dictionary*, rev. T. E. Tomlins (2 vols.; London, 1797), s.v. 'posse comitatus', 'sheriff'; *List of Sheriffs for England and Wales From the Earliest Times to AD 1831* (London, PRO, 1898); Smith, *Land and Politics*, pp. 129–30; Given-Wilson, *Royal Household and the King's Affinity*, pp. 246–54.

69. Jacob, *Law Dictionary*, s.v. 'coroner', 'escheator', 'constable'; R. F. Hunnisett, *The Medieval Coroner* (Cambridge, 1961); J. R. Kent, *The English Village Constable, 1580–1642* (Oxford, 1986).

70. This account rests on M. L. Zell, 'Early Tudor JPs at Work', *Archaeologia Cantiana*, 93 (1977), 125–43; G. C. F. Forster, *The East Riding Justices of the Peace in the Seventeenth Century* (East Yorks. Local History Society, York, 1973); J. H. Gleason, *The Justices of the Peace in England, 1558–1640* (Oxford, 1969); B. Putnam, *Early Treatises on the Practice of the Justices of the Peace* (Oxford, 1924).

71. *LP* IV. ii, nos. 3665, 3712, 3819, 3822; PRO E 36/257, art. 6; P. L. Hughes and J. F. Larkin (eds.), *Tudor Royal Proclamations*, i. *The Early Tudors* (New Haven, Conn., 1964), 172–4; *Calendar of State Papers, Venetian, 1527–33* (London, 1871), 701; G. A. J. Hodgett, *Tudor Lincolnshire* (Lincoln, 1975); M. K. Jones, 'Lady Margaret Beaufort, the Royal Council and an Early Fenland Drainage Scheme', *Lincolnshire History and Archaeology*, 21 (1986), 11–16.

72. PRO SP 1/14, fos. 108–13 (*LP* II. i, 2579*); the date is established by Henry E. Huntington Library, Ellesmere MS 2652, fo. 7.

73. Henry E. Huntington Library, Ellesmere MS 2655, fo. 15ᵛ; Ellesmere MS 2652, fo. 12; PRO C 254/161/25–6; Hughes and Larkin (eds.), *Tudor Royal Proclamations*, i. 153–4.

74. Zell, 'Early Tudor JPs at Work', pp. 126–7; Smith, *Land and Politics*, pp. 153–5, table 15.

75. *St. Pap.* iv. 155; J. A. Guy, *The Cardinal's Court: The Impact of Thomas Wolsey in Star Chamber* (Hassocks, 1977), 30–5, 72–8, 119–131.

76. Guy, *Cardinal's Court*, pp. 121–4.

77. J. G. Edwards, *The Principality of Wales, 1267–1967* (Caernarvon, 1969); T. B. Pugh (ed.), *The Marcher Lordships of South Wales, 1415–1536* (Cardiff, 1963); R. A. Griffiths, *The Principality of Wales in the Later Middle Ages: The Structure and Personnel of Government*, i. *South Wales, 1277–1536* (Cardiff, 1972); S. B. Chrimes, *Henry VII* (London, 1972; repr. 1977), 245–57; P. Williams, *The Council in the Marches of Wales under Elizabeth I* (Cardiff, 1958), 3–15.

78. *LP* VI, nos. 386 (2), 1381 (1, 3), 1382; *LP* VII, no. 781; P. R. Roberts, 'The "Acts of Union" and the Tudor Settlement of Wales', unpublished Cambridge Ph.D. dissertation (1966).

79. Roberts, 'The "Acts of Union" ', fos. 376–80; Williams, *Council in the Marches of Wales*, pp. 21–33; W. Rees, 'The Union of England and Wales', *Transactions of the Honourable Society of Cymmrodorion* (1937), 27–100.

80. R. R. Reid, *The King's Council in the North* (London, 1921; repr. 1975), 149–59; C. Haigh, *Reformation and Resistance in Tudor Lancashire* (Cambridge, 1975), 136–7; Smith, *Land and Politics*, pp. 155–9.

81. *LP* XIV. i, no. 743; J. A. Youings, 'The Council of the West', *Transactions of the Royal Historical Society*, 5th ser. 10 (1960), 41–60; D. Willen, *John Russell, First Earl of Bedford: One of the King's Men* (London, 1981), 30–1, 39, 65–8, 76–9, 81.

82. R. Harold Garrett-Goodyear, 'Revival of Quo Warranto and Early Tudor Policy towards Local governors, 1485–1540', unpublished Harvard University Ph.D. dissertation (1973), fo. 429.

83. 27 Hen. VIII, c. 24.

84. Garrett-Goodyear, fo. 561.

CHAPTER 7. POLITICS, RELIGION, WAR

1. *The Acts and Monuments of John Foxe*, ed. G. Townsend (8 vols.; London, 1843–9), v. 378, 403.

2. G. R. Elton, *Studies in Tudor and Stuart Politics and Government* (3 vols.; Cambridge, 1974–83), iii. 377–8.

3. *EHD* v. *1485–1558*, ed. C. H. Williams (London, 1967), nos. 113, 115.

4. R. Whiting, 'The Reformation in the South-West of England', unpublished Exeter Ph.D. dissertation (1977), fos. 168–78, 253–65; S. E. Brigden, 'The Early Reformation in London, 1520–1547: The Conflict in the Parishes', unpublished Cambridge Ph.D. dissertation (1979), fo. 199; P. Clark, *English Provincial Society from the Reformation to the Revolution: Religion, Politics, and Society in Kent, 1500–1640* (Hassocks, 1977), 34–68; C. Haigh (ed.), *The English Reformation Revised* (Cambridge, 1987), 12–13.

5. *EHD* v, no. 112; J. Ridley, *Thomas Cranmer* (Oxford, 1962; repr. 1966), 113–15; G. R. Elton, *Reform and Renewal: Thomas Cromwell and the Common Weal* (Cambridge, 1973), 35.

6. A. G. Fox and J. A. Guy, *Reassessing the Henrician Age: Humanism, Politics, and Reform, 1500–1550* (Oxford, 1986), 199–205.

7. *EHD* v, no. 114; Ridley, *Cranmer*, pp. 121–6.

8. Ridley, *Cranmer*, pp. 131–53. Cranmer had been married before, but his first wife had died; ibid. 16–17.

9. P. N. Brooks, 'The Principle and Practice of Primitive Protestantism in Tudor England: Cranmer, Parker and Grindal as Chief Pastors, 1535–1577', in Brooks (ed.), *Reformation Principle and Practice* (London, 1980), 121–33.

10. Brigden, 'Early Reformation in London', fos. 118–22, 142–7; S. M. Lyons, 'Conflict and Controversy: English Bishops and the Reformation, 1547–1558', unpublished Brown University Ph.D. dissertation (1980),

fos. 49–90; J. Block, 'Thomas Cromwell's Patronage of Preaching', *Sixteenth-century Journal*, 8 (1977), 37–50; Ridley, *Cranmer*, pp. 125–30.

11. A. J. Slavin, 'The Rochepot Affair', *Sixteenth-century Journal*, 10 (1979), 3–19; Whiting, 'Reformation in the South-West', fos. 36, 49.

12. J. A. Guy, *The Public Career of Sir Thomas More* (Brighton, 1980), 110–11; H. A. L. Fisher, *The History of England from the Accession of Henry VII to the Death of Henry VIII* (London, 1913), 442; Ridley, *Cranmer*, pp. 254–5; P. C. Swensen, 'Noble Hunters of the Romish Fox: Religious Reform at the Tudor Court, 1543–1564', unpublished UC Berkeley Ph.D. dissertation (1981), fos. 160–74.

13. R. J. Knecht, *Francis I* (Cambridge, 1982), 248–52; his 'Francis I, "Defender of the Faith"?', in E. W. Ives, R. J. Knecht, and J. J. Scarisbrick (eds.), *Wealth and Power in Tudor England* (London, 1978), 106–27.

14. G. Redworth, 'A Study in the Formulation of Policy: The Genesis and Evolution of the Act of Six Articles', *Journal of Ecclesiastical History*, 37 (1986), 42–67; R. B. Merriman (ed.), *Life and Letters of Thomas Cromwell* (2 vols.; Oxford, 1902), i. 233–7.

15. *Foxe*, v. 230. Christ's words at the Last Supper were, 'This is my body which is given for you' (Luke 22: 19).

16. H. M. Colvin (ed.), *The History of the King's Works*, iv. *1485–1660 (Part II)* (London, 1982), 6–7, 369–401.

17. Redworth, 'The Genesis and Evolution of the Act of Six Articles', pp. 45–67; Merriman (ed.), *Life and Letters of Thomas Cromwell*, i. 285–92.

18. Redworth, 'The Genesis and Evolution of the Act of Six Articles', pp. 42–67; Elton, *Studies*, iii. 221–2; D. R. Starkey, 'Privy Secrets: Henry VIII and the Lords of the Council', *History Today* (Aug. 1987), 30–1; S. E. Lehmberg, *The Later Parliaments of Henry VIII, 1536–1547* (Cambridge, 1977), 57–74.

19. 31 Henry VIII, c. 10; D. R. Starkey, 'The Lords of the Council: Aristocracy, Ideology, and the Formation of the Tudor Privy Council' (unpublished paper read to the 101st Annual Meeting of the American Historical Association, 27–30 Dec. 1986; I am very grateful to Dr Starkey for sending me a copy); Lehmberg, *Later Parliaments*, p. 299.

20. H. Miller, *Henry VIII and the English Nobility* (Oxford, 1986), 113–16; D. R. Starkey, 'History without Politics', *Journal of Ecclesiastical History*, 28 (1977), 397–400.

21. D. R. Starkey (ed.), *The English Court: From the Wars of the Roses to the Civil War* (London, 1987), 114–16.

22. D. L. Potter, 'Diplomacy in the Mid-Sixteenth Century: England and France, 1536–1550', unpublished Cambridge Ph.D. dissertation (1973), fos. 27–35; Merriman, *Life and Letters of Thomas Cromwell*, i. 284–5.

23. *The Lisle Letters*, ed. M. St Clare Byrne (6 vols.; Chicago, 1981), vi. 61–6.

24. Ibid. 58–9.

25. G. R. Elton, *Reform and Reformation: England, 1509–1558* (Cambridge, 1977), 290.

26. *Lisle Letters*, vi. 74–234; A. J. Slavin, 'Cromwell, Lisle and the Calais Sacramentarians: The Politics of Conspiracy', *Albion*, 9 (1977), 316–36.

27. *LP* XV, no. 850 (11).

28. *Sir Thomas Wyatt: The Complete Poems*, ed. R. A. Rebholz (London, 1978), 86.

29. Elton, *Studies*, i. 189–230; Merriman, *Life and Letters of Thomas Cromwell*, i. 285–302; G. Redworth, 'Whatever happened to the English Reformation?', *History Today* (Oct. 1987), 36.

30. J. A. Guy, 'The Privy Council: Revolution or Evolution?', in C. Coleman and D. R. Starkey (eds.), *Revolution Reassessed: Revisions in the History of Tudor Government and Administration* (Oxford, 1986), 74; A. J. Slavin, *Politics and Profit: A Study of Sir Ralph Sadler, 1507–1547* (Cambridge, 1966), 140–4; *LP* XVI, no. 394 (6).

31. Starkey, 'Privy Secrets', pp. 30–1; his 'Stewart Serendipity: A Missing Text of the *Modus Tenendi Parliamentum*', *Fenway Court* (1986), 38–49; his 'The Lords of the Council'; T. F. Mayer, *Thomas Starkey and the Commonweal: Humanist Politics and Religion in the Reign of Henry VIII* (Cambridge, 1988).

32. The other ten privy councillors attended meetings far less frequently. The nine were the earl of Hertford (admiral, 1542–3; lord great chamberlain, 1543–7; later Protector Somerset); Lord Russell (admiral, 1540–3; lord privy seal, 1542–55); Lord St John (chamberlain of the household and great master; lord president of the Council, 1545–50); Sir Thomas Wriothesley (lord chancellor, 1544–7); Stephen Gardiner (bishop of Winchester); Sir John Gage (comptroller of the household); Sir Anthony Browne (master of the horse); Sir Anthony Wingfield (vice-chamberlain of the household); and Sir William Paget (principal secretary 1543–7). Attendances were calculated from *APC* i. (London, 1890), 3–302. The value of this line of enquiry was suggested to me by Professor A. J. Slavin, to whom I am especially grateful.

33. *LP* XX. ii, pp. xxxviii–xliv.

34. *LP* XXI. i, no. 1014.

35. R. S. Schofield, 'Parliamentary Lay Taxation, 1485–1547', unpublished Cambridge Ph.D. dissertation (1963), table 40 (facing fo. 416); F. C. Dietz, *English Public Finance, 1485–1641* (2 vols.; Urbana, Ill., 1921; 2nd edn., London, 1964), i. 144–77.

36. A valuable reassessment is S. J. Gunn, 'The French Wars of Henry VIII', in *The Origins of War in Early Modern Europe* (London, 1987), 28–47.

37. Colvin (ed.), *History of the King's Works*, iv. 373.

38. J. D. Alsop, 'The Theory and Practice of Tudor Taxation', *English Historical Review*, 97 (1982), 1–30.

39. *A Discourse of the Commonweal of this Realm of England*, ed. M. Dewar (Charlottesville, Va., 1969), 36, 89; Alsop, 'Theory and Practice of Tudor Taxation', pp. 12–13.

40. Alsop, 'Theory and Practice of Tudor Taxation', pp. 19–20; D. E. Hoak, 'The Secret History of the Tudor Court: The King's Coffers and the King's Purse, 1542–1553', *Journal of British Studies*, 26 (1987), 208–31.

41. The following account is heavily influenced by the suggestive sketch in Redworth, 'Whatever happened to the English Reformation?', pp. 29–36. See also Davis, *Heresy and Reformation in the South-East*, pp. 66–97.

42. P. L. Hughes and J. F. Larkin (eds.), *Tudor Royal Proclamations*, i. *The Early Tudors* (New Haven, Conn., 1964), 349–50.

43. Redworth, 'Whatever happened to the English Reformation?', p. 34.

44. *APC* i. 127.

45. *Miscellaneous Writings and Letters of Thomas Cranmer*, ed. J. E. Cox (Parker Society, Cambridge, 1846), 83 n. 1.

46. J. A. Muller, *Stephen Gardiner and the Tudor Reaction* (New York, 1926), 104–5.

47. Lehmberg, *Later Parliaments*, pp. 186–8.

48. Ibid. 198.

49. Clark, *English Provincial Society*, pp. 60–6.

50. Muller, *Stephen Gardiner*, pp. 109–10.

51. Ibid. 110–12; Ridley, *Cranmer*, pp. 229–45; the considerable evidence is printed in *LP* XVIII. ii. 546 (pp. 291–378).

52. Clark, *English Provincial Society*, pp. 59–61.

53. For further evidence of the grass-roots Reformation beyond that supplied by Clark, see Davis, *Heresy and Reformation in the South-East*, pp. 80–97. I am extremely grateful to Professor A. J. Slavin for a discussion of the Prebendaries' plot at the Folger Institute.

54. Swensen, 'Noble Hunters of the Romish Fox', fos. 60–156, 192–208. See also Elton, *Reform and Reformation*, pp. 318–30.

55. *Foxe*, v. 464–97.

56. Ibid. 464–97, 537–50, 553–61, app. xvi; Davis, *Heresy and Reformation in the South-East*, pp. 96–7; Slavin, 'The Fall of Lord Chancellor Wriothesley', pp. 273–4.

57. The following account of Henry VIII's will and Edward VI's regency council is heavily indebted to new research by Professor Dale Hoak, in particular his discovery in the Inner Temple Library, London, of a copy of Henry's will dated 13 Dec. 1546, a version unknown to previous students of the problem. I am much indebted to Professor Hoak for allowing me to read his findings in unpublished form. See D. E. Hoak, *The Reign of Edward VI* (London, forthcoming).

58. *APC* i. 158–302; *LP* XX. ii, app. 2.

59. D. R. Starkey, 'Court and Government', in Coleman and Starkey (eds.), *Revolution Reassessed*, pp. 46–55.

60. *LP* XXI. i, no. 1537 (34).

61. This is Professor Hoak's most important discovery; see his forthcoming *Reign of Edward VI*.

62. I owe this information to the kindness of Professor Hoak.

63. *Foxe*, vi. 163–4.

64. *LP* XXI. ii. 634; H. Miller, 'Henry VIII's Unwritten Will: Grants of Lands and Honours in 1547', in Ives *et al.* (eds.), *Wealth and Power in Tudor England*, pp. 87–105; D. R. Starkey, 'From Feud to Faction: English Politics *c.* 1450–1550', *History Today*, 32 (Nov. 1982), 22.

65. Starkey, 'From Feud to Faction', p. 22. Professor Hoak kindly supplied me with the text of extracts from the will.

66. Slavin, 'The Fall of Lord Chancellor Wriothesley', pp. 268–70, 283–5.

67. D. E. Hoak, 'The King's Privy Chamber, 1547–1553', in D. J. Guth and J. W. McKenna (eds.), *Tudor Rule and Revolution* (Cambridge, 1982),

105–7; his *The King's Council in the Reign of Edward VI* (Cambridge, 1976), 118, 149–51, 260–1, 325 n. 44.

68. Hoak, *King's Council*, p. 233.
69. Slavin, 'The Fall of Lord Chancellor Wriothesley', p. 271.
70. M. L. Bush, *The Government Policy of Protector Somerset* (London, 1975), 1–6, 160–1.
71. Ibid. 7–39.
72. Ibid. 33; Dietz, i. 178–87; Alsop, 'Theory and Practice of Tudor Taxation', p. 23.
73. Bush, *Protector Somerset*, pp. 100–26; J. N. King, 'Freedom of the Press, Protestant Propaganda, and Protector Somerset', *Huntington Library Quarterly*, 40 (1976), 1–9.
74. *APC* ii. 312.
75. Brigden, 'Early Reformation in London', fos. 336, 364.
76. Bush, *Protector Somerset*, pp. 119–23.
77. J. J. Scarisbrick, *The Reformation and the English People* (Oxford, 1984), 112–31.
78. *Foxe*, v. 716–18; R. Hutton, 'The Local Impact of the Tudor Reformations', in C. Haigh (ed.), *The English Reformation Revised* (Cambridge, 1987), 114–38.
79. Hutton, 'Local Impact of the Tudor Reformations', pp. 121, 125.
80. *Foxe*, v. 716–21.
81. Bush, *Protector Somerset*, p. 103.
82. *Lords Journals*, i. 331, 343.
83. Bush, *Protector Somerset*, pp. 40–83; Elton, *Studies*, iii. 249–51.
84. Bush, *Protector Somerset*, pp. 84–99; J. Cornwall, *Revolt of the Peasantry, 1549* (London, 1977); B. L. Beer, *Rebellion and Riot: Popular Disorder in England during the Reign of Edward VI* (Kent, Ohio, 1982), 38–139; R. B. Manning, 'Violence and Social Conflict in Mid-Tudor Rebellions', *Journal of British Studies*, 16 (1977), 18–40; D. MacCulloch, 'Kett's Rebellion in Context', *Past and Present*, no. 84 (1979), 36–59; J. A. Youings, 'The South-Western Rebellion of 1549', *Southern History*, 1 (1979), 99–122.
85. Manning, 'Violence and Social Conflict', p. 28.
86. Ibid. 27.
87. Youings, 'South-Western Rebellion', pp. 103–7, 114–15, 117–19.
88. MacCulloch, 'Kett's Rebellion in Context', pp. 58–9.
89. Bush, *Protector Somerset*, p. 98.
90. PRO SP 10/8, fos. 8–11.

CHAPTER 8. REFORMATION AND COUNTER-REFORMATION

1. D. E. Hoak, *The King's Council in the Reign of Edward VI* (Cambridge, 1976), 53–5, 241–58.
2. *APC* ii. 340–5; D. E. Hoak, 'The King's Privy Chamber, 1547–1553', in D. J. Guth and J. W. McKenna (eds.), *Tudor Rule and Revolution* (Cambridge, 1982), 91, 98–102.

3. Hoak, *King's Council*, pp. 55–71; his 'The King's Privy Chamber', pp. 93–4.

4. *The Acts and Monuments of John Foxe*, ed. G. Townsend (8 vols.; London, 1843–9), vi. 287–90.

5. A. J. Slavin, 'The Fall of Lord Chancellor Wriothesley: A Study in the Politics of Conspiracy', *Albion* 7 (1975), 275; L. Stone, 'Patriarchy and Paternalism in Tudor England: The Earl of Arundel and the Peasants Revolt of 1549', *Journal of British Studies*, 13 (1974), 19–23.

6. D. E. Hoak, 'Rehabilitating the Duke of Northumberland: Politics and Political Control, 1549–53', in J. Loach and R. Tittler (eds.), *The Mid-Tudor Polity, c. 1540–1560* (London, 1980), 29–51; his *King's Council*, pp. 91–110, 142–4, 146–51, 262–8; his 'The King's Privy Chamber', pp. 97–103.

7. Hoak, *King's Council*, pp. 73–6.

8. *APC* iii. 411; Hoak, *King's Council*, pp. 150–1.

9. Hoak, *King's Council*, pp. 199–201.

10. Hoak, 'Rehabilitating the Duke of Northumberland', pp. 41–2; S. E. Lehmberg, *Sir Walter Mildmay and Tudor Government* (Austin, Texas, 1964), 28–39; W. C. Richardson, *The History of the Court of Augmentations, 1536–1554* (Baton Rouge, La., 1961), 111–96; J. D. Alsop, 'The Structure of Early Tudor Finance, *c.*1509–1558', in C. Coleman and D. R. Starkey (eds.), *Revolution Reassessed: Revisions in the History of Tudor Government and Administration* (Oxford, 1986), 135–62.

11. Hoak, *King's Council*, pp. 203–13; his 'The King's Privy Chamber', pp. 106–7; F. C. Dietz, *English Public Finance, 1485–1641* (2 vols.; Urbana, Ill., 1921; 2nd edn., London, 1964), i. 188–201.

12. *APC* iv. 109.

13. J. D. Alsop, 'The Revenue Commission of 1552', *Historical Journal*, 22 (1979), 511–33; G. R. Elton, 'Mid-Tudor Finance', ibid., 20 (1977), 737–40; his *The Tudor Revolution in Government* (Cambridge, 1953), 230–8; W. C. Richardson (ed.), *The Report of the Royal Commission of 1552* (Morgantown, W. Va., 1974); his *History of the Court of Augmentations*, pp. 197–213.

14. D. L. Potter (ed.), 'Documents Concerning the Negotiations of the Anglo-French Treaty ôf March 1550', in *Camden Miscellany, XXVIII* (Camden Society, 4th ser., 29; London, 1984), 58–180.

15. B. L. Beer, *Northumberland: The Political Career of John Dudley, Earl of Warwick and Duke of Northumberland* (Kent, Ohio, 1973), 143. The day before his death Northumberland claimed that he first embraced reformed doctrines in 1537, which presents difficulties. His 'confession' was logical in so far as it recognized Mary's supremacy and raised the hope that she might spare him. Yet Mary and Gardiner sought the duke's conversion to Catholicism for propaganda reasons. Ibid. 158–9; Hoak, *King's Council*, p. 243.

16. M. Spufford, 'Puritanism and Social Control?', in A. Fletcher and J. Stevenson (eds.), *Order and Disorder in Early Modern England* (Cambridge, 1985), 41–57.

17. R. Hutton, 'The Local Impact of the Tudor Reformations', in C. Haigh (ed.), *The English Reformation Revised* (Cambridge, 1987), 114–38;

J. Strype, *The Life of the Learned Sir John Cheke, Knight* (Oxford, 1821), 189–218.

18. Humanism was the catalyst. Protestants and Catholics both advocated welfare schemes, e.g. at Mons, Ypres, Lyons, Venice, Wittenberg, Nuremberg, and Strasburg. G. R. Elton, *Reform and Renewal: Thomas Cromwell and the Common Weal* (Cambridge, 1973); his *Studies in Tudor and Stuart Politics and Government* (3 vols.; Cambridge, 1974–83), ii. 137–54; J. A. Guy, *Christopher St German on Chancery and Statute* (Selden Society, London, 1985), 28–32.

19. P. Slack, 'Social Policy and the Constraints of Government, 1547–58', in Loach and Tittler (eds.), *The Mid-Tudor Polity*, pp. 94–115.

20. H. Davies, *Worship and Theology in England from Cranmer to Hooker, 1534–1603* (Princeton, NJ, 1970), 106–11; D. D. Wallace, *Puritans and Predestination: Grace in English Protestant Theology, 1525–1695* (Chapel Hill, NC, 1982), 3–19; H. C. Porter (ed.), *Puritanism in Tudor England* (London, 1970), 295–300.

21. The average is, in fact, distorted: 206 titles were printed in 1550, thereafter output averaged 82 per year. The Privy Council reinstituted censorship after the rebellions of 1549, naming Petre, Smith, and Cecil censors (*APC* ii. 312). J. N. King, 'Freedom of the Press, Protestant Propaganda, and Protector Somerset', *Huntington Library Quarterly*, 40 (1976), 2–8.

22. *Lords Journals*, i. 384, 387.

23. J. Ketley (ed.), *The Two Liturgies . . . in the Reign of King Edward VI* (Parker Society, Cambridge, 1844), 179; D. F. Wright (ed.), *Common Places of Martin Bucer* (Appleford, 1972), 26.

24. *Foxe*, vi. 4–7.

25. Hutton, 'The Local Impact of the Tudor Reformations', pp. 125–6.

26. I owe this information to the kindness of Dr Susan Brigden. The radicals were attacked in Mary's reign not necessarily on heresy charges, but, for instance, on sexual ones. Cf. D. M. Loades, *The Reign of Mary Tudor: Politics, Government, and Religion in England, 1553–1558* (London, 1979), 284.

27. C. Haigh, *Reformation and Resistance in Tudor Lancashire* (Cambridge, 1975), 145.

28. R. Whiting, 'The Reformation in the South-West of England', unpublished Exeter University Ph.D. dissertation (1977), fos. 295–7.

29. *APC* iii. 228.

30. F. Heal, *Of Prelates and Princes: A Study of the Economic and Social Position of the Tudor Episcopate* (Cambridge, 1980), 126–50.

31. W. S. Hudson, *The Cambridge Connection and the Elizabethan Settlement of 1559* (Durham, NC, 1980), 43–89.

32. Strype, *Life of Cheke*, pp. 69–86.

33. 5 & 6 Edw. VI, c. 1.

34. *Lords Journals*, i. 421; M. A. R. Graves, *The House of Lords in the Parliaments of Edward VI and Mary I: An Institutional Study* (Cambridge, 1981), 81, 90.

35. Davies, *Worship and Theology*, pp. 201–10.

36. *APC* iv. 173.

37. N. L. Jones, 'Fine Tuning the Reformation', in J. A. Guy and H. G. Beale (eds.), *Law and Social Change in British History* (London, 1984), 86.

38. Beer, *Northumberland*, pp. 147–66; Hoak, 'Rehabilitating the Duke of Northumberland', pp. 48–9; D. MacCulloch (ed.), 'The *Vita Mariae Angliae Reginae* of Robert Wingfield of Brantham', in *Camden Miscellany, XXVIII* (Camden Society, 4th ser. 29; London, 1984), 181–301; his 'A Rejoinder', *Past and Present*, no. 93 (1981), 172–3.

39. The standard account of Mary's reign is Loades, *Mary Tudor*; for a more favourable assessment, see J. Loach, *Parliament and the Crown in the Reign of Mary Tudor* (Oxford, 1986). Essential theses are R. H. Pogson, 'Cardinal Pole: Papal Legate to England in Mary Tudor's Reign', unpublished Cambridge Ph.D. dissertation (1972); G. A. Lemasters, 'The Privy Council in the Reign of Queen Mary I', unpublished Cambridge Ph.D. dissertation (1971).

40. PRO LC 2/4/2 (unfoliated); Loades, *Mary Tudor*, pp. 30–1, 70–100, 119, 227, 252–84, 382–3, 412, 469; A. Somerset, *Ladies in Waiting: From the Tudors to the Present Day* (New York, 1984), 48–60; D. E. Hoak, 'Two Revolutions in Tudor Government: The Formation and Organization of Mary I's Privy Council', in Coleman and Starkey (eds.), *Revolution Reassessed*, pp. 87–115. Professor Hoak is at work on the Marian Court.

41. Hoak, 'Two Revolutions', pp. 104–13; Lemasters, 'The Privy Council', app. 2; J. A. Guy, *The Court of Star Chamber and its Records to the Reign of Elizabeth I* (London, 1985), 8–9.

42. Hoak, 'Two Revolutions', p. 106.

43. Loades, *Mary Tudor*, pp. 109–39.

44. Ibid. 95–6, 124–9; D. M. Loades, *Two Tudor Conspiracies* (Cambridge, 1965), 15–127.

45. A. F. Pollard (ed.), *Tudor Tracts, 1532–1588* (London, 1903), 212.

46. Loades, *Mary Tudor*, pp. 148–77; Haigh, *Reformation and Resistance*, pp. 178–94; J. E. Oxley, *The Reformation in Essex to the Death of Mary* (Manchester, 1965), 179–209; Loach, *Parliament and the Crown*, pp. 74–90.

47. Pogson, 'Cardinal Pole', fos. 5–106; his 'Reginald Pole and the Priorities of Government in Mary Tudor's Church', *Historical Journal*, 18 (1975), 3–20; his 'Revival and Reform in Mary Tudor's Church: A Question of Money', *Journal of Ecclesiastical History*, 25 (1974), 249–65; his 'The Legacy of the Schism: Confusion, Continuity and Change in the Marian Clergy', in Loach and Tittler (eds.), *The Mid-Tudor Polity*, pp. 116–36; D. Fenlon, *Heresy and Obedience in Tridentine Italy: Cardinal Pole and the Counter Reformation* (Cambridge, 1972).

48. Pogson, 'Cardinal Pole', fos. 139–235, 261–305; his 'Pole and the Priorities of Government', pp. 8–20; Loades, *Mary Tudor*, pp. 321–55.

49. Pogson, 'Cardinal Pole', fos. 236–60; Hutton, 'The Local Impact of the Tudor Reformations', pp. 128–33; Whiting, 'The Reformation in the South-West', fos. 64–75, 205–23, 278–82; Oxley, *Reformation in Essex*, pp. 190–1.

50. Pogson, 'Cardinal Pole', fos. 71–87; J. F. Davis, *Heresy and Reformation in the South-East of England, 1520–1559* (London, 1983), 105–49; Oxley, *Reformation in Essex*, pp. 210–37; J. W. Martin, 'A Sidelight on Foxe's Account of the Marian Martyrs', *Bulletin of the Institute of Historical Research*, 58 (1985), 248–51; S. E. Brigden, 'Youth and the English Reformation',

repr. in P. Slack (ed.), *Rebellion, Popular Protest and the Social Order in Early Modern England* (Cambridge, 1984), 77–107; Loades, *Mary Tudor*, pp. 332–3, 445–8. By 1558 burnings were organized at dawn to ensure minimum publicity (ibid. 448).

51. C. H. Garrett, *The Marian Exiles: A Study in the Origins of Elizabethan Puritanism* (Cambridge, 1938; repr. 1966); K. R. Bartlett, 'The English Exile Community in Italy and the Political Opposition to Queen Mary I', *Albion*, 13 (1981), 223–41; Loades, *Two Tudor Conspiracies*, pp. 151–75; J. Loach, 'Pamphlets and Politics, 1553–8', *Bulletin of the Institute of Historical Research*, 48 (1975), 31–44; her 'The Marian Establishment and the Printing Press', *English Historical Review*, 101 (1986), 135–48.

52. Pogson, 'Cardinal Pole', fos. 108–38; Loades, *Mary Tudor*, pp. 230–3, 240, 349–50, 428–52.

53. Pogson, 'Cardinal Pole', fo. 313; Loades, *Mary Tudor*, pp. 432–6.

54. Loades, *Mary Tudor*, pp. 183–205, 291–316, 404–23.

55. Ibid. 276, 297–301, 386–7, 401 n. 116, 404–9; C. S. L. Davies, 'England and the French War, 1557–9', in Loach and Tittler (eds.), *The Mid-Tudor Polity*, pp. 179–80; J. D. Alsop, 'The Theory and Practice of Tudor Taxation', *English Historical Review*, 97 (1982), 1–30; his 'Innovation in Tudor Taxation', ibid. 99 (1984), 83–93.

56. Loades, *Mary Tudor*, pp. 204, 305–10, 414–18; Dietz, i. 208–9.

57. C. Coleman, 'Artifice or Accident? The Reorganization of the Exchequer of Receipt, *c.*1554–72', in Coleman and Starkey (eds.), *Revolution Reassessed*, pp. 163–98; Alsop, 'The Structure of Early Tudor Finance', ibid. 135–62; J. H. M. Salmon, *Society in Crisis: France in the Sixteenth Century* (London, 1975), 303–6.

58. Coleman, 'Artifice or Accident?', pp. 164–78; Alsop, 'The Structure of Early Tudor Finance', pp. 140–50.

59. Loades, *Mary Tudor*, pp. 83–4, 168–70, 270–7; Graves, *House of Lords*, pp. 58–119, 173–201; his *The Tudor Parliaments: Crown, Lords and Commons, 1485–1603* (London, 1985), 99–113; S. T. Bindoff (ed.), *The House of Commons, 1509–1558* (3 vols.; London, 1982), i. 4; D. E. Hoak, in *Parliamentary History*, 2 (1983), 232–4.

60. Loach, *Parliament and the Crown*, pp. 172–235.

61. Loades, *Mary Tudor*, pp. 274–5; J. H. Langbein, *Prosecuting Crime in the Renaissance* (Cambridge, Mass., 1974), 1–125, 202–9, 248–51.

62. J. J. Goring, 'Social Change and Military Decline in Mid-Tudor England', *History*, 60 (1975), 185–97; C. G. Cruickshank, *Elizabeth's Army* (Oxford, 1946; 2nd edn., 1966), 17–24; L. Boynton, *The Elizabethan Militia, 1558–1638* (London, 1967), 7–12; Loades, *Mary Tudor*, pp. 276, 386–7, 388–9; Davies, 'England and the French War', p. 183; Graves, *House of Lords*, pp. 135, 150, 200.

63. G. S. Thomson, *Lords Lieutenants in the Sixteenth Century* (London, 1923), 14–42; Loades, *Mary Tudor*, pp. 382–8. At first the vulnerable parts of the country were covered; on 12 Apr. 1558 Winchester was given a general commission to cover counties not already under such jurisdiction.

64. Loades, *Mary Tudor*, pp. 314, 411. I am indebted to an unpublished seminar paper by Dr Simon Adams for the number of royal ships. The

fleet in time of war mostly comprised merchantmen: 140 ships attacked Brest in 1558.

65. Guy, *The Court of Star Chamber and its Records*, p. 57.
66. Loades, *Two Tudor Conspiracies*, pp. 128–217.
67. Loades, *Mary Tudor*, pp. 234–44, 365–95; his *Two Tudor Conspiracies*, pp. 172–4.
68. Davies, 'England and the French War', pp. 159–72; Loades, *Mary Tudor*, pp. 371–6.
69. Davies, 'England and the French War', pp. 178–81; Loades, *Mary Tudor*, pp. 377–9, 389–95.

CHAPTER 9. ELIZABETH I: THE ENGLISH DEBORAH?

1. A. F. Pollard (ed.), *Tudor Tracts, 1532–1588* (London, 1903), 367–92; S. Anglo, *Spectacle, Pageantry, and Early Tudor Policy* (Oxford, 1969), 344–59; C. Haigh (ed.), *The Reign of Elizabeth I* (London, 1984), 2–3.
2. Pollard (ed.), *Tudor Tracts*, pp. 387–8.
3. Ibid. 375–6; P. Collinson, 'The Elizabethan Church and the New Religion', in Haigh (ed.), *Reign of Elizabeth I*, p. 176.
4. Historical Manuscripts Commission, *Calendar of the Manuscripts of the Most Honourable the Marquis of Salisbury* (24 vols.; London, 1883–1976), ii. 462; R. B. Wernham, *Before the Armada: The Emergence of the English Nation, 1485–1588* (New York, 1966; repr. 1972), 234; W. T. MacCaffrey, *The Shaping of the Elizabethan Regime: Elizabethan Politics, 1558–72* (London, 1969), 298–301; S. L. Adams, 'Eliza Enthroned? The Court and its Politics', in Haigh (ed.), *Reign of Elizabeth I*, pp. 72–7.
5. *Fragmenta Regalia: Memoirs of Elizabeth, her Court and Favourites* (London, 1824), 8–14.
6. MacCaffrey, *Elizabethan Regime*, p. 299; his *Queen Elizabeth and the Making of Policy, 1572–1588* (Princeton, NJ, 1981), 16, 433–5; S. L. Adams, 'The Protestant Cause: Religious Alliance with the West European Calvinist Communities as a Political Issue in England, 1585–1630', unpublished Oxford D.Phil. dissertation (1973), fos. 1–25.
7. W. S. Hudson, *The Cambridge Connection and the Elizabethan Settlement of 1559* (Durham, NC, 1980), 9–42, 75–89; MacCaffrey, *Elizabethan Regime*, pp. 27–40.
8. *Fragmenta Regalia*, p. 8.
9. Adams, 'Eliza Enthroned?', pp. 62–71; his 'Faction, Clientage and Party: English Politics, 1550–1603', *History Today*, 32 (Dec. 1982), 33–9.
10. S. Haynes and W. Murdin (eds.), *Collection of State Papers . . . left by William Cecil, Lord Burghley* (2 vols.; London, 1740–59), ii. 760–1; Folger Shakespeare Library, MS V.a.459, fo. 9.
11. Adams, 'Eliza Enthroned?', p. 67.
12. Folger Shakespeare Library, MSS Z.d.12–14, 16; MacCaffrey, *Elizabethan Regime*, pp. 27–40, 289–95; his *Queen Elizabeth and the Making of Policy*, pp. 431–62; Adams, 'Eliza Enthroned?', pp. 59–71; A. Somerset, *Ladies*

in Waiting: From the Tudors to the Present Day (New York, 1984), 61–6. I am indebted to Dr Simon Adams for a discussion of Cecil's posture as secretary.

13. Henry E. Huntington Library, Ellesmere MSS 2580, 2625 (two versions of the same document). See D. E. Hoak, 'The Secret History of the Tudor Court: The King's Coffers and the King's Purse, 1542–1553', *Journal of British Studies*, 26 (1987), 230–1 and n. 89; D. R. Starkey (ed.), *The English Court: From the Wars of the Roses to the Civil War* (London, 1987), 13–14.

14. Adams, 'Eliza Enthroned?', pp. 72–7; MacCaffrey, *Elizabethan Regime*, pp. 27–40, 126–30.

15. Somerset, *Ladies in Waiting*, p. 65; *Calendar of the Manuscripts of the Marquis of Salisbury*, i. 465; P. Wright, 'A Change in Direction: The Ramifications of a Female Household, 1558–1603', in Starkey (ed.), *The English Court*, p. 153 and n. 26.

16. Adams, 'Faction, Clientage and Party', p. 37.

17. Ibid.; Adams, 'Eliza Enthroned?', p. 63; his 'Protestant Cause', fos. 25–35; MacCaffrey, *Elizabethan Regime*, pp. 94–101, 106, 138–41, 245–54, 294–5, 301–7; his *Queen Elizabeth and the Making of Policy*, pp. 440–8, 455–62; his 'Place and Patronage in Elizabethan Politics', in S. T. Bindoff, J. Hurstfield, and C. H. Williams (eds.), *Elizabethan Government and Society: Essays Presented to Sir John Neale* (London, 1961), 108–10.

18. Folger Shakespeare Library, MS L.b.516.

19. N. L. Jones, *Faith by Statute: Parliament and the Settlement of Religion, 1559* (London, 1982), 43–7; Hudson, *Cambridge Connection*, pp. 131–7.

20. G. Burnet, *History of the Reformation of the Church of England* (3 vols. in 6 parts; London, 1820), II. ii. 450–5; Jones, *Faith by Statute*, pp. 20–30; his 'Elizabeth's First Year: The Conception and Birth of the Elizabethan Political World', in Haigh (ed.), *Reign of Elizabeth I*, pp. 32–3; Hudson, *Cambridge Connection*, pp. 111–14.

21. Hudson, *Cambridge Connection*, p. 113; Burnet, *History of the Reformation*, II. ii. 451, 454.

22. Wernham, *Before the Armada*, pp. 278–305; Jones, *Faith by Statute*, pp. 50–4.

23. Jones, *Faith by Statute*, pp. 83–103.

24. Ibid. 114–29; Hudson, *Cambridge Connection*, pp. 121–3.

25. Jones, *Faith by Statute*, pp. 129–51; his 'Elizabeth's First Year', pp. 43–8; Hudson, *Cambridge Connection*, pp. 93–9, 123–30.

26. Jones, *Faith by Statute*, p. 150.

27. Ibid. 160–8; F. Heal, *Of Prelates and Princes: A Study of the Economic and Social Position of the Tudor Episcopate* (Cambridge, 1980), 204–13.

28. Jones, *Faith by Statute*, pp. 104–12; G. Alexander, 'Bishop Bonner and the Parliament of 1559', *Bulletin of the Institute of Historical Research*, 56 (1983), 164–79.

29. *Lords Journals*, i. 568.

30. *CSPF 1558–1559*, no. 1300.

31. Folger Shakespeare Library, MS V.b.214, fos. 118–25ᵛ.

32. Adams, 'Eliza Enthroned?', pp. 63–6. Cf. MacCaffrey, *Elizabethan Regime*, pp. 93, 130–3, 154–5, 163, 169, 183, 235, 245; C. Read, *Mr Secretary*

Cecil and Queen Elizabeth (London, 1955), 211, 265–6, 342–4, 410; M. B. Pulman, *The Elizabethan Privy Council in the Fifteen-Seventies* (Berkeley, Ca., 1971), 17–63.

33. P. C. Swensen, 'Noble Hunters of the Romish Fox: Religious Reform at the Tudor Court, 1543–1564', unpublished UC Berkeley Ph.D. dissertation (1981), fos. 300–474.

34. *CSPF 1562*, no. 765.

35. *CSPF 1562*, nos. 667–74.

36. MacCaffrey, *Elizabethan Regime*, pp. 86–101.

37. G. R. Elton, *The Parliament of England, 1559–1581* (Cambridge, 1986), 363–4.

38. G. Donaldson, *All the Queen's Men: Power and Politics in Mary Stewart's Scotland* (London, 1983), 48–116; MacCaffrey, *Elizabethan Regime*, pp. 149–66.

39. J. E. Neale, *Elizabeth I and her Parliaments* (2 vols.; London, 1953–7; repr. 1969), i. 144; Elton, *Parliament of England*, p. 366.

40. PRO SP 12/28/20 (fos. 68–9); Elton, *Parliament of England*, pp. 358–63.

41. Haynes and Murdin (eds.), ii. 756, 761–2; Elton, *Parliament of England*, pp. 364–74; MacCaffrey, *Elizabethan Regime*, pp. 137–40.

42. Elton, *Parliament of England*, pp. 356–7, 369–74; Neale, *Elizabeth I and her Parliaments*, i. 151–64.

43. R. R. Reid, *The King's Council in the North* (London, 1921; repr. 1975), 191–208; L. Stone, *The Crisis of the Aristocracy, 1558–1641* (Oxford, 1965), 250–3; MacCaffrey, *Elizabethan Regime*, pp. 70, 124–5, 129, 139; P. Williams, *The Tudor Regime* (Oxford, 1979), 446.

44. M. E. James, *Society, Politics and Culture: Studies in Early Modern England* (Cambridge, 1986), 354–6; MacCaffrey, *Elizabethan Regime*, pp. 221–46.

45. James, *Society, Politics and Culture*, p. 355 n. 190.

46. Ibid. 270–307; M. E. James, *Family, Lineage, and Civil Society: A Study of Society, Politics and Mentality in the Durham Region, 1500–1640* (Oxford, 1974), 49–63; MacCaffrey, *Elizabethan Regime*, pp. 221–62.

47. James, *Family, Lineage, and Civil Society*, p. 60; Stone, *Crisis of the Aristocracy*, pp. 252–3.

48. PRO SP 12/66/45; Stone, *Crisis of the Aristocracy*, pp. 253, 737–8; Reid, *King's Council in the North*, pp. 209–30.

49. G. Parker, *The Army of Flanders and the Spanish Road, 1567–1659* (Cambridge, 1972); C. Wilson, *Queen Elizabeth and the Revolt of the Netherlands* (London, 1970); Wernham, *Before the Armada*, pp. 290–305.

50. Neale, *Elizabeth I and her Parliaments*, i. 177–234.

51. Ibid. 310–11; Elton, *Parliament of England*, pp. 374–9; M. A. R. Graves, 'The Management of the Elizabethan House of Commons: The Council's "Men of Business" ', *Parliamentary History*, 2 (1983), 24–9.

52. Wernham, *Before the Armada*, p. 317; C. Read, *Lord Burghley and Queen Elizabeth* (London, 1960), 51–108.

53. Read, *Lord Burghley*, p. 87.

54. Ibid. 87–91.

55. G. Parker, *Spain and the Netherlands, 1559–1659* (London, 1979), 65–81; MacCaffrey, *Queen Elizabeth and the Making of Policy*, pp. 157–63;

P. Zagorin, *Rebels and Rulers, 1500-1660* (2 vols.; Cambridge, 1982), ii. 51-129.

56. MacCaffrey, *Elizabethan Regime*, pp. 289-95; his *Queen Elizabeth and the Making of Policy*, pp. 431-62; Hasler (ed.), *House of Commons, 1558-1603*, ii. 276-9; Adams, 'Eliza Enthroned?', pp. 66-7.

57. Haynes and Murdin (eds.), ii. 771; MacCaffrey, *Queen Elizabeth and the Making of Policy*, pp. 431-62; Adams, 'Eliza Enthroned?', p. 63. Cf. Read, *Lord Burghley*, pp. 21-2, 40, 224-5, 227, 270, 283, 297, 345, 366-7, 401.

58. MacCaffrey, *Queen Elizabeth and the Making of Policy*, pp. 438-9.

59. C. Read, *Mr Secretary Walsingham and the Policy of Queen Elizabeth* (3 vols.; Oxford, 1925); Hasler (ed.), *House of Commons, 1558-1603*, iii. 572.

60. See pp. 335-6.

61. Read, *Lord Burghley*, p. 188.

62. Hasler (ed.), *House of Commons, 1558-1603*, iii. 572.

63. MacCaffrey, *Queen Elizabeth and the Making of Policy*, pp. 164-90, 243-301; Wernham, *Before the Armada*, pp. 324-72. In 1574 Alençon succeeded to his brother's title of duke of Anjou, but it is usual to avoid confusion by referring to him throughout by his title under Charles IX.

64. Wilson, *Queen Elizabeth and the Revolt of the Netherlands*, pp. 34-41, 129-36; *CSPF 1575-7*, nos. 567, 574, 578, 598-9, 736-7, 1037, 1042, 1321-2, 1445, 1475; Adams, 'Protestant Cause', fo. 25.

65. Read, *Lord Burghley*, p. 265; MacCaffrey, *Queen Elizabeth and the Making of Policy*, pp. 296-7.

66. MacCaffrey, *Queen Elizabeth and the Making of Policy*, pp. 302-47, 402-22; Wernham, *Before the Armada*, pp. 337-54; Read, *Lord Burghley*, pp. 256-92; J. H. Elliott, *Europe Divided, 1559-1598* (London, 1968; repr. 1977), 265-321; T. W. Moody, F. X. Martin, and F. J. Byrne (eds.), *A New History of Ireland*, iii. *Early Modern Ireland, 1534-1691* (Oxford, 1976), 104-9.

67. Parker, *Army of Flanders*, p. 241.

68. MacCaffrey, *Queen Elizabeth and the Making of Policy*, p. 338.

69. Parker, *Spain and the Netherlands*, p. 71.

70. Folger Shakespeare Library, MS V.b.214, fos. 83^v-5^v.

71. MacCaffrey, *Queen Elizabeth and the Making of Policy*, pp. 348-9; Wernham, *Before the Armada*, pp. 371-2.

72. L. Stone, *An Elizabethan: Sir Horatio Palavicino* (Oxford, 1956), 153; F. C. Dietz, *English Public Finance, 1485-1641* (2 vols.; Urbana, Ill., 1921; 2nd edn., London, 1964), ii. 40 n. 17; Adams, 'Protestant Cause', fos. 42-75; MacCaffrey, *Queen Elizabeth and the Making of Policy*, pp. 353-6.

73. Parker, *Army of Flanders*, p. 231.

CHAPTER 10. ELIZABETHAN RELIGION

1. 1 Eliz. I, c. 2.

2. W. S. Hudson, *The Cambridge Connection and the Elizabeth Settlement of 1559* (Durham, NC, 1980), 105.

3. P. Collinson, *The Elizabethan Puritan Movement* (London, 1967), 59-70.

4. H. Gee and W. J. Hardy (eds.), *Documents Illustrative of English Church History* (London, 1910), 417–42.

5. The output of the press climbed steadily under Elizabeth. The average annual volume of publications exceeded that under Protector Somerset, though it was not until after 1570 that it exceeded the peak rates of 1548 and 1550. J. N. King, 'Freedom of the Press, Protestant Propaganda, and Protector Somerset', *Huntington Library Quarterly*, 40 (1976), 1–2.

6. W. P. Haugaard, *Elizabeth and the English Reformation: The Struggle for a Stable Settlement of Religion* (Cambridge, 1970), 135–44; R. Hutton, 'The Local Impact of the Tudor Reformations', in C. Haigh (ed.), *The English Reformation Revised* (Cambridge, 1987), 114–38.

7. Hutton, 'The Local Impact of the Tudor Reformations', p. 134.

8. C. Haigh, 'The Church of England, the Catholics and the People', in Haigh (ed.), *The Reign of Elizabeth I* (London, 1984), 197; Hutton, 'The Local Impact of the Tudor Reformations', p. 135.

9. R. Whiting, 'The Reformation in the South-West of England', unpublished Exeter University Ph.D. dissertation (1977), fos. 218–26, 286–91.

10. H. Gee, *The Elizabethan Clergy and the Settlement of Religion, 1558–1564* (Oxford, 1898), 247–51.

11. H. Davies, *Worship and Theology in England from Cranmer to Hooker, 1534–1603* (Princeton, NJ, 1970), 210–19, 358–9; J. C. Cox and A. Harvey, *English Church Furniture* (London, 1907); Whiting, 'Reformation in the South-West', fos. 230–5.

12. Davies, *Worship and Theology*, p. 214; *CSPD 1547–1580*, xxxvi. 41.

13. C. Haigh, 'Anticlericalism and the English Reformation', *History*, 68 (1983), 402; D. M. Gransby, 'Tithes Disputes in the Diocese of York, 1540–1639', unpublished York University M.Phil. dissertation (1966).

14. Ibid.

15. Haigh, 'Anticlericalism and the English Reformation', pp. 404–5; W. G. Bittle and R. Todd Lane, 'Inflation and Philanthropy in England: A Re-assessment of W. K. Jordan's Data', *Economic History Review*, 29 (1976), 209.

16. Ibid.

17. Whiting, 'Reformation in the South-West', fos. 86–91, 144–52. See also P. Collinson, 'The Elizabethan Church and the New Religion', in Haigh (ed.), *Reign of Elizabeth I*, pp. 184–7.

18. R. O'Day, *The English Clergy: Emergence and Consolidation of a Profession, 1558–1642* (Leicester, 1979); P. Collinson, *The Religion of Protestants: The Church in English Society, 1559–1625* (Oxford, 1982), 94–5; his 'Elizabethan Church', p. 186; C. Hill, *Economic Problems of the Church from Archbishop Whitgift to the Long Parliament* (Oxford, 1956; repr. 1968), 207.

19. Collinson, *Religion of Protestants*, pp. 220–30.

20. Ibid. 203.

21. 1 Eliz. I, c. 2.

22. Collinson, *Religion of Protestants*, pp. 210–20.

23. P. Clark, *English Provincial Society from the Reformation to the Revolution: Religion, Politics and Society in Kent, 1500–1640* (Hassocks, 1977), 156; Collinson, *Religion of Protestants*, p. 203.

24. D. A. Spaeth, 'Parsons and Parishioners: Lay-Clerical Conflict and Popular Piety in Wiltshire Villages, 1660–1740', unpublished Brown University Ph.D. dissertation (1985), fo. 355.

25. Folger Shakespeare Library, MS L.b.215.

26. Hutton, 'The Local Impact of the Tudor Reformations', pp. 136–7.

27. Folger Shakespeare Library, MS L.b.183.

28. Collinson, *Religion of Protestants*, p. 207.

29. Gee and Hardy (eds.), *Documents*, p. 434.

30. Collinson, *Religion of Protestants*, pp. 208–9.

31. Ibid. 209–10.

32. Haigh, 'Church of England', p. 197; see also his 'The Continuity of Catholicism in the English Reformation', *Past and Present*, no. 93 (1981), 37–69.

33. D. MacCulloch, 'Catholic and Puritan in Elizabethan Suffolk', *Archiv für Reformationsgeschichte*, 72 (1981), 247–61.

34. 13 Eliz. I, cc. 1, 2.

35. P. W. Hasler (ed.), *The House of Commons, 1558–1603* (3 vols.; London, 1981), i. 329.

36. 23 Eliz. I, c. 1; J. E. Neale, *Elizabeth I and her Parliaments* (2 vols.; London, 1953–7; repr. 1969), i. 378–92.

37. C. Haigh, 'Revisionism, the Reformation and the History of English Catholicism', *Journal of Ecclesiastical History*, 36 (1985), 400–1. Cf. P. McGrath, 'Elizabethan Catholicism: A Reconsideration', *Journal of Ecclesiastical History*, 35 (1984), 414–28.

38. P. J. Holmes, *Elizabethan Casuistry* (Catholic Record Society, 67; London, 1981).

39. C. Haigh, 'From Monopoly to Minority: Catholicism in Early Modern England', *Transactions of the Royal Historical Society*, 5th ser. 31 (1981), 129–47; his 'Continuity', pp. 37–69; his 'Church of England', pp. 195–219; his 'Revisionism', pp. 394–405; his *Reformation and Resistance in Tudor Lancashire* (Cambridge, 1975), 247–315. Cf. J. A. Bossy, *The English Catholic Community, 1570–1850* (London, 1975); J. C. H. Aveling, *The Handle and the Axe: The Catholic Recusants in England from Reformation to Emancipation* (London, 1976); McGrath, 'Elizabethan Catholicism', pp. 414–28.

40. Haigh, 'Continuity', pp. 48–9; his *Reformation and Resistance*, pp. 255–9.

41. Haigh, 'Continuity', pp. 48–9.

42. Haigh, 'From Monopoly to Minority', p. 145.

43. Haigh, 'Revisionism', p. 402.

44. McGrath, 'Elizabethan Catholicism', pp. 422–5. I am grateful to Professor McGrath for advice on the status of seminary priests listed by G. Anstruther, *The Seminary Priests* (2 vols.; Ware and Great Wakering, 1969–75).

45. P. McGrath, 'A Reply to Dr Haigh', *Journal of Ecclesiastical History*, 36 (1985), 405–6.

46. P. McGrath, *Papists and Puritans under Elizabeth I* (London, 1967), 192–3.

47. Cf. Haigh, 'Revisionism', pp. 399–400; his 'Puritan Evangelism in the Reign of Elizabeth I', *English Historical Review*, 92 (1977), 30–58; his 'Church of England', pp. 195–219.

48. Haigh, 'Revisionism', p. 400.

49. Collinson, 'Elizabethan Church', p. 179.

50. J. E. Booty (ed.), *An Apology of the Church of England* (Folger Books, Charlottesville, Va., 1963; repr. 1974), 100–1, 120–1.

51. Haugaard, *Elizabeth and the English Reformation*, pp. 247–72.

52. *The Acts and Monuments of John Foxe*, ed. G. Townsend (8 vols.; London, 1843–9); W. Haller, *Foxe's Book of Martyrs and the Elect Nation* (London, 1963); Collinson, 'Elizabethan Church', p. 176.

53. W. F. Moulton, *The History of the English Bible* (5th edn., London, n.d.), 150–80.

54. Collinson, *Religion of Protestants*, pp. 232–4; his 'Elizabethan Church', p. 182; Haigh, 'Church of England', pp. 211–12; H. S. Bennett, *English Books and Readers, 1558 to 1603* (Cambridge, 1965), 146–8.

55. Collinson, *Religion of Protestants*, pp. 242–83; his *Elizabethan Puritan Movement*, pp. 159–239; his 'Elizabethan Church', pp. 187–94.

56. Collinson, *Religion of Protestants*, pp. 242–83. See also his *Elizabethan Puritan Movement*; his *Archbishop Grindal, 1519–1583: The Struggle for a Reformed Church* (London, 1980); P. S. Seaver, *The Puritan Lectureships: The Politics of Religious Dissent, 1560–1662* (Stanford, Ca., 1970).

57. C. Hill, *Society and Puritanism in Pre-Revolutionary England* (London, 1964; repr. 1966); P. Lake, *Moderate Puritans and the Elizabethan Church* (Cambridge, 1982); C. M. Dent, *Protestant Reformers in Elizabethan Oxford* (Oxford, 1983). See also Lake's review in *English Historical Review*, 102 (1987), 204–6.

58. Lake, *Moderate Puritans*, pp. 282–6.

59. Ibid.; W. Haller, *The Rise of Puritanism* (New York, Harper Torchbook edn., 1957), 83–172; D. D. Wallace, *Puritans and Predestination: Grace in English Protestant Theology, 1525–1695* (Chapel Hill, NC, 1982), 43–55.

60. See p. 259.

61. Cf. Neale, *Elizabeth I and her Parliaments*, i. 351–3, 398–404; G. R. Elton, *The Parliament of England, 1559–1581* (Cambridge, 1986), 216.

62. Collinson, *Elizabethan Puritan Movement*, pp. 159–288, 303–16; M. M. Knappen, *Tudor Puritanism* (Chicago, 1939); G. R. Elton, *The Tudor Constitution* (Cambridge, 1960; 2nd edn., 1982), 442–61; his *Parliament of England*, pp. 198–216.

63. Lake, *Moderate Puritans*, pp. 284–5.

64. D. MacCulloch, *Suffolk and the Tudors: Politics and Religion in an English County, 1500–1600* (Oxford, 1986), 192–219; his 'Catholic and Puritan', pp. 278–81.

CHAPTER 11. PRIVY COUNCIL AND PARLIAMENTS

1. M. B. Pulman, *The Elizabethan Privy Council in the Fifteen-Seventies* (Berkeley, Ca., 1971), 52–63.

2. J. A. Guy, 'The Privy Council: Revolution or Evolution?', in C. Coleman and D. R. Starkey (eds.), *Revolution Reassessed: Revisions in the History of Tudor Government and Administration* (Oxford, 1986), 59–85; D. R. Starkey

(ed.), *The English Court: From the Wars of the Roses to the Civil War* (London, 1987), 1–24.

3. J. A. Guy, *The Cardinal's Court: The Impact of Thomas Wolsey in Star Chamber* (Hassocks, 1977); D. E. Hoak, *The King's Council in the Reign of Edward VI* (Cambridge, 1976); A. G. R. Smith, *The Government of Elizabethan England* (London, 1967); Pulman, *Elizabethan Privy Council*, pp. 150–72.

4. Pulman, *Elizabethan Privy Council*, p. 156.

5. Ibid. 164–8.

6. Ibid. 53.

7. J. D. Alsop, 'The Structure of Early Tudor Finance, *c.*1509–1558', in Coleman and Starkey (eds.), *Revolution Reassessed*, pp. 156–62; Pulman, *Elizabethan Privy Council*, pp. 86–93.

8. Pulman, *Elizabethan Privy Council*, p. 90.

9. Folger Shakespeare Library, MS 459, fo. 23^v; Pulman, *Elizabethan Privy Council*, p. 87.

10. Alsop, 'Structure of Early Tudor Finance', pp. 161–2; Pulman, *Elizabethan Privy Council*, p. 87.

11. *The Egerton Papers*, ed. J. P. Collier (Camden Society, OS 12; London, 1840), 215–17; S. Haynes and W. Murdin (eds.), *Collection of State Papers . . . left by William Cecil, Lord Burghley* (2 vols.; London, 1740–59), ii. 809.

12. G. R. Elton, *The Tudor Revolution in Government* (Cambridge, 1953), 276–89; see p. 54.

13. M. Bateson (ed.), 'A Collection of Original Letters from the Bishops to the Privy Council, 1564', in *Camden Miscellany* (Camden Society, NS 53; London, 1895).

14. Pulman, *Elizabethan Privy Council*, pp. 123–30; *The Papers of Nathaniel Bacon of Stiffkey*, ed. A. Hassell Smith, G. M. Baker, and R. W. Kenny (2 vols.; Norwich, 1979–83), ii. 201–4, 237–8, 265–7, 271–2, 274–6, 281–2, 286, 310–12.

15. Pulman, *Elizabethan Privy Council*, p. 109.

16. Henry E. Huntington Library, Ellesmere MS 6206B, fos. 14–23.

17. Counties could be grouped together in twos and threes: in 1587 Burghley was named to the combined lieutenancy of Lincolnshire, Essex, and Hertfordshire, while the earl of Pembroke administered Wales and the marches. Again, one county might have two or even three lieutenants acting jointly, as did Hampshire and Sussex.

18. G. S. Thomson, *Lords Lieutenants in the Sixteenth Century* (London, 1923), 43–73; A. Hassell Smith, *County and Court: Government and Politics in Norfolk, 1558–1603* (Oxford, 1986), 112–38; E. P. Cheyney, *A History of England from the Defeat of the Armada to the Death of Elizabeth* (2 vols.; London, 1914–26), ii. 359–77.

19. Thomson, *Lords Lieutenants*, pp. 73–83; Hassell Smith, *County and Court*, pp. 127–33; C. G. Cruickshank, *Elizabeth's Army* (Oxford, 1946; 2nd edn., 1966), 19–21.

20. J. A. Youings, *Sixteenth-century England* (Harmondsworth, 1984), 254–303; Pulman, *Elizabethan Privy Council*, pp. 139–49; G. R. Elton, *The Parliament of England, 1559–1581* (Cambridge, 1986), 260–2; R. H. Tawney and E. Power (eds.), *Tudor Economic Documents* (3 vols.; London, 1924),

i. 330–4; P. L. Hughes and J. F. Larkin (eds.), *Tudor Royal Proclamations* (3 vols.; New Haven, Conn., 1964–9), ii–iii *passim*.

21. Pulman, *Elizabethan Privy Council*, p. 120.

22. Ibid. 132.

23. J. H. Langbein, *Torture and the Law of Proof: Europe and England in the Ancien Regime* (Chicago, 1977), 81–123; Pulman, *Elizabethan Privy Council*, pp. 211–12.

24. Pulman, *Elizabethan Privy Council*, pp. 176–81.

25. G. R. Elton, *The Tudor Constitution* (Cambridge, 1960; 2nd edn., 1982), 102–11.

26. Parliaments were held in 1559, 1563–7 (sessions in 1563, 1566–7), 1571, 1572–81 (sessions in 1572, 1576, 1581), 1584–5, 1586–7, 1589, 1593, 1597–8, and 1601. The longest sessions were in 1559 (15 weeks), 1566–7 (13½ weeks), 1563 (13 weeks), 1597–8 (12 weeks), 1584–5 (11½ weeks), 1586–7 (10 weeks), 1581 (9 weeks), and 1571 (8 weeks). Other sessions were 7½ weeks (1572, 1589, 1601), 7 weeks (1593), and 5 weeks (1576).

27. No session was held in the following (inclusive) years: 1560–2, 1564–5, 1568–70, 1573–5, 1577–80, 1582–3, 1588, 1590–2, 1594–6, 1599–1600, 1602–3 (Elizabeth died on 24 March 1603).

28. J. E. Neale, 'The Lord Keeper's Speech to the Parliament of 1592–3', *English Historical Review*, 31 (1916), 130; J. S. Roskell, 'Perspectives in English Parliamentary History', in E. B. Fryde and E. Miller (eds.), *Historical Studies of the English Parliament* (2 vols.; Cambridge, 1970), ii. 296–323.

29. *De republica anglorum* (Scholar Press edn., Menston, 1970), 34–5.

30. P. W. Hasler (ed.), *The House of Commons, 1558–1603* (3 vols.; London, 1981); S. T. Bindoff (ed.), *The House of Commons, 1509–1558* (3 vols.; London, 1982).

31. J. E. Neale, *Elizabeth I and her Parliaments* (2 vols.; London, 1953–7; repr. 1969), *passim*; his *The Elizabethan House of Commons* (London, 1949; rev. edn., 1963). Cf. the similar thesis of W. Notestein, 'The Winning of the Initiative by the House of Commons', *Proceedings of the British Academy*, 11 (1926), 125–76. For demolition of these views, see Elton, *Parliament of England*; his 'Parliament in the Sixteenth Century: Functions and Fortunes', repr. in his *Studies in Tudor and Stuart Politics and Government* (3 vols.; Cambridge, 1974–83), iii. 156–82; his 'Parliament', in C. Haigh (ed.), *The Reign of Elizabeth I* (London, 1984), 79–100; see also his papers linked under the title 'The Materials of Parliamentary History', in *Studies*, iii. 58–155; his 'Parliament', in *Studies*, iii. 3–21; M. A. R. Graves, *The Tudor Parliaments: Crown, Lords and Commons, 1485–1603* (London, 1985); his 'Thomas Norton the Parliament Man: An Elizabethan MP, 1559–1581', *Historical Journal*, 23 (1980), 17–35; his 'The Management of the Elizabethan House of Commons: The Council's "Men of Business"', *Parliamentary History*, 2 (1983), 11–38.

32. Elton, *Parliament of England*, pp. 378–9.

33. S. B. Chrimes and A. L. Brown (eds.), *Select Documents of English Constitutional History, 1307–1485* (London, 1961), 11–17; E. Miller, *The Origins of Parliament* (Historical Association, London, 1960; repr. 1967), 21–2.

34. H. G. Richardson and G. O. Sayles, 'Parliaments and Great Councils in Medieval England', repr. in *The English Parliament in the Middle Ages* (London, 1981), xxvi. 2.

35. *Fleta*, Bk. II, c. 2; Richardson and Sayles, xxvi. 2.

36. 'Pur voier le estat du reaume et pur treter des communes busoignes du roy et du reaume'; Richardson and Sayles, xxvi. 2 n. 1.

37. Miller, *Origins*, p. 22; Elton, *Parliament of England*, p. 378; his *Studies*, iii. 3–21.

38. Richardson and Sayles, xxvi. 19–24.

39. M. A. R. Graves, *Elizabethan Parliaments, 1559–1601* (London, 1987), 45.

40. H. Miller, *Henry VIII and the English Nobility* (Oxford, 1986), pp. 131–2, 255. Cf. Elton, *Parliament of England*, p. 378.

41. See pp. 399–402.

42. Neale, *Elizabeth I and her Parliaments*, i. 177–240; Graves, 'Management', pp. 12–13, 24; N. L. Jones, 'Fine Tuning the Reformation', in J. A. Guy and H. G. Beale (eds.), *Law and Social Change in British History* (London, 1984), 86–95.

43. Elton, *Parliament of England*, p. 376; Graves, 'Management', pp. 24–9; Neale, *Elizabeth I and her Parliaments*, i. 309–10.

44. Elton, *Parliament of England*, pp. 375–6; W. T. MacCaffrey, 'Parliament: The Elizabethan Experience', in D. J. Guth and J. W. McKenna (eds.), *Tudor Rule and Revolution* (Cambridge, 1982), 137.

45. Neale, *Elizabeth I and her Parliaments*, ii. 133.

46. Elton, *Parliament of England*, p. 343; J. S. Roskell, *The Commons and their Speakers in English Parliaments, 1367–1523* (Manchester, 1965).

47. Graves, 'Management', pp. 11–32; his 'Thomas Norton', pp. 17–35.

48. Graves, 'Management', p. 31.

49. Ibid. 16, 33 n. 35.

50. Ibid. 14; Elton, *Parliament of England*, p. 52.

51. Graves, 'Management', p. 14.

52. Data compiled from tables in *The Statutes at Large* (London, 1786 edn.). Cf. Elton, 'Parliament', in Haigh (ed.), *Reign of Elizabeth I*, p. 94; his *Parliament of England*, p. 52.

53. 5 Eliz. I, c. 3; Elton, *Parliament of England*, p. 268; J. Pound, *Poverty and Vagrancy in Tudor England* (London, 1971; repr. 1978), 45.

54. 14 Eliz. I, c. 5; Elton, *Parliament of England*, pp. 269–71; P. Williams, *The Tudor Regime* (Oxford, 1979), 200; Pound, *Poverty and Vagrancy*, pp. 47–8.

55. 18 Eliz. I, c. 3; Elton, *Parliament of England*, pp. 270–1; Williams, *Tudor Regime*, p. 200.

56. 39 Eliz. I, c. 3; 43 Eliz. I, cc. 2, 3; Pound, *Poverty and Vagrancy*, pp. 53–7.

57. 39 Eliz. I, c. 5; 43 Eliz. I, c. 4.

58. 39 Eliz. I, c. 4.

59. A. L. Beier, *Masterless Men: The Vagrancy Problem in England, 1560–1640* (London, 1985). See pp. 43–4.

60. D. Woodward, 'The Background to the Statute of Artificers: The Genesis of Labour Policy, 1558–63', *Economic History Review*, 33 (1980), 32–44.

61. Elton, *Parliament of England*, p. 265; Woodward, 'Background', pp. 34–5.

62. 5 Eliz. I, c. 4.

63. Elton, *Parliament of England*, pp. 265–7; Woodward, 'Background', pp. 41–4; C. G. A. Clay, *Economic Expansion and Social Change: England 1500–1700* (2 vols.; Cambridge, 1984), i. 230, 234–5. For indexes of wages, see above, ch. 2, table 3.

64. T. G. Barnes, 'Star Chamber and the Sophistication of the Criminal Law', *Criminal Law Review* (1977), 316–26.

65. G. R. Elton, *Reform and Renewal: Thomas Cromwell and the Common Weal* (Cambridge, 1973), 129–57.

66. J. A. Guy, *The Court of Star Chamber and its Records to the Reign of Elizabeth I* (London, 1985).

67. 5 Eliz. I, cc. 10, 16, 17; Elton, *Parliament of England*, p. 299.

68. 5 Eliz. I, cc. 9, 14.

69. Barnes, 'Star Chamber', pp. 316–26.

70. 13 Eliz. I, c. 5; 27 Eliz. I, c. 4.

71. 8 Eliz. I, c. 4; Elton, *Parliament of England*, p. 301. For the 1489 act concerning benefit of clergy, see p. 64.

72. 18 Eliz. I, c. 7; Elton, *Parliament of England*, pp. 63–6, 301–2.

73. Elton, *Studies*, iii. 12–16; his *Parliament of England*, pp. 43–61, 303–18.

74. Elton, *Studies*, iii. 14–15.

75. Elton, *Parliament of England*, pp. 44–7, 55–7.

76. Ibid. 52 and n. 46.

77. Neale, *Elizabethan House of Commons*, p. 378. I am grateful to Professor A. Hassell Smith for a discussion of this point.

78. Ibid. 369; Elton, *Studies*, iii. 16.

CHAPTER 12. THE WAR WITH SPAIN

1. PRO SP 12/174/1–11, 14–18; Folger Shakespeare Library, MS V.a.321, fos. 36ᵛ–8; *The Papers of Nathaniel Bacon of Stiffkey*, ed. A. Hassell Smith, G. M. Baker, and R. W. Kenny (2 vols.; Norwich, 1979–83), ii. 296–8; D. Cressy, 'Binding the Nation: The Bonds of Association, 1584 and 1696', in D. J. Guth and J. W. McKenna (eds.), *Tudor Rule and Revolution* (Cambridge, 1982), 217–34.

2. C. Haigh (ed.), *The Reign of Elizabeth I* (London, 1984), 17–18; J. Garrett, *The Triumphs of Providence: The Assassination Plot, 1696* (Cambridge, 1980).

3. J. E. Neale, *Elizabeth I and her Parliaments* (2 vols.; London, 1953–7; repr. 1969), ii. 13–101.

4. Henry E. Huntington Library, Ellesmere MS 1192 (draft in Popham's hand corrected by Burghley); PRO SP 12/176/22, 28–30.

5. *Correspondence of Robert Dudley, Earl of Leycester, during his Government of the Low Countries, in the Years 1585 and 1586*, ed. J. Bruce (Camden Society, OS 27; London, 1844), 342.

6. PRO SP 12/194/30.

7. Neale, *Elizabeth I and her Parliaments*, ii. 104. The trial commissioners had found Mary guilty of plotting Elizabeth's death from which it followed by the terms of the Act for the Queen's Safety that her life was forfeit.

8. Ibid. ii. 129.

9. Folger Shakespeare Library, MS V.b.142, fo. 26.

10. C. Read, *Lord Burghley and Queen Elizabeth* (London, 1960), 366–8; Neale, *Elizabeth I and her Parliaments*, ii. 139–49.

11. Read, *Lord Burghley*, pp. 366–70; Neale, *Elizabeth I and her Parliaments*, ii. 137.

12. Neale, *Elizabeth I and her Parliaments*, ii. 140.

13. W. T. MacCaffrey, *Queen Elizabeth and the Making of Policy, 1572–1588* (Princeton, NJ, 1981), 348–401; S. L. Adams, 'The Protestant Cause: Religious Alliance with the West European Calvinist Communities as a Political Issue in England, 1585–1630', unpublished Oxford D.Phil. dissertation (1973), fos. 36–103; Read, *Lord Burghley*, pp. 306–39.

14. Adams, 'Protestant Cause', fos. 52–87.

15. MacCaffrey, *Queen Elizabeth and the Making of Policy*, pp. 379–91; Adams, 'Protestant Cause', fos. 91–103; G. Parker, *The Army of Flanders and the Spanish Road, 1567–1659* (Cambridge, 1972), 241–4; J. A. Dop, *Eliza's Knights: Soldiers, Poets, and Puritans in the Netherlands, 1572–1586* (Alblasserdam, Netherlands, 1981).

16. *Spenser's Minor Poems*, ed. E. de Sélincourt (Oxford, 1960; repr. 1966), 134. The poem is mainly devoted to the honour of Leicester and Sir Philip Sidney.

17. Folger Shakespeare Library, MS G.b.5, fos. 16–20ᵛ (Spanish intelligence summary); G. Parker, *Spain and the Netherlands, 1559–1659* (London, 1979), 18–43, 135–47; his *Army of Flanders*, pp. 243–4.

18. Parker, *Spain and the Netherlands*, pp. 135–47; K. R. Andrews, *Trade, Plunder and Settlement: Maritime Enterprise and the Genesis of the British Empire, 1480–1630* (Cambridge, 1984), 230–5.

19. Parker, *Army of Flanders*, pp. 265–6.

20. Henry E. Huntington Library, Ellesmere MS 6206B, fos. 14–15, 18ᵛ–19; L. Boynton, *The Elizabethan Militia, 1558–1638* (London, 1967), 53–125; C. G. Cruickshank, *Elizabeth's Army* (Oxford, 1946; 2nd edn., 1966), 17–40.

21. Boynton, *Elizabethan Militia*, pp. 126–64; Read, *Lord Burghley*, pp. 410–36; Parker, *Army of Flanders*, p. 6.

22. *CSPF 1559–1560*, pp. cxxviii–ix.

23. Henry E. Huntington Library, Ellesmere MS 6206B, fos. 15ᵛ–16.

24. I am indebted to an unpublished seminar paper by Dr Simon Adams for numbers of royal ships. Cf. Read, *Lord Burghley*, p. 420; P. Williams, *The Tudor Regime* (Oxford, 1979), 130.

25. G. Mattingly, *The Defeat of the Spanish Armada* (London, 1959); D. Howarth, *The Voyage of the Armada: The Spanish Story* (London, 1981); D. B. Quinn, 'Spaniards at Sea', in *Times Literary Supplement* (18 Dec. 1981), 1473–4; I. A. A. Thompson, 'Spanish Armada Guns', *Mariner's Mirror*, 61 (1975), 355–71.

26. Quinn, 'Spaniards at Sea'; Mattingly, *The Defeat of the Spanish Armada*.

27. R. B. Wernham, *After the Armada: Elizabethan England and the Struggle for Western Europe, 1588–1595* (Oxford, 1984); Adams, 'Protestant Cause', fos. 104–53.

28. Wernham, *After the Armada*, pp. 93–4, 181–4, 246–9, 262–9, 412–18, 555–66; Andrews, *Trade, Plunder and Settlement*, pp. 223–55.

29. Parker, *Spain and the Netherlands*, pp. 70-3.
30. Wernham, *After the Armada*, pp. 141-5, 149-51, 161-2, 179-81, 204, 271-80, 294-301, 358, 362-4, 381, 412-16, 421, 460-1, 503, 529-34, 542-7, 554.
31. Parker, *Spain and the Netherlands*, pp. 70-3.
32. Wernham, *After the Armada*, pp. 287-91, 414-20, 488-513, 520-2.
33. Adams, 'Protestant Cause', fos. 135-45; Wernham, *After the Armada*, pp. 556-8.
34. Parker, *Army of Flanders*, pp. 185-206, 244-51, 263-8; his *Spain and the Netherlands*, pp. 45-63, 106-21; Wernham, *After the Armada*, pp. 23-47, 53-87.
35. Wernham, *After the Armada*, pp. 207-33.
36. Ibid. 407, 415-20.
37. Parker, *Army of Flanders*, pp. 245-51, 264-5; his *Spain and the Netherlands*, pp. 18-43; Wernham, *After the Armada*, pp. 563-6; F. C. Dietz, *English Public Finance, 1485-1641* (2 vols.; Urbana, Ill., 1921; 2nd edn., London, 1964), ii. 455-9.
38. Wernham, *After the Armada*, pp. 514-59; Parker, *Army of Flanders*, pp. 246-51.
39. Wernham, *After the Armada*, p. 114.
40. Ibid. 92-130; R. B. Wernham, 'Queen Elizabeth and the Portugal Expedition of 1589', *English Historical Review*, 66 (1951), 1-26, 194-218; Andrews, *Trade, Plunder and Settlement*, pp. 236-8.
41. *Adams's Chronicle of Bristol*, ed. F. F. Fox (Bristol, 1910), 137, cited by Andrews, *Trade, Plunder and Settlement*, p. 238.
42. Wernham, *After the Armada*, pp. 235-61, 445-60; K. R. Andrews, *Elizabethan Privateering: English Privateering during the Spanish War, 1585-1603* (Cambridge, 1964); his *Trade, Plunder and Settlement*, pp. 238-55.
43. Andrews, *Trade, Plunder and Settlement*, pp. 240-2; Cruickshank, *Elizabeth's Army*, pp. 251-79.
44. Andrews, *Trade, Plunder and Settlement*, pp. 242-340; his 'Elizabethan Privateering', in J. Youings (ed.), *Raleigh in Exeter: Privateering and Colonisation in the Reign of Elizabeth I* (Exeter, 1985), 1-19.

CHAPTER 13. THE MAKING OF THE TUDOR STATE

1. For the background, see Q. Skinner, *The Foundations of Modern Political Thought* (2 vols.; Cambridge, 1978; repr. 1979), ii. 349-58.
2. E. G. Salter, *Tudor England through Venetian Eyes* (London, 1930), 68-79, 117-27; *The Works of Sir John Fortescue, Knight, Chief Justice of England and Lord Chancellor to King Henry the Sixth*, ed. T. Fortescue [Lord Clermont] (2 vols.; London, 1869), i. 552.
3. *Merchant of Venice*, I. iii. 49.
4. *Henry V*, III. ii. 136.
5. S. G. Ellis, 'Crown, Community and Government in the English Territories, 1450-1575', *History*, 71 (1986), 194, 203.

6. G. R. Elton, 'Wales in Parliament, 1542–1581', in R. R. Davies, R. A. Griffiths, I. G. Jones, and K. O. Morgan (eds.), *Welsh Society and Nationhood: Historical Essays Presented to Glanmor Williams* (Cardiff, 1984), 108–21.

7. Ellis, 'Crown, Community and Government', pp. 195–6; G. J. Hand, 'Aspects of Alien Status in Medieval English Law, with Special Reference to Ireland', in D. Jenkins (ed.), *Legal History Studies, 1972* (Cardiff, 1975), 129–34.

8. M. Dewar, *Sir Thomas Smith: A Tudor Intellectual in Office* (London, 1964), 157.

9. *The Acts and Monuments of John Foxe*, ed. G. Townsend (8 vols.; London, 1843–9), iv. 447–555.

10. J. Hurstfield, *The Queen's Wards: Wardship and Marriage under Elizabeth I* (London, 1958), 257.

11. S. G. Ellis, 'England in the Tudor State', *Historical Journal*, 26 (1983), 201–12; his 'Crown, Community and Government', pp. 187–204; P. Williams, *The Tudor Regime* (Oxford, 1979), 4–6, 421–52.

12. Ellis, 'England in the Tudor State', p. 212.

13. M. E. James, *Society, Politics and Culture: Studies in Early Modern England* (Cambridge, 1986), 48–175; R. R. Reid, *The King's Council in the North* (London, 1921; repr. 1975), 147–65; Williams, *Tudor Regime*, pp. 443–7.

14. Control of the duchies of Lancaster and Cornwall, and the palatinates of Chester and Lancaster, had reverted to the Crown by 1399. The bishop of Durham had jurisdiction over a larger area than that of the modern county. Henry VIII curtailed the bishop's criminal jurisdiction in 1536, though the latter nominated JPs until 1836. K. Emsley and C. M. Fraser, *The Courts of the County Palatine of Durham from Earliest Times to 1971* (Durham, 1984).

15. S. G. Ellis, *Tudor Ireland: Crown, Community and the Conflict of Cultures, 1470–1603* (London, 1985); T. W. Moody, F. X. Martin, and F. J. Byrne (eds.), *A New History of Ireland*, iii. *Early Modern Ireland, 1534–1691* (Oxford, 1976). See also Ellis, 'Nationalist Historiography and the English and Gaelic Worlds in the Late Middle Ages', *Irish Historical Studies*, 25 (1986), 1–18.

16. S. G. Ellis, *Reform and Revival: English Government in Ireland, 1470–1534* (Woodbridge, 1986); his *Tudor Ireland*, pp. 26–30, 53–148.

17. S. G. Ellis, 'Tudor Policy and the Kildare Ascendancy in the Lordship of Ireland, 1496–1534', *Irish Historical Studies*, 20 (1977), 235–71.

18. Ellis, *Tudor Ireland*, pp. 124–9; his 'Tudor Policy and the Kildare Ascendancy', pp. 260–71; his 'The Kildare Rebellion and the Early Henrician Reformation', *Historical Journal*, 19 (1976), 807–30.

19. Ellis, *Tudor Ireland*, pp. 129–48; his 'Tudor Policy and the Kildare Ascendancy', pp. 268–71.

20. Ellis, *Tudor Ireland*, p. 137.

21. *St. Pap.* iii. 278, 323; Ellis, *Tudor Ireland*, pp. 137–40; Moody *et al.* (eds.), *New History of Ireland*, iii. 46–67; B. Bradshaw, *The Irish Constitutional Revolution of the Sixteenth Century* (Cambridge, 1979).

22. Moody *et al.* (eds.), *New History of Ireland*, iii. 51–2.

23. Ellis, *Tudor Ireland*, pp. 174–80, 228–49; Moody *et al.* (eds.), *New History of Ireland*, iii. 69–93.

24. Ellis, *Tudor Ireland*, pp. 244–74.

25. H. Mumford Jones, 'Origins of the Colonial Idea in England', *Proceedings of the American Philosophical Society*, 85 (1942), 452; N. Canny, *The Elizabethan Conquest of Ireland: A Pattern Established, 1565–1576* (Hassocks, 1976).

26. *CSPI 1509–1573* (London, 1860), 289, 298–9; Moody *et al.* (eds.), *New History of Ireland*, iii. 76–86.

27. Moody *et al.* (eds.), *New History of Ireland*, iii. 79–86.

28. Ibid. 86–100.

29. Ellis, *Tudor Ireland*, pp. 251–85; Moody *et al.* (eds.), *New History of Ireland*, iii. 94–113.

30. Moody *et al.* (eds.), *New History of Ireland*, iii. 102–9; Ellis, *Tudor Ireland*, pp. 278–85.

31. Moody *et al.* (eds.), *New History of Ireland*, iii. 109–15; Ellis, *Tudor Ireland*, pp. 285–97.

32. Moody *et al.* (eds.), *New History of Ireland*, iii. 115–27; Ellis, *Tudor Ireland*, pp. 297–303.

33. Moody *et al.* (eds.), *New History of Ireland*, iii. 122–7; Ellis, *Tudor Ireland*, pp. 302–6, 311.

34. Moody *et al.* (eds.), *New History of Ireland*, iii. 127–9; Ellis, *Tudor Ireland*, pp. 306–7.

35. Moody *et al.* (eds.), *New History of Ireland*, iii. 129–37; Ellis, *Tudor Ireland*, pp. 307–12.

36. Ellis, *Tudor Ireland*, pp. 183–223; K. S. Bottigheimer, 'The Reformation in Ireland Revisited', *Journal of British Studies*, 15 (1976), 140–9.

37. *LP* XII. i, no. 901 (p. 410).

38. G. R. Elton, *Studies in Tudor and Stuart Politics and Government* (3 vols.; Cambridge, 1974–83), ii. 55.

39. PRO SP 12/66/54 (quotations from fo. 150^{r-v}); G. R. Elton, *The Parliament of England, 1559–1581* (Cambridge, 1986), 199–216.

40. A. G. Fox and J. A. Guy, *Reassessing the Henrician Age: Humanism, Politics, and Reform* (Oxford, 1986), 151–78, 199–220; J. A. Guy, *Christopher St German on Chancery and Statute* (Selden Society, London, 1985).

41. J. A. Guy, *The Public Career of Sir Thomas More* (Brighton, 1980), 198.

42. PRO SP 2/L, fos. 203–4 (*LP* V, no. 1016 (3)).

43. *De legibus*, Bk. I, c. 8.

44. BL Cotton MS Cleopatra E.VI, fo. 28^{v}.

45. W. Ullmann, *Principles of Government and Politics in the Middle Ages* (London, 1961; 2nd edn., 1966), 176–8.

46. *Foxe*, vi. 43.

47. *The Debate betwene the heraldes of Englande and Fraunce, compyled by Jhon Coke, clarke of the kynges recognysaunce, or vulgerly, called clarke of the Statutes of the staple of Westmynster, and fynyshed the yere of our Lorde* (London, 1550).

48. E. C. Wilson, *England's Eliza* (New York, 1939; repr. 1966), 109; F. A. Yates, *Astraea: The Imperial Theme in the Sixteenth Century* (London, 1975), 29–120.

49. *St. Pap.* i. 659; iii. 323.

50. Edward Hall, *Henry VIII*, ed. C. Whibley (2 vols.; London, 1904), ii. 328. I am grateful to Professor A. J. Slavin for advice on this point.
51. Guy, *Christopher St German*, *passim*.
52. T. F. T. Plucknett and J. L. Barton (eds.), *Doctor and Student* (Selden Society, London, 1974), 327.
53. *An Answer to a Letter* (London, 1535), sigs. G5ᵛ–G6; Fox and Guy, *Reassessing the Henrician Age*, pp. 208–20.
54. Ibid. 207–10.
55. J. A. Guy, 'Law, Lawyers, and the English Reformation', *History Today*, 35 (1985), 16–22; C. S. R. Russell, 'Types of Ambiguity', *London Review of Books* (22 Jan. 1987), 15–16.
56. P. Lake, review of M. Mendle, *Dangerous Positions*, in *Parliamentary History*, 6 (1987), 336. Lake here cites an unpublished lecture by Professor Patrick Collinson.
57. *The Works of John Whitgift, D.D.*, ed. J. Ayre (3 vols.; Parker Society, Cambridge, 1851–3), i. 20–1, 372.
58. Books VI and VIII were not printed until 1648, while Book VII was unavailable until 1662.
59. *The Works of that Learned and Judicious Divine, Mr Richard Hooker*, ed. J. Keble (3 vols.; 7th edn., Oxford, 1888): *Laws of Ecclesiastical Polity*, VIII. vi. 11. See H. C. Porter, 'Hooker, the Tudor Constitution, and the *Via Media*', in W. Speed Hill (ed.), *Studies in Richard Hooker: Essays Preliminary to an Edition of his Works* (Cleveland, Ohio, 1972), 77–116.
60. *Polity*, VIII. vi. 11.
61. Ibid.
62. Ibid. ii. 13.
63. P. G. Lake, 'Calvinism and the English Church, 1570–1635', *Past and Present*, no. 114 (1987), 32–76; J. S. A. Adamson, 'The *Vindiciae Veritatis* and the Political Creed of Viscount Saye and Sele', *Historical Research*, 60 (1987), 45–63.
64. V. Morgan, 'Whose Prerogative in Late Sixteenth and Early Seventeenth Century England?', in A. Kiralfy, M. Slatter, and R. Virgoe (eds.), *Custom, Courts and Counsel* (London, 1985), 39–55.

CHAPTER 14. ELIZABETHAN GOVERNMENT

1. J. Hurstfield, *Freedom, Corruption and Government in Elizabethan England* (London, 1973), 105.
2. C. E. Challis, *The Tudor Coinage* (Manchester, 1978), 126–7, 258, 263–5, 268–74.
3. PRO SP 12/287/59; F. C. Dietz, *English Public Finance, 1485–1641* (2 vols.; Urbana, Ill., 1921; 2nd edn., London, 1964), ii. 4, 18–21, 44, 62–6, 296–301, 307–27.
4. H. M. Colvin (ed.), *The History of the King's Works*, iv. *1485–1660* (Part II) (London, 1982), 8; Dietz, ii. 34–5.
5. Dietz, ii. 22–9, 53–5, 70–2, 80–1, 380–93.
6. PRO SP 12/263/80 (fos. 113–16).

7. Ibid. (fos. 115–16).
8. For discussion of local militia rates and ship money, see pp. 385–8. J. D. Alsop, 'The Theory and Practice of Tudor Taxation', *English Historical Review*, 97 (1982), 1–30; his 'Innovation in Tudor Taxation', ibid. 99 (1984), 83–93; G. L. Harriss, 'Thomas Cromwell's "New Principle" of Taxation', ibid. 93 (1978), 721–38; G. R. Elton, *Studies in Tudor and Stuart Politics and Government* (3 vols.; Cambridge, 1974–83), iii. 216–33; his *The Parliament of England, 1559–1581* (Cambridge, 1986), 151–74; Dietz, ii. 22–4, 380–2.
9. Alsop, 'Theory and Practice of Tudor Taxation', p. 13; Dietz, ii. 380.
10. See p. 5.
11. Alsop, 'Theory and Practice of Tudor Taxation', pp. 26–30.
12. C. Coleman, 'Artifice or Accident? The Reorganization of the Exchequer of Receipt, *c.*1554–1572', in Coleman and D. R. Starkey (eds.), *Revolution Reassessed: Revisions in the History of Tudor Government and Administration* (Oxford, 1986), 195; Dietz, ii. 47–8.
13. Dietz, ii. 16.
14. R. B. Outhwaite, 'Royal Borrowing in the Reign of Elizabeth I: The Aftermath of Antwerp', *English Historical Review*, 86 (1971), 251–63; Dietz, ii. 25–9.
15. Dietz, ii. 22, 84, 382–8.
16. Ibid. i. 161–2; ii. 382–93; A. Fletcher, *A County Community in Peace and War: Sussex 1600–1660* (London, 1975), 203.
17. E. P. Cheyney, *A History of England from the Defeat of the Armada to the Death of Elizabeth* (2 vols.; London, 1914–26), ii. 214–44; Dietz, ii. 384–93; Fletcher, *A County Community*, p. 203. In 1622 Lord Treasurer Middlesex was valued for taxation at £150, but his wealth was at least £90,250. The duke of Buckingham was valued at £400, but his annual income in 1623 was £15,000.
18. Dietz, ii. 384–8; C. Russell, *Parliaments and English Politics, 1621–1629* (Oxford, 1979), 50.
19. P. Williams, *The Tudor Regime* (Oxford, 1979), 459.
20. Department of Special Collections, Spencer Library, University of Kansas, MS Q12:39 (a list of Elizabeth's debts from the papers of Sir Julius Caesar).
21. Ibid.
22. The rating system was potentially more efficient than subsidy procedure in that people were assessed for all their lands and wealth in the places where they lay; the subsidy was leviable only at the place of the taxpayer's main residence after 1559, though this whole subject requires further research.
23. C. G. Cruickshank, *Elizabeth's Army* (Oxford, 1946; 2nd edn., 1966), 17–40, 91–142; P. Williams, 'The Crown and the Counties', in C. Haigh (ed.), *The Reign of Elizabeth I* (London, 1984), 129–31; his *Tudor Regime*, pp. 76–7; P. Clark, *English Provincial Society from the Reformation to the Revolution: Religion, Politics and Society in Kent, 1500–1640* (Hassocks, 1977), 221–6; A. Hassell Smith, 'Militia Rates and Militia Statutes, 1558–1663', in P. Clark, A. G. R. Smith, and N. Tyacke (eds.), *The English Commonwealth, 1547–1640* (Leicester, 1979), 93–110.

24. A. G. R. Smith, *The Government of Elizabethan England* (London, 1967); A. Hassell Smith, *County and Court: Government and Politics in Norfolk, 1558–1603* (Oxford, 1974); D. MacCulloch, *Suffolk and the Tudors: Politics and Religion in an English County, 1500–1600* (Oxford, 1986); Clark, *English Provincial Society*; G. A. J. Hodgett, *Tudor Lincolnshire* (Lincoln, 1975); A. Fletcher, *Reform in the Provinces: The Government of Stuart England* (London, 1986), 3–5; his *A County Community*, pp. 127–9.

25. G. C. F. Forster, *The East Riding Justices of the Peace in the Seventeenth Century* (East Yorks. Local History Society, York, 1973), 12–19; Fletcher, *Reform in the Provinces*, pp. 3–11; G. R. Elton, *The Tudor Constitution* (Cambridge, 1960; 2nd edn., 1982), 464–8.

26. See pp. 315–17.

27. Williams, 'The Crown and the Counties', pp. 126–7; Hassell Smith, *County and Court*, pp. 127–31.

28. Cruickshank, *Elizabeth's Army*, pp. 17–40, 290–1; R. B. Wernham, *After the Armada: Elizabethan England and the Struggle for Western Europe, 1588–1595* (Oxford, 1984), 281, 381, 416–20, 462–3, 565–8; Cheyney, *History of England*, ii. 359–80. For the problem at a later period, see M. C. Fissel, '*Bellum Episcopale*: The Bishops' Wars and the End of the "Personal Rule" in England, 1638–1640', unpublished UC Berkeley, Ph.D. dissertation (1984).

29. Hassell Smith, 'Militia Rates and Militia Statutes', pp. 96–9; Wernham, *After the Armada*, pp. 418–19; Clark, *English Provincial Society*, pp. 221–6; M. J. Power, 'London and the Control of the "Crisis" of the 1590s', *History*, 70 (1985), 382.

30. Clark, *English Provincial Society*, pp. 221–68; but see R. Ashton's review in *Economic History Review*, 2nd ser. 31 (1978), 468–9; T. G. Barnes, *Somerset 1625–1640: A County's Government during the 'Personal Rule'* (Cambridge, Mass., 1961); Fissel, '*Bellum Episcopale*', fos. 212–403; Fletcher, *A County Community*, pp. 202–17; J. R. Kent, *The English Village Constable, 1580–1642* (Oxford, 1986); MacCulloch, *Suffolk and the Tudors*, pp. 258–82; Hassell Smith, *County and Court*, pp. 229–342; Williams, 'The Crown and the Counties', pp. 136–46.

31. *The Manuscript of William Dunche*, ed. A. G. W. Murray and E. F. Bosanquet (privately printed, Exeter, 1914); D. E. Hoak, 'The King's Privy Chamber, 1547–1553', in D. J. Guth and J. W. McKenna (eds.), *Tudor Rule and Revolution* (Cambridge, 1982), 87–108; PRO LC 2/4/2; Folger Shakespeare Library, MSS Z.d.11–14, 16–17; W. J. Tighe, 'Gentlemen Pensioners in Elizabethan Politics and Government', unpublished Cambridge Ph.D. dissertation (1983); S. T. Bindoff (ed.), *The House of Commons, 1509–1558* (3 vols.; London, 1982); P. W. Hasler (ed.), *The House of Commons, 1558–1603* (3 vols.; London, 1981); D. R. Starkey (ed.), *The English Court: From the Wars of the Roses to the Civil War* (London, 1987), 1–24, 82–92. I am particularly grateful to Dr Starkey and Professor Hoak for various discussions of this point.

32. Cheyney, *History of England*, ii. 359–75; G. S. Thomson, *Lords Lieutenants in the Sixteenth Century* (London, 1923), 68–83.

33. Thomson, *Lords Lieutenants*, pp. 77–83; Hassell Smith, *County and Court*, pp. 128–38, 246–76.

34. See the recent discussion in A. Hughes, *Politics, Society and Civil War in Warwickshire, 1620–1660* (Cambridge, 1987).

35. Hurstfield, *Freedom, Corruption and Government*, p. 106.

36. Hassell Smith, *County and Court*, pp. 303–4, 340–1; M. E. James, *Society, Politics and Culture: Studies in Early Modern England* (Cambridge, 1986) p. 425 n. 35.

37. MacCulloch, *Suffolk and the Tudors*, pp. 258–82; Williams, 'The Crown and the Counties', pp. 138–9; Hassell Smith, *County and Court*, pp. 128, 138, 277–304.

38. R. C. Braddock, 'The Rewards of Office-holding in Tudor England', *Journal of British Studies*, 14 (1975), 29–47; W. T. MacCaffrey, 'Place and Patronage in Elizabethan Politics', in S. T. Bindoff, J. Hurstfield, and C. H. Williams (eds.), *Elizabethan Government and Society: Essays Presented to Sir John Neale* (London, 1961), 95–126; L. Stone, *The Crisis of the Aristocracy, 1558–1641* (Oxford, 1965), 403–504.

39. J. E. Neale, *Essays in Elizabethan History* (London, 1958), 69–70.

40. Historical Manuscripts Commission, *Calendar of the Manuscripts of the Most Honourable the Marquis of Salisbury* (24 vols.; London, 1883–1976), iv. 364.

41. MacCaffrey, 'Place and Patronage', p. 125.

42. *CSPD Addenda, 1566–1579*, p. 46.

43. 5 & 6 Edw. VI, c. 16.

44. *Spenser's Minor Poems*, ed. E. de Sélincourt (Oxford, 1960; repr. 1966), 210.

45. Neale, *Essays in Elizabethan History*, pp. 59–81; Hurstfield, *Freedom, Corruption and Government*, pp. 137–62.

46. Coleman, 'Artifice or Accident?', pp. 163–98.

47. PRO SP 12/22/59; Coleman, 'Artifice or Accident?', p. 185.

48. Ibid. 191.

49. Ibid. 192.

50. 13 Eliz. I, c. 4.

51. Elton, *Parliament of England*, pp. 171–4.

52. Ibid. 196.

53. Ibid. 196 n. 124.

54. Folger Shakespeare Library, MSS V.a.459 (1581–2), V.a.460 (1593–4), V.a.461 (1596–8); Stonley's confession is filed in PRO E 192/3 (reference cited by Coleman, 'Artifice or Accident?', p. 191 n. 101). Mr Coleman plans to publish both a study of Stonley and an edition of the diaries. I am much indebted to him for various discussions of Stonley's affairs.

55. Folger Shakespeare Library, MS V.a.459, fos. 7, 7ᵛ, 10, 18ᵛ, 21, 21ᵛ, 24, 24ᵛ, 27, 27ᵛ, 43, 67, 91ᵛ, 92ᵛ.

56. Coleman, 'Artifice or Accident?', p. 191 n. 101.

57. Hasler (ed.), *House of Commons, 1558–1603*, iii. 450.

58. L. Stone, *An Elizabethan: Sir Horatio Palavicino* (Oxford, 1956), 271–3; Coleman, 'Artifice or Accident?', p. 197 n. 124; G. R. Elton, 'The Elizabethan Exchequer: War in the Receipt', repr. in his *Studies*, i. 355–88.

59. Historical Manuscripts Commission, *Manuscripts of the Marquis of Salisbury*, xxiii. 4.
60. Coleman, 'Artifice or Accident?', p. 197 n. 124.
61. Folger Shakespeare Library, MS V.a.460, fo. 58 (21 Jan. 1594).
62. 39 Eliz. I, c. 7.
63. Historical Manuscripts Commission, *Manuscripts of the Marquis of Salisbury*, iii. 311–12, 377; Hasler (ed.), *House of Commons, 1558–1603*, iii. 450–1.
64. J. Hurstfield, *The Queen's Wards: Wardship and Marriage under Elizabeth I* (London, 1958), 181–217; Neale, *Essays in Elizabethan History*, pp. 65–79.
65. Hurstfield, *The Queen's Wards*, pp. 266–9; Neale, *Essays in Elizabethan History*, pp. 63–4, 72.
66. *CSPD 1591–1594*, pp. 326–7; A. G. R. Smith, *Servant of the Cecils: The Life of Sir Michael Hickes, 1543–1612* (London, 1977), 66–8; Neale, *Essays in Elizabethan History*, pp. 65–6; Hasler (ed.), *House of Commons, 1558–1603*, iii. 375–6.
67. L. Stone, *Family and Fortune: Studies in Aristocratic Finance in the Sixteenth and Seventeenth Centuries* (Oxford, 1973), 56–9; Neale, *Essays in Elizabethan History*, p. 75; Hasler (ed.), *House of Commons, 1558–1603*, i. 578.
68. Neale, *Essays in Elizabethan History*, p. 77.
69. *CSPD 1591–1594*, pp. 219–20; Hasler (ed.), *House of Commons, 1558–1603*, iii. 15–17.
70. J. A. Guy, *The Court of Star Chamber and its Records to the Reign of Elizabeth I* (London, 1985); W. J. Jones, *The Elizabethan Court of Chancery* (Oxford, 1967); C. W. Brooks, *Pettyfoggers and Vipers of the Commonwealth: The 'Lower Branch' of the Legal Profession in Early Modern England* (Cambridge, 1986).
71. Williams, 'The Crown and the Counties', pp. 132–3; Hassell Smith, *County and Court*, pp. 293–302.
72. Hassell Smith, *County and Court*, p. 295.
73. J. E. Neale, *Elizabeth I and her Parliaments* (2 vols.; London, 1953–7; repr. 1969), ii. 203–15; Hassell Smith, *County and Court*, pp. 294–302; MacCulloch, *Suffolk and the Tudors*, pp. 270–1.
74. Neale, *Elizabeth I and her Parliaments*, ii. 352–6; Williams, 'The Crown and the Counties', pp. 133–6.
75. *A Dialogue between Reginald Pole and Thomas Lupset*, ed. K. M. Burton (London, 1948), 100.
76. Elton, *Parliament of England*, p. 280.
77. G. R. Elton, 'Parliament', in Haigh (ed.), *Reign of Elizabeth I*, p. 99; M. A. R. Graves, 'The Management of the Elizabethan House of Commons: The Council's "Men of Business" ', *Parliamentary History*, 2 (1983), 31.
78. Elton, *Parliament of England*, p. 278.
79. Hasler (ed.), *House of Commons, 1558–1603*, iii. 22–3, 275–6.
80. Ibid. ii. 238; iii. 661.
81. Neale, *Elizabeth I and her Parliaments*, ii. 352–62; 376; J. A. Guy, 'Law, Faction, and Parliament in the Sixteenth Century', *Historical Journal*, 28 (1985), 446 (table 1).

82. M. A. R. Graves, *The Tudor Parliaments: Crown, Lords and Commons, 1485–1603* (London, 1985), 155–6; Hasler (ed.), *House of Commons, 1558–1603*, i. 571–9; iii. 638–40.

83. Neale, *Elizabeth I and her Parliaments*, ii. 376–84; Hasler (ed.), *House of Commons, 1558–1603*, i. 571–9; iii. 638–40.

84. P. L. Hughes and J. F. Larkin (eds.), *Tudor Royal Proclamations* (3 vols.; New Haven, Conn., 1964–9), iii. 235–8; Neale, *Elizabeth I and her Parliaments*, ii. 387–8.

85. *CSPD 1601–1603*, p. 210.

86. P. Croft, 'Parliamentary Preparations, September 1605: Robert Cecil, Earl of Salisbury on Free Trade and Monopolies', *Parliamentary History*, 6 (1987), 127–32; R. Ashton, *The City and the Court, 1603–1643* (Cambridge, 1979).

87. See above, ch. 2. Cf. Power, 'London and the Control of the "Crisis" of the 1590s', p. 385; J. Walter, 'A "Rising of the People"? The Oxfordshire Rising of 1596', *Past and Present*, no. 107 (1985), 140.

88. P. Slack, 'Books of Orders: The Making of English Social Policy, 1577–1631', *Transactions of the Royal Historical Society*, 5th ser. 30 (1980), 1–22; Fletcher, *Reform in the Provinces*, pp. 43–62.

89. E. A. Wrigley and R. S. Schofield, *The Population History of England, 1541–1871: A Reconstruction* (London, 1981), 313–36, 377–84, 642–4, 645–93; E. H. Phelps Brown and S. V. Hopkins, 'Seven Centuries of the Prices of Consumables, Compared with Builders' Wage Rates', *Economica*, NS 23 (1956); J. Thirsk (ed.), *The Agrarian History of England and Wales*, iv. *1500–1640* (Cambridge, 1967), 846–50.

90. P. Slack, 'Poverty and Social Regulation in Elizabethan England', in Haigh (ed.), *Reign of Elizabeth I*, pp. 221–41; J. A. Sharpe, *Crime in Early Modern England, 1550–1750* (London, 1984), 41–72.

91. J. F. Hadwin, 'Deflating Philanthropy', *Economic History Review*, 2nd ser. 31 (1978), 112 (table 2), 117.

92. Slack, 'Poverty and Social Regulation', pp. 239–41.

93. Cf. J. S. Morrill and J. D. Walter, 'Order and Disorder in the English Revolution', in A. Fletcher and J. Stevenson (eds.), *Order and Disorder in Early Modern England* (Cambridge, 1985), 152–3.

94. M. Spufford, 'Puritanism and Social Control?', in ibid. 41–57; K. Wrightson and D. Levine, *Poverty and Piety in an English Village: Terling, 1525–1700* (New York, 1979); Sharpe, *Crime in Early Modern England*, pp. 73–93; M. K. McIntosh, 'Social Change and Tudor Manorial Leets', in J. A. Guy and H. G. Beale (eds.), *Law and Social Change in British History* (London, 1984), 73–85.

95. Walter, 'The Oxfordshire Rising', pp. 91–2; Power, 'London and the Control of the "Crisis" of the 1590s', p. 379; B. Sharp, *In Contempt of All Authority: Rural Artisans and Riot in the West of England, 1586–1660* (Berkeley, Ca., 1980), 10–21.

96. Walter, 'The Oxfordshire Rising', pp. 95–126.

97. Ibid. 127–8.

98. Ibid. 127–38; Neale, *Elizabeth I and her Parliaments*, ii. 335–51.

99. Walter, 'The Oxfordshire Rising', p. 138.

CHAPTER 15. POLITICAL CULTURE

1. J. Nichols (ed.), *The Progresses, and Public Processions, of Queen Elizabeth* (3 vols.; London, 1788–1805), ii; M. E. James, *Society, Politics and Culture: Studies in Early Modern England* (Cambridge, 1986), 419–20.

2. A. G. Fox, *Thomas More: History and Providence* (Oxford, 1982), 218–19, 223–34.

3. *The Prose Works of Sir Philip Sidney*, ed. A. Feuillerat (4 vols.; Cambridge, repr. 1962–8), iii. 22.

4. R. Strong, *The Cult of Elizabeth: Elizabethan Portraiture and Pageantry* (London, 1977), 81.

5. For texts of the 1590 and 1593 editions of *Arcadia*, see *Prose Works of Sir Philip Sidney*, ed. Feuillerat, vols. i–ii, and for the original version, see vol. iv. For the complete poetry, see W. A. Ringler (ed.), *The Poems of Sir Philip Sidney* (Oxford, 1962; repr. 1971).

6. *Spenser's Minor Poems*, ed. E. de Sélincourt (Oxford, 1960; repr. 1966), 18–28, 105–14, 195–234; A. Hume, *Edmund Spenser: Protestant Poet* (Cambridge, 1984).

7. Cf. *The Politics of Aristotle*, ed. E. Barker (Oxford, 1946; repr. 1948), 92–110.

8. Q. Skinner, 'Sir Thomas More's *Utopia* and the Language of Renaissance Humanism', in A. Pagden (ed.), *The Languages of Political Theory in Early Modern Europe* (Cambridge, 1987), 129–31; Cicero, *De officiis*, ed. W. Miller (London, 1913), 116.

9. Skinner, 'Sir Thomas More's *Utopia*', pp. 127–8; A. G. Fox and J. A. Guy, *Reassessing the Henrician Age: Humanism, Politics, and Reform, 1500–1550* (Oxford, 1986), 36.

10. *CW* iv. *Utopia*, ed. E. Surtz and J. H. Hexter (New Haven, Conn., 1965; repr. 1979), 87.

11. Ibid. 99–101; Skinner, 'Sir Thomas More's *Utopia*', pp. 132–3.

12. *A Dialogue between Reginald Pole and Thomas Lupset*, ed. K. M. Burton (London, 1948), 22; *The Book Named the Governor*, ed. S. E. Lehmberg (London, 1962; repr. 1975), 95–9; *A Discourse of the Commonweal of this Realm of England*, ed. M. Dewar (Charlottesville, Va., 1969), 16; Fox and Guy, *Reassessing the Henrician Age*, pp. 52–73; J. K. McConica, *English Humanists and Reformation Politics* (Oxford, 1965; repr. 1968), 209.

13. R. B. Wernham, *Before the Armada: The Emergence of the English Nation, 1485–1588* (New York, 1966; repr. 1972), 236–7; R. O'Day, *Education and Society, 1500–1800: The Social Foundations of Education in Early Modern Britain* (London, 1982), 128.

14. *Discourse of the Commonweal*, ed. Dewar, pp. xv–xvii; A. B. Ferguson, 'The Tudor Commonweal and the Sense of Change', *Journal of British Studies*, 3 (1963), 11–35; Q. Skinner, *The Foundations of Modern Political Thought* (2 vols.; Cambridge, 1973; repr. 1979), ii. 349–58.

15. *Prose Works of Sir Philip Sidney*, ed. Feuillerat, iii. 17; E. M. W. Tillyard, *The Elizabethan World Picture* (London, 1943; new edn., 1963, repr. 1968), 33–4.

16. J. K. McConica (ed.), *The History of the University of Oxford*, iii. *The Collegiate University* (Oxford, 1986), 707–9.

17. D. R. Kelley, *The Beginning of Ideology: Consciousness and Society in the French Reformation* (Cambridge, 1981; repr. 1983), 131–5; L. A. Knafla, *Law and Politics in Jacobean England: The Tracts of Lord Chancellor Ellesmere* (Cambridge, 1977), 40–2; McConica (ed.), *History of the University of Oxford*, iii. 713–14.

18. K. Thomas, *Religion and the Decline of Magic* (London, 1971; repr. 1978), 198–206, 681–98; *Christopher Marlowe: The Complete Plays*, ed. J. B. Steane (Harmondsworth, 1969; repr. 1977), 10–15; Skinner, *Foundations of Modern Political Thought*, ii. 275–84.

19. James, *Society, Politics and Culture*, pp. 418–21; A. B. Ferguson, *Clio Unbound: Perceptions of the Social and Cultural Past in Renaissance England* (Durham, NC, 1979); F. J. Levy, *Tudor Historical Thought* (San Marino, Ca., 1967); J. G. A. Pocock, 'The Sense of History in Renaissance England', in J. F. Andrews (ed.), *William Shakespeare*, i. *His World* (New York, 1985), 143–57.

20. *CSPD 1601–1603*, p. 15; James, *Society, Politics and Culture*, pp. 418–19, 437; Pocock, 'The Sense of History', p. 148.

21. H. S. Bennett, *English Books and Readers, 1558 to 1603* (Cambridge, 1965), 56–86; A. W. Ward and A. R. Waller (eds.), *The Cambridge History of English Literature* (15 vols.; Cambridge, 1907–27), vii. 343–4; D. M. Palliser, *The Age of Elizabeth: England under the Later Tudors, 1547–1603* (London, 1983), pp. 354–5.

22. See R. Ellrodt, 'Self-Consciousness in Montaigne and Shakespeare', *Shakespeare Survey*, 28 (1975), 37–50, and references cited.

23. *CW* ix. *The Apology*, ed. J. B. Trapp (New Haven, Conn., 1979), 13; M. Spufford, 'Schooling of Peasantry in Cambridgeshire', *Agricultural History Review*, 18 (1970), Supplement, pp. 112–47; her *Contrasting Communities: English Villagers in the Sixteenth and Seventeenth Centuries* (Cambridge, 1974), 192–209, 262–3; cf. D. Cressy, *Literacy and the Social Order: Reading and Writing in Tudor and Stuart England* (Cambridge, 1980), 44–5.

24. Cressy, *Literacy and the Social Order*, pp. 1–18, 142–74, 176; his 'Levels of Illiteracy in England, 1530–1730', *Historical Journal*, 20 (1977), 1–23. Cf. R. S. Schofield, 'The Measurement of Literacy in Pre-Industrial England', in J. Goody (ed.), *Literacy in Traditional Societies* (Cambridge, 1968), 311–25.

25. Cressy, *Literacy and the Social Order*, pp. 1–41; S. W. Hull, *Chaste, Silent and Obedient: English Books for Women, 1475–1640* (San Marino, Ca., 1982); K. V. Thomas, 'The Meaning of Literacy in Early Modern England', in G. Baumann (ed.), *The Written Word: Literacy in Transition* (Oxford, 1986).

26. Cressy, *Literacy and the Social Order*, pp. 142–64.

27. T. Harris, *London Crowds in the Reign of Charles II: Propaganda and Politics from the Restoration until the Exclusion Crisis* (Cambridge, 1987); Cressy, *Literacy and the Social Order*, pp. 65–75, 128–9, 146–7, 154–5.

28. R. B. Merriman (ed.), *Life and Letters of Thomas Cromwell* (2 vols.; Oxford, 1902), ii. 27; see also A. J. Slavin, 'The Gutenberg Galaxy and the Tudor

Revolution', in G. P. Tyson and S. S. Wagonheim (eds.), *Print and Culture in the Renaissance: Essays on the Advent of Printing in Europe* (Newark, NJ, 1986), 90–109.

29. *The Notebook of Sir John Port*, ed. J. H. Baker (Selden Society, London, 1986), 136.

30. N. Orme, *English Schools in the Middle Ages* (London, 1973), 294; J. Simon, *Education and Society in Tudor England* (Cambridge, 1966), 179–96, 215–44, 268–87; Cressy, *Literacy and the Social Order*, pp. 164–70.

31. Simon, *Education and Society*, pp. 291–316; Cressy, *Literacy and the Social Order*, pp. 34–8, 167–9.

32. Cressy, *Literacy and the Social Order*, pp. 28–41, 157–70.

33. There were ten inns of chancery in 1468, but only nine by 1540. In 1549 Strand Inn was demolished to enable Protector Somerset to build Somerset House on the site. See R. Megarry, *Inns Ancient and Modern* (Selden Society, London, 1972).

34. W. Prest, 'Legal Education of the Gentry at the Inns of Court, 1560–1640', *Past and Present*, no. 38 (1967), 20–39; J. A. Guy, 'Law, Faction, and Parliament in the Sixteenth Century', *Historical Journal*, 28 (1985), 446.

35. Simon, *Education and Society*, pp. 388–9; Palliser, *Age of Elizabeth*, p. 363.

36. McConica (ed.), *History of the University of Oxford*, iii. 645–732; L. Stone (ed.), *The University in Society* (2 vols.; Princeton, NJ, 1975), i. 3–81, 93; E. Russell, 'The Influx of Commoners into the University of Oxford before 1581: An Optical Illusion?', *English Historical Review*, 92 (1977), 721–45; Palliser, *Age of Elizabeth*, pp. 363–5.

37. Stone (ed.), *University in Society*, i. 91–2; Russell, 'The Influx of Commoners', pp. 721–45; McConica (ed.), *History of the University of Oxford*, iii. 1–68.

38. McConica (ed.), *History of the University of Oxford*, iii. 721.

39. Ibid. 465–6, 556, 633; J. C. T. Oates, *Cambridge University Library: A History From the Beginnings to the Copyright Act of Queen Anne* (Cambridge, 1986); Ward and Waller (eds.), *Cambridge History of English Literature*, iv. 422–32.

40. G. Kipling, 'Henry VII and the Origins of Tudor Patronage', in G. F. Lytle and S. Orgel (eds.), *Patronage in the Renaissance* (Princeton, NJ, 1981), 117–64; S. Anglo, *Spectacle, Pageantry, and Early Tudor Policy* (Oxford, 1969), 98–110; D. Cressy, 'Spectacle and Power: Apollo and Solomon at the Court of Henry VIII', *History Today*, 32 (Oct. 1982), 16–22; G. Wickham, *Early English Stages: 1300 to 1600* (3 vols. in 4 parts; 1959–81; vol. i, 2nd edn., 1980), i. 13–50.

41. Anglo, *Spectacle, Pageantry, and Early Tudor Policy*, pp. 266–70; Cressy, 'Spectacle and Power', pp. 16–17; Kipling, 'Henry VII and the Origins of Tudor Patronage', pp. 140–9; R. Strong, *Holbein and Henry VIII* (London, 1967), 9.

42. Anglo, *Spectacle, Pageantry, and Early Tudor Policy*, pp. 108–69.

43. Ibid. 261–80; Cressy, 'Spectacle and Power', pp. 21–2; Strong, *Holbein and Henry VIII*, pp. 14–16.

44. Folger Shakespeare Library, MSS L.b.41–2, 292, 327; Anglo, *Spectacle, Pageantry, and Early Tudor Policy*, pp. 295–343.

45. Folger Shakespeare Library, MS L.b.42, fos. 71ᵛ-2ᵛ; MS L.b.123; N. L. Jones, *Faith by Statute: Parliament and the Settlement of Religion, 1559* (London, 1982), 43; E. Welsford, *The Court Masque: A Study in the Relationship between Poetry and the Revels* (Cambridge, 1927), 149–67.

46. *Prose Works of Sir Philip Sidney*, ed. Feuillerat, iii. 39; A. Gurr, *The Shakespearean Stage, 1574–1642* (2nd edn., Cambridge, 1980), pp. 10–77; E. K. Chambers, *The Elizabethan Stage* (4 vols.; Oxford, 1923; repr. 1965) ii. 34–5.

47. Chambers, Elizabethan Stage, ii. 104.

48. Ibid. 104–15, 134–220.

49. Gurr, *Shakespearean Stage*, pp. 4–77; Wickham, *Early English Stages*, ii. II. 110–17; P. Beal, 'The Burning of the Globe', *Times Literary Supplement* (20 June 1986), 689–90.

50. Strong, *Cult of Elizabeth*, pp. 114–62; S. L. Adams, 'Eliza Enthroned? The Court and its Politics', in C. Haigh (ed.), *The Reign of Elizabeth I* (London, 1984), 72–3.

51. Strong, *Cult of Elizabeth*, pp. 134–5; M. Girouard, *Robert Smythson and the Elizabethan Country House* (London, 1983), 210–32.

52. *Bacon's Essays* (Chandos edn.), 70–1.

53. Strong, *Cult of Elizabeth*, pp. 137–46.

54. F. A. Yates, *Astraea: The Imperial Theme in the Sixteenth Century* (London, 1975), 88–111; Strong, *Cult of Elizabeth*, pp. 117, 146–51.

55. R. Strong, *Nicholas Hilliard* (London, 1975); his *Artists of the Tudor Court: The Portrait Miniature Rediscovered, 1520–1620* (Victoria and Albert Museum, London, 1983), 9–13; M. Jordan, 'Tokens of Love and Loyalty', *Times Literary Supplement* (5 Aug. 1983), 832.

56. Strong, *Nicholas Hilliard*, pp. 21–6.

57. Ibid. 14–19, 21–6; his *Artists of the Tudor Court*, pp. 9–13, 126–32.

58. Strong, *Artists of the Tudor Court*, pp. 10–11, 129–30.

59. *Prose Works of Sir Philip Sidney*, ed. Feuillerat, iii. 9; S. H. Butcher, *Aristotle's Theory of Poetry and Fine Art* (3rd edn., London, 1902), 121–36.

60. *The Book Named the Governor*, ed. Lehmberg, pp. 23–6.

61. Strong, *Artists of the Tudor Court*, pp. 97–116; his *Tudor and Jacobean Portraits* (2 vols.; London, 1969).

62. H. M. Colvin (ed.), *The History of the King's Works*, iv. *1485–1660 (Part 2)* (London, 1982), 28–31; Girouard, *Robert Smythson*, pp. 2–162.

63. Girouard, *Robert Smythson*, pp. 18–20, 144–62.

64. J. Thirsk (ed.), *The Agrarian History of England and Wales*, iv. *1500–1640* (Cambridge, 1967), 696–766; V. H. T. Skipp, 'Economic and Social Change in the Forest of Arden, 1530–1649', *Agricultural History Review*, 18 (1970), Supplement, pp. 84–111.

65. Colvin (ed.), *History of the King's Works*, iv. 17–21; Thirsk (ed.), *Agrarian History*, iv. 698–710; Girouard, *Robert Smythson*, pp. 54–65.

CHAPTER 16. THE TUDOR *FIN DE SIÈCLE*

1. P. W. Hasler (ed.), *The House of Commons, 1558–1603* (3 vols.; London, 1981), iii. 273–6.

2. S. L. Adams, 'Eliza Enthroned? The Court and its Politics', in C. Haigh (ed.), *The Reign of Elizabeth I* (London, 1984), 67–8.
3. His career was assisted by his first wife, one of the queen's gentlewomen and confidantes by 1564.
4. Hasler (ed.), *House of Commons, 1558–1603*, ii. 148–51.
5. *CSPD Addenda, 1580–1625*, p. 320; Hasler (ed.), *House of Commons, 1558–1603*, i. 571–9.
6. The youngest entrant was the fourth duke of Norfolk.
7. C. Read, *Lord Burghley and Queen Elizabeth* (London, 1960), 477.
8. J. Hurstfield, *Freedom, Corruption and Government in Elizabethan England* (London, 1973), 104–62; M. Prestwich, *Cranfield: Politics and Profits under the Early Stuarts* (Oxford, 1966), 9–48.
9. *Spenser's Minor Poems*, ed. E. de Sélincourt (Oxford, 1960; repr. 1966), 141.
10. *Epigrammes in the Oldest Cut, and Newest Fashion* (London, 1599).
11. Hurstfield, *Freedom, Corruption and Government*, pp. 126–34; M. E. James, *Society, Politics and Culture: Studies in Early Modern England* (Cambridge, 1986), 416–65; J. E. Neale, *Queen Elizabeth I* (London, 1934; repr. 1961), 343–55.
12. Hurstfield, *Freedom, Corruption and Government*, p. 127; Adams, 'Eliza Enthroned?', p. 68.
13. *CSPD Addenda, 1580–1625*, p. 320.
14. S. L. Adams, 'The Protestant Cause: Religious Alliance with the West European Calvinist Communities as a Political Issue in England, 1585–1630', unpublished Oxford D.Phil. dissertation (1973), fos. 104–18; J. E. Neale, *Essays in Elizabethan History* (London, 1958), 81–4; *DNB* s.v. Devereux, Robert.
15. Adams, 'Eliza Enthroned?', pp. 67–8; James, *Society, Politics and Culture*, p. 440; Hurstfield, *Freedom, Corruption and Government*, pp. 126–34; Hasler (ed.), *House of Commons, 1558–1603, passim*.
16. James, *Society, Politics and Culture*, pp. 440–3; M. V. Hay, *The Life of Robert Sidney: Earl of Leicester* (Folger Books, Washington DC, 1984), 163–7; Adams, 'Eliza Enthroned', pp. 67–8; Hurstfield, *Freedom, Corruption and Government*, pp. 126–34; L. L. Peck, *Northampton: Patronage and Policy at the Court of James I* (London, 1982), 13–22; Hasler (ed.), *House of Commons, 1558–1603, passim*; *CSPD 1598–1601*, pp. 545–96.
17. Hasler (ed.), *House of Commons, 1558–1603*, i. 371–3, 374–9; *Lord Burghley*, pp. 478–80.
18. R. B. Wernham, *After the Armada: Elizabethan England and the Struggle for Western Europe, 1588–1595* (Oxford, 1984), 419–20, 496; Neale, *Queen Elizabeth I*, pp. 336–7; Hasler (ed.), *House of Commons, 1558–1603*, iii. 219–20.
19. James, *Society, Politics and Culture*, pp. 427–30.
20. Ibid. 310–32, 427–34.
21. *Correspondence of King James VI of Scotland with Sir Robert Cecil and Others in England during the Reign of Queen Elizabeth*, ed. J. Bruce (Camden Society, OS 78; London, 1861), 96, 98, 102–4.
22. A. Dimock, 'The Conspiracy of Dr Lopez', *English Historical Review*, 9 (1893), 440–72.

23. Read, *Lord Burghley*, pp. 533–7.
24. Ps. 55: 23.
25. James, *Society, Politics and Culture*, p. 445.
26. Folger Shakespeare Library, MS V.a.321, fos. 1–2ᵛ.
27. James, *Society, Politics and Culture*, pp. 445–6.
28. See J. Nichols (ed.), *The Progresses, and Public Processions, of Queen Elizabeth* (3 vols.; London, 1788–1805), ii.
29. Folger Shakespeare Library, MS V.a.321, fo. 4ᵛ.
30. *CSPD 1598–1601*, p. 441; E. P. Cheyney, *A History of England from the Defeat of the Armada to the Death of Elizabeth* (2 vols.; London, 1914–26), ii. 513–15.
31. *CSPD 1598–1601*, p. 449.
32. Ibid. 450–3; James, *Society, Politics and Culture*, pp. 418–23.
33. *CSPD 1598–1601*, pp. 453–5.
34. Ibid. 573, 575; James, *Society, Politics and Culture*, pp. 419–20, 423, 446; Neale, *Essays in Elizabethan History*, pp. 83–4.
35. James, *Society, Politics and Culture*, pp. 424–6, 438–9.
36. *CSPD 1598–1601*, pp. 577–81; James, *Society, Politics and Culture*, p. 446.
37. Cheyney, *History of England*, ii. 522–7; *CSPD 1598–1601*, pp. 577–81; James, *Society, Politics and Culture*, pp. 448–51.
38. Folger Shakespeare Library, MS V.b.142, fo. 53; *CSPD 1598–1601*, pp. 549–85; James, *Society, Politics and Culture*, pp. 450–2; Cheyney, *History of England*, ii. 525–48.
39. Cheyney, *History of England*, ii. 530, 534; James, *Society, Politics and Culture*, p. 451.
40. Cheyney, *History of England*, ii. 535.
41. *CSPD 1598–1601*, pp. 545–6, 553–7, 565–8, 582–5; Folger Shakespeare Library, MS V.a.321, fos. 9ᵛ–11.
42. Hurstfield, *Freedom, Corruption and Government*, p. 129.
43. Ibid. 129–30; *Correspondence of King James VI*, pp. xxxv–vii.
44. *Correspondence of King James VI*, pp. 72–5.
45. Ibid. 47.
46. Folger Shakespeare Library, MS V.b.142, fos. 65–7.
47. J. E. Neale, *Elizabeth I and her Parliaments* (2 vols.; London, 1953–7; repr. 1969), ii. 353; his *Essays in Elizabethan History*, pp. 59–81. I inclined to this view myself before writing this book.
48. *The History of the Rebellion and Civil Wars in England* (2 vols.; new edn., Oxford, 1840), i. 2.
49. *The Book Named the Governor*, ed. S. E. Lehmberg (London, 1962; repr. 1975), 238–40.
50. H. Miller, *Henry VIII and the English Nobility* (Oxford, 1986), 130–1.
51. A. Fletcher, *Reform in the Provinces: The Government of Stuart England* (London, 1986), 44–6; Peck, *Northampton: Patronage and Policy*, pp. 84–9.
52. E. R. Foster (ed.), *Proceedings in Parliament, 1610* (2 vols.; New Haven, Conn., 1966), i. xi; Folger Shakespeare Library, MS V.b.276, fos. 41 ff.

SELECT BIBLIOGRAPHY

THIS select bibliography serves as a guide to further reading as well as to works frequently cited in the footnotes. Fuller bibliographies for Tudor England are C. Read (ed.), *Bibliography of British History: Tudor Period, 1485–1603* (2nd edn., Oxford, 1959; repr. Brighton, 1978) and M. Levine (ed.), *Tudor England, 1485–1603* (Cambridge, 1968). For books and articles published between 1967 and 1974, the *Writings on British History* series, edited by H. J. Creaton (Institute of Historical Research, London, 1982–6), provides full listings. Works published since 1975 are listed in the Royal Historical Society's *Annual Bibliography of British and Irish History* (Brighton, 1976–). Edited by Professor Sir Geoffrey Elton until 1984, and currently by Professor David Palliser, the RHS *Annual Bibliography* is as up to date and complete as possible. Any omissions or oversights are picked up in the following year. Titles of recent British dissertations, and work in progress, are listed in J. M. Horn (ed.), *History Theses, 1971–80* (Institute of Historical Research, London, 1984), and in the Institute's serial publication *Historical Research for University Degrees in the United Kingdom*. A useful supplementary guide to periodical literature is the American Historical Association's serial *Recently Published Articles*.

Acts of the Privy Council of England, ed. J. R. Dasent *et al.* (NS; 46 vols.; London, 1890–1964).

Adams, S. L., 'Eliza Enthroned? The Court and its Politics', in Haigh (ed.), *Reign of Elizabeth I*, pp. 55–77.

—— 'Faction, Clientage and Party: English Politics, 1550–1603', *History Today*, 32 (Dec. 1982), 33–9.

—— 'The Protestant Cause: Religious Alliance with the West European Calvinist Communities as a Political Issue in England, 1585–1630', unpublished Oxford D.Phil. dissertation (1973).

Alexander, G., 'Bishop Bonner and the Parliament of 1559', *Bulletin of the Institute of Historical Research*, 56 (1983), 164–79.

—— 'Bonner and the Marian Persecutions', *History*, 60 (1975), 374–91.

Allen, J. W., *A History of Political Thought in the Sixteenth Century* (London, 1928; repr. 1964).

Alsop, J. D., 'Innovation in Tudor Taxation', *English Historical Review*, 99 (1984), 83–93.

—— 'Nicholas Brigham (d. 1558), Scholar, Antiquary, and Crown Servant', *Sixteenth-century Journal*, 12 (1981), 49–67.

—— 'The Revenue Commission of 1552', *Historical Journal*, 22 (1979), 511–33.

—— 'The Structure of Early Tudor Finance, *c.* 1509–1558', in C. Coleman and D. R. Starkey (eds.), *Revolution Reassessed*, pp. 135–62.

—— 'The Theory and Practice of Tudor Taxation', *English Historical Review*, 97 (1982), 1–30.

Andrews, K. R., 'Elizabethan Privateering', in J. Youings (ed.), *Raleigh in Exeter: Privateering and Colonisation in the Reign of Elizabeth I* (Exeter, 1985), 1–20.

—— *Elizabethan Privateering: English Privateering during the Spanish War, 1585–1603* (Cambridge, 1964).

—— *Trade, Plunder and Settlement: Maritime Enterprise and the Genesis of the British Empire, 1480–1630* (Cambridge, 1984).

Anglo, S., *Spectacle, Pageantry, and Early Tudor Policy* (Oxford, 1969).

Appleby, A. B., 'Disease or Famine? Mortality in Cumberland and Westmorland, 1580–1640', *Economic History Review*, 2nd ser. 26 (1973), 403–32.

—— *Famine in Tudor and Stuart England* (Liverpool, 1978).

Aston, M., 'Lollardy and Sedition, 1381–1431', *Past and Present*, no. 17 (1960), 1–44.

—— 'Lollardy and the Reformation: Survival or Revival?', *History*, 49 (1964), 149–70.

Aveling, J. C. H., *The Handle and the Axe: The Catholic Recusants in England from Reformation to Emancipation* (London, 1976).

Baker, J. H., *The Legal Profession and the Common Law: Historical Essays* (London, 1985).

Barnes, T. G., 'Star Chamber and the Sophistication of the Criminal Law', *Criminal Law Review* (1977), 316–26.

Bartlett, K. R., 'The English Exile Community in Italy and the Political Opposition to Queen Mary I', *Albion*, 13 (1981), 223–41.

—— 'The Role of the Marian Exiles', in P. W. Hasler (ed.), *The House of Commons, 1558–1603*, i, app. xi.

Beer, B. L., *Northumberland: The Political Career of John Dudley, Earl of Warwick and Duke of Northumberland* (Kent, Ohio, 1973).

—— *Rebellion and Riot: Popular Disorder in England during the Reign of Edward VI* (Kent, Ohio, 1982).

Beier, A. L., 'The Social Problems of an Elizabethan County Town: Warwick, 1580–90', in P. Clark (ed.), *Country Towns in Pre-industrial England* (Leicester, 1981), 46–85.

—— 'Vagrants and the Social Order in Elizabethan England', *Past and Present*, no. 64 (1974), 3–29.

Beier, A. L., *Masterless Men: The Vagrancy Problem in England, 1560–1640* (London, 1985).

Bennett, H. S., *English Books and Readers, 1475–1557* (Cambridge, 1952).

—— *English Books and Readers, 1558 to 1603* (Cambridge, 1965).

Bernard, G. W., 'The Pardon of the Clergy Reconsidered', *Journal of Ecclesiastical History*, 37 (1986), 258–82.

—— *The Power of the Early Tudor Nobility: A Study of the Fourth and Fifth Earls of Shrewsbury* (Brighton, 1985).

—— *War, Taxation and Rebellion in Early Tudor England: Henry VIII, Wolsey and the Amicable Grant of 1525* (Brighton, 1986).

Bevan, A. S., 'The Role of the Judiciary in Tudor Government, 1509–1547', unpublished Cambridge Ph.D. dissertation (1985).

Bindoff, S. T. (ed.), *The House of Commons, 1509–1558* (3 vols.; London, 1982).

Bittle, W. G., and Todd Lane, R., 'Inflation and Philanthropy in England: A Re-assessment of W. K. Jordan's Data', *Economic History Review*, 29 (1976), 203–10.

Blanchard, I. S. W., 'Population Change, Enclosure and the Early-Tudor Economy', *Economic History Review*, 2nd ser. 23 (1970), 427–45.

Blatcher, M., *The Court of King's Bench, 1450–1550* (London, 1978).

Booty, J. E. (ed.), *An Apology of the Church of England* (Folger Books, Charlottesville, Va., 1963; repr. 1974).

Bossy, J. A., *The English Catholic Community, 1570–1850* (London, 1975).

Bottigheimer, K. S., 'The Reformation in Ireland Revisited', *Journal of British Studies*, 15 (1976), 140–9.

Bowker, M., 'Lincolnshire 1536: Heresy, Schism or Religious Discontent?', in D. Baker (ed.), *Schism, Heresy and Religious Protest* (Cambridge, 1972), 195–212.

—— 'The Supremacy and the Episcopate: The Struggle for Control, 1534–1540', *Historical Journal*, 18 (1975), 227–43.

—— *The Henrician Reformation: The Diocese of Lincoln under John Longland, 1521–1547* (Cambridge, 1981).

—— *The Secular Clergy in the Diocese of Lincoln* (Cambridge, 1968).

Boynton, L., *The Elizabethan Militia, 1558–1638* (London, 1967).

Braddock, R. C., 'The Rewards of Office-holding in Tudor England', *Journal of British Studies*, 14 (1975), 29–47.

Bradshaw, B., *The Irish Constitutional Revolution of the Sixteenth Century* (Cambridge, 1979).

Bridbury, A. R., 'Sixteenth-century Farming', *Economic History Review*, 2nd ser. 27 (1974), 538–56.

—— *Economic Growth: England in the Later Middle Ages* (2nd edn.; London, 1979).

Brigden, S. E., 'Popular Disturbance and the Fall of Thomas Cromwell and the Reformers, 1539–1540', *Historical Journal*, 24 (1981), 257–78.

—— 'Religion and Social Obligation in Early Sixteenth-century London', *Past and Present*, no. 103 (1984), 67–112.

—— 'The Early Reformation in London, 1520–1547: The Conflict in the Parishes', unpublished Cambridge Ph.D. dissertation (1979).

—— 'Youth and the English Reformation', in P. Slack (ed.), *Rebellion, Popular Protest and the Social Order in Early Modern England*, pp. 77–107.

Brooks, C. W., *Pettyfoggers and Vipers of the Commonwealth: The 'Lower Branch' of the Legal Profession in Early Modern England* (Cambridge, 1986).

Bush, M. L., 'The Lisle–Seymour Land Disputes: A Study of Power and Influence in the 1530s', *Historical Journal*, 9 (1966), 255–74.

—— *The Government Policy of Protector Somerset* (London, 1975).

Calendar of Letters, Despatches, and State Papers Relating to the Negotiations between England and Spain (13 vols.; London, 1862–1954).

Calendar of State Papers, Domestic: Edward VI, Mary, Elizabeth I, and James I (12 vols.; London, 1856–72).

Calendar of State Papers, Foreign: Edward VI, Mary, Elizabeth I (25 vols.; London, 1861–1950).

Canny, N., *The Elizabethan Conquest of Ireland: A Pattern Established, 1565–1576* (Hassocks, 1976).

Challis, C. E., *The Tudor Coinage* (Manchester, 1978).

Chambers, D. S., 'Cardinal Wolsey and the Papal Tiara', *Bulletin of the Institute of Historical Research*, 38 (1965), 20–30.

Chambers, J. D., *Population, Economy and Society in Pre-industrial England* (Oxford, 1972).

Chambers, R. W., *Thomas More* (London, 1935; repr. 1957).

Cheyney, E. P., *A History of England from the Defeat of the Armada to the Death of Elizabeth* (2 vols.; London, 1914–26).

Chrimes, S. B., *English Constitutional Ideas in the Fifteenth Century* (Cambridge, 1936).

—— *Henry VII* (London, 1972; repr. 1977).

—— Ross, C. D., and Griffiths, R. A. (eds.), *Fifteenth-century England: Studies in Politics and Society* (Manchester, 1972).

Clark, P., *English Provincial Society from the Reformation to the Revolution: Religion, Politics and Society in Kent, 1500–1640* (Hassocks, 1977).

—— (ed.), *The Early Modern Town* (London, 1976).

—— and Slack, P. (eds.), *Crisis and Order in English Towns, 1500–1700* (London, 1972).

Clark, P., and Slack, P. (eds.), *English Towns in Transition, 1500-1700* (Oxford, 1976).

Clay, C. G. A., *Economic Expansion and Social Change: England, 1500-1700* (2 vols.; Cambridge, 1984).

Clebsch, W. A., *England's Earliest Protestants, 1520-1535* (New Haven, Conn., 1964).

Cliffe, J. T., *The Yorkshire Gentry from the Reformation to the Civil War* (London, 1969).

Cockburn, J. S., *A History of English Assizes, 1558-1714* (Cambridge, 1972).

—— (ed.), *Crime in England, 1550-1800* (London, 1977).

Coleman, C., 'Artifice or Accident? The Reorganization of the Exchequer of Receipt, *c.* 1554-1572', in Coleman and D. R. Starkey (eds.), *Revolution Reassessed*, pp. 163-98.

—— and Starkey, D. R. (eds.), *Revolution Reassessed: Revisions in the History of Tudor Government and Administration* (Oxford, 1986).

Coleman, D. C., *The Economy of England, 1450-1750* (Oxford, 1977).

Collinson, P., 'The Elizabethan Church and the New Religion', in Haigh (ed.), *Reign of Elizabeth I*, pp. 169-94.

—— *Archbishop Grindal, 1519-1583: The Struggle for a Reformed Church* (London, 1980).

—— *Godly Rule: Essays on English Protestantism and Puritanism* (London, 1983).

—— *The Elizabethan Puritan Movement* (London, 1967).

—— *The Religion of Protestants: The Church in English Society, 1559-1625* (Oxford, 1982).

Colvin, H. M. (ed.), *The History of the King's Works*, iv. *1485-1660 (Part II)* (London, 1982).

Condon, M. M., 'Ruling Elites in the Reign of Henry VII', in C. Ross (ed.), *Patronage, Pedigree and Power* (Gloucester, 1979), 109-42.

Cooper, J. P., 'Henry VII's Last Years Reconsidered', *Historical Journal*, 2 (1959), 103-29.

—— *Land, Men and Beliefs: Studies in Early Modern History* (London, 1983).

Cornwall, J., 'English Population in the Early Sixteenth Century', *Economic History Review*, 2nd ser. 23 (1970), 32-44.

—— *Revolt of the Peasantry, 1549* (London, 1977).

—— and MacCulloch, D., 'Debate: Kett's Rebellion in Context', *Past and Present*, no. 93 (1981), 160-73.

Correspondence of King James VI of Scotland with Sir Robert Cecil and Others in England during the Reign of Queen Elizabeth, ed. J. Bruce (Camden Society, os 78; London, 1861).

Cressy, D., 'Levels of Illiteracy in England, 1530–1730', *Historical Journal*, 20 (1977), 1–23.

—— 'Spectacle and Power: Apollo and Solomon at the Court of Henry VIII', *History Today*, 32 (Oct. 1982), 16–22.

—— *Literacy and the Social Order: Reading and Writing in Tudor and Stuart England* (Cambridge, 1980).

Cross, C., *Church and People, 1450–1660* (Fontana edn., 1976).

Cruickshank, C. G., *Elizabeth's Army* (Oxford, 1946; 2nd edn., 1966).

Davies, C. S. L., 'Bishop John Morton, the Holy See, and the Accession of Henry VII', *English Historical Review*, 102 (1987), 2–30.

—— 'England and the French War, 1557–9' in J. Loach and R. Tittler (eds.), *The Mid-Tudor Polity*, pp. 159–85.

—— 'Peasant Revolt in France and England: A Comparison', *Agricultural History Review*, 21 (1973), 122–34.

—— 'Popular Religion and the Pilgrimage of Grace', in A. Fletcher and J. Stevenson (eds.), *Order and Disorder in Early Modern England*, pp. 58–91.

—— 'Slavery and Protector Somerset: The Vagrancy Act of 1547', *Economic History Review*, 2nd ser. 19 (1966), 533–49.

—— 'The Pilgrimage of Grace Reconsidered', *Past and Present*, no. 41 (1968), 54–76.

—— *Peace, Print and Protestantism, 1450–1558* (London, 1976).

Davies, H., *Worship and Theology in England from Cranmer to Hooker, 1534–1603* (Princeton, NJ, 1970).

Davis, J. F., *Heresy and Reformation in the South-East of England, 1520–1559* (London, 1983).

Dawley, P. M., *John Whitgift and the Reformation* (London, 1955).

Dent, C. M., *Protestant Reformers in Elizabethan Oxford* (Oxford, 1983).

Dewar, M., *Sir Thomas Smith: A Tudor Intellectual in Office* (London, 1964).

Dickens, A. G., 'Secular and Religious Motivation in the Pilgrimage of Grace', in G. J. Cuming (ed.), *Studies in Church History*, iv. *The Province of York* (Leiden, 1968), 39–54.

—— *Lollards and Protestants in the Diocese of York, 1509–1558* (Oxford, 1959).

—— *The English Reformation* (London, 1964; repr. 1966).

—— *The Marian Reaction in the Diocese of York* (Borthwick Institute, York, 1957).

—— *Thomas Cromwell and the English Reformation* (London, 1959).

Dietz, F. C., *English Public Finance, 1485–1641* (2 vols.; Urbana, Ill., 1921; 2nd edn., London, 1964).

Dobson, R. B., 'Urban Decline in Late Medieval England', *Transactions of the Royal Historical Society*, 5th ser. 27 (1977), 1–22.

Dodds, M. H., and Dodds, R., *The Pilgrimage of Grace, 1536–1537, and the Exeter Conspiracy, 1538* (2 vols.; Cambridge, 1915).

Donaldson, G., *All the Queen's Men: Power and Politics in Mary Stewart's Scotland* (London, 1983).

—— *The Scottish Reformation* (Cambridge, 1960).

Dop, J. A., *Elizabeth's Knights: Soldiers, Poets, and Puritans in the Netherlands, 1572–1586* (Alblasserdam, Netherlands, 1981).

Edwards, J. G., *The Principality of Wales*, 1267–1967 (Caernarvon, 1969).

Ellis, S. G., 'Crown, Community and Government in the English Territories, 1450–1575', *History*, 71 (1986), 187–204.

—— 'England in the Tudor State', *Historical Journal*, 26 (1983), 201–12.

—— 'Henry VII and Ireland, 1491–1496', in J. F. Lydon (ed.), *England and Ireland in the Later Middle Ages: Essays in Honour of Jocelyn Otway-Ruthven* (Dublin, 1981), 237–54.

—— 'Nationalist Historiography and the English and Gaelic Worlds in the Late Middle Ages', *Irish Historical Studies*, 25 (1986), 1–18.

—— 'The Kildare Rebellion and the Early Henrician Reformation', *Historical Journal*, 19 (1976), 807–30.

—— 'Tudor Policy and the Kildare Ascendancy in the Lordship of Ireland, 1496–1534', *Irish Historical Studies*, 20 (1977), 235–71.

—— *Reform and Revival: English Government in Ireland, 1470–1534* (Woodbridge, 1986).

—— *Tudor Ireland: Crown, Community and the Conflict of Cultures, 1470–1603* (London, 1985).

Elton, G. R., 'Mid-Tudor Finance', *Historical Journal*, 20 (1977), 737–40.

—— 'Parliament', in Haigh (ed.), *Reign of Elizabeth I*, pp. 79–100.

—— 'Wales in Parliament, 1542–1581', in R. R. Davies, R. A. Griffiths, I. G. Jones, and K. O. Morgan (eds.), *Welsh Society and Nationhood: Historical Essays Presented to Glanmor Williams* (Cardiff, 1984), 108–21.

—— *England under the Tudors* (London, 1955; 2nd edn., 1974).

—— *Policy and Police: The Enforcement of the Reformation in the Age of Thomas Cromwell* (Cambridge, 1972).

—— *Reform and Reformation: England, 1509–1558* (London, 1977).

—— *Reform and Renewal: Thomas Cromwell and the Common Weal* (Cambridge, 1973).

—— *Studies in Tudor and Stuart Politics and Government* (3 vols.; Cambridge, 1974–83.

—— *The Parliament of England, 1559–1581* (Cambridge, 1986).

—— *The Tudor Constitution* (Cambridge, 1960; 2nd edn., 1982).

—— *The Tudor Revolution in Government* (Cambridge, 1953).

Ferguson, A. B., 'The Tudor Commonweal and the Sense of Change', *Journal of British Studies*, 3 (1963), 11–35.

—— *Clio Unbound: Perceptions of the Social and Cultural Past in Renaissance England* (Durham, NC, 1979).

Fines, J., 'Heresy Trials in the Diocese of Coventry and Lichfield, 1511–12', *Journal of Ecclesiastical History*, 14 (1963), 160–74.

Fisher, F. J., 'Influenza and Inflation in Tudor England', *Economic History Review*, 2nd ser. 18 (1965), 120–9.

Fletcher, A., and Stevenson, J. (eds.), *Order and Disorder in Early Modern England* (Cambridge, 1985).

Foster, F. F., *The Politics of Stability: A Portrait of the Rulers of Elizabethan London* (London, 1977).

Fox, A. G., *Thomas More: History and Providence* (Oxford, 1982).

—— and Guy, J. A., *Reassessing the Henrician Age: Humanism, Politics, and Reform, 1500–1550* (Oxford, 1986).

[Foxe, John], *The Acts and Monuments of John Foxe*, ed. G. Townsend (8 vols.; London, 1843–9).

Gammon, S. R., *Statesman and Schemer: William, First Lord Paget* (Newton Abbot, 1973).

Garrett, C. H., *The Marian Exiles: A Study in the Origins of Elizabethan Puritanism* (Cambridge, 1938; repr. 1966).

Garrett-Goodyear, R. Harold, 'Revival of Quo Warranto and Early Tudor Policy towards Local Governors, 1485–1540', unpublished Harvard Ph.D. dissertation (1973).

Gee, H., *The Elizabethan Clergy and the Settlement of Religion, 1558–1564* (Oxford, 1898).

—— and Hardy, W. J. (eds.), *Documents Illustrative of English Church History* (London, 1910).

Gillingham, J., *The Wars of the Roses* (London, 1981).

Girouard, M., *Robert Smythson and the Elizabethan Country House* (London, 1983).

Goodman, A., 'Henry VII and Christian Renewal', in K. Robbins (ed.), *Religion and Humanism* (Oxford, 1982), 115–25.

—— *The Wars of the Roses: Military Activity and English Society, 1452–1497* (London, 1981).

Goring, J. J., 'Social Change and Military Decline in Mid-Tudor England', *History*, 60 (1975), 185–97.

—— 'The General Proscription of 1522', *English Historical Review*, 86 (1971), 681–705.

Gould, J. D., *The Great Debasement: Currency and the Economy in Mid-Tudor England* (Oxford, 1970).

Grace, F. R., 'The Life and Career of Thomas Howard, Third Duke of Norfolk', unpublished Nottingham MA dissertation (1961).

Gransby, D. M., 'Tithes Disputes in the Diocese of York, 1540–1639', unpublished York M.Phil. dissertation (1966).

Graves, M. A. R., 'The Management of the Elizabethan House of Commons: The Council's "Men of Business" ', *Parliamentary History*, 2 (1983), 11–38.

—— 'Thomas Norton the Parliament Man: An Elizabethan M.P., 1559–1581', *Historical Journal*, 23 (1980), 17–35.

—— *Elizabethan Parliaments, 1559–1601* (London, 1987).

—— *The House of Lords in the Parliaments of Edward VI and Mary I: An Institutional Study* (Cambridge, 1981).

—— *The Tudor Parliaments: Crown, Lords and Commons, 1485–1603* (London, 1985).

Griffiths, R. A., *The Principality of Wales in the Later Middle Ages: The Structure and Personnel of Government*, i. *South Wales, 1277–1536* (Cardiff, 1972).

—— *The Reign of Henry VI: The Exercise of Royal Authority, 1422–1461* (London, 1981).

—— and Thomas, R. S., *The Making of the Tudor Dynasty* (Gloucester, 1985).

Gunn, S. J., 'The Duke of Suffolk's March on Paris in 1523', *English Historical Review*, 101 (1986), 596–634.

Guth, D. J., 'Exchequer Penal Law Enforcement, 1485–1509', unpublished Pittsburg Ph.D. dissertation (1967).

Guy, J. A., 'A Conciliar Court of Audit at Work in the Last Months of the Reign of Henry VII', *Bulletin of the Institute of Historical Research*, 49 (1976), 289–95.

—— 'Henry VIII and the *Praemunire* Manœuvres of 1530–1531', *English Historical Review*, 97 (1982), 481–503.

—— 'Law, Faction, and Parliament in the Sixteenth Century', *Historical Journal*, 28 (1985), 441–53.

—— 'Law, Lawyers, and the English Reformation', *History Today*, 35 (Nov. 1985), 16–22.

—— 'The Privy Council: Revolution or Evolution?', in C. Coleman and D. R. Starkey (eds.), *Revolution Reassessed*, pp. 59–85.

—— 'Thomas More as Successor to Wolsey', *Thought: Fordham University Quarterly*, 52 (1977), 275–92.

—— 'Wolsey and the Parliament of 1523', in D. Loades *et al.* (eds.), *Law and Government under the Tudors* (Cambridge, 1988), 1–18.

—— *Christopher St German on Chancery and Statute* (Selden Society, London, 1985).

—— *The Cardinal's Court: The Impact of Thomas Wolsey in Star Chamber* (Hassocks, 1977).

—— *The Court of Star Chamber and its Records to the Reign of Elizabeth I* (London, 1985).

—— *The Public Career of Sir Thomas More* (Brighton, 1980).

Gwyn, P. J., 'Wolsey's Foreign Policy: The Conferences at Calais and Bruges Reconsidered', *Historical Journal*, 23 (1980), 755–72.

Hadwin, J. F., 'Deflating Philanthropy', *Economic History Review*, 2nd ser. 31 (1978), 105–28.

Haigh, C., 'Anticlericalism and the English Reformation', *History*, 68 (1983), 391–407.

—— 'From Monopoly to Minority: Catholicism in Early Modern England', *Transactions of the Royal Historical Society*, 5th ser. 31 (1981), 129–47.

—— 'Puritan Evangelism in the Reign of Elizabeth I', *English Historical Review*, 92 (1977), 30–58.

—— 'Revisionism, the Reformation and the History of English Catholicism', *Journal of Ecclesiastical History*, 36 (1985), 394–405.

—— 'The Church of England, the Catholics and the People', in Haigh (ed.), *Reign of Elizabeth I*, pp. 195–220.

—— 'The Continuity of Catholicism in the English Reformation', *Past and Present*, no. 93 (1981), 37–69.

—— *Reformation and Resistance in Tudor Lancashire* (Cambridge, 1975).

—— (ed.), *The English Reformation Revised* (Cambridge, 1987).

—— (ed.), *The Reign of Elizabeth I* (London, 1984).

Haller, W. (ed.), *Foxe's Book of Martyrs and the Elect Nation* (London, 1963).

—— *The Rise of Puritanism* (New York, Harper Torchbook edn., 1957).

Harris, B. J., *Edward Stafford, Third Duke of Buckingham, 1478–1521* (Stanford, Ca., 1986).

Harrison, C. J., 'Grain Price Analysis and Harvest Qualities, 1465–1634', *Agricultural History Review*, 19 (1971), 135–55.

—— 'The Petition of Edmund Dudley', *English Historical Review*, 87 (1972), 82–99.

Harrison, S. M., *The Pilgrimage of Grace in the Lake Counties, 1536–7* (London, 1981).

Harriss, G. L., 'Thomas Cromwell's "New Principle" of Taxation', *English Historical Review*, 93 (1978), 721–38.

Hartley, T. E. (ed.), *Proceedings in the Parliaments of Elizabeth I*, i. *1559–1581* (Leicester, 1981).

Hasler, P. W. (ed.), *The House of Commons, 1558–1603* (3 vols.; London, 1981).

Hassell Smith, A., 'Militia Rates and Militia Statutes, 1558–1663', in P. Clark, A. G. R. Smith, and N. Tyacke (eds.), *The English Commonwealth, 1547–1640* (Leicester, 1979), 93–110.

Hassell Smith, A., *County and Court: Government and Politics in Norfolk, 1558–1603* (Oxford, 1974).

Hatcher, J., *Plague, Population and the English Economy, 1348–1530* (London, 1977).

Haugaard, W. P., *Elizabeth and the English Reformation: The Struggle for a Stable Settlement of Religion* (Cambridge, 1970).

Hay, M. V., *The Life of Robert Sidney: Earl of Leicester* (Folger Books, Washington DC, 1984).

Haynes, S., and Murdin, W. (eds.), *Collection of State Papers . . . left by William Cecil, Lord Burghley* (2 vols.; London, 1740–59).

Heal, F., 'The Bishops and the Act of Exchange of 1559', *Historical Journal*, 17 (1974), 227–46.

—— *Of Prelates and Princes: A Study of the Economic and Social Position of the Tudor Episcopate* (Cambridge, 1980).

—— and O'Day, R. (eds.), *Church and Society in England: Henry VIII to James I* (London, 1977).

Heath, P., *The English Parish Clergy on the Eve of the Reformation* (London, 1969).

Heinze, R. W., *The Proclamations of the Tudor Kings* (Cambridge, 1976).

Hexter, J. H., *Reappraisals in History* (London, 1961).

Hicks, M., 'Attainder, Resumption and Coercion, 1461–1529', *Parliamentary History*, 3 (1984), 15–31.

Hill, C., *Economic Problems of the Church from Archbishop Whitgift to the Long Parliament* (Oxford, 1956; repr. 1968).

—— *Society and Puritanism in Pre-Revolutionary England* (London, 1964; repr. 1966).

Historical Manuscripts Commission, *Calendar of the Manuscripts of the Most Honourable the Marquis of Salisbury* (24 vols.; London, 1883–1976).

Hoak, D. E., 'Rehabilitating the Duke of Northumberland: Politics and Political Control, 1549–53', in J. Loach and R. Tittler (eds.), *The Mid-Tudor Polity*, pp. 29–51.

—— 'The King's Privy Chamber, 1547–1553', in D. J. Guth and J. W. McKenna (eds.), *Tudor Rule and Revolution* (Cambridge, 1982), 87–108.

—— 'The Secret History of the Tudor Court: The King's Coffers and the King's Purse, 1542–1553', *Journal of British Studies*, 26 (1987), 208–31.

—— 'Two Revolutions in Tudor Government: The Formation and Organization of Mary I's Privy Council', in C. Coleman and D. R. Starkey (eds.), *Revolution Reassessed*, pp. 87–115.

—— *The King's Council in the Reign of Edward VI* (Cambridge, 1976).

Hodgett, G. A. J., *Tudor Lincolnshire* (Lincoln, 1975).

Holmes, P. J., 'The Great Council in the Reign of Henry VII', *English Historical Review*, 101 (1986), 840–62.

—— *Elizabethan Casuistry* (Catholic Record Society, 67; London, 1981).

—— *Resistance and Compromise: The Political Thought of the Elizabethan Catholics* (Cambridge, 1982).

Horowitz, M. R., 'Richard Empson, Minister of Henry VII', *Bulletin of the Institute of Historical Research*, 55 (1982), 35–49.

Hoskins, W. G., 'Harvest Fluctuations and English Economic History, 1480–1619', *Agricultural History Review*, 12 (1964), 28–46.

—— *The Age of Plunder: The England of Henry VIII, 1500–1547* (London, 1976).

Houlbrooke, R. A., *Church Courts and the People during the English Reformation, 1520–1570* (Oxford, 1979).

House, S. B., 'Sir Thomas More and Holy Orders: More's Views of the English Clergy, both Secular and Regular', unpublished St Andrews Ph.D. dissertation (1987).

Howarth, D., *The Voyage of the Armada: The Spanish Story* (London, 1981).

Hudson, W. S., *The Cambridge Connection and the Elizabethan Settlement of 1559* (Durham, NC, 1980).

Hughes, P., *The Reformation in England* (3 vols.; London, 1950–4).

Hughes, P. L., and Larkin, J. F. (eds.), *Tudor Royal Proclamations* (3 vols.; New Haven, Conn., 1964–9).

Hurstfield, J., *Elizabeth I and the Unity of England* (London, 1960).

—— *Freedom, Corruption and Government in Elizabethan England* (London, 1973).

—— *The Queen's Wards: Wardship and Marriage under Elizabeth I* (London, 1958).

Hutton, R., 'The Local Impact of the Tudor Reformations', in C. Haigh (ed.), *The English Reformation Revised*, pp. 114–38.

Ives, E. W., 'Faction at the Court of Henry VIII: The Fall of Anne Boleyn', *History*, 57 (1972), 169–88.

—— *Anne Boleyn* (Oxford, 1986).

—— *The Common Lawyers of Pre-Reformation England* (Cambridge, 1983).

James, M. E., 'Obedience and Dissent in Henrician England: The Lincolnshire Rebellion, 1536', *Past and Present*, no. 48 (1970), 3–78.

—— 'The Concept of Order and the Northern Rising, 1569', *Past and Present*, no. 60 (1973), 49–83.

—— *Change and Continuity in the Tudor North: The Rise of Thomas, First Lord Wharton* (Borthwick Institute, York, 1965).

—— *Family, Lineage and Civil Society: A Study of Society, Politics and Mentality in the Durham Region, 1500–1640* (Oxford, 1974).

James, M. E., *Society, Politics and Culture: Studies in Early Modern England* (Cambridge, 1986).

Johnson, P., *Elizabeth I: A Study in Power and Intellect* (London, 1974).

Jones, N. L., 'Elizabeth's First Year: The Conception and Birth of the Elizabethan Political World', in Haigh (ed.), *Reign of Elizabeth I*, pp. 27–53.

—— 'Fine Tuning the Reformation', in J. A. Guy and H. G. Beale (eds.), *Law and Social Change in British History* (London, 1984), 86–95.

—— 'Profiting from Religious Reform: The Land Rush of 1559', *Historical Journal*, 22 (1979), 279–94.

—— *Faith by Statute: Parliament and the Settlement of Religion, 1559* (London, 1982).

Jones, W. J., *The Elizabethan Court of Chancery* (Oxford, 1967).

Jordan, W. K., *Edward VI: The Threshold of Power. The Dominance of the Duke of Northumberland* (London, 1970).

—— *Edward VI: The Young King. The Protectorship of the Duke of Somerset* (London, 1968).

—— *Philanthropy in England, 1480–1660* (London, 1959).

Kelly, H. A., *The Matrimonial Trials of Henry VIII* (Stanford, Ca., 1976).

Kelly, M. J., 'Canterbury Jurisdiction and Influence during the Episcopate of William Warham, 1503–1532', unpublished Cambridge Ph.D. dissertation (1963).

Kent, J. R., *The English Village Constable, 1580–1642* (Oxford, 1986).

Kerridge, E., *Agrarian Problems in the Sixteenth Century and After* (London, 1969).

King, J. N., 'Freedom of the Press, Protestant Propaganda, and Protector Somerset', *Huntington Library Quarterly*, 40 (1976), 1–10.

Kipling, G., 'Henry VII and the Origins of Tudor Patronage', in G. F. Lytle and S. Orgel (eds.), *Patronage in the Renaissance* (Princeton, NJ, 1981), 117–64.

Knappen, M. M., *Tudor Puritanism* (Chicago, 1939).

Knecht, R. J., 'The Episcopate and the Wars of the Roses', *University of Birmingham Historical Journal*, 6 (1957–8), 108–31.

Knowles, D., 'The Matter of Wilton', *Bulletin of the Institute of Historical Research*, 31 (1958), 92–6.

—— *The Religious Orders in England*, iii. *The Tudor Age* (Cambridge, 1959; repr. 1971).

Kreider, A., *English Chantries: The Road to Dissolution* (Cambridge, Mass., 1979).

Lake, P. G., 'Calvinism and the English Church, 1570–1635', *Past and Present*, no. 114 (1987), 32–76.

—— *Moderate Puritans and the Elizabethan Church* (Cambridge, 1982).

Land, S. K., *Kett's Rebellion* (Ipswich, 1977).

Lander, J. R., *Conflict and Stability in Fifteenth-century England* (London, 1969).

—— *Crown and Nobility, 1450–1509* (London, 1976).

—— *Government and Community: England, 1450–1509* (London, 1980).

Langbein, J. H., *Prosecuting Crime in the Renaissance* (Cambridge, Mass., 1974).

—— *Torture and the Law of Proof: Europe and England in the Ancien Regime* (Chicago, Ill., 1977).

Lehmberg, S. E., *Sir Thomas Elyot: Tudor Humanist* (Austin, Texas, 1960).

—— *Sir Walter Mildmay and Tudor Government* (Austin, Texas, 1964).

—— *The Later Parliaments of Henry VIII, 1536–1547* (Cambridge, 1977).

—— *The Reformation Parliament, 1529–1536* (Cambridge, 1970).

Leonard, E. M., *The Early History of English Poor Relief* (Cambridge, 1900).

Letters and Papers, Foreign and Domestic, of the Reign of Henry VIII, ed. J. S. Brewer, J. Gairdner, R. H. Brodie, *et al.* (21 vols. and *Addenda*; London, 1862–1932).

Levy, F. J., *Tudor Historical Thought* (San Marino, Ca., 1967).

Loach, J., 'Pamphlets and Politics, 1553–8', *Bulletin of the Institute of Historical Research*, 48 (1975), 31–44.

—— 'Parliament: A "New Air"?', in C. Coleman and D. R. Starkey (eds.), *Revolution Reassessed*, pp. 117–34.

—— 'The Marian Establishment and the Printing Press', *English Historical Review*, 101 (1986), 135–48.

—— *Parliament and the Crown in the Reign of Mary Tudor* (Oxford, 1986).

—— and Tittler, R. (eds.), *The Mid-Tudor Polity, c.1540–1560* (London, 1980).

Loades, D. M., 'Anabaptism and English Sectarianism in the Mid-sixteenth Century', in D. Baker (ed.), *Reform and Reformation: England and the Continent, c.1500–c.1750* (Oxford, 1979), 59–70.

—— 'The Enforcement of Reaction, 1553–1558', *Journal of Ecclesiastical History*, 16 (1965), 54–66.

—— *Politics and the Nation, 1450–1660* (London, 1974).

—— *The Oxford Martyrs* (London, 1970).

—— *The Reign of Mary Tudor: Politics, Government, and Religion in England, 1553–1558* (London, 1979).

—— *The Tudor Court* (London, 1986).

—— *Two Tudor Conspiracies* (Cambridge, 1965).

Lupton, J. H., *A Life of John Colet* (London, 1887; 2nd edn., 1909).

Lusardi, J. P., 'The Career of Robert Barnes', in *The Complete Works of St Thomas More*, viii. *The Confutation of Tyndale's Answer*, ed.

A. Schuster, R. C. Marius, J. P. Lusardi, and R. J. Schoeck (New Haven, Conn., 1973), pt. 3, pp. 1365–1415.

Luxton, I., 'The Reformation and Popular Culture', in F. Heal and R. O'Day (eds.), *Church and Society in England*, pp. 57–77.

Lyons, S. M., 'Conflict and Controversy: English Bishops and the Reformation, 1547–1558', unpublished Brown Ph.D. dissertation (1980).

MacCaffrey, W. T., 'Parliament: The Elizabethan Experience', in D. J. Guth and J. W. McKenna (eds.), *Tudor Rule and Revolution* (Cambridge, 1982), 127–47.

—— 'Place and Patronage in Elizabethan Politics', in S. T. Bindoff, J. Hurstfield, and C. H. Williams (eds.), *Elizabethan Government and Society: Essays Presented to Sir John Neale* (London, 1961), 95–126.

—— *Exeter, 1540–1640* (Cambridge, Mass., 1958; 2nd edn., 1975).

—— *Queen Elizabeth and the Making of Policy, 1572–1588* (Princeton, NJ, 1981).

—— *The Shaping of the Elizabethan Regime: Elizabethan Politics, 1558–72* (London, 1969).

McConica, J. K., *English Humanists and Reformation Politics* (Oxford, 1965; repr. 1968).

—— (ed.), *The History of the University of Oxford*, iii. *The Collegiate University* (Oxford, 1986).

MacCulloch, D., 'Catholic and Puritan in Elizabethan Suffolk', *Archiv für Reformationsgeschichte*, 72 (1981), 232–89.

—— 'Kett's Rebellion in Context', *Past and Present*, no. 84 (1979), 36–59.

—— (ed.), 'The *Vita Mariae Angliae Reginae* of Robert Wingfield of Brantham', in *Camden Miscellany, XXVIII* (Camden Society, 4th ser. 29; London, 1984), 181–301.

—— *Suffolk and the Tudors: Politics and Religion in an English County, 1500–1600* (Oxford, 1986).

McFarlane, K. B., *England in the Fifteenth Century: Collected Essays* (London, 1981).

McGrath, P., 'A Reply to Dr Haigh', *Journal of Ecclesiastical History*, 36 (1985), 405–6.

—— 'Elizabethan Catholicism: A Reconsideration', *Journal of Ecclesiastical History*, 35 (1984), 414–28.

—— *Papists and Puritans under Elizabeth I* (London, 1967).

McKenna, J. W., 'How God Became an Englishman', in D. J. Guth and J. W. McKenna (eds.), *Tudor Rule and Revolution* (Cambridge, 1982), 25–43.

Manning, R. B., 'The Crisis of Episcopal Authority during the Reign of Elizabeth I', *Journal of British Studies*, 11 (1971), 1–25.

—— 'Violence and Social Conflict in Mid-Tudor Rebellions', *Journal of British Studies*, 16 (1977), 18–40.

—— *Religion and Society in Elizabethan Sussex* (Leicester, 1969).

Marius, R., *Thomas More* (New York, 1984).

Martin, J. W., 'A Sidelight on Foxe's Account of the Marian Martyrs', *Bulletin of the Institute of Historical Research*, 58 (1985), 248–51.

—— 'The Marian Regime's Failure to Understand the Importance of Printing', *Huntington Library Quarterly*, 44 (1980–1), 231–47.

Mattingly, G., *The Defeat of the Spanish Armada* (London, 1959).

—— (ed.), *Further Supplement to Letters, Despatches and State Papers Relating to the Negotiations between England and Spain* (London, 1940).

Mayhew, G. J., 'The Progress of the Reformation in East Sussex, 1530–1559: The Evidence from Wills', *Southern History*, 5 (1983), 38–67.

Merriman, R. B. (ed.), *Life and Letters of Thomas Cromwell* (2 vols.; Oxford, 1902).

Metzger, F., 'Das Englische Kanzleigericht Unter Kardinal Wolsey 1515–1529', unpublished Erlangen Ph.D. dissertation (1976).

Miller, H., 'Henry VIII's Unwritten Will: Grants of Land and Honours in 1547', in E. W. Ives, R. J. Knecht, and J. J. Scarisbrick (eds.), *Wealth and Power in Tudor England* (London, 1978), 87–105.

—— 'London and Parliament in the Reign of Henry VIII', *Bulletin of the Institute of Historical Research*, 35 (1962), 128–49.

—— *Henry VIII and the English Nobility* (Oxford, 1986).

Moody, T. W., Martin, F. X., and Byrne, F. J. (eds.), *A New History of Ireland*, Vol. iii. *Early Modern Ireland, 1534–1691* (Oxford, 1976).

Moran, J. A. H., *The Growth of English Schooling, 1340–1548: Learning, Literacy and Laicization in Pre-Reformation York Diocese* (Princeton, NJ, 1985).

[More, Thomas], *Yale Edition of the Complete Works of St Thomas More* (15 vols.; New Haven, Conn., 1963–).

—— *The Correspondence of Sir Thomas More*, ed. E. F. Rogers (Princeton, NJ, 1947).

Morgan, V., 'Whose Prerogative in Late Sixteenth and Early Seventeenth Century England?', in A. Kiralfy, M. Slatter, and R. Virgoe (eds.), *Custom, Courts and Counsel* (London, 1985), 39–64.

Morris, C., *Political Thought in England: Tyndale to Hooker* (London, 1953; repr. 1965).

Muller, J. A., *Stephen Gardiner and the Tudor Reaction* (New York, 1926).

Mumford Jones, H., 'Origins of the Colonial Idea in England', *Proceedings of the American Philosophical Society*, 85 (1942), 448–65.

Murphy, V. M., 'The Debate over Henry VIII's First Divorce: An Analysis of the Contemporary Treatises', unpublished Cambridge Ph.D. dissertation (1984).

Neale, J. E., 'The Lord Keeper's Speech to the Parliament of 1592–3', *English Historical Review*, 31 (1916), 128–37.

—— *Elizabeth I and her Parliaments* (2 vols.; London, 1953–7; repr. 1969).

—— *Essays in Elizabethan History* (London, 1958).

—— *Queen Elizabeth I* (London, 1934; repr. 1961).

—— *The Elizabethan House of Commons* (London, 1949; rev. edn., 1963).

Nichols, J. (ed.), *The Progresses, and Public Processions, of Queen Elizabeth* (3 vols.; London, 1788–1805).

Nicholson, G. D., 'The Nature and Function of Historical Argument in the Henrician Reformation', unpublished Cambridge Ph.D. dissertation (1977).

O'Day, R., *Education and Society, 1500–1800: The Social Foundations of Education in Early Modern Britain* (London, 1982).

—— *The English Clergy: Emergence and Consolidation of a Profession, 1558–1642* (Leicester, 1979).

—— and Heal, F. (eds.), *Continuity and Change: Personnel and Administration of the Church of England, 1500–1642* (Leicester, 1976).

Orme, N., *English Schools in the Middle Ages* (London, 1973).

Outhwaite, R. B., 'Royal Borrowing in the Reign of Elizabeth I: The Aftermath of Antwerp', *English Historical Review*, 86 (1971), 251–63.

Oxley, J. E., *The Reformation in Essex to the Death of Mary* (Manchester, 1965).

Palliser, D. M., 'Dearth and Disease in Staffordshire, 1540–1670', in C. W. Chalklin and M. A. Havinden (eds.), *Rural Change and Urban Growth, 1500–1800: Essays in English Regional History in Honour of W. G. Hoskins* (London, 1974), 54–75.

—— 'Tawney's Century: Brave New World or Malthusian Trap', *Economic History Review*, 2nd ser. 35 (1982), 339–53.

—— *The Age of Elizabeth: England under the Later Tudors, 1547–1603* (London, 1983).

—— *Tudor York* (Oxford, 1979).

Parker, G., *Spain and the Netherlands, 1559–1659* (London, 1979).

—— *The Army of Flanders and the Spanish Road, 1567–1659* (Cambridge, 1972).

—— *The Dutch Revolt* (London, 1977).

Phelps Brown, E. H., and Hopkins, S. V., 'Seven Centuries of the Prices of Consumables, Compared with Builders' Wage Rates', *Economica*, NS 23 (1956), 296–314.

Pickthorn, K., *Early Tudor Government: Henry VII* (Cambridge, 1934).

Pocock, J. G. A., 'The Sense of History in Renaissance England', in J. F. Andrews (ed.), *William Shakespeare*, i. *His World* (New York, 1985), 143–57.

Pogson, R. H., 'Cardinal Pole: Papal Legate to England in Mary Tudor's Reign', unpublished Cambridge Ph.D. dissertation (1972).

—— 'Reginald Pole and the Priorities of Government in Mary Tudor's Church', *Historical Journal*, 18 (1975), 3–20.

—— 'Revival and Reform in Mary Tudor's Church: A Question of Money', *Journal of Ecclesiastical History*, 25 (1974), 249–65.

—— 'The Legacy of the Schism: Confusion, Continuity and Change in the Marian Clergy', in J. Loach and R. Tittler (eds.), *The Mid-Tudor Polity*, pp. 116–36.

Pollard, A. F., *Henry VIII* (London, 1902; new edn., 1951, repr. 1963).

—— *Wolsey* (London, 1929).

Pound, J., *Poverty and Vagrancy in Tudor England* (London, 1971; repr. 1978).

Power, M. J., 'London and the Control of the "Crisis" of the 1590s', *History*, 70 (1985), 371–85.

Prest, W. R., 'Legal Education of the Gentry at the Inns of Court, 1560–1640', *Past and Present*, no. 38 (1967), 20–39.

—— *The Inns of Court under Elizabeth and the Early Stuarts, 1570–1640* (London, 1972).

Prior, M. (ed.), *Women in English Society, 1500–1800* (London, 1985).

Pugh, T. B. (ed.), *The Marcher Lordships of South Wales, 1415–1536* (Cardiff, 1963).

Pulman, M. B., *The Elizabethan Privy Council in the Fifteen-Seventies* (Berkeley, Ca., 1971).

Pythian-Adams, C., *Desolation of a City: Coventry and the Urban Crisis of the Late Middle Ages* (Cambridge, 1979).

Quinn, D. B., *England and the Discovery of America, 1481–1620* (New York, 1974).

Ramsay, G. D., *English Overseas Trade during the Centuries of Emergence* (London, 1957).

Read, C., *Lord Burghley and Queen Elizabeth* (London, 1960).

—— *Mr Secretary Cecil and Queen Elizabeth* (London, 1955).

—— *Mr Secretary Walsingham and the Policy of Queen Elizabeth* (3 vols.; Oxford, 1925).

Redworth, G., 'A Study in the Formulation of Policy: The Genesis and Evolution of the Act of Six Articles', *Journal of Ecclesiastical History*, 37 (1986), 42–67.

Rees, W., 'The Union of England and Wales', *Transactions of the Honourable Society of Cymmrodorion* (1937), 27–100.

Reid, R. R., *The King's Council in the North* (London, 1921; repr. 1975).

Rhodes, J., 'Private Devotion in England on the Eve of the Reformation', unpublished Durham Ph.D. dissertation (1974).

Richardson, W. C., *The History of the Court of Augmentations, 1536–1554* (Baton Rouge, La., 1961).

—— *Tudor Chamber Administration, 1485–1547* (Baton Rouge, La., 1952).

—— (ed.), *The Report of the Royal Commission of 1552* (Morgantown, W. Va., 1974).

Ridley, J., *Thomas Cranmer* (Oxford, 1962; repr. 1966).

Riegler, E. G., 'Printing, Protestantism and Politics: Thomas Cromwell and Religious Reform', unpublished UCLA Ph.D. dissertation (1978).

Roberts, P. R., 'The "Acts of Union" and the Tudor Settlement of Wales', unpublished Cambridge Ph.D. dissertation (1966).

Robertson, M. L., 'Thomas Cromwell's Servants: The Ministerial Household in Early Tudor Government and Society', unpublished UCLA Ph.D. dissertation (1975).

Rose-Troup, F., *The Western Rebellion of 1549* (London, 1913).

Roskell, J. S., 'Perspectives in English Parliamentary History' in E. B. Fryde and E. Miller (eds.), *Historical Studies of the English Parliament* (2 vols.; Cambridge, 1970), ii. 296–323.

Ross, C. D., *Edward IV* (London, 1974).

—— *Richard III* (London, 1981).

Rowse, A. L., *The England of Elizabeth* (London, 1950; repr. 1953).

—— *Tudor Cornwall* (London, 1941; 2nd edn., 1969).

Rupp, E. G., *Studies in the Making of the English Protestant Tradition* (London, 1947).

Russell, E., 'The Influx of Commoners into the University of Oxford before 1581: An Optical Illusion?', *English Historical Review*, 92 (1977), 721–45.

Scarisbrick, J. J., 'Cardinal Wolsey and the Common Weal', in E. W. Ives, R. J. Knecht, and Scarisbrick (eds.), *Wealth and Power in Tudor England* (London, 1978), 45–67.

—— 'Clerical Taxation in England, 1485 to 1547', *Journal of Ecclesiastical History*, 11 (1960), 41–54.

—— 'The Pardon of the Clergy, 1531', *Cambridge Historical Journal*, 12 (1956), 22–39.

—— *Henry VIII* (London, 1968).

—— *The Reformation and the English People* (Oxford, 1984).

Schofield, R. S., 'Parliamentary Lay Taxation, 1485–1547', unpublished Cambridge Ph.D. dissertation (1963).

—— 'The Measurement of Literacy in Pre-Industrial England', in J. Goody (ed.), *Literacy in Traditional Societies* (Cambridge, 1968), 311–25.

Seaver, P. S., *The Puritan Lectureships: The Politics of Religious Dissent, 1560–1662* (Stanford, Ca., 1970).

Sharp, B., *In Contempt of All Authority: Rural Artisans and Riot in the West of England, 1586–1660* (Berkeley, Ca., 1980).

Sharpe, J. A., *Crime in Early Modern England, 1550–1750* (London, 1984).

Simon, J., *Education and Society in Tudor England* (Cambridge, 1966).

Skinner, Q., 'Sir Thomas More's *Utopia* and the Language of Renaissance Humanism', in A. Pagden (ed.), *The Languages of Political Theory in Early Modern Europe* (Cambridge, 1987), 123–57.

—— *The Foundations of Modern Political Thought* (2 vols.; Cambridge, 1978; repr. 1979).

Skipp, V. H. T., 'Economic and Social Change in the Forest of Arden, 1530–1649', *Agricultural History Review*, 18 (1970), Supplement, pp. 84–111.

Slack, P., 'Books of Orders: The Making of English Social Policy, 1577–1631', *Transactions of the Royal Historical Society*, 5th ser. 30 (1980), 1–22.

—— 'Mortality Crises and Epidemic Disease in England, 1485–1610', in C. Webster (ed.), *Health, Medicine and Mortality in the Sixteenth Century* (Cambridge, 1979), 9–59.

—— 'Poverty and Social Regulation in Elizabethan England', in Haigh (ed.), *Reign of Elizabeth I*, pp. 221–41.

—— 'Social Policy and the Constraints of Government, 1547–58', in J. Loach and R. Tittler (eds.), *The Mid-Tudor Polity*, pp. 94–115.

—— 'Vagrants and Vagrancy in England, 1598–1664', *Economic History Review*, 2nd ser. 27 (1974), 360–79.

—— *The Impact of Plague in Tudor and Stuart England* (London, 1985).

—— (ed.), *Rebellion, Popular Protest and the Social Order in Early Modern England* (Cambridge, 1984).

Slavin, A. J., 'Cromwell, Lisle and the Calais Sacramentarians: The Politics of Conspiracy', *Albion*, 9 (1977), 316–36.

—— 'Lord Chancellor Wriothesley and Reform of Augmentations: New Light on an Old Court', in Slavin (ed.), *Tudor Men and Institutions* (Baton Rouge, La., 1972), 49–69.

—— 'The Fall of Lord Chancellor Wriothesley: A Study in the Politics of Conspiracy', *Albion*, 7 (1975), 265–86.

—— 'The Gutenberg Galaxy and the Tudor Revolution', in G. P. Tyson and S. S. Wagonheim (eds.), *Print and Culture in the Renaissance: Essays on the Advent of Printing in Europe* (Newark, NJ, 1986), 90–109.

—— 'The Rochepot Affair', *Sixteenth-century Journal*, 10 (1979), 3–19.

—— *Politics and Profit: A Study of Sir Ralph Sadler, 1507–1547* (Cambridge, 1966).

534 *Select Bibliography*

Smith, A. G. R., *Servant of the Cecils: The Life of Sir Michael Hickes, 1543–1612* (London, 1977).

—— *The Emergence of a Nation State: The Commonwealth of England, 1529–1660* (London, 1984).

—— *The Government of Elizabethan England* (London, 1967).

Smith, L. B., *Henry VIII: The Mask of Royalty* (London, 1971).

Smith, R. B., *Land and Politics in the England of Henry VIII: The West Riding of Yorkshire, 1530–46* (Oxford, 1970).

Somerset, A., *Ladies in Waiting: From the Tudors to the Present Day* (New York, 1984).

Somerville, R., 'Henry VII's "Council Learned in the Law" ', *English Historical Review*, 54 (1939), 427–42.

Spufford, M., 'Puritanism and Social Control?', in A. Fletcher and J. Stevenson (eds.), *Order and Disorder in Early Modern England*, pp. 41–57.

—— *Contrasting Communities: English Villagers in the Sixteenth and Seventeenth Centuries* (Cambridge, 1974).

Starkey, D. R., 'Court and Government', in C. Coleman and Starkey (eds.), *Revolution Reassessed*, pp. 29–58.

—— 'From Feud to Faction: English Politics c. 1450–1550', *History Today*, 32 (Nov. 1982), 16–22.

—— 'Representation through Intimacy: A Study in the Symbolism of Monarchy and Court Office in Early Modern England', in I. Lewis (ed.), *Symbols and Sentiments: Cross-cultural Studies in Symbolism* (London, 1977), 187–224.

—— 'The King's Privy Chamber, 1485–1547', unpublished Cambridge Ph.D. dissertation (1973).

—— 'Which Age of Reform?', in C. Coleman and Starkey (eds.), *Revolution Reassessed*, pp. 13–27.

—— (ed.), *The English Court: From the Wars of the Roses to the Civil War* (London, 1987).

—— *The Reign of Henry VIII: Personalities and Politics* (London, 1985).

State Papers during the Reign of Henry VIII (11 vols.; Record Commission, London, 1830–52).

Stone, L., 'Patriarchy and Paternalism in Tudor England: The Earl of Arundel and the Peasants Revolt of 1549', *Journal of British Studies*, 13 (1974), 19–23.

—— 'Social Mobility in England, 1500–1700', *Past and Present*, no. 33 (1966), 16–55.

—— *An Elizabethan: Sir Horatio Palavicino* (Oxford, 1956).

—— *Family and Fortune: Studies in Aristocratic Finance in the Sixteenth and Seventeenth Centuries* (Oxford, 1973).

—— *The Crisis of the Aristocracy, 1558–1641* (Oxford, 1965).

—— *The Family, Sex and Marriage in England, 1500-1800* (London, 1977).

—— and Fawtier Stone, J. C., *An Open Aristocracy? England, 1540-1880* (Oxford, 1983).

—— (ed.), *The University in Society* (2 vols.; Princeton, NJ, 1975).

Storey, R. L., *Diocesan Administration in Fifteenth-century England* (Borthwick Institute, York, 1959; 2nd edn., 1972).

—— *The Reign of Henry VII* (London, 1968).

Strong, R., *Nicholas Hilliard* (London, 1975).

—— *The Cult of Elizabeth: Elizabethan Portraiture and Pageantry* (London, 1977).

Swales, T. H., 'The Redistribution of the Monastic Lands in Norfolk at the Dissolution', *Norfolk Archaeology*, 34/1 (1966), 14–44.

Swensen, P. C., 'Noble Hunters of the Romish Fox: Religious Reform at the Tudor Court, 1543–1564', unpublished UC Berkeley Ph.D. dissertation (1981).

Sylvester, R. S., and Harding, D. P. (eds.), *Two Early Tudor Lives* (New Haven, Conn., 1962; repr. 1969).

Tawney, R. H., and Power, E. (eds.), *Tudor Economic Documents* (3 vols.; London, 1924).

Thirsk, J. (ed.), *The Agrarian History of England and Wales*, iv. *1500-1640* (Cambridge, 1967).

Thomas, D., 'Leases in Reversion on the Crown's Lands, 1558–1603', *Economic History Review*, 2nd ser. 30 (1977), 67–72.

Thomas, K., *Religion and the Decline of Magic* (London, 1971; repr. 1978).

Thompson, I. A. A., 'Spanish Armada Guns', *Mariner's Mirror*, 61 (1975), 355–71.

Thomson, G. S., *Lords Lieutenants in the Sixteenth Century* (London, 1923).

Thomson, J. A. F., *The Later Lollards, 1414-1520* (Oxford, 1965).

Thornley, I. D., 'The Destruction of Sanctuary', in R. W. Seton-Watson (ed.), *Tudor Studies Presented to A. F. Pollard* (London, 1924), 182–207.

Tighe, W. J., 'Gentlemen Pensioners in Elizabethan Politics and Government', unpublished Cambridge Ph.D. dissertation (1983).

Tillyard, E. M. W., *The Elizabethan World Picture* (London, 1963; repr. 1968).

Tittler, R., *The Reign of Mary I* (London, 1983).

Ullmann, W., ' "This Realm of England is an Empire" ', *Journal of Ecclesiastical History*, 30 (1979), 175–203.

Vale, M., *The Gentleman's Recreations: Accomplishments and Pastimes of the English Gentleman, 1580-1630* (Ipswich, 1977).

[Vergil, Polydore], *The Anglica Historia of Polydore Vergil*, ed. D. Hay (Camden Society, 3rd ser. 74; London, 1950).

Walker, G., *John Skelton and the Politics of the 1520s* (Cambridge, 1988).

Wallace, D. D., *Puritans and Predestination: Grace in English Protestant Theology, 1525–1695* (Chapel Hill, NC, 1982).

Walter, J., 'A "Rising of the People"? The Oxfordshire Rising of 1596', *Past and Present*, no. 107 (1985), 90–143.

Ward, A. W., and Waller, A. R. (eds.), *The Cambridge History of English Literature* (15 vols.; Cambridge, 1907–27).

Warnicke, R. M., 'Sexual Heresy at the Court of Henry VIII', *Historical Journal*, 30 (1987), 247–68.

Weiss, R., *Humanism in England during the Fifteenth Century* (Oxford, 1941; 2nd edn., 1957).

Wernham, R. B., 'English Policy and the Revolt of the Netherlands', in J. S. Bromley and E. H. Kossmann (eds.), *Britain and the Netherlands*, 1 (Groningen, 1960), 29–40.

—— 'Queen Elizabeth and the Portugal Expedition of 1589', *English Historical Review*, 66 (1951), 1–26, 194–218.

—— *After the Armada: Elizabethan England and the Struggle for Western Europe, 1588–1595* (Oxford, 1984).

—— *Before the Armada: The Emergence of the English Nation, 1485–1588* (New York, 1966; repr. 1972).

—— *The Making of Elizabethan Foreign Policy, 1558–1603* (Berkeley, Ca., 1980).

Whibley, C. (ed.), *Henry VIII* [an edition of Hall's *Chronicle*] (2 vols.; London, 1904).

Whiting, R., 'Abominable Idols: Images and Image-Breaking under Henry VIII', *Journal of Ecclesiastical History*, 33 (1982), 30–47.

—— ' "For the Health of my Soul": Prayers for the Dead in the Tudor South-West', *Southern History*, 5 (1983), 68–94.

—— 'The Reformation in the South-West of England', unpublished Exeter Ph.D. dissertation (1977).

Wilkie, W. E., *The Cardinal Protectors of England: Rome and the Tudors before the Reformation* (Cambridge, 1974).

Wilks, M., '*Reformatio Regni*: Wyclif and Hus as Leaders of Religious Protest Movements', in D. Baker (ed.), *Schism, Heresy and Religious Protest* (Cambridge, 1972), 109–30.

Willen, D., *John Russell, First Earl of Bedford: One of the King's Men* (London, 1981).

Williams, C. H. (ed.), *English Historical Documents, 1485–1558* (London, 1967).

Williams, N., 'The Risings in Norfolk, 1569 and 1570', *Norfolk Archaeology*, 32 (1961), 73–81.

—— *Thomas Howard, Fourth Duke of Norfolk* (London, 1964).

Williams, P., 'Court and Polity under Elizabeth I', *Bulletin of the John Rylands Library*, 65 (1983), 259–86.

—— 'The Crown and the Counties', in Haigh (ed.), *Reign of Elizabeth I*, pp. 125–46.

—— *The Council in the Marches of Wales under Elizabeth I* (Cardiff, 1958).

—— *The Tudor Regime* (Oxford, 1979).

Wilson, C., *Queen Elizabeth and the Revolt of the Netherlands* (London, 1970).

Wolffe, B. P., 'Henry VII's Land Revenues and Chamber Finance', *English Historical Review*, 79 (1964), 225–54.

—— *The Crown Lands, 1461–1536* (London, 1970).

—— *The Royal Demesne in English History: The Crown Estate in the Governance of the Realm from the Conquest to 1509* (London, 1971).

Woodward, D., 'The Background to the Statute of Artificers: The Genesis of Labour Policy, 1558–63', *Economic History Review*, 33 (1980), 32–44.

Woodward, G. W. O., *The Dissolution of the Monasteries* (London, 1966; repr. 1969).

Wormald, J., 'James VI and I: Two Kings or One?', *History*, 68 (1983), 187–209.

—— *Court, Kirk and Community: Scotland, 1470–1625* (London, 1981).

Wrightson, K., *English Society, 1580–1680* (London, 1982).

—— and Levine, D., *Poverty and Piety in an English Village: Terling, 1525–1700* (New York, 1979).

Wrigley, E. A., and Schofield, R. S., *The Population History of England, 1541–1871: A Reconstruction* (London, 1981).

Wyndham, K. S. H., 'Crown Land and Royal Patronage in Mid-sixteenth-century England', *Journal of British Studies*, 19 (1980), 18–34.

Yates, F. A., *Astraea: The Imperial theme in the Sixteenth Century* (London, 1975).

Youings, J. A., 'The Council of the West', *Transactions of the Royal Historical Society*, 5th ser. 10 (1960), 41–60.

—— 'The South-Western Rebellion of 1549', *Southern History*, 1 (1979), 99–122.

—— 'The Terms of Disposal of the Devon Monastic Lands, 1536–58', *English Historical Review*, 69 (1954), 18–38.

—— *Sixteenth-century England* (Harmondsworth, 1984).

—— *The Dissolution of the Monasteries* (London, 1971).

Youngs, F. A., *The Proclamations of the Tudor Queens* (Cambridge, 1976).

Zagorin, P., *Rebels and Rulers, 1500–1660* (2 vols.; Cambridge, 1982).

Zeeveld, W. G., *Foundations of Tudor Policy* (Cambridge, Mass., 1948).

Zell, M. L., 'Early Tudor JPs at Work', *Archaeologia Cantiana*, 93 (1977), 125–43.

GLOSSARY

THE definitions here are not intended to be exhaustive, but rather to provide accessible explanations for some of the technical terms used in the book.

Admonition controversy. Debate over church government and organization begun when the Cambridge presbyterian Thomas Cartwright published the *Second Admonition to the Parliament* (1572) in support of the *First Admonition* issued earlier the same year by John Field and Thomas Wilcox.

advowson. Right of presentation to an ecclesiastical benefice.

almoner. Official whose task it is to distribute the king's alms.

anabaptists. Comprehensive term covering radical Protestants who refused to allow their children to be baptized and who reinstituted the baptism of believers. The term implied commitment to social revolt and other evil intentions.

Arminian. Follower of the Dutch theologian Jacobus Arminius (1560–1609). More generally, Protestant theologians who insisted that divine sovereignty was compatible with free will in man. By extension the term described the anti-Calvinist bishops and clergy in seventeenth-century England.

assizes. Sessions held twice a year in each county in England by justices acting under special commissions.

attainder. Deprivation of rights (including those of heirs) consequent upon conviction of treason or felony.

attorney-general. The Crown's legal representative in the courts of law.

bail. The freeing of a person who had been arrested or imprisoned upon a civil or (more usually) criminal charge on surety taken for his subsequent appearance at a stated place and time.

bailiff. Servant or agent for the management of a landed estate; a county official subordinate to the sheriff.

benefit of clergy. Privilege of exemption from trial by a secular court allowed in cases of felony to clergy or by extension to persons who could read by virtue of immunity granted to the church by the Crown since the Compromise of Avranches (1172).

benevolence. Non-parliamentary tax levied under the guise of a voluntary loan.

bill of complaint. Plaintiff's petition addressed to the lord chancellor requesting the grant of a writ of subpoena and a hearing in the court of chancery or star chamber.

bond. Written obligation binding one person to another to perform some specified action or to pay a sum of money.

bull. Leaden or other metallic seal, or (usually) a papal letter sealed therewith.

caesaropapism. The absolute authority which a theocratic king has as God's 'vicar' over the church and clergy within his dominions.

chamber. The main state room at Court where the king sat under a canopied throne on days of estate and received ambassadors, etc. The lord chamberlain's department within the royal household.

champerty. A corrupt bargain with a litigant to maintain a lawsuit in exchange for a share of the land, debt, or other thing sued for.

chantry. Endowment for the singing of masses for the souls of the dead.

cloth of estate. The rich cloth which formed the decorative canopy above the throne in the king's chamber, House of Lords, privy chamber at Whitehall, inner star chamber, and elsewhere.

commission of the peace. Authority given by the Crown to persons empowered to act as justices of the peace in specified districts.

commissioner of sewers. Local official appointed by the Crown to supervise the repair of sea-banks and sea-walls, and the cleansing and drainage of rivers, streams, ditches, etc.

consiliarius natus. In baronial theory a magnate who believed that he was entitled to membership of the King's Council by right of high birth.

covin. Deceit.

culverin. Long-range gun: range 12,500 feet; approx. weight 4,500 lb.; calibre 5 ins.; weight of shot 15–20 lb.

demi-culverin. Middle-range gun; range 8,500 feet; approx. weight 2,500 lb.; calibre 4½ ins.; weight of shot 9–11½ lb.

dispensation. An exemption from an obligation of ecclesiastical law.

embracery. Attempt to influence a jury corruptly by means of promises, bribes, entreaties, etc.

engrossing. The buying up of large quantities of foodstuffs with intent to sell them again at a higher price.

escheat. Forfeiture of lands and tenements to a feudal lord either on failure of issue of the tenant dying seised, or on account of his attainder for treason or felony.

escheator. Local official concerned with Crown revenues derived from escheat, wardship, and other feudal incidents.

excommunication. Exclusion from communion of the church.

exemplification. Certified and official copy of a document.

fee farm. Perpetual rent imposed on the grantee of land held by feudal service.

felony. General term of law including all capital crimes below that of treason.

femme couverte. Married woman whose property is vested in her husband.

feudal incidents. The feudal rights of the Crown which included reliefs, escheats, the profits of wardships, and the rarely recurring right to a feudal aid. This last was asserted only once during the Tudor period, when Henry VII claimed (in Prince Arthur's case posthumously) feudal aids in respect of the knighting of his eldest son and the marriage of his eldest daughter.

first fruits and tenths. Ecclesiastical taxes originally paid to the papacy which were annexed to the Crown by statute in 1534, and remained part of the royal revenue until 1703, when they were assigned to the augmentation of clerical stipends.

forestalling. The buying of, or contracting for, cattle or foodstuffs before they came to the market, or dissuading persons from marketing their goods or provisions, in order to enhance the price.

groom of the stool. The king's most intimate personal attendant and *de facto* head of the privy chamber; after 1540 the groom was senior of the two chief (later four principal) gentlemen of the privy chamber.

guild. Association of craftsmen, traders, or other persons for socio-religious or professional purposes.

hundred. A subdivision of a county or shire.

impositions. Additional customs, over and above those granted to the Crown at the beginning of a reign, imposed by virtue of the royal prerogative over trade.

in chief (*in capite*). A term describing feudal land held by a tenant direct from the Crown without the inter-position of a mesne tenant.

indictment. The legal document con-taining a formal accusation presen-ted by or preferred to a grand jury.

indulgence. Remission (after absol-ution by the church) of punishment due to sin.

inquisition *post mortem*. Inquiry before the escheator and a jury on the death of a landowner who was believed to hold freehold land in chief of the Crown. The purpose of the inquiry was to entitle the Crown to the feudal incidents due to it.

jury. Panel of men sworn to answer truly upon some question or ques-tions officially referred to them. A grand jury numbered from twelve to twenty-three 'good and lawful men of the county' returned by the sheriff to present, receive, and inquire into indictments. They were asked to decide whether or not bills of indictment were in their opinion 'true' before the accused persons were committed for trial, and to perform such other duties as were submitted to them. A petty jury was the 'trial jury' which subsequently tried the final issue of

fact and pronounced its decision in a verdict upon which the court gave judgment. After the pleadings in a case were concluded, the jury was required to consider its verdict, and was to be kept without meat or drink until members were unani-mously agreed.

justice of the peace. Member of the commission of the peace; a number of JPs presided over quarter sessions and performed adminis-trative duties in their districts.

king's serjeants. Senior barristers retained by the king for his legal service and therefore forbidden to advise or plead against the Crown in any court of law.

letters patent. Parchment letters under the great seal embodying a grant by the Crown of land, office, right, liberty, or the monopoly of some trade or invention.

liberty (franchise). Privilege enjoyed locally by a subject by way of grant or prescription; a district exempt (usually before 1536) from the jurisdiction of the sheriff.

livery. The delivery of possession of land held by knight's service to the person who had the right to it.

lord-lieutenant. A nobleman or privy councillor given overall adminis-trative authority in a specified district especially in military matters.

maintenance. The unlawful upholding of litigation to which one is not directly a party.

misprision of treason. Failure to reveal knowledge of treason; 'bare' knowledge or concealment of treason by a person who did not assent to, and who was not involved in, the treasonable act itself.

muster. Assembly for the inspection of men eligible for military service, together with their arms.

neck-verse. A verse of the Bible placed before a person claiming benefit of clergy, by reading which he might save his neck.

ordnance. Military stores, munitions.

oyer et terminer. Commission directed to justices and others empowering them to 'hear and determine' indictments on a specified crime or crimes committed within a particular area.

pell. Parchment or 'skin' (*pellis*) containing a record of money paid or received.

praemunire. The criminal offence of introducing into England or otherwise acknowledging foreign (usually papal) jurisdiction, contrary to royal prerogative and Crown jurisdiction.

prescription. A title or right acquired by use and time, and allowed by the law.

presentment. Denunciation of jurors or peace officers of an offence inquirable in the court where it is presented; an information made by a grand jury to a court of law.

privy chamber. The king's private chamber at Court (in practice the term increasingly described a suite of rooms) where the king lodged and retired for his private affairs. The privy chamber was under the groom of the stool until 1603.

probate. Certificate of an ecclesiastical court having jurisdiction that a will had been proved and might be executed.

proclamation. Notice or command publicly given by the Crown and proclaimed in London and the localities.

prohibition. Writ forbidding an inferior court from taking cognizance of a particular case.

purveyance. The right of the Crown to purchase supplies or to obtain transport for the royal household at prices fixed below prevailing market rates.

quarter sessions. General court held four times a year by the justices of the peace in every county to hear and determine matters concerning the breach of the peace and to deal with any other legal or administrative business specified by statute or ordered by the Crown or Privy Council.

real presence. Comprehensive term covering theological doctrines that assert the *actual* presence of Christ in the Eucharistic sacrament, as against doctrines maintaining that Christ is present only figuratively or symbolically.

recognizance. Formal acknowledgement of a debt or some other obligation, with sureties and penalties for enforcement.

recusant. A person (Catholic) who denied the royal supremacy or refused to attend the services of the Anglican Church.

regalian rights. Royal rights over the church (especially fiscal rights).

regrating. The buying of corn or foodstuffs in any market, and selling them again in the same market or within 4 miles.

regular clergy. Clergy who were members of religious orders.

relief. Sum of money which the tenant holding land by knight's service, grand serjeanty, or other tenure for which homage or legal service was due, paid to the Crown or to a lesser feudal lord at his admission to his tenure on the death of his ancestor.

rood-loft. The rood-screen separated the chancel of a pre-Reformation church or cathedral from the nave and (sometimes) completed the side enclosures of the chancel. The loft or upper gallery above the rood-beam was used for preaching or reading prayers. The screen was surmounted by a crucifix flanked by carved images of the Virgin Mary and St John which faced the congregation.

sacramentarian. A Protestant who denied the real presence of Christ in the Eucharist.

secular clergy. Clergy who lived and worked outside the monastic cloister.

serjeant at law. Barrister admitted to the 'order of the coif' and permitted to plead in the court of common pleas.

sheriff. Originally the principal agent of the Crown in the county for administrative and financial purposes.

sign manual. Handwritten signature, especially of the sovereign.

signet. Small personal seal, especially the king's smallest seal used by his secretary.

signification. Legal process ordering the detention by the secular juris-diction of a person named in a bishop's certificate of excommuni-cation.

stannary. Privileged tin-mining area (in Devon or Cornwall).

subornation. Secret underhand preparing, instructing, or bringing in false witness in a court of law.

subpoena. Writ requiring under penalty that a defendant appear in chancery or star chamber.

subsidy. Tax granted to the Crown in Parliament to be levied on taxpayers according to the value of their lands or goods.

surety. A person who makes himself liable for the behaviour or default of some other person.

temporalities. The secular possessions (e.g. lands) of a bishop or other ecclesiastical dignitary held by the Crown during a vacancy.

tithe. One-tenth of the produce of land and livestock, and also of the profits of labour, originally payable to the rector (ecclesiastical or lay) of each parish for the maintenance of a priest. Many tithes had become commuted for fixed cash payments by 1603, but commutation was a contentious business since lay tithe payers aimed to increase commutation at less than market prices, while tithe owners (especially lay owners) resisted the same.

transubstantiation. Theological doctrine explaining how the whole substance (i.e. every particle) of the bread and wine in the Eucharist is converted into the whole sub-stance of the body and blood of Christ, only the accidents (i.e. the appearances of the bread and wine) remaining.

traverse. Formal denial or dispute of a legal inquisition made of lands or goods.

trespass. A civil action which sought to determine liability and secure damages for a wrong or injury.

villein. A bondman; a servile tenant who was bound to perform such services as his lord commanded.

visitation. Inspection of a church or religious house by the bishop or his representative, by the authorities of a religious order, or by Crown commissioners.

wardrobe. The royal department which purchased and administered all dry stores, e.g. cloths, silks, cloth of gold, upholstery, furni-ture, carriage supplies, harness, and saddle goods. It was based at the Tower of London and was separate from the wardrobe of the household which travelled with the Court under the clerk of the wardrobe of the household or cofferer.

wardship. The right of the Crown or a lesser feudal lord to govern the person and administer the estates of a person under the age of twenty-one who was the heir to one of the lord's landholders.

INDEX

IN sub-headings alphabetical order is followed, except where this violates the chronology of the Tudor monarchs. Where the monarchs are in the sub-headings, they appear first, in order, followed by the other sub-headings in alphabetical order.

Kings, emperors, dukes, counts, and theological *auctorites* (e.g. Henry of Langenstein) with the same name are indexed according to royal and noble precedence, and chivalric and personal dignity, as was recognized in the Tudor period. Henry II (king of England) is followed by Henry II (king of France).

Peerages are numbered in order of creation, descent, and re-creation (where the last applies) according to the dates of the royal letters patent establishing the title.

OXFORD

MORE OXFORD PAPERBACKS

This book is just one of nearly 1000 Oxford Paperbacks currently in print. If you would like details of other Oxford Paperbacks, including titles in the World's Classics, Oxford Reference, Oxford Books, OPUS, Past Masters, Oxford Authors, and Oxford Shakespeare series, please write to:

UK and Europe: Oxford Paperbacks Publicity Manager, Arts and Reference Publicity Department, Oxford University Press, Walton Street, Oxford OX2 6DP.

Customers in UK and Europe will find Oxford Paperbacks available in all good bookshops. But in case of difficulty please send orders to the Cash-with-Order Department, Oxford University Press Distribution Services, Saxon Way West, Corby, Northants NN18 9ES. Tel: 01536 741519; Fax: 01536 746337. Please send a cheque for the total cost of the books, plus £1.75 postage and packing for orders under £20; £2.75 for orders over £20. Customers outside the UK should add 10% of the cost of the books for postage and packing.

USA: Oxford Paperbacks Marketing Manager, Oxford University Press, Inc., 200 Madison Avenue, New York, N.Y. 10016.

Canada: Trade Department, Oxford University Press, 70 Wynford Drive, Don Mills, Ontario M3C 1J9.

Australia: Trade Marketing Manager, Oxford University Press, G.P.O. Box 2784Y, Melbourne 3001, Victoria.

South Africa: Oxford University Press, P.O. Box 1141, Cape Town 8000.

OPUS

General Editors: Walter Bodmer,
Christopher Butler, Robert Evans,
John Skorupski

CLASSICAL THOUGHT

Terence Irwin

Spanning over a thousand years from Homer to Saint Augustine, *Classical Thought* encompasses a vast range of material, in succinct style, while remaining clear and lucid even to those with no philosophical or Classical background.

The major philosophers and philosophical schools are examined—the Presocratics, Socrates, Plato, Aristotle, Stoicism, Epicureanism, Neoplatonism; but other important thinkers, such as Greek tragedians, historians, medical writers, and early Christian writers, are also discussed. The emphasis is naturally on questions of philosophical interest (although the literary and historical background to Classical philosophy is not ignored), and again the scope is broad—ethics, the theory of knowledge, philosophy of mind, philosophical theology. All this is presented in a fully integrated, highly readable text which covers many of the most important areas of ancient thought and in which stress is laid on the variety and continuity of philosophical thinking after Aristotle.

HISTORY IN OXFORD PAPERBACKS

THE STRUGGLE FOR THE MASTERY OF EUROPE 1848–1918

A. J. P. Taylor

The fall of Metternich in the revolutions of 1848 heralded an era of unprecedented nationalism in Europe, culminating in the collapse of the Hapsburg, Romanov, and Hohenzollern dynasties at the end of the First World War. In the intervening seventy years the boundaries of Europe changed dramatically from those established at Vienna in 1815. Cavour championed the cause of *Risorgimento* in Italy; Bismarck's three wars brought about the unification of Germany; Serbia and Bulgaria gained their independence courtesy of the decline of Turkey—'the sick man of Europe'; while the great powers scrambled for places in the sun in Africa. However, with America's entry into the war and President Wilson's adherence to idealistic internationalist principles, Europe ceased to be the centre of the world, although its problems, still primarily revolving around nationalist aspirations, were to smash the Treaty of Versailles and plunge the world into war once more.

A. J. P. Taylor has drawn the material for his account of this turbulent period from the many volumes of diplomatic documents which have been published in the five major European languages. By using vivid language and forceful characterization, he has produced a book that is as much a work of literature as a contribution to scientific history.

'One of the glories of twentieth-century writing.' *Observer*

ILLUSTRATED HISTORIES IN
OXFORD PAPERBACKS

THE OXFORD ILLUSTRATED HISTORY
OF ENGLISH LITERATURE

Edited by Pat Rogers

Britain possesses a literary heritage which is almost
unrivalled in the Western world. In this volume, the
richness, diversity, and continuity of that tradition
are explored by a group of Britain's foremost literary scholars.

Chapter by chapter the authors trace the history
of English literature, from its first stirrings in Anglo-
Saxon poetry to the present day. At its heart towers
the figure of Shakespeare, who is accorded a special
chapter to himself. Other major figures such as
Chaucer, Milton, Donne, Wordsworth, Dickens,
Eliot, and Auden are treated in depth, and the story
is brought up to date with discussion of living
authors such as Seamus Heaney and Edward Bond.

'[a] lovely volume . . . put in your thumb and pull
out plums' Michael Foot

'scholarly and enthusiastic people have written in-
spiring essays that induce an eagerness in their readers to return to the writers they admire' *Economist*

A Very Short Introduction

CLASSICS

Mary Beard and John Henderson

This *Very Short Introduction* to Classics links a haunting temple on a lonely mountainside to the glory of ancient Greece and the grandeur of Rome, and to Classics within modern culture—from Jefferson and Byron to Asterix and Ben-Hur.

'This little book should be in the hands of every student, and every tourist to the lands of the ancient world . . . a splendid piece of work'
Peter Wiseman
Author of *Talking to Virgil*

'an eminently readable and useful guide to many of the modern debates enlivening the field . . . the most up-to-date and accessible introduction available'
Edith Hall
Author of *Inventing the Barbarian*

'lively and up-to-date . . . it shows classics as a living enterprise, not a warehouse of relics'
New Statesman and Society

'nobody could fail to be informed and entertained—the accent of the book is provocative and stimulating'
Times Literary Supplement

ARCHAEOLOGY

Paul Bahn

'Archaeology starts, really, at the point when the first recognizable 'artefacts' appear—on current evidence, that was in East Africa about 2.5 million years ago—and stretches right up to the present day. What you threw in the garbage yesterday, no matter how useless, disgusting, or potentially embarrassing, has now become part of the recent archaeological record.'

This Very Short Introduction reflects the enduring popularity of archaeology—a subject which appeals as a pastime, career, and academic discipline, encompasses the whole globe, and surveys 2.5 million years. From deserts to jungles, from deep caves to mountain-tops, from pebble tools to satellite photographs, from excavation to abstract theory, archaeology interacts with nearly every other discipline in its attempts to reconstruct the past.

'very lively indeed and remarkably perceptive ... a quite brilliant and level-headed look at the curious world of archaeology'
Professor Barry Cunliffe,
University of Oxford

OPUS

TWENTIETH-CENTURY FRENCH PHILOSOPHY

Eric Matthews

This book gives a chronological survey of the works of the major French philosophers of the twentieth century.

Eric Matthews offers various explanations for the enduring importance of philosophy in French intellectual life and traces the developments which French philosophy has taken in the twentieth century from its roots in the thought of Descartes, with examinations of key figures such as Bergson, Sartre, Marcel, Merleau-Ponty, Foucault, and Derrida, and the recent French Feminists.

'*Twentieth-Century French Philosophy* is a clear, yet critical introduction to contemporary French Philosophy. . . . The undergraduate or other reader who comes to the area for the first time will gain a definite sense of an intellectual movement with its own questions and answers and its own rigour . . . not least of the book's virtues is its clarity.'
Garrett Barden
Author of *After Principles*

WORLD'S ✿ CLASSICS

PRINCIPLES OF HUMAN KNOWLEDGE AND THREE DIALOGUES

GEORGE BERKELEY

Edited by Howard Robinson

Berkeley's idealism started a revolution in philosophy. As one of the great empiricist thinkers he not only influenced British philosophers from Hume to Russell and the logical positivists in the twentieth century, he also set the scene for the continental idealism of Hegel and even the philosophy of Marx.

There has never been such a radical critique of common sense and perception as that given in Berkeley's *Principles of Human Knowledge* (1710). His views were met with disfavour, and his response to his critics was the *Three Dialogues* between Hylas and Philonous.

This edition of Berkeley's two key works has an introduction which examines and in part defends his arguments for idealism, as well as offering a detailed analytical contents list, extensive philosophical notes and an index.

OXFORD

RETHINKING LIFE AND DEATH
THE COLLAPSE OF OUR TRADITIONAL ETHICS

Peter Singer

A victim of the Hillsborough Disaster in 1989, Anthony Bland lay in hospital in a coma being fed liquid food by a pump, via a tube passing through his nose and into his stomach. On 4 February 1993 Britain's highest court ruled that doctors attending him could lawfully act to end his life.

Our traditional ways of thinking about life and death are collapsing. In a world of respirators and embryos stored for years in liquid nitrogen, we can no longer take the sanctity of human life as the cornerstone of our ethical outlook.

In this controversial book Peter Singer argues that we cannot deal with the crucial issues of death, abortion, euthanasia and the rights of nonhuman animals unless we sweep away the old ethic and build something new in its place.

Singer outlines a new set of commandments, based on compassion and commonsense, for the decisions everyone must make about life and death.

Oxford
Paperback
Reference

THE CONCISE OXFORD DICTIONARY
OF POLITICS

Edited by Iain McLean

Written by an expert team of political scientists from Warwick University, this is the most authoritative and up-to-date dictionary of politics available.

* Over 1,500 entries provide truly international coverage of major political institutions, thinkers and concepts

* From Western to Chinese and Muslim political thought

* Covers new and thriving branches of the subject, including international political economy, voting theory, and feminism

* Appendix of political leaders

* Clear, no-nonsense definitions of terms such as veto and subsidiarity

The South East Essex
College of Arts & Technology
Carnarvon Road, Southend-on-Sea, Essex SS2 6LS
Phone 0702 220400 Fax 0702 432320 Minicom 0702 220640